MASTERPLOTS II

SHORT STORY
SERIES

MASTERPLOTS II

SHORT STORY
SERIES

5

Pru-Ter

Edited by
FRANK N. MAGILL

SALEM PRESS

Pasadena, California   Englewood Cliffs, New Jersey

3-89   Publ 3500

Library of Congress Cataloging-in-Publication Data
Masterplots II: Short story series.
Bibliography: p.
Includes index.
Summary: Examines the theme, characters,
plot, style and technique of more than 700 nine-
teenth- and twentieth-century works by prominent
authors from around the world.
1. Fiction—19th century—Stories, plots, etc. 2.
Fiction—19th century—History and criticism. 3.
Fiction—20th century—Stories, plots, etc. 4. Fic-
tion—20th century—History and criticism. 5.
Short story. [1. Short stories—Stories, plots, etc. 2.
Short story] I. Magill, Frank Northen, 1907-   .
II. Title: Masterplots 2. III. Title: Masterplots two.
PN3326.M27 1986   809.3   86-22025
ISBN 0-89356-461-3 (set)
ISBN 0-89356-466-4 (volume 5)

LIST OF TITLES IN VOLUME 5

page

Prussian Officer, The—*D. H. Lawrence* 1859
Psychiatrist, The—*Joaquim Maria Machado de Assis* 1862
Pupil, The—*Henry James* 1865
Purloined Letter, The—*Edgar Allan Poe* 1868

Queen of Spades, The—*Alexander Pushkin* 1872

Ragman's Daughter, The—*Alan Sillitoe* 1876
Raid, The—*Leo Tolstoy* 1880
Rain—*W. Somerset Maugham* 1883
Rainy Moon, The—*Colette* 1887
Ram in the Thicket, The—*Wright Morris* 1890
Ransom of Red Chief, The—*O. Henry* 1894
Rappaccini's Daughter—*Nathaniel Hawthorne* 1897
Rashōmon—*Ryūnosuke Akutagawa* 1901
Real Thing, The—*Henry James* 1905
Reasonable Facsimile, A—*Jean Stafford* 1908
Recluse, A—*Walter de la Mare* 1913
Red Leaves—*William Faulkner* 1918
Red-Headed League, The—*Arthur Conan Doyle* 1922
Rembrandt's Hat—*Bernard Malamud* 1926
Report to an Academy, A—*Franz Kafka* 1929
Resemblance Between a Violin Case and a Coffin, The—
   Tennessee Williams 1933
Return of a Private, The—*Hamlin Garland* 1937
Return of Chorb, The—*Vladimir Nabokov* 1941
Revelation—*Flannery O'Connor* 1945
Revenant, A—*Walter de la Mare* 1948
Rich Boy, The—*F. Scott Fitzgerald* 1952
Rip Van Winkle—*Washington Irving* 1957
Rise of Maud Martha, The—*Gwendolyn Brooks* 1961
Ritter Gluck—*E. T. A. Hoffmann* 1964
Road to the Isles—*Jessamyn West* 1968
Rocking-Horse Winner, The—*D. H. Lawrence* 1971

page

Roman Fever—*Edith Wharton* 1974
Rope—*Katherine Anne Porter* 1978
Rosa—*Cynthia Ozick* 1982
Rose for Emily, A—*William Faulkner* 1986
Rose in the Heart of New York, A—*Edna O'Brien* 1990
Rothschild's Fiddle—*Anton Chekhov* 1994
Round by Round—*Conrad Aiken* 1998

Sad Fate of Mr. Fox, The—*Joel Chandler Harris* 2002
Sailor Off the *Bremen*—*Irwin Shaw* 2005
Saint Augustine's Pigeon—*Evan S. Connell, Jr.* 2008
Saint Marie—*Louise Erdrich* 2012
Sanatorium Under the Sign of the Hourglass—*Bruno Schulz* 2016
Sandman, The—*E. T. A. Hoffmann* 2020
Saturday Night—*James T. Farrell* 2025
Scandal in Bohemia, A—*Arthur Conan Doyle* 2029
Scandalous Woman, A—*Edna O'Brien* 2033
Scapegoat, The—*Paul Laurence Dunbar* 2037
Schreuderspitze, The—*Mark Helprin* 2041
Sculptor's Funeral, The—*Willa Cather* 2045
Seaton's Aunt—*Walter de la Mare* 2049
Secret Integration, The—*Thomas Pynchon* 2053
Secret Life of Walter Mitty, The—*James Thurber* 2057
Secret Sharer, The—*Joseph Conrad* 2061
See the Moon?—*Donald Barthelme* 2064
Shape of Light, A—*William Goyen* 2068
Sheriff's Children, The—*Charles Waddell Chesnutt* 2072
She-Wolf, The—*Giovanni Verga* 2076
Shoemaker Arnold—*Earl Lovelace* 2080
Short Friday—*Isaac Bashevis Singer* 2084
Short Happy Life of Francis Macomber, The—*Ernest Hemingway* ... 2088
Shot, The—*Alexander Pushkin* 2093
Shower of Gold—*Eudora Welty* 2097
Sick Call, A—*Morley Callaghan* 2101
Sick Child, The—*Colette* 2104
Silent Snow, Secret Snow—*Conrad Aiken* 2108
Silver Dish, A—*Saul Bellow* 2112
Silver Mine, The—*Selma Lagerlöf* 2116
Simple Heart, A—*Gustave Flaubert* 2120
Sisters, The—*James Joyce* 2124
Sky Is Gray, The—*Ernest J. Gaines* 2128
Slide Area, The—*Gavin Lambert* 2132

LIST OF TITLES IN VOLUME 5

page

Small, Good Thing, A—*Raymond Carver* 2135
Smallest Woman in the World, The—*Clarice Lispector* 2138
Smell of Death and Flowers, The—*Nadine Gordimer* 2142
Smiles of Konarak, The—*George Dennison* 2146
Snake Charmer, The—*Varlam Shalamov* 2150
Sniper, The—*Liam O'Flaherty* 2154
Sniper, The—*Alan Sillitoe* 2158
Snow-Storm, The—*Leo Tolstoy* 2163
Soldier's Embrace, A—*Nadine Gordimer* 2166
Soldier's Home—*Ernest Hemingway* 2170
Some Like Them Cold—*Ring Lardner* 2173
Some of Us Had Been Threatening Our Friend Colby—
   Donald Barthelme 2177
Something Out There—*Nadine Gordimer* 2182
Sonny's Blues—*James Baldwin* 2186
Sorrow-Acre—*Isak Dinesen* 2190
South, The—*Jorge Luis Borges* 2194
Southern Thruway, The—*Julio Cortázar* 2198
Spinoza of Market Street, The—*Isaac Bashevis Singer* 2202
Split Cherry Tree—*Jesse Stuart* 2206
Spotted Horses—*William Faulkner* 2210
Spring Victory—*Jesse Stuart* 2214
Sredni Vashtar—*Saki* 2217
Station-master, The—*Alexander Pushkin* 2220
Steppe, The—*Anton Chekhov* 2224
Stick of Green Candy, A—*Jane Bowles* 2228
Stone Boy, The—*Gina Berriault* 2232
Storm, The—*Kate Chopin* 2235
Story by Maupassant, A—*Frank O'Connor* 2238
Story of an Hour, The—*Kate Chopin* 2241
Story of My Dovecot, The—*Isaac Babel* 2244
Story of Serapion, The—*E. T. A. Hoffmann* 2248
Strange Ride of Morrowbie Jukes, The—*Rudyard Kipling* 2252
Street of Crocodiles, The—*Bruno Schulz* 2256
Strong Horse Tea—*Alice Walker* 2259
Suicide Club, The—*Robert Louis Stevenson* 2262
Summer Evening—*Kay Boyle* 2267
Summer Night—*Elizabeth Bowen* 2271
Summer of the Beautiful White Horse, The—*William Saroyan* 2275
Sun—*D. H. Lawrence* 2278
Supper at Elsinore, The—*Isak Dinesen* 2281
Supremacy of the Hunza, The—*Joanne Greenberg* 2285

MASTERPLOTS II

page

Sur—*Ursula K. Le Guin* 2288
Sweat—*Zora Neale Hurston* 2293
Swimmer, The—*John Cheever* 2297

Tables of the Law, The—*William Butler Yeats* 2300
Tatuana's Tale—*Miguel Ángel Asturias* 2305
Tell Me a Riddle—*Tillie Olsen* 2308
Tell-Tale Heart, The—*Edgar Allan Poe* 2312
Tender Shoot, The—*Colette* 2316
Territory—*David Leavitt* 2320

MASTERPLOTS II

SHORT STORY
SERIES

THE PRUSSIAN OFFICER

Author: D. H. Lawrence (1885-1930)
Type of plot: Psychological realism
Time of plot: 1914, prior to World War I
Locale: Germany
First published: 1914

> *Principal characters:*
> THE CAPTAIN, about forty years old
> SCHÖNER, his orderly, about twenty-two years old

The Story

In this classic story of sexual repression and tension which, when released, explodes into maddened violence, D. H. Lawrence examines the psychology of two men, both German soldiers. The captain, a Junker aristocrat, tall, muscular, and an expert horseman, is accustomed to domineering his soldiers just as he subjugates horses. He is, however, isolated from the vital life of other soldiers; fortyish and unmarried, he has had occasional mistresses, but has always returned from their arms with greater tension and irritability after he resumes his military duties. Cold, impersonal, harsh, he is subconsciously tormented by repressed homoerotic desire for his young orderly, Schöner, whose name means "more beautiful" in German, and whose vigorous physical presence is "like a warm flame upon the older man's tense, rigid body."

In the most extensive section of the story, part 1, Lawrence develops the theme of conflict between these men, who are locked in a fatal struggle for domination of both body and spirit. With mounting fury, the captain attempts to break down his orderly's will. At one point, he demands to know why Schöner has a piece of pencil stuck behind his ear. When he learns that the young man has been writing a letter to his sweetheart, the officer humiliates the youth. By the end of this section, the two men are driven by hatred and self-loathing.

In part 2, the psychological conflict reaches a climax through physical release in a scene of terrible intensity. Watching with hypnotic fascination while the captain drinks a mug of beer, Schöner is maddened by the sight of the older man's throat; he lunges toward the captain, strangles him against a sharp-edged tree base, and stares in shocked horror—but also satisfaction— as the older man expires.

In part 3, Schöner stumbles through forest brakes to a high mountain range; his vision clouded by delirium, he perceives a landscape transmogrified into sinister colors and vague shapes. Sick from fever, probably "brain fever," he twists in a paroxysm on the grass until his eyes go black, so that he cannot see the distant, gleaming mountains.

In the briefest section, part 4, Schöner is discovered, barely alive, by soldiers who drop his body in horror when they gaze upon the youth's open, black mouth. Later, the remains of the two men are placed at the mortuary, side by side: one rigid and the other young and unused, almost as though he might be roused from a slumber. In death they are not divided.

Themes and Meanings

This story of elemental attraction and repulsion between two men of different temperaments can be understood on at least three levels of meaning. On the simplest level, the captain and his orderly are locked in a struggle for domination on the one hand, for submission on the other. At the beginning of the story, the captain persecutes Schöner; his brutal will focused upon breaking the spirit of the young man, he achieves his goal of mastery in the letter scene, but his victory leaves him depressed rather than elated. In the second section, Schöner, the former victim of persecution, turns about to strangle his adversary, but his brief triumph brings no joy, for in a vertigo of dizzying emotions, he falls prey to delirium and madness.

On a more complex level, the struggle between antagonists is a classic exposition of sadism and masochism, the two forces seemingly opposed but actually correlative. At first, the captain is the sadist; later, Schöner reverses his role to take the captain's. Even so, can either man be understood as a masochist—one who takes psychological pleasure in abuse? Schöner's suffering under the blows of his superior officer cannot be avoided; as a soldier, his power to disobey his leader is limited. Nevertheless, Lawrence allows the reader clues to perceive that, even in his misery, Schöner is mysteriously attracted to the captain. The older man's domination touches in him the quick of his erotic energy. Similarly, Lawrence allows the reader scope to observe how the captain, in his death throes from strangulation, is curiously submissive, as though his body were pressed beneath the weight of his lover.

On the highest level of abstraction, the struggle can be seen as one involving the repressed homoerotic (not explicitly physical homosexual) urges of two men, each transforming desire into hatred, hatred into desire. The captain's erotic attachment to the youth is more nearly evident, although Lawrence's exposition of that compulsion is subtle and indirect. Unable to express openly his suppressed passion for the youth, the captain is filled with self-disgust. Schöner's reciprocation of this passion—which he similarly represses—is less evident, even from a close reading of the text. Nevertheless, by murdering the captain in a way that grotesquely parodies an act of love, he releases himself briefly from the tension of his erotic constraints and is "satisfied"; then, in madness, he destroys himself through repressed grief over the loss of his hated-beloved. In death the two men are laid body to body, their passion never achieved, their vitality wasted.

Style and Technique

In this story of compulsion, Lawrence creates a mood of nearly intolerable tension, broken at last, suddenly and elegiacally, at the conclusion. He sustains this mood, at least in part, by symbolic use of three repeated words: neck (or throat), dryness (or thirst), and the color red (contrasted at times with black or green). The three symbols are presented together in the first section, when the orderly drinks a bottle of red wine, some of which spills upon the tablecloth. Gazing with hatred at this innocent act, the captain subconsciously identifies the wine with blood, the neck and throat of the young man with erotic tenderness. Later, in part 2, the captain's repressed sexuality is symbolized by the dryness of his own throat, which Lawrence describes as "parched." While Schöner watches the captain drink, in a reversal of the earlier scene, his mind snaps, his repressions explode into furious action, and he springs for the older man's throat. Finally, in part 3, the horror of the soldier's panic is represented by his own parched throat, "thirst burning in his brain." The glistening, green corn that he views (contrasted against the image of a woman with a black cloth on her head) represents his decline into madness. Lawrence's symbolism for green in this context is not, as is common in other writers (or, for Lawrence, in other contexts), luxuriant growth or vitality, but irrationality and terror (as in Vincent van Gogh's green billiard table in *The Night Café*, 1888). In the final scene, the three dominant symbols come together. Schöner is discovered desiccated, "his black hair giving off heat under the sun." His mouth is open, but not red with the promise of life; instead it is open (dry) and black. Through these persistent symbols, operating powerfully below the level of awareness, Lawrence unifies the conflicting emotions of the story and concentrates them with great force.

Leslie B. Mittleman

THE PSYCHIATRIST

Author: Joaquim Maria Machado de Assis (1839-1908)
Type of plot: Social satire
Time of plot: Early nineteenth century
Locale: Itaguaí, a town near Rio de Janeiro
First published: "O alienista," 1881-1882 (English translation, 1963)

> *Principal characters:*
> DR. SIMÃO BACAMARTE, the psychiatrist
> DONA EVARISTA DA COSTA E MASCARENHAS, his wife
> CRISPIM SOARES, a druggist, one of Bacamarte's closest
>   friends
> FATHER LOPES, the vicar
> PORFÍRIO CAETANO DAS NEVES (STEWED CORN), a local barber

The Story

According to the town chronicles, Simão Bacamarte, one of the greatest doctors in Europe, turned down two extremely prestigious crown appointments to return to his native Itaguaí and devote his life to science. He settled there and married Dona Evarista, the story goes, not for love, but because she seemed to him a biologically promising specimen to mother his children.

When the children fail to come, Bacamarte dedicates himself to an exhaustive study of sterility. Realizing the therapeutic value of study itself, he hits on psychopathology, a then-unknown specialty in the realm, as a way not only to contribute to science but also to alleviate his disappointment in not having an heir.

He appeals to the town council for aid, and, to support him, it enacts a tax on the plumes on the horses which pull funeral carriages. With this money, Bacamarte erects the Green House, which will be both asylum and laboratory for his studies of mental illness. Within months, the Green House is home for madmen and madwomen of all varieties. Bacamarte becomes so involved in his studies of these pathetic cases that he ignores all else in life, and he finally has to send Evarista on her longed-for journey to Rio de Janeiro to keep her happy. Now free to labor without interruption, he develops a new theory that the slightest sign of lack of equilibrium is proof of madness, and by the time Evarista returns from Rio de Janeiro, the Green House is full to the rafters with people who have loaned away an inheritance, demonstrated excessive interest in a house ("petrophilia"), or are unfailingly polite.

Almost everyone in town by now has a relative or loved one behind bars, and a minor revolt led by the barber Porfírio (called "Stewed Corn") thus swells to a mob and storms Bacamarte's house. A troop of dragoons arrives to quell the disorder, but many of its number defect to the "Stewed Corners," and in a matter of minutes the barber has taken over the town and deposed the council. Porfírio goes to see Bacamarte and offers a compromise, which prompts another barber, João Pina, to depose Porfírio. Government troops finally arrive to restore order, whereupon Bacamarte commits Porfírio and fifty of his followers to the asylum. Within months, the psychiatrist discovers some flaw in most of the population, including his wife (who, he finds, exhibits "vestimania," or excessive preoccupation with clothing), his friend Crispim Soares, and the president of the town council. With four-fifths of the population interned, he comes to the realization that his theory is flawed, and he now decides that complete equilibrium, not its lack, is proof of madness. He releases the patients and starts his search for persons of irreproachable virtue, starting with Father Lopes (the vicar) and the only honest councilman, and ending with Porfírio, who has refused to lead a new revolt.

Such chronic virtue, the psychiatrist soon discovers, is easily cured, and in the end he has effected a cure on every one of the perfectly balanced persons in town—until he realizes that he himself is above reproach. He interns himself in the Green House and dies before finding a cure for his indefectibility.

Themes and Meanings

The arbitrary line which society draws to separate those mad from those sane is clearly the essence of this story, but the story is also an ironic study of credulity, vanity, and humankind's chronic weakness for simple solutions. The general theme of madness versus sanity has a long literary history, and it is one that Machado de Assis explored in other short stories and at least two of his major novels. Since the theme is simply one of the declensions of the larger theme of appearance versus reality, it is probably fair to say, in fact, that it appears in some form in most of his fiction.

In the context of time and place, the irony is especially acute, since Brazil was a country in which faith in the ability of science to solve any problem had great currency in the late nineteenth century. Indeed, positivism became a sort of second national religion, and it contributed the national motto "Order and Progress," which still appears on the Brazilian flag and which still seems to hold great appeal for Brazilians. Critics have noted the particular relevance of Machado de Assis' treatment of the psychiatrist here because of Brazilians' fondness for, and obeisance to, any high-sounding credential.

Bacamarte initially appears to be not much more than a charlatan, but since he is not even aware of the misery which results from his unremitting egotism, he is oddly naïve as a villain. What he turns out to be is a sort of embodiment of the eccentric but dedicated scientific spirit, ready to make any sacrifice in the name of the advancement of knowledge. Since, like all the other characters, his actions are at the same time guided by his colossal vanity, the story stands not only as an ironic inquiry into the mind of a megalomaniac but also as a commentary on the chronic human problem of self-delusion.

Style and Technique

Machado de Assis is considered the most "English" of Brazilian writers because of his subtle and often biting sense of humor and because of his laconic and understated diction. In part for the same reasons, he is a writer almost impossible to insert neatly into general observations of Brazilian literary history; his novels and short stories have none of the quality of datedness which is so evident in the works of most of his contemporaries. Though uncommonly long for a Brazilian short story, "The Psychiatrist" is an example of Machado de Assis' skill as an illusionist. The story is ostensibly drawn from a documentary source, the town's chronicles, which makes of the entire tale a single preterit narrative block, a piece of history. Though there are numerous characters, only one, Bacamarte, is of real importance. Time is repeatedly compressed by summaries in which months of time are reduced to a single line. These manipulations all contribute to a very tight narrative scheme which in fact obeys the classic reductionist form of the genre.

Machado de Assis is also a master stylist. His narrator is privy to the contents of the chronicles on which he bases the story, but he never betrays any of the credulity the characters all show as a fundamental trait. The narrator consistently employs euphemisms, multiple adjectivation, and pseudophilosophical asides to create the illusion of an elegant and cultured style, but what these devices really create is a narrative style just a shade too grand for the implausible sequence of events. The result is that Bacamarte (the name means "blunderbuss") is constantly seen in the light of a not altogether gentle irony, so that at the end, the cause of his death, like the cause of everything else, seems to be a simple case of incurable vanity.

Jon S. Vincent

THE PUPIL

Author: Henry James (1843-1916)
Type of plot: Domestic realism
Time of plot: The 1850's
Locale: Nice, Venice, and Paris
First published: 1891

> *Principal characters:*
> PEMBERTON, the tutor
> MORGAN MOREEN, his adolescent pupil
> MR. MOREEN, Morgan's father
> MRS. MOREEN, Morgan's mother

The Story

Needing money, Pemberton agrees to become the resident tutor of the eleven-year-old Morgan Moreen, whose heart condition prevents him from attending school. Pemberton's initial impression of Morgan is not favorable; though the child seems intelligent, he is not physically attractive and looks as if "he might be unpleasant."

Soon, though, Morgan is the only member of the family whom Pemberton does like. He must threaten to leave before the Moreens pay him even a portion of the salary they owe him, and eventually he tutors for free simply because he has grown fond of his pupil. They become so close that Pemberton suggests that they "ought to go off and live somewhere together."

Morgan is as eager as Pemberton to leave his family, whom both recognize as adventurers, gypsies who repeatedly move from city to city and hotel to hotel because they cannot or will not pay their bills. The family finances eventually become so desperate that, in Venice, Mrs. Moreen asks Pemberton to lend her sixty francs. Pemberton can only laugh. "Where in the world do you suppose I should get sixty francs?" he asks.

Immediately afterward, Pemberton is invited to return to England to tutor a rich but dull youth whose parents want to prepare him for Balliol College, Oxford. Pemberton accepts the appointment, at Morgan's urging, because he hopes to earn enough money to allow him to support Morgan.

The new post does indeed pay well, but Pemberton abandons it when Mrs. Moreen writes to him that Morgan is desperately ill. Arriving in Paris, Pemberton realizes that he has been tricked; Morgan has indeed been ill, but not so "desperately" as his mother pretended.

Despite the deception, Pemberton resumes his nonpaying post as tutor, though without enthusiasm. One afternoon in the winter, Pemberton and Morgan go for a walk. When they return, they find the Moreen family in turmoil, for they are being evicted for failing to pay their hotel bills. Mr. and

Mrs. Moreen offer Morgan to Pemberton, for they no longer want the expense of rearing the child.

For Morgan, this rejection by his parents is the fulfillment of his dreams. He has never liked their ways and has yearned to go off with his tutor. His joy, however, is short-lived; the excitement kills him. True to their characters to the last, Mrs. Moreen blames Pemberton for having taken the child on too long a walk, and her husband claims that Morgan's heart was broken over the prospect of leaving his parents.

Themes and Meanings

Morgan's death sadly vindicates Pemberton's observation that his pupil is "too clever to live." Morgan is the most perceptive of the story's characters, and that clear-sightedness produces both his charm and his undoing. His parents and siblings see and feel nothing and never show embarrassment. Even when their world crumbles about them at the end of the story, they feel no shame; they bear the death of Morgan like "men of the world." In contrast, as soon as Morgan realizes that his parents are being evicted, he blushes "to the roots of his hair" at their "public exposure."

For Morgan's parents, life is surface and appearance. They are always "looking out," which means that they are never introspective. Their only concern is to make a good show. Hence, they spend no money on Morgan's clothes: He never appears in public. Their very name suggests this focus on the outside, for moreen is a coarse fabric with a smooth exterior.

Even Pemberton, supposedly Morgan's tutor, proves himself less perceptive than his charge. When he is first hired, he fails to draw any conclusions from the fact that Mrs. Moreen says nothing about paying him, nor does he realize that her soiled gloves suggest the state of the Moreen family finances. When Morgan interrupts this first interview to say, "We don't mind what anything costs—we live awfully well," Pemberton does not understand that the Moreens care nothing for cost because they never pay their bills.

Pemberton is more sympathetic than the elder Moreens. He willingly divides his limited funds with his pupil, even buying clothes for him since Morgan's parents will not. Yet he does not measure up to his pupil in wisdom or generosity. Morgan is prepared to give Pemberton his very life, but Pemberton does not want it.

Pemberton realizes that the Moreens cannot continue to live like gypsies indefinitely, and he expects that when the end comes, each family member will try to save himself without regard to the needs of the others. He is correct in this assessment; in the final scene, the older son, Ulick, has already vanished, the daughters are nowhere in sight, and the parents try to dispose of Morgan without consulting him. Yet Pemberton, too, behaves like "a man of the world." He is not pleased when Morgan finally is offered to him because he worries about practical matters: "Where shall I take you, and how?" He does not relish the role of "a floating spar in case of a wreck." Though his generosity is not put to the test, one is not certain that Pemberton would have accepted the child.

Early in their relationship, when Pemberton claims to find Morgan's parents charming, the child, recognizing that his tutor is merely trying to be polite, tells him, "You're a jolly old humbug!" In the end, Pemberton does prove to be a humbug; after raising Morgan's hopes of escape, he shrinks from the opportunity and responsibility.

Style and Technique

James tells the story objectively from Pemberton's perspective, never intruding his own opinions. Yet irony abounds to highlight the discrepancies between appearance and reality. Thus, Pemberton accepts the position of tutor because he needs money to pay his hotel bill, yet in the course of his employment he will, together with his employers, avoid many another such charge. Though Pemberton is nominally the tutor and Morgan the pupil, the child proves to be the more clever of the two.

He also seems older and more experienced. Indeed, while he is the youngest member of the household, he notes that his older brother imitates him, and he refers to himself as if he were the patriarch of the family: "I'll take their affairs in hand; I'll marry my sisters," he reassures Pemberton. Such a self image is not wholly fanciful, since his parents do behave like irresponsible children and only he shows concern for their reputation.

Yet another irony is Morgan's weak heart. Of all the characters, he is the most generous. He repeatedly urges Pemberton to leave his family because he knows that he never will earn any money from them, and he is willing to give away his very life. All the others are more or less self-centered; even Pemberton's heart is not as great as Morgan's.

The numerous ironies not only emphasize the deceptiveness of appearances but also add an element of humor that diminishes the sense of tragedy. Pemberton laughs when he is asked to give money to the people who should be paying him. Pemberton agrees to work for free if he can tell Morgan that the Moreens are not paying him; immediately afterward, Pemberton discovers that Morgan already knows this "secret." These repeated reversals distance the reader by giving him a sense of superior knowledge or insight. He is thus able to judge the characters dispassionately.

Perhaps James has in this way introduced a final irony. The reader responds to Morgan's death, as the Moreens do, like "a man of the world." Has James tricked his audience into becoming like these unsavory characters? Pemberton succumbs to their spell; he really does find them charming and finally behaves like them. Since Morgan's death does not seem tragic, is the reader, too, composed of moreen?

Joseph Rosenblum

THE PURLOINED LETTER

Author: Edgar Allan Poe (1809-1849)
Type of plot: Mystery
Time of plot: Nineteenth century
Locale: Paris, France
First published: Unauthorized, 1844; enlarged and authorized, 1845

> *Principal characters:*
> C. AUGUSTE DUPIN, an amateur detective and friend to the
> narrator
> THE NARRATOR, a friend to Dupin who serves as the auditor
> for most of the details of the narrative
> MONSIEUR G——, the prefect of the Parisian police, who has
> failed to secure the stolen letter
> MINISTER D——, the one who steals the letter and from
> whom Dupin steals it in turn

The Story

The unnamed narrator and his friend, C. Auguste Dupin, are interrupted by the intrusion of the prefect of the Parisian police, who bursts in to tell the tale of the theft of a compromising letter from the bedroom of the queen by the unscrupulous Minister D——. The contents of the letter are never made known, but the prefect avers that he has been charged with retrieving it, and he further reveals that so long as the letter remains in the minister's possession, he will hold the queen in his power. The prefect details to the narrator and Dupin the extent of his searches of the minister's apartments, and confesses that even though he and his assistants have searched in every possible place, leaving no place unexamined, all of their efforts have been in vain. The letter remains concealed in a place undiscoverable by anyone.

Dupin questions the prefect closely about the methods and the places of his search, suggesting that it would appear that the letter is no longer in the minister's apartments. He nevertheless advises the prefect to search them once more, inquiring as he does about the exact physical appearance of the letter, as well as its contents. The prefect departs in despair, and the story shifts immediately to his return to Dupin's apartment a month later, at which time the letter remains, as far as the prefect can discern, in the possession of the minister. Dupin inquires as to the amount which the prefect would be willing to give to possess the letter, and when the latter names the sum of fifty thousand francs, Dupin offers to produce the letter for the sum named. He does so, much to the astonishment of both prefect and narrator (who is present at this second meeting as well), and after the departure of the prefect, tells the narrator how he came to recover the letter from the minister.

The secret of Dupin's success, he asserts, lay in his capacity to read the intentions of the minister more accurately than the Parisian police. Briefly, Dupin realizes that rather than hiding the letter in some ingenious contraption or out-of-the-way place, the minister would realize that all such efforts would be fruitless in concealing the item from the searches that were bound to ensue upon his having stolen it. Consequently, Dupin surmises that the minister would hide the letter in plain sight. In a visit to the latter's apartments, and under the cover of wearing dark glasses, Dupin surveys the sitting room and notices the letter dangling from a ribbon in the center of the mantelpiece, even though its outward appearance is such as to deny this possibility. Leaving a gold snuffbox in the minister's quarters, Dupin thus provides himself with an occasion to return on the following day, at which time he arranges for a diversion that allows him deftly to substitute a facsimile of the letter for the authentic article and thus to possess himself of the letter and earn the reward. The tale ends with Dupin's account of his previous relations with the minister, and the revelation of the message which Dupin had inscribed on the inside of the facsimile. The words are a citation from an eighteenth century play about the legend of the house of Atreus: "So funereal a design, if it is not worthy of Atreus, is worthy of Thyestes."

Themes and Meanings

"The Purloined Letter" has been the subject of considerable commentary, most interestingly as the bone of contention between two of the more prominent contemporary French thinkers, the philosopher Jacques Derrida and the psychoanalyst Jacques Lacan, who have argued about the story's pertinence to the themes and significance of psychoanalysis. It would require considerable space to lay out the complicated arguments that each of these thinkers mounts in reading Poe's tale, but one could characterize this debate briefly as signifying the difference between a reading of the story as presenting readers with a definite and finitely circumscribed set of meanings (roughly Lacan's position) and one that denies categorically, on behalf of Poe's story, the possibility that any definitive interpretation of the elements in this or any narrative can ever be produced. One could say, perhaps too schematically, that Derrida's claim rests primarily upon the fact that the precise contents of the letter are never revealed, and that therefore the letter itself becomes an emblem of the indeterminacy in meaning which the tale enacts. Certainly the central tension in the story between the calculating and rationally motivated Dupin and the more shadowy narrator—whose relation to Dupin is established in prior stories, "The Mystery of Marie Rôget" and "The Murders in the Rue Morgue"—as well as the difficulty of knowing precisely how to apply the closing citation to the case of the minister and his actions, suggests that Lacan's more or less straightforward symbolic interpretation of the tale as an allegory of sexuality misses many of the subtlest discriminations which the narrative establishes. Once one has opened up the possibility that all is not as it seems—and this is the very possibility upon which the plot turns, since it is the appearance of the letter itself which is crucial to its concealment by the minister—it is not simple to begin to pin down the meaning of individual elements. Nor is it absolutely certain at the end that Dupin has in fact delivered the original letter to the prefect, since he might, with the knowledge of the original's contents, have prepared a facsimile and retained the original for purposes which he does not here reveal. In truth, the reader knows little more about the facts of the matter at the end than he did at the beginning, although he has been initiated into an astonishingly intricate web of intrigues, stratagems, and motivations.

Style and Technique

Like many of Poe's tales, this one is written in a complex idiom that smacks of archaism—and did so even at the moment of his writing. The language tends to be somewhat stilted, and the insertion here of foreign phrases (mostly, although not exclusively, French) puts the situation and the characters at some distance from the average reader. Poe is careful to set the tale in a distant and alien locale, the ambience of which is minutely evoked, with precise references to quarters of Paris, to articles of clothing and furniture, and to the whole unfamiliar business of court intrigue. The net result of these distancing effects is to render the tale more exotic, and to make the preternatural powers of observation and ratiocination exhibited by Dupin appear plausible in the context. To the extent that the world of the story is clearly not one familiar to any of Poe's readers, contemporary with the tale or subsequent, it can be argued that the extraordinary events of the plot seem less fantastic. In such a world, such characters may be said to make sense.

The narrative itself is so constructed as to reinforce the sense of mystery which pervades this world, as the position of the narrator remains entirely obscure from beginning to end. He never reveals anything substantive about himself, and one might surmise that he is merely a formal device for getting the story told, a means for introducing the real protagonist, Dupin, and for giving the latter an occasion to speak, since it would be unlikely, given the discretion of Dupin's character, that he would readily tell his own story. Yet one is led always to speculate on the motivations of this character, on his precise relationship to Dupin, and on the degree of knowledge to which he himself can with justice lay a certain claim. It would be mistaken simply to slot him into the position of the Sherlock Holmes foil, the ingenuous Dr. Watson. By framing his tale in the discourse of this elusive narrator, Poe inaugurated what would become an important tradition in European and American short fiction, visible, for example, in the works of Henry James, where the relationship between narrator and what is narrated is often problematic and somewhat mysterious. While it is generally thought that the genre of detective or mystery fiction, which Poe with considerable warrant has often been said to have initiated, issues in definite solutions to the crimes or other enigmas that form the basis of the plot, one is left wondering in the case of Poe just what it is that has been revealed. Certainly one would want to know the contents of the purloined letter of the title, but this is precisely what is never revealed. It may be a mark of Poe's genius that he recognized as an intrinsic property of narratives what Diane Arbus once remarked of photographs: that they are secrets about secrets; the more they tell you, the less you know. Such might be the very motto of Dupin, or even of the narrator, for it is in the relation between their two tellings that the structure of this story resides.

Michael Sprinker

THE QUEEN OF SPADES

Author: Alexander Pushkin (1799-1837)
Type of plot: Psychological realism
Time of plot: The 1830's
Locale: St. Petersburg
First published: "Pikovaya dama," 1834 (English translation, 1896)

>Principal characters:
>   HERMANN, the protagonist, a Russian officer of German
>   descent
>   THE COUNTESS, an aged noblewoman
>   ELIZAVETA IVANOVNA, the poor ward of the Countess
>   PRINCE PAVEL TOMSKY, the grandson of the Countess
>   CHEKALINSKY, the proprietor of a gambling parlor

The Story

As the story opens, a group of young military officers are playing cards into the early morning. One officer remarks that Hermann, an officer in the Engineer Corps, likes to watch the others play, but he himself does not play. The prudent and industrious Hermann replies that he is attempting to build a fortune and does not want to risk the essential in order to gain the superfluous. Prince Pavel Tomsky changes the conversation by telling the story of his grandmother, a strong-willed socialite when she was younger. While on a trip to France, the young beauty lost a large sum at cards, a sum which her long-suffering husband refused to give her in order to honor her debt. The Countess ran to a friend, the Count St. Germain, who gave her the secret of victory at cards. The Countess returned to the tables the next evening, regained the money which she had lost, and settled her debts.

The officers who have listened to the story react to it in different ways. One believes that the story is fantasy, another that the cards were marked, and a third that the victory was a result of pure chance. Although Tomsky cannot explain what happened, he believes that a secret exists and that his grandmother has been derelict in not passing it on to her family. On this note, the officers break up their card game as the sun begins to rise.

The narrative changes to the Countess, who is now an elderly lady unable to do much but terrorize her domestic staff. Elizaveta Ivanovna is a ward of the Countess and completely dependent upon the old lady for her sustenance. Elizaveta's life is difficult, as she endures the conflicting orders and irrational opinions of the Countess and can find no way out of her predicament.

One afternoon, Elizaveta looks out the window as she is sewing and spies a young officer standing on the corner and staring at her window. It is Hermann, who was strongly impressed by Tomsky's story about his grandmother and wishes to learn the secret of the cards before the Countess dies. He stands on the corner and dreams of ways to enter the house and confront the Countess. When he notices Elizaveta Ivanovna at the window, an idea comes to him. He sends letters to her, some taken word-for-word from German novels, in which he professes his love and importunes her for a meeting. After an initial reluctance, Elizaveta Ivanovna, viewing the young officer as a potential deliverer from her dreary existence with the Countess, concocts an elaborate plan to let the young officer into the house and into her room for a private meeting.

All goes according to plan; Hermann sneaks into the house while the Countess and Elizaveta are at a ball. Instead of going to Elizaveta's room, however, he enters the room of the Countess, hiding until her return. Hermann surprises the old lady and pleads for the secret. The Countess refuses to divulge the secret, and Hermann, losing patience, threatens her with a pistol. Seeing the gun, the Countess gives a start and dies, presumably of fright. Hermann sneaks off to Elizaveta's room, informing her of events and explaining why he had gone to the Countess' room. Elizaveta is broken-hearted, as she realizes that Hermann was cultivating her friendship in order to gain money, not because of love.

Although Hermann's conscience is dulled by his obsession and his main regret is the loss of the secret, he still feels obligated to attend the old lady's funeral. As Hermann looks into the casket to pay his last respects, the Countess seems to open her eyes and wink at him. Taken by surprise, he falls backward to the floor and has to be helped up. Unnerved by this experience, he decides to eat a good meal and drive away his fright with wine.

After coming home and falling into a deep sleep induced by the wine, Hermann awakens at three in the morning. He looks at the window and sees a face looking at him. The face disappears; then Hermann hears the door to his anteroom being opened. A ghostly apparition slides into his room, and Hermann realizes that the Countess is paying him a visit. The old lady tells a frightened Hermann that she has been commanded to reveal to him the secret which he desired: He is to play a three, seven, and ace three nights in a row, and then never play again. The apparition disappears; Hermann, now fully awake, finds his valet asleep and the outer door locked. Was it a vision or a dream?

Hermann's life now takes a new turn. Thoughts of the Countess are displaced by an obsession with three, seven, ace; even women and inanimate objects begin to look like one of the three numbers. Hermann debates whether to resign from the army and go to the great gambling halls of Paris; meanwhile, a renowned Moscow gambler, Chekalinsky, opens a gambling parlor in St. Petersburg. His decision thus made for him, Hermann is introduced to Chekalinsky by a friend and is allowed to play. He bets his patrimony, forty-seven thousand rubles, and plays a three. Hermann wins, and Chekalinsky, ever affable, pays the young officer. The large bet of the first evening attracts a small crowd when Hermann returns on the second evening, places ninety-four thousand rubles on the table, and wins with a seven. A bit distressed, Chekalinsky pays Hermann.

On the third evening, Hermann returns to the gambling hall. He places all of his winnings on the table and prepares to play. The other gamblers cease their play and surround the table of Hermann and Chekalinsky, who is visibly nervous. The suspense builds as the play commences. Hermann, desiring to play the ace, inadvertently and possibly through excitement pulls out the Queen of Spades by mistake and loses everything. As he stares at the Queen, it seems to wink at Hermann, who remembers the wink of the Countess in the casket. He leaves the hall as play resumes, and Chekalinsky begins smiling again. In an afterword, Pushkin informs the reader that Hermann is now insane, confined to a hospital. Elizaveta has married and is supporting a poor ward.

Themes and Meanings

Alexander Pushkin's "The Queen of Spades" is considered one of the seminal short stories of Russian literature, the beginning of a rich tradition. The main theme, however, is a moral borrowed from the ancient heritage of Latin and Greek literature: the golden mean. Hermann is a Russified German, a device in Russian literature used to depict the virtues of prudence, moderation, and hard work—the opposite of another stock device, the Russian who goes to extremes and lives life to the fullest. Obsession with winning money deflects Hermann from the correct path and disaster ensues; he goes broke and mad at the same time. The obsession also kills his humanity as he callously misuses Elizaveta, is responsible for the death of the Countess, and then represses any feeling of remorse which he felt for this act.

Another view sees the story as the depiction of the power of the supernatural. If man tempts fate, then he is liable to punishment. The game is a symbol of life governed by fate; Hermann tries to short-circuit the process by using the secret and is destroyed.

A third view sees the Queen of Spades as the Countess' revenge upon Hermann for being frightened to death. Perhaps all three views are valid interpretations of the tale.

Style and Technique

Pushkin lived in a time of transition for Russian literature, from Romanticism to realism. This story is a Romantic tale of fantasy told in a realistic manner. The author employs the techniques of classicism that would become the staple of the realistic short story: economy of words, elimination of superfluous detail, and emphasis upon a single theme. As a result, the story moves quickly and keeps the reader's attention directed to the main point.

The interest of the reader is also kept alive by the inclusion of elements of fantasy, especially the vision of the Countess after her death. It is unclear whether the Countess really appears or whether the drunken Hermann is merely imagining the entire episode. If the vision is a figment of his imagination, how is he able to win the first two times? Is it mere chance? Pushkin leaves clues, such as repeating, "It seems as. . . ." The puzzle is not conclusively answered, however, and each reader is able to draw whatever conclusion he or she wishes. By means of this technique, Pushkin not only retains one's interest during the story but also keeps one thinking about the story long after the original reading.

Philip Maloney

THE RAGMAN'S DAUGHTER

Author: Alan Sillitoe (1928-   )
Type of plot: Social criticism
Time of plot: The 1950's and 1960's
Locale: Nottingham, England
First published: 1963

> *Principal characters:*
> TONY, the narrator, a loader in a warehouse, formerly a petty
>   thief
> DORIS, the schoolgirl daughter of a scrap merchant

The Story

As Tony, the narrator of the story, is leaving the warehouse where he works as a cheese loader, the police question him about a suitcase that he is carrying out. It is empty, as it happens—returned by a friend who had borrowed it and had been hoping to keep it for himself.

This short opening episode, embellished with some pithy references to the police, economically establishes that Tony and his workmates are no respecters of private property and that the police are their common enemy. Tony elaborates his attitude toward the law in a comic account of cheese stealing and of the relish with which he and his family savor the stolen food, thus revealing himself as a married man who is poorly paid and has a history of lawbreaking.

He then looks back to his childhood and explains his development as a habitual thief, starting with his experience in the infants' school when, sensing something morally wrong with the idea of a "buying and selling" lesson, he pocketed the token coins without detection or punishment. Subsequent childish experiments taught him that, although "money was trouble," it was safer to steal money than things, and that it was best to keep silent. Petty thieving soon became a way of life.

Tony's account of the delight with which he used to plunge the goods he had stolen into the river demonstrates his contempt for possessions and consumerism and, by implication, for an unjust and hypocritical society. He expresses his notions of an ideal society, in which everyone is equally provided for and equally treated, in the only terms with which he is familiar: like a prison, but with everyone free.

The evolution of his antiauthoritarian philosophy is essential to an understanding of his relationship with Doris, whom, in the recollected part of the narrative, he meets at a fish-and-chip shop, and who agrees to accompany him on his thieving "expeditions" (her word). Doris, who is still at school, has no need to steal; her father is a prosperous scrap merchant. She does it "for kicks."

From their first joint expedition, Tony recognizes Doris as the ideal partner in crime. Unlike the lads who have occasionally joined him, she is deft, quiet, and efficient. The excitement of the theft is transformed into sexual excitement: Tony is in love.

The quality of his love is highlighted in a dramatic description of Doris' arrival on horseback at the backyard of his run-down street, to the astonishment of the neighbors. Doris, "all clean and golden-haired on that shining horse," as he recalls in a later part of the story, symbolizes Tony's aspirations for a freer life-style—something of the reverse, perhaps, of the knight in shining armor whisking the lady away in traditional legend.

Tony and Doris get into the habit of depositing the goods they steal in back gardens or through mailboxes, to give the finders happy surprises. With his accumulation of stolen money, Tony buys a motorcycle and whisks Doris off for rides in the industry-scarred countryside—a token of his dream of a shared country life with her.

The sequence of successful expeditions, in which their love is consummated with mounting passion, leads to a heady climax, which takes place in the storeroom of a shoe shop they have broken into. Inching his way around in the dark, Tony finds the till and proceeds to fill his pockets with bank notes.

Suddenly Doris switches on the lights. She tries on shoe after shoe, tossing them across the room as she rejects them, while Tony acts as her wild and willing shop assistant. It is a gesture of defiance, a consummation of "living for kicks." When Tony, sensing danger, switches the lights off, the darkness brings them back to reality. With the inevitable arrival of a policeman, Tony's ability to ensure that Doris escapes and that the bank notes are "posted" in the mailbox of a nearby house before he is arrested shows that his code of morality can be sustained even at the moment of crisis.

During three years at Borstal (a reform institution for young offenders), he hears nothing from Doris and is tortured by doubt about whether she—and the liberating future she represents—will still be there when he is released. The news, on his release, that she has been married, has given birth to his son, and has been killed with her husband in a motorcycle crash is a mortal blow to his aspirations. It sends him on a senseless thieving trip which lands him back in jail. In the last incident of the recollected narrative, he glimpses his son, playing in the woods with Doris' father—a poignant reminder of what might have been.

This brings Tony back to the present and explains why, despite his challenging attitude toward life, he has become a conventional family man and has "gone straight"—except that, like his workmates, he keeps himself, his wife, and his two children eating well by stealing food from the warehouse.

Themes and Meanings

Like many of the antiheroes of Alan Sillitoe's early stories and novels, Tony is a young, working-class man who is alienated by the harsh conditions of his neighborhood and the false values of the world outside.

Social class is a key element in the story, as its title emphasizes. Had Doris been, for example, a banker's daughter, she would have been beyond Tony's reach and would not, in any case, have visited the fish-and-chip shop, a central feature of the British working-class life-style. Her father's trade is also a working-class symbol; Tony can identify with and even envy a person who started out as a humble rag-and-bone man and grew prosperous on other people's throwaways.

Although Tony has developed his own moral code in direct conflict with orthodox morality, he is not an outsider. References to a shared class attitude to private property run throughout the narrative, from the man at the beginning who had hoped to keep the borrowed suitcase, to the woman toward the end who, finding the stolen bank notes pushed through her mailbox, spends the money on pleasure (as Tony rejoices to discover later) and tells everyone that it came from a loving relative. Tony carries this attitude to its extended conclusion by destroying or giving away the consumer goods he steals.

At the time of his narrative, he has learned enough to be sharply critical of contemporary society—the inequalities, dishonesties, and obsession with possessions which he has observed. Unlike Sillitoe, however, he does not think in political terms. When he describes his vision of an ideal society and adds that he does not know what it would be called, Sillitoe is in effect inviting the reader to make a political judgment by recognizing a naïve version of socialism.

The story is both a criticism of contemporary society and a moving personal tragedy. The feeling that life could and should be different runs all through Tony's account of himself and shapes his private dream of a wandering country life with Doris, with her crisp, cool looks, her yellow hair, and her liberated spirit. After her death, he recalls the moment when he switched out the lights in the shoe shop. "We both went into the dark," he says, "and never came out." The ultimate tragedy, in Sillitoe's terms, is not that Doris died, but that Tony's aspirations died with her.

Style and Technique

Sillitoe's use of the first-person narrative form establishes the story's tone of gritty realism, which was a strong characteristic of the upsurge of regional literature in the 1950's and 1960's—a movement in which Sillitoe played a leading role.

Born and brought up in the industrial, mid-England city of Nottingham, Sillitoe is one of the few contemporary British writers with a solidly working-class upbringing and work experience. His reproduction of the local patterns of speech is therefore very authentic.

He uses two styles of vernacular in this story: The pithy, working-class slang and idiom of Tony's direct narrative is a little more self-conscious than the broad Nottingham dialect in which Tony recounts his bantering conversations with neighbors and friends.

The idiomatic narrative style that Sillitoe has given to Tony is very economical. Ideas are encapsulated in a few choice words, and each sentence is taut with meaning. Tony is able to share his assumptions about life with the reader by using crisp, vivid similes which are culled from his own experiences but have universal nuances.

The use of Tony as narrator also enables Sillitoe to present him from two points of view—as Tony sees himself in the very specific context of his own experiences and comprehensions, and as he appears in the broader and more generalized context which Sillitoe, through occasional small nudges, invites the reader to provide.

Nina Hibbin

THE RAID
A Volunteer's Story

Author: Leo Tolstoy (1828-1910)
Type of plot: Romantic realism
Time of plot: The 1850's
Locale: The Russian Caucasus
First published: "Nabeg: Razskaz volontera," 1853 (English translation, 1909)

> *Principal characters:*
> THE NARRATOR, unnamed
> CAPTAIN PAVEL HLOPOV, a Russian army officer stationed in
> the Caucasus
> MARYA IVANOVNA HLOPOV, the captain's aged mother
> ENSIGN ANATOLE IVANOVICH ALANIN, a soldier in the captain's
> regiment
> IVAN MIHAILOVICH HASANOV, a Russian cavalry officer
> LIEUTENANT ROSENKRANZ, a Russian officer

The Story

The anonymous narrator begins by describing how a certain Captain Pavel Hlopov visits him in his hut in the Russian Caucasus to inform him of an impending Russian military action against the native Tatar tribesmen. As a consequence of their conversation, the two men begin to discuss the concept of bravery. Captain Hlopov offers a definition of bravery which reminds the narrator of Plato's definition; the captain says quite concisely: "He's a brave man who behaves as he ought." The narrator adds that the man who risks his life out of vanity, or curiosity, or greed cannot be called brave, while a man who refuses to face danger out of duty to his family or on conscientious grounds cannot be called a coward.

The narrator is a former neighbor of Captain Hlopov's mother, whom he visited before coming to the Caucasus. The old lady, Marya Ivanovna Hlopov, worships her son and has prayed for him since he went into the service eighteen years ago. The captain was wounded severely four times but has kept this information from his mother, who thinks that he has been safe all the while. Although the captain rarely writes and never visits his mother, he does send her money every year. Before the narrator departed for the Caucasus, he had agreed to deliver a black religious amulet from the mother to her son. When he arrives in the Caucasus, the narrator delivers the gift, which deeply touches the captain.

The next day, at four in the morning, the captain arouses the narrator and invites him to join the military operation. As they ride, the narrator is impressed by the splendid scenery and fauna and flora of the mountain setting. A young ensign in the captain's regiment, Alanin by name, overtakes them and rides by, delighted at his first chance to be in a real battle. The young soldier's romantic attitude toward battle mildly annoys Captain Hlopov.

The narrator gives a detailed profile of a Lieutenant Rosenkranz, a romantic type who often assumes a kind of Byronic pose—distant, contradictory, and misunderstood by those around him. The narrator notes with interest the prebattle activities of the soldiers—playing cards, telling jokes and stories, and singing. "It was as though no one could conceive that some of them were destined not to come back along that road."

The narrator describes in detail the life at the Russian fort and is struck again by the casual attitude of everybody toward the upcoming battle against the Tatars. Nature in the mountains is so picturesque and splendidly romantic that it is hard to imagine the possibility of danger and death so close at hand. He sums up the paradox: "Everything evil in the heart of man ought, one would think, to vanish in contact with Nature, in which beauty and goodness find their most direct expression."

Soon Tatar torchlights are seen in the distance, signaling other tribesmen that the Russians are approaching. The Russians ford a river and are soon exchanging gunfire with the Tatars. The Tatars fall back, and the Russians advance, shelling a Tatar village with artillery.

The Tatar village is sacked by the Russians, and one old Tatar is taken prisoner. As the Russians advance beyond the village, the enemy's resistance becomes stronger. The real confrontation begins. Lieutenant Rosenkranz and the young Ensign Alanin are in the thick of battle and are enjoying it. Only Captain Hlopov calls a Russian retreat and offers no excuses or explanations for his seemingly cowardly actions. "This, to my thinking, is the peculiar and noble characteristic of Russian courage," observes the narrator.

As if fulfilling the captain's prophecy that the ensign's fear of nothing is immature and foolish, Alanin is wounded and carried off for treatment. The doctor is not able to stablilize the young man, and Ensign Alanin dies. The detachment marches back to the fortress singing in the moonlit Caucasus night, their mission accomplished.

Themes and Meanings

In "The Raid" (subtitled "A Volunteer's Story"), Tolstoy offers a fictional elaboration of Plato's theory of courage. For Tolstoy, real bravery is in the knowledge of what one should and what one should not fear. Contrary to more typically romantic notions of bravery, in which the hero is the one who goes against exaggerated odds with no rational thought of the consequences (as does, for example, Ensign Alanin), Tolstoy defines bravery as the ability to size up a situation and act logically (as does Captain Hlopov). More elaborate, but similar, examples of Tolstoy's theory of courage are found frequently in his later fiction, especially in *War and Peace* (1865-1869).

In a broader sense, "The Raid" is a compelling account of men's fear, anxiety, and cowardice in the face of death. Tolstoy is particularly interested in describing different men's reactions to war and combat, especially how they deal with the ever-present possibility of being killed. Although Tolstoy himself later became a pacifist and an active opponent of war and the use of force that war represents, there is in "The Raid" praise (sometimes subtle, more often overt) for such values as patriotism, loyalty to country and comrades in arms, and duty. Tolstoy moralizes very little about the horrors of war. Instead he approaches war as a kind of necessary category of history. As such, it is philosophically neutral, beyond good and evil. Although the lives of some are winnowed away in war, those who survive have added another dimension of valuable experience to their personal lives, which have been enhanced by the exposure to danger and uncertainty, ultimately resulting in an increased love of life.

Style and Technique

The Caucasus frequently served as a backdrop for Russian Romantic writers in the early decades of the nineteenth century. Tolstoy, well aware of this tradition, infused his lyrical passages describing nature with a touch of irony, trying to bring out the paradox of war and killing in a perfectly peaceful and majestic setting. The narrator describes the local color in vivid detail but is somehow unable to reconcile completely the gratuitous killing and carnage of war within such a unique and beautiful setting. The narrator has very keen senses, and describes the sounds, smells, and sights of the harmonious nature around him. At the same time there is no sentimentality about the narrator's feeling toward nature; he simply is impressed and enjoys the new experience in his life. Finally, the contrast between the tranquillity of nature and the violence of war becomes so strong that Tolstoy as narrator is able to "estrange" the reader's perception of the paradox.

R. E. Richardson

RAIN

Author: W. Somerset Maugham (1874-1965)
Type of plot: Cultural realism
Time of plot: During or just after World War I
Locale: Pago-Pago, American Samoa
First published: 1921

> *Principal characters:*
> SADIE THOMPSON, a prostitute
> THE REVEREND MR. DAVIDSON, a missionary
> DR. MACPHAIL, a physician
> MRS. MACPHAIL, his wife
> MRS. DAVIDSON, the Reverend Mr. Davidson's wife, also a
> missionary

The Story

When a measles epidemic temporarily prevents the Davidsons and the Macphails from continuing their journey to Apia, Western Samoa, they find themselves stranded in Pago-Pago. Though the two couples have socialized on shipboard, they are very different: The Davidsons, who have been absent from their medical and religious mission north of Samoa for a year, are religious zealots whose single aim in life is to convert natives to Christianity. They are a drab and humorless pair who associate with the Macphails only because the rest of the ship's passengers seem "fast" by comparison. Though the women find much to talk about, the men share only an association with medicine, for Dr. Macphail is a shy, contemplative man to whom religion means little. When it is announced that they will be unable to leave the island for at least ten days, the energetic Davidsons take action. Through his influence with the governor, Davidson is able to find them rooms in the establishment of Mr. Horn, a local trader. Mrs. Davidson, with characteristic efficiency, helps the rather ineffectual Macphails settle into the boardinghouse, determined to make the best of things in spite of the bleak environment.

Soon Macphail learns that another of their shipmates will be lodging at Horn's, a second-class passenger named Sadie Thompson. Sadie, en route to Apia where a job supposedly awaits her, has been judged "fast" by Mrs. Davidson and Mrs. Macphail for dancing with the ship's quartermaster at the shipboard party the night before the landing at Pago-Pago. Vulgar in appearance and speech, Sadie is a friendly and vivacious sort who seeks, in the ensuing days, to enliven the depressing boardinghouse by giving frequent parties, loud and raucous affairs attended solely by the island's sailors. One evening the couples' dinner conversation is interrupted by especially loud noises coming from Sadie's room on the floor below. As they try to talk over

the din, Davidson has a sudden revelation: Sadie, who boarded the ship at
Honolulu, must be a denizen of Iwelei, that city's notorious red-light district,
which has only recently been shut down through the efforts of Hawaiian
missionaries. Further, she must be plying her trade here in Pago-Pago—just
below them in her room at Horn's.

Over the objections of Macphail, who considers Sadie's actions none of
their business, Davidson insists on storming into her room and trying to
break up the party. As his wife and the Macphails listen, Davidson is thrown
out of the room by the sailors. After the Davidsons go to their room, the
party starts up again, even louder than before.

The arrival of the ship in Pago-Pago has coincided with the beginning of
the tropical rainy season, and rain falls almost ceaselessly during the time
period covered by the story—torrential, oppressive rain, which depresses the
Macphails and greatly adds to the sense of claustrophobia that permeates the
story. During a rare dry spell on the day after Sadie's party, Mrs. Macphail
and Mrs. Davidson twice encounter Sadie, who treats them rudely. Mrs. Davidson is certain that Sadie will regret having made an enemy of Davidson,
who is tireless and vengeful in his battle against sin, but when he announces
later that day that he intends to try to save the prostitute's soul, even his wife
is shocked: Surely the woman has sunk too low to be reformed. Davidson's
reply that no sinner is beyond God's mercy leaves little doubt of his confidence that Sadie can be converted, and he has his first session with her that
very day. It seems to be a standoff. Sadie is coarse, brazen, unrepentant; the
Reverend Mr. Davidson is determined.

Time passes on the island and the rain seems as though it will never stop.
The weather, the climate, and the natives are grating on Macphail's nerves.
One day Sadie calls him to her room, where she discloses that Davidson has
convinced the governor to force her to leave on the next boat. Unfortunately
for her, its destination is San Francisco, to which she does not want to return.
She asks Macphail to speak to the governor for her: Why cannot she be
allowed to leave on the next boat for Sydney instead? Sympathetic to her
plight and irritated by Davidson's lack of compassion, Macphail agrees. The
governor stands by his decision, however, obviously intimidated by the
missionaries' influence in the region. Macphail is disgruntled and more disgusted than ever with Davidson's intractability.

That evening, a distraught and disheveled Sadie comes to plead with Davidson for mercy. She admits that she is wanted by the police in San Francisco, and begs Davidson not to make her return. The missionary remains
unmoved, however, despite Macphail's pleas on her behalf. When Sadie
becomes hysterical, Macphail helps her to her room. Later that evening,
after Davidson has led the group in praying for her soul, the calmed and
ostensibly contrite Sadie sends for Davidson, saying that she is ready to
repent. Davidson stays with her until two o'clock the next morning and

declares the next day that he has brought her to the Lord.

Sadie's sessions with Davidson continue for several days, during which time the rain, the heat, and the mosquitoes make life on the island nearly intolerable. Macphail looks forward to the day when Sadie's departure will break the tension that her religious conversion has brought to the boarding-house. Davidson, exhausted from spending much of each night with Sadie, is nevertheless in a state of spiritual rapture. Sadie seems to have accepted the fact that she must return to the United States to face her punishment. This uncomfortable state of affairs continues until the morning that Sadie's ship is to sail for San Francisco. Just after dawn, Macphail is awakened by Horn, who tells him that his services are needed. Horn leads him to the beach, where a group of natives stand huddled around a body. Macphail is shocked to find that the dead man is Davidson, who still holds the razor with which he has slit his throat. After making arrangements with the police, Macphail returns to Horn's and asks his wife to break the news to Mrs. Davidson. Abnormally calm, Mrs. Davidson asks to see the body.

On the way back from the mortuary, the Macphails and Mrs. Davidson are startled by the sound of Sadie's gramophone, which had been silent since her supposed conversion. Sadie herself has reverted to her former ways: Dressed in her old flashy costume and heavily made-up, she is entertaining a sailor. When she sees Mrs. Davidson, she spits at her. Mrs. Davidson hurries to her room, and Macphail chastises Sadie. What does she think she is doing? Fixing him with a look of intense hatred, Sadie gives Macphail the key to Davidson's suicide: "You men! You filthy, dirty pigs! You're all the same, all of you. Pigs! Pigs!" Macphail realizes in a flash the reason for the guilt that has driven Davidson to kill himself.

Themes and Meanings

Setting is central to the effectiveness of "Rain." Probably the most famous of W. Somerset Maugham's numerous tales set in the tropics, "Rain," like others of its kind, is an exploration of what happens when East meets West in a tropical setting. The clash between Pacific and European cultures informs every aspect of "Rain," and for each Anglo-Saxon character, the tropics represent some different and alien reality. The Davidsons see the South Seas as a vast pagan chaos waiting to be colonized and Christianized. For Sadie Thompson, the islands represent an escape, a place to begin life anew, far away from the repression exercised by Davidson and his kind. Even the even-tempered Macphail is affected by the strange world of the tropics: Appalled by the squalor and disease of Pago-Pago, he is driven to distraction by the unremitting rain. Much like "The Letter" and "The Outstation," two of Maugham's other South Seas tales, "Rain" is a study of the bizarre behavior that results when a European temperament must face prolonged exposure to tropical climates and customs.

"Rain" is also a bitter indictment of intolerance, both political and religious. The Davidsons are self-righteous and authoritarian, accomplished destroyers of native culture. Mrs. Davidson is a cold and prudish woman to whom even European-style dancing is immoral, and it is little wonder that Davidson seeks sexual satisfaction from a prostitute. Davidson himself is merciless in his cruel insistence that Sadie return to the United States; he is a single-minded bigot whose suicide is the product of an unbearable but self-imposed religious guilt. In that it criticizes and exposes the colonizers who would transform the tropics into a morally upright and repressive extension of the West, who seek to impose white culture and religion on the world at large, "Rain" is a powerful critique of American and Western European imperialism.

Style and Technique

"Rain" is told primarily from the point of view of Macphail, an intelligent and modest man to whom the world of the Samoan Islands is entirely unfamiliar. Thus, the reader shares with Macphail the sense of newness, of exoticism of setting and climate so central to the story's effectiveness. Macphail's viewpoint controls the reader's perceptions in other ways as well, particularly as concerns the relationship between Sadie and Davidson: Since Macphail is basically an agnostic, willing to live and let live, he serves as an obvious foil to Davidson, and the reader comes to share with Macphail an impatience with the missionary's religious authoritarianism. Like Macphail, the reader ignores hints of what is going on between Davidson and Sadie until the end of the story when, with Macphail, the reader must reinterpret past events in the light of Davidson's suicide. This masterful use of a limited point of view ensures that the surprise ending delivers a strong perceptual shock.

Maugham's prose is famous for its directness, its urbanity, and its polish. Like much of his fiction, "Rain" is written with a minimum of ornamentation, concentrating almost unflinchingly on the narrative line. Maugham thought of himself primarily as a storyteller rather than as a literary artist, but "Rain" belies such modesty. Not only is it a highly entertaining morality play about temptation, sin, and salvation, but also, at its best, it is an incisive and even allegorical critique of the white man's colonial impulse.

J. D. Daubs

THE RAINY MOON

Author: Colette (Sidonie-Gabrielle Colette, 1873-1954)
Type of plot: Horror
Time of plot: Mid-twentieth century
Locale: Paris
First published: "La Lune de pluie," 1940 (English translation, 1959)

> *Principal characters:*
> THE NARRATOR, an author
> ROSITA BARBERET, her typist
> DÉLIA ESSENDIER, Rosita's married sister

The Story

The narrator of the story, an author, comes for the first time to the apartment of her new typist, Mlle Rosita Barberet. The typist's apartment is situated on Montmartre, where the narrator herself once lived. Yet there have been many changes since the narrator resided on the Butte: Some of the street names have been changed, and buildings have been repainted or torn down altogether. During the course of their conversation, the author goes to the window to inspect the view; unconsciously, her hand rests upon the window catch. The unusual catch—a cast-iron mermaid—jars her memory, and suddenly the author realizes that she used to live in this very apartment.

She does not reveal this discovery to the efficient, birdlike Rosita, but instead asks her to retype a page, stalling for time to inspect the room. The author is especially curious to see again her old bedroom and, as she leaves, pretends to mistake the bedroom door for the door to the corridor. Before she can twist the knob, however, Rosita bars the way.

On her next visit, the author learns (through unsubtle questioning of the typist) that Rosita's sister lives in the bedroom. Apparently, the sister has been "ill" and confined to the room. The author's romantic imagination paints a picture of a young woman forsaken by her lover, pining away in the same bed where the author herself once pined for a departed man.

Her guess is actually close to the truth. When the author next comes to the apartment, Rosita is distraught and weepy. The typist confesses that her sister's character has changed for the worse since her husband, "the faithless Essendier," deserted her. The author decides not to pursue the matter; yet, as she is leaving, a small rainbow appears on the wall, a reflection caused by the sun hitting an imperfection in the window pane. The author is again reminded of her past—she had called the reflection her "rainy moon," greeting it as an optimistic sign. Rosita confides, however, that her sister considers the little fan of colors a bad omen. Her curiosity again aroused, the author bluffs her way into the bedroom and meets the beautiful, cold Délia Essendier, who has taken to bed not to pine, as the writer had fancied, but to sulk.

Annoyed yet intrigued by this saturnine young woman, the author asks her why she does not work like her sister does.

> "I work too," she said stiffly. "Only nobody sees what I do. I wear myself out; oh, I wear myself out. In there. . . . In there. . . ."
> She was touching her forehead and pressing her temples.

Nevertheless, the challenge affects Délia, for one day shortly thereafter the author arrives to find her engaged in needlework. Délia remarks that it is good for her to handle pointed things. The author makes a joke of this seemingly inane comment and goes out to make a purchase from a street vendor. As she rushes back inside, she bumps into a fatigued-looking man who is staring fixedly at the Barberet window.

Rosita—seeming suddenly aged herself—explains what has been "wearing out" her sister: Délia has been convoking, or summoning through intense concentration, her husband. Supposedly, the result of convocation is, for her husband, death. When Colette expresses disbelief in convocation, Rosita assures her that it is quite common, citing several examples even in the same neighborhood.

Although not convinced, the author is disgusted by this evil endeavor and vows never to return to the Barberet apartment. Yet weeks later, she begins haphazardly running into Délia, whose confinement has apparently ended. The young woman "looked pale and diminished, like a convalescent who is out too soon, pearly under the eyes, and extremely pretty." Finally, the author catches sight of Délia at a fried-potato stand. Ravenously eating potato chips, Délia is now dressed all in black, wearing the widow's crepe.

Themes and Meanings

With its voodoo overtones and macabre O. Henry ending, "The Rainy Moon" is a tale told primarily for impact. Délia's convocations, her "need" to handle pointed things (suggesting that she is either mentally or actually gouging her husband's likeness), and the transfixed man in the street escalate the reader's suspense. Although in the story the symbolic nature of the rainy moon is uncertain (the author sees it as a good sign; Délia labels it bad), Colette explains elsewhere that she meant the ephemeral image to suggest the iridian halo around the moon foretelling foul weather. Despite all these ill tidings, the conclusion is still surprising. Perhaps the reader, like the narrator, makes the mistake of deciding too quickly what is possible and what is not.

Yet the bizarre finale should not overshadow the original weird coincidence. Not only does the author return unknowingly to her old apartment, but there she finds a seeming time twin: a young woman deserted by her man, taking refuge in her bed, and even wearing the same type of tassled slippers that the author used to wear. Is this not a coincidence as disturbing as the "coincidence" that Délia convokes her husband and her husband dies? Colette's point is not that voodoo works or that there are supernatural forces in play because an author once lived in her typist's apartment, but rather that no one really knows what exists beneath the veneer of a "coincidence." There may be other powers at work, or there may not be. It might be unwise to discount any possibility.

Style and Technique

In "The Rainy Moon," the writer's style and the character of the narrator-author are practically indistinguishable. Both are reticent, seemingly disinterested, and intuitive.

Colette's style is reticent because, although she offers many details about her personal life, the reader nevertheless completes the story feeling as though he really knows very little about her. With scant preamble, she makes a baldly honest and self-astute comment such as " . . . a solitude that bore no resemblance to peace had wiped all the life and charm out of my face." Then she withdraws from her statement as precipitously as she introduced it, leaving the reader to speculate on why she was solitary and discontent. Just as Colette the character does not bother to share with Rosita the astonishing discovery that she used to inhabit this very apartment, neither does the narrator Colette share explanations with the reader. Her reticence implies that some things are inexplicable, while other things are explicable yet better left unexplained.

Feigning disinterest, the author barges into Délia's bedroom on the pretext of aiding the young woman. Yet her true purpose is to satisfy her own curiosity about this virtual specter of her former self. Similarly, Colette's style is superficially disinterested. She renders a seemingly dispassionate and cool record of events; yet there is an undercurrent of deep sensitivity, if not deep emotionality, constantly held in check, running through her work. Her disinterest is but a façade; no one in the story has greater emotional investment in the events in the Barberet apartment than does the author.

Lastly, Colette is an intuitive writer rather than an empirical one. Some of her intuitive flights could be termed "digressions." In the middle of recounting the Barberet tale, she suddenly talks of the pleasantness of picnics in the Bois, her mother's perspective-restoring visit, or an eventless dinner in a neighborhood café. Although ostensibly discursions, these snapshots serve several important purposes. Scenes of normalcy provide contrast for the culminating evil in the Barberet apartment and, at the same time, add to the tale a journal-like realism, intimating that, no, this is not a contrived story but simply a diary of events. Ideally, these "digressions" beguile the reader into identifying with the author's "normal" life, then whisper to him, *See what eerie and unexplainable things lurk close to you.*

Susan Davis

THE RAM IN THE THICKET

Author: Wright Morris (1910-   )
Type of plot: Domestic realism
Time of plot: June 23, in a year near the end of World War II
Locale: A town in Pennsylvania
First published: 1948

> *Principal characters:*
> ROGER ORMSBY, the protagonist, a storekeeper
> VIOLET ORMSBY, his wife, whom he calls "Mother," founder of
>   the League for Wild Life Conservation, secretary for the
>   League of Women Voters, and an activist
> VIRGIL ORMSBY, their son, killed in the war, a hero

The Story

"The Ram in the Thicket" falls into three sections, each distinguished by the point of view assumed by the third-person narrator: In the relatively long first section, told from the point of view of Roger Ormsby, he awakens in the morning, prepares breakfast, and calls Violet, his wife, of whom he habitually thinks as "Mother"; in the second section, told from Mother's point of view, she arises and dresses; in the third section, which returns to Mr. Ormsby's point of view, the two of them eat breakfast and prepare to leave for the ceremony at which Mother will sponsor the USS *Ormsby*, named in honor of Virgil Ormsby, their dead son. Although the external action is slight, psychological action is dense with conflict, implication, and irony.

As the story opens, Mr. Ormsby is dreaming. He has been staring at a figure on a rise with the head of a bird; the figure is casually holding a gun, and above his extended right arm hovers an endless procession of birds. Mr. Ormsby, though his wrists are bound, reaches out to the friendly birds and with that gesture becomes free. The first thing he sees when he awakens is a photograph of his son Virgil, referred to throughout as "the boy," standing on a rise and casually holding a gun, thus identifying the boy with the figure in the dream. The gun, which he holds as though it were a part of his body, is clearly phallic.

In his waking ruminations, Mr. Ormsby recalls having years before given the boy a gun "because he had never had a gun himself. . . . " The boy's relationship to his gun was remarkably natural, but Mother disapproved. A founder of the League for Wild Life Conservation, she ironically stands against things natural. Though she is skilled in identifying birds, it is the boy who is, implicitly, identified with them as free, natural creatures. In sharp contrast to the boy's naturalness, Mr. Ormsby recalls that "Mother had slept the first few months of their marriage in her corset—as a precaution and as an aid to self-control." As he dresses and shaves, Mr. Ormsby thinks of Mother's obsessive neatness, which has made the house barely habitable. When the boy was young, the house was redecorated and Mother covered everything with newspaper, at which time Mr. Ormsby began having his pipe in the basement, and the boy took to the outdoors.

After tiptoeing downstairs, Mr. Ormsby begins preparing breakfast, but, when he feels a stirring in the bowels, he retires to his basement toilet, a quiet dark place that gives him the privacy he wants. Once, when the boy accidentally discovered him on the stool and said "et tu, Brutus," they laughed until their sides ached, and he felt closer to the boy than at any other time in his life. Upstairs, continuing to prepare breakfast, Mr. Ormsby is diverted again, this time by a stench from the jars of leftovers in the refrigerator that Mother will not allow him to throw away. When the boy was quite young, he went into the living room filled with Mother's guests and displayed something in a jar. Mother, suspecting a frog or something of the sort, was horrified, but after the boy announced that it had come from the icebox, she never forgave him. The moldy food is one of many images of ugliness beneath a pleasing surface, suggesting the falsity of the Ormsbys' lives and the repressions that fill their subconscious minds. Breakfast almost prepared, Mr. Ormsby calls, like an invocation, "Ohhh Mother!"

The second and much briefer section of the story shifts to Mother's point of view. She rises like a goddess, but comic incongruities undercut her grandiose pretensions: After having groped about for her corset and wriggled into it in the dark, she intones "Fiat lux" as she turns on the light. In the locked bathroom, she turns on the water before she sits on the stool and, when she is finished, simulates a shower, including a dampened shower cap, to cover up the flush of the toilet. Since Mr. Ormsby, as the reader has already learned, is acutely aware of her subterfuges, she ironically dramatizes what she intends to cover up.

The concluding section returns to Mr. Ormsby's point of view. In the course of breakfast, he timidly ventures an opinion. Mother at first ignores him, but, when he dares to repeat it, her mustache begins to show, and he knows that she is angry. Saying that he can go to the ceremony without her, Mother leaves him in helpless torment, but she relents. Despite her personal feelings, she explains, she has responsibilities and cannot, like some people, simply act as she pleases, which, of course, is exactly what she is doing.

Themes and Meanings

The story explores male-female relationships in contemporary society. Mother and the boy embody antithetical attitudes and values, with Mr. Ormsby caught between his feelings of kinship with the boy and his subservience to Mother. Mother, of course, is clearly the ascendant figure in the household; moreover, she enjoys comparable social status as a community leader, indicating that her values reflect the prevailing values of society.

Mother stands for, among other things, decorum, control, and purity. Her values may have merit, but she pursues them in defiance of nature. Her unnaturalness is evident in the corset she wears to enforce sexual restraint, in elaborate subterfuges to cover up bodily functions, and in self-identification with the Diety. The boy, in contrast to Mother's prudish, sterile femininity, stands for masculinity and is associated with the out-of-doors, nature, freedom, heroism, and mortality. Just as Mother denies the flesh, the boy accepts it.

Mr. Ormsby, caught between the values embodied by Mother and by the boy, yields to Mother's power and thereby betrays his own masculinity. When the boy is killed, so is a part of Mr. Ormsby, and though it is the boy who is dead, Mr. Ormsby is not quite alive. The title, "The Ram in the Thicket," alludes to the story of Abraham and Isaac. Abraham, about to sacrifice his son Isaac in obedience to God's commandment, is spared at the last moment by an angel sent from God and offers up instead "a ram caught in a thicket" (Genesis 22:13). Mr. Ormsby worships the goddess Mother, a mortal creature who ludicrously presumes to unnatural perfection. Despite the affection he feels, he allows his son to be driven from his home and he sacrifices his own masculinity in subservience to Mother. Unlike Abraham, he will not be the father of many nations.

Style and Technique

To compensate for the paucity of dramatic action, Morris uses a variety of stylistic devices and techniques to enrich and enliven his story. Vivid images and provocative symbols abound—guns, birds, Mother's corset, and moldy leftovers are examples—and language is dense with implication, such as Mr. Ormsby's effort "to keep the springs quiet" when he rises so as not to disturb Mother. Reversals and surprises keep the reader's attention, as when Mr. Ormsby lights a match in his basement cell to read the telegram about the boy's death and discovers Mother's hoard of illegal canned goods. Interruptions and delays create suspense, as when Mr. Ormsby is about to venture an opinion but must help with the dishes and defer to Mother's observation of a thrush before he finishes his thought. Even within sentences Morris creates suspense through interrupted constructions: "The way the boy took to the out-of-doors—he stopped looking for his cuff links, began to look for pins— was partially because he couldn't find a place in the house to sit down." The substitution of the comma for a conjunction after "links" keeps the sentence moving and is another typical stylistic device.

Much of the impact of the story is shaped by various ironic contrasts. Some, not placed in direct opposition to one another, are relatively subtle, such as Mother's creation of light in the attic in contrast to Mr. Ormsby's striking matches in his basement cell. Others are immediately apparent, as when Mother grandly writes on a note pad "Ars longa, vita brevis" while sitting on the toilet stool. The story repeatedly juxtaposes things natural to things unnatural, contrasts underscored by a cliché to which Mr. Ormsby has frequent recourse: "It was only natural."

Jerome Cartwright

THE RANSOM OF RED CHIEF

Author: O. Henry (William Sydney Porter, 1862-1910)
Type of plot: Comedy
Time of plot: Early twentieth century
Locale: Summit, Alabama
First published: 1907

> *Principal characters:*
> SAM, the narrator
> BILL DRISCOLL, his confederate
> JOHNNY DORSET "RED CHIEF," the kidnaped boy
> EBENEZER DORSET, Johnny's father

The Story

The pattern of "The Ransom of Red Chief" is suggested by the first sentence of the story: "It looked like a good thing: but wait till I tell you." The story is essentially ironic; in a series of comic reversals, the expected event is replaced by its opposite. From the name of the town where the story takes place, Summit, which is perfectly flat, to the end of the story, where a fat man outruns the thin narrator, what the narrator anticipates never does occur.

The "good thing" which Sam and Bill have planned is a kidnaping. Early in the story, they select a quiet, sleepy town, a wealthy man with an only son, and a cave where they can keep their victim. They rent a buggy and approach the small boy with the promise of candy and a buggy ride. At this point, the first reversal occurs. Instead of sweetly climbing into the buggy, Johnny Dorset hits Bill Driscoll with a brick and fights violently when the two men drag him into the buggy. Although Sam and Bill get the boy to their cave hideout, another reversal occurs while Sam is returning the buggy and walking back. During Sam's absence, the captor and the captive change roles, seemingly only in play but actually in real control of the situation. When Sam returns to the cave, he finds Bill, badly battered, playing the captured trapper to Johnny's heroic Indian, who calls himself "Red Chief." Appropriating Sam for his game, Johnny announces that Bill is to be scalped and Sam burned at the stake.

From this time on, Johnny is in power, annoying his captors with chatter and questions, keeping them from sleeping, terrifying Bill with an attempted scalping at daybreak—followed by an attack with a hot potato and later with a rock—and generally enjoying himself so much that he seems disinclined to return home. Finally, Sam mails the ransom note, but the reply makes it clear that Ebenezer Dorset recognizes his son's power. The father demands a ransom of $250 from the kidnapers, in return for which he will take Johnny back. Bill, who has already tried to send Johnny home, begs his confederate to agree, and Sam himself is now willing to pay to get rid of the child whom the con men had abducted. Johnny, however, does not wish to leave his captors. They must scheme to get him back to his father as once they had schemed to get him away from home, and finally, they must run at top speed to escape the boy who does not wish to lose his new playmates, the would-be kidnapers who have become his victims.

Themes and Meanings

"The Ransom of Red Chief" is not simply a story in the O. Henry tradition of surprise endings; it is also a story in the pattern of classical comedy, which assures the reader that sometimes in this world the underdog can win. Generally, however, slaves or servants, wives or lovers, have prevailed by outwitting their masters. In "The Ransom of Red Chief," the kidnapers are defeated not by any scheme devised by Johnny but simply by his nature. Johnny is, himself, the ultimate ten-year-old terror, certainly worse than most small boys his age but not so unlike them as to be a monster. Part of the humor of the story comes from Johnny's relationship to the generic ten-year-old boy. Like the generic boy, he asks questions, rambles, fantasizes, and enlists playmates. While Sam and Bill could have coped with the average ten-year-old, they are helpless in Johnny's hands because Johnny is not average. He is tougher, meaner, and wilder than the ten-year-old whom these street-smart criminals thought they were victimizing.

A second element in the underdog theme involves the city and the country. The sophisticated con men, Sam and Bill, select Summit, Alabama, for the scene of their crime because they think that the country bumpkins will be easy to fool: their law officers inept, their bloodhounds lazy, their weekly rural newspapers ineffectual. Sam's visit to the bewhiskered, tobacco-chewing citizens of Poplar Grove is related with unconcealed contempt. Yet a small rural boy and his practical father defeat the crooks without even resorting to the law or the newspapers. The implication is that just as some children are tougher than adults, some rural people are tougher than city people. Sam and Bill have erred in selecting underdogs.

They have certainly erred in casting Ebenezer Dorset as an underdog. Their original information should have warned them. The man is stingy and mean, a "mortgage-fancier," a "forecloser." Yet Sam and Bill think of him only as a father, who customarily is indeed the underdog when his only child has been kidnaped. The father, however, knows his son, knows him well enough to insist that he be returned when the neighbors could not object. A tough man himself, he does not underestimate the toughness or the nastiness of his only son, a boy whom even he can control for no more than ten minutes. Furthermore, Ebenezer Dorset knows what things are worth, and he can estimate the value to the kidnapers of being relieved of Johnny.

The rural father and the rural son, then, do not need to outwit the kidnapers. They simply outwait them. To the reader's delight, the story suggests that a kidnap victim and his father can be the instruments of poetic justice, leaving the criminals both physically and financially defeated by their seeming inferiors.

Style and Technique

"The Ransom of Red Chief" derives from the tall tale so familiar in American humor. Ordinarily, the tall tale answers a question: "How big was the ox?" "How slow was the horse?" In this story, the question is, "How bad was the ten-year-old boy?" Thus, the tall tale simply exaggerates reality; in this case, the reality is the average ten-year-old boy, and the exaggeration is Johnny Dorset.

The narrative technique of the story is also reminiscent of the tall-tale tradition. Sam, the leading con man, speaks in the first person, as if relating his story to an audience: "Wait till I tell you," "Yes, sir, that boy seemed to be having the time of his life." He is given to malapropisms, such as "philoprogenitoveness," and to literary words, such as "sylvan" and "dastardly," which suggest that he is overreaching his real capacities, as he does in the story. Yet both Sam and Bill can use the language of frontier America, too, comparing Johnny to a "welter-weight cinnamon bear" or a "two-legged skyrocket" when they choose to exaggerate, saying that Johnny has "somewhat got on my nerves," in a comic understatement.

Nor is the story without its scenes of comic pathos, all related by Sam, as when Bill apologizes for releasing Johnny, then turns to find the boy behind him and seems for a time to be losing his sanity. It is Sam who describes Bill's pleas, which finally result in a "getaway" from the kidnaped boy and in paying the "ransom" to his father.

Because the story is written in the comic tradition, it lacks the sentimentality which has dated some of O. Henry's other stories. Fusing as it does the elements of classical comedy and those of the American tall tale, "The Ransom of Red Chief" is one of the writer's most successful productions.

Rosemary M. Canfield-Reisman

RAPPACCINI'S DAUGHTER

Author: Nathaniel Hawthorne (1804-1864)
Type of plot: Gothic
Time of plot: Late eighteenth century
Locale: Padua, Italy
First published: 1844

>*Principal characters:*
>GIOVANNI GUASCONTI, the protagonist, a student at the
>   University of Padua
>DAME LISABETTA, his landlady
>DR. GIACOMO RAPPACCINI, a scientist and physician
>BEATRICE RAPPACCINI, his daughter
>DR. PIETRO BAGLIONI, a professor of medicine at the
>   university

The Story

A young man named Giovanni rents a room in an old edifice belonging to a family whose ancestor was listed among the sufferers in Dante's *Inferno*. It looks down on a luxuriant inner garden belonging to a neighbor, Dr. Rappaccini. The garden is brilliant with exotic blooms, the most spectacular, a shrub growing by a ruined fountain. It is covered with rich purple blossoms. Dr. Rappaccini is often tending the garden, but he is always protected by heavy gloves and sometimes a face mask. His lovely daughter, Beatrice, takes no such precautions, however, and she is the only one who touches the handsome plant with the purple blooms. She tends it as though it were a beloved sister.

Giovanni has a letter of introduction to a Dr. Pietro Baglioni, a professor of medicine at the university, who once knew his father. Dr. Baglioni warns him to keep away from Rappaccini, a brilliant scientist but one inclined to sacrifice anything and anyone to his scientific experiments. He is an expert in poisons and is known to have developed new varieties of herbs more poisonous than those in nature.

Such information lends substance to Giovanni's lurid imaginings about the garden and the girl. He had once thrown her a bouquet that had seemed to wilt the moment she picked it up. He also fancied that a butterfly that hovered close to her face had died suddenly in midflight.

These forebodings do not prevent him from entering the garden when his landlady, Lisabetta, offers to show him a secret door into the inner courtyard. Beatrice comes out to meet him, and they are drawn to each other immediately. When he asks for a blossom from the shrub at the ruined fountain and reaches out to pluck it, Beatrice cries out in alarm, seizes his hand,

and warns him never to touch it. The next morning, the place where she grasped his hand is painful and inflamed.

Giovanni continues to visit Beatrice, until he notices with horror that flowers will no longer remain fresh in his own hands. As an experiment, he exhales a long breath on a spider that is industriously weaving a web in his room: The spider curls up and dies immediately. Tortured now by fear and resentment, Giovanni paces the streets of Padua, where Dr. Baglioni sees him and divines the reason for his distraction. Dr. Baglioni brings him a silver vial containing an antidote which was originally created to counteract the poisons of the Borgias. He instructs Giovanni to give the antidote to Beatrice to counteract the deadly fumes in which she has lived.

When Beatrice again calls from the garden, he goes down to her with hatred and resentment in his heart, instead of love. He curses her for contaminating him with her poison. Beatrice is crushed by his cruel words, having always assumed that he was safe so long as he did not touch her or the flowers. He accuses her of deliberately trapping him to share in her isolation from the world. This she passionately denies, "I dreamed only to love thee and be with thee a little time, and so let thee pass away. . . ; for Giovanni, believe it, though my body be nourished with poison, my spirit is God's creature and craves love as its daily food."

Giovanni is somewhat mollified and tells her of the antidote that Dr. Baglioni provided. Perhaps they can both escape the garden. Beatrice agrees, but adds emphatically, "I will drink; but do thou wait the result." She does so and dies at the feet of Giovanni and her father.

Themes and Meanings

This parable of the Fall from Innocence in a poisonous garden of Eden has several levels of meaning, not all of them explicitly stated. The Eden analogy is certainly clear, and one may assume that the garden, with its ruined fountain, is in some sense a microcosm of the fallen world cursed by sin and death. Perhaps it is the world that might ensue if scientists value knowledge and power more than human love.

Hawthorne suggested in other stories as well, such as "The Birthmark" and "The Great Carbuncle," that the scientist in his intellectual pride might destroy the natural blessings that God has provided. This sentiment was a fairly common one at the time. The technique of grafting was recently discovered and widely distrusted as an impious if not dangerous interference with God's intentions. While such processes seem innocent enough today, readers may certainly recognize the "mad scientist" motif still popular in science fiction.

The imagery of the story, however, is primarily religious and moral. Granted Rappaccini's malevolent impact, Giovanni falls from Grace not entirely through the machinations of a Satanic scientist. To be sure, the young man seems to have been lured deliberately into the garden by the doctor, not by Beatrice herself, to serve as a companion for the isolated girl. He falls not because of Beatrice's evil nature, but because of his own shallow capacity for love. Giovanni's shortcomings in the face of an admittedly tainted world are repeatedly suggested: "His love grew thin and faint as the morning mist," "that cunning semblance of love which flourishes in the imagination, but strikes no depth of root into the heart." Before he descends to the garden on the last occasion, he mutters venomously, "She is the only being whom my breath may not slay! Would that it might!" Given this preliminary evidence of Giovanni's malice, the dying words of Beatrice ring true: "Farewell, Giovanni! Thy words of hatred are like lead within my heart; but they, too, will fall away as I ascend. Oh, was there not, from the first, more poison in thy nature than in mine?"

If Beatrice, unlike Giovanni, is innocent of malice, that sin most damned in Dante's *Inferno*, the moral status of Dr. Baglioni, giver of the antidote that kills, is most ambiguous. Dr. Baglioni stands in a godlike position above the garden in the closing scene calling down his judgment from the balcony: "Rappaccini! Rappaccini! and is *this* the upshot of your experiment!" That would seem to reflect God's moral indignation, except that Dr. Baglioni is also suspect as harboring considerable malice for Rappaccini as a professional rival. Moreover, there is a distinct implication that Dr. Baglioni knew that his antidote would kill, not cure, Rappaccini's daughter. This ambiguity may suggest simply that the real world of Dr. Baglioni and the untested Giovanni is already contaminated, or it may suggest that God himself, who created a garden with the foreknowledge of man's fall, is somehow implicated in the sin and death that inevitably follow.

Style and Technique

This story is obviously replete with literary symbols, some of them pointing in seemingly opposite directions. Although the function of Beatrice suggests Eve, often blamed for Adam's fall, her name recalls that other Beatrice who rescued Dante from sin and escorted him into Heaven.

If one looks at the story from the viewpoint of Freudian psychology, one might suspect that the "original sin" of this virginal Eve is simply her inborn sexuality and the "original sin" (though not the final sin) of Giovanni is plain lust. One might even imagine that the lethal, purple plant so close to the fountain of life might signify, in dream language, the female sexual parts which he must not touch. Nowhere is that inelegant word "lust" used, yet the description of his obsession seems to convey it:

> "She had at least instilled a fierce and subtle poison into his system. It was not love, although her rich beauty was a madness to him; nor horror, even while he fancied her spirit to be imbued with the same baleful essence that seemed to

pervade her physical frame; but a wild offspring of both love and horror that had each parent in it and burned like one and shivered like the other."

Seldom has the forbidden term "lust" been evoked in such rich and gothic prose.

The deliberate mention of Dante at the beginning, the viewpoint of Giovanni from his balcony looking down as into a pit, the poisonous vapors presumably arising from it, all suggest the ledge overlooking deepest Hell where Dante and Vergil discussed the different degrees of sin, beginning with lust and ending with malice and betrayal.

Yet, at the bottom of this pit, at the center, is not Lucifer, or even Rappaccini, presumably his agent, but a fountain. There is no evidence that the water itself is polluted. Beatrice's innocent spirit is several times likened to a fountain:

Many a holy and passionate outgush of her heart, when the pure fountain has been unsealed from its depths and made visible in its transparency to his mental eye; recollections which, had Giovanni known how to estimate them, would have assured him that all this ugly mystery was but an earthly illusion.

Thus, the traditional association between evil and physical nature, magnified in the story, may seem real or illusory, depending on the purity of the human heart.

Katherine Snipes

RASHŌMON

Author: Ryūnosuke Akutagawa (1892-1927)
Type of plot: Fable
Time of plot: Late twelfth century
Locale: Kyoto, Japan
First published: 1915 (English translation, 1930)

Principal characters:
AN UNEMPLOYED SERVANT
AN OLD WOMAN

The Story

In "Rashōmon," Ryūnosuke Akutagawa depicts the plight of an out-of-work servant who ponders his fate at Rashōmon Gate, a dilapidated building in twelfth century Kyoto. The servant knows, or believes, that in order to survive he must resort to theft, but he is at first reluctant to steal. In the course of the story, however, his encounter with an old woman, herself a thief, causes him to change his mind, or it enables him to rationalize resorting to theft as a way of life. His decision to steal is undoubtedly influenced not only by the unsettled times, but also by the deathly atmosphere of the Rashōmon Gate. It was precisely that setting which appealed to Akira Kurosawa, the film director who used the Rashōmon Gate to convey a sense of corruption and decay in his film *Rashomon* (1950), which has as its sources not only Akutagawa's "Rashōmon," but also his "In a Grove."

The Rashōmon Gate, with its peeling paint and weather-beaten pillars, serves as a symbol for the ruins of Kyoto, which has been plagued by a series of disasters such as earthquakes, fires, tornadoes, and famines. The gate has become a refuge for wild animals and thieves, a depository for unclaimed bodies, and a haunt for crows, which feed off the bodies. In this gloomy setting—it is dusk, and a steady rain is falling—a dismissed servant thinks about his future and reluctantly concludes that if he is to survive he must steal. In an effort to find better shelter from the rain and the cold he climbs a ladder into the loft, where he sees a light. As he approaches the light, he sees that it is held by an old woman, who is pulling the hair out of the head of one of the decaying corpses.

As he watches the woman, the servant grows increasingly angry and self-righteous until he finally gains the courage to confront her. Sword in hand, he springs into the loft, blocks the woman's escape, asks her what she is doing, and throws her to the floor of the loft. When he realizes that she is at his mercy, he assures her that he is not a policeman and again demands to know what she is doing in the corpse-filled loft. This time she gasps out the answer that she uses the hair to make wigs. The woman, who fears for her life, desperately tries to justify her action by stating that she is sure that the dead would not mind her taking their hair, and then she adds that the woman before her had committed the crime of selling snakes as dried fish. Comparing her crime to the dead woman's, the old woman explains that no "wrong" was involved since both would have starved otherwise and that both consequently had no choice. She ends by reiterating her belief that the dead woman would forgive her.

The old woman's justification of her actions ironically serves in turn to justify the servant's decision to steal from her because he, too, would otherwise starve. He rips off her kimono, flings her among the corpses, and flees into the night and into obscurity. After he leaves, the old woman recovers, crawls to the loft ladder, and stares into the darkness.

Themes and Meanings

In "Rashōmon," Akutagawa probes the subtle relationship between setting and character. Twelfth century Kyoto becomes an emblem for desolation, decay, and death: The entire city has been plagued by natural disasters (earthquakes, tornadoes, and fires) and by famine, but the spiritual "famine" is no less important. In order to survive (and the story concerns the conflict between morality and survival), people have smashed the Buddhist icons and sold the pieces for firewood. In effect, then, Akutagawa indicates that in desperate situations people not only abandon morality, but also use and exploit it as they would any other material at hand. Given his need to survive, the servant who steals the kimono is merely acting as the townspeople have acted.

Set against this general picture of physical and spiritual desolation is Rashōmon Gate, which represents the entire city. With its peeling paint and weather-beaten pillars, the dilapidated structure serves as a haven for wild animals and thieves and as a repository for unclaimed corpses. The only other visitors are the crows, which feed on the dead bodies. Thus, in his description of the gate, Akutagawa has provided images of decay, immorality, and predatory behavior. The crows prey on the dead bodies; the old woman preys on dead bodies; the dead woman had preyed on her customer; the servant preys on the old woman—all in the name of survival. (In fact, the servant's dismissal may have been caused by his master's need to survive financially.)

Other negative images pervade Akutagawa's description of Rashōmon Gate: the overgrown tall weeds, the crumbling stone steps, and the white bird droppings—all attest Kyoto's decline, so widespread that the servant's dismissal seems trivial by comparison. In fact, the individual seems insignificant against the backdrop of physical, cultural, and moral bankruptcy. Adding to the general gloom are the dusk, with its associations of death and ambiguity, and the steady rain, which has forced the servant to seek shelter. In one sentence, Akutagawa combines the dusk and rain with a sense of the ominous: "As evening descended, a low cloud, dark and foreboding, loomed heavily above the corner rooftiles."

Because the setting is so negatively described, the servant is understandably pessimistic about his fate. Cold, wet, and hungry, he has no prospects of gaining employment and can see only his impending death, unless he resorts to theft. Stealing is, he believes, the "only way out," but he cannot "bring himself to do it," primarily because of his weakness: He is a coward who quickly resolves to steal but lacks the will or courage to do it. Because he fears the dead, he clutches the sword at his side; it is only when he sees the old woman, not a strong young man, that he decides to "summon his strength" and attack her. Before he can act, however, he must abhor the old woman's action so that he can rationalize his action as being motivated by principle. The author thereby establishes the servant as a weak person who seeks both a suitable victim and a justification for his crime. In effect, while the setting does provide a backdrop against which his action seems consistent, the servant does have a choice and cannot evade responsibility for his actions by comparing his crime to the old woman's or her victim's.

Style and Technique

In the course of the story, Akutagawa uses imagery not only to establish the setting, but also to portray his characters. The servant is first compared to the lone cricket, which "clings" to the pillar but later abandons his "perch"—much like the fleeing servant. When he climbs up the loft ladder, the servant is "quiet as a lizard" and stealthy "as a cat." He fears that his corpse will be thrown into the loft as would a "stray dog's." The old woman's arm is like a chicken's, and she is twice compared to a monkey. Through his imagery, Akutagawa suggests that these two characters have forsaken their humanity and have become caught up in a struggle for survival. When he describes the old woman's eyes as being those of a "bird of prey," he also ties the characters to the crows that prey on the dead.

Even though such imagery does not present the characters favorably, Akutagawa treats the old woman and the servant with light irony: The author is rather condescending, but he is not harsh or contemptuous of the thieves. For the most part, Akutagawa uses the third-person point of view but filters much of the story through the mind of the servant. On the other hand, the narrator occasionally editorializes about the servant so that his audience will not have any doubts about the servant's motives or his self-deception. The narrator uses the phrases "in fact" and "the truth is that" when he first discusses the servant's desperate plight. When the servant grows increasingly angry with the old woman's theft from the dead, he is being a hypocrite, for he has already decided to steal to survive. The narrator points out the hypocrisy: "He had, of course, already forgotten that only a few minutes earlier he himself had made up his mind to become a thief." From this point on the narrator suggests that the servant, knowing he controls the situation, manipulates his emotions in order to justify his actions: "His hatred returned, only this time he controlled it." When he uses the old woman's rationalization, the servant joins her in the predatory behavior symbolized by the crows and encouraged by the setting of death and decay. The servant's moral decay is his inner corruption, which is mirrored by his physical corruption and affliction: On his cheek there is a festering pimple which oozes "red pus." Until he finds the rationalization he seeks, the servant picks at his cheek; he uses that same hand to steal from the old woman when he is finally free of nagging moral scruples.

Thomas L. Erskine

THE REAL THING

Author: Henry James (1843-1916)
Type of plot: Social and psychological realism
Time of plot: The 1890's
Locale: London
First published: 1892

> *Principal characters:*
> THE NARRATOR, an artist
> MAJOR and MRS. MONARCH
> ORONTE and MISS CHURM, professional models

The Story

An artist is visited one day in his studio by a middle-aged couple, Major and Mrs. Monarch. At first the artist assumes that they have come to commission a portrait, but he soon learns that they want, instead, to pose as paid models. He observes that the Monarchs, though on the edge of poverty, are an eminently respectable pair, well-mannered, immaculately poised—in effect, as their name suggests, the very embodiment of taste, refinement, and class.

Hoping that they might prove ideal subjects for a series of illustrations he is engaged in creating for a publisher, the artist agrees to hire them, though their very authenticity causes him to have vague misgivings. They are the "real thing," but they are still amateurs, and the artist is more confident of his ability to work with his professional models, Oronte and Miss Churm.

Miss Churm is an ill-mannered cockney who "couldn't spell and loved beer" but who can represent anything from an aristocrat to a beggar. The artist regards her as an excellent model. As for Oronte, he is an Italian vagrant who found his way to the artist's studio and who has become as good a model, in the artist's eyes, as Miss Churm. He is, the narrator relates, as good at posing as an Englishman as Miss Churm is as an Italian.

Against these two, the Monarchs must compete for the artist's favor, though at first they assume that their own credentials as aristocrats will be warrant enough for their success. Try as he might, however, the artist cannot do anything with them. He draws Mrs. Monarch many times, in many ways, always failing to capture what he wants. With Major Monarch the situation is worse, his representation being always gigantic and out of scale. Eventually the artist manages several drawings with both husband and wife and sends them to the publisher for approval.

Meanwhile, a fellow artist and friend of the narrator has returned from Paris, where he has studied some of the great works and where he has, as the narrator says, "gotten a fresh eye." Viewing some of the artist's illustrations with the Monarchs as models, the friend expresses his disapproval. The artist

1906   *Masterplots II*

insists that the illustrations are good, but his friend counsels him to get rid of the models or risk his career.

Despite his friend's remonstrances, the artist continues to keep the Monarchs as models, not so much out of respect for their gentility as out of compassion for their impoverishment. Ultimately the artist rejects them by working exclusively with Oronte and Miss Churm. "I can't be ruined for *you*," he tells the major, petulantly.

In a final humiliation, the Monarchs plead for a position, even offering to act as servants. For almost a week the artist keeps them on, but in the end, saddened by their failure, he pays them off and never sees them again.

Themes and Meanings

"The Real Thing" is an extraordinarily subtle work demanding, like much of the work of Henry James, sensitivity and perceptiveness from the reader. The theme, one of James's recurring preoccupations, is the artist's honest struggle with his material, a struggle to render a subject in all of its multifaceted meaning. The Monarchs are the real thing, but their very authenticity, their very perfection is somehow not enough for the artist to capture. As the ideal, they are easily recognizable yet just as elusive. The artist's struggle to paint them ends in failure because, though it is the nature of art to be always striving for perfection, on the human level of the artist, it must always miss—perfection being beyond human attainment.

In this sense, "The Real Thing" is suggestive of a short story by Nathaniel Hawthorne, a writer whom James admired and about whom he published one of the first critical studies (1879). In that Hawthorne story, "The Artist of the Beautiful," Owen Warfield—whose name signifies the artist's dilemma, the warfare between ideality and reality—strives for the perfection of his art, but in the struggle destroys his creation. So too, in "The Real Thing," the artist is unable to capture fully what the Monarchs are and must turn them away, although, as he says, he was happy "to have paid the price— for the memory."

In this sense, too, the characters of Oronte and Miss Churm amplify the meaning. Unlike the Monarchs, they are not the aesthetic ideal, but the mundanely real, the concrete, the actual; these qualities the artist is most successful in dealing with. The question becomes, then, whether the artist's achievement is in the ability to capture the ideal on its own terms, or, rather, is in the ability to shape phenomena into a form that merely suggests or approaches the ideal. Significantly, the artist in James's story is engaged in a series of illustrations for a magazine called *Cheapside*, a wonderfully apt appellation, connotative of quality as well as locale: The artist is a commercial success; he is becoming popular and is fearful for his reputation. Pursuit of the Monarchs (as Owen Warfield's invention was a mechanical butterfly) means failure. Working comfortably, risk-free, with his professional models ensures success in the marketplace. He is, in this light, a second-rate artist, having, in his own words, "an innate preference for the represented subject over the real one."

Finally, a second theme runs simultaneously along with that of the artist's struggle with his material: the demise of the aristocratic class in a society more and more fluid, increasingly amenable to the rising lower orders who make things work. The Monarchs can be seen as anachronisms, unable in their effete gentility to compete with the aggressive versatility of the worldly middle class. So ill-equipped are they for survival in the society of shifting values that they fail even at being domestics, unable even to serve where once they were so obviously served.

Oscar Wilde perceived the decay of the aristocracy in his brilliant comedy of the same period, *The Importance of Being Earnest: A Trivial Comedy for Serious People* (1895), in which aristocratic drawing-room manners and life-styles are parodied into absurdity. In one scene, for example, Lady Bracknell sums up her nephew's attributes thus: "He looks everything but has nothing." If the same could be said of the Monarchs, it is a declaration less humorous and more pitiful.

Style and Technique

Published a few years before the great novels of James's so-called late style, characterized by rhetorical complexity, "The Real Thing" is interesting as an example of its author's successful use of the "popular" style to convey the more serious meanings already discussed.

The story moves quickly, gracefully, with an elegant, precise prose recall-ing the sparkle of James's earlier works such as *Daisy Miller* (1879) and *The Portrait of a Lady* (1881). The first-person narration is successful in establish-ing a central point of view—James's trademark—while maintaining the lively, spontaneous tone. Additionally, by allowing the artist to speak for him-self, James brings his dilemma into sharper focus, making it a personal drama rather than a dry monologue or a mere critique of aesthetic theory disguised as a story. The artist's personality is keenly felt—his wit, his compassion, even his delusion of someday capturing the real thing.

Finally, and characteristically, the story is marked by an intriguing use of names, an almost Dickensian exuberance and unabashed simplicity. The name "Monarch" is obviously suggestive. So too is the grossly discordant "Churm" and the shallow flashiness of "Oronte." The name of the artist's friend, Claude Rivet, suggests the iron-bound commercialism by which the Monarchs are judged. Even the title of the novel for which the artist is providing illustrations, *Rutland Ramsey*, suggests a mild parody of James's own first novel of artists in Rome, *Roderick Hudson* (1876).

Edward Fiorelli

A REASONABLE FACSIMILE

Author: Jean Stafford (1915-1979)
Type of plot: Sketch
Time of plot: Mid-twentieth century
Locale: Adams, Colorado, a fictional composite of the towns of Boulder and
   Colorado Springs
First published: 1957

> *Principal characters:*
> DR. WOLFGANG BOHRMANN, a graciously aging philosopher, a
>   retired academic, a prodigious correspondent, and an
>   uncommonly generous man
> MRS. PRITCHARD, Dr. Bohrmann's loyal housekeeper
> HENRY MEDLEY, the insufferable interloper, the uninvited
>   and protracted houseguest of his intellectual mentor Dr.
>   Bohrmann
> GRIMALKIN, the ginger cat, lord of the manor
> HEDDA BOHRMANN, Dr. Bohrmann's deceased but fondly
>   remembered wife

The Story

"Change is the only stimulus," insists Dr. Wolfgang Bohrmann upon retiring from a career of teaching at Nevilles College in Adams, Colorado. Instead of resigning himself to spending the remainder of his allotted years in quiet retirement, Dr. Bohrmann embarks upon a variety of engrossing pursuits, not the least of which is having a new house built for himself, a "house of tomorrow—cantilevered, half-glass—six miles out on the prairies." From his position on one of the house's many decks, the enthusiastic professor *emeritus* can command an expansive view of the Rocky Mountains and the ever-changing panorama of cloud and sky: "there dark rain, here blinding sunshine, yonder a sulphurous dust storm, haze on the summit of one peak, a pillow of cloud concealing a second, hyaline light on the glacier of a third." From his aerielike perch, Dr. Bohrmann inhales the invigorating air of freedom; loosed from his career bonds, he is free to explore the numerous hobbies which intrigue his curious mind. A man of wide-ranging interests, he occupies his time studying Japanese, learning the art of engraving, exploring the mysteries of mycology, and growing Persian melons. Having carved his own private space within a landscape that he loves, Dr. Bohrmann is not prepared for the sudden arrival of a young Easterner, Henry Medley, who informs the old gentleman of his intention to pay him a prolonged visit so that the two may get to know each other personally after having corresponded for some years. Dr. Bohrmann, astonished at the prospect of having a houseguest ("not through any want of hospitality but because it was a matter that had never arisen"), nevertheless rallies to the occasion and has his housekeeper, Mrs. Pritchard, prepare the spare room for his visitor.

The ubiquitous Mrs. Pritchard, "shaped like a pear" and having "a blue mustache under a fleshy and ferocious bill," harbors a deep suspicion that the arrival of the professor's disciple may not be a very pleasant event. Indeed, when Henry Medley, true to his name, unloads his gear from the taxi (a pup tent, a portable grill, a sleeping bag, "two bulging Gladstones, a type-writer, a tennis racket, a pair of skis, a rifle, a fishing rod and tackle box, a recorder . . . and two large boxes of cuttings of field flowers from the Hudson Valley . . ."), Mrs. Pritchard senses that his will be no abbreviated visit, for skis cannot be used, even in the mountains near Adams, until late fall or early winter at best. Dr. Bohrmann, whose magnanimous hospitality be-comes taxed by Medley's invasion of his home, tries to maintain his habitual friendly demeanor, but as days pass, it becomes clear that the overbearing English teacher plans to stay.

The drama of the story builds as Dr. Bohrmann, urged on by Mrs. Pritchard's concerned prodding, attempts to free himself from Medley's grasp. He longs for his highly prized solitude, which Medley has broken by his noisy, persistent presence. Perhaps the most overwhelmingly unbearable aspect of Medley's omnipresence is his infatuation with his mentor, which leads him to agree, wholeheartedly and constantly, with whatever Dr. Bohr-mann says. Although Bohrmann scolds Medley for his sin of "impassioned, uncritical agreement," he soon discovers that the young man simply has no ideas of his own. While overtly brilliant, for Medley "had apparently read everything and forgotten nothing," Bohrmann's protégé "was so unself-centered that Dr. Bohrmann began to wonder if he had a self at all." In short, Henry Medley is an intellectual robot, a "reasonable facsimile" of the true intellectual and spiritual offspring that Dr. Bohrmann once desired more than anything else in the world.

Once Dr. Bohrmann realizes that Medley must go—must be evicted, al-beit gently, if need be—the focus of the story turns to a most essential yet rather unusual character, Bohrmann's cat, Grimalkin. As fate (or fortune) would have it, Henry Medley suffers an excruciating allergy to cats, and even though the professor has agreed to restrict Grimalkin to the outdoors during Medley's stay, Mrs. Pritchard intervenes, allowing the animal to slip into the house just long enough to keep the dander level painfully high. Finally, in a voice punctuated with explosive sneezes and with an expression dampened by tears of allergic agony, Medley announces his intention to depart. No char-acter is more pleased than Grimalkin, who, having been unceremoniously ousted by Medley's arrival, equally unceremoniously deposits a farewell gift on the mat outside Medley's door as he prepares to leave—a dead gopher. With a sense of unspeakable relief, Dr. Bohrmann returns to the life he most

enjoys, free from the "sapping tedium of Medley's monologues and inter-
rogations" which had seemed to rob him of his own personality.

Themes and Meanings

Jean Stafford is fond of exploring the parallel between the landscape of
the Rocky Mountain West and characters indigenous to that region. She
believes that the Colorado spirit is reinforced by a strength of character, an
inimitable independent personality, which makes people straightforward,
resilient, and above all intrigued by life's potential. As Dr. Bohrmann himself
observes, there is a special ingredient found in the Rocky Mountains that
gives characters a certain Western charm. "Once they were out in the world,
they seldom came back to Adams, and when they did, they were not the
same, for they had outgrown their lucubrations; they were no longer so fer-
vent as they had been, and often their eyes strayed to their wristwatches in
the midst of a conversation." Just as Stafford herself never returned to the
Rocky Mountain West to live after leaving the area when she finished her
university education, other characters who move away in her fiction seldom
come back to live. Yet those who remain, like Dr. Wolfgang Bohrmann,
epitomize a certain quality not to be found elsewhere.

Another theme frequently found in Stafford's short stories and novels is
the importance of a character's past experiences on his present life. Often her
characters seem anachronisms in the society in which they live. Dr. Bohrmann, for example, relishes his retirement in his new house, but he also fills
the new space with artifacts of his past, symbols of a former life which he
would never forsake simply because it was out of date. Stafford recognizes
the universality of human experience and urges readers to become aware of
the value of the past.

Stafford echoes the theories of Virginia Woolf and D. H. Lawrence with
regard to the centrality of character in fiction, insisting that her characters be
above all dynamic, believable, and real for the reader. In a letter to the Pul-
itzer Committee in 1969, Stafford wrote: "I want, in a novel, a tarnished,
perhaps, but nonetheless sterling hero or heroine; I don't want everybody to
be a simon-pure alloy of base metals. . . ." Thus, in her collection of short
stories entitled *Bad Characters* (1964), she portrays individuals whose lives
are far from perfect but who nevertheless live determinedly. Stafford's devotion to physical and psychological realism gives her fiction the solid, earthy
quality so integral to the American literary tradition.

Style and Technique

Critics have long credited Jean Stafford with having a vivid, descriptive
style which shows her deep reverence for the power of the English language.
When "A Reasonable Facsimile" appeared in print, Stafford's acquaintance
Eudora Welty commended her story, writing, "Oh, Jean, I love all the detail

and the splendor." Saul Bellow, another admirer of Stafford's writing, sent her a congratulatory note, remarking: "I liked *all* the stories, but the one about the old professor and the young know-it-all best." Through her elaborate descriptions of characters and settings, Stafford is able to create an atmosphere as realistic as, for example, many found in Charles Dickens' novels. In "A Reasonable Facsimile," Stafford presents the professor so thoroughly that the reader really feels as though he has met the old gentleman. The narrator pulls the reader into the actual theater of the story: "Imagine, then, this character, with his silver beard, wearing a hazel coat-sweater from J.C. Penney. . . . Or look at him pottering in his pretty Oriental garden. . . . See him in his sleek, slender blond dining room eating a mutton chop or blood pudding with red cabbage. . . ." Stafford's style also develops a firm sense of place, for she uses actual and specific locations to give her fiction that local-color flavor most often found in realistic fiction. As a result, her fiction presents an atmosphere which becomes more crucial than plot itself; her characters emerge as sculptured identities rather than mere outlines of personalities. Reading Stafford's short stories gives one the ability to journey deep inside the souls of her characters and to cheer with glee when Dr. Bohrmann finally boots that upstart Medley right out the door.

Another stylistic element characteristic to Stafford's fiction is her use of an exhaustive and intricate vocabulary which makes heavy demands on the contemporary reader. Her style challenges the reader to accompany her narrators on journeys of language exploration. Few modern readers would be able to grasp Stafford's vocabulary at first glance; for example, when one learns that Dr. Bohrmann's retirement activities include the study of "mycology, and mycophagy as well," one knows that this is a man who is not content with studying the mundane disciplines of scholarship. The professor's "monograph on Maimonides for the *Hibbert Journal*" tempts even the most hasty reader to reach for the nearest dictionary. In addition to her use of elaborate descriptions, Stafford also reveals a marvelous ear for the varieties of speech which enrich the English language. Who is able to resist a smile at Dr. Bohrmann's reaction to Medley's annoying, exhaustive commentary: "I think you have made a Jungfrau out of the hill of a pygmy mole." Medley himself is described as "brilliant, though undisciplined and incorrigibly highfalutin' . . . ," and even minor characters speak with genuineness as they describe the main character: "You should have seen *mein Herr Doktor Professor* this morning, with his cat and his fiddle, ready to hop right over the moon." One can certainly see the truth in Stafford's comment to one of her editors: "My mother tongue has been, from the beginning of my life, my dearest friend."

Stafford strove throughout her life to defend the language against the destructive influences of cant and imprecision. Readers soon discover that Stafford's language is as elaborate as her subjects are diverse, and that her ability to expand the language rather than to reduce it (as did many modernist writers) makes her fiction a study in the limitless power of the human imagination.

Mary Davidson McConahay

A RECLUSE

Author: Walter de la Mare (1873-1956)
Type of plot: Ghost story
Time of plot: The 1920's
Locale: Rural England
First published: 1926

Principal characters:
CHARLES DASH, a young man, the narrator
A HORSEMAN, unnamed
MR. BLOOM, owner of Montrésor
S. S. CHAMPNEYS, Mr. Bloom's late secretary

The Story

In spite of Mr. Charles Dash's promise to make his record "as full, concise and definite as possible," this story, like the estate Montrésor, wears "a look of reticence." The plot is straightforwardly, even naïvely, developed, but as the events of the story unfold with increasing complexity, the reader is sent back to earlier parts of the story or out of the story altogether by allusions— to symbolic forms, to folkloric associations, to literary and extraliterary sources. Though on a first reading the story seems all too clearly banal, further perusals fascinate—trap—the reader by revealing ever more frustrating (thus interesting) patterns of inconclusiveness, loose ends not explained by any authorial intervention and beyond the explanatory powers of the narrator, Mr. Dash.

The story proceeds simply enough, Mr. Dash making only the most superficial connections between its parts. His initial musings on life's "edges"— Walter de la Mare included this story in his collection *On the Edge* (1930)— give haphazard rise to memories of Mr. Bloom of Montrésor, whose estate is for sale, and to the question, "But was it discreet of them to describe the house itself as an *imposing* mansion?" This question tells the reader much about Mr. Dash, especially in readerly retrospect, for his quibble and his off-hand reason for it—"A pair of slippers in my possession prompts this query"—reveal a fastidious but superficial intellect, quite ready to cry *Distinguo!* but rarely if ever prepared to follow up. In a more serious way, this tendency is revealed in his excessive relief to be gone from the "dismal reminders" of death afforded by his convalescing friend; Mr. Dash notices all the right things but knows the significance of none, as shown further by his comment on the gray-faced horseman: "So far as I can see he has nothing whatever to do with what comes after—no more, at most, than my poor thin-nosed, gasping friend." These are to Mr. Dash all oddities, remarkable, and so remarked upon, but no more.

At first, the reader sees no further than Mr. Dash does, but as this superficial narrator's observations accumulate, the reader's role becomes more and more active. As Mr. Bloom remarks in contempt of Mrs. Altogood, vaunting his own occult attainments, "There are deeps, and vasty deeps." It is an ambiguous comment, yet ambiguity befits a story whose depths remain largely undefined, but whose very lack of definition asks readers to try to plumb those depths, to create them, as it were, in the very act of reading.

Mr. Dash's actual encounter with Mr. Bloom is compounded of numerous tiny suspenses, each contributing to the almost overwhelming suspense of the story itself, which is then anticlimactically dissipated by the indefiniteness of the apparition seen and by the final paragraph about Mrs. Altogood and her "gallipot of 'tiddlers.'" The initial empty appearance of the house is answered by the emptiness of Mr. Dash himself, though the narrator is typically quick to pull back from what his observation might imply: "His house had suggested vacancy, so did he—not of human inmate, that is, but of pleasing interest!" He returns to this idea later, when he is less inclined to soften its significance: "What was wrong with the man? What made him so extortionately substantial, and yet in effect, so elusive and unreal? What indeed constitutes the reality of a fellow creature in himself? The something, the someone within, surely, not the mere physical frame." Unlike the story's author, who was willing to admit the impossibility of answering most questions yet pursued them all of his life, Mr. Dash believes that answers are available but allows his odd blend of skepticism and civility to prevent their active pursuit. Pushed by his exigent situation to admit the questions, Mr. Dash's tendency is to comment on the absurdity of the situation, and his admission that his sensations of distaste "lie outside the tests even of mighty Science" is for Mr. Dash a dismissal, not an opportunity for a broader or deeper mind.

The reader, meanwhile, accumulates the ingredients of horror: the silence surrounding Montrésor, the missing key, the "dead-white" lake, Mr. Bloom's odd hesitations at doors, the flatness of his voice and the immobility of his face, his obvious expectation and fear of only he knows what, hints at deaths and hauntings, the yellow dog that skulks from the corner just when the reader expects something else, finally the voices and footsteps, the "hallucination" in Mr. Bloom's bed, and the narrator's dash to safety. These and the other richly contiguous particulars of "A Recluse" pull the reader through the story and set him on a hunt for patterns and connections. Mr. Dash's final misgivings, however, even his notion that he ought to have made "amends" for his running away from Montrésor, are formulated conventionally (Mr. Bloom "has gone home," he has "taken his wages") and though Mr. Dash takes more seriously than heretofore the reality of a less physically tangible world than the one he sees, his mind remains superficial: "I know of no harm he *did*."

Themes and Meanings

Doris Ross McCrosson has written of Walter de la Mare: "Should anyone be looking for answers, he has none.... He questioned everything, never arrogantly, however, because he believed—in fact, it was the only thing he seemed certain of—that all of life is shot with strangeness and mystery...." The story "A Recluse" bears out this assertion, but it makes certain distinctions: The narrator, Mr. Dash, recognizes the predominance of questions in the story he tells, yet the story does not ask the reader therefore to consider him a mouthpiece for the author, one appropriately aware of the difficulty of what de la Mare called "the whole question of the relation between the living and the dead." Mr. Dash, as his name suggests, retreats from the truth of what confronts him—an ironic retreat, since he has accused Mr. Bloom of "showing himself incapable of facing facts." De la Mare's use of such a narrator forces the reader also to choose between running away and facing facts. The story offers this choice in the form of loose ends, a series of inconclusive elements simply presented by Mr. Dash, but forming patterns of significance—though no firm answers—for the reader.

The gray-faced horseman is one of the first inconclusive elements in the story. Here Mr. Dash, as usual, notices all the right things, even makes some appropriate connections, but adds, "Why I have mentioned him I scarcely know, except that there he was, for an instant, at those gates." Later he suspects that Montrésor's effect on him has something to do with "the queer gesture and the queerer looks of my cardboard-boxed gentleman on horseback," but he finds little further reason in the odd encounter. The reader finds himself at first in much the same situation, but hindsight provides a context of significance for the "pseudo-miller" of Montrésor. Horsemen are often messengers or otherwise portentious, and this one mutely fulfills the expected function with his dismissive gesture of "unnecessary violence." Then Mr. Dash's quotation of the old song introduces into the picture the traditional association between millers and the Devil, and though it is merely the "indiscriminately hairy face" that brings this ditty to the narrator's mind, the association raised suggests some connection with the theme of death running through the later parts of the story: On the one hand, one thinks of the vision of Saint John: "I saw ... a pale horse, and its rider's name was Death, and Hades followed him...." (Revelation 6:8); on the other hand, the mysterious cardboard box this horseman carries suggests secrets and the possibility of their revelation—Pandora's Box, perhaps, and its association with the mysteries of the human unconscious. These allusions give the horseman a more exact function as messenger (though neither a strictly theological nor a rigorously psychological one), for they portend the hauntedness of Montrésor, its aura of present death, and the challenge these present to Mr. Dash's persistently flippant externality.

More significant and comprehensive as an inconclusiveness is the matter of the dead secretary, S. S. Champneys, particularly since Mr. Dash believes that he has himself been invited somehow to take Mr. Champneys' place in the household at Montrésor. Mr. Bloom's apparently ingenuous remarks about his former companion's death do not seem to arouse Mr. Dash's suspicion that anything out of the way has happened here; indeed, he considers that though "lung trouble" appears to have killed Mr. Champneys, "exasperation and boredom alone would have accounted for it." Neither do Mr. Bloom's references to his personal wishes—"to go quickly"—even accompanied as they are by Mr. Bloom's startling gestures of head and eyes. Nor, finally, do Mr. Bloom's rather threatening references to Mr. Dash's own death.

These unrecognized or unacknowledged threats, coupled with Mr. Bloom's apparent desire to keep Mr. Dash at Montrésor, suggest that Mr. Dash is similarly incorrect in his failure to connect Mr. Bloom more than casually with Mr. Champneys' death or with any irregular disposal of his remains. That Mr. Champneys' death has something to do with Mr. Bloom's occult experiments is suggested by Mr. Dash's remark that "this house was not haunted, it was infested. Catspaw, poor young Mr. Champneys may have been, but he had indeed helped with the chestnuts." The more immediately horrible inference is not even hinted at by the narrator, yet the surprise entrance of Chunk, the dog, and "the crunching of teeth on bones" are accompanied by this odd exchange:

> "You greedy! You glutton!" Mr. Bloom was cajoling him. "Aye, but where's Steve? An animal's intelligence, Mr. Dash"—his voice floated up to me from under the other side of the table—"is concentrated in his belly. And even when one climbs up to human prejudices one usually finds the foundation as material."

A moment later: "'That animal could tell a tale.' The crunching continued. 'Couldn't yer, you old rascal? Where's Steve; where's Steve?'" The reader naturally wonders who Steve is and later learns that Mr. Champneys' initials are "S. S." His mother addressed him as "Sidney"; did Mr. Bloom call him "Steve"?

Style and Technique

De la Mare's employment of loose ends extends to the witty diction of "A Recluse," where wordplay sets up patterns of verbal echo in the text. The word "imposing" in the story's second paragraph is a good limited example. Here Mr. Dash is quibbling with the auctioneers' use of the term, suggesting that it is an indiscretion. In its usual sense, though, the word cannot be called indiscreet: Montrésor is plainly an impressive sight. Mr. Dash, however, suggests the word's less pleasant senses with his equivocation, and his entire story ostensibly springs from a desire to explain that the word is indiscreet because Montrésor is not what it seems, is in fact a mansion "practising imposture" (as the *Oxford English Dictionary* defines a no longer current meaning of "imposing").

Again, in his final comments on Mrs. Altogood as "a Thomasina Tiddler"—a trifler, that is, not up to the seriousness of Mr. Bloom's occult researches—Mr. Dash employs his terms equivocally. He also considers Mrs. Altogood to be dabbling in "those obscure waters" and leaning "over a gallipot of 'tiddlers'"—a small container, that is, of small fish. Mr. Dash's pun is an obvious one, but it establishes an inescapable contrast with Mr. Bloom's "vasty deeps," suggesting that Mr. Bloom has so far accustomed himself to the "Serpentine" (in contrast to Mrs. Altogood's "gallipot") that he has become master of the big fish—perhaps one of the big fish himself (in contrast to Mrs. Altogood's "tiddlers"). Here Mr. Dash provides as well the watery imagery of the human unconscious, which he has chosen to ignore.

The word "edge," finally, creates a more extensive verbal ambiguity. It opens the story, of course, but Mr. Dash dismisses it as too vague and prefers "the central." Yet the concept appears repeatedly in the story, both in its primary sense—besides "edge," the terms "borderline" and "Jordan" refer in this story to the boundary between life and death—and in two others. During the evening, Mr. Dash says, his host "would . . . edge off toward the door," move furtively to listen for noises. More important, Mr. Bloom is "on edge" and even acknowledges his "edginess." He is upset, but the word also suggests the ambiguity of Mr. Bloom's relationship to life (in Mr. Dash's sense) and the "other side." Such cases of verbal indeterminateness are the particular exemplars of de la Mare's style of inconclusiveness in the story, by which he invites the reader to participate with him in the act of establishing significance and at the same time challenges the concreteness of the categories cherished by every Mr. Dash.

Jonathan A. Glenn

RED LEAVES

Author: William Faulkner (1897-1962)
Type of plot: Satiric realism
Time of plot: The nineteenth century, before the Civil War
Locale: Yoknapatawpha County, Mississippi
First published: 1930

> *Principal characters:*
> HERMAN BASKET, a Chickasaw Indian
> LOUIS BERRY, another Chickasaw Indian
> THE BLACK MAN, a body servant to the dead chief
> MOKETUBBE, the new Chickasaw chief
> ISSETIBBEHA, the recently deceased chief
> DOOM, the chief before Issetibbeha
> OLE GRANDFATHER, a snake

The Story

The situation at the beginning of "Red Leaves" is presented in a dialogue between sixty-year-old Herman Basket and his companion Louis Berry. The two are carrying out an assignment demanded by the age-old custom of some Mississippi Indians of burying slaves with the body of a chief. The two Indians are looking for the body servant of Chief Issetibbeha, who has just died under questionable circumstances. The servant is a black slave from Guinea. In mock-heroic tone and diction, the seekers discuss the fact that the man does not want to die. Bits of information regarding the past history of three successive chiefs and the Chickasaw Indians' keeping of black slaves are shared.

Part 2 gives more detailed information on the chiefs, from Doom, the father of the dead chief, to his son Issetibbeha, and finally to Moketubbe, the son of Issetibbeha and the newest chief. More information is given on the relationship between the Indians and their slaves. For example, Doom hunted his slaves as if they were animals; Issetibbeha mated with a slave and sired Moketubbe. The conversation in this section is an earlier version of the one between Basket and Berry in Part 1: The slaves are a burden, but they are too valuable to get rid of; they could be eaten, but they probably do not have a good taste. Of special interest is the story of the origins of the palace, a river steamboat brought on rollers by slave labor from the river some miles away. Again, there is reference to the slippers with the red heels, brought from Paris some years before by Issetibbeha: They serve the same purpose for the chiefs as a crown for a king. The picture of 250-pound, five-foot Moketubbe forcing the slippers on his too large feet is ludicrous, and his wearing the slippers while his father is still alive bodes ill for Issetibbeha. The digression continues with the fact that Issetibbeha lived for five more years and then he died. It ends with a return to the story's present with the words "That was yesterday."

Part 3 of "Red Leaves" resumes the dialogue between Basket and Berry. They are concerned that the chase will be too long, that the chief's body will begin to smell, and that the food for the many celebrants of the occasion will give out too soon. Their mock-heroic style continues as they blame the white man for all of their troubles—blame him, that is, for foisting the blacks on them. The two report to the indolent Moketubbe, who will lead the hunt.

Part 4 shifts attention to the black body servant. He is described as forty years old, his having served the chief for twenty-three years. A slight time shift relates his observations on the day the chief lay sick. From a hiding place in the loft, he has followed closely the reports of the illness and the death of Issetibbeha, listening after dark to the sound of the drums. He also hears the sound of "two voices, himself and himself," discussing the fact that he, too, is dead. He begins his flight, stopping at the plantation to receive assistance from the other blacks there, then plunging into the wilderness. On two occasions he is nearly apprehended by Indians. At sunset he is slashed by a cottonmouth moccasin, which he treats as a totem animal: He addresses it as "Ole Grandfather" and touches its head, letting it strike him again and again. He contemplates once more the fact that he does not wish to die.

Part 5 continues the chase but shifts to a less serious tone. The huge Moketubbe is being carried on a litter by alternating crews of Indians as he leads the pursuers. Again, he is a ludicrous figure as he tries to wear the royal slippers; the similarity to the plight of Cinderella's big-footed stepsisters is too obvious to miss. The hunt goes on into the sixth day, with the predicted shortage of food for the guests and the odor of the dead chief both coming to pass. Another odor is also of concern: that of the body servant with snake's venom in his veins. Will he be of any use to Issetibbeha in the Happy Hunting Grounds? The slave is told that he has nothing to be ashamed of, that he has run well. His shouting, talking, and singing have ceased as he quietly watches his captors.

Part 6 concludes the story in three pages covering the return to the plantation. The man stalls for time, asking for food, which he unsuccessfully tries to eat, and water, which he goes through the futile motions of drinking. His cry of "ah-ah-ah" is answered by the last word of the story when Basket says "come."

Themes and Meanings

Treated from various viewpoints is the primitive ritual of human sacrifice as practiced by these Indians. Reference is made to a now discarded ritual of cannibalism, but the ritual of burying the chief's servant with him is at the time of the story still practiced, although some of the superstitious feeling for it has disappeared. Where the viewpoint is that of the Indians, the attitude is one of complaining about the inconvenience of such ritual, as if to say, "let's get on with it before the body becomes too rank." The chief is much too fat and lazy to lead the hunt as tradition demands he must; the sixty-year-old Herman Basket would much prefer not to be in the position of organizing the expedition; there is even a statement or two blaming blacks for the inconvenience. The Indians never question directly their belief in Happy Hunting Grounds or in the idea that chiefs need a horse, a dog, and a servant to hunt there, yet the implication of their attitude is that of doubt, perhaps disbelief; the ritual is continued because it is a tradition honored by time—thus the many references to past observances.

When the viewpoint is that of the body servant, there is a realistic facing of the inevitable while regretting and trying to postpone if not prevent it. No longer is there speculation on customs or inconveniences: The vital matter of life and death dominates every concern, a matter that has been treated by Basket and Berry somewhat flippantly at times, casually or realistically at others. The tone, when the focus is on the slave is always deadly serious.

Style and Technique

William Faulkner has woven into "Red Leaves" two stories carefully unified into one. The first is a humorous narrative of Indians honoring an outdated ritual. The treating of such serious matters as the poisoning of chiefs and the burying of men who, at least for the moment, are still alive, would suggest a lofty, solemn tone. Faulkner indeed assumes such a tone in the lofty diction of the Indians, a style suggestive of the King James Bible, and in the dutiful manner in which Basket and Berry carry out their responsibilities. Yet the underlying tone is ironic: What the Indians say is not in harmony with the way they say it. Frequent references to the incongruities in the lives and persons of the three chiefs contribute to this undertone. The fact that none of them is a full-blooded Chickasaw, that the newest chief is half black but no more than one-eighth Chickasaw, raises doubts as to the legitimacy of the succession. The strong suggestions of royal poisonings confirm such suspicions. The use of a deteriorated steamboat for a palace and ill-fitting slippers for a crown reinforce the opinion that these are not legitimate chiefs; yet their credentials are impressive enough to qualify them for a dog, a horse, and a servant in the Happy Hunting Grounds. The ambiguous attitude toward the keeping of black slaves also suggests humor and irony.

The other story, the wilderness tale of a runaway slave being pursued by his Indian masters so that he can become a human sacrifice to their timeworn superstition, lacks the glibness of humorous speech. The slave is often silent; when he speaks, the words are agonizingly forced; at times they are incoherent. His plight is real; his fear is genuine; his emotions are intense. The wilderness through which he flees is also realistic, even naturalistic, for in spite of his valiant effort, he knows his doom is inevitable. The fear, the darkness, the exhaustion, the beat of the drums—all reflect an attitude in complete contrast to that of the Indians.

Faulkner frequently found opportunity to use his stories more than once. "Red Leaves" was published originally in 1930 in *The Saturday Evening Post*. The next year it was included in his first collection of stories, *These 13*. In 1950 he included it in his most complete collection, *Collected Short Stories of William Faulkner*, edited by Joseph Blotner and published by Random House (this is the edition followed herein). Five years later he revised the story of the servant's flight through the wilderness for his collection of hunting stories entitled *Big Woods*.

George W. Van Devender

THE RED-HEADED LEAGUE

Author: Arthur Conan Doyle (1859-1930)
Type of plot: Detective story
Time of plot: 1890
Locale: London, England
First published: 1891

> *Principal characters:*
> SHERLOCK HOLMES, the world's greatest detective
> DR. JOHN H. WATSON, his friend and biographer
> MR. JABEZ WILSON, the owner of a small pawnshop
> JOHN CLAY, alias VINCENT SPAULDING, his assistant

The Story

When Dr. Watson visits the apartment of his friend Sherlock Holmes, he finds the world's first consulting detective in conference with a client with bright red hair, Mr. Jabez Wilson. Holmes invites Watson to remain and to hear the client's unusual story. Wilson, a man of about sixty, is a not very successful small businessman; the most noteworthy thing about him is the flaming color of his hair. After introductions all around, Wilson explains how upset he has been by a recent incident, so upset that he has come to Holmes for his help.

Wilson says that he is a man of very settled habits, a bachelor who almost never deviates from the daily routine of running his pawnshop. At least, he never deviated until he heard of the Red-Headed League. One day in his shop, his assistant, Vincent Spaulding, called his attention to an advertisement in the newspaper that announced an opening in the Red-Headed League. The announcement promised a salary of four pounds a week (about twenty dollars at the time of the story) for "purely nominal services" to the candidate who was accepted. The amount was a considerable sum at the time, especially if the duties were slight, and Spaulding urged Wilson to apply. The timid pawnbroker did so, but only after Spaulding practically took him to the office mentioned in the ad.

There Wilson heard the story of an eccentric American millionaire who had left a fortune to provide an income for Londoners with red hair as bright as the millionaire's had been. Wilson was accepted into the League. He learned that the nominal duties consisted only of his coming to the office from 10:00 A.M. until 2:00 P.M. each day and copying out the *Encyclopaedia Britannica* in longhand. Since most of Wilson's business was done in the evening, he was delighted at the chance to supplement his income. This he did for eight weeks, getting well into the "A" volume, until one day he arrived at the office to find it closed, with a notice on the door that the Red-Headed League had been dissolved. He was so disturbed by the thought that someone had been playing a practical joke on him that he came to Holmes for a solution.

Holmes points out that Wilson has lost nothing—indeed, has made thirty pounds—but says that the case is remarkable. Holmes soon discovers that Spaulding, who encouraged Wilson to apply, is not all that he seems. The assistant came to Wilson recently for half-wages, claiming to want to learn the business. Although perfectly satisfactory as an assistant, Spaulding has an interest in photography, has set up Wilson's cellar as a darkroom, and is down in the basement every minute that Wilson does not need him in the shop above. Holmes promises to look into the case, and Wilson leaves.

Holmes and Watson first visit the district in which Wilson's shop is located, where Holmes does some mysterious things: He asks directions from a clerk at the pawnshop; he taps the street outside with his walking stick and remarks that the case is complicated by the fact that it is Saturday. Later, he asks Watson to meet him at Baker Street that evening at ten, and to come armed. When Watson arrives, he finds two other men there: Peter Jones, an inspector from Scotland Yard, and a Mr. Merryweather, a bank director. Holmes takes them to a branch of the City and Suburban Bank, a branch located in the same district as Wilson's pawnshop. There they enter the vaults of the bank, where Merryweather shows them a shipment of thirty thousand gold coins they have recently received from the Bank of France. Holmes says that they may have some time to wait, and they sit quietly in the dim vault.

After about an hour, they see a glint of light from the floor: A paving stone moves, and a man's face appears from the hole. He climbs out, and Holmes and the inspector seize him.

Holmes later explains his reasoning: He became suspicious when first he heard that Vincent Spaulding had taken Wilson's job offer at less than the normal wages. His time in the cellar suggested that there would be found the real interest of Spaulding. The business of the Red-Headed League seemed to be a trick to get the sedentary Wilson out of the shop for some hours each day so that Spaulding and his confederates could do whatever they were up to, unobserved. When, on his visit to the area, Holmes tapped the pavement and heard a hollow sound, he concluded that they were tunneling beneath the street to the branch bank in question. When he asked the pawnbroker's clerk, Spaulding himself, for directions, Holmes recognized him as John Clay, a notoriously cunning criminal. The rest was the simple matter of gaining entrance to the bank vault—Holmes reasoned that the robbers would strike on Sunday, when the bank was closed—and waiting for them to appear.

Themes and Meanings

Arthur Conan Doyle wrote so many Sherlock Holmes stories, all of which can be found in collected editions, that it is hard to imagine a time when the character of the famous detective was new and fresh in the public imagination. Two novels featuring Holmes, *A Study in Scarlet* (1887) and *The Sign of Four* (1890), were published with only mild success. It was not until the publication of the first Holmes short story, "A Scandal in Bohemia," in 1891, that the detective became immensely popular. It was to capitalize on this public demand that Doyle wrote "The Red-Headed League."

The story is above all a vehicle to display the remarkable reasoning ability of Sherlock Holmes, a man who is able to impose order on a seemingly meaningless jumble of experience. Experience in the Holmes stories only seems, however, to be meaningless: For someone who, like the detective, observes closely and interprets correctly, the world is a book to be read.

In "The Red-Headed League," the character of Holmes is the theme, and in the story Doyle continues to supply information about the background, tastes, and habits of his greatest creation. It is in this story that the reader learns that Holmes has a "poetic and contemplative" side to his nature, one that is illustrated when Holmes interrupts his detective work to attend a violin concert. One finds out as well that Holmes himself is a musician and a composer "of no ordinary merit." Through the almost casual introduction of details such as these, Doyle created a character who escapes the bounds of fiction, becoming almost lifelike in his solidity.

A subsidiary theme may be present, too, represented in the adage "You can't cheat an honest man." Throughout the story, Doyle delicately hints at Wilson's greed. The most telling example of that greed is his hiring of Vincent Spaulding only because Spaulding agrees to work for half-pay. From that bad decision, all of Wilson's troubles spring.

Style and Technique

The style of the story is one that was to become customary in the Holmes adventures: Watson narrates the tale from his viewpoint as an on-the-spot observer. He provides Holmes (and Doyle) with the means to build suspense because, although Watson is present to see all of Holmes's actions, he does not understand their significance. Thus, the unlocking of the mystery is postponed until the end, when Holmes explains his actions.

The technique of building suspense by holding off the explanation is usually employed several times in a typical Sherlock Holmes story, and this one is no exception: First, there is the small demonstration of Holmes's ability when Wilson first enters the Baker Street flat and Holmes deduces many facts about him from his appearance. The postponement is only momentary in this prelude, so to call it, because Holmes explains the inferences he draws from watch chains and calluses and the like. Nevertheless, the technique has been used to show Holmes's powers, and his revelation at the end of the story of a greater chain of inferences has been prepared for by the less important scene at the beginning.

"The Red-Headed League" was a story of which Doyle himself was proud: At the conclusion of a contest held by *Strand* magazine, asking readers to pick their favorite Sherlock Holmes stories, Doyle contributed a list of his own, on which "The Red-Headed League" ranked second only to "The Adventure of the Speckled Band"; Doyle rated it so high, he said, because of the originality of the plot. It is hard to argue with the author's recommendation: The cleverness of the trick to remove Wilson from the scene of the crime and Holmes's equal cleverness in preventing the crime continue to make the story memorable.

Walter E. Meyers

REMBRANDT'S HAT

Author: Bernard Malamud (1914-1986)
Type of plot: Psychological realism
Time of plot: The 1960's
Locale: New York City
First published: 1973

> *Principal characters:*
> ARKIN, an art historian at a New York art school, age thirty-four
> RUBIN, a sculptor and teacher at the same art school, age forty-six

The Story

After his wife left him, Rubin, the sculptor, took to wearing various odd hats. Now, at age forty-six, he favors a visorless, soft, round white cap. Arkin, the art historian at the New York City art school where Rubin also teaches, thinks that the hat "illumines a lonely inexpressiveness arrived at after years of experience." He tells Rubin that the hat resembles Rembrandt's hat—the one that Rembrandt wears in the profound self-portraits of his middle age. The day after Arkin makes this remark, Rubin stops wearing the hat and begins to avoid him.

Arkin—"a hypertensive bachelor of thirty-four"—has considered himself friendly with Rubin, although they are not really friends. Arkin has been at the school for seven years, having left an art curator's job in St. Louis to come to New York. Arkin could never get Rubin to say anything at all about his artwork. Arkin remembers that when he first arrived, Rubin was working in wood, altering driftwood objects with a hatchet. At that time Rubin was persuaded by the director of the art school to present an exhibition—his only one. The exhibit was not a success, and Rubin spent the time sulking in a storage room at the rear of the gallery. Recently, Arkin suggested that it might be a good idea for Rubin to show his new work, which is constructed from welded triangular pieces of scrap iron. The suggestion obviously irritated Rubin.

After the hat remark, months pass during which Rubin avoids Arkin. After a while Arkin, too, becomes irritated, reasoning that "he didn't like people who didn't like him." He usually worries, however, that it might be his fault. He decides that he has probably done three things to alienate Rubin: not mentioning Rubin's driftwood show; suggesting the possibility of a new show that Rubin obviously does not want; and commenting on Rubin's white cap. He makes up his mind to apologize to Rubin and to put their acquaintanceship back on its normal track.

Before he is able to apologize, Arkin receives a present for his thirty-fifth birthday from one of his students: a white ten-gallon Stetson hat. Immediately after Rubin sees the Stetson, it is stolen. Arkin realizes that Rubin is the thief. Even though they try to avoid each other, they begin to encounter each other everywhere they go. At this point, "The art historian hated Rubin for hating him and beheld repugnance in Rubin's eyes." After a yelling scene between the two in front of the art school, Arkin again realizes that he should apologize, "if only because if the other couldn't he could."

Half a year after the yelling scene, on his thirty-sixth birthday, Arkin decides to visit Rubin's studio to look around for his Stetson. He inspects Rubin's work in welded triangular iron pieces, set amid broken stone statuary he has been collecting for years. Rubin has come from abstract driftwood sculptures to figurative objects such as flowers and busts of men and women colleagues. He discovers only one lovely piece: a sculpture of a dwarf tree. Arkin begins to understand why Rubin does not like to talk about a new exhibition of his work—for there is only the one fine piece.

Several days later, Arkin is preparing a lecture about Rembrandt's self-portraits. In doing so, Arkin realizes that it is not Rembrandt's hat that resembles Rubin's white cap; rather, it is the expression in the artist's eyes that is similar: "the unillusioned honesty of his gaze." Rembrandt's expression is "magisterially sad," as Arkin notes. Realizing this, Arkin decides to put himself in Rubin's position. He realizes that his previous remark about the hat was too much for Rubin to bear, because it forced him to ask himself once too often: "Why am I going on if this is the kind of sculptor I am going to be for the rest of my life?"

Finally realizing this, Arkin goes directly to Rubin's studio. Shortly afterward, Rubin enters, and the first thing Arkin says concerns the dwarf tree: "It's a beautiful sculpture, the best in the room I'd say." At this, Rubin stares at him in anger. Arkin then apologizes for his earlier remarks, and Rubin beings to cry. Arkin immediately leaves.

After this, the two men stop avoiding each other. They speak pleasantly when they meet, which is not often. One day Rubin reappears in his white cap—the one that seemed to resemble Rembrandt's hat. The narrator's concluding remark is "He wore it like a crown of failure and hope."

Themes and Meanings

Bernard Malamud presents the idea that art and beauty are difficult taskmasters. When Rubin measures himself as an artist, what scale is he to use—perfection in beauty and form? Indeed, is he to compare himself with one of the world-acclaimed master painters, Rembrandt? If these are to be his standards, then how is Rubin to measure up? In case he should try to stop thinking about the quality of his art, the comic Arkin is sent to keep him on his toes. Here Arkin serves much the same purposes as the troublesome

Susskind in Malamud's "The Last Mohican."

Arkin reminds Rubin about Rembrandt, hence of Rembrandt's beautiful achievements in art as well as the recognition the world has accorded Rembrandt. Rubin, on the other hand, has had only one exhibition of his work—seven years ago—and has produced little or nothing of merit since then. Rubin is painfully aware of this himself. At forty-eight years of age toward the story's end, Rubin has few years left to produce beautiful work, and somehow his welded iron triangles do not produce much hope in the reader's mind. This is the reason for the sadness Arkin notices in Rubin's eyes. Since Rubin shares his pursuit of beauty with some of the greatest artists of the past, however, perhaps one may hold out hope for him. At the least, perhaps the pursuit of the beautiful is its own reward.

A second theme that Malamud pursues is the difficulty of human relationships. Arkin, a well-meaning fellow if ever there was one, despite his best intentions frequently wounds Rubin. When he finally realizes, however, that he is responsible for alienating Rubin, Arkin apologizes and asks forgiveness. Thus, Malamud demonstrates effectively that despite their difficulty, human relationships are possible so long as one is willing to make the effort and take the responsibility.

Style and Technique

Although "Rembrandt's Hat" uses a third-person narrator to present the characters, much of the story is built around Arkin's interior monologues. These monologues, delivered by the super-sensitive art historian, add a special comic touch to the story. The monologues, as well as the dialogue, are presented in the Jewish idiom of New York City.

Malamud's title secures the reader's attention at the outset, and he focuses the opening two pages of the story on this white cloth hat. The third-person narrator says that "Rubin wore it like a crown"; the last line in the story, describing the hat as a "crown of failure and hope," returns to this image, investing it with a deeper understanding of the artist's quest.

Malamud keeps a sharp thematic focus on the two men; indeed, they are the only characters who appear in the story at all except for the two-sentence appearance of an art student who gives Arkin the cowboy hat. The only aspect of the men that is mentioned is their mutual interest in art and in each other. Arkin's thoughts—through which the reader sees Rubin for the most part—are kept focused on Rubin and on their strained relationship. In this way, Malamud keeps the reader focused on his main interest: the difficulties of a life devoted to art.

A. Bruce Dean

A REPORT TO AN ACADEMY

Author: Franz Kafka (1883-1924)
Type of plot: Animal tale
Time of plot: Early twentieth century
Locale: Perhaps Hamburg
First published: "Ein Bericht für eine Akademie," 1917 (English translation, 1946)

Principal character:
ROTPETER, the narrator and protagonist, an ape that is becoming human

The Story

Asked by a scientific academy to report on his former life as an ape, Rotpeter responds by saying that his development into a human being during the last five years has erased virtually all memories of his youth in the Gold Coast. In his address to the distinguished gentlemen of the academy, he concentrates instead on his penetration into the human world, where he now feels well established as an accomplished artist in variety shows.

According to his captors, he was shot twice by members of an expedition of the Hagenbeck circus, on the cheek and below the hip. The first wound gave him his name, Rotpeter ("Red Peter"), which he finds distasteful but which differentiates him from a trained ape named Peter that has recently died. He is not at all bashful about showing his second wound to journalists, especially those who claim that he has not completely suppressed his ape nature. In the interest of truth, he believes that he may take down his pants whenever he wishes to reveal his well-groomed fur and the maliciously inflicted wound.

His first memories stem from the time of his captivity in a small cage in the Hagenbeck steamship. Overwhelmed by distress at not having a "way out" for the first time in his life, he was unusually quiet, which was taken as a sign that he either would die soon or could be easily trained. Realizing that he could not live without some kind of way out, he decided to cease being an ape. This solution meant, however, neither escape nor desire for freedom "in all directions," a quality he perhaps knew as an ape and for which some humans long. Freedom is among the noblest of human self-deceptions, comparable in his mind to the precarious movements of trapeze artists in the variety theaters.

The quiet that the ship's sailors afforded Rotpeter allowed him to observe them carefully. They moved slowly, often sitting in front of his cage, smoking and watching him in turn. He began to imitate them, first spitting in their faces, then smoking a pipe. It took him weeks to bring himself to drink schnapps. One sailor in particular persisted in giving him drinking lessons. Rotpeter watched attentively as the man uncorked a bottle and repeatedly set it to his lips. Eager to imitate him, Rotpeter soiled his cage, to the sailor's great satisfaction. Then, with an exaggerated didactic gesture, the sailor emptied the bottle in one gulp and ended the "theoretical" part of the instruction by rubbing his stomach and grinning. It was now the ape's turn, but despite all of his efforts, he could not overcome his aversion to the smell of the empty bottle when he brought it to his lips.

One evening, the ape grabbed a schnapps bottle that had been left in front of his cage. It was perhaps during a party—a gramophone played—and a number of spectators gathered around as he uncorked the bottle, raised it to his mouth, and emptied it without hesitation. He then threw away the bottle, not in despair but as an artist. His senses intoxicated, he called out suddenly "Hallo," and with this cry "leaped into the human community." Although his voice failed him for months afterward and his disgust at the schnapps bottle increased, he had found his way out: He would imitate humans.

After his arrival in Hamburg for training, he did not hesitate to choose between the two paths open to him: zoo or variety stage. The zoo was only a different sort of cage. Wearing out many instructors in the process, he learned rapidly how to abandon his ape nature. When he became more confident of his abilities and the public began to follow his progress, he hired his own teachers, placed them in five neighboring rooms, and learned from them simultaneously by jumping from one room to another without interruption.

Looking back on his development, Rotpeter is relatively happy with the gains he has made, yet he is also aware that his enormous exertion has given him only the "average culture of a European." Nevertheless, it has provided him with his way out, his human way out. He has "taken cover"; this was his only path, for he could not choose freedom.

During the day, he lounges in his rocking chair and looks out the window. His impresario sits in the anteroom and waits for his ring. In the evening there is the performance, followed by social or scientific gatherings. Afterward, he comes home to a small, half-trained chimpanzee, with whom he takes his pleasure according to the manner of apes, yet whose sight he cannot stand in the daytime.

On the whole, he has achieved what he had set out to achieve. He does not want any human judgment of his efforts, but rather wishes only to spread knowledge and to report. To the distinguished gentlemen of the academy as well, he has only reported.

Themes and Meanings

In the fall of 1916, six months before the composition of "A Report to an Academy," Kafka wrote Felice Bauer, the woman to whom he was engaged twice and who played such a major and traumatic role in his life from 1912 to 1917, that he had an "infinite desire for autonomy, independence, freedom in all directions." Torn between the demands of artistic freedom on the one hand and ties to his family, work, and possible marriage on the other, Kafka insisted on the former in order to pursue his writing. While Rotpeter, in his report, adamantly denies himself such a desire for limitless freedom, he also vividly demonstrates the weaknesses of his artistry and the extent to which he has compromised his life. Yet given his capture and the loss of his original freedom, Rotpeter's ruthless pursuit of his way out of captivity has succeeded in gaining for him freedom of movement, respect, and fame.

Rotpeter remains peculiarly suspended outside both the ape and the human communities, and his case eludes human judgment, which he does not want anyway. As he well knows, he is not a human, but only mimics human behavior as a means of remaining on the path that he has chosen for himself. In human terms, his art is not true art (but rather imitative and neither original nor creative), and his measure of freedom is not true freedom (he has sacrificed his real self for the sake of his career). In his own terms, however, especially compared to his first days of captivity in the steamship, he has achieved an astounding degree of success: He can read and write and think rationally and has become a moderately cultivated and sophisticated being. Although commentators have often understood the story as a satire of conformity and accommodation to a superficial culture, the ape in fact remains a critical outsider; whatever laughter his report engenders comes less at his expense than at that of the civilization which has forced him into such narrow choices.

Style and Technique

The virtues and shortcomings of Rotpeter's talent as a mimic are readily apparent in the language and style of his address, which is an unconscious yet masterful parody of academic oratory. Its comic incongruities arise from the fact that he is so unaware of how empty and hollow his high-flown phrases sound. In proper deference to his learned audience, Rotpeter uses a considerable amount of metaphor, philosophical reflection, complex sentence structure, exclamation, and wit to tell his life story. Thus, he speaks of the five years that divide him from his apehood as "a time that is perhaps short when measured on the calendar, but infinitely long when galloped through as I did, accompanied in stretches by admirable men, advice, applause, and orchestral music, but basically alone, for all accompaniment kept itself—to keep to the image—far in front of the gate." Elsewhere, he speaks of the drunken sailor wanting to "resolve the riddle of my soul," of how his "ape nature raced rolling over itself out of me and away, so that my first instructor almost became apish as a result," of his intellectual progress as a "penetration of the rays of knowledge from all sides into the awakening brain." These rhetorical flourishes underscore both his shrewd verbal dexterity and the superficial and trivial speech of those whom he mimics so well.

Peter West Nutting

THE RESEMBLANCE BETWEEN A VIOLIN CASE
AND A COFFIN

Author: Tennessee Williams (1911-1983)
Type of plot: Domestic realism
Time of plot: c. 1923
Locale: Clarksdale, Mississippi
First published: 1950

> *Principal characters:*
> Tom, the narrator, a boy about twelve years old
> Tom's sister, unnamed in the story, who is two years older
> than he
> Tom's mother, also unnamed
> Grand, Tom's grandmother
> Richard Miles, a handsome seventeen-year-old boy who
> plays the violin
> Miss Aehle, a music teacher from whom Tom's sister and
> Richard Miles take lessons

The Story

Tom, the twelve-year-old narrator, is bewildered because suddenly his sister is receiving all the attention from his mother and grandmother. The girl is said not to be feeling well, a euphemism for the fact that the physical manifestations of her passage from childhood to womanhood have just begun to show themselves. When Tom becomes frustrated with the situation and yells at his sister, his grandmother, who usually treats him with great gentleness, twists his ear. Tom wants his sister to go out and play but is told that she must practice her piano, which she starts to do. When Tom asks Grand why his sister cannot practice later, the girl flees from the piano in tears and goes to her bedroom. Tom does not know what to make of any of this.

The girl's rites of passage are symbolized by her being taken downtown by her mother on an expedition from which Tom is excluded. When his sister and mother return, the girl's long hair has been cut: "The long copperish curls which had swung below her shoulders, bobbing almost constantly with excitement, were removed one day." Tom's relationship with his sister has changed in ways that he cannot quite fathom.

Tom's sister takes piano lessons from Miss Aehle, a spinster who is extremely encouraging of all of her students' abilities, regardless of whether they are gifted. She need not exaggerate, however, to praise the musical virtues of Tom's sister, who is a quite gifted pianist for her age. Soon, Miss Aehle's students are to give a concert in the parish hall of Tom's grandfather's church. Tom's sister and Richard Miles are to play a duet: she at the piano, Richard at the violin. The two practice constantly, both alone and together, in preparation for the event. These are troubling days for Tom's sister, because her musical talent seems to be declining. She has great trouble remembering the music, and her fingers are not working well.

Richard, who is handsome, talented, and sensitive, has obviously stolen the heart of Tom's sister, and Tom also feels a sexual attraction to Richard. He is disturbed at the awakening of his own sexuality: "How on earth did I explain to myself, at that time, the fascination of his [Richard's] physical being without, at the same time, confessing to myself that I was a little monster of sensuality?" Not only has Tom lost his sister as a playmate, but he also finds himself in an unmentionable and, at the time in which the story is set, unthinkable competition with her for the affections of the same boy.

The concert takes place, and Tom's sister, almost pathologically shy and sensitive, nearly goes to pieces before it. She complains that her hands are stiff. She fills her room with steam from the bath and opens the windows, which Grand closes, saying that the girl will catch her death of cold, whereupon the girl uncharacteristically snaps at the grandmother. Finally, she gets to the parish hall, however, and tries to play her duet with Richard. She is so nervous that she cannot remember the piece beyond the first few pages, so she keeps returning to the beginning. Richard follows skillfully and does what he can to be understanding and encouraging. He plays loudly when she is making mistakes, and the pair receives an ovation, largely because of Richard's skillful handling of a tense situation.

On the drive home from the parish hall, Tom's family remains silent. Soon the family moves from the South. They learn that Richard, who had always seemed too good to be real, has died of pneumonia. The narrator muses on how Richard's violin case had looked like a little black coffin made for a child or a doll.

Themes and Meanings

Tennessee Williams is said to have used his short stories as sketch pads for his plays. Certainly, in the case of "The Resemblance Between a Violin Case and a Coffin," the situation is reversed; it is the story in the Williams canon most closely related to *The Glass Menagerie* (1944). The story is autobiographical in all of its details, although the time sequence and locales are slightly distorted.

Williams' own sister Rose was the very essence of Tom's sister in this story, a beautiful but wretchedly insecure adolescent who grew into a neurotic and, finally, psychotic woman. Rose eventually had to be institutionalized and have a lobotomy, which required her to have custodial care for all of Williams' lifetime. In actuality, Rose played the violin, not the piano, as the sister in the story did; in *The Glass Menagerie*, Rose fantasized about her collection of glass animals, the only things with which she felt safe and somewhat secure.

Williams constantly explored the question of what inroads the real world makes upon the psyches of sensitive people. The Blanche DuBois–Stanley Kowalski relationship in *A Streetcar Named Desire* (1947) centers on this same consideration. Blanche is the typical idealized Southern woman who, like the women in Williams' own family, has retained the gentility of the South's vanished glory but has fallen on hard times. Stanley Kowalski represents the modern industrial age that will bring the gentle Southerners to their knees, but in *A Streetcar Named Desire*, at least, not without the connivance and enticement of these Southerners. In "The Resemblance Between a Violin Case and a Coffin," the unfeeling world is more vague than it is in some of Williams' other work, but it is still devastating to the sensitive.

Williams is concerned with sexual pressures as a root cause of human tensions, and "The Resemblance Between a Violin Case and a Coffin" clearly illustrates the effect that these pressures have on the central characters in the story. Yet Williams also drops hints about the effects that such pressures have upon the parents in the story. Williams writes of the mother, "Upstairs my mother began to sing to herself which was something she only did when my father had just left on a long trip with his samples and would not be likely to return for quite a while."

Obviously, the parents in the story do not have a close or loving relationship. As the story unfolds, Tom is systematically excluded from the family, a boy among three women—a grandmother, a mother, and a sister—who whisper among themselves about confidences to which the boy is not privy. The healthiest person in the story, Richard Miles, is ironically the one who does not live to maturity. One senses some kind of perverse divine retribution in the fact that the sister lives on with her great emotional pain, that Tom lives on with his unresolved guilt and his feeling of detachment from those he loves, while Richard, who seems well adapted to his world, is taken from it.

The theme of personal isolation pervades the story, for despite the fact that members of families cling to one another, the individual members of the family are very much isolated in their own discrete worlds. Tom's sister, as she is seen here, is in the process of constructing around herself the wall behind which she will spend her life. In *The Glass Menagerie*, the wall becomes so strong as to be virtually impenetrable, and so did it come to be in the case of Williams' own sister.

Style and Technique

Williams' style in this story is one of surface gentleness which masks the great cruelties of life that lurk just below the surface. In this story, having assumed the persona of a pubescent boy, the author never deviates from that point of view. Readers see the world that Williams is revealing to them just as a twelve- or thirteen-year-old child would see it. No omniscient insights destroy the illusion Williams initially creates.

Williams' women cannot accept realities. They have enough of the Southern lady about them to be exceedingly vulnerable to the hurts that are a part of daily life for most people. They agonize over what to most people would seem to be routine events. In dealing with her daughter's first menstruation, Tom's mother (and the grandmother as well) makes of it something almost mystical rather than something quite natural. The message the young girl derives from this is that women are supposed to be sickly during their menstrual period. She learns quickly that her expected behavior must demonstrate her delicacy, and in meeting her parental (and grandparental) expectations, she sows the seeds for a life of emotional delicacy and physical weakness.

In this story, one sees the interplay of love and death that Leslie Fiedler finds at the heart of much American fiction. The title bears the suggestion, and the story carries it through. One might ask, "Who is dead?" Is Tom's sister really not more dead than Richard Miles? She has experienced a death of the soul, while Richard has lived his life vitally, self-assuredly. He remains a vivid memory in the minds of those whose lives he touched.

R. Baird Shuman

THE RETURN OF A PRIVATE

Author: Hamlin Garland (1860-1940)
Type of plot: Domestic realism
Time of plot: 1865
Locale: Near LaCrosse, Wisconsin Territory
First published: 1891

> *Principal characters:*
> PRIVATE EDWARD SMITH, the hero, a sickly Civil War veteran returning home after four years
> EMMA SMITH, his young wife, who has cared for their three children and the farm in his absence
> WIDOW GRAY, also called "Mother Gray," a kindly neighbor
> JIM CRANBY and
> SAUNDERS, two veterans who served with Private Smith and are also returning home

The Story

"The Return of a Private" begins on a train from New Orleans carrying Northern veterans back to the Midwest. They are among the last to leave the South; sickness and wounds delayed their departure until August. Only four or five are left to get off the train at LaCrosse. One of them, Private Edward Smith, still suffers from fever and ague. It is two o'clock in the morning, and rather than spend their money for a hotel room, Smith and two compatriots decide to bed down in the train station. The two other veterans arrange their blankets so that their sickly friend might be more comfortable, but Private Smith has trouble sleeping. The war has left him worn out and infirm and in no shape to care for his heavily mortgaged farm or to provide for his young wife and their three children.

As Sunday morning dawns, the three veterans look across the Mississippi River and to the hills beyond, invigorated by a familiar landscape that they have not seen for several years. They buy some coffee, eat their army hardtack, and then begin walking along the road toward the hills and home, stopping now and again to let Private Smith rest. Jim Cranby, the oldest of the three, expects that he will get home just in time to surprise his boys at evening milking. Private Smith muses aloud that Old Rover will no doubt be the first of his household to run out to meet him, but when he mentions Emma, his voice breaks and is silenced by emotion. Saunders, the youngest of the three, seldom says a word. His wife will not be waiting for him; she died the first year of the war, having caught pneumonia laboring in the autumn rains to bring in the harvest. The veterans know one another well; it is a friendship born in the hardships of war.

Coming to a fork in the road, Private Smith says farewell to his friends; they promise to keep in touch, and he reassures them that he will be all right walking alone. They stop and wave at a distance, and Private Smith thinks of the good times they have had in the midst of the terrible war. He also thinks about Billy Tripp, his best friend from home, and how Billy was laughing one minute and dead from a "minie" ball the next. Billy's mother and sweetheart will want him to tell them all about the untimely death of handsome young Billy Tripp. Private Smith walks on slowly.

The scene now shifts several miles up the road to the little valley, or coulee as it is called, where Emma Smith is beginning another Sunday morning worrying about her husband and their uncertain future. Six weeks before, Edward wrote that he would shortly be discharged but has sent no other word since. She thinks about the farm he had labored so diligently to keep up. It is a shambles. Before leaving for war, Edward had contracted with a man to take care of the farm, but the man ran away in the night, stealing some farm equipment in the process. The neighbor who is now renting the land is naturally harvesting his own crops first. Thinking about her three children, Emma looks around her and weeps. Rather than be overcome by despair, she hastily dresses nine-year-old Mary, six-year-old Tommy, and four-year-old Ted, and they go down the road to Mother Gray's.

Widow Gray has a house full of children and a heart full of love. Worn down by constant labor, she is happiest when she is sharing what little she has. It is Sunday, and her girls are expecting their beaux; son Bill and his family arrive for dinner, and Widow Gray is beside herself with joy to see Emma and her little brood coming down the road. The Gray household is filled with a contagious conviviality that makes Emma momentarily forget her sadness. The dinner itself is a farmer's feast, with platters of corn and potatoes and pies of various kinds. After the meal, the women linger at the table, and Widow Gray reads the tea leaves, producing shrieks and gales of laughter from her daughters as she predicts the coming of handsome callers. Turning to Emma, she says that a soldier is on his way to her. Just then, Widow Gray looks out the window and sees what appears to be a soldier walking up the road just beyond the house. Emma tries to get his attention, but he seems not to hear.

Running up the road toward her farm, Emma is not sure that the soldier standing by the rail fence is really her husband Edward. He is so thin and pale. They suddenly recognize each other, kiss, and reunion of husband and wife, father and children, begins. The reader is told that it is a sight which Tommy, the six-year-old, will always remember with affection. As Emma takes Edward inside and prepares some biscuits, he is overcome with joy and relief at being home with his beloved wife and children. Here is his life, his happiness, in this run-down little cabin.

The homecoming is presented in bittersweet terms to the reader. The familial affection is almost overpowering, and yet the trials and tribulations that await both Private Smith and Emma are everywhere lurking in the background. Private Smith knows the hardships that are before him, but "his heroic soul did not quail." In prose that reaches poetic eloquence, the narrator relates that Private Smith fights a hopeless battle against injustice and the harshness of nature. Nevertheless, there is dignity in his struggle.

Themes and Meanings

Hamlin Garland was at the forefront of the realist movement. He called it "veritism," and it led him to reject virtually all the romance and sentimentality that had traditionally clothed stories about the farm family. Garland knew the poverty, injustice, and dullness of rural life at first hand and conveyed that understanding with exceptional clarity in his early writings. "The Return of a Private" is a case in point. Although the focus here is on the homecoming itself, the hardships of working the land are always present. The land is not kind, and nature takes her toll, in terms of worn-out bodies and shattered dreams; as Widow Gray makes clear, though, the generosity of the human spirit is able to prevail under even harsh conditions.

Garland was a critic of land speculation and banks. A follower of economist Henry George, he saw the ubiquitous mortgage as the primary reason for the poverty of farm life. At one point in this story, the narrator even contrasts the sacrificing patriotism of Private Smith, who left his farm, wife, and babies to fight for the North, with the selfish millionaires who sent their money to England for safekeeping. Private Smith is constantly aware of the insatiable mortgage, ever threatening to devour all that he has worked for, including the security of his family. The injustice of it all is palpable, and it is relieved only slightly by the strength of character of the victims themselves. There are glimpses of a depressing determinism that presages the naturalism of later writers such as Stephen Crane and Theodore Dreiser.

Despite the cultural and material poverty he describes, Garland affirmed the dignity and nobility of the human spirit. Conditions might be harsh, but tenderness and family affections still survive, as does the struggle of the father and the mother to make a better life for their offspring. Still, there is no retreat to sentimental optimism. One finishes the story convinced that the protagonist and his family are good, loving, and deserving. Yet it is clear that they cannot overcome the drabness and harshness of their environment. Their joys, whether visiting Widow Gray or simply resting together outside by the well, are all the more poignant because they are so few.

Style and Technique

Clear, concise descriptions of people and places are hallmarks of Garland's style. The story indicates that the narrator is the son Tommy, now grown up and looking back on the return of his father and the futile struggles that the entire family waged against poverty that stifled both body and soul. This revelation adds to the basic credibility and realism of the story. Saying just so much but never too much is a technique that Garland mastered early, especially in presenting his characters or describing the landscape. The characters are ordinary, rather drab, and yet so sympathetic that their plight reaches out to the reader.

Garland was a precise recorder of life on the prairie, and he wrote as one who loved it and yet deplored it. Dramatic contrasts are everywhere to be found demonstrating the poverty of the environment and the goodness of the people. Intimate details are also added at the right time in the story—it might be Edward saying goodbye to Cranby and Saunders, or coaxing his shy children to him with three red apples, or Emma fixing biscuits and blushing at her husband's compliments. The author also captured the dialect of the Middle Borders with remarkable felicity.

In "The Return of a Private," Garland wove together theme, character, and landscape into a powerful statement about the ordinary and sometimes forgotten people of the prairie. Indeed, not the least of his contributions to literature is his wholehearted devotion to American themes. He took the trials and tribulations of the common people and rendered them in starkly realistic prose. In this and other stories, Garland followed his own injunction to portray life as it is.

Ronald W. Howard

THE RETURN OF CHORB

Author: Vladimir Nabokov (1899-1977)
Type of plot: Psychological realism
Time of plot: 1920
Locale: A German city
First published: "Vozvrashchenie Chorba," 1925 (English translation, 1976)

> *Principal characters:*
> CHORB, a destitute Russian émigré and litterateur
> MR. KELLER and MRS. KELLER, his Russo-German in-laws

The Story

The Kellers, smug, prosperous philistines, return home after an evening at the opera and a nightclub. The maid tells them that their son-in-law, Chorb, supposedly on his honeymoon in the south of France, has paid a call, saying that his wife is ill. He is staying in the same disreputable hotel where he and his bride spent their wedding night, after fleeing the elaborate reception arranged by her dismayed parents. Although Chorb has promised to call in the morning, the alarmed couple immediately sets out for the hotel.

The wife is in fact not ill, but dead. Nearly a month earlier, the laughing girl had accidentally touched a fallen roadside power line. Chorb's world has ceased to exist:

Her death appeared to him as a most rare, almost unheard-of occurrence; nothing . . . could be purer than such a death, caused by the impact of an electric stream, the same stream which, when poured into glass receptacles, yields the purest and brightest light.

The young husband wishes to possess his grief alone, "without tainting it by any foreign substance and without sharing it with any other soul." For this reason, Chorb has not informed the parents but rather has undertaken a ritualistic return journey.

The bereaved bridegroom decides to re-create, to immortalize, the image of his dead wife by retracing step-by-step their long, autumn-to-spring honeymoon journey. The re-created image will, he hopes, replace his bride. Starting from the place of her death, Chorb attempts to relive each of their memories, the small shared perceptions with which they delighted each other: the oddly marked pebble found on a Riviera beach, the winter in Switzerland, the autumn walks in the Black Forest where they saw an iridescent, dewdrop-covered spiderweb radially spanning two telegraph wires, perhaps, Chorb now thinks, prefiguring his bride's fate. Completing his reverse journey, Chorb has arrived back at their starting point.

The young writer checks into the same disreputable hotel and by chance gets the same shabby room which he recognizes by the picture over the bed. He also recognizes the green couch upon which he spent their chaste first night while she slept in the bed. He recalls his bride's amusement at the seedy establishment and their glee at having escaped her stuffy parents and their reception. The room seems haunted: A mouse rustles behind the wallpaper, and the light bulb hanging from the ceiling sways gently. Though exhausted by his sleepless, three-week journey, Chorb is too distraught to rest and sets out for a nocturnal walk. As he wanders, he recalls a wedding-eve stroll with his laughing, skipping bride. Finding himself at the house of his in-laws, he learns from the maid that they are at the opera and leaves word that their daughter is ill.

Chorb realizes that he is now back at the source of his recollections. He needs only to spend one night in their former hotel room, and the ordeal will be over. Her image will be complete. He senses, however, that he cannot spend the night alone in the haunted room. He must have a companion. At length, he finds a prostitute, who accompanies him to the room where she has spent other nights. Chorb, to the surprise of the untouched girl, immediately falls asleep. The prostitute prowls about the room, fingers the dead wife's clothes in a trunk, and finally goes to sleep. The air is rent by a visceral scream. Chorb has awakened to find his "wife" beside him in the bed. The terrified girl leaps up and turns on the lamp to find Chorb huddled in the bedclothes with his hands over his face, through which one eye can be seen burning "with a mad flame." Chorb gradually recognizes the prostitute and gives a sigh of relief. His ordeal is now over. He moves to the green couch and gazes at the girl with "a meaningless smile." Still terror-stricken, she scrambles to dress.

Voices and steps are heard in the corridor, and there is a knock on the door. The girl flings it open to meet the stupified gazes of Keller and his wife. Responding to a signal from the hotel employee, she bolts out as the in-laws enter. The door closes. The girl and the bellboy wait at the door, listening. Silence reigns.

Themes and Meanings

Nabokov's title, "The Return of Chorb," points to his major theme. Chorb's return takes place on two levels: the geographical and the psychological. The former merely frames and provides a set of cues for the latter's world of memory. Nabokov's central theme, one common to much of his work, is the relationship of the memory of things past to present reality. If Chorb succeeds in re-creating his bride in memory, he thinks, he will have exorcised the tragedy and possess her forever; he will be able to live again. This is the goal of his reverse journey through space and time. Yet reality proves him wrong. Although momentarily relieved of his tragic burden when he awakes, he immediately faces the tragicomic denouement with his in-laws. One cannot successfully live in a world of idyllic memories, no matter how richly reconstituted.

The story also has a subtle undercurrent of the supernatural. The bride dies the purest of deaths, killed by that same stream of electricity that pours into glass bulbs and gives the brightest light. It is not by chance that Chorb is unaccountably distressed by the gently swaying light bulb in his hotel room. As Nabokov once remarked in a discussion of the occult: "Electricity. Time. Space. We know *nothing* about these things." The always laughing wife may have returned to play a joke on the husband (the comic fiasco of the ending) or to try to jolt him into the loving realization that he must live in the present, not in shared memories of their brief past.

Chorb is perhaps not fated to be a great writer, for he lacks the toughness of mind to live in the present. There is a hint that his mind has snapped as he sits peeping out with his mad, flame-filled eye and then gazes at the prostitute with "a meaningless smile."

Style and Technique

Nabokov was one of the great twentieth century masters of structure and style, in both his Russian and his English works. "The Return of Chorb" is a good example. Nabokov employs an omniscient narrator who focuses upon the Kellers in the opening and closing sections (both set in the present) and on Chorb in the longer middle section, which alternates between the present of Chorb's return and the past of his memories. Events in the present trigger memories of related scenes from the past. The mention of the wife's "illness" evokes Chorb's reminiscence of her death and his slow return journey, the picture in the grubby hotel room, the lovers' wedding and flight to the hotel, and Chorb's walk, his wedding-eve stroll with his fiancée. The striking thing about Nabokov's narrative technique is that it proceeds in two directions at once. The present-tense narration, beginning with Chorb's return, moves in the normal forward direction; the past-tense narration stages Chorb's tragedy in reverse order: the death and return trip, the wedding night, the wedding-eve stroll. The two time-lines proceed in opposite directions and are linked by the web of memories just as in the image of the two telegraph lines spanned by the iridescent spiderweb.

Nabokov's development of the characters is also noteworthy. The narrator's contempt for the unimaginative, bourgeois Kellers is evident. Both are stout, and Herr Keller's face is "simian." Their level of taste is satirically reflected in the slippers (hers red, with cute little pom-poms) placed by the newlyweds' intended bedside on the throw rug, with its incongruous but prophetic motto, *"We are together unto the tomb."* They stand in grotesque contrast to the sensitive Chorb, an artist caught up in his subtle perception of the wonder of reality. This sense of wonder is shared by his laughing, nameless bride, who is mysteriously and fatally linked with images of electricity and falling leaves.

Nabokov is justly famed as a master of the precise verbal detail ("The same black poodle with apathetic eyes was in the act of raising a thin hindleg near a Morris pillar, straight at the scarlet lettering of a playbill announcing *Parsifal*"). Detail is also sometimes used for narrative purposes. A good example is the "lovely blond hair" found in the hotel room's washbasin by Chorb's bride. The hair belongs to the blonde prostitute, a frequent "guest" at the hotel, who later spends the night with Chorb. There is even a faint suspicion that Keller may have been her client at the time the hair was left. Also to be noted is the humorous irony in which the narrative's elegiac tone is deliberately shattered by the abrupt if understated comic fiasco of the ending.

D. Barton Johnson

REVELATION

Author: Flannery O'Connor (1925-1964)
Type of plot: Psychological realism
Time of plot: The 1950's
Locale: Georgia
First published: 1964

> *Principal characters:*
> MRS. RUBY TURPIN, a self-righteous woman
> CLAUD TURPIN, her husband
> MARY GRACE, a Wellesley student

The Story

While Mrs. Turpin and her husband Claud are waiting in the doctor's office for treatment of Claud's bruised leg, Mrs. Turpin strikes up a conversation with some of the other patients, but becomes annoyed with a Wellesley student, whom she thinks is fat and ugly and who scowls at her. Mrs. Turpin notices that the girl, Mary Grace, seems to be staring at her malevolently, and when she tries to engage the girl in conversation, she is snubbed. As she sizes up the people in the doctor's office, Mrs. Turpin classifies them, as is her wont. She thinks that Mary Grace's mother is stylishly dressed and pleasant, in contrast to the woman with the small child sitting nearby, whom she regards as white trash.

While talking to Mary Grace's mother, Mrs. Turpin concentrates her attention on herself. As the reader soon learns, she is normally preoccupied with herself. She thinks about how fortunate she is to be who she is, rather than being black or merely white trash. Just as she comments to the others on how grateful she is for all she is and has, she is suddenly assaulted by Mary Grace—struck by the book that she has been reading. As she struggles to escape, Mrs. Turpin feels as if she is watching the event from far away. When Mary Grace is sedated, Mrs. Turpin asks her what she has to say for herself and waits as if for a revelation. Mary Grace calls her a warthog and tells her to go back to Hell.

Because she believes that Mary Grace had something to say to her rather than any of the others in the doctor's office, who were more deserving of such reprobation, Mrs. Turpin sees herself as being singled out to be given a special message. As she thinks over the revelation later, she becomes angry, and it continues to prey on her mind.

Later, while talking to the black women who work for her husband, Mrs. Turpin relates the incident, and the women commiserate with her, telling her how sweet and nice she is. Still, she realizes how empty their sympathy is, recognizing the accustomed role blacks play in their dealings with whites. As she goes out to water down the pig parlor, she continues to mull over the incident in her mind. She speaks to God, asking why He sent such a message to her when there are so many others more deserving, ending with asking God just who He thinks He is.

Finally she has a vision of a bridge that extends from the earth through a fire, and on the bridge are troops of souls whom she recognizes as blacks and white trash being washed clean for the first time in their lives. At the end of the procession, she sees staunch, respectable middle-class people such as Claud and herself, and she sees by the shock on their faces that these people have had their virtues burned away. As she turns off the water and slowly walks back to the house, she hears only the voices of the souls in her vision singing hallelujah.

Themes and Meanings

Though the message of "Revelation" is clear, its impact is underplayed; the reader is left unsure about what Mrs. Turpin has learned from the revelation she has received. It is through the title and the name of the girl, Mary Grace, and chiefly Mrs. Turpin's reactions that the revelation that comes to her is emphasized.

The revelation is prepared for by the author's exposition of the character of Mrs. Turpin at the start of the story. The story is narrated from the third-person limited-omniscient point of view: Events are narrated in the third person for all the characters in the story, except for Mrs. Turpin. Others are described as Mrs. Turpin perceives them. Interspersed with the narrative are the thoughts of Mrs. Turpin about how superior Claud and she are to others and how she likes to classify people.

The narrator speaks of how Mrs. Turpin is accustomed to lying in bed at night, contemplating the virtues of different people. In her classification, she puts blacks on the bottom (she usually refers to them as "niggers" not with malice, but through custom), white trash next, then homeowners, followed by "home-and-land owners, to which she and Claud belonged," ending with people with a large amount of money, who should be beneath Claud and her. At this she thinks of a black dentist who unaccountably has more material possessions than she and Claud do. When she contemplates these values while lying in bed she usually falls into utter confusion trying to figure out why Claud and she are not at the top: "All the classes of people were moiling and roiling around in her head, and she would dream they were all crammed in together in a box car, being ridden off to be put in a gas oven."

The author's language gives several clues about Mrs. Turpin. First, her phrase "she and Claud" shows her self-centeredness because she places herself before Claud, contrary to proper usage. Later, she compounds this error with the phrase, "Above she and Claud," an error made by those who think they are more educated than they are.

More telling is the final metaphor of confusion used by the author. The obvious association with the Holocaust in Nazi Germany passes an unequivocal judgment on the kind of morality that is represented by Mrs. Turpin. Although Mrs. Turpin is sometimes troubled by the contemplation of her role on earth, she has a closed mind about her sense of superiority. Yet she is forced to confront her self-concept, and with the final revelation it is uncertain how she will react to this knowledge—whether she has acquired a new awareness of herself and a new humility. Judging from Flannery O'Connor's penchant for stories of "redemption through catastrophe," it is probable that such is the intended theme.

Style and Technique

As noted above, Mrs. Turpin's thoughts are conveyed by an omniscient narrator who otherwise narrates the events of the story from the third-person point of view, picking up Mrs. Turpin's judgments of most of the events. The reader cannot be certain whether Mary Grace, as Mrs. Turpin believes, is really fixing her eyes on Mrs. Turpin in hatred. What is important is that Mrs. Turpin thinks so, and this belief leads her to expect some sort of revelation from the girl. The girl's name is also important (as is the title, which gives the reader the main clue to the theme of the story), combining the word "grace" with the holy name Mary, an indication of the grace that Mrs. Turpin receives in gaining a revelation which can lead to her redemption.

At the same time, the point of the story is not overly emphasized by the author. Rather, the theme arises naturally, as O'Connor presents objective details through the consciousness of Mrs. Turpin, letting the reader decipher what impact the events finally have on her.

Roger Geimer

A REVENANT

Author: Walter de la Mare (1873-1956)
Type of plot: Ghost story
Time of plot: 1932
Locale: Wigston, England
First published: 1936

> *Principal characters:*
>   PROFESSOR MONK, a man of letters, lecturing to a small literary society
>   THE GHOST OF EDGAR ALLAN POE, a member of the audience
>   THE REVEREND MR. MORTIMER, the chairman of the lecture
>   A YOUNG GIRL, unnamed, a member of the audience

The Story

Though the title "A Revenant" proclaims that this is a ghost story—and it is—it reads more like an essay, a discourse more on ideas than on events or characters. In this aspect, its structure is twofold: It is a duel of intellects between Professor Monk and the ghost of Edgar Allan Poe, the professor's assertions about Poe followed by Poe's rebuttal. The story is also a study of Professor Monk—limited as his character is by academic habits of mind and waffling prudery—and as such its structure, like the professor's lecture, is fourfold: a lengthy introductory section establishing time, place, and characters; a synopsis of the professor's lecture up to 8:46 P.M., when the present action of the story begins; the continuation of the lecture to its end; and two responses, the chairman's public response followed by Poe's private one.

The introductory section establishes two sides to Professor Monk's character: his habitual complacency and his present profound disquietude. The former is revealed in the professor's preference for "a sober and academic delivery," in his rejection of gestures and any sort of staginess, in his determination to appeal to the intellect alone, in his "modest satisfaction" with this lecture and its systematic organization. His disquietude is expressed by his sudden sharp awareness of where he is, his acute sense that he is alone, and the "amazing rapidity" of the speculations that agitate his thoughts. Mediating between these two aspects of Professor Monk's state of mind is the "challenge" offered by the darkly cloaked stranger at the back of the hall, of whose presence, apparently, only Professor Monk is aware.

The professor's lecture seems an odd tissue of qualifications, full of "but" and "though," "on the other hand," and "nonetheless." In the portion of the lecture preceding 8:46 P.M., summarized here by the narrator, Professor Monk focuses largely on Poe's character ("arrogant, fitful, quarrelsome, unstable") and on his failure to find material success. What little the professor does say about Poe's work itself is done briefly and apparently contradictorily, announcing that "craftsmanship, artistry . . . [are] vital alike in prose and verse" and proceeding directly to fault Poe's poems for their "flawless mastery of method." Like an anatomist with the human body, the professor fails to deal creatively with the whole of the phenomenon his lecture purports to treat, yet he does not realize why he finds Rembrandt's *Anatomy Lesson of Dr. Nicolaes Tulp* (1632) flickering through his mind; his statements, like Rembrandt's painting, remain "curiously detached"—that is, curiously disconnected—and his intellect falls somehow between the two sides of his own advice: "Life, like a lecture, is a succession of moments. Don't pay too extreme an attention to any one or two; wait for the end of the hour." He takes his lecture, for its own sake, too seriously, failing to take its subject seriously enough; his lecture, consequently, fails to make sense of the writings he purports to be expounding or of the man he actually treats. Professor Monk's lecture continues after 8:46 P.M. as a series of discrete comments—contiguous but barely linked—and turns ever and again from Poe's writings to Poe the man.

If the professor has erred on the side of "academic mouthings and nothings," as Poe's ghost later claims, the lecture's chairman, the Reverend Mr. Mortimer, misses any point a literary lecture may have, his ignorance illustrating one argument against what the professor has offered his audience: The chairman seizes on all the least relevant points in the lecture and fluently constructs from them an "urgent lesson." Probably the only person who has had an actual literary experience at this lecture is the schoolgirl who asks for Professor Monk's autograph, and she has attained her experience by ignoring most of what the lecturer says, concentrating instead on the loveliness of the poems she has learned in class.

The encounter that follows with the ghost of Edgar Allan Poe is the crisis of Professor Monk's life, for Poe's rebuttal is at once so incisive and so acid that it completely changes Professor Monk's "view of himself and even of his future." He may continue to insist on existing "within strict limits," and he understands what has happened to him as "a piece of mere legerdemain," yet his final "Ah, yes" seems at least to acknowledge the truth of what Poe's ghost has said:

Opinions, views, passing tastes, passing prejudices—they are like funguses, a growth of the night. But the moon of the imagination, however fickle in her phases, is still constant in her borrowed light, and sheds her beams on them one and all, the just and the unjust.

Themes and Meanings

As an essay, "A Revenant" opposes two viewpoints, Professor Monk's and Edgar Allan Poe's. The professor's position is equivocal, however, for his theory and his practice are at odds. "He preferred," the narrator explains, "facts to atmosphere, statements to hints, assumptions, 'I venture's', and dubious implications." Yet his lecture is compounded largely of atmosphere, hints, assumptions, and all the rest. His sober academic manner has been, even by the professor himself, mistaken for scholarly method, the dryness of his delivery for depth of understanding, and the constant qualification of his statements for critical acumen. His unfitness—and, by extension, the unfitness of many academics—to venture into the world of literary criticism is evidenced by his discontent with the nature of its subject: "Poetry may, and perhaps unfortunately, *must* appeal to the emotions and the heart."

Ironically, Poe's ghost seems to agree with the remainder of the professor's statement, that "the expounding of [poetry] is the business of the head." Quoting Poe's own essay on "The Poetic Principle," the ghost asserts that "we must be cool, calm, unimpassioned." In a sentence deleted from the ghostly quotation, Poe wrote, "We need severity rather than efflorescence of language." At the same time, however, the specter insists on the aspect of the poetic impulse that Professor Monk finds so unfortunate; he argues, indeed, that "imagination" is no "mere faculty," but is a "sovereign power," a "divine energy." Poe's ghost further demands of the professor a definition of poetry, or at least some reference to Poe's own definition. The ghost thus calls into question the professor's ability even to speak of poetry, since he seems unable to appreciate it, and the acuity of his intellectual method, since he has failed even to define his terms.

The method followed by the ghost in his rebuttal is simpler yet more comprehensive than the professor's own lecture. He begins by summarizing Professor Monk's attitude toward his subject by adducing "the tone, the flavour, the accent" of the lecture and noting how poor a basis for the critical endeavor such an attitude is. He proceeds to critique the lecturer's treatment of Poe the man, noting that he has turned tragedy into melodrama and that his words have revealed his feelings, hinting at opinions such as "mountebank, ingrate, wastrel, fortune-hunter, seducer, debauchee, dipsomaniac." The specter prepares for his next point by finding an area of common ground and then attacking the professor from that vantage:

> Oh yes, I agree that a man's writings indelibly reflect him and all of him that matters most. And since your poet's are all that is left of him in the world, and they alone are of lasting value, should we not look for him there? Did you attempt to depict, to describe, to illuminate that reflection? No: for that would have needed insight, the power to divine, to re-create. *You* are a stern and ardent moralist, Professor. But since when has the platform become the pulpit? It needs, too, little courage to attack and stigmatize the dead.

Again the ghost calls into question the professor's intellectual acumen by reminding him of the title of his paper—"The *Writings* of Edgar Allan

Poe"—and by using such terms as "groping" and "fatuous" to describe the professor's treatment of poetic technique; his "remarks on the art of writing," the specter adds, "were nothing short of treason to the mind. They were based on inadequate knowledge, and all but innocent of common sense."

Walter de la Mare's discursive intention may, perhaps, be found in the specter's suggestion that "man's feeblest taper [is] . . . a *dual* splendour—of heat *and* light." Professor Monk professes but half that formula—light—and he fails even there because of the confusions he entertains, the distinctions he does not make, and the knowledge he simply does not have.

Style and Technique

De la Mare's discursive intentions have been tempered in "A Revenant" by the machinery he employs to lend both mystery and importance to the presence of a ghost at Professor Monk's lecture. His gradual introduction of the stranger, for example, piques the reader's interest primarily by what is not told. Initially, no reason is offered for the professor's disquiet, but a series of incomplete ideas leads to the latecomer's introduction; "one single exception," "he knew why," "Then what was wrong?" are offered, paragraphs apart, without completion, raising questions in the reader's mind: Who is the exception? What is the reason the professor knows? Why does he not answer the question?

Again, Professor Monk's "*punctual* interruption" is presented in terms appropriate to the occasion. The story's first notice of the "sudden, peculiar, brief, strident roar" describes it thus: "On his way to the Hall he had noticed—incarnadining the louring heavens—what appeared to be the reflected light from the furnaces of a foundry. Possibly it was discharging its draff, its slag, its cinders." The next explicit notice of this infernal interruption occurs when it takes the position of a place-name in the specter's statement, "I am from. . . ." It is noticed again as Professor Monk hesitates before leaving the anteroom of the lecture hall. This foundry's presence, then, provides a structurally significant objective correlative for the revenant's larger meaning when he asks, "Is there not a shade of the Satanic in these streets?"

Finally, the "piercing cold" of the specter's hand acts on Professor Monk as spiritual shock therapy: "A sigh shook him from head to foot. A slight vertigo overcame him. He raised his hand to his eyes. For an instant it seemed to him as though even his sense of reality had cheated him—had foundered." De la Mare has, then, used the ambivalent reality of life and death, waking and sleeping, to call into question the limitedness of Professor Monk's sense of the reality of art and the imagination; the ghost of Edgar Allan Poe is sent to remind Professor Monk—and the reader—that logic is only half the tale and that the transcendent invites "cachinnation" only from "fools."

Jonathan A. Glenn

THE RICH BOY

Author: F. Scott Fitzgerald (1896-1940)
Type of plot: Psychological realism
Time of plot: The 1920's
Locale: New York and Florida
First published: 1926

Principal characters:

ANSON HUNTER, an attractive, charming, but arrogant young
man from a wealthy and prestigious family

PAULA LEGENDRE, a beautiful, wealthy young woman who
falls in love with Anson but later marries another man

DOLLY KARGER, an attractive young woman from new money
who is attracted to men who are not attracted to her

AUNT EDNA, Anson's aunt by marriage

CARY, the young lover of Edna

THE NARRATOR, an unidentified friend of Anson

The Story

Anson Hunter, the rich boy for whom the story is named, aptly portrays
Fitzgerald's fascination with an analysis of the rich as

> different from you and me. They possess and enjoy early, . . . [which] makes
> them soft where we are hard, and cynical where we are trustful. They think,
> deep in their hearts, that they are better than we are because we had to dis-
> cover the compensations and refuges of life for ourselves.

As a child, Anson is cared for by a governess and is secluded from contact
with his social peers. His fraternizing with the local town children helps instill
his feeling of superiority. His education is completed at Yale, where he makes
connections in the business and social worlds. He establishes himself in a
New York brokerage firm, joins the appropriate clubs, and commences to
maintain an extravagant life-style, arrogantly frowning on excessive behavior
in others which he finds acceptable for himself.

Anson serves in the Navy but is not changed by the experience. While in
Florida at a training base, he meets Paula Legendre, a woman of his class
and social standing. As he himself admits, their relationship is superficial,
based on common upbringing and expectations. Paula and her mother
accompany him north, and while there he arrives at their hotel one evening,
inebriated. Paula and her mother react negatively to this improper behavior,
but Anson never apologizes. Later, when he becomes drunk and fails to keep
a date with Paula, she breaks the engagement. Anson, however, continues to
believe that he has control over Paula, that she will, in fact, wait for him for-

ever. When he and Paula meet again, his arrogance prevents him from recognizing Paula's weakening attraction and patience toward him: "He need say no more, commit their destinies to no practical enigma. Why should he, when he might hold her so, biding his own time, for another year—forever?" Because of this attitude, Anson loses her. He receives word that she will marry someone else.

His loss of Paula shocks him, but he continues his wild life and becomes involved with Dolly Karger. His relationship with Dolly is gamelike; when she tries to make him jealous, he purposely wins her back, only to show her who is in control, and then promptly rejects her. When she accompanies him to the country for the weekend, he goes to her in her bedroom, but at the last minute, the image of Paula intervening between them, he, close to tears and projecting his anger on Dolly, breaks away from her: " . . . I don't love you a bit, can't you understand?"

Anson prides himself on his ability to control the lives of other people, and when he learns that his Aunt Edna is having an affair, he informs her and her lover that it must end. He states that failure to do so will cause him to inform his uncle and the young man's father. This threat gains the result he desires. He gives his motivations as the prevention of a scandal, which would reflect on him as well as on the rest of the family, and the protection of his uncle. Primarily, however, it is simply a way for him to assert his superiority. The lover dies, either by accident or by suicide, but Anson feels no remorse. He is banned from his uncle's house, an act which Anson believes is unjustified.

As Anson approaches thirty, he becomes more conscious of his position in society; he teaches Sunday school, sponsors young men for various clubs, and, with the deaths of his mother and father, becomes head of the family, assuming responsibility for his brothers and sisters, particularly financially and socially. He continues to give advice to his friends, especially to those recently married. Despite his continued drinking and partying, the older generation considers him reliable and safe because of the air of self-assurance which he exhibits. Finally though, his friends establish their own lives and interests and find him less necessary.

His loneliness becomes evident to him one evening at the beginning of summer when he tries to find someone in New York with whom to spend the evening, and everyone he knows, including people he has not seen since college, is either busy or out of town. The thought of being alone frightens him, and he glimpses the emptiness of his life. On this evening he accidentally meets Paula, recently remarried and pregnant. They travel up to the country for the weekend, and, after a pleasant meal, the husband leaves them alone to catch up on old times. When Anson learns from Paula that she never loved him, that she is now happy with her husband, Anson is devastated. He returns to the city but breaks into tears easily and seems unable to go on with his life. Although Anson is certainly upset about Paula, it is typical of him that he is not upset that Paula is married or pregnant or happy; his pride is wounded because she had not loved him as he assumed she had.

His work suffers, and his colleagues become worried about him. They urge him to take a voyage and, accompanied by a male friend, the narrator, he plans to depart. Several days prior to their departure, Anson learns that Paula has died during childbirth; nevertheless, he departs for Europe as planned. On the voyage, Anson takes up with another young woman, reverting to his old ways, without benefitting from his experiences. The narrator-friend concludes, "I don't think he was ever happy unless someone was in love with him, responding to him like filings to a magnet, helping him to explain himself, promising him something. . . . Perhaps they promised that there would always be women in the world who would spend their brightest, freshest, rarest hours to nurse and protect that superiority he cherished in his heart."

Themes and Meanings

Fitzgerald depicted the life-style of the Lost Generation of the 1920's, those rich young people who blamed the evils of the world on the previous generation and rejected their parents' value system of duty to society and family but also failed to establish a new system. Instead they adopted an irresponsible, cynical, extravagant way of life, which Fitzgerald recognized as essentially devoid of meaning or fulfillment. Certainly Anson is depicted as a superficial character who has no concern for anyone other than himself and who consistently fails to learn from his experiences. Fitzgerald's belief that the rich pay a price for their self-imposed isolation is demonstrated in "The Rich Boy." Anson is rich and different, and the penalty that he pays for his sense of superiority is that he never achieves a meaningful relationship with anyone. Fitzgerald explored the basic psychological drives and how they are satisfied by the very rich. He learned that the possession of wealth was bought at the price of individualism and of increased responsibility to others. His character Anson never learns this lesson. He refuses to take responsibility for his own actions, never considering his effect on the lives of others. Anson is a user of people; he views them as merely objects upon which to exert his influence, thus reinforcing his sense of superiority, as exemplified particularly by his treatment of women: Paula, Dolly, and Aunt Edna.

As a child, Anson recognizes the unchallenged superiority of the rich, and "he accepted this as the natural state of things, and a sort of impatience with all groups of which he was not the center—in money, in position, in authority—remained with him for the rest of his life." Yet this superiority has its price; closeness to other people becomes unavailable to him. His relationship with Paula illustrates this. Anson admits "that on his side much was insincere, and on hers much was merely simple," thus indicating his lack of true involvement as well as his feeling of superiority toward her. Yet Paula is drawn to Anson:

> [He] . . . dominated and attracted her, and at the same time filled her with anxiety. Confused by his mixture of solidity and self-indulgence, of sentiment and cynicism—incongruities which her gentle mind was unable to resolve—Paula grew to think of him as two alternating personalities. When she saw him alone, or at a formal party, or with his casual inferiors, she felt a tremendous pride in his strong, attractive presence, the paternal, understanding stature of his mind. In other company she became uneasy when what had been a fine imperviousness to mere gentility showed its other face. The other face was gross, humorous, reckless of everything but pleasure.

Anson believes that Paula will wait for him forever, but he is mistaken. He claims that it is Paula's action in ending their relationship, rather than his own which necessitated it, which has made him a cynic, thus refusing to take responsibility for the demise of their relationship.

This arrogance surfaces again in his affair with Dolly and his cruel treatment of her: "He was not jealous—she meant nothing to him—but at her pathetic ruse everything stubborn and self-indulgent in him came to the surface. It was a presumption from a mental inferior and it could not be overlooked. If she wanted to know to whom she belonged she would see."

There is no compassion in Anson. He firmly believes that he knows best for everyone, or that whatever is best for him is what must be, despite the effects on others. He does not merely offer advice to friends and family; he forces it upon them. Understandably people begin to resent this and withdraw from the area of his control. After he totally humiliates Aunt Edna and her lover and destroys any hope of happiness for them, he calmly returns home, believing that he has done the right thing, even feeling self-satisfied with his actions.

Despite his experiences, Anson never changes. On a superficial level he adopts the responsibilities of head of his family, of church member, and of civic leader, but morally he remains unconcerned with the welfare of anyone other than himself. This arrogance and selfishness lead him into an empty, cynical, and callous way of life. This is aptly illustrated when, on the trip abroad after Paula's death, he bounces back to his irresponsible, charming, witty self as he makes the acquaintance of yet another beautiful young woman.

Style and Technique

The story is told by a first-person observer-narrator, who identifies himself as a friend of Anson. As Anson's confidant, the narrator is privy to Anson's thoughts, yet he is able to relate his perception of events objectively, particularly as one who has not been reared in wealth. Thus, he is the persona of

Fitzgerald and is able to interpret the effects of Anson's actions objectively, though with more compassion toward Anson than Anson exhibits toward others; thus, the narrator also serves as a foil to Anson.

The psychological realism evidenced in "The Rich Boy" is accomplished through Fitzgerald's close attention to detail and through a consistent, believable portrayal of the characters' thoughts, actions, and personalities. He divulges to the reader the inner workings of the mind of a wealthy, arrogant young man and the social influences which have formed him.

Jane B. Weedman

RIP VAN WINKLE

Author: Washington Irving (1783-1859)
Type of plot: Tale
Time of plot: Late eighteenth century
Locale: The Catskill Mountains of New York
First published: 1819

> *Principal characters:*
> RIP VAN WINKLE, the protagonist, a village ne'er-do-well
> DAME VAN WINKLE, Rip's shrewish wife
> JUDITH VAN WINKLE GARDENIER, Rip's daughter

The Story

Rip Van Winkle is a good-natured but unassertive descendant of the Dutch settlers who assisted Peter Stuyvesant in his military exploits. Every small community has a Rip: the entertainer of local children, the willing helper of his neighbor, the desultory fisherman—but a man constitutionally unable to work on his own behalf. Rip's farm falls into ruin, his children run ragged, and his wife's bad temper mounts. He takes refuge from Dame Van Winkle in protracted discussions at the village inn, all-day fishing expeditions, and rambles in the mountains with his dog Wolf. It is on one of these occasions that he encounters a company of antique Dutchmen who are playing at ninepins in a natural amphitheater high in the Catskills.

Offered liquid refreshment, Rip drinks himself to sleep, from which he awakens the next morning, as he supposes, to find everything inexplicably changed: his dog gone, a worm-eaten gun in place of the one he had brought, no trace of the bowlers or of their bowling alley. Descending to the town, he finds his old dog strangely hostile, his house abandoned, and even the village inn replaced by a large new hotel.

The first person Rip actually recognizes is his daughter, now a young wife and mother; she kindly takes the perplexed old man home to live with her family. He learns of the death of many of his old friends and of his wife, for whose demise he feels nothing but relief. When he sees his son Rip slouching against a tree, looking much as he himself did "yesterday"—actually twenty years ago—he briefly doubts his own identity.

The larger changes in society are yet more profound. Rip went to sleep a subject of George III and has awakened a citizen of the United States of America under the leadership of George Washington. Although Rip soon falls into his old loitering ways, justified now by his white beard and the absence of matrimonial demands, it takes him some time to absorb the Revolution that has run its full course while he slept. The town has learned to accommodate the new republic, and all the changes lend charm to Rip's fresh recollections of the old order. Rip tells and retells his story, which is accepted most readily by the older Dutch villagers, who have kept alive a legend that Hendrick Hudson's men keep a vigil in the nearby mountains and play at ninepins there regularly in the afternoon. Rip prefers the company of the young, however, not so much to be in touch with the new as to preserve the old in a relentlessly changing world.

Themes and Meanings

Irving was a nostalgic man in whom a touch of Rip Van Winkle persisted. Like Rip, he was away from home for many years. He was in the earlier years of a seventeen-year sojourn in England when he wrote *The Sketch Book of Geoffrey Crayon, Gent.* (1819-1920) with its two narrative master-pieces, this story and "The Legend of Sleepy Hollow." A conservative who enjoyed the old ways, Irving wrote best when he juxtaposed old and new, tradition and change. His friend Sir Walter Scott encouraged him to rum-mage in European folklore. Both of the famous stories in *The Sketch Book* are based on German tales; by adapting them, Irving helped to create a distinctively American fiction. Whereas earlier American imitators of Euro-pean romances and gothic horror stories had suffered from the lack of convincing settings in a land without ancient abbeys and castles, Irving rea-lized the possibilities inherent in the Hudson River Valley, only a day's jour-ney from New York but teeming with romantic possibilities and local tradi-tions which, although they did not date from medieval times, nevertheless went back a respectable two centuries.

In "Rip Van Winkle," Irving seized upon the venerable theme of the hen-pecked husband who turns the tables on his tyrannical wife, a feat Rip achieves by simply outlasting her—with a bit of preternatural help from the crew of Hudson's *Half Moon*. Rip merely desires a leisurely, casual, convivial life, but his wife calls him home from the congenial atmosphere of the inn and lectures him in bed at night. Irving never, however, permits Dame Van Winkle's point of view to obtrude; she does not speak in the story, and Irving elicits no sympathy for her. She is the enemy partly because she embodies a whole culture that is at odds with Rip's values: that of the tidy, thrifty, ambi-tious Dutch.

Despite the story's German source and its setting in a Dutch-American community, Irving domesticates his material very successfully. First, he deftly captures the beauty of a recognizably American region. The rather brief scene in which the mountains become the setting for fantasy is sandwiched between two thicker slices of late eighteenth century American village real-ity. By the very act of passing over a signal event in American history, the story draws attention to it. Rip returns to find people talking of the heroes of the late war (some of his friends fought and one died in it), the new form of government (the village schoolmaster is now in something called "Congress"), and national political parties (almost immediately he is asked whether he is a Federalist or a Democrat).

Rip has paid heavily for his secure leisure, for he has lost what should have been the years of his mature vigor and all opportunity to participate in the great events of his lifetime. While loving freedom, Rip placidly endured the tyranny of Dame Van Winkle and King George and has escaped playing any role in the forging of American liberty. He has avoided the tribulations of family life by losing all title as husband and becoming dependent on his daughter, while he has sloughed off his responsibilities as patriot by choosing "overnight" status as a senior citizen.

His easygoing philosophy is completely at odds with that of the great architects of American freedom, including Benjamin Franklin, whose almanac *Poor Richard's* (first issued in 1732) stands at a pole opposite to Rip's sluggishness. Irving even uses Franklin's idiom to describe Rip, who "would rather starve on a penny than work for a pound." Rip would also rather starve himself of any satisfaction for accomplishment such as that permeating Franklin's much admired *Autobiography* (1771-1788).

The other Founding Father prominent in the story is George Washington, whose image has replaced that of King George in front of the new hotel. By virtue of exchanging the life of a country gentleman for the dangers and deprivations of military service in wartime, Washington became "the Father of his country," while Rip's children have in effect grown up fatherless. After the war, Washington, presumably about Rip's age, did not recede into the past but accepted eight years of further responsibility as president.

Irving, named for Washington, was, like Rip, a man who spent much of his life telling stories, but the one he labored at most diligently through his late years was his five-volume biography of Washington, the man after whom neither Rip nor his creator could pattern himself. In Rip, Irving created a character whom the reader can envy—but only by ignoring the implicit reminders of a far nobler type of American.

Style and Technique

Irving erected an elaborate façade for the book in which this story first appeared. Purporting to be the work of "Geoffrey Crayon, Gentleman," *The Sketch Book* featured primarily literary "sketches" of the type popularized by Joseph Addison a century earlier and influenced writers as late as Charles Dickens. Irving's sketches are chiefly travel essays of an American in England, written in a graceful, well-bred manner calculated to appeal to the English gentleman as well as his American readers. As a result, Irving became the first American literary man widely read abroad.

Irving further distanced himself from his narrative by means of a headnote alleging the story to be a posthumously discovered work of "Diedrich Knickerbocker, an old gentleman of New York" and a postscript to the effect that

Knickerbocker himself had it from a "German superstition," though Irving more or less retracts this suggestion by including a note reputed to be Knickerbocker's own in which the old gentleman claims to have talked with the real Rip Van Winkle himself.

This sort of elaborate hocus-pocus was common in American fiction up to about the middle of the nineteenth century, and readers may compare Irving's frame for this story with Nathaniel Hawthorne's lengthy customhouse essay at the head of *The Scarlet Letter* (1850). Common to both works is a desire both for the freedom from any obligation to respect prosaic everyday life and for an air of authenticity these writers seemed to feel readers of the time required.

Unlike Hawthorne, however, Irving does not aspire to profundity, and his style is much more colloquial and familiar. The dialogue is extremely simple and straightforward, and the descriptions, while effective, are rather understated. Irving's simplicity, which has helped make his tales enduringly popular school texts, is somewhat deceptive, for although Irving is not an ambitious artist, he has an artful way of suggesting more than he seems to say. Thus, the allusions to Franklin and Washington establish the standards of duty and accomplishment against which Rip's withdrawal from responsibility is to be measured. Unlike his greatest American contemporary in fiction, James Fenimore Cooper, Irving seldom overwrites. By describing his mountaineers very little and keeping them absolutely silent, he creates the desired atmosphere of enchantment. He understands the value of describing Dame Van Winkle indirectly through her effect on Rip. In a century of writers always poised to spin great webs of words, Irving demonstrates the virtues of an economical and unpretentious style.

For all its derivative nature, simplicity, and modest statement, "Rip Van Winkle" achieves universal significance. It depicts the pastoral contentment yearned for in a society aware of its own increasing complexity but shows this peace to be purchased at the expense of the protagonist's full manhood and maturity. With considerable justification, "Rip Van Winkle" has been called the first successful American short story.

Robert P. Ellis

THE RISE OF MAUD MARTHA

Author: Gwendolyn Brooks (1917-   )
Type of plot: Psychological realism
Time of plot: c. 1955
Locale: Chicago
First published: 1955

> *Principal characters:*
> MAUD MARTHA, who is newly widowed
> MRS. PHILLIPS, her mother-in-law
> BELVA BROWN, her mother

The Story

"The Rise of Maud Martha," a very brief and deceptively simple story, opens as a pastor observes the departure of a funeral procession and closes only a short time later, the moment Maud Martha begins crying as they lower her husband Paul into his grave. With the precision of the poet she is and the insight of the sensitive observer of human behavior she has always been, Gwendolyn Brooks joins the procession through the thoughts and observations of Maud Martha as she rides in the first car with her mother, Belva Brown, and Paul's mother, Mrs. Phillips. Each carefully detailed picture conveys the life-style in which Maud Martha finds herself, from the opening details of the "big and little and few" wreaths with "fresh and barely fresh" flowers, through the placement of Maud Martha in "the longest and shiny-blackest of the long black cars," to the image of an "after-funeral white cake" which closes the story.

Equally vivid are the flashback observations of Paul's death as one of "30-odd" passengers burned in the crash of a streetcar with a gas truck. Ironically, the streetcar was a new model, and its sealed windows sealed the fate of its unfortunate passengers as well.

The violent tragedy is not, however, the focus of Brooks's story. Rather, it is "the women in the street"—from the grieving wives to the high school girl in the crowd "enjoying herself. Seeing Life." Brooks may focus on Maud Martha, but she uses a wide-angle lens, taking in the many faces of grief and contrasting the "'dreadful' blackness" of charred bodies with the formerly "known and despised" blackness of race.

Next Brooks narrows her lens to the three women in the head car and turns up the sound, as Mrs. Phillips eulogizes her son and patronizes her daughter-in-law. Criticism disguised as faint praise fails to provoke a rise from either Maud Martha or her mother, Belva, although Belva does have to snap her lips shut at one point. Maud Martha's only response is "I understand," ambiguously acknowledging Mrs. Phillips' request for visits and her own growing understanding of the real meaning of Paul's death for her.

Reminiscent but not derivative of Kate Chopin's "The Story of an Hour," Brooks's story presents a newly widowed wife who is looking for the feelings which she has been taught to expect from herself but who finds instead inescapable and unpredicted realities. Instead of the self-pity of the abandoned love, Maud Martha discovers in herself only pity for Paul's loss of the physical beauty he loved so dearly. As does Chopin's character, Maud Martha feels in herself a release of freedom and power: "She could actually feel herself rising." The tears which come in time to please the relatives are not for Paul.

Themes and Meanings

Gwendolyn Brooks had introduced her readers to Maud Martha two years before the publication of this story with her novella *Maud Martha* (1953). The young black woman who wanted to "found tradition" for herself, for Paul, and for little Paulette now finds herself caught in and measured by the narrow expectations of physical existence. Mrs. Phillips praises her for giving Paul hot meals: "That's what makes for a healthy man." Blind to the spiritual values Maud Martha might hope to instill in her household, the mother-in-law goes on to suggest that letting ten-year-old Paulette leave school to baby-sit for the smaller children and getting a job would have been the right way for Maud Martha to help Paul.

Like his mother, Paul had loved physical existence and had offered little but "vicissitudes" to his wife. If love makes a man "more than a body" to a woman, Maud Martha realizes, then even when he "happens to be dead, he is still what you love." Physical values, though, are easily and surprisingly turned into "a fire-used, repulsive thing": The body cannot be protected from life's vicissitudes. Even the young girl observing the grief of others is not envied by Maud Martha; she, too, will know loss in time.

For Maud Martha, life with Paul had become dominated by the physical limits of childbearing and problem-solving; he "had made her feel like a pumpkin." Now his death offers Maud Martha another opportunity to "found tradition"; she realizes that her children's lives and her own are now "in her individual power." The physical realities do not go away—the tears and the white cake will both come—but Maud Martha is ready to rise to the challenge once more. In a world that still approves of her because of her tears, the physical sign of grief, the story of her rising has yet to reach the surface of her life.

Style and Technique

With the eye and the language of a poet, Brooks offers a surface of social realism within which the psychological realities of Maud Martha's thoughts are probed. The opening paragraph describing the pastor watching the departure of the funeral procession has already suggested the shallow reality of surfaces. "It was impossible to tell just what he was thinking," Brooks reminds the reader as she re-creates him; her suggestions range from thoughts about death or its accoutrements to the irrelevance of "strawberries."

Even language can be as shallow as visual surfaces if one does not plumb its depths, and Brooks forces one to read every word of her story thoroughly before exhausting it of meaning. Again, the first paragraph introduces this stylistic density as she describes the quiet closing of the casket lid "to avoid jarring the family." Not only does this shift the reader's focus from the dead man to the surviving family, where it belongs, but it also contains the double meanings for "jar" of upsetting or enclosing. Maud Martha has been "jarred" in her marriage and is about to be "jarred" out of it.

In a story thematically concerned with the limits of physical reality, Brooks also conveys the power of that reality as she personifies the fire as an "invader" eating the trapped "flesh" of the streetcar passengers. The emotions of the women are similarly given physical reality as "ripped-open wounds" and "sores." Yet already the reader is offered the values that negate physical realities, as what is considered physical beauty or ugliness becomes its opposite through the intense grief of the women. Establishing physical correspondence for the nonphysical realities with which she confronts the reader allows Brooks to reveal a physical world inseparable from the spiritual. On the other hand, the spiritual is so independent of the physical that when a man is loved, "his physical limits expand, his outlines recede, vanish."

Brooks is not, however, writing a poem here, whatever poetic demands she makes on language. She is telling a story, and her setting provides the backdrop for the inner and outer dialogues that convey the story. Mrs. Phillips is revealed culturally through her dialect as she describes her "boy" as "a-laughin'" and "a-jokin'"; she is revealed psychologically as she qualifies her "praise" of Maud Martha in every sentence until it becomes blatant criticism. Belva Brown reveals her character by what she does not say, and by the struggle she has to keep from saying it.

To understand Maud Martha, the psychological center of the story, however, one must go into her thoughts, even before she has had them. Brooks carefully stretches the limits of the third-person limited perspective to anticipate the realization that is rising in Maud Martha and to trace its growth. Even when Maud Martha has had her epiphany, Brooks phrases it ambiguously: "She felt higher and more like a citizen of—what?" Whereas the physical can reach its final expression in death, the spiritual reality comes in hints. If physical limits seal one in a jar where one can be destroyed by fire, spiritual realization offers one choices. It promises Maud Martha neither approval nor success—merely that "a road was again clean before her."

Thelma J. Shinn

RITTER GLUCK

Author: E. T. A. Hoffmann (1776-1822)
Type of plot: Fantasy
Time of plot: 1809
Locale: Berlin
First published: 1809 (English translation, 1969)

> *Principal characters:*
> A MAN, one who claims to be the great German composer
> Christoph Willibald Ritter von Gluck (best-known as
> Christoph Gluck, 1714-1787)
> THE NARRATOR, a connoisseur of music

The Story

On a beautiful fall afternoon, the first-person narrator, a passionate lover of music, sits in one of Berlin's well-known cafés, desperately trying to escape from the "cacaphonic racket" of its obligatory music into the world of pleasant reveries. Brought back from his dreams by the offensive tune of a particularly vile waltz, he suddenly notices that an older man of strikingly mysterious countenance and demeanor has joined him at his table. In an ensuing conversation, the stranger disagrees with the narrator's harsh criticism of the musicians and, to prove his point, asks them to play the overture to Christoph Gluck's opera *Iphigenia in Aulis* (1774). The narrator is quickly caught up in his companion's intense delight and is finally able to hear the heavenly beauty of the composition in spite of the pitiful performance it receives at the hands of the little orchestra.

At the end of the music, the stranger admits that he himself is a composer and proceeds to recount with evergrowing exaltation his way from his boyhood music lessons to the frightening but enchanting realms of music to his final, mystical encounter with the truth of all art. This truth revealed itself to him under the symbol of the sun as an ineffable harmony, a musical triad "from which the chords, like stars, shoot out and entwine you with threads of fire." Overcome by the wild enthusiasm of his own story, the stranger abruptly gets up and vanishes.

That same night, the narrator runs into the mysterious composer for the second time. Fascinated by the extraordinary aura of this man, he invites him to his apartment for a further exchange of ideas. Now it is the older of the two who castigates with great bitterness Berlin's theatrical practice of lavishing all care on the ostentatious production of operas while neglecting their musical integrity. The atrocious liberties directors have taken in the staging of Gluck's works are singled out for particularly impassioned censure. Paroxysms of emotion, this time pain and frustration clearly dominant, finally drive the unhappy man back into the night. Again he departs without a good-bye.

A third meeting comes to pass several months later as the narrator finds his eccentric friend in a state of bewildering excitement outside a theater in which a performance of Gluck's opera *Armida* (1777) is taking place. This time the curious stranger insists on inviting the narrator to his own apartment, which the visitor finds filled with old-fashioned furniture belonging to the era of Gluck rather than that of the early nineteenth century. The host now suggests that he will play the music to *Armida* on his piano and that his guest should turn the pages for him. These pages are, however, to the young man's total consternation, completely blank. The agitated stranger proceeds, nevertheless, to play Gluck's music from the empty pages and does so with a fervor and with numerous, brilliant variations which for the mesmerized listener seem to outshine the genius of Gluck's original. When the performance has come to an end, the stunned visitor begs to know to whom he is talking. The host disappears for a while into an adjacent room, only to reappear in the embroidered court dress of an eighteenth century chevalier. The young man stands paralyzed at the sight. The last words belong to the mysterious man, who now politely introduces himself by saying: "I am Ritter Gluck!"

Themes and Meanings

"Ritter Gluck" was Hoffmann's first tale and marked his emergence as one of German Romanticism's most important and influential writers. For many years Hoffmann thought his true calling to be that of a composer or conductor. In 1809, when "Ritter Gluck" was published, he served as orchestral director in the small southern town of Bamberg, and it must have seemed only natural to him to submit his short tale to Germany's leading musical journal, the *Allgemeine musikalische Zeitung*. Hoffmann's preoccupation with music is still quite obvious in the story, and literary critics have occasionally tried to dismiss it for that reason as little more than a barely disguised essay in musical criticism. Yet in spite of several musical references which the uninitiated reader today will find difficult to understand or appreciate, "Ritter Gluck" is now widely recognized as one of the finest examples of Hoffmann's literary genius, an amazingly concise prefiguration of several of his most obsessive themes.

The outward, historical circumstances of the modest plot are taken from Hoffmann's stay in Berlin between 1807 and 1808 and, more specifically, center on a performance of Gluck's opera *Armida* which Hoffmann attended and whose staging convinced him of the abominable tastes of Berlin's musical circles. On this experience, Hoffmann built a story which proclaims the fundamental incompatibility between artistic creativity and bourgeois receptivity. This insurmountable conflict between an artist and his audience is heightened by the fact that it merely reflects on a social level an even deeper conflict within the artistic process itself. The true tragedy of the artist must arise out of the recognition that what he perceives in moments of creative vision belongs to the realm of the inexpressible—no artistic realization can fully recapture such an experience in its original beauty and intensity.

The mysterious stranger of "Ritter Gluck" escapes his insensitive social environment through ever more self-absorbing flights of the imagination until in a moment of untrammeled exaltation he enters a world of harmony in which the division between nature and art has been overcome. The frustration inherent in such mystical immediacy is that its very essence forbids adequate artistic formulation. Despair thus becomes the inevitable result of any experience of the ultimate. The gifted composer of Hoffmann's tale tries to compensate for his own inability to give voice to the ecstatic harmonies of his mind by employing and improving on the work of another artist, by assuming the identity of the successful composer Christoph Gluck.

The paradox of Hoffmann's position seems to be that precisely those artists who experience most deeply will, of necessity, be driven into artistic impotence which, in turn, must lead to madness and self-destruction. Hoffmann explored these frightful consequences in much greater detail in such characters as the painters Traugott, Berklinger, and Berthold in "The Artus Exchange" and "The Jesuit Church in G." as well as in the fate of the musician Kreisler, the hero of his last novel *Lebensansichten des Katers Murr, nebst fragmentarischer Biographie des Kapellmeisters Johannes Kreisler in zufälligen Makulaturblättern* (1820-1822; *The Life and Opinions of Kater Murr, with the Fragmentary Biography of Kapellmeister Johannes Kreisler on Random Sheets of Scrap Paper*, 1907).

Style and Technique

Many of Hoffmann's most prominent stylistic devices can be identified in this, his first tale. Central among these is what has been called his style of two worlds: the unmediated juxtaposition of the ordinary and the extraordinary, the everyday and the uncanny. Again and again, Hoffmann lures the unsuspecting reader with descriptions of great precision into chains of perceptions which, in the end, leave him helplessly stranded in a world of fantastic unreality. The figure of the curious Ritter Gluck is only the most obvious instance of Hoffmann's grotesque integration of mutually exclusive perspectives. Is this man a figment of the narrator's imagination, is he the ghost of the historical Gluck, or is he simply a deranged artist? Evidence is presented in support of each of these contradictory explanations.

In the same vein, Hoffmann blurs the distinction between the arts. That he uses words to describe a musical world seems unavoidable. Yet when he conveys the ultimate mysteries of musical harmony in the highly visual images of sun and flower, he consciously aims at an artistic vision that would transcend the limits of man's divided sensorium.

The narrative technique with which "Ritter Gluck" is told seems only to intensify the resulting disorientation. Though the story provides few actions, the speed with which dialogues develop and scenes follow one another provides a dramatic tension that leaves the reader breathless in his bewilderment. For Hoffmann, in everything there lurks its opposite: sanity in madness, madness in sanity. It is the unhappy fate of the sensitive soul to be torn apart by being attuned to the fiendish transparence of all reality. Clear outline and identity, mainstays of a secure existence, reveal themselves from this vantage point as nothing but the dubious prerogatives of one-dimensional mediocrity.

Joachim J. Scholz

ROAD TO THE ISLES

Author: Jessamyn West (1907-1984)
Type of plot: Psychological realism
Time of plot: The last Thursday and Friday in January
Locale: Tenant City
First published: 1948

> *Principal characters:*
> JOHN DELAHANTY, the father
> GERTRUDE DELAHANTY, the mother
> CRESS DELAHANTY, the daughter
> BERNADINE "NEDRA" DEEVERS, Cress's friend

The Story

Cress Delahanty, a remedial dance student, is chosen to appear in the Tenant City High School Folk-Dance Festival. The fourteen-year-old girl is thrilled that she has been selected to dance alongside Bernadine Deevers, Tenant City High School's most gifted dancer, in the dance number "Road to the Isles." She has a vision of dancing "not only the outward steps of the 'Road to the Isles' but its inner meaning." Cress feels that she has achieved one of the two great goals in the life of a Tenant High School student, the other being to have Bernadine for a friend. Now that Bernadine is coming to spend the weekend with her, Cress feels as if all of her life's dreams are coming true.

Every winter, since there is little work on the ranch, Mr. Delahanty embarks on a self-improvement program, an idea suggested and nurtured by Mrs. Delahanty. Then every spring he abandons the project as if he had never begun. Last year it was "A Schedule of Exercises to Ensure Absolute Fitness"; this schedule involved running six times around the orchard in short pants, his arms flailing and chest pumping—an embarrassing sight for Cress.

This year Mr. Delahanty's schedule is a reading program from an encyclopedia for the purpose of acquiring all "Human Knowledge in a Year." Mrs. Delahanty is always trying to help Mr. Delahanty to stay on his schedule—before breakfast, before lunch, before supper, and before bedtime. Cress is ashamed of this business of schedules: Her friend Bernadine is far too sophisticated for schedules, and Cress wants to see her parents become what Bernadine would want them to be. Further, Cress is worried that her father might mispronounce the dance numbers and embarrass her in front of Bernadine. Meekly, Mr. Delahanty suggests that he will not open his mouth in the presence of Cress's friends.

Cress reminds her parents that they should address Bernadine as Nedra on Fridays. Naturally, her parents are inquisitive. Cress explains to them about the dubious origin of "Nedra": Bernadine's boyfriend Neddy, who owned two drugstores and to whom Bernadine said no on a Friday, died the following Friday. The Delahantys are amused and skeptical.

Bernadine comes the next day, Friday, to spend the weekend with Cress. They are getting ready for the folk-dance festival. While getting her costume on, Bernadine confides in Cress: Her parents also used to be like Cress's. They went where Bernadine went and she stayed with them all the time. This year, however, she will not let them go with her to the dance festival because her father made a spectacle of himself, to her shame and chagrin, when he awkwardly danced the Hopak with Miss Ingols, the gym teacher. Bernadine now wants Cress to warn her parents not to make fools of themselves on the dance floor with Miss Ingols in public.

Cress goes to the kitchen to warn her parents. As she is about to open the kitchen door to the porch, she overhears her father and mother talking about her. Unseen by them, she listens. Her parents, especially her father, are very worried about her. Mr. Delahanty is afraid that his daughter, being clumsy in footwork, might make a fool of herself in public by falling on her ear during the dance. He could not bear it if his daughter should experience such a humiliation.

As Cress traces her steps back to her friend, she looks at herself in the bathroom mirror. "I look different," she tells herself. She looks at her image again—it is blurred, wavering, and doubtful; it is no longer the triumphant face she imagined.

Cress tells Bernadine everything about her parents; indeed, she is proud of them; she is no longer apologetic about her parents; she is not afraid to admit that her father keeps schedules. She proudly announces that her parents are concerned and worried about her because they care. Cress is no longer worried about what Bernadine thinks about her parents. When Bernadine tries to make fun of her father, she tells her to shut up. Cress has grown up.

Themes and Meanings

Growing up through the process of change is what this story is about. There are two groups of people involved in this maturation process: two adults and two adolescents.

Of the two adults, one, Mrs. Delahanty, tries futilely and mistakenly to help Mr. Delahanty grow up physically and mentally. Since Mr. Delahanty is a mature adult, Jessamyn West implies, he should not be forced or nudged by his wife to change; his strenuous running and his intellectual schedule-keeping merely make him look ridiculous in the eyes of his adolescent daughter. On the other hand, Mrs. Delahanty does not try to change herself. It is interesting to note that Mr. Delahanty does not try to change his wife at all; he knows that he should not force change upon another adult.

The two adolescents, Cress and Bernadine, try to change their parents, who they think are ignorant of the ways of the modern world and naïve in social graces. Bernadine shuts her parents out of her life and refuses to accept their advice. She simply refuses to change her ways and to grow up. Cress, on the contrary, keeps an open mind and remains open to change. In only two or three minutes of conversation heard through a back porch door, Cress gets to know her parents better, and the change in perspective gives her a newfound maturity.

Jessamyn West seems to imply that refusal to grow up and change is a destructive process. Bernadine is described as a "femme fatale": Bernadine is capable of performing only Salome's dance of death; she is also somehow involved in the death of her boyfriend Neddy.

Style and Technique

The consistent and clever use of the journey motif is the means whereby Jessamyn West achieves unity and coherence in the story. This is best illustrated by the story's title, "Road to the Isles," by the movement involved in the dance routine, by the trip to the festival, and by the transportation to the out-of-town game.

One important characteristic of Jessamyn West's style in this story is that she portrays the world as an adolescent, Cress Delahanty, sees it. The reader is given the realistic impression that he or she is an unobserved spectator of the unfolding drama of Cress's psychological development. In this regard, the reader is like Cress, who, unseen, listens in on her parents' conversation about Bernadine and Cress.

Zacharias P. Thundy

THE ROCKING-HORSE WINNER

Author: D. H. Lawrence (1885-1930)
Type of plot: Fantasy
Time of plot: 1920
Locale: England
First published: 1926

Principal characters:

PAUL, the protagonist, a preadolescent boy
HESTER, Paul's mother, a beautiful, dissatisfied woman
OSCAR CRESSWELL, Hester's brother, Paul's uncle and
confidant
BASSETT, the gardener, an avid horse-racing enthusiast and
gambler

The Story

"The Rocking-Horse Winner" relates the desperate and foredoomed efforts of a young boy to win his mother's love by seeking the luck which she bitterly maintains she does not have. By bringing her the luxurious life for which she longs, Paul hopes to win her love, to compensate her for her unhappiness with his father, and to bring peace to their anxious, unhappy household. He determines to find luck after a conversation with his mother, in which she tells him that she is not lucky, having married an unlucky husband, and that it is better to have luck than money because luck brings money. In response, Paul clearly accepts the unspoken invitation to take his father's place in fulfilling his mother's dreams of happiness. His purpose seems to be fulfilled when, with the help of Bassett, the gardener, he begins to win money betting on horse races. Shortly thereafter, he confides in his uncle Oscar, whom he also considers lucky because Oscar's gift of money started his winning streak. Paul, Oscar, and Bassett continue to bet and win until Paul has five thousand pounds to give his mother for her birthday, to be distributed to her over the next five years. When she receives the anonymous present, his mother does not seem at all happy but sets about arranging to get the whole five thousand pounds at once. As a result, Hester becomes even more obsessed with money, increasingly anxious for more. Also, the house, which previously seemed to whisper "There *must* be more money! There *must* be more money!" now screeches the same refrain.

Paul, unable to perceive that his mother is insatiable, redoubles his efforts to win more money for her. He hides himself away, alone with his secret source of information on the outcome of the races. This secret, which he has shared with no one, is his mysterious, nameless rocking horse, which he rides frenziedly until he gets to the point at which he knows the name of the winner in the next big race. Desperate to know the name of the winner in the derby, he urges his parents to take a brief vacation. Summoned back to Paul by a strange sense of foreboding, Hester returns to see Paul fall from his horse after a frenzied ride, stricken by a brain fever from which he never recovers. While Bassett runs to tell Paul that he has successfully guessed the derby winner and is now rich, Paul tells his mother, "I *am* lucky," and then dies. Thereupon his uncle comments, "he's best gone out of a life where he rides his rocking-horse to find a winner."

Themes and Meanings

This story is Lawrence's strongest indictment of materialism and his strongest demonstration of the incompatibility of the love of money and the love of human beings. In Paul's unhappy family, his parents' marriage is unsatisfactory. His mother is sexually frustrated: "She had bonny children, yet she felt they had been *thrust* upon her." Clearly, she feels not fulfilled, but violated.

Yet she does not seek the cause of the failure of her marriage inside herself, but rather outside herself, claiming that she and her husband have no luck. In confiding her disappointment to her son, she seductively invites him to take the father's place in her life by finding luck for her. This task he sets out to accomplish. Thus, the preadolescent boy, who should feel sufficiently secure in his mother's love and in the stability of his family so that he can seek outside relationships and embark on his own sexual course, is arrested in his development. Stuck in an Oedipal bind with his mother, he regresses from adolescent sexuality into sexual infantilism. Instead of riding his own horse, symbol of male sexual power, he rides a rocking horse, an activity which, in its frenzy and isolation, suggests masturbation rather than fulfillment with a partner.

Throughout, Lawrence condemns the modern notion that luck and happiness come from the outside, rather than from within; that happiness must take the form of money and goods rather than of erotic, parental, and filial love.

Lawrence also points out, with psychological astuteness, that to supplant love with money is a deception through which everyone can see. In the story, no one is fooled. The mother, whose heart is too hardened to love her children, tries to compensate them with presents and solicitousness, but the children and the mother know the truth: "They read it in each other's eyes."

To give and to receive love, the only true fulfillment in life, is, as Lawrence points out, to relate to but never to control another human being: The loved one always remains mysterious, unknown, unpredictable. Thus, love, freely given and received, is the very opposite of Paul's desperate need to know, to force knowledge, and to predict the future.

Although the reader never discovers how Paul learns the names of the winners, Lawrence hints, at various points in the story, that Paul may be trafficking with false and evil gods. This suggestion is made through his repeated descriptions of Paul's eyes as looking demoniac: "his uncanny blue eyes" that had "an uncanny cold fire in them"; "his eyes were like blue stones." This idea is also suggested by the religious language that surrounds Paul's gambling. Bassett repeatedly refers to Paul's correct prediction by saying, "It's as if he had it from heaven"; "his face terribly serious, as if he were speaking of religious matters"; his manner "serious as a church."

Style and Technique

The story begins with the deceptively simple and formulaic language of the fairy tale: "There was a woman who was beautiful, who started with all the advantages, yet she had no luck." This language underscores the inappropriateness of a life lived, as Hester lives it, in the belief that just as in fairy tales, luck and happiness are unpredictable because they come from the outside rather than being matters over which the individual exercises some control.

The supernatural elements in the story, rather than providing an opportunity for escape, augment its sense of reality. The futility of the materialistic quest, and its lack of destination, are well symbolized in Paul's frantic riding of his rocking horse. That the house whispers "There must be more money" seems not so much a supernatural or magical element as a brilliantly sustained metaphor for the unspoken messages that shape and often take over the life of a family. In all, the story is a brilliant study in the sustained use of symbolism to suggest with bold economy the death-dealing consequences of the substitution of money for love.

Carola M. Kaplan

ROMAN FEVER

Author: Edith Wharton (1862-1937)
Type of plot: Ironic epiphany
Time of plot: The 1920's
Locale: Rome
First published: 1933

>   *Principal characters:*
>   MR. DELPHIN (ALIDA) SLADE, a middle-aged American
>   tourist
>   MRS. HORACE (GRACE) ANSLEY, another middle-aged
>   American tourist, a longtime acquaintance of Mrs. Slade

The Story

As the story begins, two old friends, Alida Slade and Grace Ansley, are finishing lunch on the terrace of a Roman restaurant and move to the parapet, where they benignly contemplate the magnificent ruins of the Palatine and the Forum. Remarking that the scene below is the most beautiful view in the world, the two ladies agree to spend the afternoon on the terrace. Alida arranges with the waiter to permit them to stay until evening. They hear their respective daughters, Barbara Ansley and Jenny Slade, departing to spend the afternoon with two eligible young Italian men, and Grace remarks that the young women will probably return late, flying back by moonlight from Tarquinia. It becomes evident at this point that Grace has a closer relationship with her daughter than Alida has with Jenny, because Alida did not know where the girls were going. Also, Barbara remarks a bit ruefully to Jenny as the two of them depart that they are leaving their mothers with nothing much to do.

At that point, Alida broaches the subject of emotions by asking Grace if she thinks that their daughters are as sentimental, especially about moonlight, as they once were. Grace responds that she does not know at all about the girls' sentiments and adds that she doubts that the two mothers know much about each other either. The two women sit silently for a while, thinking about their perceptions of each other.

Alida's perceptions of Grace are recounted as an interior monologue, which continues throughout the story, interspersed with passages of dialogue. As she reflects, she also reveals the circumstances of the years since she first met Grace. Grace had been married to Horace Ansley shortly before Alida had married Delphin Slade. Alida considered the Ansleys nullities, living exemplary but insufferably dull lives in an apartment directly across the street from the Slades in New York City. They had been superficial friends, and Alida had rather closely observed the irreproachable events of the Ansleys' lives for a number of years before her very successful lawyer husband made a big coup in Wall Street, and the Slades moved to a more fashionable Park Avenue address. She prided herself on the lively social life that she and Delphin enjoyed, and especially on her own skills as a hostess and a brilliant personality. Both women were widowed only a few months before the time of the story, and have renewed their friendship in the common bond of bereavement.

Alida's envy of Grace, despite her disparaging assessment of her, emerges in her thoughts at this time. She wonders how the Ansleys could have produced such a vivid and charming daughter, when her own Jenny seems by comparison so dull. She recalls that Grace was exquisitely lovely in her youth as well as charming in a fragile, quiet way. She reflects that she herself would probably be much more active and concerned if she had Barbara for a daughter.

Grace, for her part, has a mental image of Alida as a brilliant woman, but one who is overimpressed by her own qualities. She remembers Alida as a vivid, dashing girl, much different from her pretty but somewhat mousy daughter. She views Alida's life as sad, full of failures and mistakes, and feels rather sorry for her. Thus, in part 1 of the story, the setting, the situation, and the attitudes of the two women are presented in a manner which suggests a placid, if superficial, friendship of many years' standing, with both of the women secretly feeling some pity for each other's past life.

Part 2 begins with the tolling of the five o'clock bells and the decision of the two women to remain on the terrace rather than going in to play bridge. As Grace Ansley knits, Alida Slade reflects that their own mothers must have had a worrisome task trying to keep them home safe despite the lure of the romantic evenings in Rome. Grace agrees, and Alida continues with speculations about the probability that Barbara will become engaged to the attractive, eligible young Roman pilot with whom she is spending the evening, along with Jenny and the second young man. Jenny, Alida reasons, is only a foil for Barbara's vivacious charm, and Grace may be encouraging the companionship for that very reason. She tells Grace of her envy, stating that she cannot understand how the Ansleys had such a dynamic child while the Slades had such a quiet one. Alida recognizes in her own mind her envy, and also realizes that it began a long time ago.

As the sun sets, Alida recalls that Grace was susceptible to throat infections as a girl and was forced to be very careful about contracting Roman fever or pneumonia. Then she recalls a story of a great-aunt of Grace, who sent her sister on an errand to the Forum at night because the two sisters were in love with the same man, with the result that the unfortunate girl died of Roman fever. Alida then reveals that she used a similar method to eliminate the competition she believed existed between herself and Grace when, as young women in Rome, they both were in love with Delphin Slade. She cruelly reveals that she wrote a note to Grace imploring a rendezvous in the Colosseum by moonlight, and signed it with Delphin's name.

Revealing her hatred further, she gloats about how she laughed that evening thinking about Grace waiting alone in the darkness outside the Colosseum, and how effective the ruse had been, for Grace had become ill and was bedridden for some weeks. Grace is at first crushed to learn that the only letter that she ever received from Delphin was a fake, but then turns the tables on Alida by assuring her that she had not waited alone that night. Delphin had made all the arrangements and was waiting for her.

Alida's jealousy and hatred are rekindled as she realizes that she has failed to humiliate Grace Ansley, especially when Grace states that she feels sorry for Alida because her cruel trick had so completely failed. Alida protests that she really had everything: She was Delphin's wife for twenty-five years, and Grace has nothing but the one letter that he did not write. In the final ironic epiphany, Grace simply replies that she had Barbara. Then she moves ahead of Alida toward the stairway.

This battle of the two women for the integrity of their own status with respect to the man they both loved ends with the complete victory of the woman who has appeared to be the weak, passive creature. She moves ahead because she is now dominant. The source of Barbara's sparkle is now revealed, and Grace is also now shown to be a woman who defied conventional morality and social restrictions to spend a night with the man she loved. Alida Slade is left only with the dismaying knowledge that she, in her attempt to be hateful and cruel, actually brought about the meeting which produced the lovely daughter she envies her friend having.

Themes and Meanings

The title of the story refers to malarial fever, which was prevalent in Rome prior to the draining of the swamps around the early nineteenth century. This fever was much feared by American tourists, especially those who had young, fragile daughters who might succumb to the ravages of the disease. The chances of contracting the disease were increased greatly after dark, when the mosquitoes which spread the infection were most active. Symbolically, the title also refers to the fever pitch of the passions that were engendered in the two women when they visited Rome as nubile young girls. The surface serenity and static nature of the plot provide ironic contrast to the gradual revelation of the intense emotions that the two women experienced when they were in Rome before.

The story contrasts the abiding hate of Alida Slade with the abiding love of Grace Ansley. Alida's cruelty and hatred, aroused by her fear that Delphin might be attracted to Grace, prompts her finally to reveal her trickery to the other woman. Her intention was clearly to humiliate the other, and to bask in her triumphant superiority. Grace reveals, at Alida's goading, that the trickery not only did not work but also was actually the impetus for the birth of Barbara, the child for whom Alida has envied Grace ever since the child was an infant.

Friendship and companionship are superficial social amenities as depicted in this story. Strong emotions are suppressed or at least concealed in favor of outward tranquillity and smooth social relations. Yet the deep, hidden emotions have nevertheless driven these women to actions which shaped their lives and characters in profound ways.

Style and Technique

The style of the story in its serenity, its quiet setting, and its almost total lack of action well matches the calm control exhibited by Grace Ansley, who turns out to be the victor in the contest initiated by Alida Slade. Although the reader is told that Alida is the dominant, vivid personality, and she clearly takes charge of both the activities (or lack thereof) and the conversation, her attacks on Grace are quietly rebuffed, and she is finally the loser as they mutually reveal information about their past activities.

The story is carefully wrought, so that the shift in sympathy to the timid Grace occurs fairly early, and it comes as a surprise to learn that she was so unconventional in her behavior as to undertake an assignation with another woman's fiancé. Then the final surprise, which is so quietly, and characteristically, announced to the arrogant Alida, serves to end the story with a dramatic flourish that has even more impact because it is so subdued.

Betty G. Gawthrop

1978

ROPE

Author: Katherine Anne Porter (1890-1980)
Type of plot: Psychlogical realism
Time of plot: The 1920's
Locale: The South, a house in the country
First published: 1928

> *Principal characters:*
> "HE," the husband
> "SHE," the wife

The Story

Katherine Anne Porter's simple plot structure belies an insightful render-ing of an embittered and ambivalent relationship between a husband and wife, who have recently moved to the country from their apartment in town. Despite the generic pronominal references and an ambiguous locale (South-ern regionalism more in spirit than in fact), her characters are more fully rea-lized than the reader may at first suppose—indeed, each will flesh out his or her personality by degrees after the inward turning of the first paragraph.

Returning from a four-mile walk through heat and dust, the husband is first greeted by his wife with affection; they exchange playful remarks about their unfamiliar circumstances: She resembles "a born country woman"; he seems like "a rural character in a play." Swiftly, the narrator plunges inside to reveal the essence of what each says to the other. This narrational viewpoint (narrated monologue) involves, at times, not only a rapid switch between characters but also a greater degree of editorializing by the narrator as the tempo of their argument increases.

At first, she is mildly disappointed that he has forgotten her coffee; then she spies the broken eggs in the sack—caused by a twenty-four-yard coil of rope; the eggs will have to be used right away, and her plans for dinner are spoiled. Soon, they are arguing with a surprising vehemence, considering the trivial cause. Her passion for order is, in his view, "an insane habit of chang-ing things around"; she, however, "had borne all the clutter she meant to bear in the flat in the town." For the most part, her emotional outbursts are inflected with her own idiom, thinly disguised by the narrator's mediation, but it becomes evident that the pressure of the past is on the point of over-whelming her. Deeper plunges by the narrator inside his character reveal how wide is the discrepancy between what he thinks is wrong with her and what her own near-the-surface reflections reveal.

The rope, which keeps getting underfoot in a figurative sense, lends a bit of grotesque comedy, causing the reader to ponder its obvious symbolic aspects. Although the taunts fly between them, it is clear that they cannot articulate the most deeply rooted sources of their discontent. Aside from the poverty and drudgery of their marriage, she chafes at the housework, even though "getting the devilish house ready for him" pleases her. They are childless, but he cruelly taunts her infertility, wishing she had "something weaker than she was to heckle and tyrannize over." She is also tortured by jealousy and the likelihood that he may have been unfaithful during his stay in town the summer before; he cavalierly dismisses her fear; "It may have looked funny but he had simply got hooked in, and what could he do?"

In contrast to her bitterness, he seems smugly indifferent to probing his own responsibility, exploding in wonderment and fury: "What *was* the matter, for God's sake?" He knows that it cannot be "only a piece of rope that was causing all the racket," but he deflects her barbs with those of his own by threatening to leave her "with a half-empty house on her hands." Less fragile than she, he assumes a kind of mordant pose about it all: "Things broke so suddenly you didn't know where you were."

He tries to placate her by returning to the village for the coffee, as if that were the source of contention, but she complains that he is deserting her: "Sometimes it seemed to her he had second sight about the precisely perfect moment to leave her ditched." Then she collapses into a fit of hysterical laughter, from which he has to revive her by a violent shaking, and she sends him and his rope down the road with a curse. Alone with his thoughts, he consoles himself with more philosophy: "Things accumulated, things were mountainous, you couldn't move them or sort them or get rid of them."

Upon his return—again with the rope, which he had hidden and retrieved—he sees his wife waiting; the air is cool and carries the smell of broiling steak; she is attractive, beckoning—and he runs to her. Together, embracing, they return to the house; he playfully coos baby talk to her, and he pats her stomach—a gesture that elicits "wary smiles" from them both. She admires an out-of-season whippoorwill calling its mate (she thinks), and the narrator concludes on an ironically detached note, giving the reader a last glimpse of his mind: Oblivious to the day's strife, he tells himself that he understands her: "Sure, he knew how she was."

Themes and Meanings

The rope is the story's central symbol: It binds and oppresses; it lashes and it strangles. Tied together as this couple is, the reader may wonder whether the equilibrium restored to their marriage at the end is merely a temporary respite: Is their need for each other sufficient to overcome the inertia of this kind of anger and bitterness? Like the crab apple fruit itself, the marriage of this pair may well survive on the strength of these intense emotions: Hatred, for them, may be the obverse side of love's coin. In any case, the narrator remains detached from commentary, and the reader must accept the ambiguity of the conclusion. Certainly, their marriage is a hell of their own making.

Porter had married at sixteen and was divorced several years later, so she knew well the forms of dissension that can alienate a couple's affections despite the intimate bond of marriage. The wife of this story, however, is not up to the standards of her later, more fully developed female figures, for example, Miranda of "Pale Horse, Pale Rider" or Laura of "Flowering Judas." For one thing, the wife in "Rope" is not possessed of their powers of self-awareness or their discriminating sensibilities. Strong forces are at work inside her, to be sure, but the narrator will merely report their superficial consequences—for example, she "grew livid about the mouth" and "looked quite dangerous . . . her face turned slightly purple, and she screamed with laughter." Despite her husband's glib confidence that he understands her, the reader cannot so easily reconcile the disproportionate gap between what she says and what she knows to be true in the story world.

Style and Technique

The most significant technique is the superb control over point of view, so that characters reveal themselves at the moments of greatest stress. The editorializing function of the narrator is therefore all-important, but it must not seem to be too heavy-handed in manipulating the narrative voice. Porter ensures that the characters' points of view are woven into the narrative in a manner that is consistent and artful. In the first place, she uses narrated monologue rather than other forms of interior monologue, pruning away the unnecessary tags of thinking and saying as well as the signals of quotation. The end result is that the reader "hears" the man and woman in their private voices, when in fact what constitutes the narrative transmission is an aggregate of points of view that mixes the narrator's and characters' voices and which is richly composed of idiom and colloquialism, exclamations, repetitions, and circumlocutions—in short, all the features of a mind instantly verbalizing. In this way, the reader experiences with freshness and immediacy the thoughtless ease with which they wound each other: "Oh, would he please hush and go away, and *stay* away, if he could, for five minutes? By all means, yes, he would. He'd stay away indefinitely if she wished."

Ultimately, language itself becomes both the theme and the style, causing them to merge into each other with precise diction and economy of choice so that—for all its density and capacity to communicate—the reader experiences this vitriolic exchange of language and realizes that these two cannot say what they most want to say, and that language is itself the source and barrier to a true communication. To this end, Porter makes use of a wide array of the forms of language: from mild profanities (emblematic of their hellish relationship), through a kind of subvocal level (indicated by the narrator's allusions to her feline responses of hissing and clawing), to, finally, that level of self-communion in which the husband will seek to explain his wife's behavior and their crumbling marriage to himself.

Last, there is the narrator's ambiguous silence, looking on dispassionately, allowing things as well as characters to speak for themselves; perhaps this is best exemplified in the lonely bird in the crab apple tree with all its bittersweet allusiveness, suggestive of another Garden and expulsion from it into a hostile and disorderly world.

Terry White

ROSA

Author: Cynthia Ozick (1928-   )
Type of plot: Sociopsychological realism
Time of plot: 1977
Locale: Miami, Florida
First published: 1983

Principal characters:

ROSA LUBLIN, the protagonist, a fifty-eight-year-old Polish
    Jewish woman, a survivor of a Nazi concentration camp
MAGDA, her infant daughter who perished in the camp, to
    whom Rosa nevertheless writes and confides her thoughts
STELLA, Rosa's niece, who is still living in Brooklyn, also a
    camp survivor
SIMON PERSKY, a retired button manufacturer who gradually
    becomes Rosa's friend

The Story

From the very beginning of the story, Rosa Lublin is described as a madwoman; indeed, the world she inhabits seems composed of as much illusion as reality. After destroying her junk shop in Brooklyn, she has exiled herself to Miami, which she envisions as a sort of Hell of the elderly. She lives in a sordid hotel room with a disconnected phone and keeps as much to herself as possible. Her main form of communication is letter writing; yet her long-dead daughter Magda, to whom she pens lengthy and intimate thoughts in "excellent literary Polish," seems to have more substance for Rosa than the long-suffering niece Stella, who actually supports Rosa and to whom Rosa writes in "crude" English.

When Simon Persky bursts upon Rosa's solitude in a laundromat one morning and attempts to lure her back to the world of the living, she repels his advance, even rejecting their common origins in Warsaw. Rosa insists, "My Warsaw isn't your Warsaw." She pictures his Warsaw as one of alleys strung with cheap clothing and "signs in jargoned Yiddish," while hers was Polish, a place of "cultivation, old civilization, beauty, history." Her parents mocked Yiddish, and the young Rosa was preparing to become another Marie Curie. Persky treats her to a meal in the Kollins Kosher Kameo, which she grudgingly endures, preferring her lonely exclusivity.

When she returns to her hotel, the mail has arrived: Stella's letter announcing that she has finally sent the shawl Rosa requested, and a package which Rosa imagines contains the shawl of her dead infant Magda. Before she can open it, however, she must purify her room and herself; justifying her motives in a long letter to a perfect and adult Magda, she emphasizes the purity of Magda's heritage. Then Rosa ventures out into the dusk in search of a pair of lost underpants that she imagines Persky has "stolen" from her, causing her to feel shamed and degraded. During the search she becomes entrapped on a private hotel beach, behind a barbed-wire fence; she finally gets free but registers her complaint with the hotel's manager, who as a Jew, she reminds him, ought to know better: "In America it's no place for barbed wire on top of fences."

"Cleansed" by the outburst, she returns to her hotel to find Persky waiting in the lobby, and they have tea in her room. Feeling already exposed to Persky, the imagined possessor of her underwear, she opens in front of him, first her thoughts and then the package. To her disappointment it contains, instead of the shawl, only a scientific book. In a fury, Rosa smashes up the tea party, and Persky dashes out.

The next day she has her telephone reconnected, and the real shawl arrives in the mail, though it is now colorless, like an old bandage, and does not immediately evoke Magda's presence for her, as it usually does. Not until Rosa phones Stella "long distance" does Magda come magically to life. Rosa composes another letter to her in which she relates the story of her family's degradation in wartime Warsaw, when Jews were imprisoned in the Ghetto and her family was forced to live among the poor and ignorant in crowded, unbelievably squalid conditions. Through the center of the Ghetto ran the city tram because it could not be economically rerouted around the Ghetto. While people in the Ghetto were prevented from getting on the tram, common Polish working-class citizens, passing from one side of Warsaw to the other, rode through each day, "straight into the place of our misery," to witness her family's shame. One day Rosa noticed an ordinary woman riding the tram with a head of lettuce showing out of the top of her shopping sack. Now, she concludes in the letter to Magda, she has herself become like that ordinary woman with the lettuce in the tramcar. At that point Magda disappears, because the telephone rings to announce Perksy's arrival in the lobby downstairs, and Rosa invites him to come up.

Themes and Meanings

It would be simple enough to read this as a tale of psychic wounds borne by a survivor of the Holocaust, particularly as "Rosa" is a sequel to an earlier story, "The Shawl," which provides an account of a particular experience in the concentration camp involving Rosa, Stella, and Magda and lays groundwork for a probable cause of guilt on Rosa's part.

This would seem further supported by Rosa's explanation of time as a structuring device dividing people's lives into "before," "after," and "during" the Holocaust. Just as the "before" is a dream, she says, the "after" is a joke: "Only the during stays." She condemns those who try to forget the "during," as if she were trapped in that time of horrifying experience, which had the power to transform "before" into "after," or "dream" into "joke."

Yet Rosa is trapped not in time but in pride. Although her mind seems often to dwell in the "before," she insists that she does not want to return to that actual time. Her memories serve, rather, to recall the privileged potential that she once enjoyed and to give imaginative shape to the potential perfection that Magda (as Rosa's single accomplishment of any value) might have attained had she only survived, for Magda, too, has the power to transform: Like "the philosophers' stone that prolongs life and transmutes iron to gold," Magda can, through the material agency of the shawl, transform her ordinary mother into "a Madonna." Rosa believes not in God but in "mystery" and attributes such power to the shawl that the object becomes almost a sacred relic in and of itself: "Your idol," mocks Stella, whom Rosa often calls the Angel of Death.

The real means of Rosa's transformation, however, is her pride, her readiness to be recognized as special, if only by Magda. Rosa cannot bear to be thought ordinary; that Persky would take her for "another button"; that Stella would have her "recuperated" or healed of her "craziness," which, if nothing else, sets Rosa apart from the "ordinary."

This same pride is also her cage, her trap, in that it not only holds her apart from her fellowman but also prevents her from recognizing that the distance and misperceptions between herself and others are at least partially of her own making. While she can admit "how far she had fallen . . . nobility turned into a small dun rodent," she does not see that her fallen state comes, ironically, from having set herself so high above her fellowman, past and present. She has discovered the "power to shame" other Jews who did not experience the Holocaust and does not hesitate to hold it over them: "Where were you when we was there?" Yet even after having shared a ghastly fate with those other Jews imprisoned with her family back in the Warsaw Ghetto, she can look back now only with contempt and shame at the squalor they imposed on her delicate and sensitive family.

It is, finally, from this same memory—in particular the metaphor of the tram which ran through the center of the walled-off Ghetto with the woman aboard, carrying the lettuce—that Rosa at last draws the key which may release her from her trap of pride. Cynthia Ozick, in "The Moral Necessity of Metaphor," has written, "Metaphor is the reciprocal agent, the universalizing force: it makes possible the power to envision the stranger's heart." When Rosa admits, in her last letter to Magda, "Now I am like the woman who held the lettuce in the tramcar," she has clearly begun to understand, it would seem, what it means to be a stranger, an ordinary stranger, traveling temporarily into a place of "misery," and how she must appear to those less free than she, those others too "deaf" to understand. Rosa, having suffered both humiliation and persistent compassion from Persky, decides finally to reconnect her telephone and invites Persky to "come up" to her room, suggesting both that she is admitting him to her rarefied environment and that she is deliberately reaching out to another human being.

Style and Technique

Because Rosa's version of truth is often at odds with other information presented in the story, it is clear that Ozick intends for the reader to question Rosa's reliability. The discrepancies range from something as minor as two different accounts of Rosa's age to the crucial question of whether Magda actually lives, and much ground in between remains open to interpretation. At times the charge of madwoman appears warranted, yet at other times Rosa's faculties seem too accurately to record the cultural and spiritual wasteland around her for her to be anything but painfully sane. Even in acknowledging that some people live only in their thoughts, she seems ironically aware of her own delusions.

The net effect of these conflicting accounts, while demonstrating in an abstract sense the subjectivity of truth, is to establish between the reader and the story's "reality" a tension parallel to that between Rosa and her environment. As he participates in Rosa's isolation from an uncertain world with which she is out of step, the reader's sense of reality, as defined by "fact," is undermined.

Rosa's unreliable accounts also cast doubt over the past from which she has "fallen," however, and threaten the very underpinnings of her pride. She seems to protest too much, for example, offering so elaborate an explanation that Magda's father was not a German Nazi that the reader may suspect the opposite to be true. Moreover, Rosa's act of smashing up her antique shop— literally destroying "other people's history"—speaks plainly enough not only of her own subjective view of the past but also of the inadequacy of factual (material) minutiae as a basis for truth. As Rosa fleshes out Magda's "life" with conflicting details, the reader might well question how much of Rosa's own reconstructed past is to be trusted. What, then, of Rosa is true?

This subverting of factual detail finally lessens the reader's dependency on fact as a reliable tool for discovering truth and brings into focus, at the same time, the concept of Rosa's truth as composed of universals—of fatal flaws and qualities of character, of fallen states and states of redemption, of the human need to be accepted, connected, and lovingly interpreted—the truths of myth and metaphor, and of lives taken on faith.

Sally V. Doud

A ROSE FOR EMILY

Author: William Faulkner (1897-1962)
Type of plot: Southern gothic
Time of plot: c. 1865-1924
Locale: Jefferson, Yoknapatawpha County, Mississippi
First published: 1930

> *Principal characters:*
> MISS EMILY GRIERSON, a Southern lady
> THE UNNAMED NARRATOR, a citizen of Jefferson
> HOMER BARRON, Emily's Yankee lover
> TOBE, Emily's black servant
> EMILY'S FATHER, an aristocrat
> COLONEL SARTORIS, the onetime mayor

The Story

Although an unnamed citizen of the small town of Jefferson, in Yokna-patawpha County, Mississippi, tells the story of the aristocratic Miss Emily Grierson in a complicated manner, shifting back and forth in time without trying to make clear transitions, the story line itself is quite simple. Miss Emily's father dies when she is a little more than thirty, in about 1882. For three days she prevents his burial, refusing to accept his death. He had driven off all of her suitors; now she is alone, a spinster, in a large house.

In the summer after the death of her father, Miss Emily meets Homer Barron, the Yankee foreman of a crew contracted to pave the sidewalks of Jefferson. They appear on the streets in a fancy buggy, provoking gossip and resentment.

Two female cousins come to town from Alabama to attempt to persuade Miss Emily to behave in a more respectable manner. Emily buys an outfit of man's clothes and a silver toilet set. To avoid the cousins, Homer leaves town. Miss Emily buys rat poison from the druggist. The cousins leave. Homer returns; he is never seen again.

A foul odor emanates from Miss Emily's house. After midnight, four citizens, responding to complaints made by neighbors to Judge Stevens, the mayor, stealthily spread lime around the house and in her cellar. In a week or so, the smell goes away.

In 1894, Colonel Sartoris, the mayor, remits Miss Emily's taxes. For about six or seven years, while in her forties, she gives china-painting lessons to the young girls of the town. Then for many years she is seen only at her window. Townspeople watch her black servant Tobe going in and out on errands. A new generation comes to power; they insist that Miss Emily pay taxes on her property. When she fails to respond, a deputation calls on her, but she insists that she owes no taxes, as Colonel Sartoris will tell them (he has been dead ten years).

In about 1925, Miss Emily dies. On the day of her funeral, the towns-people, including some old Civil War veterans, invade the house. Tobe leaves by the back door and is never seen again. One group breaks into a locked room upstairs and discovers the corpse of Homer Barron, which has moldered in the bed for forty years. On a pillow beside him, they find "a long strand of iron-gray hair," evidence that Miss Emily had lain down beside him years after she poisoned him.

Themes and Meanings

Miss Emily's story is certainly bizarre, suspenseful, and mysterious enough to engage the reader's attention fully. She is a grotesque, Southern gothic character whose neurotic or psychotic behavior in her relationships with her father, her lover, and her black servant may elicit many Freudian interpreta-tions. For example, her affair with Homer Barron may be seen as a middle-aged woman's belated rebellion against her repressive father and against the town's burdensome expectations. That Faulkner intended her story to have a much larger dimension is suggested by his choice of an unnamed citizen of Jefferson to tell it.

The narrator never speaks or writes as an individual, never uses the pro-noun "I," always speaks as "we." As representative of the townspeople, the narrator feels a compulsion to tell the story of a woman who represents something important to the community. Black voices are excluded from this collective voice as it speaks out of old and new generations. Colonel Sartoris' antebellum generation is succeeded by one with "modern ideas": "Thus, she passed from generation to generation."

Even though Miss Emily was a child during the Civil War, she represents to generations past and present the old Deep South of the Delta cotton-plantation aristocracy. She is a visible holdover into the modern South of a bygone era of romance, chivalry, and the Lost Cause. Even this new South, striving for a prosperity based on Northern technology, cannot fully accept the decay of antebellum culture and ideals. Early, the narrator invokes such concepts as tradition, duty, hereditary obligation, and custom, suggesting a perpetuation in the community consciousness of those old values. The community's sense of time is predominantly chronological, but it is also like Emily's, the confused, psychological time sense of memory. Like many women of the defeated upper class in the Deep South, Miss Emily withdraws from the chronological time of reality into the timelessness of illusion.

Miss Emily is then symbolic of the religion of Southernness that survived military defeat and material destruction. The children of Colonel Sartoris' generation are sent to learn china-painting from Miss Emily in "the same spirit that they were sent to church." It is because "we" see her as resembling "those angels in colored church windows" that her affair with a Yankee makes her "a bad example to the young people."

Given the fact that the Yankee colonel who made the deepest raid into Rebel territory was named Grierson, Faulkner may have intended Emily's family name to be ironic. The insanity of clinging to exposed illusions is suggested by the fact that Miss Emily's great-aunt went "crazy" and that Miss Emily later appears "crazy" to the townspeople. Ironically, even within aristocratic families there is division; her father fell out with Alabama kinsmen over the great-aunt's estate.

Immediately after the narrator refers to Miss Emily as being like an "idol" and to her great-aunt as "crazy," Faulkner presents this image, symbolic of the aristocracy: "We had long thought of them as a tableau, Miss Emily a slender figure in white in the background, her father a spraddled silhouette in the foreground, his back to her and clutching a horsewhip, the two of them framed by the back-flung front door." Her father's rejection of her suitors is like the defeated aristocracy's rejection of new methods of creating a future. Emily's refusal to accept the fact of her father's death suggests the refusal of some aristocrats to accept the death of the South even when faced with the evidence of its corpse. Perversely, "She would have to cling to that which had robbed her, as people will." Yet the modern generations insist on burying the decaying corpse of the past.

Miss Emily preserves all the dead, in memory if not literally. "See Colonel Sartoris," she tells the new town fathers, as if he were alive. The townspeople are like Miss Emily in that they persist in preserving her "dignity" as the last representative of the Old South (her death ends the Grierson line); after she is dead, the narrator preserves her in this story. The rose is a symbol of the age of romance in which the aristocracy were obsessed with delusions of grandeur, pure women being a symbol of the ideal in every phase of life. Perhaps the narrator offers this story as a "rose" for Emily. As a lady might press a rose between the pages of a history of the South, she keeps her own personal rose, her lover, preserved in the bridal chamber where a rose color pervades everything. Miss Emily's rose is ironically symbolic because her lover was a modern Yankee, whose laughter drew the townspeople to him and whose corpse has grinned "profoundly" for forty years, as if he, or Miss Emily, had played a joke on all of them.

Style and Technique

The extraordinary degree to which the young Faulkner managed to compress into this, his first published story, many of the elements that came to be characteristic of his fiction is the effect of his unusual use of the first-person point of view and his control of the motifs that flow from it.

By confining himself to the pronoun "we," the narrator gives the reader the impression that the whole town is bearing witness to the behavior of a heroine, about whom they have ambivalent attitudes, ambiguously expressed. The ambiguity derives in part from the community's lack of access to facts, stimulating the narrator to draw on his own and the communal imagination to fill out the picture, creating a collage of images. The narration gives the impression of coming out of a communal consciousness, creating the effect of a peculiar omniscience. An entire novel could be developed from the material compressed into this short story.

Is the narrator telling the story in the Southern oral tradition or is he or she writing it? To ask basic questions about this unusual collective mode of narration—who, what, where, when, and why—is to stir up many possibilities. The oral mode seems most appropriate, but the style, consisting of such phrases as "diffident deprecation," suggests the written mode.

A pattern of motifs that interact, contrasting with or paralleling one another, sometimes symbolically, sometimes ironically, flows naturally from the reservoir of communal elements in the narrator's saturated consciousness as he tells the story: the funeral, the cemetery, the garages, cars, cotton gins, taxes, the law, the market basket and other elements of black existence, the house, its front and back doors, its cellar and upper rooms, the window where Emily sits, the idol image that becomes a fallen monument, images that evoke the Civil War, images of gold, of decay, the color yellow, dust, shadows, corpses and bodies like corpses, the smells, the breaking down of doors, the poison, and the images of hair.

To lend greater impact to the surprise ending and to achieve greater artistic unity and intensity of effect, Faulkner uses other devices: foreshadowing, reversal, and repetition. Most of the motifs, spaced effectively throughout, are repeated at least three times, enabling the reader to respond at any given point to all the elements simultaneously.

Imitators of the surprise-ending device, made famous in modern times by O. Henry, have given that device a bad name by using it mechanically to provoke a superficial thrill. In raising the surprise-ending device to the level of complex art, Faulkner achieves a double impact: "The man himself lay on the bed" is shock enough, justified by what has gone before, but "the long strand of iron-gray hair," the charged image that ends the story, shocks the reader into a sudden, intuitive reexperiencing and reappraisal of the stream of images, bringing order and meaning to the pattern of motifs.

David Madden

1990

A ROSE IN THE HEART OF NEW YORK

Author: Edna O'Brien (1930-   )
Type of plot: Domestic realism
Time of plot: The 1930's to 1970's
Locale: Rural Ireland
First published: 1978

> *Principal characters:*
> THE DAUGHTER, the unnamed protagonist, a member of a
> rural Irish family
> THE FATHER, a violent drunkard
> THE MOTHER, with whom the daughter is obsessively close

The Story

"A Rose in the Heart of New York" chronicles several decades in the lives of a rural Irish family, focusing principally on the daughter, who is born in the story's first scene, and the mother, who is buried in the last. This one turn in the ancient cycle of birth and death constitutes a vivid and moving struggle by both to understand their relationship with each other and with the culture that inevitably shapes them.

If intensity of devotion is a reliable gauge of a happy relationship, then mother and daughter must have been happy indeed. The daughter follows her mother everywhere, watching each of her movements, absorbing her manners and attitudes. The mother dotes on her daughter, sacrificing for her, "spoiling" her as much as their poverty will allow. There is a thin line, however, between healthy devotion and something closer to unnatural obsession, and the reader finds that this line is approached perilously near, if it is not actually crossed.

When the daughter is sent to a convent, she is forced to find some way of living apart from her mother. Her solution to this forced separation is to adopt a nun as a sort of surrogate mother, lavishing her with praise, presents, and devotion and receiving the same in return. That their relationship is unnaturally and unhealthily intense is indicated by the disapproval of the convent superiors. Chastised, the two decide to "break up." Out of the convent, the daughter's life is not so different from many another young woman's; she has affairs, marries "in haste," separates, has more affairs, becomes an independent career woman, and so on. Throughout, her mother never quite leaves her thoughts; in fact, she tends to see her own affairs and life in the light of her mother's life and attitudes. The last scene between mother and daughter occurs when they go on a brief vacation together. They are closer, physically, than at any time since the daughter left home, but closeness brings no revelation. Indeed, they are struck by how little they understand of each other.

In the brief final section, the daughter learns that her mother has died. She rushes home just in time for the funeral. Afterward, she rummages around in her mother's things and finds a letter that her mother had written to an old beau whom she had met while living in New York as a girl. Later, she finds an envelope addressed to her in her mother's handwriting; inside are a few trinkets and a small amount of money. The reader can be forgiven for expecting the letter and the envelope to contain the key to the whole, to provide the revelation or epiphany with which many short stories culminate. O'Brien, however, avoids easy resolutions. The letter is sadly banal; the envelope contains not a word, not a clue to the mystery. The story ends with the daughter farther than ever from understanding her mother or herself.

Themes and Meanings

Labeling "A Rose in the Heart of New York" a "feminist" story should not be construed as reducing it to a simplistic set of assumptions about life and literature. Rather, it powerfully and movingly dramatizes exactly what it means to be a woman in modern rural Irish society. The story's feminist theme can best be seen in what the women devote themselves to but what fails or even enslaves them: men, the Church, other women.

Men are less an outright evil than they are facets of a brutal, unyielding landscape. The dominant male figure in the story is the father, a violent drunkard who "takes" the mother in scenes of intercourse more reminiscent of impalement than love or even lust. Two of the daughter's most vivid memories are of the time when the father went after the mother with a hatchet and a later episode when he tried to shoot her. His mellowing with age is less a sign of growing tenderness than growing senility. If the men in the daughter's life are less violent, neither are they much more satisfying. Her first sexual encounter is banally sordid. She marries a man who dominates every facet of her life, even down to how she should fold her clothes. Rather than a relationship of mutual growth and sharing, her marriage feels "like being in school again." Subsequent affairs bring mostly guilt. In short, not a single man in the story brings to the mother or the daughter the slightest modicum of happiness.

Historically, especially in Ireland, when all else fails, the woman can take solace in the Church. Such is hardly the case in "A Rose in the Heart of New York." Religion is not an overt theme in the story, but a rich pattern of religious imagery shows how subtly important it is in women's lives—and how decidedly it fails them. The first mention of religion is the bottle of holy water that the midwife brings, along with her gauze and other medical supplies. These she administers to the laboring mother who is "roaring and beseeching to God." Does God hear? No one can say, but in her agony the mother drops the crucifix, then dents it by biting down on it in pain. The mother, indeed, is invested with more religious imagery than anything else in the story. Being stitched up after delivery is her "vinegar and gall." She finally rises from bed after the third day. Later, she is attacked by her husband on a hill under three trees—a scene suggesting Christ's crucifixion on Golgotha. Significantly, the nun who replaces the mother in the daughter's affections is seen by her as an "idol," whose gift of a tiny Bible, unreadable, is cherished by the daughter as "a secret scroll in which love was mentioned."

Perhaps mother and nun achieve such godlike status in the daughter's eyes because the traditional religious figures—Father, Son, Holy Ghost, Mary, and so on—offer only false hope. What can be said with certainty is that at no time in the story—at birth, death, or anywhere in between—does religion ease the woman's lot.

Other women offer no more hope than do men or religion. Other than her mother, no woman makes any significant impression on or achieves a lasting relationship with the daughter. Her relationship with her mother, too, comes to seem a kind of death. As a child she wishes to go to Heaven with her mother; after her divorce, her mother writes that her one wish is that they be buried together. Yet their last visit concludes with the daughter openly hating her mother and resolving that they will never be buried together.

O'Brien clearly believes that death is less horrible than being buried alive: "buried" by poverty, ignorance, the false hope of religion, sexual dominance, suffocating love. If by the end the daughter has learned that lesson, painful as it is, then perhaps "A Rose in the Heart of New York" should be seen as more affirmative than a catalog of its grim specifics would seem to suggest.

Style and Technique

The most interesting technical feature of a story powerful in its simplicity is one that generally is considered a flaw: that is, a lack of foregrounding.

A term appropriated from painting, "foregrounding" refers to the added "weight"—length of discussion, intensity of emotion—given to certain scenes that the author considers, and wants the reader to consider, more important than others. Foregrounding may seem especially crucial in a long story such as O'Brien's, one that spans four decades in the lives of its characters, but "A Rose in the Heart of New York" unfolds largely without major scenes upon which to hinge the action. The daughter's first sexual encounter, for example, is related in part of a sentence, less space than is devoted to baking a cake. Her marriage transpires and expires in little more than a page, not many more lines than O'Brien devotes to the mother and daughter mending broken water pipes.

One effect of this lack of foregrounding is that the reader infers that, for the woman, such daily minutiae as baking a cake or fixing a leaking pipe are as important—perhaps *more* important—than often brief and unsatisfying encounters with men. Another effect is the precipitous quality given the action. The mother's and daughter's lives slip by them in a rush, with no heightened scenes to provide revelation, only the understanding that too often women are born and die with precious little joy in between.

Dennis Vannatta

ROTHSCHILD'S FIDDLE

Author: Anton Chekhov (1860-1904)
Type of plot: Psychological realism
Time of plot: The 1890's
Locale: Western Russia
First published: "Skripka Rotshilda," 1894 (English translation, 1915)

Principal characters:

YAKOV IVANOV, the protagonist, an elderly, impoverished
coffin maker
MARTHA, his wife
ROTHSCHILD, a Jewish village musician
MAXIM NIKOLAICH, an ignorant but haughty doctor's assistant

The Story

The setting of "Rothschild's Fiddle" is a squalid little village where Yakov Ivanov, a Russian coffin maker, and Rothschild, an equally poor Jewish musician, both live. Yakov lives in a one-room hut, which contains his gloomy wares as well as his humble domestic possessions. Childless, the dour Yakov barely notices Martha, his downtrodden wife of fifty years. Yakov has an unexpected side to his character, for he is a gifted, if rude, violinist who is sometimes invited to join the local Jewish orchestra to play for weddings. Although the coffin maker needs the occasional money, he dislikes the Jewish musicians—especially the flutist Rothschild, who turns even the merriest songs into lugubrious plaints. Yakov abuses Rothschild and is once on the point of beating him. The quarrel ends Yakov's association with the orchestra, apart from rare occasions when one of the Jews cannot perform.

Yakov sees his life as an endless succession of "losses." Sundays and holidays when he cannot work represent losses; a wedding without music represents a loss; a rich man who inconsiderately dies and is buried out of town is another loss. Yakov keeps an account book of his losses, even calculating the interest he might have received on his lost opportunities. At night he arises from his sleepless bed and seeks relief by playing his violin.

One morning Martha feels ill but carries on with her chores while her husband plays his fiddle and gloomily calculates ever new and more distressing imaginary losses. That night the wife cries out that she is going to die. Her feverish face gives the impression that she looks forward to deliverance from her hard, loveless lot and Yakov's endless "losses." Horrified, the coffin maker takes her to a hospital, where the medical assistant shrugs her off as hopeless, refusing Yakov's pleas that he bleed her as he would a rich patient. Realizing the worst, Yakov takes his wife's measurements and begins work on a coffin, duly entering the loss in his account book—two rubles, forty kopecks. Before her death, the wife calls Yakov to her bedside and asks whether he remembers the baby with curly golden hair that God had given them fifty years before. The couple would take the child down to the river bank, sit under the willow, and sing. Yakov has no recollection of the dead child or the willow. That night, Martha dies, and Yakov arranges a miserly funeral, admiring the coffin as he takes final leave of his wife.

Yakov, feeling unwell as he walks home from the cemetery, reflects on his lifelong neglect of his wife in spite of her uncomplaining labor and help. At this point, a nervously bowing and scraping Rothschild approaches with a message from the Jewish orchestra leader, inviting Yakov to play for a wedding. The coffin maker once again abuses and threatens the cowering flute player, who flees pursued by a horde of small boys screaming "Jew, Jew!" Yakov now walks down by the river for the first time in many years, where he, too, is heckled by the village boys who address him by his nickname, "Old Man Bronze." Suddenly he comes upon the willow and recalls the dead child. Yakov now falls into regretful reflection of his lost opportunities. Nothing waits ahead of him, and there are only losses behind. Now, however, Yakov's distress over his losses takes a new turn: " . . . why shouldn't men live so as to avoid all this waste and these losses?" He belatedly regrets his harsh treatment of his wife and the Jew: "If it were not for envy and anger [men] would get great profit from one another."

In the morning, seriously ill, Yakov returns to the "doctor." As the sick man walks home, he bitterly thinks that after his death he will "no longer have to eat and drink and pay taxes, neither would he offend people any more, and, as a man lies in his grave for hundreds of thousands of years, the sum of his profits would be immense." He concludes that life is a loss; death, a profit. Yakov is not sorry to die but regrets leaving behind his violin. At home he sits on the threshold and plays his violin with tears streaming down his face. Once again, a quivering Rothschild approaches Yakov on behalf of the orchestra director. This time, however, the Jew is greeted kindly. Yakov tells him that he is ill and continues to play. So plaintive is his song that Rothschild also begins to weep as he leaves. Later that day, when the village priest asks the dying man if there is any particular sin of which he wishes to repent, Yakov asks that his violin be given to Rothschild.

Time passes, and the townsfolk begin to wonder where Rothschild obtained the violin that he now plays instead of the flute. An even greater mystery is the source of the song he plays, which is so entrancingly sorrowful that wealthy merchants vie in having him come to their homes to play it over and over again.

Themes and Meanings

Chekhov's major theme in this, as in many others of his works, is the isolation of the individual within himself and his often vain attempts to break out of his shell and establish meaningful contact with others. Yakov's anti-Semitism is but a particular example of this more general malaise. Yakov finally succeeds in reaching out to others and does so in the form of his music: first to his archenemy Rothschild through his death song and the gift of his violin, and then through Rothschild, who brings Yakov's harrowing melody to many others. Art is the means by which the two men, both deeply unattractive characters, surmount their isolation and manifest their shared humanity.

The theme of Yakov's losses is also important. "Losses" is the most frequently used word in the story, and through repetition it assumes symbolic meaning, referring to far more than Yakov's hypothetical financial setbacks. He is obsessed with his so-called losses. They have poisoned his life, and he has lost the capacity for love and simple pleasures (apart from his music). In fact, the death of his wife is the sole real loss that Yakov suffers, and it is only with this that he begins to reflect on his profitless, ill-spent life and his ill-treatment of his wife and Rothschild. This realization, especially in the face of his own imminent death, leads to his remorse and his final haunting melody. The final irony is that it is the Jew Rothschild rather than Yakov himself who profits and recoups the coffin maker's "losses."

Style and Technique

The story is told by an omniscient narrator the year after Yakov's death. Its formal structure is tripartite: the brief introduction which establishes the setting and the hero; the story itself, that is, the relationship between Yakov and Rothschild and the deaths of the wife and husband; and the ironic, bittersweet ending in which Rothschild plays Yakov's song. As in many Chekhov stories, a key event (Yakov's interaction with Rothschild) is repeated three times. The first two encounters are hostile, while the third depicts a reversal of the earlier ones. The last carries the story's message—the breaking down of the isolation of the two men through art and the establishment of their shared humanity.

The narrative technique through which Chekhov makes his thematic statement should be noticed. Superficially, Yakov and Rothschild seem very different: The coffin maker is big, strong, and aggressive, while Rothschild is gaunt, frail, and cowering; Yakov prefers merry songs, Rothschild, mournful ones; the Christian Yakov despises Rothschild the Jew. The narrative, however, poses a series of parallels that point to their essential sameness. Yakov is obsequious to the "educated" medical assistant, just as Rothschild is to Yakov. Also noteworthy are the parallel scenes in which the Jew fleeing from Yakov's fists is jeered by the village boys, who moments later jeer the bereaved Yakov. Both are "outsiders." The most important parallel scene, the one demonstrating their common humanity, is that in which the two men cry together as Yakov improvises his own death dirge. This evolving pattern ends in the identification of the former enemies, each of whom had lived in his own profitless prison of the self.

Chekhov's language is sometimes considered rather "flat," a feature of much realistic prose. On close inspection, however, Chekhov's language is not, in fact, "realistic" but rather evocative and impressionistic. The reader comes to know characters and their lives not through accumulated description but through the carefully chosen, evocative detail which suggests far more than it says. Similarly, the carefully elaborated formal structure contributes to the reader's sense of a meaning that goes far beyond the limits of the brief tale.

D. Barton Johnson

ROUND BY ROUND

Author: Conrad Aiken (1889-1973)
Type of plot: Social realism
Time of plot: c. 1935
Locale: A large Midwestern city
First published: 1935

> *Principal characters:*
> THE NARRATOR, a sports reporter for a large newspaper
> CUSH, an entertainment reviewer for the same newspaper

The Story

As the story opens, the narrator, a reporter, sits at his typewriter, composing an account of the title fight he has just watched, working from shorthand notes and drinking whiskey as he types. Cush, an entertainment reviewer for the newspaper, enters, drops his coat at his desk, and asks the reporter how the fight went. The reporter replies that it was great but he "wasn't looking," and offers Cush a drink. Cush tells him that the new musical he attended that evening was exactly like all the others, but adds that reviewers are not able to tell the truth about what the audience really goes to see anyway. He points out that both mayor and censor were there.

The reporter continues to read his notes and compose his story, remembering while doing so details that will not get into the account—such as the behavior of the fiancée of the champion, Zabriski. Cush, now working at his own typewriter, asks how the fight came out. The reporter tells him that there is a new champion, that the fight was a classic example of science over strength, but that he "wasn't there." Cush figures out that the reporter means that Ann, his girlfriend, has dropped him, not for the first time. He asks who she is now dating.

The reporter does not answer right away, turning instead to his notes, his copy, and his memories of the fight. Finally he states that it was not only one man. Cush asks why he keeps after her, and suggests that a chorus girl would be more faithful. The reporter answers that no one is faithful anymore; the psychologists have brainwashed everyone into believing that it is enough to be yourself. Ann is herself with everyone.

The reporter goes to the window to adjust the shade, but it flies out of his hand to the top of the roller. He looks down to a desolate alley forty feet below, only to conclude that jumping would do him no good. He does not want to die; he only wants Ann to be there with him to share this glimpse of modern life.

In the next section, the reporter returns to his whiskey and his story; again his account of the action mingles with his memories of the atmosphere. The story shows the challenger, Romero, to be taking command of the fight by outmanuevering the champion. Meanwhile, the reporter sees again in his mind the hoodlums in the crowd, the actions of the seconds, the new warning buzzer, the forty-light canopy illuminating the ring, the two great overhead clocks. He wonders how much action he has missed while looking at the time. He sees that he has notes for every second of the fight, except for two rounds, for which he borrowed notes.

Cush complains again about the quality of current shows. The reporter offers to swap their next assignments and to throw Ann in for good measure. Cush asks where she is. The reporter replies that he does not know; the friend who was supposed to be covering for her missed the signals. He returns to his memory of the fight, especially of the byplay between the champion's girlfriend and four tough kids who harass him.

Suddenly he stops typing and glances up at a small photograph of the James family—the writer Henry, the philosopher William, and their sister Alice—sitting in an English garden. The picture strikes him because of the extraordinary integrity, the "profound and simple honesty" of their faces. They seem to him to be contemplating the truth of things in perfect serenity as they peer into and beyond the camera.

He returns to his typewriter, again combining an objective account of the fight with his subjective responses to the behavior of the crowd. Cush complains that no one seems to care anymore about keeping things as they belong. He asks the reporter for a ride home, but learns that he is walking.

In the third section, both men continue working in silence. The reporter once more calls to mind the fiancée, a hard-bitten woman who remains true to her man, cheering him on to the end. The fight is now in the eleventh round. The reporter senses a mesmerizing, snakelike quality in the challenger's jab; he keeps fending off the clumsy rushes of the champion with the easy confidence of superior intelligence or planning. The fiancée's enthusiasm wanes, and the crowd begins to back Romero. He only has to keep boxing.

Cush interrupts his memories by asking if he has heard of a mutual acquaintance, whose drinking has finally led to a breakdown. The two men sympathize with his wife, who stayed by him to the end.

The reporter returns to the fight, now in the final round. The boxers slug it out toe-to-toe. Romero continues to block and make Zabriski miss, while scoring himself. The final round, and the fight, are his. Two images remain: Romero doing a knock-kneed dance of victory around the ring; Zabriski lying on a training table laconically commenting that he waited too long to make weight, that it would not happen again. His fiancée is still with him. The reporter hands his copy to Cush as the latter prepares to leave, and says that he is staying to write a letter.

In the fourth section, instead of writing immediately, he gets up and looks at the photograph again. What he has to tell Ann has something to do with that. He begins by saying that he is not going to write an ordinary letter, or argue as he has so often that he cannot accept her habit of casual flirtation. He senses a wide gulf between them; neither seems to hear what the other is saying. The rift deepens every time he sees her yield to the caresses of simple acquaintances. His feeling is not jealousy or prudery, as she has suggested; it is rather that he cannot divorce body and spirit as she tries to wedge them apart. For him, body and soul are integrated like two dancers; when they part, something fragments, and that fragmentation affects both. Body and soul united make love—and life—possible; separating them can produce only sainthood or evil, but not love. The photograph in front of him illustrates that kind of union, that integrity.

He breaks off in despair, knowing that he cannot explain these things to her. Either one feels them or one does not. Lacking that shared feeling, they are doomed to continue quarreling as they have, as the fighters are doomed to combat, and there will never be an end.

Themes and Meanings

Aiken's story centers on human conflict and the possibility of cooperation, and it develops this focus on several levels of human interaction. To begin with there is the fight itself, the subject of the reporter's story. As he writes about it, he realizes that it is not a simple combat, not simply one man pitted against another, but an entire network of interlocking conflicts. There is, on the simplest level, the participation of the crowd, from those who go implicitly to see someone physically beaten, to those who side with one fighter or the other, to those who bait the loser, to the fiancée who stands by her man. There is also in the match more than mere physical competition: Will contends with will, intelligence with intelligence. Finally, the match is not over at the end; the fighters are not even particularly hostile to each other: Fighting is their business, and they immediately look ahead to the rematch. The conflict thus becomes self-perpetuating; further, it is peculiarly human.

Aiken brings this into contrast with three other elements in the story: the relationship between the reporter and his colleague Cush, the photograph of the James family, and the frustration of the reporter with his girlfriend. First, he and Cush work together in fellowship, sharing whiskey, problems, common interests, and common pursuits. Though their work could bring them into competition, they respect and help each other. The photograph deepens this sense of the possibility overcoming the limitations of the self. No conflict is apparent here; the figures are serene in repose, sympathetic to the pangs of existence, but somehow capable of transcending them and uniting with all humanity. This kind of peace is available only to those who enter imaginatively into the souls of others.

His conflict with his girlfriend does not have this kind of intuitive understanding. Because it lacks this, it parallels the physical combat of the fight; it has rounds and bouts, with temporary winners and losers, but it can never be resolved and will never end.

Style and Technique

The most conspicuous characteristic of this story is the unconventional use of plot. The central interest lies in the relationship between the reporter and his girlfriend, but they do not occupy center stage, they do not interact, and the relationship does not change from beginning to end. What changes is his consciousness of the relationship, and this change is brought about by his experience of the fight and his appreciation of the photograph. Through them, he gains an understanding of the roles of body and soul in human conflict, but that understanding brings him no closer to her.

Structurally, the story could be termed cinematic. Aiken cuts irregularly from one level of action to another, often in the middle of a paragraph. This allows him to depict what is proceeding in the reporter's consciousness, to whom all these levels are present simultaneously. The opening of the story sets up this focus: The reporter states that it was a great fight, but he "wasn't there"; yet the details show that he saw every second of it, even that he saw some things without registering them distinctly, such as the reactions in the crowd. He means that his attention was on something else: His body was involved, but not his soul. This technique reinforces the major themes: the difficulty of integrating body and soul in any human endeavor and the difficulty of transcending the natural tendency of all men to conflict.

James L. Livingston

THE SAD FATE OF MR. FOX

Author: Joel Chandler Harris (1848-1908)
Type of plot: Animal fable
Time of plot: After the Civil War
Locale: The Deep South
First published: 1880

> *Principal characters:*
> UNCLE REMUS, an aged black man and former slave, who tells
> the story
> MISS SALLY'S SEVEN-YEAR-OLD SON, an appreciative audience
> BRER FOX, the villain/victim in this story
> BRER RABBIT, the trickster-protagonist
> MISS FOX, the wife of Brer Fox
> TOBE, Brer Fox's son

The Story

"The Sad Fate of Mr. Fox," the last of Uncle Remus' tales in *Uncle Remus: His Songs and Sayings* (1880), marks the end of Mr. Fox, as well as the end of the book. It is, as Uncle Remus says, "de las'row er stumps, sho." For this reason, Uncle Remus is more serious when the evening storytelling session begins, and he states at the beginning that Brer Fox dies in this tale.

The focus of the tale, however, is, as usual, Brer Rabbit. Hoping to share Brer Fox's dinner, he tells Brer Fox that his wife is sick and his children are cold, but Brer Fox offers him only a piece of fire to take home. Frustrated, but not defeated, Brer Rabbit returns to Brer Fox under the pretense that the fire went out. When he asks the fox about the beef that he is cooking for dinner, the fox offers to show him where he, too, can get as much meat as he wants. The next morning, Brer Fox takes Brer Rabbit down by Miss Meadows' place, where a man keeps a special cow. When called by name, "Bookay," this cow will open her mouth and let the fox (and the rabbit) inside her body where they can cut away as much meat as they can carry.

Inside this magical cow, they begin to cut off pieces of beef, but Brer Fox warns Brer Rabbit not to cut the "haslett" (the edible viscera of an animal such as the heart and lungs). When Brer Rabbit hacks the haslett, the cow dies. Brer Rabbit hides in the gall, Brer Fox in the maul. The next morning, the owner of the cow, upset to discover his cow dead, cuts her open to see who or what killed her. Brer Rabbit jumps out of the gall and tells the man that the killer of the cow is hiding in the maul. Immediately the man takes a stick and begins to beat the stomach of the dead cow, killing the fox hiding there.

Yet the death of his old enemy is not enough for Brer Rabbit. He asks the man for the head of Brer Fox, which he takes to Miss Fox, telling her that it is a good piece of beef but that she should not look at it until after she cooks and eats it. Her son, Tobe, curious and hungry, looks in the pot and tells his mother what he sees. The angry Miss Fox and her dogs trap Brer Rabbit in a hollow log. Unfortunately, she leaves Tobe to guard the rabbit while she goes to fetch the ax. Tobe is no match for the wily rabbit, who tricks him into going to the nearby stream for water. When Miss Fox tries to whip Tobe for being so stupid, he too runs off through the woods, where he meets Brer Rabbit. While they are talking, Miss Fox catches them both and declares she will kill the rabbit and whip her son.

This time Brer Rabbit has another suggestion: He urges her to grind off his nose with the grindstone so that he will not be able to smell after he is dead. Hopping up on the grindstone, the cooperative, clever rabbit suggests that Tobe can turn the handle while Miss Fox gets water for the stone. The gullible widow agrees, and the rabbit escapes again. At this point the story ends. The little boy asks if that is the last of Brer Rabbit. Uncle Remus now bows to oral tradition and tells the child that the truth is hard to determine. Some people, he says, claim that Brer Rabbit actually married Miss Fox; others say that the rabbits and the foxes became friends. Uncle Remus does not take a stand. Instead he carries the little boy piggyback up to the big house for bedtime. Readers of the Uncle Remus tales need not despair. *Nights with Uncle Remus*, published in 1883, contains seventy-one more stories in which both Brer Rabbit and Brer Fox figure prominently.

Themes and Meanings

The violence in this story is startling. In contrast to stories such as "The Wonderful Tar-Baby Story," "The Sad Fate of Mr. Fox" seems harsh and unexpected. The understatement of the word "sad" is gravely humorous, and the moral advice found in many of the other tales is reduced here to Phineas Taylor Barnum's epitaph for suckers: "There's one born every minute." Certainly one is appalled by the fate of Mr. Fox. Harris' story, however, does not stop with the horror of the Fox's head in his wife's stew pot. He goes on to detail the incredible stupidity of the widow and her son as they try in vain to capture the clever rabbit. What does this reveal about the characters and the worldview of Uncle Remus? There is no doubt that it is the persona of the black slave, in the guise of the physically weak but clever rabbit, that escapes from the clutches of the more powerful, but slow-witted foxes, which are obvious symbols of the dominating white man. Indeed, escape is not enough; Brer Rabbit seeks and finds revenge. Yet the story does not celebrate death or revenge; it is a story of survival, the survival of the feisty spirit of Brer Rabbit. Although the main characters, Brer Fox and Brer Rabbit, seem to cooperate, there is no compromise. Even though they share the same beef, there is no honest connection or communion between them. Thus, Brer Rabbit has no qualms about betraying the fox. Revenge is sweet, no matter how horrible it may seem to the outsider. No matter how sad the fate of Mr. Fox may seem, this story is not tragic; the foolishness of the foxes is funny. Nor is the narrator a grim applauder of cruelty and trickery, for he himself would not do the terrible things that the characters do. He further distances himself from the reality of the story by suggesting that there are several optional conclusions for the irrepressible Brer Rabbit. "The Sad Fate of Mr. Fox" reveals more clearly than some of the other tales the depth of anger that the slave felt against white society—a society made up of "foxes" and "wolves" who maintained the power, the money, and the status that could never be his. The moral of this fable may simply be a warning: In an unfair world, only the clever survive.

Style and Technique

Joel Chandler Harris' attempt to reproduce the dialect in which he heard these stories told presents a literary hurdle for some readers. When read aloud, however, the story is clear and sensible. The oral nature of the story is also emphasized by the frame in which it is set: the old man telling stories to a young boy who asks questions at the beginning and end of the tale. The genres of the animal fable and the trickster tale, common in West African storytelling, are adapted to and reflective of the social experience and the anger of the Afro-American slave. Because this anger is so violently expressed in this story, the double barrier of the dialect and the framework of the storytelling situation protects the reader from the horror of Mr. Fox's sad fate. Harris further tempers the effect by continuing to speculate on what eventually happened to Brer Rabbit and Widow Fox. There are few realistic touches in this story; instead, the plot borrows from the supernatural as the rabbit and the fox climb into the mouth of the willing cow, Bookay, in order to cut away pieces of beef. This "unreality" also softens the implication of cannibalism in Brer Rabbit's revenge. Although humorous in presentation, "The Sad Fate of Mr. Fox" is a serious and rather grim tale for the end of the first published collection of Uncle Remus tales. The specter of malicious mischief out of control may explain why this story did not achieve the degree of popularity of others such as "The Wonderful Tar-Baby."

Linda Humphrey

SAILOR OFF THE *BREMEN*

Author: Irwin Shaw (1913-1984)
Type of plot: Social realism
Time of plot: The 1930's
Locale: New York City
First published: 1939

> *Principal characters:*
> ERNEST, an artist and a Communist
> SALLY, his wife
> CHARLEY, his brother
> LUEGER, a steward on the liner *Bremen*
> PREMINGER, a Communist deck officer

The Story

Ernest, an artist, is beaten and disfigured (losing an eye and his front teeth) when he participates in a Communist demonstration aboard the ocean liner *Bremen*. As the story opens, his friends and family gather in his kitchen to hear Preminger, a Communist deck officer aboard the *Bremen* (and a witness to the incident) explain what happened. Ernest's brother, Charley, a college football player, decides to take revenge on Lueger, the German steward who beat Ernest. Ernest, however, despite his injuries, remains committed to the Communist ideal and objects on the grounds that taking revenge on Lueger will serve no purpose. He is overruled by Charley and by his wife, Sally, and they tell him to leave the room while they plot against Lueger. They decide to lure him to the waiting Charley by using Sally as bait. She is to let him pick her up and to pretend to bring him home with her, and Charley is to ambush him in the street.

When the *Bremen* returns to New York City, Sally is briefed over and over on the plan. Lueger takes Sally to see a film and then is concerned only with reaching her apartment (she has told him she lives alone), but she stalls him with the offer of drinks to keep the plan on schedule. She begins to have second thoughts about delivering Lueger, and almost backs out completely because, even though she hates him, he is "a human being and thoughtless and unsuspecting and because her heart was softer than she had thought." He chooses this moment, however, to hurt her, and she is strengthened in her resolve to carry out the plot. Lueger is taken by surprise, and Charley is savage in his treatment of Lueger, almost killing him with his bare hands.

The last scene is tinged with irony, as Preminger, who identified Lueger as Ernest's assailant in the story's opening scene and later pointed out the steward to Charley, must make another identification, this time to the staff at the hospital where Lueger is taken and to the detective who is investigating the incident. In a masterpiece of dramatic irony, Preminger offers a pat explanation for Lueger's fate: "You must be very careful in a strange city."

Themes and Meanings

Irwin Shaw was considered a very political writer, often with leftist overtones in his work, but in "Sailor Off the *Bremen*," his thrust is simply anti-Fascist, not necessarily pro-Communist. He seems, instead, to point to a happy medium between the two political extremes as the ideal for political thought.

Fascism is made repulsive by its representative in the story, the Nazi Lueger. Preminger (a German Communist, and thus diametrically opposed to the German Nazi Party) may be prejudiced, but the reader must concur with his judgment where Lueger is concerned. Preminger, in reporting Ernest's beating, observes that the other stewards charged with breaking up the demonstration at least "were human beings. [Lueger] is a member of the Nazi party." To further emphasize Lueger's repugnance, Shaw hints that the Nazi is also a sadist, particularly in the scenes in which he and Sally walk through the streets alone; he takes pleasure in hurting her, pinching her arm, kissing her harshly. Lueger and, by representation, Fascism are thus portrayed by Shaw as being evil and, as he attempted to warn in this story in 1939, the time of the story's appearance, dangerous.

Although Fascism is bad, Communism is not necessarily good, as the Communists are seen as impotent to act against Lueger. It is Charley, the football player, the thoroughly American man (whose only philosophy, according to Ernest, is "Somebody knocks you down, you knock him down, everything is fine"), who takes matters into his own hands and acts while the Communists can only talk. Only after he has taken the initiative do Ernest's Communist friends follow him. Preminger even delineates the concern for Party over person when, "as a party member," he agrees with Ernest that no point can be served by paying Lueger back for the loss of his eye, but "as a man" he advises Charley to "put Lueger on his back for at least six months." He cannot have personal thoughts if the Party is uppermost in his mind, and only when he thinks for himself does he admit that a wrongdoer must be punished, that some sort of action must be taken.

The sympathy of the reader is clearly with Charley and Sally, the Americans who are not affiliated with either political extreme, whose concern is not some lofty ideological goal, but rather the simple human concern of seeing that justice is done—literally an eye for an eye in this case. Through this sympathy for the middle course, Shaw points at the necessity of taking violent action against Fascism, but also seems to say that neither Fascism nor Communism measures up to American democracy.

Style and Technique

The most interesting aspect of Shaw's style in "Sailor Off the *Bremen*" is his construction of the story. The reader's attention must be concentrated on the violent confrontation between Charley and Lueger, between the United States and Germany, so rather than depicting the action which leads up to Ernest's beating, which would have robbed the story's climax of much of its novelty as the most active portion of the story, Shaw introduces it through Preminger in the kitchen-table discussion in the opening scene. The demonstration and the violence that follow it are reduced to expository elements which cannot rob the climax of the reader's full and undivided attention, and Shaw manages to place importance where he felt it most belonged, in the retribution against the Nazi Lueger.

Greg T. Garrett

SAINT AUGUSTINE'S PIGEON

Author: Evan S. Connell, Jr. (1924-   )
Type of plot: Satire
Time of plot: The early 1960's
Locale: New York City
First published: 1965

> *Principal characters:*
> KARL MUHLBACH, an executive with the Metropolitan Mutual
>   Insurance Company, a widower more than forty years old
>   and the father of two children
> MRS. GRUNTHE, his housekeeper, a guardian of domestic
>   order and virtue
> EULA CUNNINGHAM, a stout spinster intent upon becoming
>   the second Mrs. Muhlbach
> ROUGE, a teenage girl whom Muhlbach meets in Washington
>   Square
> PUIG, Muhlbach's college roommate, a career officer in the
>   United States Navy

The Story

Karl Muhlbach decides, after reading a passage from Saint Augustine's *Confessions* (c. A.D. 397-400) dealing with the tension between flesh and spirit, that the celibacy enforced by the death of his wife should end. Barely more than forty years old, Muhlbach rebels against his ordered, ascetic life, presided over by his housekeeper, Mrs. Grunthe, and decides to cross the river into Manhattan one Saturday evening in search of a mistress. His choice of that word is significant; it reveals how out of touch with the mores of his society Muhlbach has become.

The carefully structured life that Muhlbach leads, with dinner each night at eight and wine with it only on Sundays, stifles both body and soul. He silently assures Mrs. Grunthe that he intends this evening to go to hell. Showering in preparation for the journey, Muhlbach admits that he looks "professorial" but hopes that his chances will be improved by the fact that he has plenty of money in his pockets. He is looking for a sophisticated woman, somebody uninhibited sexually. Muhlbach admits that what he wants is a companion as unlike himself as possible. With his children Donna and Otto safely occupied and Mrs. Grunthe prepared to mount guard over the home, Muhlbach takes the first step on his descent into the underworld by taking a subway ride to Manhattan.

Muhlbach is convinced that the type of woman for whom he is looking is not that represented by Eula Cunningham, who had called while he was in the shower. Eula confesses to thirty-two but reminds him of thirty-eight, and Muhlbach finds her too ordinary and domestic to tempt him. Getting off the subway, he thinks that he sees the profile of Blanche Baron, an elegant redhead whose husband has killed himself. The sight of her sparks his imagination, so Muhlbach telephones her apartment. The fact that a man answers the phone discomfits him a bit, but it also encourages him in his quest. If Blanche Baron can find a new companion, so can Karl Muhlbach. It is clear, however, that he has no strategy in mind to accomplish this purpose. Muhlbach is carried along the street by the crowd and ends up in a bar on Lexington Avenue that he has not visited for nearly a year. There he is eyed by a Hollywood actress whose name he cannot quite remember, but he recognizes that she has no real interest in him. Her glance suggests that he must content himself with somebody ordinary and unimaginative, such as Eula Cunningham.

Stung by this rejection, Muhlbach takes a bus to Washington Square to try his luck among the bohemians of Greenwich Village. He literally bumps into a teenage girl named Rouge, who takes him to a coffee shop called the Queen's Bishop. Both confused and attracted by her language, a mixture of French and contemporary English slang, Muhlbach accepts Rouge's challenge to play chess. He recognizes too late that she wants to win the game. He initially thinks that the hamster nibbling his trouser cuff is Rouge's foot expressing sexual interest. He takes the appearance of her friends Quinet and Meatbowl as a sign of acceptance. The shop manager brings four bowls of soup, and Muhlbach takes this as an indication that he has fit in at the Queen's Bishop—until the manager makes it clear that he is expected to pay for all the food. Muhlbach concludes that he is paying for intruding into a place where he does not belong. A passage from Saint Augustine's *Confessions* comes to his mind. It discusses serving one's fellows, seeing them as pilgrims like oneself, in order to live in God's sight.

Outside the coffee shop, Muhlbach feels a renewed sense of sexual deprivation, and it seems to him a kind of illness. "Yet the cure is absurdly simple," he thinks: "The body of a woman, that is all." Muhlbach takes a taxi to the Club Sahara, where exotic dancers with names such as Nila, Lisa, and Riva perform for patrons in need of fantasy. He finds these performers, especially Nila, attractive; they appeal to his imagination as much as to his sexual appetite. As time passes and he continues to drink, their attraction diminishes, so Muhlbach leaves the Club Sahara, meeting on the street his old college roommate, Puig, a career navy officer out on the prowl for a woman.

Puig does not have scruples about his behavior nor does he worry about his dignity. As a result, when Muhlbach and he go to another bar, Puig finds a woman named Gertie who, despite her drunken claim that all men want is sex, leaves the bar with him. Muhlbach admits to himself that he would have shared her bed if he had been asked, and he recognizes how far toward Hell he has descended during this evening's journey. The driver of the taxi Muhlbach finds outside this bar, looking "like a messenger of God," takes him back uptown toward Times Square. Muhlbach recalls another passage from Saint Augustine, this one about the imperfectness of perception through the flesh, and finds its truth confirmed by the fact that his wallet is missing. Only by reassuming his identity as an insurance company executive and insisting that the desk clerk at the Tyler Plaza awaken the manager to authorize cashing a check does Muhlbach begin the upward journey back toward the world that he normally inhabits.

His night in the hotel is a painful one. Resolving to drown his lust in alcohol, Muhlbach goes to the cocktail lounge and makes a pass at a waitress named Carmen. His attempt to restore pride and self-confidence leads to a potentially violent confrontation with her boyfriend Porfirio, and Muhlbach recognizes, in Saint Augustine's words, that he has exceeded the limits of his own nature. The next morning, he sees Rouge and her companions Quinet and Meatbowl outside a bookstore across the street from the Tyler Plaza, and he hurries toward her, in a final attempt to make a connection with some woman, only to have a pigeon relieve itself upon his hat. Rouge and her two friends laugh hysterically, and Muhlbach's illusions about himself come to an end.

Themes and Meanings

The pigeon, referred to in the title of the story, makes a final satiric comment on the self-deceiving romanticism of Muhlbach. His need for companionship, both physical and emotional, is so great that he finds the potential for passion in the most unlikely situations. Muhlbach admits that he is immature, even adolescent, in terms of his sexual fantasies. He is also unrealistic in his expectation that sophisticated women would find him attractive. References to his balding head, diffident manner, and awkwardness while making conversation suggest that Connell intends Muhlbach to appear like the title character of T. S. Eliot's "The Love Song of J. Alfred Prufrock."

The central thematic point of "Saint Augustine's Pigeon" arises from the juxtaposition of Muhlbach's conscious descent into the hell of New York City's nightlife and his unintentional ascent from this dark world by the assistance of Saint Augustine's *Confessions*. The satire to which Connell subjects Muhlbach depends upon awareness of the aptness of the passages he quotes from the *Confessions*, and it further depends upon recognition that Muhlbach misreads, at times deliberately, Saint Augustine's meaning. The confusion of body and soul that he experiences leads him to find justification in the *Confessions* for a conscious choice of sin, and it is only through the agency of the saint's pigeon that Muhlbach attains a truer insight. "I have spent one whole night attempting to distort the truth which was born in me," he concludes; "now I have learned."

The truth Muhlbach recognizes may be something as simple as the necessity of being true to one's own nature. Muhlbach, from the very start of the story, is an unlikely actor in the drama he imagines for himself. Recognition of the fact that he may have to content himself with Eula Cunningham would come hard, but it would confirm his acceptance of the truth conveyed by the pigeon's action. The message from Saint Augustine may also have something to do with Muhlbach's need to accept the loss of his wife, Joyce, whose illness and eventual death are the subject of an earlier story entitled "Arcturus," published in Connell's *The Anatomy Lesson and Other Stories* (1957).

Connell also treats Muhlbach as a character in two stories called "The Mountains of Guatemala" and "Otto and the Magi," both reprinted with "Saint Augustine's Pigeon" in *At the Crossroads* (1965), and in the novels *The Connoisseur* (1974) and *Double Honeymoon* (1976).

Style and Technique

The chief stylistic device at work is Connell's use, as the major structural pattern, of a variation on the descent into Hell common in epic literature. The journey takes place without the formal guide characteristic of some of the epic models, but Muhlbach's frequent quotations from the *Confessions* serve to cast Saint Augustine in that role. It is appropriate, therefore, in the light of his guide's long service in Africa, that Muhlbach goes to Club Sahara. It also makes sense that Rouge's name evokes the fires of Hell, that the taxi driver taking him away from Greenwich Village looks like an angelic messenger, and that the bird which brings the message of truth to Muhlbach is a pigeon or dove. Connell's details allow for a fairly thorough allegorical reading.

Nevertheless, as the limited third-person narrator makes clear, it is Muhlbach who sees the trip into New York City in these terms. He is the one, not Connell or the narrator, making these associations, for the journey occurs as much in his consciousness as in the actual city. As a result, the conclusions that Muhlbach reaches about himself at the end of the story seem to develop out of his personality and the situation rather than being imposed on him by the narrator or the author.

Robert C. Petersen

SAINT MARIE

Author: Louise Erdrich (1954-   )
Type of plot: Comedy
Time of plot: 1934
Locale: North Dakota
First published: 1984

> *Principal characters:*
> MARIE LAZARRE, the narrator and protagonist, about
>   fourteen years old at the time of the story
> SISTER LEOPOLDA, a demented nun, Marie's mentor and foe

The Story

Marie Lazarre is reliving the day that she tried to join the nuns in the Convent of the Sacred Heart. Walking to the door, she considers her motives: to be respected, even revered, by the nuns, who look down on her because she is from the reservation (even though she does not "have that much Indian blood"), and to get away from "the bush" and into town. She also remembers the day Sister Leopolda, hearing the "Dark One" in the coat closet, hurled a long hooked pole through the closet door, then made the terrified Marie stand in the dark closet because the girl had smiled.

Sister Leopolda shows Marie in by the back door, then takes her to the larder and lets the girl see the rich food reserved for the priest. She feeds Marie goat cheese and talks to her while they mix and knead bread. Marie challenges the nun, asserting that she will inherit her keys to the larder, and Leopolda says that she can see the Devil in Marie's soul. When a cup rolls under the stove, Leopolda makes Marie reach under with her arm rather than the poker to retrieve it. As the girl lies on the floor, the nun places her foot on Marie's neck, pouring boiling water on her back and shoulders to warm her heart with devotion. Finally letting the girl rise, Leopolda assures Marie that she has prayed for her.

As Marie eats cold mush, waits for the bread to rise, and listens to the nuns eating their sausage, she has a vision: She has been transformed into gold, her breasts tipped with diamonds, and she walks through panes of glass which Leopolda must swallow. Two French nuns enter the kitchen, ask if Marie belongs to Leopolda, and compliment the girl on her docility; they help rake coals into the oven. While the bread bakes, Leopolda takes Marie to her room and puts salve on the girl's back; Marie sees her vision again and tells Leopolda that it is the nun who is caught by the Dark One. When they return to the kitchen, Leopolda, fork and poker in hand, orders Marie to help take the bread out of the oven. When the nun opens the oven door, Marie tries to kick her into the hot oven, but the nun's outstretched poker causes her to rebound out. She turns and impales Marie's hand on the fork, then knocks her out with the poker.

About half an hour later, Marie awakens, lying on clean sheets on a couch. All the nuns, including Sister Leopolda, are kneeling in attitudes of reverence around her. Marie lifts her bloody, bandaged hand and calls Leopolda to her in the voice of a saint. Leopolda says that she explained to the nuns that Marie had received the stigmata and then fainted. Marie laughs, then blesses Leopolda. Yet seeing the emptiness and hunger for love underlying the nun's depravity, she cannot relish her triumph as she had expected.

Themes and Meanings

"Saint Marie," the second in the cycle of fourteen linked stories that make up Louise Erdrich's novel *Love Medicine* (1985), centers on the complex relations between Indians and non-Indians, a theme which runs throughout the book. Marie in this story and the next, "Wild Geese" (which takes place on the same day, as Marie leaves the convent), is a tough, intelligent, willful daughter of adversity. The nuns look down on her as "Indian," whereas her future husband, Nector Kashpaw, regards her as merely a "skinny white girl" from a family of drunken horse thieves. She is truly an orphan.

Marie Lazarre is engaged in an archetypal quest for a mother. Seeking a better home than that of her own impoverished family, she enters the convent as the protégée (though really, it is suggested, the slave) of Sister Leopolda. As if in a fairy tale, Sister Leopolda turns out to be a wicked stepmother: Like Cinderella, Marie must dress poorly (not like the other sisters), sleep behind the stove, and eat meager and coarse food. Worse yet, Sister Leopolda physically mistreats the girl, and when, like the heroine in "Hansel and Gretel," Marie attempts to thrust her tormentor into the oven, the witch rebounds and stabs Marie.

The central conflict resembles a legendary joust: Leopolda sees herself as fighting the Devil for control of the girl's soul and insurance of her salvation, while Marie perceives that to be thus controlled is to perish. The contest is imaged in parodies of chivalric legend, first Leopolda's lance hurled at the Devil in the closet, then hand-to-hand fencing with poker and fork—albeit both weapons are in Leopolda's hands, while Marie's hand triumphs through a wound. This wound gives the girl her final, bittersweet, triumph: Even as she relishes the comedy of Christian forgiveness that signifies her supposed saintliness, she recognizes in Leopolda the voracious hunger for love that makes the nun a fellow human rather than solely a devilish adversary. Only then can she escape.

Marie's battle with Sister Leopolda also encapsulates the inherent absurdity of assimilationist doctrines: the attempt to "kill the Indian in order to save the person." The contradictory aims of Christian colonizers have been to maintain the lowly status of the colonized peoples while claiming to elevate them as "brothers in Christ." It may be no accident that Sister Leopolda is named for the king who presided over one of the most oppressive colonial empires in Africa.

Style and Technique

Marie Lazarre's narration is down-to-earth, laden with pungent metaphor and psychologically acute. In a manner reminiscent of Huckleberry Finn, she moves between the language of the unlettered country girl ("They don't want no holy witness to their fall") and the astuteness of the clinician: "Veils of love which was only hate petrified by longing—that was me." Both statements epitomize the story's multiple levels of meaning. The drunkards do not want the nuns to see them literally falling down outside the bar, nor, thinks Marie, do they want witnesses to their "fall from grace." The veils remind the reader of the nun's veil to which Marie aspires (to hide her origins?), but the veils are really stone, that frozen immobility of hate and longing that barricades and conceals the vulnerable and misused little girl.

Christian themes and allusions enrich the story. Sister Leopolda's hooks, first on the long oak window-opening pole and then on the poker, recall two biblical hooks: the shepherd's crook, adopted as a symbol of bishops' guidance and authority, and fishhooks, reminiscent of the New Testament passage in which the apostles are to become "fishers of men" and "catch" souls for Heaven. Marie compares herself in her naïve faith to a fish that has taken bait, and at the end of the story squirms like a gaffed fish in her recognition of Sister Leopolda's pathetic hunger for love.

This comparison is one of many references to food and eating throughout the story. Further paralleling the comparison of fish's bait to the "lure" of faith is Marie's allusion to Indians who had eaten the smallpox-infected hat of a Jesuit; instead of receiving what they thought was healing power, they consumed infection. (There are many accounts of the "white man's gift" of smallpox; sometimes trade blankets have been deliberately infected, sometimes a box is the receptacle, and so on.) In "Saint Marie," the image is a central metaphor for relations between Sister Leopolda's Christianity and the powerless children she teaches. In a parody of the Sacrament of Holy Communion, which to believers imparts life and healing, the Indians swallow disease; Leopolda fasts herself gaunt but is herself consumed by madness, which Marie interprets as the Devil possessing her.

While Marie's and Leopolda's job ("the Lord's work," Leopolda says) is baking bread, Marie does not eat bread in any communion with the nuns; rather, the nun feeds the girl first stolen goat cheese (recalling the reference to Judgment Day and separation of the sheep from goats) and then cold mush. Marie's initiation into the Christian life of the convent also includes a blasphemous "baptism," as Sister Leopolda first pours scalding water over the girl and then rubs her back with salve. Marie's eventual triumph also begins with an image of eating, when she envisions Leopolda following her, swallowing the glass she walks through.

In addition to references to the Sacraments, traditional Christian iconography and familiar superstitious practices appear in the story. When Leopolda places her foot on Marie's neck, she is imitating a popular representation of the Virgin Mary in which the Madonna is shown to be standing with her foot on the neck of a serpent representing Satan. Related to this powerful Madonna is the woman clothed with the sun described in the book of Revelation, which pious art frequently identifies with the Virgin Mary, and which resembles Marie's vision of herself as transfigured in gold and diamonds. Finally, there is the stigmata: the belief that the bodies of certain holy individuals spontaneously reproduce the wounds of Christ. Marie, seeing that Sister Leopolda has used the appearance of stigmata to avoid having to admit that she stabbed the girl's hand, ironically colludes with Leopolda in deceiving the naïve nuns.

Helen Jaskoski

SANATORIUM UNDER THE SIGN OF THE HOURGLASS

Author: Bruno Schulz (1892-1942)
Type of plot: Fantasy
Time of plot: 1937
Locale: A mythical town, suggestive of the narrator's small Polish hometown
First published: "Sanatorium pod klepsydrą," 1937 (English translation, 1978)

> *Principal characters:*
> JOSEPH, the narrator and protagonist, a young man living in a
>   dreamworld
> FATHER, Joseph's deceased father, who is kept alive in the
>   dreamworld Sanatorium
> DR. GOTARD, the head of the Sanatorium

The Story

Joseph arrives by train in a small, strangely dark town to visit his father, who is staying at a hotel called the Sanatorium. From the beginning, however, the reality of everything is in question. The physical world itself is shaky, shifting, and fluid. The Sanatorium is run by Dr. Gotard, a difficult man to find. The only other visible member of the staff is a chambermaid, a hardly less elusive figure.

Joseph anxiously inquires whether his father is still alive. Dr. Gotard replies that from a certain perspective, his father is dead, and "This cannot be entirely remedied. That death throws a certain shadow on his existence here." Nevertheless, in the Sanatorium, they have put back the clock. "Here your father's death, the death that has already struck him in your country, has not occurred yet."

Guests of the Sanatorium sleep most of the time. No one suggests to them that they are, so to speak, dead. Time itself is confused by the perpetual darkness, in which it is difficult to distinguish between night and day. Thus the guests are kept, in a certain sense, alive.

Dr. Gotard invites Joseph to stay in Father's room. There is only one bed in it, and Father is fast asleep, filling the room with "layers of snoring." Joseph climbs in with him and falls asleep too. In the morning, he wakes to see Father sitting up, drinking tea, and making plans for the day.

Joseph's father leaves briskly, telling Joseph to drop by later at a store that the old man has just opened in town. Left on his own, Joseph explores the town, struck by its remarkable resemblance to his own native city. He easily finds his father's new dry-goods shop. Already, a parcel has been delivered to Joseph there (as his father informs him disapprovingly). Instead of the pornographic book that Joseph had expected, a folding telescope has been substituted. As Joseph gazes through the telescope, he has the sensation of sitting in a limousine. The slight touch of a lever causes the now-enormous black telescope-limousine, with Joseph seated in it, to roll out the door. Everyone watches disapprovingly.

Joseph stays in the Sanatorium, losing all sense of time. Mysteriously, his mother appears once but cannot speak and remains out of reach. Living conditions steadily deteriorate. The room is never cleaned. The other guests and the staff seem to have left. Food is to be had only in town.

The very landscape grows darker, and the country is overrun by packs of dogs. At the Sanatorium itself, one enormous, vicious dog is kept on a chain.

One day war breaks out, to universal consternation. "A war not preceded by diplomatic activity? A war amid blissful peace?" The enemy is greeted by discontented townspeople who now come out in the open to terrorize their neighbors. "We noticed, in fact, a group of these activists, in black civilian clothing with white straps across their breasts, advancing in silence, their guns at the ready."

Joseph's father resolves to push through the mob to reach his store. He orders Joseph back to the Sanatorium. Joseph obeys him, he says, from "cowardice."

When Joseph gets back to the Sanatorium, he must face the chained dog alone. He is terrified, but seeing the dog up close, he makes an astounding discovery.

> How great is the power of prejudice! How powerful the hold of fear! How blind had I been! It was not a dog, it was a man. A chained man, whom, by a simplifying metaphoric wholesale error, I had taken for a dog.

In fact, the creature actually is still a dog, but in human shape. With his yellow, bony face and black beard, he might be taken for Dr. Gotard's elder brother, but he is a fanatic, "a tub-thumper, a vocal party member," and it was his passion and violence "that made him a hundred per cent dog."

Yet Joseph pities the dog, unchains him, and takes him back to his room in the Sanatorium. Meanwhile, he notices the glare of a fire over the town. He guesses that Father is "somewhere in the thick of a revolution or in a burning shop."

Joseph tricks the dog into staying locked in his room while he himself escapes. For a moment, he feels remorse at the danger that Father will face. Then he remembers: "Luckily, in fact, Father was no longer alive; he could not really be reached."

Leaving the dark and menacing town, Joseph boards the same train on which he came. He never leaves the train again, but rides it forever, turning into a pathetic beggar in a torn black hat.

Themes and Meanings

Initially, in view of the narrator's childlike personality and his tremendous dependence upon his father, the story reads like a pure psychological exploration of a son's relationship to his father. The author is now an adult, but he is reaching back into childhood to recapture the essence of his feelings and need for his parent. The relationship is not one of pure mutual admiration. Father shows disapproval of the son's pornographic book order (which is magically turned into a telescope). Though the son loves his father, he ultimately does abandon him and only after the fact consoles himself with the thought that Father is, after all, dead. The son's guilt and fear at letting Father go even in death form the very foundation of the plot: The Sanatorium exists precisely in order to give dead people only a little more time to continue living.

Yet the theme of a son's grief, guilt, and poor adjustment to his loss by no means exhausts the story's message. The outside world intrudes in the form of a war, "not preceded by diplomatic activity," in which discontented local people actively collaborate with the invaders. The black clothing worn by the inhabitants of this dreamworld after death acquires other than funereal significance. Those who collaborate with the enemy wear black clothing crossed with white straps. As they march through the streets carrying rifles, they flash "ironical dark looks" in which there is "a touch of superiority, a glimmer of malicious enjoyment." When this story appeared in 1937, such an image could only be a very transparent—and indeed, very bold—reference to Nazism.

More than bold, the story was prophetic. The Holocaust had not yet reached Poland in 1937, yet how uncannily Schulz describes the process of relentless circumscription, relinquishment, and slow death. Joseph's father, a dead man who has not yet died, has opened a tiny shop in this dream-ghetto (from which he will never escape). Joseph finds the old man's behavior strange, "yet what could one expect of Father, who was only half real, who lived a relative and conditional life, circumscribed by so many limitations!"

The name of the narrator, Joseph, was not chosen by chance, but is very much part of Schulz's traditions. The name harks back to the Old Testament's Joseph, the prophetic dreamer and seer.

Style and Technique

Schulz is a consciously symbolic writer. As he stated in another story, "Spring," "Most things are interconnected, most threads lead to the same reel." Any detail in the universe may be relevant to any puzzling question in the universe.

The most visible symbol in "Sanatorium Under the Sign of the Hourglass" is the color black. It is found everywhere: on the mysterious train, in clothing, leaves, beards, the telescope, and the eyes of the terrible dog. There is a crescendo of black, enhancing the impact of the last three scenes: the outbreak of war (the black uniforms), the unchaining of the dog-man (black eyes and beard), and Joseph's end (a beggar in a black hat). In a similar manner, other recurring images also help to unify the story's tone and structure.

Schulz also practices a technique of extended and vivid metaphor that is uniquely his, and hints at his other craft (he was a painter and art teacher):

> I broke a twig from a roadside tree. The leaves were dark, almost black. It was a strangely charged blackness, deep and benevolent, like restful sleep. All the different shades of gray in the landscape derived from that one color. It was the color of a cloudy summer dusk in our part of the country, when the landscape has become saturated with water after a long period of rain and exudes a feeling of self-denial, a resigned and ultimate numbness that does not need the consolation of color.

D. G. Nakeeb

THE SANDMAN

Author: E. T. A. Hoffmann (1776-1822)
Type of plot: Fantastic realism
Time of plot: Early nineteenth century
Locale: Germany
First published: "Der Sandmann," 1816 (English translation, 1844)

> *Principal characters:*
> NATHANAEL, a student at the University of G.
> CLARA, a distant cousin and Nathanael's fiancée
> LOTHAR, her brother
> COPPELIUS, a lawyer
> GIUSEPPE COPPOLA, a trader in barometers, eyeglasses, and
> optical instruments
> SPALANZANI, a professor of physics
> OLIMPIA, Spalanzani's "daughter," a doll

The Story

In the first of the three letters that open the story, Nathanael writes Lothar, a distant cousin who lives with his sister Clara and Nathanael's mother, of the distress he has felt following the recent visit to his room by an instrument trader named Giuseppe Coppola. Nathanael is convinced that Coppola is the lawyer Coppelius, who was responsible for the death of Nathanael's father years earlier during his childhood. As a child, Nathanael believed Coppelius to be the Sandman, who, according to a nursemaid's fairy tale, threw sand into children's eyes when they did not want to go to bed, causing their eyes to spring bloodily out of their sockets. One evening Nathanael decided to investigate the Sandman's activities in his father's room and hid himself behind a curtain in his father's closet. When the Sandman entered the room and Nathanael discovered that it was Coppelius, an old lawyer who occasionally had dinner with the family and whom the children found ugly and repulsive, Nathanael was transfixed. As the two men worked on a steaming experiment, his father suddenly appeared to him to be Coppelius' satanic double. When Coppelius shouted "Eyes here, eyes here," Nathanael fell out of his hiding place onto the floor, whereupon Coppelius threatened to burn out his eyes, causing Nathanael to faint. A year or so later, during Coppelius' next visit, an explosion in the laboratory killed the father.

Nathanael has addressed the letter by mistake to his fiancée, Lothar's sister, Clara, who tries to reassure Nathanael in the story's second letter that all the horrible things he experienced existed only in his imagination and not in reality. She recommends that he forget all about Coppelius and Coppola and adds that by recognizing them as phantoms of his real self he will be free of their evil influence over him.

A somewhat more sober Nathanael tells Lothar in the third letter of his acquaintance with a new physics professor by the name of Spalanzani, who has known Coppola for years and claims that Coppola has left the city. Nathanael now doubts that Coppola and Coppelius are identical, yet insists that he cannot rid himself of the image of Coppelius' hideous bearing. He also mentions that on the way to Spalanzani's lecture he caught sight of the professor's daughter Olimpia, whom Spalanzani keeps locked in a glass cabinet behind closed curtains. Her eyes seemed to stare at him, though she appeared not to see him.

At this point, the narrator breaks in to say that he has prefaced his own narration with these three letters because he knows of no other beginning that could adequately reflect the ardent intensity of Nathanael's story. The narrator then continues with Nathanael's return home, where the coolly rational Clara again tries to dismiss Nathanael's demoniac visions as imaginary. The ill effect of Coppola's visit on Nathanael, however, is apparent to everyone. In a long, murky poem, he depicts how Coppelius was destroying their love. According to the poem, at their marriage Coppelius touched Clara's eyes, which sprang into Nathanael's chest "like bloody sparks," and then threw Nathanael into a rapidly turning circle of fire. When Clara tells him to destroy the poem, he responds by calling her a lifeless "automat" (automaton). Lothar arrives and in a heated exchange of insults challenges Nathanael to a duel, which ends, however, with apologies and a reconciliation.

Nathanael returns to G. and finds his apartment destroyed by fire. His new room is across from Professor Spalanzani's house, and he can see into the room where Olimpia remains seated motionless for hours; he is not, however, moved by her steadfast gaze toward him. Just as he is writing to Clara, Coppola appears at his door and pulls thousands of eyeglasses out of his pockets. Nathanael is overwhelmed by the flickering lenses, which seem like a thousand eyes staring at him. As Coppola lays more glasses on the table, "flaming glances" leap around and shoot "their blood-red rays into Nathanael's chest." Nathanael, however, calms down enough to persuade Coppola to remove the glasses and settles instead for a small telescope. Involuntarily he looks into Olimpia's room with the telescope. At first her eyes seem fixed and dead, but then they become more and more lively the closer he looks at them. Coppola demands his money and leaves, laughing loudly. In the next few days, Nathanael thinks only of Olimpia and sees her image everywhere except in her room, where the curtains have been closed.

Spalanzani gives a ball and concert in order to introduce his daughter to the public. Olimpia is beautifully dressed and has a wonderful figure, though her movement is a bit measured and stiff. She plays the piano with great skill and sings with a bright, though brittle, voice. Nathanael stands at the back of the room and uses his pocket telescope to see her better. He becomes inflamed with longing and yells out her name, to the consternation of those around him. When her concert ends, he races up to her to invite her to dance. Although her dancing is rather mechanical and his heated advances are met with cold and laconic responses, he falls so deeply in love with her that he is oblivious to the snickering of the young people behind his back or the end of the ball. Spalanzani is delighted with Nathanael's interest in his daughter and invites him back any time.

Nathanael now lives only for Olimpia and reads to her from his writings for hours in her room, while she sits passively staring him in the eye. Her only words are "ah, ah" and an occasional "good night, my beloved." One day Nathanael decides to go over and propose to her, but on the stairs to Spalanzani's study he hears a horrible banging, swearing, and arguing. It is the voices of Spalanzani and the dreaded Coppelius. Nathanael bursts into the room and sees Spalanzani and Coppola fighting over Olimpia's body. Coppola wrests her away, hits the professor with her, and runs off laughing madly with her on his shoulder. Nathanael notices that her face has no eyes, only empty sockets. Spalanzani implores Nathanael to run after Coppelius, who is stealing his best automat and ruining twenty years of work. A pair of bloody eyes lie on the floor. Spalanzani picks them up and throws them at Nathanael, who tries to strangle him but is restrained and taken to an insane asylum.

When Nathanael regains consciousness, he is in bed at home, with Clara, Lothar, and his mother standing nearby. Nathanael appears to be fully recovered from his bout of madness and is now quieter. The family is preparing to move to a new house, and Nathanael intends again to marry Clara. In town one day, the lovers decide to climb the tower of the city hall. Nathanael pulls out his telescope and by chance looks at Clara, whose eyes suddenly seem to spew fire. He leaps wildly at her and tries to kill her, but Lothar manages to get her away from Nathanael and back down to safety. Nathanael meanwhile begins racing around the gallery of the tower, screaming, "Turn, circle of fire." A crowd gathers below, and when Nathanael sees Coppelius among them, he leaps to his death. Several years later, people claim to have seen Clara and a new husband playing with their two lively young boys in front of a country house.

Themes and Meanings

"The Sandman," like all of E. T. A. Hoffmann's tales, deals with the unsettling disparity between the self and the external world. For Hoffmann there were three possibilities for facing the basic disharmony between internal and external reality: Like Nathanael, one may allow the inner visions and feelings to predominate, leading eventually to madness; like Clara, one may insist on the primary importance of everyday, factual reality; or, like the Romantic writer, one may accept this dualism and try to transcend it with ironic detachment.

Nathanael's early childhood experiences (the nursemaid's story of the Sandman, Coppelius' threat to his eyes, and his father's death) make him susceptible to the destructive workings of his imagination. His obsession with losing his eyes and his fear of the evil father-substitutes, Coppelius and Coppola, destroy his love for Clara and make him easy prey for Spalanzani's and Coppelius' suggestive manipulations. The pocket telescope further distorts his vision, for instead of bringing external objects nearer and into sharper focus, it only magnifies their effect on his soul.

In Olimpia he discovers a mirror of his involuntary emotional responses. His statement to a friend that "only in Olimpia's love do I find my own self again" is a telling expression of his latent narcissism. He fails to take seriously Clara's sensible advice and becomes very upset when she sharply criticizes his premonitory poem about Coppelius' destruction of their love. It is easier for him to retreat into his private world and converse with a mechanical doll than to develop an open, unselfish relationship with Clara.

Nevertheless, the narrator's and Hoffmann's sympathies lie with Nathanael, for he is the one who recognizes the deeper creative and destructive powers that are hidden behind everyday experience. Nathanael, however, fails both as a poet and as an individual because he is unable to communicate his dark and esoteric visions with the least bit of distance and objectivity. The persistent motif of eyes and seeing emphasizes all the more the tragedy of Nathanael's blindness to his own drives and desires.

Style and Technique

At the beginning of his tale, Hoffmann provides no stable base of objective reality with which to distinguish between Nathanael's delusions and actual events. The narrative perspective constantly shifts between impartial observation and empathetic closeness. Although the three opening letters give the tale a documentary quality, the narrator's humorous digression on his difficulties in telling the story leave the reader in doubt as to how seriously to take Nathanael's anxious concerns. Furthermore, Clara's rational interpretation of Nathanael's stories is just as unsatisfactory an explanation of Coppelius' hold over him as Nathanael's own understanding of the childhood events.

In order to blur the boundary between appearance and reality, Hoffmann seems to want to disorient the reader. Thus, Coppola's true identity remains uncertain until the climactic fight between Spalanzani and Coppelius; Olimpia's dollhood, though hinted at, is not revealed earlier, for she is described solely from the perspective of Nathanael, for whom she is a more loving and deeply spiritual being than Clara; Coppelius' final "giant" appearance in the crowd in front of the city hall may or may not be a product of Nathanael's madness. The author and narrator play both sides of the story—the psychological and demoniac, realistic and fantastic—against each other, and in the end give neither more credence than the other.

Peter West Nutting

SATURDAY NIGHT

Author: James T. Farrell (1904-1979)
Type of plot: Psychological realism
Time of plot: 1929
Locale: Chicago
First published: 1947

> *Principal characters:*
> JOSEPH "DOPEY" CARBERRY, an unemployed high school
>   dropout, in his mid-twenties
> MICHAEL "MIKE" McGUIRE, his uncle
> ANNA McGUIRE, his aunt
> KATE CARBERRY, his sister
> PHIL GARRITY, the rebuffed suitor of Kate
> JACK KENNEDY and
> RED MURPHY, Dopey's and Phil's pals

The Story

From a detached and rather cool third-person point of view, the reader observes Joseph "Dopey" Carberry shamble into the dining room of his Uncle Mike's and Aunt Anna's home and sit down to eat, only to begin yet another Saturday night of bickering and blathering with his relatives. Dopey and his two sisters have been living with their aunt and her brother since their father remarried. He is harangued by all assembled for his shiftlessness. His Aunt Anna directs the abuse, "We've helped him, fed him, clothed him, waited on him, coddled him, tried to point the right way out to him, but it's just not in his bones." Dopey hardly listens; he silently laments his lack of "two bucks to lay on Red Pepper after Len had come around the corner with that hot tip," earlier in the day. He eventually offers some excuses and evasions for his lack of energy, and his aunt retorts, "Yes, I know what you want. A banker's job from twelve to one, with an hour for lunch." Given the brevity of the scene, there is more satire displayed than bathos, and the bigotry and corruption of their milieu are deftly sketched.

In the second scene (there are ten in all, matching the straightforward chronology of the evening), Uncle Mike counsels young Joe (who, after quitting high school has had a number of jobs—one of which he describes as "a slave factory for dopes"—and a period of vagabondism) to change his ways, and Dopey tells him, "I'd like to go back to sea or else be a bookie." Through a ruse, Dopey then manages to borrow five dollars from his uncle.

Phil Garrity arrives in the fourth scene, looking like a "Big Shot," as Dopey's sister Kate tells him. "Why, Phil, you're all togged out like Joe College." Phil has just made a large amount of money "legit," playing the stock market with money from his La Salle Street job and has just purchased a new used car, a Lincoln. He is attracted to Kate, but has not gone out with her for six months. He and Kate banter about dating, but Phil is not able to extract a commitment from her. He and Dopey go out for a night on the town and, through scenes five and six, the third-person point of view severs its attachment from Dopey and secures itself to Phil, who thenceforth assumes the position of protagonist. Farrell manages this switch rather smoothly, since it coincides with a change of location, from inside to outside.

Phil and Dopey drive to the corner of Sixty-third and Stony Island, where it is "bustling with Saturday-night activity, crowded with people, noisy with the traffic of automobiles and streetcars." They join a crowd outside a drugstore, and Phil muses on his lack of success with women, his hopes for marriage to Kate, her lack of interest in him, wishing all the while that he could be "wild, carefree, dashing, romantic, brave, a guy who didn't care two hoots in hell for anything in the world."

After picking up some speakeasy gin, as well as another friend, Marty, they "put their liquor in their pockets and left to see Jack Kennedy." Kennedy's apartment, where "most of the space is taken up by a wide in-a-door bed, which was unmade," is full of the din of single young men recounting old times and former glories, their unsatisfying work and lack of money. The dialogue is brisk and fresh throughout. Phil yearns for Kate and is sent out to buy more liquor.

After his return, Phil, Dopey, and Jack set off for the whorehouses of Twenty-second Street and Red Murphy, another acquaintance of their big-city—yet excruciatingly tiny and parochial—world, staggers up to them as they are getting into Phil's new car. As Phil drives badly down the Midway, the essential realism of Farrell's style keeps this foreshadowing from being too heavy-handed when the remains of an earlier car wreck catches their eyes and they stop and survey the debris. "There's a lot of blood in one person. This blood might mean just one poor sonofabitch killed," Red comments.

The drunken men arrive at the "Sour Apple" on the near North Side, a tearoom and dance hall with a bohemian reputation. Phil hesitantly asks a young woman for a dance and she "acted as if she had not heard him. He repeated it, humiliation eating inside of him." Rejected, he retreats into further reveries of Kate and unintentionally insults a husky lad by telling him that he "can't dance to the Notre Dame *Victory March*." A brawl commences. When the club's proprietor asks what started the fight, a denizen of the Sour Apple explains, "Four drunken Irishmen with liquor, four sober Irishmen with girls."

Unable to secure pickups at the Sour Apple, the four friends depart and find the brothels on Twenty-second Street closed by an unexpected police raid. They do manage to pick up four older women who are leaving a nearby dance hall. With Phil at the wheel, they drive out to the country fields.

"Large shadows raked the road, and the car whipped on." After a few miles it smashes head-on into a Cadillac "going as swiftly as Phil's Lincoln." Phil and one of the young women disentangle themselves from the wreckage, and Phil drags her, dazed and drunk, into the fields, where they are found later by the police with their britches down—an effective, if moralistic, yoking of sex and death. "You ought to swing for this, you sonofabitch," the cop tells Phil. The dead bodies of Jack and Dopey are pulled out of the car. Phil is left delirious and uncomprehending.

Themes and Meanings

"Saturday Night" repeats many of Farrell's central concerns and subjects. His fictional world, the cosmology it describes, echoes, in many ways, the teaching that was instilled in him as a boy growing up in a Roman Catholic family and attending parochial schools on the South Side of Chicago in the early twentieth century. There is a sense of predestination and original sin with which all his characters come equipped, though Farrell's own attitude seems to be one of alternating cynicism toward and respectful anger at this worldview. Dopey does not elicit much sympathy in Farrell's depiction; his death, though, is a consequence of his closest friendship, albeit a friendship of convenience and exploitation on Dopey's part. Phil is trapped in his own unrequited longings and sexual inexperience and ambivalence, the perpetual boyishness visited upon most of Farrell's male characters, and he becomes the agent of destruction. Farrell has retained a good bit of the Catholic puritanism of his youth. Phil's sexual initiation is only accomplished at dire cost. Both society and Farrell disapprove of the boys' behavior.

Farrell reveals his own ambivalence as a left-wing social critic in "Saturday Night." The most amusing lines are given to Aunt Anna, a conservative scold, and to the *habitué* of the Sour Apple, Wolcroft, a self-proclaimed poet. In addition, Danny O'Neill, Farrell's closest counterpart in the O'Neill pentalogy of novels, is spoken of at Kennedy's apartment as a "cracked socialist" who "was trying to write books," and the terrible fate of the young friends is presented not in the language of Marxist determinism (these young men all being sacrifices to alienated labor and the inexorable march of capitalism) but according to Farrell's own personal determinism, which he is exercising over the blockheads of his youth who did not appreciate the special young man whom they had in their midst. The Sour Apple, indeed: "Saturday Night" could be described as a mixture of sour grapes and bad apples.

Style and Technique

James T. Farrell has never been praised as a stylist; in fact, he is often described as an undistinguished writer of prose. His power comes, as it does with many American writers, from sheer force and accumulation, the command and sweep of factual material which does not need or solicit strenuous interpretation (though the car crash could be viewed as an allegory for the stock-market crash to come). Farrell overwhelms the reader with the visceral, with what he describes, somewhat mockingly, in "Saturday Night," through the words of poet Wolcroft, as not just "realism. That's old-fashioned. My poetry, now, it's superrealist." Farrell's early naturalistic writing was in the mainstream and remained fashionable until that stream was thoroughly diverted and rechanneled after World War II.

Farrell, though he wrote many short stories, was not so much a master of the form as its earnest supplicant. The stories he wrote that were short enough became short stories instead of novels. Farrell had a novelist's skill at synthesizing, but also the novelist's appetite for size, for the repetitive scene; the short story form does not profit from that sort of segmentation. Farrell's stories are often novels in miniature, rather than short stories in full bloom—although "Saturday Night" is one of his most effective, rich with humor, energy, and life, and not simply scenes from a novel writ small.

William O'Rourke

A SCANDAL IN BOHEMIA

Author: Arthur Conan Doyle (1859-1930)
Type of plot: Detective story
Time of plot: c. 1888 or 1889
Locale: London, England
First published: 1891

> *Principal characters:*
> SHERLOCK HOLMES, the world's greatest detective
> DR. JOHN H. WATSON, his friend and biographer
> IRENE ADLER, a beautiful young operatic soprano
> WILHELM, KING OF BOHEMIA

The Story

Soon after his first marriage, Dr. John Watson leaves the Baker Street flat which he has shared with Sherlock Holmes and returns to private medical practice. In the course of his calls, he passes through Baker Street one day, sees Holmes pacing before the window, and on an impulse walks up to visit his friend. Holmes tells him that a client is expected that evening, one whose case may be interesting to Watson in his capacity as Holmes's chronicler. The client arrives, a huge man, richly and garishly dressed and wearing a mask. Holmes quickly penetrates the disguise, however, and identifies the man as King Wilhelm of Bohemia. The surprised king unmasks and tells Holmes why he has come.

It seems that some years earlier, the king fell in love with a young soprano named Irene Adler; the woman is not only beautiful but also possessive: The king's engagement to another woman, a princess, will soon be announced, and Irene Adler has sworn to stop the wedding. She threatens to publish a compromising photograph of her and the king, thereby creating a scandal that will lead the bride's family to call off the wedding. She refuses to sell the photograph to the king; twice, burglars have failed to find it in her house; her luggage has been searched without success; and on two occasions robbers have stopped her, but without finding the picture. The king lays the matter in Holmes's hands, begging for his help.

The next morning, Holmes disguises himself as a seedy-looking groom and goes to the neighborhood around Miss Adler's house to see what gossip he can pick up. There he not only learns that Miss Adler has an admirer, Godfrey Norton, but also becomes involved in an incident that amuses as well as enlightens him. He sees both Norton and Miss Adler set off in carriages for a nearby church. When he follows them there, the disguised Holmes is commandeered as a witness for their wedding. Now that Irene Adler is married, Holmes expects her to leave London at any moment. He must therefore act, and do it swiftly.

On the following day, Holmes again disguises himself, this time as a clergyman, and requests Watson's help for his scheme. They go to Adler's house separately. Once there, Watson sees Miss Adler arrive, and she is immediately beset by a crowd of loafers. Holmes, in disguise, comes to her aid, is attacked and apparently wounded by the crowd, and falls to the ground. He is carried into Adler's house and laid on a couch near a window where Watson can see him. On Holmes's signal, Watson throws a smoke bomb through the window, and the people on the street outside begin to cry "Fire!" After the tumult which follows, Holmes joins Watson outside, and on their walk back to Baker Street, explains what has happened.

Reasoning that Miss Adler had the photograph well hidden somewhere in her house and that she would immediately go to it in an emergency, Holmes stage-managed the little scene outside her house to see where she would run in such a case. The plan worked, and now he knows where the photograph is hidden. On the morrow he plans to go to the house with the king and take the photograph while Miss Adler is not in the room. As Watson and Holmes pause at Holmes's door, a short, cloaked figure passes them on the street and wishes Holmes good evening.

The next morning, all goes as planned until Holmes and the king reach Adler's house. There, an old woman tells them that Miss Adler and her husband have left for their honeymoon and that she expected Holmes to arrive. Alarmed, the two men are shown into the drawing room. Holmes goes at once to the secret compartment that held the photograph but instead finds there a photograph of Miss Adler herself and a letter addressed to him. The letter explains that she had been warned that the king might use an agent. After Holmes, dressed as a clergyman, was brought into her house, she began to have suspicions. She left the room, put on a disguise of her own as a man, and followed Holmes and Watson back to Baker Street. She says further that now that she loves a better man than the king—Godfrey Norton—the king need not worry any longer about their photograph: She will not hinder his marriage.

The astonished and relieved king thanks Holmes for his services and offers him a ring from his finger as reward. Holmes refuses, however, and asks for something else—the photograph of Irene Adler, which the king gives him.

Themes and Meanings

"A Scandal in Bohemia" was the first Sherlock Holmes short story that Doyle published. Two earlier novels, *A Study in Scarlet* (1887) and *The Sign of Four* (1890), had already introduced the great detective to the public, but largely in the character of, as Watson says, "the most perfect reasoning and observing machine that the world has seen." A theme that runs throughout the Holmes stories is that reason is a trusted guide through the confusion of everyday life. As Holmes says to Watson, representative of the ordinary person, "You have not observed. And yet you have seen." For those who both see *and* observe—such as Holmes—even an apparently meaningless detail speaks volumes—and the trained mind is a reliable guide. Yet there is something mechanical about the way that Holmes is presented in the two long stories that introduced him, and Doyle both modifies his theme and amplifies the character of Holmes in "A Scandal in Bohemia."

The story's first sentence says of Irene Adler, "To Sherlock Holmes she is always *the* woman"; the last sentence is almost identical: It says that Holmes always refers to her "under the honorable title of *the* woman." In this story, if Sherlock Holmes is the intellect, Irene Adler is clearly the emotions. Watson emphasizes this interpretation by stating Holmes's aversion to all emotions as disruptive of the working of his mind, comparing a strong emotion in Holmes to a piece of grit in a delicate machine. Here again the reader sees the image of the machine used to describe Holmes. Yet to make Holmes only a machine denies him his full humanity; he is indeed capable of powerful feelings, as the story shows.

"A Scandal in Bohemia" might loosely be called the most feminist of the Sherlock Holmes tales. Holmes is something of a misogynist in many of the stories, often scorning what he regards as a feminine tendency to emotionalize life. He frequently makes generalizations about women that seem glib from one who lacks everyday contact with them. That a woman could outreason Holmes, could see one step further than he has, and could anticipate his next move teaches him a lesson that he does not forget: As Watson says near the conclusion, "He used to make merry over the cleverness of women, but I have not heard him do it of late." Holmes has discovered humanity both in women and in himself.

Style and Technique

"A Scandal in Bohemia" was Doyle's first attempt at a new literary form: a self-contained short story with a continuing character at the center of it. Although Holmes appeared twice before, it was in novels. The usefulness of a familiar character in a series of short stories is immediately obvious, once one considers it: In a short story, an author must either give a very sketchy portrait of the main characters or violate the dictum of Edgar Allan Poe that a short story must aim at producing a single effect without one wasted word. If the character is already known to the public from earlier stories, however, the author can begin with the plot at once. So effective was this technique, especially for the detective story, that many later authors followed the same practice, writing a series of stories about a detective—Nero Wolfe or Ellery Queen, for example. The character of the detective was built up throughout the series, producing a much more lifelike character than would have been possible in a single story.

"A Scandal in Bohemia" also introduced the structural pattern that Doyle was to use again and again in the Holmes stories. The mystery is first revealed at Holmes's apartment at Baker Street with the arrival of the client. Holmes demonstrates his powers, to the amazement of the client, by revealing something about the client that Holmes has not yet been told. By this means, Holmes also gains the confidence and respect of his employer. Next, both Holmes and Watson journey at least once to another location; there Holmes acts mysteriously, but this time he does *not* explain. Finally, Holmes, Watson, and the other principals gather for a "revelation scene," in which both the mystery and Holmes's method are explained.

Doyle used all these elements over and over again, keeping the stories fresh by inserting new mysteries into this setting or by occasionally adding some detail about the character of Holmes or Watson. The technique was to make Doyle one of the most popular writers of his time on both sides of the Atlantic, and it was a technique first employed in "A Scandal in Bohemia."

Walter E. Meyers

A SCANDALOUS WOMAN

Author: Edna O'Brien (1930-   )
Type of plot: Domestic realism
Time of plot: The 1930's or 1940's
Locale: Rural Ireland
First published: 1974

Principal characters:
EILY HOGAN, the teenage daughter of a farming family
THE NARRATOR, Eily's schoolfriend, the daughter of a
   neighboring family named Brady
JACK, a young bank clerk in the village
EILY'S FATHER

The Story

A grown woman recalls her friendship with Eily Hogan, and from the opening paragraph, the reader is alerted by her remark that she has been "connected" with Eily's life. At first, that connection takes the form of romantic admiration. The narrator sees Eily as a high-spirited person who brings excitement into their dull lives. Their childhood bond, based on play, soon becomes a bond of collusion when Eily begins a sexual relationship with a bank clerk. The narrator helps Eily to cover her tracks when she goes out into the woods to meet Jack, whom they call Romeo, and their shared sense of the danger and sinfulness of what they are doing colors the romantic glow with foreboding. Images of violence and guilt have been prominent from the beginning, even in their childhood games of hospital. This first phase ends in a triumphant scene in which the girls meet in a meadow and Eily produces a bottle of perfume. The narrator's most intense pleasure in their friendship is focused on this moment when childhood romance is balanced with adult sensuality.

When the bank clerk ends the liaison rather brutally, the girls enter a new phase of their collusion. The narrator tries to calm Eily's suicidal thoughts, and together they visit a fortune-teller. This unpleasant and witchlike character encourages Eily to believe that the dream of Jack's return will come true. Overlooking the sinister note in the witch's words, "You'll end your days with him," they return home in joyful anticipation of a reunion with Jack. The joy is short-lived, for Eily's father comes upon the lovers one evening. This insanely violent man imprisons Eily in a room, and the narrator's loyalty is tested as she must deny all knowledge of Eily's earlier meetings.

The bond between the girls is broken when it becomes apparent that Eily is pregnant, and the Hogan and Brady parents begin to coerce Jack to marry her. They succeed, but in the process, the narrator observes the destruction of Eily's joyous spirit. It appears that Jack is marrying Eily in hatred and frustration, and the narrator realizes that Eily and other women also are trapped victims of a crude male power structure.

In later years, the narrator's memories of her affection for Eily return, prompted by glimpses of her. Broken in spirit, she has become the mother of three children in four years, and as her husband prospers in business, she slides into a breakdown. Many years later, the narrator visits and finds her functioning competently in her husband's business but without feeling or affection except for the narrator's child. Worse still, she has lost all memory of their joy together as schoolgirls, and the story ends with an expression of the narrator's grief and anger at the destruction of so many women by her native countryside.

The "connection" of the narrator's life to this image of youthful vitality so brutally destroyed is not made clear, but it is implied that the narrator's sense of life has been overshadowed by these memories. The "spark" of joyous pleasure of which she became aware was extinguished for her also, and it is hinted that no later experience has given her the same intensity of pleasure or of love. She appears to have married a man who is indifferent to her feelings and lavishes his affections on his vintage car.

Themes and Meanings

The general theme is evident: Woman's capacity for finding joy and pleasure is destroyed at an early age by an environment in which all relationships are colored by the fear of punishment. This feminist theme takes on a local significance, however, in the Irish peasant setting with its closely knit family and community ties through which the intimidation of dogma and physical violence is transmitted.

The fathers in the story live close to the land, and the grim regime of hard physical work for long hours makes life a matter of joyless endurance. Their closeness to the animals which breed and are bought and sold influences their ways of thinking about sexual relationships and marriage. Taciturn and abusive, the men seem to control relationships by provoking fear and repression. Mothers cater to them, and daughters too, and the prominence of Catholic teaching seems to extend the power of the father into the social arena; the father's authority seems to have social and divine sanction. What the girls fear most, discovery, is connected with public disgrace and with a fear of final damnation. Sin and guilt are associated with disobedience, and so the girls are led to doubt their own feelings and impulses. Their pleasures and their innocent play are a self-defeating mixture of escape and submission and prayer. When the narrator is held down so that Eily's sister can pretend to be the doctor about to remove her female parts, the hopelessness and humiliation surface in the bewildered comment, "For some reason I always looked upward and backward." It is not surprising that Eily's craving for romantic adventure leads her to an indifferent exploiter who fits well into her father's code of behavior, even when he is being bullied into marriage.

The girls are trapped in another way: by their religious and literary education. Eily believes that "the god Cupid is on our side," and the narrator dramatizes herself as a Shakespearean heroine. Their favorite perfume, "Mischief," creates an atmosphere "of mystery and sanctity," and the sacred and the profane are again confused when the chapel is "better than the theatre," the "rosary beads . . . were as dazzling as necklaces," and the mission priest is imagined as a lover. The overactive imaginations of the girls veil the reality of their circumstances from them, even as imagination is their means of transcending the impoverishment of their environment.

It is only at the end of the story that the narrator acknowledges the prosaic tragedy that has overtaken Eily; her youthful revolt has embedded her even more deeply in this environment that kills individual feeling and joy. The narrator wants the little luxury of re-creating in memory "the good old days," but Eily tells her that "they're all much of a muchness." Repression has flattened her affective life, killing even her memories.

Style and Technique

The story is told in an apparently effortless, episodic recollection and then, suddenly, ends with a howl of despair at the destruction of the innocent joy which was re-created in the narrative: "I thought that ours indeed was a land of shame, a land of murder, and a land of strange, throttled, sacrificial women." The role of storyteller seems to remove the narrator from the category of "throttled" women, but the anger which issues directly here is present throughout under the calm surface. The style blends a wide-eyed innocence appropriate to the age of the schoolfriends with a bitter irony and a grotesque humor which are suited to the exposure of that horrific reality which the girls in their innocence do not consciously oppose. By entering fully into the girls' earlier experience, the narrator tells the story with a surprising acceptance of the horrific reality which is part of things as they are in the world.

Sometimes the irony is directed against the children's way of observing and of expressing themselves. "She would work like a horse to get to the main road before dark to see the passerby"; such a sentence captures the grim routine of the farm, which turns Eily into a workhorse, and also her craving for excitement or release. This is a typical, understated sentence, apparently factual but catching a raw quality of the life there. The next sentences deepen the insight which was dropped so casually: "She was swift as a colt. My father never stopped praising this quality of her and put it down to muscle." The humor of this innocent and ignorant commentary is prominent and heightens a grimmer irony which underlies it. The father's sense of an affective response to life's possibilities issues in animal images which are demeaning; when Eily is pregnant, he says she has "a porker in her."

Grotesque humor is again unintentional on the part of the narrator and serves to underline the pervasive violence and repression which is accepted as bland fact. The blandness and the horror are wonderfully captured in a sentence such as this: "As usual, my mother ate only the pope's nose, and served the men the breasts of chicken." At a turning point in the story, poignancy and comedy blend with the grotesque. Eily's secret pregnancy becomes public knowledge at a religious service attended by the entire community, and she is taken outside the church. The narrator's overly literary manner reports: "They bore her aloft as if she were a corpse on a litter." The narrator appears not to realize the irony of her metaphors.

The style in which Edna O'Brien reveals her world owes much to James Joyce's early fiction; in "Araby" and "The Boarding House," Joyce used a similar mixture of styles to convey the sinister ordinariness of a life which is a form of death. O'Brien adapts Joyce's style to her country world and gives it a nostalgic innocence and humor.

Denis Sampson

THE SCAPEGOAT

Author: Paul Laurence Dunbar (1872-1906)
Type of plot: Sketch
Time of plot: c. 1900
Locale: Cadgers, a fictional American city
First published: 1904

> *Principal characters:*
> ROBINSON ASBURY, a leader in Cadgers' black community
> SILAS BINGO, his political rival
> ISAAC MORTON, a school principal, a political tool, and later rival of Bingo
> JUDGE DAVIS, an old white judge, a loyal supporter of Asbury

The Story

The story opens with a brief survey of Robinson Asbury's rise from a bootblack to an owner of a barbershop-social club for blacks in the town of Cadgers. With this shop as a base, Asbury becomes politically visible and, with the patronage of party managers, the town's recognized black leader. Since Asbury has further ambitions, he studies law on the side and, with the help of Judge Davis, a white man and the only member of the political establishment with moral principles, is admitted to the bar. Rather than leave the black district and enter the elite class, Asbury opens up a law office next to his barbershop, declaring a loyalty to the black people who gave him his success.

At this point, Dunbar introduces the antagonist, Silas Bingo, and the central conflict of the story. Bingo and Latchett, partners in a black law firm and envious of Asbury's rise to power, plot his downfall by creating a new faction within the political party, by gathering all the "best people" to their side, and by co-opting an innocent school principal, Isaac Morton, to be their figurehead. At the Emancipation Day celebration, during which the black leader Asbury heads a procession, the Bingo faction tries to compete with Asbury by organizing a counterprocession but fails. Asbury thus becomes the party's candidate in the next spring election. When Ashbury wins the election, the defeated party cries fraud. In order to clear its name, the winning party searches for a scapegoat. Only Asbury himself has the prominence to ensure a complete purgation. Tried and convicted, he begins his revenge even before his sentence. He makes a public statement at the trial naming all the political leaders as being guilty of criminal acts—all but Judge Davis. Against his own conscience and wishes, Davis sentences his friend to one year in prison. Bingo had betrayed Asbury by joining forces with his accusers, and now he tries to capitalize on Asbury's absence, but his bid for popular support must contend with a scapegoat suddenly turned martyr.

The second part of the story treats Asbury's political life after his release from prison. Amid speculation over what he intends to do, Asbury turns his law office into a "news-and-cigar stand" and declares that he is no longer engaged in politics, a stance that pleases and convinces Bingo. As Emancipation Day once again approaches, Bingo, now the black leader, must face a faction headed by Isaac Morton, who resents being used earlier by Bingo. While the contest for leadership is still close, Asbury visits Bingo to offer his support, but when the day of the procession comes, Bingo discovers that Asbury has tricked him and gained revenge for past betrayals. Behind the scenes, Asbury has turned practically the entire black community, including the leadership, against Bingo. Even his law partner, Latchett, abandons him. At the spring elections, everyone in the party organization who was in power when Asbury was convicted is defeated at the polls. Asbury has mobilized the entire black vote to defeat the party machine. Still, he declares to a reporter after the election is over, " 'I am not in politics, sir.' "

Themes and Meanings

The idea of a scapegoat has a long literary tradition and has taken various forms. Oedipus, though guilty of punishable crimes, is himself a victim whose suffering and exile purify the city of Thebes. Hamlet, who is a more innocent example, still must die for Denmark's corrupt state to be redeemed. Shirley Jackson's "The Lottery" offers a twentieth century version of the ancient ritual sacrifice. In all three works, the scapegoat dies or suffers excruciating pain. Paul Laurence Dunbar's scapegoat is a sociopolitical figure, at least on the surface; Asbury has none of the deep, mythical, religious, and cultural significance that one attaches to these other examples, or to the goat that the Jewish high priest sent off into the wilderness. He neither dies nor suffers— at least Dunbar does not show the suffering. Instead he chooses to show Asbury's triumph, strength, and self-confidence. Within the structure of the story, Asbury remains a scapegoat for only a few moments; afterward he is unquestionably and permanently a martyr. The martyr chooses his fate, and while Hamlet, too, makes such a choice toward the end of his play, Asbury is a martyr who remains alive and enjoys privately the fruits of victory. Dunbar creates a man willing to submit to social ostracism and even to self-exile from public honors. What he will not give up, however, are his principles and the power that derives from them. He consistently abides by the principle of democratic rule—one person, one vote; he remains loyal to the people; most important, he does not define the best people according to wealth and status. Such a presentation of the scapegoat suggests an unexpected optimism in a black writer at the turn of the century: Goodness will out, even in politics; the truly good man will, in the end, receive his due. What he must be willing to sacrifice are vanity and material success.

Behind this political story, however, lies a hint of racial comment. The final statement in the story, "Cadgers had learned its lesson," may have implications beyond the political one that the will of the people must not be violated. Dunbar is speaking specifically to the black community as a political block capable of challenging white supremacy. His specific advice is to black leaders who use the people to get power, then abandon them, and perhaps even to white leaders who underestimate minorities. That Dunbar's story is a form of protest literature should be clear from the beginning. In his initial paragraphs Dunbar describes the demographics of American cities: with the "usual tendency [of blacks] to colonize, a tendency encouraged, and in fact compelled, by circumstances, they had gathered into one part of the town. Here in alleys, and streets as dirty and hardly wider, they thronged like ants." When Asbury goes into business for himself, he puts up "the significant sign, 'Equal Rights Barber-Shop.'" Together with this protest, however, Dunbar insists on a pragmatic deception in achieving ends. Isaac Morton begins his political career as "an innocent young man," whose "ideals . . . should never have been exposed to the air." He eventually becomes more adroit, and Asbury's own success relies on the principle of deception.

Style and Technique

As a black writer at the turn of the century, Dunbar had a problem, to some extent imposed upon him by William Dean Howells—whether to write in dialect and meet certain expectations of a white audience, or to write in standard English, which he preferred, because he wanted to deal with "serious" issues. While he could not see dialect as a medium for serious poetry or fiction, he did write numerous stories in the plantation tradition, concentrating on rural blacks. Most are pleasantly nostalgic (though even here he does reveal his concern with racial injustice in the South). His identification with the rural poor and his feeling for their plight are also in the urban tale "The Scapegoat," but well in the background. In the foreground are a language that is standard American English, and an argument that is serious enough, perhaps, but mild-mannered and apparently innocuous.

It should not be surprising to find a black writer at that time, a writer anxious to succeed as a professional, choosing indirectness rather than an overtly revolutionary style. If he were to register a protest or assert any political ambition in the name of black people, he would do it subtly. If such thoughts are in "The Scapegoat" at all, they would be hidden. As with almost all black literature in America, not only with Dunbar, there is an underlying irony, a second perspective that lies just beneath the surface. One is tempted to see it even in the name of the hero as a whimsical play on words: the man who is "black as a berry" and the living man who acts as though he were buried. The title leads one to expect death or suffering, but instead one gets ultimate victory in this life: an ironic incongruity. Dunbar also uses verbal irony within the story. In one notable instance, as Asbury plots with Bingo, he actually plots against him. Asbury's language reveals one thing to Bingo and another to the careful reader: "I don't want to appear in this at all. All I want is revenge. You can have all the credit, but let me down my enemy." While Bingo applies "enemy" and "revenge" to Isaac Morton, his opponent, Asbury is actually referring to Bingo himself.

Yet the main ironies in the story lie in the incongruities of the story and the character of Asbury. The surface calm in Dunbar's tone, the quiet confidence of a man betrayed, do not jibe with the realities of such a situation. The ultimate victory may be at a deeper cost after all. Asbury allows the public to see only what Dunbar himself allows the reader to see. In this short sketch of Cadger life, the real face of Asbury never appears from behind the mask. Dunbar remains true to the words in his most famous poem, "We wear the mask that grins and lies" (which is itself an ironic violation of the deception principle), by not permitting his audience to "be overwise." In "this debt" that Dunbar "pays to human guile," one wonders what "tortured soul" might have resided in that "news-and-cigar stand"; one wonders what resemblance there was between Asbury's hermitlike existence and Dunbar's own private thoughts. Perhaps the irony turns back on itself, and "The Scapegoat" turns out to be an acutely appropriate title.

Thomas Banks

THE SCHREUDERSPITZE

Author: Mark Helprin (1947-   )
Type of plot: Fable
Time of plot: Unspecified
Locale: Munich and the German Alps
First published: 1977

>*Principal characters:*
>WALLICH, the protagonist, a commercial photographer
>WALLICH'S WIFE and SON, both deceased
>FRANZEN, a commercial photographer

The Story

From the first sentence ("In Munich are many men who look like weasels"), "The Schreuderspitze" is pervaded by a sense of strangeness and mystery. As the story opens, one of these weasel-like men, a commercial photographer named Franzen, is rejoicing at the disappearance of Wallich, a rival photographer. Franzen regards Wallich with a mixture of respect and scorn: While Wallich is capable of taking beautiful pictures, he lacks the drive that would make him successful. He probably fled to South America or jumped off a bridge, Franzen suggests, because he was too weak to face himself and understand "what sacrifices are required to survive and prosper. It is only in fairy tales that [the weak] rise to triumph." If that is so, "The Schreuderspitze" is itself a fairy tale. Franzen disappears from the story; Wallich, the protagonist, emerges triumphant, though not in a way that his earthbound rival would be able to understand.

Wallich has disappeared to try to adjust to the death of his wife and son in an automobile accident. Only once before has he left Bavaria, on a week-long honeymoon in Paris, and even then he was homesick. Now he seeks a place where he can be alone, yet where he will "have to undergo no savage adjustments." He finds it in the Alpine village of Garmisch-Partenkirchen, close to the German border, which he is afraid to cross. By the end of the story, a fable of mystical transformation, he will cross a border more profound than any national boundary.

He goes in October, and, in response to the railroad agent's warning about snow, claims on the spur of the moment that he is a mountain climber. In fact, he has always been poor at sports and "would close his eyes in fear when looking through Swiss calendars." Yet "why was he going to Garmisch-Partenkirchen anyway, if not for an ordeal through which to right himself?" That ordeal, mad as it seems for one with neither talent nor experience, will be to attempt a five-day ascent of the nearly vertical west face of the

Schreuderspitze, the most imposing peak in the area.

In the village he feels too awkward to eat in restaurants and so almost haphazardly begins to starve himself. He begins to exercise; at length the noise he makes gets him evicted from his hotel room, and he moves up the valley to the even smaller village of Altenburg–St. Peter—another significant stage in his journey. By the end of February, five months after his arrival, he is doing 250 pushups four times a day, 150 of them on his fingertips; he runs for four hours every night, "sometimes in snow which had accumulated up to his knees." Meanwhile, he has been reading mountaineering manuals— determined to press on despite their graphic warnings against climbing without proper training—and ordering the finest equipment.

So far, his movement has been exclusively upward and outward, away from humanity. Now, in May, he sees his reflection in a shop window and finds that his face has grown hard and lean, lacking gentleness. He buys a radio and listens to music by Ludwig van Beethoven to bring himself back into balance, knowing that "unmitigated extremes are a great cause of failure." At the railway station, awaiting the arrival of a rope he has ordered, he encounters an attractive family—father, mother, two small daughters— which appeals to him greatly. At this point, just over halfway through the story, he begins to dream. The remainder of "The Schreuderspitze" consists largely of detailed depictions of his mysterious dreams.

At first, inspired apparently by the encounter at the station, the dreams unfold "like the chapters in a brilliant nineteenth century history." It is "as if the mountains and valleys were filled with loving families of which he was part." He dreams then of his wife, who embraces him and then parts from him. Then begin the dreams of climbing. He feels light and strong, "as if he had quickly evolved into a new kind of animal suited for breathtaking travel in the steep heights." In his dreams as in his waking life, he is becoming a new man.

Earlier, in a high meadow, he had fugitive glimpses of a boy whom he comes to believe is his dead son. He finds that in certain conditions of light he can see and sense miraculous things, hints of the world beyond. Again he dreams of climbing in the pure world of ice and reaches the summit of the Schreuderspitze. Meanwhile, down below, he has packed up his gear, readying himself to return to Munich without having attempted a physical ascent. In a final dream he finds himself again at the summit in a mighty storm. He sees that the mountain is far higher than he thought: "The Alps were to it not even foothills." He has a mystic vision of the world, with Munich at its center, "shining and pulsing like a living thing." He longs for the city now, and returns to it ready to resume his work, having "found freedom from grief in the great and heart-swelling sight he had seen from the summit" of the Schreuderspitze. He realizes that soon enough he will be reunited with his wife and son in the world of light.

Themes and Meanings

"The Schreuderspitze" is a quest story: the story of a man, wounded by the loss of his loved ones, who undertakes a physical and spiritual journey and returns triumphant, born anew. The weasel-like photographer, Franzen, who appears in the opening section, ironically is blind to everything except the requirements of commerce, and this tunnel vision enables him to get ahead in the world. Wallich, on the other hand, is less successful materially precisely because he has an eye for beauty, for the rich and grand possibilities depicted in fairy tales. It is this vision which saves him in his hour of need. It drives him up into the mountains where he can be alone and discover the meaning of life and death. The Schreuderspitze, as he prepares to climb it, has a perilous beauty for him, for, as the story makes clear, to attempt a physical ascent would be to die, despite all his valiant preparations. Yet, having lost his wife and son, he is more than half in love with death.

He is saved finally by his openness to the world of human life: the Beethoven symphonies to which he listens, the family on the platform. Thus, he is able to climb to the summit, the world of ice and pure radiant light, in his dreams (as a result of his arduous preparations), yet he is anchored to the world as a mountaineer is anchored by his ropes and pitons. The journey is circular, as it must be. Franzen, who stands for all who neither think nor see, will never understand him. Yet Wallich, an unassuming, not very successful little man to those who know him in Munich, is a true hero. Having stood at the border, seen the light, come so close to being reunited with his wife and son, he yet returns willingly to "struggle at his craft." In that he is most heroic of all.

Style and Technique

"The Schreuderspitze" is not realistic, in the sense of depicting ordinary events in the waking lives of ordinary people, nor is it intended to be. Rather, it is a fable whose purpose is to compel belief in, or at least open the reader's mind to, extraordinary spiritual phenomena. A fable is not limited in subject matter as a realistic story is; it can contain, as this one does, the stuff of dreams. Much is customarily taken for granted. Here, for example, there is no close-up psychological examination of Wallich's grief; it is simply a given. The fabulist has two methods of persuading the reader to believe in the strange events he depicts. One is the copious use of highly specific detail; the other, the use of a calm, authoritative, rather formal and distanced narrative voice.

The use of specific detail, while important throughout, is especially noteworthy in Mark Helprin's descriptions of Wallich's climbing dreams: "Anchoring two pitons into the rock as solidly as he could, he clipped an oval carabiner on the bottom piton, put a safety line on the top one, and lowered himself about sixty feet down the two ropes." This kind of sentence is common, and it serves an important thematic function. To the reader, as to Wallich himself, the ascent is absolutely real, even though Wallich never climbs the mountain in body. Thus, by the end, the distinction between spiritual and bodily ascent becomes insignificant. Wallich has climbed the Schreuderspitze in the only sense that matters.

The voice must be established at the beginning, as it is here, so that the reader will at once be inclined to trust the author and listen openly to whatever he has to say. "In Munich are many men who look like weasels," the first sentence of the story, is on the face of it a very odd statement. Yet Helprin goes on to expand on it—the possible causes of such a phenomenon—as if it were a simple matter of fact, readily verifiable. For the purposes of the story it becomes true, then, just as it is true later on that Wallich runs for four hours nightly through knee-deep snow (a feat beyond the strength of a world-class athlete), that high in the Alps he receives clear signals from a Berlin radio station, or (more crucially) that he has elaborate dreams which he remembers in perfect detail. There is no question of deceit between author and reader; the reader simply agrees to believe in order to be led, finally, to a profound and liberating idea about the nature of human life.

Edwin Moses

THE SCULPTOR'S FUNERAL

Author: Willa Cather (1873-1947)
Type of plot: Satire
Time of plot: Late nineteenth century
Locale: Sand City, a small Kansas town
First published: 1905

Principal characters:
HARVEY MERRICK, a sculptor
JIM LAIRD, a local lawyer
PHILIP PHELPS, a local banker
HENRY STEAVENS, one of the sculptor's pupils
ANNIE MERRICK, the sculptor's mother

The Story

Harvey Merrick, a distinguished sculptor, has died of tuberculosis at the age of forty. As the story opens, a group of townsfolk waits for the arrival of the night train that is bringing Merrick's body back from the East for burial in the small Kansas town where he grew up. The conversation among those waiting reveals the small-mindedness of their assessment of Merrick. When the train pulls in, Jim Laird, a local lawyer, drunk as usual but seemingly the only person who has a real purpose in being at the station, leads the group of waiting men to the express car. There they find Henry Steavens, a young apprentice of Merrick, who has traveled from the East with the coffin. Steavens, who worshiped his master, is stunned by the apparent lack of any connection or similarity between Merrick and the men who have come to collect the body. He watches them gaze with curiosity but without comprehension at the palm that lies across the coffin lid, a symbol of Merrick's distinction as an artist.

When the coffin reaches Merrick's home, his mother rushes out into the yard, screaming for her dead son. Steavens tries to see some evidence of kinship between her and his idol, but he is appalled by her look of violence and fierce passion, as well as by the power she wields over everyone around her. Steavens is equally appalled by the cheap vulgarity of taste which is everywhere apparent in the decor of the house and can scarcely believe that Merrick could ever have had any connection with this place. Despite her show of pious grief and decorous behavior, Mrs. Merrick stages a horrifying tantrum when her servant makes a small mistake, and it is evident that only this same servant, along with Mrs. Merrick's weak, worn-out husband, actually feels any sorrow for the dead man. Steavens' distress at the abysmal family situation finds an echo in the expression he sees on the dead sculptor's face, which looks "as though he were still guarding something precious and holy, which might even yet be wrested from him."

Steavens begins for the first time to see the full significance of Merrick's achievement. The sculptor's accomplishments now take on a near-miraculous aspect, especially when seen against the background of his dreadful family and the physically difficult and culturally impoverished life of this small frontier town. Steavens also begins to understand the connection between the tragedy of Merrick's personal life (that is, the sculptor's deep introversion and reluctance to be involved in personal relationships), and his past life as a boy in Sand City.

Steavens joins the group of watchers in the dining room, who are as dreadful a collection of small-town types as can ever have been gathered together into one room. Everything they say reveals their pettiness and sordid materialism. The banker Phelps, representative of the mean-spirited callousness of all the watchers, discusses usury law with another banker. To these men, Merrick was a failure, and they dismiss him contemptuously for his lack of material success, his straining of the family resources for the purpose of financing his education, his inability to deal with the practical aspects of farm life, and his effeminacy.

Just as Steavens is wondering how much more he can take, Jim Laird bursts into the room. Despite the fact that he is a drunkard, Laird is a strong and intelligent man, as well as a shrewd lawyer, and Steavens has already recognized the fact that he is the only person in Sand City who has any understanding or appreciation for Harvey Merrick. Laird launches into a bitter tirade against those assembled in the dining room and everything for which they stand. In this climactic moment of the story, Laird reveals his own stature as a human being as well as the vision of greatness which he and Merrick shared as young men. Merrick was able to achieve his vision, it is implied, only because he never returned to Sand City. Laird, on the other hand, who did return, found that the town did not want great men but only "successful rascals," which is what he became. Laird confesses that he had felt shamed at times by Merrick's success, but at other times proud that Merrick, at least, had escaped. The next day, Laird is too drunk to attend the funeral, and, in a final moment of irony, Cather relates that he died the following year of a cold he caught in the Colorado mountains. One of Phelps's sons had been involved in criminal activity, and Laird had gone out to defend him, thereby upholding to the end his image of himself as a successful rascal. In what has clearly been his finest hour, Laird defends his old friend Harvey Merrick from the vicious attacks of Phelps and the others, but it is too late for him to salvage any kind of meaningful life for himself. Merrick's death, on the other hand, although it has tragically cut short a life of great achievement and promise, affirms the values for which that life stood, despite the failure of the people of Sand City to understand or cherish those values.

Themes and Meanings

Many of Cather's early stories probe in a highly self-conscious manner the relationship between the artist and society. Despite her own statement that the world was tired of stories about artists, Cather returned to the subject over and over again, indicating clearly her passionate concern with it. In "The Sculptor's Funeral," the clash of values between Harvey Merrick, the artist figure, and the inhabitants of the frontier town to which he returns only in death, is absolute. Only by escaping to the East, representative of older, more civilized traditions and values, has Merrick been able to achieve artistic fulfillment, and even then the fulfillment is premised on a total sacrifice of self.

For Cather, the artist represents everything that is beautiful and noble in terms of human endeavor, and yet artistic achievement is seldom acknowledged or even recognized by ordinary people. In the case of Harvey Merrick, the ultimate irony lies in the failure of the artist's own family and fellow citizens to understand the value of his art. Life is too harsh and demanding in the primitive conditions engendered by pioneer society, to support anything except a crass materialism which blights any appreciation for the creative spirit. Although Cather came to believe later that she had been overly harsh in her condemnation of western society in this story, the intensity of her commitment to art and her desire to defend its value against the encroachment of vulgar materialism remained with her during her entire life.

Style and Technique

The deliberate choice of rendering the events of the story through the point of view of Steavens, Harvey Merrick's young apprentice, strongly colors the reader's response to those events. An unworldly young man whose chief characteristic is his admiration for the dead sculptor, Steavens looks on Merrick's family and the inhabitants of Sand City with such horror and scorn that they take on the aspects of caricature at times. There is no indication that Cather does not share the views of Steavens, but she does complicate matters with her portrayal of Jim Laird, who is by far the most interesting character in the story. The biting and to some degree simplistic satire on small-town life, the descriptive style which verges at times on the naturalistic, despite Cather's avowed distaste for this term, are qualified by the figure of Laird. Laird's physical appearance (he is large, redheaded, bearded) and vitality make a strong impression, and in one scene, in which he opens with one blow of his fist a window that Steavens has been unable to move, there is a suggestion that this strength is not simply physical. The speech he makes in response to the petty criticisms the townsfolk have leveled at Merrick, is a set piece which rather too clearly expresses the views of Willa Cather herself. Yet it is also a moving testimony to what remains noble and visionary in Laird. He is a lost soul, one who sees the truth but has not been able to follow it himself. Cather clearly intends the reader to view him sympathetically. The beauty of the prairie landscape, along with Cather's portrayal of Jim Laird, suggests the possibility of a less monolithic vision of pioneer life than the story, for the most part, offers, and one that would shape Cather's later work.

Anne Thompson Lee

SEATON'S AUNT

Author: Walter de la Mare (1873-1956)
Type of plot: Domestic realism and horror
Time of plot: c. 1890 and c. 1900
Locale: Gummidge's preparatory boys' school in rural England, London, and
Seaton's country home
First published: 1923

> *Principal characters:*
> WITHERS, the narrator, a British schoolboy of about twelve,
> later a young man
> ARTHUR SEATON, his schoolmate
> SEATON'S AUNT, actually his half-aunt and guardian
> ALICE OUTRAM, later Seaton's fiancée

The Story

Withers, the story's narrator and central consciousness, is first aware of
Seaton as an unpopular schoolfellow at Gummidge's. Seaton has money, but
he is unattractive and unskillful at games, and he is often the butt of practical
jokes. Nevertheless, he manages to persuade Withers to spend the half-term
holiday with him at his aunt's.

When they arrive, Seaton dawdles rather than entering the house directly,
acting as if vaguely afraid of something. Finally they approach the house to
find his aunt watching them ominously from an upper window as if brooding
over them. When she meets them she mispronounces Withers' name but
overwhelms him with attention, in marked contrast to her disdainful treatment of Seaton, of whom she says, "Dust we are, and dust we shall become."
She presides over a lavish and sumptuous lunch, which she attacks with
gusto, while Seaton merely nibbles. Taking Withers to a neatly appointed
bedroom, she speaks slightingly of her nephew.

That afternoon, during which she pointedly ignores the boys, Seaton confesses uneasily that she sees and knows everything—that she is "in league
with the devil." He adds that she is not his real aunt, that the estate is actually his. At tea she mocks him again, referring to him as "that creature."
Later she deliberately prolongs a chess match with Withers, carefully avoiding mate while praising his play, and sweeping the board clear so that play
cannot be resumed. She seems to be toying with him.

That night Seaton awakens Withers shortly after they retire. He hints that
the house is full of ghosts, all at his aunt's command. He suggests further that
his aunt was responsible for his mother's death and that she has the power to
suck souls dry. He fears she intends that fate for him. Suddenly he freezes;
he has sensed her eavesdropping at the door.

Believing that Seaton is simply trying to scare him, Withers bets that the aunt is still in bed. Seaton takes up the challenge, and the two set off. Noises in the house seem to reinforce Seaton's fears of ghosts, and when they reach the bedroom, after passing a labyrinth of shadowy corridors, the bed is empty. Worse, they hear her coming. They hide in a cupboard; through a crack they watch her enter. After what seems hours they manage to sneak out, but Seaton seems drained by the experience. Withers helps him back to his dingy, littered, uncomfortable bedroom, then hides underneath the bedcovers. The following morning, Withers finds it easy to believe that Seaton's aunt knows every word and movement that occurred.

On their return to school, Withers drops Seaton, who shortly thereafter leaves. Their next encounter takes place by chance several years later in London; Seaton announces that he has come to town to buy an engagement ring. He admits that he and his aunt have lost much money and that she has aged. He also implies that Withers continues to discount their boyhood experience and invites him to come down to meet his fiancée and confirm his earlier impressions. Withers reluctantly agrees.

Shortly afterward, Withers returns to find the place considerably run down. When pressed, Seaton states that he finds the deterioration fitting: Man brings ruin in his wake. Withers rejects this philosophy. The two lunch, then play a desultory chess match, interrupted by the arrival of Alice Outram, Seaton's fiancée. The couple spend the rest of the afternoon discussing their future, but without animation, as if they sense futility in the face of an unseen destructive force.

They join Seaton's aunt for dinner; she seems older, but more massive and powerful than before. The meal itself is stupendous, though poor; her appetite remains voracious. She manages the table conversation brilliantly but directs implicit sarcasm at Seaton. Among other topics, she singles out marriage as a refuge for fools and evolution as a reservoir of degeneration, and she hints darkly at the "spiritual agencies" to which the truly superior have access. The two ladies withdraw.

Seaton confides that he fears leaving Alice alone with his aunt. When Withers attempts to downplay these fears by suggesting that the old lady's spite proceeds from feeling neglected, Seaton insists there are unseen forces and that his aunt makes use of them to gain control over others, fattening herself on their souls. When they rejoin the ladies, his aunt asks the betrothed couple to promenade in the moonlit garden while she plays the piano for Withers. Her playing is diabolic: First she inverts and parodies the romantic sentiments of the *Moonlight Sonata*, then transforms the simple hymn "A Few More Years Shall Roll" into a commentary on the bitterness and squalor of life. When she finishes, she speaks briefly on the beauty of darkness: "dark hair, dark eyes, dark cloud, dark night, dark vision, dark death, dark grave, dark DARK!" She suggests that she will not be lonely after Seaton's marriage because she will have her memories for company, and she hints at her awareness of everything said and done in the garden during her playing. Withers invites Seaton to join him in town before the wedding.

Yet Withers loses touch with Seaton. That autumn, realizing that he must have missed the marriage, he rushes off to make amends. Once there, he finds himself reluctant to enter the house. The housekeeper tries to fend him off but finally admits him. Seaton's aunt seems to have faded in the interim. She tells him that Alice has gone to Yorkshire, and she is evasive about Seaton. She accuses her nephew of having spread lies about her; when Withers asks directly where he is, she stares him down, mumbles incoherently, and leaves.

Withers remains alone until it is dark. Finally resolving to depart, he finds his way to the front hall, where he makes out Seaton's aunt peering down from the landing. She calls for Arthur; then, recognizing Withers, says that he is disgusting and orders him out.

He runs from the house, not stopping until he reaches the village. There he asks the butcher if Mr. Seaton still lives with his aunt. The butcher's wife replies that he has been dead and buried these three months, just before he was to be married. Withers is stunned; finding no course of action, he leaves with the reflection that Seaton "had never been much better than 'buried' in my mind."

Themes and Meanings

Though ostensibly a subdued horror story of the vampire or diabolic possession variety, "Seaton's Aunt" is in many respects rather an inversion of the narrative of coming of age—a failed rite of passage. To that extent it traces the life of one who does not pass through boyhood through adolescence to maturity, and it focuses on some of the fears and perils of that passage.

At the beginning of the story, Seaton is the prototypical "odd boy," inexpert at all the skills that constitute social acceptance in boyhood. He is not good at games, does not mix well with others, and depends on his extra money to buy companionship. As Withers gets to know him better, he discovers further disadvantages. Seaton's parents are dead; his guardian aunt is unsympathetic at best; finally, as the reader learns at the outset, he has to leave school in semidisgrace. His very beginnings are clouded.

Further shadows appear in the peculiarities of his relations with his aunt. It is not only that she continually denigrates him—though that is significant, for nothing can grow if it is routinely stifled—but also that she is hostile to life in ways both real and symbolic. She takes delight in humiliating others, in strenuously asserting her own superiority; she toys with others, letting them live only because her own life is drawn out of theirs. She is more than the older generation suppressing the younger; she is the bloated ego glorying in the failure of others, the cannibal feeding on the young, in the process destroying life itself.

In this way she becomes the embodiment of many standard adolescent fears. She is the evil stepmother, who succeeds first in depriving Seaton of his childhood, then of his estate, then of his fiancée, and finally of his life. She controls evil forces, robbing others of their souls. In the end she becomes the spider to which Seaton has likened her, surrounded only by the desiccated husks of those upon whom she has preyed and dismissing Withers (note the name) as a "dreadful creature" because she has no power over him.

Style and Technique

De la Mare diffuses the real horrors of this rather horrible story by his choice of point of view and by a deliberate use of parellelism. Withers is presented as the commonplace "regular guy," both at school and in early manhood; thus he is both significantly different from Seaton and enough like him to sympathize distantly with his distress. From the beginning he sees Seaton as a failure, in the way that boys rate their schoolfellows as if gauging their chances of surviving adolescence. By all the signs, Seaton will not make it, and that causes Withers some discomfort. Yet he cannot identify with Seaton, in the way of friends—Seaton is at first too unprepossessing, later too "sensitive," or "imaginative," or simply embarrassing, for that.

In this way, Withers—and the reader—are spared the full horror of Seaton's fate. He tells the story as if he were relating the curious story of someone else, of one of the others, those who are not quite like us. By the end, he comes close to accepting what happened as something predestined for those like Seaton—but not for him and, by inference, not for the reader. Thus he does not finally assent to Seaton's version of the events, with its overtones of evil spirits, diabolic possession, and occult influences; he remains free to believe that Seaton's aunt is merely conventionally rather than unconventionally evil—the parent who blights the child by indifference and hostility, the egotistical bully, rather than the demon who sucks souls. He leaves with the safe observation that Seaton had been buried all of his life.

James L. Livingston

THE SECRET INTEGRATION

Author: Thomas Pynchon (1937-   )
Type of plot: Psychosocial commentary
Time of plot: The early 1960's
Locale: Mingeborough, Massachusetts, in the Berkshires
First published: 1964

> *Principal characters:*
> GROVER SNODD, a "boy genius"
> TIM SANTORA, his friend
> ETIENNE CHERDLU, another friend
> HOGAN SLOTHROP, a nine-year-old reformed alcoholic
> CARL BARRINGTON, their black friend
> MR. MCAFEE, a black musician

The Story

"The Secret Integration" takes place among a group of children living in Mingeborough, a small but growing Berkshire community. Led by Grover Snodd, "a boy genius with flaws," the group includes Tim Santora; Hogan Slothrop, at nine already a reformed alcoholic and a member of Alcoholics Anonymous (AA); Etienne Cherdlu, a notorious practical joker; and Carl Barrington, a child in a black family which has recently moved to town. In addition to dabbling with Grover's experiments and listening to the radio that he has built, the children spend time exploring the abandoned Gilded Age mansions around the town and working on "Operation Spartacus," the annual dry run for a projected anarchistic uprising.

The children of Berkshire find their projects disturbed, though, by two events. One, which takes place a year before the second, occurs when Hogan is called by AA to sit with Mr. McAfee, a black musician passing through town. Although Mr. McAfee recognizes that Hogan has been sent as a joke by white men who do not want to help a black man, the boy and his friends do their best. They sit through the night with the musician, listening to his anecdotes and trying to reach his girlfriend on the telephone. Eventually, though, the police come and take McAfee away. The children never learn what has happened to him, but they retaliate by staging a raid on the local train at night, using green lights and masks and costumes to scare the passengers.

The second event has been caused by the arrival in town of the Barringtons, Carl's parents. The white adults in town are fiercely opposed to any integration in their community, and Tim catches his mother making an anonymous threatening call to the black couple. The children are confused by these events and make vague plans to help the Barringtons, but their projects are cut short. Finding garbage dumped all over the Barringtons' lawn, the boys recognize trash from their own houses, and the Barringtons angrily send them away when they offer to help.

As the group walks home from this disturbing event, Carl offers to "lay low" for a while, and the other children agree that he should leave. It is only then that the reader discovers that Carl is not real, but is, rather, an imaginary friend whom these young people can no longer support. Tim, Grover, and Etienne then all head to the comfort of their homes and families and "dreams that could never again be entirely safe."

Themes and Meanings

This story is overtly concerned with racism in American life, not only in itself but also as an example of how a society's dominant mores and ideologies seek to reproduce themselves in succeeding generations. The children of "The Secret Integration" are innocent in that they lack an understanding of the terms and behavior of the adult world. They recognize, though, that forces are at work that seek to modify and control their behavior and way of thinking. They know that something is being plotted against them at PTA meetings and dispatch Hogan to infiltrate the adult group (although he is thrown out). Grover keeps coming across Tom Swift books, which he is convinced are planted to indoctrinate him with a notion of how boy geniuses are supposed to behave and with the racism which Tom manifests in the book.

It is this threat from the adult world that has led the boys to create "Operation Spartacus," inspired by the Kirk Douglas film about an uprising of Roman gladiators. Although it is Grover who conceives of this "conspiracy," the others share his motivations: They find the adult world threatening in its blandness, conformity, and lack of purpose or surprise. The old Gilded Age estates are contrasted with a new housing development called "Northumberland Estates" which lacks not only the grandeur of the old mansions but also the hiding places and mysteries that surround them. The adults seem content to stay within their houses, sitting in front of their television sets, all tuned to the same channel despite the vague discontent about their lives and jobs that Grover senses.

Racism is seen as one more example of the blandness of white adult life, which seems opposed to any form of color; when Tim asks his father if they can have a color television, he is told that "black and white is good enough." The Barringtons represent the kind of difference and surprise that the town of Mingeborough seems determined to eradicate. Tim thinks of the imaginary Carl "as not only 'colored' himself, but somehow more deeply involved with *all* color." Racism, then, is portrayed as not merely an aberration within American culture but as a symptom of a larger malaise.

The children in the story represent hope for the future, but that hope has definite limits. First, the children are, after all, children, and they are limited in the scope of their knowledge. Tim does not understand the word "nigger," and Grover admits that the only integration of which he has ever heard is the mathematical term. More important, when these children have to choose between Carl and their families, between their vague vision of a better society and the safety and comforts of the present order, the families win. Still, with "dreams that could never again be safe," there is at least the hint that these children may remember some of what they have believed and learned.

Style and Technique

The great technical strength of "The Secret Integration" lies in the story's seeming simplicity. Although the characters of these children and their friends are sketched out in engaging detail, they lack the self-seriousness and artificiality of the characters in most of Pynchon's early works. While clearly unusual by the standards of realistic fiction, they are still recognizable in behavior and thought as children and as individuals, plotting conspiracies at one moment and splashing in puddles the next.

Similarly, Pynchon's setting comes alive through his detailed descriptions of the landscape and its past. Combining aspects of his own Long Island home and the Berkshires as described in a regional guide put out in the 1930's, Pynchon gives a tangible presence to the story's surroundings. The descriptions of Tim riding a bicycle down a hill, of Mr. McAfee's hotel room, and of a lavish party hosted a century before in one of the mansions portend Pynchon's startling re-creation of World War II London in his 1973 novel *Gravity's Rainbow*. (The town of Mingeborough reappears in that book as well, as the boyhood home of the novel's main character, Tyrone Slothrop, who is the uncle of Hogan Slothrop in "The Secret Integration.")

As in much of his other fiction, Pynchon makes use of technology and science to provide images and metaphors. Here again, though, he does so more subtly than in such earlier works as "Entropy." The major metaphor in "The Secret Integration" is the term as it is understood by Grover, from mathematics. Drawing a graph for Tim, Grover sketches out a y-axis, an x-axis, and a curve and explains integration as theoretically infinite segments of x which are drawn vertically on the graph. Although they look like the bars on a jail cell, Grover explains that they never fill in completely solidly, so that if someone "could make himself any size he wanted to be, he could always make himself skinny enough to get free."

Although integration is the mathematical opposite of differentiation, it is clear that racial integration is an admission and acceptance of difference. The mathematical model, though, also seems to suggest that no matter how much a society tries to impose its hegemony on individuals, there is always the possibility of escape, of getting out from behind the bars. It is that possibility with which Pynchon leaves the reader as the children return to the safety of their homes, which will not be as safe for them again as they once were.

Donald F. Larsson

THE SECRET LIFE OF WALTER MITTY

Author: James Thurber (1894-1961)
Type of plot: Comic psychological realism
Time of plot: The late 1930's
Locale: Waterbury, Connecticut
First published: 1939

> *Principal characters:*
> WALTER MITTY, the protagonist, a middle-aged, henpecked
>   husband who is unhappy with his life
> MRS. MITTY, Walter Mitty's assertive and domineering
>   middle-aged wife

The Story

Although Walter Mitty's daydream life has much exciting action, his waking life, as recounted in the story, is routine, uneventful, and, at a deep subconscious level, unsatisfying. In his waking life, Mitty motors on a wintry day with his wife into Waterbury for the regular weekly trip to shop and for Mrs. Mitty's visit to the beauty parlor. After dropping his wife off at the salon, Mitty drives around aimlessly for a brief time, then parks the car in a parking lot, purchases some overshoes at a shoe store, with some difficulty remembers to buy puppy biscuit, and goes to the hotel lobby where he always meets his wife. After a short time Mrs. Mitty appears, complaining to Mitty about the difficulty of finding him in the large chair where he has "hidden" himself, and then for a "minute" (actually much longer) leaves Mitty standing in front of a nearby drugstore while she goes to accomplish something she forgot. Interspersed with these events are Mitty's five daydreams or fantasies, which not only are induced by the events of his waking life but also affect them.

Themes and Meanings

James Thurber's expression through his characterization of the protagonist of the ineptitude, oppression, and disappointment nearly all human beings at some time feel in their lives in the real world (particularly in middle age) is so universally applicable that the name "Walter Mitty" has been canonized as an official term in the English language denoting these ideas by inclusion in the *Webster's Third New International Dictionary* (1971) and *Webster's Ninth New Collegiate Dictionary* (1984).

The story's four main themes are the contrast between a human being's hopes for life and its actuality, the power of the mind or imagination, the conflict between the individual and authority, and the ascendancy of technology and materialism in the twentieth century.

These themes are conveyed through the deflating disparity between

Mitty's heroic ability and stature in his five daydreams and his hesitancy, servility, and ineptitude in real life. Mitty's first fantasy of captaining a hydroplane in a terrible ice storm is shot down, so to speak, by his domineering wife, who says that Mitty is driving the car too fast on the icy highway into town. Mitty's second fantasy, of being a published, world-renowned medical specialist and surgeon, is punctured by having been evoked by a double subordination, to his wife and to the family doctor; in subconscious reaction to his wife's patronizing attitude in her response to his highway driving—"It's one of your days. I wish you'd let Dr. Renshaw look you over"—the daydreaming Mitty becomes a medical authority, a commanding figure to whom Dr. Renshaw, in the fantasy, is obsequious. In his third daydream, Mitty, the defendant in a murder trial, is yet in control in the courtroom, bravely exploding his attorney's alibi that Mitty's right arm was in a sling the night of the murder (Mitty boldly announces his expert ambidextrous marksmanship) and with youthful virility adroitly punching the chin of the district attorney, who has physically accosted Mitty's beautiful young beloved on her headlong rush to join Mitty on the witness stand. The immediately preceding scene, however, which stimulates the daydream, shows Mitty as manually incompetent (unable to park his car properly or remove tire chains), helplessly subordinate to both the parking attendant and the garage mechanic who removes the tire chains, and dimly and unhappily aware of being middle-aged in contrast to the cocky youths taking charge of his automobile. To the more subtle domination of his wife's making him wait in the hotel lobby, Mitty's subconscious counters with the fourth fantasy of being a forceful, dauntless, and insouciant World War I British aviator. Finally, to the minor humiliations of being disregarded by his wife and told like a child to wait in front of the drugstore, his imagination replies with the last fantasy of Mitty's being the victim of a firing squad, physically under some restraint but still in control of the situation by his proud and disdainful bearing.

Beyond Mitty's subconscious search in his daydreams for power, freedom, and authority in his relations with people is a quest for mastery over technology, one of Thurber's perceptively prophetic themes in this 1939 story. In all daydreams except the last, Mitty can expertly manipulate some technological instrument, whose complexity is usually emphasized in the description of it: the hydroplane with its "row of complicated dials," the "huge, complicated" anaesthetizer with its "row of glistening dials," any firearm (and especially the Webley-Vickers 50.80), and the two-man bomber, which "Captain" Mitty can heroically pilot alone. A motif of the same sound emitted by the various machines in each of the fantasies, "pocketa-pocketa," emphasizes their technological presence. Mitty seeks power and control over technology in daydreams because he is subject to it and to its controllers in real life, as exemplified by his various difficulties with his automobile. Even the more primitive technological device of the hotel's revolving door seems in conspiracy to mock or subordinate him, for as he leaves, it makes a "faintly derisive whistling sound." Besides its onomatopoeic aptness in conveying the sound of machinery, the "pocketa" motif may also suggest Mitty's feeling of confinement or restraint by technology, of enclosure as if in a pocket.

Mitty's feeling of oppressive enclosure in his life is expressed by the buildings of Waterbury "rising up" and "surrounding him" after his third fantasy, and the sergeant's remark "the box barrage is closing in" in the fourth fantasy as well as Mitty's echo, "things close in," when rudely jolted awake by his wife in the hotel lobby. The prevalent references to flying in his fantasies are not accidental, for they reflect Mitty's desires for escape and freedom; the magazine that he casually scans in the hotel lobby, which is the immediate cause of his fourth fantasy, has the appropriate title *Liberty*. In one sense, the overall pattern of Mitty's five fantasies is unhappy, since their trend is toward an increasingly certain death of the fantasy protagonist, which suggests that Mitty's hope and the reader's for him are waning. Near the story's conclusion, Mitty's wife, who perhaps could aid him, does not. In response to an unexpected though oblique assertiveness from her husband, she continues in her failure to achieve sympathetic understanding of what ails her spouse. Instead, she remains aligned with the oppressive forces of technology and materialism, failing to sense that her husband is not suffering from a physical or material ailment, and so does not need to see Dr. Renshaw or to have his temperature taken, her materialistic solutions proposed at the story's beginning and ending. Rather, with some pathos, Mitty remains alone, awaiting his daydream firing squad; he is "inscrutable," because no one around him recognizes his inner frustration and pain. Yet his daydreams, paradoxically, do allow a measured triumph as well. In a sense he is a limited victor in his fantasies, but a victor, even in the last, which recalls a similar idea in Thurber's fable "The Moth and the Star"—that triumphs of the imagination have their own compelling reality.

Style and Technique

One admirable component of the story is Thurber's keenly observed, often ironic, small detail of human action that reveals personality. Almost imperceptible is the detail of Mitty racing the car motor when told by his wife that he needs overshoes because he is no longer a young man—a response which suggests Mitty's furtive defiance. Another such detail is Mitty's reaction to a police officer's curt command "Pick it up, brother" at a traffic signal that has changed. Mitty first put on his gloves in the car as ordered by his wife, took them off when she was out of sight, but now puts them back on, suggesting that he equates the traffic officer with his wife as an authority figure, to whom he has been guiltily disobedient in the matter of his gloves. Though merely ordered to move on now that the traffic signal has turned green, Mitty (whose last name recalls the sort of gloves imposed on children) acts to rectify all misbehaviors. Mitty's subdued rebellion is also glimpsed in carrying his new overshoes out of the store in the box rather than wearing them, for which his wife later scolds him. Still another unobtrusive detail is Mitty's going not to the first A & P grocery store available but to a smaller one farther up the street in his quest of puppy biscuit (a particularly unheroic task). Earlier, Mitty was embarrassed by a woman's laughter at his isolated utterance "puppy biscuit" on the street and thus wants to gain as much distance as possible from the site of his shame.

The story, as might be expected from one of America's premier humorists, is constantly amusing. Mitty continually misapplies melodramatic film clichés (from war films, courtroom dramas, and the like) in his fantasies, creating, for example, a comically exaggerated Englishman whose understatement in response to an explosive demolition of the room in which he is standing, "a bit of a near thing," is enjoyably ludicrous, as is the British "Captain" Mitty's attempt at carefree profundity: "We only live once . . . or do we?" Other amusing touches include the hydroplane commander's full-dress uniform in the midst of a storm and his nonsensical orders about a turret, Mitty's made-up medical jargon for his hospital fantasy, and marksman Mitty's incredibly exaggerated claim of how far he can accurately shoot (with any firearm) and mention of an impossible caliber.

Yet the comic exaggeration—Mitty's fixing a complex machine with a fountain pen, being the only one on the East Coast who can make the repair, or having as his patient not only a millionaire banker (a point needlessly repeated in the fantasy except as a bolster to Mitty's ego) but a personal friend of President Roosevelt—like the other elements of humor in the story, has a serious point. At heart, all human beings need respect, dignity, and freedom. Walter Mitty is a comic Everyman.

Norman Prinsky

THE SECRET SHARER

Author: Joseph Conrad (Józef Teodor Konrad Korzeniowski, 1857-1924)
Type of plot: Adventure
Time of plot: 1880
Locale: The Gulf of Siam
First published: 1912

> *Principal characters:*
> THE CAPTAIN, the narrator and protagonist, a young man in command of his first ship
> THE CHIEF MATE, an elderly, simple man
> THE SECOND MATE, a slothful, insolent young man
> LEGGATT, the first mate of the *Sephora*, a neighboring ship, who has committed a murder
> ARCHBOLD, the captain of the *Sephora*, an obstinate man who always goes by the rules

The Story

As the story opens, the young protagonist, having suddenly been given his first command of a ship, feels a stranger to the ship, to the crew, and to himself. Untested by the rigors and responsibilities of command, he wonders to himself "how far I should turn out faithful to that ideal conception of one's own personality every man sets up for himself secretly." He has not long to learn, for no sooner does he assume his duties as captain than he spies, one night while on watch, a young swimmer hanging onto the ship's rope ladder. He hauls the swimmer on board, only to learn that the young man is Leggatt, the former first mate of the *Sephora*, who has escaped after killing a sailor in an angry outburst at the sailor's ineptitude. His rescuer feels an immediate affinity with Leggatt, so much so that he hides him in his own cabin, at great personal risk. During his infrequent, whispered conversations with Leggatt, he learns that they both come from similar homes, have been graduated from the same naval school, and share the same values and outlook on life. Often the captain feels so great a kinship with his stowaway that he believes that they are doubles or even two halves of the same person.

In the second half of the story, the captain's complicity in Leggatt's escape deepens when the captain of the *Sephora* visits him to question him about the escaped man. In response to these questions, the young captain goes to great lengths to protect, hide, and lie about Leggatt. All this while, his officers and men are becoming distrustful of his odd, erratic, and agitated behavior, while Leggatt remains remarkably cool and self-possessed.

Finally, Leggatt suggests a plan to the young captain: He asks the captain to drop him off in the dead of night on one of the small nearby islands. The captain does so, at great risk to his ship and crew. This expedition is so hazardous that the ship nearly founders on the land. Desperately seeking an object by which to steer the ship, he spots in the water a white hat, the very hat he had given his secret visitor to protect him from the elements in his place of refuge. Satisfied that Leggatt has escaped and sure of his bearings, the captain successfully guides the ship away from land, certain of his ability to make the lonely decisions and to fulfill the individual responsibilities of command. He is satisfied as well that he has helped Leggatt to make a free decision about his own fate.

Themes and Meanings

This story, like many of Conrad's tales, subjects a young, untested man to the rigors and responsibilities of leadership. Through a crisis, which tests him to the limit, he learns who he is and what he is capable of doing. Some men, such as Jim in *Lord Jim* (1900), fail this test, despite great promise and public favor. Others, such as the young captain of "The Secret Sharer," arouse the suspicion and criticism of others, yet, by taking full responsibility for their actions, they rise to the demands of their office and prove themselves fit adversaries of the sea, which relentlessly waits to claim them.

What distinguishes the young captain from Jim is his ability to recognize and accept the darker possibilities within his own soul, possibilities which he embraces in his admission of kinship with Leggatt. He understands that he, like Leggatt, is capable of murder. Were he in similar circumstances to those Leggatt described, burdened with a good-for-nothing sailor, hampering him from performing the one action that could save the ship in a gale, he too might have killed the man.

Recognizing as well that the murderer must be punished, he knows that he would demand, like Leggatt, to find punishment at the hands of his peer or peers—not a land-bound jury of tradesmen but a wellborn sailor like himself, who shares his background, education, and values. Thus, the captain willingly risks his ship and his men, in a questionable series of actions, in order to offer Leggatt the punishment of exile rather than of hanging. The captain has earned the right to make this difficult decision through full acceptance of responsibility for it: He thus claims for himself the unique privileges as well as the great burdens of command.

The tale celebrates the coming of age of a young man at his first command. It also tacitly posits an aristocratic code of behavior for the young captain, which repudiates the apparent democratic brotherhood of all naval officers. The tale maintains that the greatest commanders must be judged by different standards than those used for other officers, that such leaders are entitled to take greater risks because they are able to make finer choices.

Style and Technique

This story shows Conrad's finest use of the doppelgänger, or double, a symbolic figure who serves to show the true character of the protagonist by exhibiting the darker, more unsavory sides of his nature. Thus, Leggatt, who shares the middle-class background, naval training, morals, and assumptions of the young captain, forces the captain to admit that he, too, is a potential murderer and therefore less than the perfect hero that he originally hoped to be. In other words, Leggatt and the captain are alter egos, dark and light sides of the one self. In fact, the impression that the two of them together form a single complete person, both good and evil, is reinforced by the fact that only one of them has a name.

Conrad's style is also very rich in pictorial description. He masterfully uses setting to suggest the possibilities and meanings of human action: Thus, the water, like the green young captain, at the beginning of the story is remarkably calm. Similarly, the life-threatening gale during which Leggatt commits the murder suggests the psychological and moral turbulence of that episode in his life.

In addition, Conrad's narration emphasizes the larger moral and social issues which give dimension to what otherwise would be merely a fine tale of adventure and suspense. Accordingly, as the protagonist is assured of Leggatt's successful escape, he expresses satisfaction that "the secret sharer of my cabin and of my thoughts, as though he were my second self, had lowered himself into the water to take his punishment: a free man, a proud swimmer striking out for a new destiny."

Finally, Conrad suggests to the reader the magnitude and the justice of the young captain's decision by having him narrate this tale of his youth at a much later period of his life. Thus, his story gains distance and dimension.

Carola M. Kaplan

SEE THE MOON?

Author: Donald Barthelme (1931-   )
Type of plot: Antistory
Time of plot: c. 1965
Locale: The narrator's house
First published: 1966

> *Principal characters:*
> THE UNNAMED NARRATOR, an eccentric intellectual
> SYLVIA, his first wife
> ANN, his current wife
> GREGORY, his seventeen-year-old son

The Story

The form of this story is that of a monologue in which the speaker's perceptions and revelations are the primary content. The speaker, or narrator, would seem to be confiding his deepest apprehensions and ambitions, along with much of his life history to an interlocutor of some sort, a visitor or friend, or perhaps even a psychiatrist, since the narrator's personality is, to say the least, odd. He claims to be conducting "very important lunar hostility studies," although his methods "may seem a touch light-minded. Have to do chiefly with folded paper airplanes." Indeed, he confesses to "a frightful illness of the mind, light-mindedness" while at another point he asserts that he is nevertheless "riotous with mental health."

To a literal-minded reader, the narrator may seem simply to be insane. In the world of this story, however, conventional standards of neither sanity nor fictional form have much relevance. The narrator's obsession with the moon and its possible negative influence implies inevitably the origins of the word "lunatic." The implication is more than likely ironic and intentional on the author's part, for if the narrator is a "lunatic," he is certainly a brilliant one whose provocative observations cannot be dismissed merely as the product of a deranged mind.

During the course of the disjointed, meandering narration, a coherent autobiography emerges, fragment by fragment. The narrator was in the late 1940's a very promising student at an unnamed university on the Gulf Coast. He was drafted into the United States Army upon graduation, however, and sent to Korea. Upon his return to civilian life, he was hired by his alma mater as an assistant to its president with the primary responsibility of writing "poppycock, sometimes cockypap" for the president's speeches. He married Sylvia, and they had a son, Gregory. Within a few years he became disillusioned with his work at the university; rearing a child proved to be a further stress; he resigned from his job, and his marriage ended in divorce.

At the time of the story, Gregory is a freshman at Massachusetts Institute of Technology (M.I.T.) Obsessed by his own quest for selfhood, Gregory makes frequent, unexpected telephone calls to his father with questions out of the blue such as "Why did I have to take those little pills?" or "What did my great-grandfather do?" The narrator has meanwhile remarried in middle age, and his current wife, Ann, is pregnant with a child whom they call Gog—a name whose apocalyptic associations seem, in this instance, bizarrely incongruous.

Although it is hard to say what the narrator at this point actually does for a living, a bohemian life-style is rather obviously implied. An eccentric freelancer, he devotes his "moonstruck" brilliance to various "little projects" such as the aforementioned lunar hostility studies and the equally eccentric pursuit of "cardinalogy"—a taxonomical study of cardinals of the Catholic Church, "about whom science knows nothing."

In the concluding section of the story, the narrator addresses his monologue to his unborn child. It appears now that the story also represents the father's concern for (and need to justify himself to) his offspring—as he says, "You see, Gog of mine, Gog o' my heart, I'm just trying to give you a little briefing here. I don't want you unpleasantly surprised. . . ." Thus, to help forestall "unpleasant surprises" in life for his new child, he has presented the truth (whatever that is) of the world as he knows it: the report of a traveler to someone beginning the journey. Beyond human understanding, though, there are realms of terror and fascination that no "reports of travelers" can describe. In the narrator's mind, the bright, austere face of the moon is equated with the threat and the allure of the unknown mysteries of life; in the climactic next-to-last line of the story, he voices the resolve to protect his child by making "sure no harsh moonlight falls on his new soft head."

Themes and Meanings

The narrator's autobiographical revelations bear a strong resemblance to the author's own life. Like his protagonist, Barthelme was a brilliant student at a Gulf Coast university (the University of Houston) in the late 1940's and early 1950's, was drafted and served in Korea, returned to civilian life as a writer and editor for his alma mater, and by the early 1960's had moved to New York, staking his career on his unconventional, radically creative intellect and imagination. Given this sort of clear authorial presence in the story, as well as the quirky incisiveness of the narrator's commentary, the reader may reasonably enough identify the narrator with the author. Yet it is probably more accurate to think of the narrator as a persona, or character mask, through which the author speaks (and thus the "you" to whom the narrative is addressed is also the reader in addition to some hypothetical listener within the story). The effect of montage, or overlapped planes of meaning, is central to Barthelme's method and outlook. Nothing is ever quite literally itself in a Barthelme story, because, for the author, fact and illusion, appearance and reality are not absolute, mutually exclusive categories. Truth, if it can be known at all, must be approached obliquely through satire, irony, and ambiguity. Thus, the author leads the reader, like Alice through the looking glass, into a strange world of whacky events and imaginings, non sequiturs, and unsettling parody of contemporary society.

The thematically most significant aspect of the story lies in its application to America's quest to reach the moon in the 1960's. Published in 1966, on the eve of the Apollo program, which led to the lunar landings three years later, the story raises fundamental questions about the nature of this quest—the motives involved; the unforeseen dangers and consequences to human society; the mythic dimension of the whole enterprise. Such concerns tend to be obscured within the community of technical expertise because of its preoccupation with method and quantitative judgment—not the "why" of things, but the "how." In this story, Gregory (the promising M.I.T. student) clearly is identified with this community. Yet his competence in arcane subjects such as "electron-spin-resonance spectroscopy" is ironically undercut by the naïveté and urgency of his personal quest for self-knowledge. The narrator, in contrast, knows that all mortals are fallible; that the truth is never quite as clearcut as the scientific approach assumes; and that even the current technological quest for the moon is really an aspect of mankind's age-old fascination with the heavens. Thus, his "moonstruck" obsession with the moon may be more "sane" than is the scientist's linear, one-dimensional understanding of this momentous undertaking.

Style and Technique

A key to Barthelme's fictional approach lies in a statement that occurs twice in this story: "Fragments are the only forms I trust." If the term "montage" applies to Barthelme's overlapping planes of narrative perspective, then "collage" aptly describes the effect of his narrative style. His stories generally, and this one most assuredly, seem assembled from a jumble of unrelated materials: pedantic literary allusions, current events, scraps of scientific jargon, profound philosophical issues, trendy pop culture. Moreover, the tone of his writing oscillates freely from hysterically comic to sad, from whimsical to deadpan earnest.

Thus, to take but one significant example, the narrator calls his unborn child "Gog," using the name of the biblical monster and legendary English giant in a humorously ironic way. The sound of the name in turn prompts an allusion to the old sentimental tune "Peg o' My Heart." The parents' apprehensions about the impact the child will have on their lives leads to an extended, metaphorical comparison of the child to a battleship. Finally, the narrator's hopes for a bright, intelligent child who will mature into wisdom leads to a reference to Pallas Athena, the Greek goddess of wisdom, who according to myth leaped fully armed from her father Zeus's head ("in another month Gog leaps fully armed from the womb").

The zany collage style of the story reflects Barthelme's postmodernist sensibility. Like so many contemporary artists, Barthelme seeks to create a coherent vision of life yet profoundly mistrusts the conventional techniques of "serious" art. Thus, his kaleidoscopic manipulations of thought and language are central to his artistic purposes: Only by such unconventional means can a valid image of life in the contemporary world be presented. The narrator, in justifying his self-revelations, also would seem to be speaking for the author when he says, "It's my hope that these . . . souvenirs . . . will someday merge, blur—cohere is the word, maybe—into something meaningful."

Charles Duncan

A SHAPE OF LIGHT

Author: William Goyen (1915-1983)
Type of plot: Mythopoeia
Time of plot: Long ago and many years later
Locale: There, in a Southern town, and here, in a city
First published: 1952

> *Principal characters:*
> BONEY BENSON, a seeker after the mysterious shape of light
> ALLIE BENSON, his forsaken wife
> THE NARRATOR, a later seeker, and a shaper of the record of
> Boney's quest
> YOU, a counterpart of the narrator, "kite-maker and kite-
> flyer," to whom part of the story is addressed

The Story

Boney Benson, a man obsessed with a singular quest, lived in a town where it was his job to flag the midnight trains with a red lantern. Wizened, scary, almost ghostlike in appearance, but gentle, he awakened the imagination of the town. The people would whisper his story, passing down what they knew to the younger generation. Some said he spent his days in the graveyard, sprawled on the earth over the place where Allie, his wife, and their unborn child lay buried. It was said that the baby murdered Allie, that in the last month of her pregnancy the child had risen in her body until it lodged beneath her heart and nested there, a kind of vampire, until Allie could not breathe. Allie died in terror, fighting for air without knowing what was strangling her. It might have been her husband, for all she knew, for he often left her without warning, to pursue "a lighted shape, much like a scrap of light rising like a ghost from the ground." They might be sitting at the supper table when the powerful urge to follow the light would strike him, and then he would rise, go saddle his purple horse, King, and be off, to wander over the countryside all night long, until, at daybreak, the light vanished into the ground.

In a fit of conscience, Boney turned against himself and mutilated his body; he buried his severed member in the grave with his wife and child. It was said that the child was born in the grave and lived underground, like a mole, but rose each night in the shape of a ball of light. Mexicans who lived at the edge of the graveyard first saw the specter. Fishermen and campers also reported an eerie shape of floating light. When Boney heard about the haunting, he attempted to seal the light in the dirt with a slab of slate, holding it down with the weight of his body. Finding it impossible to contain the light, he began to wait in the graveyard each night, mounted on King, for the light to rise. Then he followed it wherever it led. Three young men, who went with Boney on one of his nightly journeys, reported having followed the shape of light to a field of grave-children, and beyond, through a phantasmagoric landscape riddled with nursing mothers, martyrs, hermits, "wings and limbs of a lost son falling from the sky," and lovers mating like strange insects. They followed Boney, who followed his light, into another country, where the wearied young men turned back, and Boney died. He was returned home and buried alongside Allie, but the destructive-creative light continued to rise for someone to give his life over to following it.

This skeleton of Boney Benson's tale can be pieced together from the two sections of "A Shape of Light": "The Record" and "The Message." Yet to exhume a plot from Goyen's poetic narrative hardly conveys the archetypal force of the story or its haunting effect. At the heart of "The Message," in a city, long after the life and death of Boney, his image surfaces from the past, through the retelling and fabulation of his tale, to claim the imagination of a "kite-maker and kite-flyer," addressed only as "you." This character replaces the narrator of "The Record" and seems at times to be both author and reader, or a figure for a type of messenger-message relationship, like that of writer and story. Boney appears, "his face, swimming and dipping and bowing and rising and darting, looking down at you . . . his kite face . . . *send up a message!* You had built kite and kite had taken his message and delivered it. Now you must shape him, like kite, and send his message back to him." This writer's story attempts to give shape to something essentially inexpressible through the quest of Boney Benson and the appearance of the light. It seems to have been written, in part, to exorcise ghosts of memory which would overshadow the artist if the story could not be told. Not only the kite-maker but also the kite itself, the artist must look down and confront his mooring, the power holding the string, which is his own past: "You turned and called out, man now and no longer child, speaker now and no longer listener, asking man's question, crying man's cry. . . . Now Boney Benson was all your question and all your pain; and tell it." Out of grief and guilt, out of what has been forever lost to memory, out of the failure of language to communicate, the messenger must find the perfect vehicle for his message. The obsession of the kite-maker to shape a story out of the wreckage of memory and words parallels the seeker after the light who must surrender himself and live separate from the world in order to fulfill his quest.

Themes and Meanings

This complex story traces the ancient pattern of the journey in parallel narratives, one about the seeker, Boney Benson, and another interwoven narrative about the process of discovering truth through fiction-shaping. Partially, it is a traditional coming-of-age story, for the shift from listener to teller completes the artist's passage into manhood, and in the writing of the story he is able to shed the ghosts of his memory which threaten to strangle his power of expression. The figure of Boney, whose very name holds a foreboding of mortality, and the shape of light he must follow against reason reveal the story's true message.

Boney has been touched, poisoned, or made crazy by the light. Once he is converted to the light he no longer belongs to the world. He lives apart from the rest of the town. As a "follower" of the light, he must abandon everything else and look to the light alone for meaning in his life.

> He had to give himself wholly, unafraid, surrendered to it. He had to leave things behind . . . and this was his life, bearing, suffering the found-out meaning of what he was involved in, haunted by it, grieved by it, but possessing it— and watching it continue to grow, on and on, into deeper and larger meaning.

The Christian parallels both in pattern and in language are so strong that they become the real center of the story. In this light, the initiation pattern is subsumed into the conversion experience.

Just as there is no reasonable explanation for the events of Boney's life, there is no proof of God or of Jesus' life and Resurrection, except through faith. Jesus said, "I am the light of the world. Whoever follows me will never walk in darkness, but will have the light of life" (1 John 8:12). Boney's dedication to the light seems to predicate a post-Pentacostal world, when the Holy Ghost, set loose in the world as guide and comforter, has taken the place of Jesus the man and teacher, and conversion must be wholly a matter of faith in the unseen.

Another name for Jesus, found in the beginning of the Gospel of John, is the Word, the incarnate Word of God. It is these dual aspects of God, light and word, that Goyen's story about dual quests attempts to express, always aware in the telling of what words can never say. In the face of the inexplicable and inexpressible, words are ever more precious to bridge the dark silence between humankind and Creator.

The image of the kite-message, with its crossed sticks stretched over with fragile paper, becomes an emblem for Jesus. In the same way that this kite enables the artist to find his voice, the mystery aglow in the world illuminates the smallest details of "the frail eternal life of the ground." Some of Goyen's most impressive writing goes into descriptions of this natural wonderland, which needs only to be apprehended to be celebrated. Once illumined, one is made aware of the world's intimate beauty of design, evidenced in living forms, and once one has seen, one must tell it. Like Boney, who still sees and must follow the light where it leads, even after blinding himself to escape it, the converted will never be free of the force of that illumination. Yet they, like the artist, do not wish to be apart from what defines them, even though they can never really be part of the world in the same way again.

Style and Technique

Goyen's distinctive style permeates any other investigation into his fiction, be it for character, for plot, or for theme. The surface of his language is inescapable, seeming to envelop the reader in a lyrical web which can best be approached as a kind of spoken music, a cadenced, colloquial music put down in words from deep attention to the rhythms and repetitions of a regional, yet interior, voice. Goyen's voice, a blend of Texan and Mexican and rural tongues, touched by the King James Bible and the Romance languages, cannot be located in the mapped world; his language charts its own place, becomes a world at times so heady that a single sentence tumbles through so many transfigurations of simile that anyone in search of a regular story would feel lost and perhaps even fatigued by the force and passion in the prose.

As in much of Goyen's fiction, someone in "A Shape of Light" struggles to listen, to comprehend, and then to set down for others a story essentially too complicated to be told. Much of the experience that seems worthy of being passed on is noncorporal, or spiritual, in nature and therefore doomed to find only partial expression in language. The effect of this visible effort is nearly magical; the complexity of overlapping texts, of records and messages, retellers and relisteners, brings to light what cannot otherwise be spoken. To simplify stylistically would be a lie in the face of the mystery. In this way, Goyen's voice embodies both a fictional territory all his own and a very intense struggle to make lasting shapes, to "tell it" against the destructive intrusions of time and death.

Cathryn Hankla

THE SHERIFF'S CHILDREN

Author: Charles Waddell Chesnutt (1858-1932)
Type of plot: Social realism
Time of plot: Late nineteenth century
Locale: A county seat in rural North Carolina
First published: 1899

> *Principal characters:*
> COLONEL CAMPBELL, the protagonist, a county sheriff
> POLLY CAMPBELL, his daughter
> TOM, his illegitimate mulatto son

The Story

An unfamiliar event, the murder of an old Civil War veteran, has roused a placid North Carolina village. Within twenty-four hours, the sheriff and his posse have captured a suspect, a young mulatto, who is unknown to any of them. Disappointed that the preliminary hearing will not take place for another week, a crowd gathers around a whisky jug and plans to lynch the suspect, but Sheriff Campbell, an educated and socially prominent man, is tipped off and proceeds to hold the mob at bay.

After their initial retreat, the sheriff takes up a position in the prisoner's cell as the best position for keeping an eye on them. He removes the handcuffs and fetters from his prisoner to give the man a chance in case his protector is killed, although he feels nothing but "contempt and loathing" for the suspect. When a gunshot from nearby woods whistles through the window and distracts the sheriff, the prisoner seizes a revolver that the lawman, armed with a shotgun, has left on a nearby bench. As the sheriff lays aside his shotgun, the prisoner, regarded as too cowardly and lacking in initiative to pose a threat, takes the sheriff prisoner.

Although he insists that he did not kill the old war veteran but merely stole a coat from him, the young man knows that he has no better chance with a jury than with the mob, and so he forces the sheriff to unlock the cell and front doors and prepares to kill him. When the sheriff exclaims, "You would not kill the man to whom you owe your own life," the prisoner informs him that he has spoken more truth than he realizes, for the young man is the sheriff's own son Tom by one of his slaves from prewar days. Campbell sold the mother and son south to a rice plantation in Alabama. "You gave me a white man's spirit, and you made me a slave, and crushed it out," his son censures him.

He promises not to kill his father if the latter will promise to delay attempts to recapture him until the following morning; when the sheriff hesitates, Tom raises his arm to fire only to have the weapon shot out of his hand by Polly, the sheriff's daughter, who has silently entered the jail during the confrontation. The sheriff binds the wound, tells his son that he will have the doctor attend him more thoroughly in the morning, locks him back up, and goes home to examine his conscience. Rejecting the idea of allowing Tom to escape as incompatible with his duty, he decides to devote all of his energies to securing an acquittal. Upon his return to the jail in the morning, he discovers that Tom has torn the bandage off his wound and bled to death during the night.

Themes and Meanings

In some ways, Chesnutt's fiction anticipates that of William Faulkner and other later Southern writers. He immediately establishes the pervasiveness of the Civil War even among Southerners who lived far from the principal action. In a simpler way than Faulkner, he presents the evil that continues to flow from slavery and particularly from miscegenation under the slave system. Furthermore, Chesnutt depicts the conflict between educated but guilt-ridden Southern leaders and a citizenship generally marked by ignorance and insensitivity to the claims of the law.

Yet, Chesnutt's purposes in this and other stories of "the color line" are quite different from Faulkner's. As a black who had grown to manhood and trained for the law during Reconstruction, Chesnutt felt keenly the failure of that program and the blighting of the hopes of the immense majority of less fortunate blacks after the earlier promise of the Emancipation Proclamation. Tom is intelligent and well educated but has turned into a petty criminal facing the prospect of hanging for stealing a coat, and desperate enough to kill his father. His fate is not that of a typical freed plantation hand in a segregated society but that of a man who has no place in society, a man who has learned enough to interpret his situation and feel the full bitterness of unfulfilled human aspirations.

The author also wishes to explore the conscience of the ruling class. From the time he first appears in the story, the focus is on the sheriff. He represents statutory law in its conflict with lynch law; in addition, he must endure the inner conflict between the claims of duty and those of blood. Tom has brought forcibly back to him the fact that instead of freeing his son, as he might have done, he pursued the expedient course of selling him into the Deep South.

The sheriff is a fundamentally decent man, prejudiced but determined to carry out his duty at the risk not only of his popularity but also of his life. He hopes to establish his son's innocence of the murder charge and then find some way to atone for his past injustice, which he recognizes as a sin against his son, society, and God. Chesnutt leaves the reader to surmise the thoughts of Tom, who is unaware of his father's resolve and who would probably be unable to believe in it or in its efficacy even had he known. It is easy to see, however, that Tom reaches the very pit of despair before his death.

The author has created a vivid picture of a man's past moral failing return-ing to haunt his later life. Unless his resolution to make amends is itself his salvation, the evil he has done is irreversible. He, not the mindless, would-be lynchers, is the measure of justice available to black citizens in a society un-willing to take the risks involved in acknowledging its moral responsibility to secure the full liberty of its newly enfranchised citizens.

Style and Technique

Chesnutt aimed to counter the sentimental version of slavery so popular in fiction of the late nineteenth century. Sensing the unwillingness or inability of white America to come to terms either with the historical reality of slavery or with the failure of Reconstruction, he attempted to show the harsh reality of both pre– and post–Civil War society. His description of his mythical county has almost a documentary quality. His use of Sheriff Campbell as protagonist shows how easy it was for even a conscientious man to acknowledge his past irresponsibility. By depicting him as assuming an ingrained inferiority in his prisoner, Chesnutt exemplifies the attitude that institutionalized second-class citizenship for blacks from the late 1870's until long after the author's death.

The title of the story is clever. Although only one child is introduced early in "The Sheriff's Children," the author establishes that Sheriff Campbell had been one of the few people in the region to own numerous slaves before the war, and thereby hints at the significance of the title. The sheriff survives his ordeal because one of his children disarms the other. Chesnutt does not develop the character of the quietly resourceful daughter very amply, how-ever, and he does not permit her father to reveal to her the prisoner's iden-tity. Because of his decision to confine the moral conflict to the father, he establishes no relationship between the children.

The author reveals the sheriff's chief failing to be a lack of imagination. Unable to imagine a black fugitive enterprising and daring enough to appro-priate an unguarded revolver in the midst of the threat from the mob outside, he exposes himself to capture. The same lack of moral imagination creates the very possibility of such a predicament, for although his stated motives for selling Tom and his mother were a quarrel with her and temporary financial difficulties, a man such as Campbell would be more likely to anticipate embarrassment from a freed slave or a favored one on his own property than to expect any threat from a boy banished to a rice paddy. Once he deter-mines to make amends, he cannot grasp the state of mind of the recaptured son after all his hopes of escape have faded, and thus the son's act of self-destruction surprises him completely.

In arranging this ironic retribution on the father, Chesnutt did not provide Tom with a plausible motive for returning to his native region. The fact of the son developing into an articulate and thoughtful young man, while unlikely, has the virtue of illustrating the bitter truth that even a black man of considerable attainments might well wind up a vagabond and outlaw. Yet the author does not make clear why Tom, if he returned to make a claim on his father, would go elsewhere first and steal a coat. Unless Tom's motive was simple retaliation—and there is nothing in the story to suggest that it is—or moral suasion, it is difficult to see why he came back to North Carolina at all. The reader may also wonder why the author, having decided to give Tom's half-sister an important role, did not involve her in the horror of the family situation.

Despite these problems, the story holds the reader's interest with its frank portrayal of the conflict within the sheriff and its tense struggle of sheriff versus mob and sheriff versus prisoner. The author presents the sheriff in an evenhanded way and understands white society, even to its paradoxical tendency to choose the best person in it to lead and then to resist that leadership. He knows that the black man, on the other hand, remains a mystery to the best of white men in such a society; thus the reader sees Tom only as his father sees him. Nevertheless, the reader can sense the anguish in Tom. It is doubtful that any white writer in 1899 could have presented the struggle within a white father such as Sheriff Campbell and the embitterment of a black son such as Tom as powerfully as Chesnutt does in this story.

Robert P. Ellis

THE SHE-WOLF

Author: Giovanni Verga (1840-1922)
Type of plot: Italian verism
Time of plot: The late 1800's
Locale: A rural Sicilian community
First published: "La lupa," 1880 (English translation, 1896)

> *Principal characters:*
> GIUSEPPINA, the She-wolf and protagonist
> MARICCHIA (diminutive of Maria), her daughter
> NANNI, a young local man

The Story

The villagers have given Giuseppina the nickname "the She-wolf" "because she never had enough—of anything. The women made the sign of the Cross when they saw her pass," and even the parish priest lost his soul for her. Maricchia, her daughter, bemoans her own fate: No one would want the daughter of such a woman as his wife, even though her dowry and land-holdings are the match of any young woman in the town.

When Nanni, a young man of the village, returns from his compulsory military service, the She-wolf falls desperately in love with him. Much older than he, with the telltale pallor of malaria on her face, she nevertheless presents an imposing and handsome figure that belies her age, with piercing, black eyes and lips that devour men with their intense color. Her passion for Nanni, however, is thwarted. Nanni will have the daughter, not the mother, and so he tells her, directly and laughingly. A few months later, she offers Maricchia to him; the dowry is discussed, and the She-wolf tells him to come at Christmastime to arrange the marriage.

Maricchia is repelled at the sight of Nanni when she first sees him, oily and dirty after his labors, but her mother imperiously forces her to marry him, threatening to kill her if she does not. After some years have passed, Maricchia is occupied with her children, while the She-wolf, almost destroyed by her continuing passion for Nanni, seems to have lost her energy and will. Nanni, now quite satisfied with his life, laughs in her face when she looks at him, while Maricchia, who has grown to love her husband intensely, reviles her mother, "her eyes burning with tears and jealousy, like a young she-wolf herself." The She-wolf continues to visit Nanni in the fields. He chases her away again and again, yet, she returns, like an ill-treated dog, only to be chased away again. Finally, however, Nanni falls prey to the She-wolf. Maricchia senses what is happening, and even threatens to make her own humiliation public by reporting the situation to the police. This she does eventually, but the She-wolf refuses to give up the corner of the house that she has reserved for herself with the married couple.

A short time later, Nanni almost dies after being kicked in the chest by a mule. The parish priest refuses to give him the Final Sacraments unless the She-wolf leaves the house. He recovers, performs an act of public penance, and again begs the She-wolf to leave him alone, this time threatening to kill her if she comes to him again. "Kill me, then," she responds, "for it makes no difference to me; without you I have no desire to live." This chilling rejoinder immediately precedes the final paragraph, in which she does, indeed, seek out Nanni one final time as he is working the soil of a vineyard. As she approaches him, devouring him with her black eyes, a mass of red poppies in her hands, Nanni leaves off his work, picks up his ax and watches her draw nearer, cursing her soul in a stammering voice as the She-wolf comes toward him.

Themes and Meanings

The She-wolf is dominated by a single, overriding passion that ultimately destroys her and those closest to her, yet it is a passion that remains true to its own nature throughout, giving her an exalted role in what might otherwise be an undistinguished rustic domestic drama. Nanni stammers out his final curse; he is unable to cry out with the same strength of resolve that characterizes the sure, determined movement of the woman who faces him. Does he kill her? The author does not say, because ultimately it is not important. What is important is that the She-wolf has no power over the forces that have brought her to this point, nor can Nanni resist her. They are both victims of a tragedy that is played out over and over again in every age and in all socioeconomic circumstances. There are crucial differences, however, between the two: The She-wolf is as proud in her strength as she is unswerving in her purpose; Nanni's weakness is as inevitable and inexorable as is the She-wolf's obsession.

Adhering to the Verist canon of impersonality, Verga insisted that the work of art must rise spontaneously, naturally: It should appear "to have made itself," the hand of the author never seeming to interfere. It must be a human document, direct, unadorned, plunging directly into "the necessary development of passions and facts leading to the denouement, which is thus rendered less unforeseen, less dramatic, perhaps, but not less fatal." This briefest among Verga's greatest short stories gives full credence to his doctrine. This simple peasant woman, perhaps his finest creation, expresses both the power and the vital force of a cultural entity that had been denied a voice in Italian literature before the 1800's, before Verga. The She-wolf, transformed by her passion, establishes a terrible superiority of isolation over the common tenor of communal life that levitates against her. Its structures, its mores, and its punishments are fixed; thus, the outcome of the story will be fatal, whatever form that fatality may take. The She-wolf plays out her tragic drama in every gesture and every linear action which she initiates. She *is* the parched fields under a blazing summer sun, the desire of the new plant for life in a harsh terrain. Although she knows that she is a sinner and accepts her fate, she is, at the same time, an awesome, albeit oblique, example of integrity, of purity.

Deterministic in every detail, the story moves immediately to the level of the deepest implications of desire and despair, to those places in the heart where differences of class and status have no meaning. The violent truth of the She-wolf's tortured soul takes her beyond the specific Sicilian setting to achieve the stature of the Greek heroines who have reappeared in every succeeding epoch, beyond the consolations of religion, beyond plaint.

In the introduction to another story from the collection in which "The She-Wolf" first appeared, "Gramigna's Mistress," Verga asks the question: "Shall we ever reach such perfection in the study of passions that it will become useless to continue in this study of the inner man?" His answer is that of the artist who captures a reality and presents it in the form of a modern myth, remaining true to his theory of the human document, enhancing it with the subtlety of his art.

Style and Technique

Identifying as much as possible with his characters, Verga entered their world through the cadence of a language as closely mimetic of their speech as can be achieved without actually using Sicilian dialect. He explained the genesis and effectiveness of this technique following his chance discovery of a ship captain's log, written in the abrupt and truncated manner of one little practiced in the art of writing, with the day's events recorded and chronicled in a straightforward and rough-hewn language, asyntactic but effective—a language, in short, consonant with the individual's thoughts and ability to express those thoughts. As a logical extension of this pattern, dialogue predominates over description, and where description is necessary, it springs directly from the characters' perception, the narrator himself taking on the identity of a character in the story, an anonymous fellow villager. This identity is heightened, and the factual reality of the events underlined, through the specific use of proverbs or proverbial statements that recapitulate every pattern of behavior, every expression of feeling, in a traditional and formulaic saying. Only the She-wolf ventures out "in those hours between nones and vespers, when no good woman goes roving around. . . ." To express her feeling for Nanni, the She-wolf uses an old Sicilian simile: "It's you I want. You who are as beautiful as the sun, and sweet as honey." After Maricchia and Nanni are married and the She-wolf is sick with longing, "the people were saying that when the devil gets old, he becomes a hermit."

The brief descriptions focus on the inclement contrasts that dominate both the landscape and human passions. The cold winds of January are no harsher than the August sirocco, the thirsty and immense fields no more mournful than the howling dogs at night in the vast, dark countryside. Nor will the She-wolf sate her thirst while working next to Nanni in the fields, for she does not want to leave his side even for a minute.

There is no intervention on the part of the author. The narrator is part of a dialogue that involves the characters and the reader equally. At moments, this dialogue becomes an interior monologue, penetrating primitive needs and becoming the voice of a primordial world, conforming dramatically to the nature of that world.

I. T. Olken

SHOEMAKER ARNOLD

Author: Earl Lovelace (1935-   )
Type of plot: Social realism
Time of plot: A New Year's Eve in the 1950's
Locale: A rural village in Trinidad
First published: 1982

> *Principal characters:*
> ARNOLD, a fifty-year-old shop-owner
> NORBERT, a twenty-nine-year-old employee in Arnold's shop
> OLD MAN MOSES, a solitary charcoal burner
> BRITTO, the owner of a bar

The Story

The third-person omniscient narrator of this brief tale opens the story with a compressed exposition of Arnold's character and background. The shoemaker is a proud man, recognized by the villagers for his "undefeated stubbornness," his "unrelenting cantankerousness," and his "readiness for confrontation." No one contests his freely expressed opinions; he is master of his world, the shoemaker's shop. So difficult to live with is Arnold that, years before, his wife and three children "had moved not only out of his house but out of the village." Maintaining his solitary pride, Arnold refuses to accept even his own sexual needs, admiring but resisting village girls in a "testing relationship of antagonism and desire." Young men in the village fare no better; his apprentices never satisfy him, and they can seldom tolerate him long enough to learn the trade.

The village is shocked, then, when Arnold hires—and retains—Norbert, who is a drifter, drinker, and gambler. He disappears from the shop for weeks at a time, but Arnold always takes him back, albeit with a severe scolding. He steals money, providing his friends with free shoes and drinking sprees. In short, Norbert is "so indisputably in the wrong" that he is "exactly the sort of person that one did not expect Arnold to tolerate for more than five minutes." This puzzling about-face in Arnold's attitude leads the villagers to believe that Arnold wishes to demonstrate "one of his rare qualities, compassion." Whenever Arnold welcomes Norbert back to his shop, Arnold basks in a self-congratulatory "idea of his own goodness," feeling that no one in the world is "more generous a man than he."

Norbert, however, does have redeeming qualities beyond those of his zest for spontaneous revelry. He works hard when he works. Having left the shop for a piece of ice two weeks before Christmas, Norbert did not return for three weeks; yet on New Year's Eve, when others would not have bothered to return, Norbert is back and "working like a machine to get people's shoes ready." Arnold admires Norbert for being "faithful," for returning on "Old Year's Day" to finish repairs due before New Year's Day. He does not scold him, deciding that Norbert "shows appreciation" for him. Appreciation, Arnold thinks ironically, is all too rare an attribute among people.

As Arnold contemplates Norbert's appreciation while looking down the street from his shop's door, he sees Old Man Moses, the charcoal burner, dozing on a donkey cart with a small boy riding in back as it meanders up into the bush. Realizing that it will soon rain, Arnold complains to Norbert that Moses should not be getting soaked but should be feasting with his family for the New Year: "That is how we living. Like beast." Ignoring Arnold's outrage in his metaphor of people as orphans, Norbert responds only briefly, saying, "Maybe he want to go up in the bush" in order to protect his coals from burning down into powder; yet Arnold ignores the suggestion that Moses may be doing what he wants to do. As an analogue for Arnold and Norbert, Moses and the boy evoke Arnold's impulse to order the world around him; his own loneliness, his fear of solitary aging, and his foreboding "sense of the approaching new year hit him." He tells Norbert that "the world have to check up on itself," oblivious to the irony that he must examine his own life, and introduces the subject of Norbert's recent unexplained absence.

In the conversation that follows, Arnold's deep cynicism becomes apparent. He fears both a useless life and a living death, bemoaning his own drinking and justifying his habitual lecturing: "What else to do but drink and waste and die. That is why I talk." Norbert contributes only his blunt remark, "We dying," again and again, to Arnold's question, "You think we living?" When Arnold learns how much older he is than Norbert and considers Norbert's "condition," his despair that "life really mash you up" disturbs Norbert to the point that he reminds Arnold that they have three more pair of shoes to finish, Arnold having thrown down the pair which he was fixing. Arnold's genuine concern for Norbert—and for himself—is broken abruptly when two girls arrive to pick up Synto's shoes.

Arnold responds harshly to the girls as he demands that they enter the shop while waiting for him to finish. With Synto's niece is a girl "who reminded him of rain and moss and leaves." Distracted by her alluring presence and aware of his own gruff manner, Arnold asks, "You fraid me?" Hoping that he sounds tough, Arnold is not surprised when the girl confesses that she is afraid, "A little." Norbert is shocked at Arnold's next gesture: He offers her a chair, "dusting it too." A peaceful, calm ambience fills the shop as he repairs the shoes for the waiting girls. In further kindness, Arnold carefully wraps the shoes in a newspaper which he had been saving to read. When the girl thanks him as she is leaving, her voice "made something inside him ache"; she leaves behind the "breathlessness" of "the scent of moss and aloes and leaves" as "if all his work was finished." Then Arnold offers to buy Norbert "a nip," returning Norbert's earlier offer.

When Norbert returns with the rum, Arnold's usual tough mask of self-righteousness has fallen completely. His longing for intimacy, his desire for community, and his need for renewal have led him to comprehend "how he could leave everything just so and go" as Norbert had done. Arnold tells Norbert, "I dying too," admitting that perhaps he does frighten people.

When they close the shop that evening, Arnold and Norbert go to Britto's bar. There they share in the revelry with Britto, his family, and his friends. As Norbert sings along with the band's traditional songs, Arnold wishes "he could cry." Later, after singing, drinking, eating, and dancing, Norbert draws Arnold's attention as he opens another bottle of rum; hesitating before he drinks, Norbert looks at Arnold and says, "Let me dead." Arnold, thinking about the girl in the shop, believes that if she were "sitting there beside him he would be glad to dead too." Arnold, perhaps for the first time in his life, acknowledges the joy in living.

Themes and Meanings

Earl Lovelace offers in "Shoemaker Arnold" a character study in which personal identity is reconciled with the spirit of place, in the sense of both nature and culture. Arnold's consciously fashioned identity consists primarily of self-sufficient, tough masculinity. Seeking self-respect just to survive in a poverty-ridden rural village, Arnold has held the world at bay with his frightening mask, but he has done so at the cost of alienating much of the community, including his own family. His incessant talking achieves little authentic dialogue; consequently, the very expression in which genuine intimacy is grounded further isolates him: He has tolerated no voices other than his own. As the mask of self-sufficiency drops in order for Arnold to understand Norbert's spontaneity and as the mask of masculinity falls in order for him to show kindness to the girls, Arnold discovers his own neediness. With the masks removed, Arnold can then participate fully in the community's life and joy, which he does at Britto's celebration.

With Arnold's reconciliation of his own social needs also comes his acceptance of the consoling power of nature and sexuality. Although nature here is not transcendent, it does offer the renewal of rain and green leaves, metaphors for the regenerative power of the young girls as well as that of Norbert. Despite a fallen nature in the figure of Norbert and the fecund island world, the death present in this world is still capable of renewing life just as Norbert attempts to show Arnold that Moses' life, apparently beastly, may be a choice to tend his coal, heat for cooking and warmth out of dead trees. Arnold seems to fear weakness, aging, and death, but, in actuality, he fears the strength and youth of life itself. Ironically, when Britto greets him as a "man now," thinking that he acknowledges Arnold's tough image, he greets an Arnold who is discovering that masculinity consists of intimacy and compassion rather than unconscious fears.

Norbert's theft in generosities to friends, his penchant for leaving spontaneously with friends, his prodigal returns to the coarse Arnold, and his "appreciation" for Arnold all embody the "faith" of the people in one another. Even amid Norbert's awareness that "we are dying," he gives himself to a faith in the life of the community. It is this faith that Arnold embraces when he realizes that Norbert leaves work for "something deeper, a call," not merely "a good time." That faith is the freedom of spirit within both nature and culture: It is Arnold's salvation from the desperation of his loneliness and the alienation of his neediness.

Style and Technique

Lovelace's story succeeds in his capacity for compact but complex characterization. Arnold and Norbert come fully alive through descriptive exposition and dialect: They sound like a crusty, aging shoemaker and his carefree assistant. The dialogue is rapid; Arnold displays his propensity for outraged rambling, and Norbert delights in what he suspects may be a profound idea, that one must accept death in order to live completely. West Indian rural English echoes throughout sentence fragments without subjects and patois variants of subject-verb agreement. Even the closing sentences' use of the noun *dead* instead of the verb *die* (first in Norbert's final remark and again in the narrator's assumption of Arnold's sensibility) helps unify characterization with theme. As the narrative voice develops, the point of view and the use of dialect in the narration mingle increasingly with that of the characters' dialogue: A community of characters and narrator results, and the omniscience of the narrator is no longer detached but found now among the characters.

To further complicate the characterization, Lovelace reverses roles for Arnold and Norbert. This reversal occurs when Arnold's cynical despair causes him to throw down his shoes while Norbert works on, reminding him of the remaining repairs. The reversal unifies theme with character development; by exchanging their customary roles of diligence and indifference, Arnold and Norbert complement each other in a microcosm of community. When the girls enter, Arnold continues the reversal in his attention to them, enlarging the metaphor for the community to include an implicit sexual (hence, natural) basis. The reversal proceeds when Arnold buys the rum, and, by the time they reach Britto's celebration, both enter fully into that yet larger community, one founded on family and tradition. Subsequently, the reversal strengthens the renewal of both men, a renewal symbolized by New Year's Eve and the scent of aloes (a plant with healing properties). In the closing moment of the final scene, Arnold and Norbert stand out in relief, whole individuals yet intimate members of a vital community.

Michael Loudon

SHORT FRIDAY

Author: Isaac Bashevis Singer (1904-   )
Type of plot: Fable
Time of plot: Unspecified
Locale: The village of Lapschitz
First published: "Der Kurtser Fraytik," 1945 (English translation, 1964)

> *Principal characters:*
> SHMUL-LEIBELE, a simple but devout tailor
> SHOSHE, his pious wife

The Story

Shmul-Leibele is a simpleton, unsuccessful but honest in his trade. Although he is not scholarly, he is expert at following the basic tenets of his religion. His wife, Shoshe, is a meticulous homemaker and more competent in her trade than her husband in his. Together they create a life, a marriage, and a home devoted to the observance of Jewish ritual and customs.

The couple's commitment to making and keeping the Sabbath is unequivocal. A recognition of the day on which God rested after completing the Creation, the Sabbath represents the culmination of the devout couple's daily spiritual strivings. Shmul-Leibele ceases work at noon every Friday, takes a ritual bath, and aids in the temple's preparation for the Sabbath prayers. Shoshe purchases special foods to cook and prepares herself and her home in royal fashion. Both attempt to create an earthly paradise in which to experience, as best they can, the divine presence.

On one winter Friday, the shortest Friday of the year, the couple's preparatory rituals begin in customary manner, but the elements of nature effect change. A severe snowstorm hampers movement outside and makes it difficult to distinguish day from night. The rooster's morning crow is not heard and the couple arise late. Shmul-Leibele decides not to work his half-day, spending the day instead at the bathhouse and in study.

When he returns home, however, the candles that announce the Sabbath's official arrival are lit and the home, as usual, sparkles with a spiritual essence. Shoshe is dressed beautifully, adorned with her wedding necklace and a polished wedding band. Despite the physical manifestations of winter, to Shmul-Leibele the experience is particularly enchanting. He leaves for the synagogue, where his prayers seem assuredly to transcend his earthly lips and find an audience with God's ears.

After temple, Shmul-Leibele tries to hurry home to Shoshe, anxious that some ill may have befallen her. Instead, she greets him looking radiant; their home sparkles with a Sabbath glow and the scents from the Sabbath meal are alluring. Having fulfilled the ritual obligations to partake of their dinner, the couple intersperse their meal with Sabbath hymns, chants, and prayer. Finally, exhaustion overcomes Shmul-Leibele, who falls quickly asleep, with Shoshe following shortly thereafter.

Sometime later, Shmul-Leibele awakens, eager to satisfy his physical desires for his wife. After fulfilling the proper observations regarding marital sex (that his wife has attended the ritual bath signaling her preparedness for sexual relations; that he speak first of his love for her and his hope that their mating may produce an offspring), the couple consummates the sexual act. Despite Shoshe's warning that something may be burning in the oven and that the flue is closed, they fall immediately asleep.

Both awaken from dreams of death and burial. Shmul-Leibele believes he has had a terrible nightmare but alters his perceptions upon hearing that Shoshe has had the same experience. They realize that they cannot either move or hear sounds, and come to understand that they have died, perhaps by asphyxiation. First with a sense of alarm and then with pious acceptance, the couple prepares to greet the angel of God who will come to lead them into paradise.

Themes and Meanings

This is a story about a love and marriage, a life and death, enhanced and embraced by spirituality. Here the daily laws, rituals, and customs of Judaism provide two simple and ordinary people the opportunity to rise above the mundane trappings of the physical world and to sanctify their humble lives.

A portrait of simple but beautiful piety, "Short Friday" examines the role of faith and religion in one's life. All aspects of life are included: Shmul-Leibele and Shoshe apply their beliefs to their work, their marriage, their sexual relationship, and ultimately their death.

A slow and sloppy tailor, Shmul-Leibele uses only the strongest thread, the finest materials, and returns scraps to his clients. Shoshe not only keeps a proper home but also acquires additional money from outside sources. Having married each other for their serious and pious natures, the couple achieves a love so great that not even their inability to bear children (one of God's commandments) threatens their future together.

Shmul-Leibele remembers the Law even during moments of great passion for Shoshe. Aware that the sexual act is intended for procreation, he nevertheless permits himself to experience pleasure from caressing and exploring Shoshe's physical beauty. "The great saints also loved their wives," he maintains, planning to attend the ritual bath the following morning in recognition of any transgression. For Shoshe, Shmul-Leibele's praise of her worth each Sabbath is truly God's blessing: "Here am I, a simple woman, an orphan, and yet God has chosen to bless me with a devoted husband who praises me in the holy tongue."

As the couple allow no aspect of life to pass without an attempt to render it holy, so do they embrace their sudden death. Despite Shoshe's initial alarm and confusion ("We went to sleep hale and hearty. . . . We were still young people. . . . We arranged a proper Sabbath. . . ."), and encouraged by Shmul-Leibele's acceptance of their fate ("Yes, Shoshe, praised be the true Judge! We are in God's hands. . . ."), the couple recall their final act of devotion as they prepare to give accounts of themselves to the angel of God.

The contrasts and parallels between the physical and spiritual worlds dominate the story. An examination of the story's title itself suggests one such link: In the physical realm, it is on the shortest Friday of the year, when daylight fades rapidly, that the couple's life also ends. Concurrently, it is on their holiest day of the week, the Sabbath, which begins on Friday evening and ends the following night, that Shmul-Leibele and Shoshe are called upon to make a new beginning together.

This Friday is particularly dark, cold, and foreboding, whereas the Sabbath glow permeates the auras of Shmul-Leibele and his wife. In their home, the physical warmth from Shoshe's oven and the spiritual warmth of the Sabbath combine to bring a sense of beauty, calm, and peace to an otherwise harsh existence. Ironically, it is Shmul-Leibele's love of warmth that causes both his neglect of Shoshe's warning that there is food still in the oven and, finally, his death.

A story that seeks to define even its readers' faith, the appeal of "Short Friday" is the comprehension of universal themes linked by a common spiritual thread. One is encouraged to study and understand how to achieve meaning in life; how to approach death; how to prioritize opportunity and experience; how to create and recognize the spiritual dimensions of the physical world; how to consider religious teachings for a morally uplifting life.

Style and Technique

The style of "Short Friday" is that of the fable or folktale. The language is simple and direct; the natural and the supernatural (the couple's awareness after their death) are treated on the same plane.

A significant example of the story's fabulistic style is the use of foreshadowing to prepare for the couple's fate. On the Friday of their death, a portrait is painted of an exceptionally cold and bleak day in which darkness and daylight are indistinguishable. As the evening and the beginning of the Sabbath approach, the sky grows clear and a full moon arises. The author describes the scene:

> The stars on this Friday seemed larger and sharper, and through some miracle Lapschitz seemed to have blended with the sky. Shmul-Leibele's hut . . . now hung suspended in space, as it is written: "He suspendeth the earth on nothingness."

Clearly, this Friday is marked by divine intervention; the town and the heavens have merged and the couple's home is at the mercy of God. What is perhaps being suggested is that, ultimately, all return to God.

It is noted that Shmul-Leibele loves warmth, and for this he pays a dear price. In another allusion to fire, at the bathhouse Shmul-Leibele uses a willow broom against his skin "until his skin glowed red."

Premonitions of death and danger are present as well throughout the story within the context of the couple's marriage. After Sabbath services, Shmul-Leibele hastens home because he worries that Shoshe may be in trouble. The couple speak often of their fate should one die before the other. It is clearly a dreadful thought for Shmul-Leibele: "God forbid! I would simply perish from sorrow. They would bury us both on the same day." He need not have feared, for in death as in life they are united.

Shelly Usen

THE SHORT HAPPY LIFE OF FRANCIS MACOMBER

Author: Ernest Hemingway (1899-1961)
Type of plot: Adventure
Time of plot: The 1920's
Locale: Africa
First published: 1936

> *Principal characters:*
> FRANCIS MACOMBER, a wealthy American sportsman
> MARGOT MACOMBER, his beautiful wife
> ROBERT WILSON, a white hunter

The Story

While on safari in Africa with Robert Wilson, a professional hunter and guide, Francis Macomber shows cowardice in the face of a charging lion. The story opens at noon as Macomber, his wife, and Robert Wilson are having a drink before lunch. The atmosphere is tense, though Wilson and the native porters try to act as if everything were normal. Macomber is very upset because of his earlier behavior, while Margot, his wife, ranges in her reaction from tears to merciless criticism. As Macomber tries to apologize for his failure, Wilson becomes increasingly impatient, not so much because of the events of the morning but because Macomber insists on talking about them. The final insult to Wilson comes when Macomber asks for reassurance that he will not talk about the incident when they return to civilization. Just as he has decided to break any social contact with Macomber for the remainder of the safari, the latter apologizes in such forthright terms for not understanding the custom of not talking about failures that Wilson cannot simply dismiss him. As their conversation finishes, Wilson suggests that Macomber might make up his failure with the lion when they hunt buffalo the next morning.

That night, Macomber is haunted by memories of the lion hunt as he relives it in his mind. After having listened to the lion roar and cough all night, Macomber is unnerved the next morning, even before they start out for the hunt. Not knowing, as an old Somali proverb says, that "a brave man is always frightened" when he sees a lion's track, hears him roar, or confronts him, Macomber loses confidence in himself. When they go after the lion, Macomber is nervous to the point of being reluctant to leave the car in which they are traveling to take his shot. Ordered out by Wilson because it is unsporting to shoot from the vehicle, Macomber shoots badly, wounding the animal, which retreats into the bush.

Macomber does not want to pursue the lion into the dangerous bush, and even suggests that they simply leave him. Wilson, the professional, is shocked at this suggestion, but he does tell Macomber that he need not go in after the wounded animal if he does not wish to do so. Macomber, though frightened, does want to go, so together they enter the tall grass. Hearing them coming, the lion charges. "They had just moved into the grass when Macomber heard the blood-choked coughing grunt, and saw the swishing rush in the grass. The next thing he knew he was running; running wildly, in panic in the open, running toward the stream." Wilson kills the lion, and Macomber senses the contempt of the hunter and the native gun bearers. Most contemptuous is Margot Macomber, who witnessed the entire scene from her place in the car. As they await the gun bearers, who are skinning the lion, Macomber attempts to take her hand, but she draws it away. Then, "while they sat there his wife had reached forward and put her hand on Wilson's shoulder. He turned and she had leaned forward over the low seat and kissed him on the mouth."

Macomber believes that his wife is through with him, but in a short sketch of their marriage, Hemingway points out that these two are inextricably bonded. Macomber is so very wealthy that his wife will never leave him. Though she is still very beautiful, Margot "was not a great enough beauty any more . . . to be able to leave him and better herself and she knew it and he knew it." She knows that he is not successful with other women, so she does not worry about him leaving her either. "All in all they were known as a comparatively happily married couple, one of those whose disruption is often rumored but never occurs." On the night of the lion hunt, Macomber awakens and realizes that Margot has left their tent to sleep with Robert Wilson. He confronts her on her return, insisting that she had promised not to be unfaithful if they made this trip. She blames him, saying that he spoiled the trip by the lion episode.

After an awkward breakfast the following morning, they go in search of buffalo. Three bulls are discovered and chase is given in the car. As the buffalo are overtaken, Macomber seems to lose his fear. He shoots well and drops all three bulls with only minor help from Wilson. Yet as they are celebrating their luck, a gun bearer brings news that the first of the three bulls that they shot has got up and made its way into the bush. "Then it's going to be just like the lion," Margot says, but Wilson answers, "It's not going to be a damned bit like the lion." Macomber "expected the feeling he had had about the lion to come back but it did not. For the first time in his life he really felt wholly without fear." Macomber is transformed by this experience, and it is a different man who follows Wilson into the bush after the buffalo.

Macomber is eager to go in after the bull, even urging Wilson to action before he is ready. As they wait, Macomber tells Wilson, "You know, I don't think I'd ever be afraid of anything again," and proposes that they might go after another lion because, "after all, what can they do to you?"

"That's it," said Wilson, "Worst one can do is kill you. How does it go? Shakespeare. Damned good. See if I can remember. Oh, damned good. Used to quote it to myself at one time. Let's see. 'By my troth, I care not; a man can die but once; we owe God a death and let it go which way it will he that dies this year is quit for the next.' Damned fine, eh?"

He was very embarrassed, having brought out this thing he had lived by, but he had seen men come of age before and it always moved him. It was not a matter of their twenty-first birthday.

As Wilson and Macomber move into the bush, the bull charges. Macomber and Wilson both shoot, and Macomber can see fragments fly as his bullets bounce harmlessly on the boss of the large horns. He stands his ground in the face of the charge, calmly firing until "he felt a sudden white-hot, blinding flash explode inside his head and that was all he ever felt." Margot Macomber had shot at the buffalo to protect her husband, and the bullet had struck him in the head.

The ending of the story is only slightly ambiguous. Though Wilson reiterates several times that the shooting was accidental, the reader comes away with little doubt that Margot has shot her husband deliberately. "That was a pretty thing to do," he says to her, then adds, "he *would* have left you too." The story ends as Margot begs Wilson to stop his accusations.

Themes and Meanings

"The Short Happy Life of Francis Macomber" includes several of Hemingway's important themes and introduces characters typical of his work. This is a story of a man's coming of age, but it also presents something of Hemingway's attitude toward "the code" for which he is famous, his views on women, and the value he placed on the life of action. Each of the main characters can illustrate one of these themes.

Robert Wilson, the white hunter, is an archetypal Hemingway hero. He lives a life of action—a manly life—that is governed by a code that he never states, but which is his standard for judging his own as well as others' behavior. Sportsmanship, courage, and "grace under pressure" are the hallmarks of Wilson's behavior. His professionalism is more than simply an attitude; it is a philosophy that governs his life. To him, it is morally unthinkable that he might leave a dangerously wounded animal in the bush, talk about his clients behind their backs, or otherwise violate the unspoken contracts of his trade. His philosophy, however, is expressed in action, not words, and he is suspicious of those who, like Macomber, ruin an experience by too much talk. He respects men who, like himself, can face danger courageously, certain that death is less to be feared than a coward's life.

Francis Macomber is described as one of "the great American boy-men," the sort of men who are likely to remain immature throughout their lives. Untested under pressure, he "had probably been afraid all his life" until the buffalo hunt. In the buffalo hunt, things happen so fast that he does not have time for fear to manifest itself, and he is transformed by the event. As Wilson puts it, Macomber would "be a damn fire eater now. . . . More of a change than any loss of virginity. Fear gone like an operation. Something else grew in its place. Main thing a man had. Made him into a man. Women knew it too. No bloody fear." The title of the story refers to those few minutes between the time Macomber shoots the three buffalo and the moment Margot's bullet crashes into his brain when he does savor life fully as a man.

Margot Macomber is perhaps the least attractive of Hemingway's women characters, many of whom share characteristics with her. She is spoiled, selfish, domineering, and castrating on the one hand, insecure and frightened on the other. Such women are able to control weak men, as Macomber was at the beginning of the story, but cannot work their wiles on the strong. Wilson takes her casually in his tent partly because he shares her contempt for her husband. After Macomber's death, however, it is he who reminds her that she would have been left had she not killed him. The relationship between Macomber and Margot is based on their mutual weaknesses, and could not have survived his maturity. Knowing this, Margot kills him as a perverse act of self-preservation.

Style and Technique

Hemingway is the best-known stylist in modern American literature, and this story is an excellent example of his method. Understatement is the best term to characterize his writing. Using simple, declarative sentences, he avoids elaborate description, allowing exact physical details to suggest the settings, backgrounds, and implications of his stories. The reader is never told, for example, that Robert Wilson is British, but careful examination of his dialogue reveals his origins. Similarly, in the opening passages of the story, only the words "pretending that nothing had happened" alert the reader to anything out of the ordinary, yet by the time the reader learns that Macomber had been a coward, it comes as no surprise. Through slight intonations of dialogue and description, Hemingway has "shown" its effects before he "tells" about Macomber's failure.

Hemingway rarely uses symbols overtly, yet subtly they are embedded in the story. Wilson's admiration of the beasts he hunts, usually expressed in such terse lines as "damned fine lion" or "hell of a good bull," suggest that these animals embody the qualities that he, and Hemingway, admire most: courage, strength, honesty, and grace under pressure. Ritual is important, too, in Hemingway's work, and is most emphasized in the hunt itself, which brings out the best in man and animal. In other ways as well, small rituals bring order into the story and structure life into a meaningful whole.

Finally, attention should be paid to Wilson's speech when he says, "Doesn't do to talk too much about all this. Talk the whole thing away. No pleasure in anything if you mouth it up too much." Hemingway shares this basic distrust of language, especially abstract language, so he allows as nearly as possible the action of the story to speak for itself. In "The Short Happy Life of Francis Macomber," his technique succeeds in heightening the power of the story.

William E. Grant

THE SHOT

Author: Alexander Pushkin (1799-1837)
Type of plot: Sketch
Time of plot: c. 1815, c. 1821, and c. 1826
Locale: The fictitious villages of N—— and R—— in Russia
First published: "Vystrel," 1831 (English translation, 1875)

> *Principal characters:*
> IVAN PETROVICH BELKIN, the compiler
> LIEUTENANT-COLONEL I. L. P., the narrator
> SILVIO, a former officer in the Russian hussars
> R——, a lieutenant in the infantry
> COUNT B——, a former officer in the hussars
> MASHA, his wife

The Story

This double story-within-a-story is presented by Ivan Petrovich Belkin, a gregarious but even-tempered army officer who committed to paper much of what others had told him before his untimely death. The first of his tales, which was related to him by Lieutenant-Colonel I. L. P., takes place among the garrison stationed in the village of N——. At the outset, so the story goes, all present in the garrison are awed and mystified by one Silvio; generous without any thought of recompense, he has retired at an early age from the hussars and exists on an uncertain income. His skill at pistol shooting has taken on nearly legendary proportions. It is said that he can take a loaded pistol and shoot a fly dead from across a room. Already rumors are current that he is troubled by some past dueling incident.

More enigmatic is Silvio's curt dismissal of an episode which the others consider to be manifestly grounds for a duel. During a game of cards, another officer, Lieutenant R——, twice challenges Silvio's scorekeeping, and thus, his reckoning of the money stakes; after two silent rebuffs, he hurls a candlestick at their host. In a cold fury, Silvio demands that he leave. The others expect a formal test of honor and are greatly surprised when Silvio later accepts a slight apology.

One day Silvio receives a letter and immediately begins to pack his possessions. He holds a final dinner for the regiment, and afterward he requests the narrator to stay behind. Pallid, preoccupied, but with devilish coolness, Silvio remarks upon the general puzzlement when he did not duel with the unruly officer. Then he informs his guest that six years before, he had fought another hussar, who was also left alive. He shows the narrator a red cap from his previous regiment, with a bullet hole above the forehead.

Embarking on his story, Silvio recounts how he was stationed in a garrison town on the frontier; among his comrades he enjoyed an unrivaled reputation for gallantry, drinking capacity, and dueling skill. A newcomer to the regiment, Count B——, from a well-born family, outdid Silvio in cleverness and was more successful with the ladies. At a formal ball, Silvio sought out his rival and whispered an insult into his ear. When the count slapped his face, a duel was arranged for the following dawn. At the appointed place, his opponent, calmly eating cherries, put the first shot through Silvio's cap. Perturbed beyond measure by the other's nonchalant impudence, Silvio elected not to continue. He has now received an announcement of the other's betrothal to a young and beautiful lady in Moscow.

Following the telling of Silvio's story, five years pass. The narrator has moved to R——, another country village. A nobleman has purchased an estate in the area, and when the narrator comes calling, he is struck by the opulent furnishings. His attention is drawn to a painting of a Swiss scene, with two bullet holes in it right against each other. When the conversation turns to pistol shooting, the narrator lets slip Silvio's name; Count B——, for it is he, is thunderstruck. He completes the story of the interrupted duel. Quite unexpectedly, Silvio appeared at the estate, dusty from a long ride, and demanded of the count the shot he had not taken before. Then, unwilling to fire on an unarmed man, Silvio proposed that they draw lots; with a diabolical smile that the count shall never forget, he announced that, as before, his opponent had the first shot. Unnerved, the count sent his bullet into the picture. Silvio took aim just as Masha, the count's wife, entered the room. Wildly he proclaimed the entire confrontation a joke—just as the original duel and the count's errant shot had been in jest. Then, taking heed of the count's visible consternation, he paused for a moment and pronounced himself satisfied; he measurably struck fear into his adversary, and that will always remain on the count's conscience. As Masha fell into a faint, Silvio turned to go; then, at the doorway, he drew back his pistol and almost effortlessly sent a second bullet into the picture beside the first shot.

The narrator has also heard somewhere that, upon the outbreak of the Greek revolution, Silvio commanded a detachment of volunteers and was killed in action against Ottoman forces.

Themes and Meanings

The modern reader is at first taken aback at the melodramatic quality of this story; the narrative as it unfolds also seems to a great extent to depend upon coincidence. There is, however, a clear though indirectly stated thematic intent. Certain virtues of the military officer—stoicism, indifference to danger, and an unyielding sense of personal honor—are first set forth and then called into question where they appear to excess. At the outset, Silvio appears to be the embodiment of this heroic, valorous type, the more so for the aura of mystery that enshrouds much of his past. With calm and controlled dignity, he dismisses the offending officer from their game of cards; yet he does not, as many would have, pursue the matter to a formal duel. The narrator is even more astonished when he learns that Silvio's conscience is troubled, not by a victim of his extraordinary skill, but by memories of the effrontery of an opponent who ridiculed the fears most men inwardly suffer when dueling.

The count's story casts the issue in a different light. Although there is still the image of Silvio as mercurial and diabolically impulsive, marriage and the passage of time have tempered the count's carefree fatalism. Thus, he was betrayed by his visible agitation when, six years later, Silvio came to finish the duel. That the count had no interest in continuing indicates the degree to which his new station in life has instilled in him responsibility and a greater value for life and security.

The grounds, or indeed pretexts, mentioned here for dueling seem slight if not altogether frivolous. The narrator suggests that only the young can take them seriously. Silvio seems to acknowledge that some grievances are transitory when he refuses to challenge another officer over a disputed score in a card game; he confesses to the narrator that, when he originally insulted the count, his calculated provocation was intended explicitly to incite the other man to a challenge and a formal test of honor. The actual outcome of the duel was of little consequence; what seemed to matter was that each man was able to face imminent death with apparent indifference. Indeed, this open and feckless disregard for personal safety appears to be even more highly esteemed than marksmanship; neither of the parties seemed intent on actually wounding or killing his opponent. The two duels in part seem to have taken place within each participant, who in each case put his own presence of mind and coolness under fire to the test and then evidently abjured the practice. Indeed Silvio, though he pursued the count six years after their suspended duel, eventually enlisted his energies in a larger cause and died fighting for the liberation of Greece.

Style and Technique

This work derives much of its impact from the way in which it is told, and notably from the author's ability to fuse several points of view and to join tales from periods years apart into a single narrative with its own internal logic. The style, while often richly descriptive and evocative, is terse, and the mannerisms of the two duelists who tell their own tales blend imperceptibly with the narrator's anecdotal approach. Each episode arouses the narrator's, and the reader's, attention and points the way for the unfolding story of Silvio's duel in two parts with the count. The incident of the duel that was never fought, with Lieutenant R——, prods Silvio into revealing details of the unsettled confrontation from his past. A chance conversation about marksmanship, commenced just as the narrator realizes Count B——'s identity, then leads to the story about the second half of Silvio's duel.

Characterization heightens the reader's interest, for the tale hangs above all upon the qualities of reckless valor often displayed in dueling. Silvio is depicted as taciturn and moody; at one juncture the narrator describes him as conjuring up images of the diabolical. Similar imagery is used when the count discusses Silvio' challenge to him; whether the satisfaction he has ultimately obtained has tempered Silvio is left unstated. His dark and brooding qualities are offset by the more outgoing traits of the narrator, and by the count's balanced maturity, which during the years since his first duel has come as a result of ripening experience. Eventually for him dueling stories become merely examples of youthful ardor carried to extremes, which then are told to call back vanished rivalries.

J. R. Broadus

SHOWER OF GOLD

Author: Eudora Welty (1909-   )
Type of plot: Realism
Time of plot: Early twentieth century
Locale: Morgana, Mississippi
First published: 1948

> *Principal characters:*
> MRS. FATE RAINEY "Miss Katie," the narrator
> SNOWDIE MCLAIN, the wife of King McLain
> KING MCLAIN, a traveling man

The Story

Mrs. Fate Rainey is talking to an implied listener, a visiting stranger in Morgana, Mississippi. After Snowdie McLain comes for her butter and leaves, Mrs. Rainey begins to tell Snowdie's unusual story. It is the story of how badly King McLain treats his wife and how well she takes it, a private story, though everyone knows it. "But," Mrs. Rainey says, "I could almost bring myself to talk about it—to a passer-by, that will never see her again, or me either." Mrs. Rainey then relates several astonishing incidents from Snowdie's married life.

First, she explains the inexplicable marriage between King McLain, the most desirable man in the area, notorious for the number of children he is supposed to have fathered, and Snowdie Hudson, a teacher and the albino daughter of a respectable family. In Mrs. Rainey's opinion, King has wanted to shock the community, to keep it off balance.

This desire also accounts for King's staying away from Snowdie for long periods. Though he works as a traveling salesman, he is gone too often and too long. The next astonishing incident occurred after his longest absence to that date. He sent Snowdie a note asking to meet her in Morgan's Woods. Though it is quite difficult to construct an accurate chronology from Mrs. Rainey's account, it appears that Snowdie's twin sons were conceived under the tree where she met King, and that King departed immediately afterward, leaving his hat on the bank of the Big Black River to make it appear that he had drowned. Yet it may be that he impregnated Snowdie and left his hat on the river bank at a later date.

Mrs. Rainey's characterization of the town's reactions to these strange events is amusing. It ranges from a kind of wondering, almost admiring acceptance of the inevitable in King's behavior, on the one hand, to a kind of outraged sympathy for poor Snowdie, on the other. Though the women of Morgana should think King a scoundrel, they find him irresistibly attractive. Though they want to pity Snowdie, she seems irrepressibly happy. When

Snowdie announces her pregnancy to Mrs. Rainey, she is radiant: "She looked like more than only the news had come over her. It was like a shower of something had struck her, like she'd been caught out in something bright." Snowdie seems to find joy in her life despite King's supposed death. King continues to fascinate the town. No one seems really to believe that he is dead.

The story's second part centers on the most recent astonishing event, the apparent return of King to Morgana on Halloween, when his sons are about eight years old. No one sees his visit except an ancient black man, Plez, whose testimony is impeccable, and King's two sons, who confront him on the front steps of his house, wearing outlandish costumes and roller skates. Plez's account of the antic meeting suggests that it is a sort of exorcism, and the boys report that they have frightened off a "booger." Though no one in town will tell Snowdie the full account, all know it. Mrs. Rainey knows that Snowdie believes that King came that day, and she believes that Snowdie holds it against her that she was there at the time, somehow preventing the desired meeting.

Mrs. Rainey finishes her narration, regretting that her friendship with Snowdie has cooled since that day, and reflecting, "With men like King, your thoughts are bottomless. . . . But I bet my little Jersey calf King tarried long enough to get him a child somewhere." Finally, she expresses amazement at her ability to say such things.

Themes and Meanings

"Shower of Gold" opens *The Golden Apples* (1949), a collection of stories which has much of the unity of a novel. It can be argued that the collection has a kind of lyrical form. Eudora Welty describes the pervading impulse of the collection when she describes her motive for writing as a lyrical impulse "to praise, to love, to call up, to prophesy." Some of the meanings of "Shower of Gold" emerge from examining the allusions to myths.

The title alludes to the story of Zeus's intercourse with Danaë, mother of Perseus. According to Ovid, Perseus was "conceived in joy beneath a shower of gold." Snowdie is similar to Danaë, whose father did not want her to bear children, in that the people of Morgana see her as fated to remain single because she is an albino. King is like Zeus in his reputation for fornication and, later, for adultery. That their children are twins suggests an allusion to the union of Zeus with Leda, which produced two pairs of twins. By associating King with Zeus and Snowdie with at least two of Zeus's mortal lovers, Welty sets up an opposition which gives meaning to the story and which is elaborated in the other stories of *The Golden Apples*.

To Mrs. Rainey, one of the mysteries of the McLain marriage is that Snowdie is quite happy to be abandoned with only her children. During King's absence, she lives contentedly, "taking joy in her fresh untracked rooms and that dark, quiet, real quiet hall that runs through her house." This happiness arises from the opposition between Snowdie and King. This opposition may be described with the terms "Apollonian" and "Dionysian" as Friedrich Nietzsche uses them in *The Birth of Tragedy* (1872).

Snowdie is Apollonian, preferring a quiet, orderly, and stable life. She is willing and happy, on the whole, to live her life in the narrow, intensely rule-governed town of Morgana, where public opinion rigidly enforces social and sexual morality. King is Dionysian, a wanderer of the fields and of the world, lawless, promiscuous, and fascinating. His principle of being seems to require that he flout rules and upset categories. Snowdie's happiness is a product of her marriage to this wild man. Without his unpredictable returns, the sexual pleasure he provides, and the children he fathers, Snowdie's life would be unbearable, too orderly and fixed. Because of his wildness, she is virtually immune to the oppressive pity of Morgana. The McLain marriage is filled with creative and fulfilling tension, a source of renewal which prevents stagnation.

This pattern of necessary opposition is central to *The Golden Apples*. Characters in the other stories suffer because of imbalances between these opposing forces and, in various ways, seek out the kind of balance that will make their lives seem meaningful and complete. Though the opposition in this story is between a man and a woman, parallel oppositions in other stories take multiple forms, between friends of the same sex, within individual characters, and between Dionysian women and Apollonian men. "Shower of Gold" may be seen to introduce the volume by presenting an example of a balanced opposition against which the central conflicts of the following stories may be judged.

Style and Technique

One of the most interesting aspects of technique in this story is Welty's use of first-person narration. Mrs. Rainey draws the reader directly into the story, requiring that one imagine oneself a stranger passing through town and, somehow, finding oneself in Mrs. Rainey's dairy. Like many of Welty's first-person narrators, Mrs. Rainey is not very careful to remember her listener's ignorance of town affairs. As a consequence, Mr. Rainey repeatedly runs ahead of her story and must go back to fill in details. "Shower of Gold," like "Why I Live at the P.O." and "Petrified Man," requires the reader to make careful and sometimes complex inferences in order to follow the narration successfully. Finally, however, all the pieces are given, even if their order seems idiosyncratic. Welty is a master of this sort of narration, which gives so convincing an illusion of hearing the actual voice of a speaking character. Reading this story is at first like plunging into an alien world, but as the reader rereads and contemplates the narration, that world becomes increasingly familiar, convincing, and rich.

Another effect of this mode of narration is humorous irony. Mrs. Rainey, like Snowdie and most of Morgana, does not understand the story she tells. She tells it precisely because it is beyond her how this marriage can continue to satisfy both parties. She responds to the attractiveness of King and Snowdie, perceives the balance that they achieve, yet cannot understand how it works, because it so clearly offends conventional morality. Mrs. Rainey's perpetual amazement at the McLain marriage provokes laughter and delight.

Terry Heller

A SICK CALL

Author: Morley Callaghan (1903-   )
Type of plot: Domestic realism
Time of plot: 1932
Locale: An unspecified city in North America
First published: 1932

> *Principal characters:*
> FATHER MACDOWELL, a kind old priest
> ELSA WILLIAMS, a sick parishioner
> JOHN WILLIAMS, her husband
> JANE STANHOPE, Elsa's sister

The Story

Father Macdowell is an old, slightly deaf priest who always has "to hear more confessions than any other priest at the cathedral." His vast tolerance and slight deafness seem to account for his popularity as a confessor, yet his massive size hints at another dimension to his character: He is gentle, but he is also formidable in the exercise of his priestly office.

One day, after hearing confessions for many hours, he is reading in the rectory when the house girl informs him that a woman is waiting to see him about a sick call. The tired, old priest asks hesitantly if he was specifically requested—he was. So he goes to the waiting room.

Miss Jane Stanhope, a fine-looking young woman, is there crying. She explains that her sister Elsa is seriously ill, perhaps dying, and wishes to received the Sacrament of Extreme Unction. In the Roman Catholic Church, this sacrament is administered to those in danger of death and involves the priest's anointing of the sick person with oil blessed by the bishop. Father Macdowell replies that he hopes the situation is not so critical as to call for the last rites of the Church and offers to go with her and hear Elsa's confession. Just before they set out from the rectory, Jane reveals the complication that explains why she was particular about seeing him and no other priest. Her sister's husband, John Williams, is not a Catholic; the couple was married outside the Catholic Church two years ago; John is against religion in general; and the girl's family, except for Jane, has ostracized them. Father Macdowell assures her that all will be well, and they set off.

During the short walk, Jane offers additional information about the situation. The two young people have been exceptionally happy together. Nevertheless, Jane has just come from Elsa, who desperately wants to see a priest but fears that her husband will find out that she asked for one; just before Jane left for the rectory, John threatened violence if a priest were brought in. Father Macdowell radiates confidence and warmth, and proceeds on his mission.

When they knock on the door, John opens it and is fiercely indignant at the sight of a priest with his sister-in-law. He rebukes her for bringing him and stands obviously poised in expectation of a counterattack from the massive old man. Father Macdowell smiles serenely at him, nods his head, complains of the disadvantages of his deafness, and slides by the astonished young man into the hallway.

As Father Macdowell starts down the hall, he asks John to speak louder so that he can hear him. John stops him again and tries to make it clear that he is not wanted there. John still is expecting, even longing for, a direct confrontation, partly to relieve his pent-up anger and pain. Yet Father Macdowell once again disarms his rage with a gentle request to see the sick girl. Without waiting for a reply, he sets off down the hall, looking for her. Now John grabs his arm and restrains him physically. Once again, Father Macdowell refuses to meet anger with anger. He tells John that he is very tired and would merely like to sit a moment with the girl and rest. John hesitates to deny so modest a request from such a poignant figure; while he fumbles for a reply, Father Macdowell finds the girl's room. John comes in after him.

Elsa is lying in bed. She avoids making eye contact with her husband and barely speaks to the priest. The little she does say, however, makes it clear that she desires the priest's blessing but fears it because it means expressing sorrow for the sin of marrying outside the Church. In other words, she must express sorrow for placing human affection for John before religious duty.

The conflict of wills between Father Macdowell and John goes on as before, but this time John seems in control. He absolutely refuses to leave the room so that the priest can hear his wife's confession. She weeps, seems resigned to the situation, and asks merely for the priest to pray for her. Father Macdowell, too, seems resigned to the situation. He kneels and prays silently for the girl's recovery. While he prays, he comes to realize that John is even more afraid of losing his wife to the Church than to death. He also realizes that Elsa was willing to give up everything—friends, family, religion—to marry John. He has a glimpse here of their conjugal love and is surprised by its intensity.

Father Macdowell tricks John into leaving the room briefly to get him a drink of water, and in the interlude he hurriedly hears Elsa's confession. John returns just as the priest is giving his blessing at the end. He is stunned to find that his wife needed something beyond his love, protection, and understanding.

Father Macdowell and Jane leave the house. For a moment, he is exultant that he rescued the soul of a girl in such peril. Then he feels some slight qualms about his pious duplicity in dealing with John. Finally, he wonders if he came between John and Elsa in any way: He marvels at the beauty of their staunch love for each other, tries to dismiss this beauty as "pagan," but ends by feeling "inexpressibly sad."

Themes and Meanings

The story provides a convincing dramatization of the moral complexity of life, even for someone as saintly as Father Macdowell. As an elderly priest who is well acquainted with the stratagems by which people seek to excuse wrongdoing, Father Macdowell would certainly agree with the maxim that the ends do not justify the means. Hence, it is ironic, if somewhat comic, that the priest is forced into a mild deception in order to carry out his mission of mercy.

Thematically more interesting is the story's contrast between priestly and conjugal love. In Father Macdowell's scale of values, love of God is preeminent. Although he does not overlook or despise the temporal world, his eyes are fixed on eternity. There is something both wonderful and frightening about this single-mindedness. He is a kind and tolerant priest. Yet he allows nothing to stand in his way when it comes to the dictates of his religion.

Contrasted with his love for God is the love of John and Elsa for each other. There is something both wonderful and frightening about this love as well. It has the power to transform and enrich human life. They, however, have made gods of each other, and this exclusive devotion seems destined for tragedy, given human frailty and limitations. Thus, there is considerable insight into complex human emotions in this story, which at first glance might appear to be no more than an anecdote about an ordinary incident in a priest's life.

Style and Technique

The story is written in Callaghan's usual reportorial style, with succinct character sketches and highly selective physical details, providing the necessary context for dialogue that serves to propel the narrative forward. The third-person narration is coyly noncommittal about the old priest's thoughts and feelings until the very end of the story. Nothing "seemed" to shock Father Macdowell; he walked "as if" his feet hurt; he "didn't seem to hear"; he sighed "as if" he were tired. The prose style is evasive, in a sense, and prepares the reader to accept Father Macdowell as both a sincere priest and as a consummate actor who can adapt himself to different situations.

Callaghan's muted style gives the effect of looking through the narrative directly into unmediated reality. Part of the reason for Callaghan's success in conveying a sense of reality or authenticity in his writing is that he gets the details right when he describes a particular occupation or activity. Father Macdowell is a completely convincing portrait of an old priest, and one of the more memorable clerics in literature.

Michael J. Larsen

THE SICK CHILD

Author: Colette (Sidonie-Gabrielle Colette, 1873-1954)
Type of plot: Psychological realism
Time of plot: Unspecified
Locale: Paris
First published: "L'Enfant malade," 1942 (English translation, 1950)

> *Principal characters:*
> JEAN, a ten-year-old boy stricken with poliomyelitis
> MADAME MAMMA, his mother

The Story

The sick child of the title is ten-year-old Jean. His legs are semiparalyzed, and he is extremely weak and emaciated, but pallor has given him an ethereal beauty. From the beginning of the story, the reader is led to expect that he will die. The description of the sickroom suggests a prosperous and cultured background.

The first part of the story establishes a delicate relationship between the sick child and his widowed mother, whom he calls "Madame Mamma." He tries to conceal his pain from her; she tries to conceal her anxiety from him. They both know that they are deceiving each other in their determination to protect each other from the truth.

There is another and more compelling reason—which becomes the central part of the narrative—for Jean to keep his mother distanced from his real thoughts. He is conserving his daytime energy so that at night he can indulge in fantastic journeys of the imagination, which have become the reality of his sickbed existence. To conceal this reality from his mother, he has adopted a slightly mocking approach toward her, which gives him some power over her.

His long-drawn-out illness has made him hyperreactive to sensations, with all the senses intermingled: He can hear smells, taste sounds, smell textures. He has become intensely involved with words and uses a secret vocabulary to describe the people and the everyday things around him.

His nighttime journeys are often sparked by his power to animate the everyday objects or sensations within his bedroom. The scent of lavender, sprayed by his mother, becomes a cloud of fragrance on which he can ride through the skylight into the world beyond. He can fly freely and flowingly, above fields and pastures, with complete control over his adventures and over everything within them. He laughs as he flies, although he never laughs in bed. He dreads landing back in bed, for he often bumps himself on the iron frame and wakes up in pain. He denies the pain that he feels, however, when

Madame Mamma questions him.

Besides his mother, the most frequent visitor to the sickroom is the maid Angelina, whom he has rechristened "Mandora." He loves Mandora because she radiates a profusion of colors, sounds, and feelings. His least favorite visitor is the doctor, whom he finds patronizing and cold. He regards the children who visit him—his cousin Charles, with his scratched knees and hobnail boots, and a little girl who talks about her ballet lessons—as tolerable daytime irritations, for he knows that when night falls, he can find true enjoyment by flying away on one of his adventures again.

One night, Jean's voyage ends when he comes down to earth and hears some words that he cannot quite grasp. The reader understands them as "crisis" and "poliomyelitis." Jean hears them in the shape of people's names and conjures up visions of their owners.

In a protracted period of delirium, the boy's fantasies take on a different and more disturbing texture. Inanimate objects, which were previously at his beck and call, begin to defy him. He finds himself in the grip of unfamiliar presences and sensations. He wants to cry out to Madame Mamma, but an invisible wall separates him from her.

As the fever mounts, strange feelings assail his legs, as if they are being assaulted by ants; menacing forces attack him with burning heat and icy cold. A sudden calm and sadness indicates to the reader that Jean is close to death. His hallucinations become increasingly disoriented. Occasionally, consciousness breaks through as he hears, in distorted form, the sound of bedside voices.

Still struggling to take command of the situation, he at last succumbs to tears. He feels the touch of soft flesh and hair and falls asleep with the knowledge that he is nestling on his mother's shoulder. When he awakens, he has regained enough of his old self to greet her with one of his slightly mocking comments.

In a state of blurred consciousness, he politely asks Madame Mamma to scratch his calves as the "ants" are plaguing him again. This indication that he has regained some feelings in his legs causes excitement among the adults at his bedside, but he becomes conscious of a hateful presence among them and tries to use his powers to abolish it. He discovers that it is the doctor and that the doctor's eyes are filled with tears.

The following weeks bring a muddled and lethargic succession of short and long sleeps, sudden awakenings, and small treats of jelly and vanilla milk. As the "ants" become increasingly active and his appetite returns, Jean's powers decrease until he is no longer able to conjure up his cherished visions. Inanimate objects refuse to obey him. He can no longer fly.

He has defeated death. He is on the mend and is sleeping well at night, but the nights are without marvels. The final word of the final sentence indicates that, contrary to the reader's expectations, Jean is disappointed.

Themes and Meanings

Colette's sensitive, subtle, and unsentimental perception of childhood, which is evident in her factual stories about her own child, is refined and developed to the farthest limits in "The Sick Child" by her penetration of the mind of a boy brought close to death by poliomyelitis. The delicate borderline which she traces between imagination and reality reflects the boy's own subjectivity in which his nighttime fantasies become his reality, compensating for the daytime torment of confinement and helping him to make some sense of the pain. In more general terms, Colette is examining the gap which she perceives between a child's and an adult's reality.

At first, the deception which mother and child practice on each other seems no more than a form of courtesy. As the narrative unfolds, however, the gap between them is shown to be of more fundamental significance. In a revealing passage expressing his innermost thoughts, Jean ponders over the impossibility of explaining to Madame Mamma that a sick and suffering child can be actually happy: far less unhappy, he reflects, than when he was being pushed about in a wheelchair, with everyone staring or asking questions.

The quality of his happiness (or, more precisely, his lack of unhappiness) is a key to the story's deepest interior observation. Jean's dislike of the doctor is associated with the doctor's patronizing attempt to get him to pass the time by sketching. Jean, although absorbed by reading, which feeds his imagination, has already rejected the idea of drawing; he has found that it demands a daunting revelation of truths he prefers not to reveal or to face. There is a similar train of thought in Colette's story, "The Seamstress," about her nine-year-old daughter; the child's imagination flows freely when she is reading but is channeled into more intimidating areas when social pressures force her to learn to sew.

Jean's disappointment at the end of "The Sick Child" can therefore be understood not simply in terms of his own loss of imaginative power, or in the more generalized terms of the final paragraph which considers "children whom death lets go," but as Colette's bitter protest against the pressures of the adult world which extinguish the free, untrammeled imagination of childhood and alter the quality of childhood perception.

Style and Technique

The story is unfolded in a prose style of exquisite delicacy. In the child's world of imagination, the senses are blended with one another; objects transform themselves into different shapes and textures; fantasy merges with reality. The images take on an even greater plasticity in the nightmare of high fever and in the child's gradual, fluctuating return to consciousness.

The free-ranging, protean dynamic of the fantasy passages contrasts with the more formal style used to describe the actual events in the sickroom and the exchanges between the sick child and Madame Mamma (names are seldom used). Although the narrative is developed mainly through the child's subjective vision, the structure of the story, in which the adult reality of the sickroom keeps entering his consciousness in a blurred and distorted form, enables the reader to understand the progress of the illness much more clearly than Jean himself does, and to visualize the comings and goings in the sickroom.

At the same time as being deeply involved in the child's private experiences, one must inevitably identify with the adults' desperate hope for his recovery, a hope that has been made fragile by repeated references to Jean as "the child who was going to die" or "the child promised to death."

By establishing this shifting center of sympathy, Colette is able, at the end, to swing the reader from one reaction to its opposite—first relief that the boy has unexpectedly recovered, then dismay and shock at the finality of the word "disappointed." This unstressed and rather gentle word at the very end of the story commands a reinterpretation of all that has gone before.

Nina Hibbin

SILENT SNOW, SECRET SNOW

Author: Conrad Aiken (1889-1973)
Type of plot: Psychological realism
Time of plot: c. 1920
Locale: An unspecified American town
First published: 1932

> *Principal characters:*
> PAUL HASELMAN, the protagonist, a young boy who suffers
> from "daydreams"
> MR. HASELMAN
> MRS. HASELMAN
> MISS BUELL, Paul's teacher
> THE DOCTOR
> DEIDRE, one of Paul's classmates

The Story

In "Silent Snow, Secret Snow," Conrad Aiken describes the increasing emotional isolation of a boy, Paul, who prefers his imaginative world of silence and retreat to the real world of parents and teachers. Aiken limits his third-person point of view to Paul, through whose eyes readers view corruption and authority, as well as serenity, peace, and perhaps insanity.

The story begins with Paul in the classroom of Miss Buell, the geography teacher, who instructs her students in the different regions of the globe. As she conducts her class, Paul muses about his secret, the world of snow that is slowly replacing the real world. Every day, Paul senses that the snow, which exists only in his own mind, is getting deeper. As the snow deepens, Paul has more difficulty hearing the postman's steps, which he believes are muffled by the snow: The first day, he first hears the postman's step six houses away; the next day, five houses away; eventually, he will not hear the postman's step at all. Although he realizes that his daydreaming distresses his concerned parents, who seek physical reasons for his preoccupation, he treasures his secret world and fears to reveal his secret to them. Miss Buell also senses Paul's inattention, but she seems more concerned with humiliating him than with helping him. When she asks Paul a question, he does manage to answer correctly, but only with a large amount of effort.

On his "timeless" walk home from school, Paul sees through the "accompaniment, or counterpoint, of snow" a series of items of "mere externality" (internal matters are more important to Paul). As he approaches his street, he anticipates seeing the snow and reviews its progress, suddenly realizing with disappointment that in fact he had not heard the postman's steps that morning until he knocked at his family's door. He wonders, "Was it all going to happen, at the end, so suddenly?"

That evening, the doctor arrives and gives Paul a physical examination to determine the cause of his problem. After Paul reads a passage from Sophocles, the doctor concludes that there is nothing wrong with his eyes and that the cause is "something else." When he asks about Paul's worries, Paul becomes evasive and retreats into his snow world, where he receives reassuring promises from the "voice" of the snow. The doctor continues to probe, and Paul's parents become impatient with him when he will admit only that he thinks about the snow. When he refuses to divulge more information, his father, who has grown increasingly exasperated, uses his "punishment" voice. At this point, Paul escapes by running upstairs to his room, where the snow engulfs the furnishings and speaks to him of peace, remoteness, cold, and white darkness. When his mother suddenly enters the room, he sees her as a hostile presence that threatens his world. He cries out, "Mother! Mother! Go away! I hate you." Those words solve everything, for the snow resumes its speech about peace, cold, remoteness, and, finally, sleep.

Themes and Meanings

Aiken's "Silent Snow, Secret Snow," like Willa Cather's "Paul's Case," concerns a boy's emotional and psychological estrangement from the real world. Although some critics have seen the retreat to the snow world as representative of a death wish, it seems more to represent schizophrenic detachment into a fantasy world. Psychological criticism of the story is almost inevitable because Aiken himself was much influenced by Sigmund Freud, whose theory of the Oedipal complex seems related to the conflict between Paul and his father. (The passage Paul reads for his eye test is from *Oedipus at Colonus*, 401 B.C.) Psychological readings are further encouraged by events in Aiken's life: As an eleven-year-old, he had seen his father kill his mother and then commit suicide.

The story, however, is more than a clinical case study of a person who is suffering from a psychological disorder. Aiken's background is literary as well as psychological, and his story relies heavily on the theme of "two different worlds," a theme that is reinforced through imagery of geography and exploring. Paul tries to lead a double life (a "public life" and the "life that was secret") in two worlds, but he also is aware of the necessity of keeping a balance between those worlds. His mother expresses her concern about his living in another world, and when he realizes the depth of the snow on the sixth day, he understands that the "audible compass of the world" is thereby narrowed as the snow world supplants it. As the story progresses, Paul loses his balance (on the homeward walk he notices the egg-shaped stones which are mortared "in the very act of balance") and falls, albeit willingly, into the snow world, which he has been determined to explore: "He had to explore this new world which had been opened to him."

In fact, Aiken's story abounds with references to explorers: Robert Edwin Peary, Robert Falcon Scott, Sir Ernest Henry Shackleton, Christopher Columbus, and Henry Hudson. These references are instructive: Scott reached the South Pole but perished on the return trip; Hudson searched for the Northwest Passage to the Orient, a region as exotic as the snow world, but Paul observes that Hudson was disappointed. Explorations of the new worlds may seem promising and exciting, but those journeys also end in disappointment, death, or dead ends. The inner geography is mirrored by the geography lesson being taught by Miss Buell, who first talks about the equator and then about the North Pole, the "land of perpetual snow."

Paul's exploration becomes in part 2 a kind of odyssey, a journey homeward, not necessarily to his parent's home (he asks himself, "Homeward?"), but to another home. The journey to the snow world that is completed when the "bare black floor was like a little raft tossed in waves of snow" actually starts in the classroom, where Paul is also adrift. Like a captain at sea, he charts his course by the stars, in this case the "constellation of freckles" on the back of his classmate Deidre's neck. In effect, Deidre serves as a guide, a reference point by which he can calculate his position. When class is over, he follows her in rising from his seat.

Style and Technique

Aiken's story relies on both literary and psychological symbolism. By forcing the reader to adopt Paul's point of view, Aiken encourages his audience to identify with the boy, who seems locked in conflict with his father in a classical Oedipal situation. Paul mentions his conflict with his father and mother, but he only speaks of talking with his mother. When the examination (the "inquisition" as seen by Paul) occurs, Paul hears his father's soft and cold voice of "silken warning"; later, Paul hears the "resonant and cruel" punishment voice. In fact, Paul cannot meet his father's gaze, for he sees only his father's brown slippers, which come closer and closer.

Not only does the reader adopt Paul's perspective (the examination is an "inquisition" and a "cross-examination," both of which imply Paul as persecuted victim), but also the reader shares Paul's thoughts as Aiken moves from third-person limited point of view to an even more intimate stream-of-consciousness narration. As a result, Paul's interpretation of the events seems so convincing that a concerned mother's visit becomes an invasion by an "alien," that a cruel "I hate you!" becomes an exorcising phrase. (The references to "exorcism" and "inquisition" suggest that Paul's world has become a religion for him.)

Aiken's style also involves the use of imagery which suggests corruption and the failure of relationships. As he walks home, Paul notices "items of mere externality" that comment ironically on his internal state: a dirty newspaper touting an ointment for eczema, a physical corruption; "lost twigs descended from their parent trees," surely a reference to his own relationship to his father; a piece of gravel on the "lip of a sewer," balanced like Paul between two states; "a fragment of eggshell," which suggests birth and a divided personality; and a gateway with balanced egg-shaped stones, thereby connoting an entrance to another world while referring again to birth and potential development. Perhaps because of his relationship with his father, he also pauses at the empty birdhouse, which obliquely relates to his own home. That the mere details are meant to represent the real world seems obvious since Aiken uses large-scale terms with small objects: There is a "continent of brown mud" and a "delta" near the gutter. What Paul sees is a microcosm of the macrocosm, the real world.

Compared to this world of "the usual, the ordinary," Paul's snow world is understandably appealing, because it is a combination of "ethereal loveliness" and terrifying beauty. Aiken observes that no fairy story Paul had ever read could compare to it, and, ironically, when the snow speaks, it is in terms of a fairy tale, which can also be beautiful and terrifying (and many deal with failed family relationships): "I will tell you a better story than Little Kay of the Skates or the Snow Ghost." In the familiar guise of a fairy tale, the snow draws Paul into a story of a flower becoming a seed. Rather than stressing growth and development, the story describes regression and withdrawal from the real world.

Thomas L. Erskine

A SILVER DISH

Author: Saul Bellow (1915-   )
Type of plot: Psychological realism
Time of plot: Mid-twentieth century
Locale: Chicago
First published: 1978

> *Principal characters:*
> WOODY SELBST, a businessman
> MORRIS SELBST, his deceased father
> MRS. SKOGLUND, a wealthy widow

The Story

After his father's death, Woody Selbst feels a yawning emptiness in his life. At the age of sixty, he is deeply disturbed by questions about the meanings of life and death. In his period of mourning, he recalls a trip to the White Nile, where he had seen a buffalo calf being seized by a crocodile while the parent buffaloes looked on without understanding what was happening. Their brute grief now helps him to cope with his own.

As Woody reflects on his own life, his father's, and their unusual relationship, the story reveals the contours of Woody's imagination and the travails of his experiences. His present life is full of cares, for he supports his invalid mother and two insane sisters, one of whom he has committed to a mental institution; a wife, from whom he has been separated for fifteen years; a mistress; and, now, his father's widow, Halina, and her son, who plays the organ at games in the stadium. Despite the number of dependents whom he has accumulated, Woody lives alone, working as a tile contractor.

As a youth, Woody grew up fast, and his spirit has remained independent; at the funeral parlor, he insisted on dressing the corpse for burial, and at the funeral, he rolled up his sleeves and shoveled the dirt himself. There is no harm in Woody, yet his self-respect has not allowed him to live entirely within the law and has led him, over the course of his life, into theft, smuggling, procuring, and adultery. Still, he is moved by honesty, he hates faking, and he has always held in his heart both a belief in love and "a secret certainty that the goal set for this earth was that it should be filled with good, saturated with it."

Woody's memories and reflections probe these elements of his personality. His parents exerted very different influences on him. His mother had been converted to Christianity by Aunt Rebecca's husband, the Reverend Dr. Kovner, himself a converted Jew, whose ministry was financed by a wealthy widow, Mrs. Skoglund. Kovner imparted his fervor to Woody and "taught him to lift up his eyes, gave him his higher life." After the boy accepted Jesus as his personal redeemer, he was paid fifty cents to stand up in churches and give his testimony.

Though not a very devout Jew, Morris Selbst was increasingly alienated from his converted family. He considered Kovner a fool and resented the way his wife and daughters were being turned into "welfare personalities" who would lose their "individual outlines." Standing for "real life and free instincts, against religion and hypocrisy," he tried to rescue his son from their religion and hypochondria. Under their influence, he believed, Woody would not "even understand what life is. Because they don't know—those silly Christers."

Morris was an earthy, common, thick, physical man, "like a horseman from Central Asia, a bandit from China." He had fallen in love with a refined English girl in Liverpool, in whose cellar he had slept, having been abandoned at the age of twelve by his family of Polish Jews on their way to America. Then, at sixteen, he scabbed his way onto a ship during a seaman's strike and brought Woody's mother with him to Brooklyn. Settling eventually in Chicago, he pursued horses, cards, billiards, and women, always living life in "his own vital, picturesque, original way."

Woody remembers one spring afternoon when his father deserted the family and took off with a married woman, Halina Bujak, who worked in his shop. "From now on you're the man of the house," Morris told his fourteen-year-old son before asking him for money to buy gasoline.

Woody's central memory involves the time his father stole a silver dish and the two came to blows over the theft. They had braved a blizzard to come to Mrs. Skoglund's home in Evanston to ask for fifty dollars, which Morris said he needed to keep his business going. While the old lady and her servant withdrew to pray over the matter, Morris shocked his son by picking the lock on a cabinet, taking out a silver dish, and stuffing it into his trousers. Woody begged him to put it back, but he would not, so Woody wrestled his father to the floor, receiving several blows to the face, enough to rattle his teeth, before the ladies returned.

They left with the silver dish and a check for fifty dollars. Later, after the theft had been discovered and Morris had fallen under suspicion, Woody stoutly maintained his father's innocence, on pain of being expelled from the seminary where Mrs. Skoglund had been paying his tuition.

Father and son debated the episode "in various moods and from various elevations and perspectives for forty years and more, as their intimacy changed, developed, matured." After the funeral, Woody reflects on how his father, with a silver dish, had defeated his mother's influence and "carried him back to his side of the line, blood of his blood."

Indeed, when Woody became a man, he chose to live his life imaginatively, expensively, as his self-willed father might. On vacations, he traveled to such places as Mexico, Uganda, Istanbul, Delphi, Burma, and Jerusalem. In

Japan, he saw the temple gardens, the holy places, and "the dirtiest strip show on earth." In Addis Ababa, he lured an Ethiopian beauty from the street into his shower. He taught American obscenities to a black woman in Kenya.

The story ends with Woody's memory of his father's death. The old man was writhing in his hospital bed, trying to rip out the intravenous needles. Woody astonished the nurses by climbing into bed with his father to soothe and still him. While he held him in his arms, he felt his father's body growing colder and colder as life left it.

Themes and Meanings

Written at a time when Americans, young and old, were perplexed by "the generation gap," this story explores relationships between the generations of a quintessentially American family. Like many characters in ancient and modern literature, Woody finds the search for his identity inextricably tangled with his genealogical roots. From his parents, he inherits seemingly incompatible impulses toward sincerity and mischief, instinct and refinement, recklessness and responsibility. Woody is "leading a double life," the narrator says, "sacred and profane."

Coming to terms with his own identity is, therefore, largely a matter of reaching an understanding of his father's vices, an understanding which goes beyond the righteous scorn or kind forgiveness of his mother and her circle. The episode involving the silver dish brings Woody's emotional conflicts into sharpest relief; he gathers from it a comprehension not only of his father's energetic though immoral imagination, but also of his female relatives' insipid religiosity. His immediate reaction to the theft was like theirs, but ultimately he sided with his father against them.

Perhaps the most intriguing insight in this study of generations is the way the author has made the father more immature than the son. Morris' impulsiveness, his puerile sinning, and his financial irresponsibility often seem more juvenile than Woody's foibles: Consider the irony of a son physically punishing his father for stealing; imagine a fourteen-year-old boy financing his own father's desertion. Often the child plays father to the man.

For all the individuality with which these two characters are drawn, they assume mythic dimensions inasmuch as they stand for two of the nation's most interesting generations, those that made the 1920's roar and the 1960's soar. An immigrant, Morris is a typical burly, passionate, broad-shouldered Chicagoan who survived the Great Depression. He wants his son to be "like himself, an American." By the time his father dies, Woody has grown "fleshy and big, like a figure for the victory of American materialism." With his Lincoln Continental, his tile business, and his foreign vacations, Woody typifies mid-century generations of Americans who brought seeds planted by indigent immigrants to fruition. Born a Jew, converted to Christianity, and finally lapsed into agnosticism, Woody embodies the dynamic religious mélange of American culture. The tensions and anxieties he suffers from the competing claims of these traditions are those of the nation as a whole.

Style and Technique

While this story belongs to the tradition of American realism, its technique should be distinguished from the more external, hard-boiled objectivity of realists such as Ernest Hemingway. This story is more concerned to reveal the inward thoughts and feelings of its characters than to present them in a succession of dramatic incidents. Characters' reactions to events are as important as the events themselves. The story is based on Woody's memories and mental reflections, but is does not plunge the reader into a stream of consciousness. Thoughts and actions are presented objectively rather than subjectively, through the words of a narrator who refers to Woody in the third person. Such narratorial objectivity may blunt the lyricism of Woody's plaint, though it absolves him of much of the onus of self-pleading.

Convincing characterizations are achieved through ingenious selection of revelatory detail, such as Morris' theory of breast cancer, the image of Mrs. Skoglund's servant wiping the doorknobs with rubbing alcohol after guests had left, or the mention of Woody's wife still not being able to shop for herself though she had lived alone for fifteen years.

The style is, for the most part, casual and plain. The diction is generally less crude than that of most men such as Morris and Woody, but dialogue is rendered naturally, without obtrusive literary elevation.

The sound of bells is perhaps the most delicately drawn image in the story. Woody believes that their "vibrations and the banging did something for him—cleansed his insides, purified his blood." Connected as they are with churches, bells recall the religious agony at the center of Woody's life. They also symbolize the honesty that Woody and his father valued so highly, for, as the narrator says, "A bell was a one-way throat, had only one thing to tell you and simply told it." Woody's soul is perhaps best described by the narrator's epithet, "bell-battered."

John L. McLean

THE SILVER MINE

Author: Selma Lagerlöf (1858-1940)
Type of plot: Moral fable
Time of plot: 1788
Locale: Dalecarlia, Sweden
First published: "Silvergruvan," 1908 (English translation, 1910)

> *Principal characters:*
> KING GUSTAF THE THIRD OF SWEDEN
> THE PARSON OF DALECARLIA
> THE MINERALOGIST
> OLAF and
> ERIC SVARD, who are soldiers
> ISRAEL PER PERSSON, a peasant
> STEN STENSSON, an innkeeper who discovers (with the parson,
> the Svards, and Persson) the silver mountain

The Story

As a result of King Gustaf's demands that it go faster, his coach, traveling on a poor rural road of Dalecarlia, breaks down. The king's will is thus proved limited, unable to control objective reality. While his coach is being repaired, the king visits a church, where he beholds what he takes to be "the finest lot of folk he had ever seen . . . with intelligent and earnest faces." He is prompted to appeal for their help in his war against the Russians and Danes, but the peasants shift the burden of a response to their pastor. In the vestry, a rugged and rough peasant greets the king, who, again judging on the basis of outward appearance, snubs the peasant (who is in fact the pastor). Instead of immediately identifying himself, the peasant-pastor provokes the king to reveal his elitist bias, his contemptuous attitude, to the peasantry.

The peasant explains to the king that the pastor may be able to procure money for the king by narrating the story of how the parson, together with four hunters from the parish, stumbled on a hidden silver mine and how these "dignified and excellent men" were corrupted by the prospect of so much wealth. Confronted with the ensuing moral degeneration of the parishioners, the parson resolves that he will not reveal to anyone the whereabouts of the silver and that if the people persist in their evil ways, he will leave them.

Given the parson's tested virtue of self-abnegation, the king doubts if he could convince him to reveal the secret treasure. The peasant (whose alternate identity as parson the king fails to discern) makes an exception if the silver were used to save the Fatherland. This subordination of the peasantry's welfare to the nation triggers a sudden illumination in the king, who changes his haughty stance and now acclaims the evasive congregation as "a beautiful

sight" totally gratifying for Sweden's king. The pastor's practice of not exalt-
ing himself above his flock quickens "all that was noble and great within" the
king.

The reader senses at this point that the king has already intuited the pastor behind the poor peasant's unassuming but astute "disguise." Despite the
danger besetting the kingdom, the king formulates the moral decision that
"the kingdom is better served with men than with money."

When the king is asked by a peasant outside the church whether the pastor gave their collective response, the king replies yes. No doubt the community's trust in their pastor, based on an actualized egalitarian principle, contrasts with their suspicion of the king, whose army, riddled with traitors,
signifies the king's morally questionable rule. This episode of moral instruction through a didactic recollection of a past incident suggests the need for a
democratic mutuality of concern and the abolition of class distinctions if justice and compassion are to prevail.

Themes and Meanings

It is clear that the salient thematic issue involves the blindness of the king
(monarchical authority) to the plight of his subjects, the injustice of a hierar-
chical, feudal system based on private ownership of property (land, in particular) which fosters violent competition, and the priority of the spiritual good
of the community over the claims of the wealth-seeking individual. On the
surface, it is easy to reduce such a complex web of thematic motifs to the
simplistic idea that money, or speculation of property, corrupts; that wealth is
the root of all evil. If one reflects further, however, one can see that it is on
the problematic relation between the king and the parson, who represents
the peasantry or common people, that the text focuses. While the prospect of
owning the silver ruins the people, the parson believes that it can do good in
the service of the country.

When the king inquires if the pastor is ready to be responsible for surren-
dering that wealth to the Fatherland no matter what happens to the parishioners, he says that he is, and that the fate of his flock "can rest in God's
hand." This demonstrates the pastor's independence of mind, his strong
faith, and his loyalty to the welfare of the nation. He is therefore selfless
both as peasant and as pastor in relation to a larger good to which, he
believes, even the king should submit. This value the king confirms when he
decides to preserve the integrity of the peasants: "Inasmuch as you have labored and starved a lifetime to make this people such as you would have it,
you may keep it as it is."

Connected with this paternalistic care for the spiritual health of the peasants is the king's conservative attitude that these subjects should not disturb
the status quo or rebel against the present social arrangement. The silver
mine betokens disruption and subversion of the existing class system. The

fratricide committed by Olaf Svard (recounted in the parson's story told to the king) and the promise Svard exacts from the parson before he is hanged (that nothing of the mine be given to his children) proves this unsettling effect of the possibility of access to power through wealth.

The fact that the peasantry delegates their right of representation to the pastor may argue for their conservatism, their habit of allowing others to speak and make decisions for them. Because of his poverty and honesty, however, the pastor demonstrates the unifying and stabilizing practice of democracy: He refuses to make his wisdom dominate his flock. He subordinates himself to his parishioners. In contrast, the king maintains his aristocratic distance up to the end, refusing even to acknowledge openly his mistake in not recognizing the pastor underneath the peasant, even though he affirms the superior value of such "men" over money. The king reconfirms the pastor's role of "spiritual adviser" in this validation of unflinching self-denial of which the pastor is the model.

Where, then, is the criticism of hierarchy? It appears in the pastor's decision not to reveal himself to the king and simply deal with him as a peasant, forcing the king to regard him seriously for what he has to say. The king not only ignores the peasants but also despises them. By expressing his criticism of the pastor as "a bit arbitrary" and authoritarian because he "wants to be the only one to counsel and rule in this parish," preaching "a pure and clear gospel," the peasant detaches himself from his assigned role as pastor and indirectly voices the protest of the dispossessed subjects and plebeians against indifferent rule. The king's patronizing approval of the pastor as portrayed by the peasant sanctions the fact of class division: "'Then, at all events, he has led and managed in the best possible way.' He didn't like it that the peasant complained of one who was placed above him. 'To me it appears as though good habits and old-time simplicity were the rule here.'" "Good habits" and "simplicity" imply submission to an unjust social order. It is only through this ruse, an example of peasant cunning, that the peasant succeeds in bringing the king to listen to him and realize that the dominated class has something that equals if not transcends the honor and aristocratic learning of the privileged nobility.

Yet this project of the narrator-peasant to engage in dialogue with the king and teach him a lesson is accomplished at the expense of maintaining the peasants' poverty as their only resource, the sole guarantee of their virtue. So long as the king represents the Fatherland, his right to rule is not questioned—but then the peasants in the beginning do not really recognize him. In effect, the king has not earned the right to exercise kingly authority, and he remains powerless at the end, even though he may have gained insight into the humanity of his peasant subjects. His rule remains arbitrary; the "silver" quality of the people remains hidden, unexplored and untapped. The egalitarian peace and communal wholeness of such rural retreat, with nature and religion blended together, will endure despite intrusions of arbitrary power and the seductions of the individualistic, war-ridden world.

Style and Technique

The structure of the narrative comprises three parts: the breakdown of the king's coach caused in part by the poor country roads, the king's speech to the Sunday worshipers in which he tells a lie, and the king's reception of the pastor's narrative of the silver and its lesson. Employing a third-person point of view moving from the king to the pastor, the narrative progresses from description of the king's accident, over which he has no control, to his enforced listening to the parson's narrative of the accidental finding of the mountain and the subsequent ordeal of the people. This progression suggests the influence of inscrutable fate, of a providential force that guides human destiny.

The two principal protagonists dramatize the disparity and conflict between the peasantry and the monarchy. They conform to the conventional view that attributes taciturn cunning and prudential calculation to the oppressed peasantry, and paternalistic if arbitrary nobility to the king. Here, however, such feudal obligation is amiss: The peasants never expect a visit from the king. The king's remark to the parson's disclosure of the people's plight captures the king's indifference: " 'Human beings here would certainly be no better than others if this world's temptations came closer to them.' " said the parson. " 'But there's no fear of anything of the sort happening,' said the King with a shrug."

The narrator's characterization of the pastor is a subtle embodiment of the fundamental moral problem of how an oppressed class can make its voice heard. The whole point of the story-within-a-story framework, which contains the people's answer to the king's appeal, becomes clear: Fiction, the imagination which imbues the storyteller with a magical power, enables him to project the exemplary role of the pastor whose mind and actions coalesce in a way that condemns the king's duplicity. That framework traps the king in the tangle of suspense, even though at the end the king redeems himself by generously acknowledging the intrinsic worth of his dominated subjects.

Selma Lagerlöf concentrates on delineating a few gestures and remarks loaded with meaning, relying on actions which imply considered moral thought and judgment. The parson's story suggests that a selfless will can prevent fate and social norms from destroying humans; it delivers a whole philosophy, a utopian vision of community, exceeding the utilitarian demand of the king. By incorporating the parson's sacrifice into the routine event of a king's unexpected stopover, Lagerlöf suggests that an unjust society can be saved and renewed by mobilizing the spiritual strength and shrewdness of the peasantry.

E. San Juan, Jr.

A SIMPLE HEART

Author: Gustave Flaubert (1821-1880)
Type of plot: Psychological realism
Time of plot: The nineteenth century
Locale: The French province of Normandy, in and around Pont-l'Évèque, Trouville, and Honfleur
First published: "Un Cœur simple," 1877 (English translation, 1903)

> *Principal characters:*
> FÉLICITÉ BARETTE, the protagonist and "simple heart" of the title, an orphaned farm girl who spends her life as a domestic in Pont-l'Évèque
> MME AUBAIN, Félicité's widowed employer
> THÉODORE, Félicité's early suitor
> PAUL AUBAIN and
> VIRGINIE AUBAIN, children of Félicité's employer, age seven and four, respectively, at her arrival in the household
> VICTOR LEROUX, Félicité's nephew

The Story

"A Simple Heart" embraces in only a few pages the story of an entire life, that of a woman born into the most unfortunate and narrowest of circumstances, a woman who lives within the narrowest frame of reference. The story is divided into five distinct sections. The first gives an overview of the Aubain household and the daily routine of Félicité Barette. For fifty years, the surrounding world sees her as a possession of Mme Aubain, a paragon of domestics: frugal, hardworking, unchanging. She seems an automaton, a wooden woman. The human being behind the mask is seen in the subsequent parts of the story.

Félicité, an orphan reared haphazardly as a barnyard laborer, exposed to want and abuse, is without personal attractions or affections. She is courted briefly by a brusque young farmer who is looking for an establishment and safety from the draft. When he marries a wealthy, older widow, Félicité spends one night in the fields, weeping, then gives notice and leaves her farm for the small town of Pont-l'Évèque. In front of the inn there, she meets the young Mme Aubain, a widow in reduced circumstances, and is engaged as a domestic after a brief conversation, because she is full of such goodwill and makes so few demands, although she is very ignorant. Félicité's early involvement with the Aubain household centers on her affection for the children of her employer. She also orients herself within a weekly round of visits from a set circle of acquaintances of Madame and occasional idyllic visits to the Aubain property in the countryside. On one such visit, Félicité saves the family from a charging bull, bravely holding it at bay until all escape. She ignores her newfound reputation for heroism. A more far-reaching concern is Virginie Aubain's resulting nervous invalidism, treated by ocean baths at Trouville. There Félicité is reunited with a long-lost sister and meets her young nephew Victor, another child for her to love. This second part of her story ends with the breaking of the Aubain family circle as Paul is sent away to school.

Virginie is now sent to catechism lessons, in preparation for her first Communion, and Félicité is introduced to the world of religious faith, which she accepts, despite her years, in a childlike manner. She trembles in sympathy with each step of Virginie's initiation into the Church, feeling more of a thrill as the beloved child accepts the Host than when she herself goes to Communion. Yet Virginie, in her turn, must go away to school and Félicité is desolate. She and Mme Aubain lead parallel but nonintersecting affectionate lives. Madame can attempt to fill the void with letters, but the illiterate Félicité invites her nephew Victor and lavishes her love on him. As he grows older, he becomes a sailor, bringing her small gifts from his first short voyages. His first long voyage takes him to Havana. Félicité, with her childlike vision of the world, cannot comprehend the distances involved, does not understand when shown a map, imagines a world of cigars and cartoon blacks. Virginie Aubain's worsening illness obscures Félicité's anxieties over Victor. When he dies of fever and poor doctoring in Havana, her grief is enormous, but she stifles its expression and continues her round of work. Virginie's death at the convent school prostrates her mother. It is the servant who must care for the little body, praying over her darling and wishing for a miracle, Félicité who must care for and groom the little grave. In time, Mme Aubain recognizes this silent anguish, and her acceptance of Félicité's grief in one moment of sympathy binds the servant to her in a devotion that is quasi-religious.

The fourth part of the story is dominated by Loulou, a parrot that is swept into the domestic backwater of the Aubain household by faraway political events. Bright in color, quaint in his actions, he fascinates Félicité and fills her life with affection again. The details of his life absorb her. When he escapes, briefly, she devotes such fervor to searching for him that she catches a severe chill, suffers from angina, and eventually loses her hearing. The parrot's shrill voice becomes her only link to the world of sound, but in 1837, he dies, during a severe cold spell. On Mme Aubain's suggestion, Félicité sends Loulou to Le Havre to be stuffed. On his return, he becomes her idol, placed in her small room along with all the religious and personal relics of her life. Here, with the passage of time and her increasing isolation from the world, the parrot comes to represent the Holy Spirit. She sleepwalks through life, rousing only to preparations for the yearly celebration of the Feast of Corpus Christi. The even tenor of the years is broken by three events: Paul Aubain marries, the old family lawyer kills himself amid shameful circumstances, and Mme Aubain, disheartened by both events, sickens and dies. Félicité is deprived all at once of her reasons for living; she remains in the Aubain home, maintained in her attic room by a legacy from Mme Aubain, but Paul sells the other contents of the home and leaves it empty, up for rent or sale. Life is narrowed to the smallest scope possible, and many years pass with no change in externals, except that the house grows more and more dilapidated. One damp, cold winter, Félicité coughs blood, and around Easter, develops pneumonia.

The final movement of "A Simple Heart" brings the death and transfiguration of Félicité, lying blind, deaf, cared for out of charity by a kind neighbor. The temporary altar used for display of the Host during the procession of Corpus Christi has been built in the Aubain courtyard, and Félicité has sent her only treasure, Loulou, to adorn it. She creates the procession, the gay sights and sounds in her mind as she lies dying, the typical small-town personalities amid the excitement and flowers of the early summer festival. When the neighbor climbs up and peeks out Félicité's attic window, Loulou is seen, a brilliant blue patch amid the surrounding profusions of flowers, laces, and personal treasures given to enrich the altar. Félicité smells the incense rising to her room, and in communion with the festival below, slips gently out of life into a Heaven whose opening skies reveal a gigantic parrot hovering in welcome.

Themes and Meanings

Flaubert uses the story of Félicité to study the transcendence of the qualities of love, courage, and faith in a life firmly anchored in the most tragic, sordid, and limited circumstances. Félicité has no pretensions to beauty or intellect, and every aspect of her life has its burden of sorrow. She has glimpses of the tragically barren nature of her life in general, forever a servant, her loves lost to death or betrayal. Yet her own capacity to love and serve beautifies and transforms this life. It is impossible to discuss Félicité without reference to the strong Christian framework given by the writer, both through Félicité's faith and through her embodiment of an ethic expressed in the Gospels. She is a loving, suffering servant, feeding the hungry, caring for the dying, ever humble and childlike in her faith.

The parrot, Loulou, invested by Félicité with qualities of a religious image, embodies the paradox of Félicité's faith. There is much that is comical and grotesque in the old servant's love for the gaudy bird. Yet there is also an element of purest mysticism, which transforms Loulou into a fully satisfying symbol of the divine in Félicité's life, the power of the Holy Spirit, imperfectly understood yet leading the soul to transcendence. The reader shares Félicité's deathbed vision and trusts its clarity as the heavens open before her.

It has been suggested that Flaubert based the characters and plot of this story on autobiographical elements. Félicité corresponds to Julie, a faithful servant in his mother's house; Mme Aubain resembles the author's mother; geographical names and descriptions are those of Flaubert's youth; and some specific incidents of the plot, such as the death of Virginie Aubain, parallel events in the life of the author's family. Such biographical details, however, are not essential to an understanding of "A Simple Heart," and, in fact, may detract from the impact of the story. By the power of art, deeply felt, intimately personal material is generalized and transformed, and the transfiguration of the simple Félicité parallels the reweaving of Flaubert's story into hers.

Style and Technique

An omniscient, third-person narrator leads the reader into the world of Félicité and the Aubain family, laying out the vignettes of daily life which finally combine to form a portrait complete in all particulars. Great care is taken to produce an impression of point-to-point congruence with reality, as if one is reading a biography. Thus, many dates are explicit; the reader learns that M. Aubain died in 1809, that Victor Leroux sailed for Havana in 1818, and that Loulou died in 1837. Yet although these dates are scattered throughout the story, they serve as points of reference for an orderly narration and do not overpower it. The tone of "A Simple Heart" is always even, unemotional, even in dealing with the most touching of scenes. Dialogue is seldom used, and, among the sparse numbers of phrases cited directly, it is the ordinary, simple expression that predominates. The author's eye is avid for the homely detail; he exhibits Félicité as she eats her meals, slowly and deliberately, picking up the crumbs of her bread with a moist fingertip, Félicité cherishing little Virginie's moth-eaten hat as a holy relic, Félicité wearing a traditional Norman headdress whose wings mimic those of the parrot Loulou.

Flaubert's description of Félicité is framed by his evocation of her whole milieu, with pithy descriptions of typical characters such as the family lawyer, an aged veteran of the Terror of 1793, and Mme Aubain's daughter-in-law. The reader sees the Norman countryside, breathes the sea air with Virginie, attends catechism class in the country church, and joins the procession on the feast of Corpus Christi. Flaubert is known as a great stylist, forever dedicated to the search for *le mot juste*, the right word. Here, this famous search produced clear and pungent images, compact yet satisfying, which continue to bring readers into the world of Félicité Barette.

Anne W. Sienkewicz

THE SISTERS

Author: James Joyce (1882-1941)
Type of plot: Domestic realism
Time of plot: 1895
Locale: Dublin, Ireland
First published: 1904

Principal characters:
THE NARRATOR, an adult recalling a childhood experience
THE BOY'S AUNT
ELIZA FLYNN, the sister of Father Flynn
NANNIE FLYNN, the sister of Father Flynn

The Story

In this opening story from James Joyce's *Dubliners* (1914), the unnamed narrator is an adult recalling his first direct experience with death when he was a boy in Dublin in 1895. He tells of passing on several evenings the house in which a retired old priest, who was his mentor, lay dying. Then, when the boy, who lives with his aunt and uncle, comes down to dinner one night, he hears them and a neighbor talking about the priest, who has just died.

Old Cotter, the neighbor, says that "there was something queer... something uncanny about him" and refers to the priest as "one of those... peculiar cases." The uncle recalls that Father Flynn taught the boy "a great deal... and they say he had a great wish for him." Yet the "wish," or respect, that the priest had for the boy does not impress old Cotter and the family, for they are anti-intellectual and indifferent to education. The uncle even disparagingly refers to his nephew as "that Rosicrucian," and agrees with Cotter that youngsters should focus on physical activities.

During their conversation, the adults talk about the boy as if he were not present, though they closely observe him. Knowing this, the boy continues eating "as if the news had not interested [him]." Actually, he becomes increasingly upset by the comments and crams his mouth with porridge to keep from venting his anger.

The next morning, he goes to the New Britain Street house, where the priest lived with his two sisters above a drapery shop, and the bouquet and card on the door confirm for him the fact that his old friend indeed has died; therefore, he does not want to knock. Wandering about Dublin in the wake of this decision, he remarks to himself that neither he nor the day "seemed in a mourning mood" and that he felt "a sensation of freedom as if... freed from something by his death." Though he does not comprehend what is happening, he is, for the first time, seeing that the world at large is unaffected by one person's death and that life goes on. In other words, the death of his mentor—or surrogate parent—is a major event in his progress toward maturity. As he continues to walk through sunny Dublin (the narrator mentions the sun twice in this context, as if emphasizing the indifference of the world to Father Flynn's death), the boy remembers what the priest had taught him, including "stories about the catacombs and about Napoleon Bonaparte, and . . . the meaning of the different ceremonies of the Mass and of the different vestments worn by the priest."

That evening, accompanied by his aunt, he visits "the house of mourning," climbing a narrow staircase "towards the open door of the dead-room," which he hesitates to enter until one of the priest's old sisters beckons to him repeatedly. There Father Flynn is lying, "solemn and copious, vested as for the altar, his large hands loosely retaining a chalice." When the three kneel at the foot of the bed to pray, the boy cannot "because the old woman's mutterings distracted [him]." At this point, about two-thirds through the story, the focus shifts to Nannie and Eliza, the priest's old sisters.

Nannie leads the guests to the sitting room, where she serves wine and crackers, and then sits on a sofa and falls asleep, having fulfilled her duties as hostess and having introduced the boy to the mysteries of the "dead-room" and welcomed him into the fraternity of adults with the sherry. Gently prodded by the boy's aunt, Eliza (sitting "in state" in her late brother's armchair) tells about Father Flynn's last days. Among other things, she recalls noticing "something queer coming over him latterly" and mentions that she would "find him with his breviary fallen to the floor, lying back in the chair and his mouth open." Then Eliza gets to more substantive matters, which in the aggregate clarify the veiled comment ("something queer . . . something uncanny . . . peculiar . . .") that old Cotter made about Father Flynn.

Eliza begins by saying, "The duties of the priesthood was too much for him. And then his life was, you might say, crossed." His problem started, she says, when he broke the chalice. Others said that it was "the boy's fault," that is, the carelessness of the acolyte who assisted the priest at the altar, and the people made light of the incident, since the chalice "contained nothing," the wine already having been transubstantiated into Christ's body and blood. According to Eliza, however, the incident "affected his mind," and "he began to mope by himself, talking to no one and wandering about by himself."

The crucial incident, which presumably led to Father Flynn being relieved of his duties and retired, occurred one night when he was needed to make a call, perhaps on a dying parishioner. "They looked high up and low down," Eliza tells the boy and his aunt, and finally tried the locked chapel. There two priests and the clerk found him alone in his dark confessional "wide awake and laughing-like softly to himself." Clearly, "there was something gone wrong with him. . . ." Eliza has the last word, for the story concludes with this statement.

Themes and Meanings

The first three of the fifteen stories that compose the collection *Dubliners* deal with youngsters and are initiation works, narrative pieces about different aspects of the rite of passage, the progress from childhood to adulthood. Since it is the opening story in the book, "The Sisters" has the youngest hero, and it shows him confronting directly for the first time the reality of death. The story also develops the archetypal motif of the search for a father. The boy, apparently an orphan (he lives with an aunt and uncle), finds in the priest a substitute father, a kindly man who teaches him about many things, nurturing his intellect and preparing him for the future; yet Father Flynn himself is an imperfect, eventually demented, man—and priest—who is unable to face his own faults and inadequacies and ends up going mad in his own confessional.

The third theme is that of paralysis, which Joyce introduces in the first paragraph, when the boy, gazing up at the dying priest's window, says *"paralysis"* to himself, a word that "had always sounded strangely in [his] ears," like *"gnomon* in the Euclid" and *"simony* in the Catechism." Linked as it is with the other two words, "paralysis" refers to more than the priest's physical imperfection, which is the result of the debilitating stroke he has suffered; it also calls to mind his spiritual and social imperfections. Further, Joyce's introduction of the paralysis motif in the first paragraph of this opening story also signals its general significance for the entire volume.

In a 1904 letter, Joyce speaks of writing a group of stories: "I call the series Dubliners to betray the soul of that . . . paralysis which many consider a city." Indeed, the fourteen stories that follow "The Sisters" introduce characters from many walks of life who are frustrated with their lives but unable to effect change. Personally, socially, and vocationally or professionally, these Dubliners—young as well as old—are paralyzed, ineffectual failures. The story, then, can be interpreted as the first of Joyce's fifteen visions of Dublin, the capital of Ireland, which he left for good on October 8, 1904, to live the remainder of his life on the Continent.

Style and Technique

Despite the obvious symbolism, Joyce's style in this story and elsewhere in *Dubliners* is straightforward and realistic (some have even said naturalistic), and it has been compared to that of Anton Chekhov, Guy de Maupassant, and Émile Zola.

Any such indebtedness notwithstanding, Joyce conceived of "The Sisters" (like the rest of *Dubliners*) as an "epiphany," a story in which a character experiences a "sudden spiritual manifestation." In this story, the boy gains enlightenment, learning the truth about Father Flynn; significantly, at the very moment of the revelation, when Eliza pauses for a bit, the boy rises, goes to the altarlike table where Nannie has laid out the refreshments, and tastes his sherry, a conscious ceremonial gesture in the concluding act of this particular rite of passage.

Eliza is the third medium through which Joyce develops Father Flynn's character in the story. First there is the narrator, who recalls his experiences when a boy with the priest; second, there is the dialogue between Cotter and the boy's uncle, who raise questions and speak negatively about Father Flynn. The sympathetic attitude of the boy, called into question by the mutterings of the neighbor and uncle, finally is placed in the proper perspective by Eliza's testimony.

Gerald H. Strauss

THE SKY IS GRAY

Author: Ernest J. Gaines (1933-   )
Type of plot: Realism
Time of plot: World War II
Locale: Bayonne, Louisiana
First published: 1963

> *Principal characters:*
> JAMES, the narrator, an eight-year-old black boy
> OCTAVIA, James's mother
> ROSE MARY, his aunt
> MONSIEUR BAYONNE, a black folk doctor
> HELENA and "ALNEST," an old white couple who keep a store
>   in Bayonne
> A STUDENT, a young black man

The Story

As the narrative opens, James and his mother, Octavia, are waiting by the roadside for the bus that will carry them to Bayonne. The weather is cold and James knows that his mother will be worried that her family lacks wood to keep them warm until her return. She worries about other things as well, especially when James is not there to assume the man's role in her absence. James is instinctively drawn to his mother and feels the urge to put his arm around her, but he restrains himself, knowing that she regards such a display of affection as weakness and "crybaby stuff."

James has been silently suffering for some time with a toothache, about which he told no one, since he knew that there was no money for the dentist. James's aunt first became aware that he was in pain, but he swore her to secrecy. She did send for Monsieur Bayonne, a folk healer, to treat the tooth, but his remedies were ineffective. The pain became so unbearable that it could no longer be kept secret from James's mother, so now they are on their way to have it removed. They have money "enough to get there and get back. Dollar and a half to have it pulled," and fifty cents left over to buy a "little piece of salt meat."

As they prepare for the day, James recalls the time before his father went off to the war, when things were better for the family. He also recalls when his mother made him kill two redbirds caught in the traps that he and his brother set for owls and blackbirds. James did not want to kill the redbirds, but his mother killed the first one and then demanded that he kill the other. He refused, and she beat him until he gave in. Afterward, as they ate the tiny morsels, James felt the pride the others had in him for providing even this small meal. He later understood that his mother's stern discipline was preparing him in case he had to carry on in her stead.

The ride to town on a Jim Crow bus is uneventful except for James's self-conscious flirtation with a small girl, which amuses the other passengers. Alighting in Bayonne, James becomes aware of the penetrating cold, which seems more intense than at home. They make their way to the dentist's office, where James listens to an exchange between a preacher who believes it best not to try to understand suffering, and a young, educated black man who insists that people should "question everything. Every stripe, every star, every word spoken. Everything." These two exchange views on religion, which the young man rejects. Growing angry and frustrated at the young man's calm rejection of Christian complacency, the preacher finally strikes him twice in the face. The young man merely sits down and reads as the preacher bolts out the door. Later, the young man has a similar exchange with a woman to whom he says, "Words mean nothing. Action is the only thing. Doing, that's the only thing." James observes these scenes without comment, but clearly he is impressed by the contrast in values and attitudes between the old and new generations of black Southerners. He thinks, "When I grow up I want be just like him. I want clothes like that and I want keep a book with me too."

The nurse announces that the dentist will see no more patients until after one o'clock, and that all those waiting must leave and return then. Having no place to go to escape the bitter cold, James and his mother walk, window-shopping. When James's eyes are drawn to a café where white people are eating, his mother insists that he keep his eyes to the front. After walking the length of Bayonne and back, they enter a hardware store, where James has a chance to get warm while his mother pretends to examine ax handles. Soon after returning to the street, James is cold again. Hunger gnaws at him. The courthouse clock shows a quarter to twelve—another hour and a quarter before they can return to the warmth of the dentist's office. It has now begun to sleet.

After desperately trying to get into the closed dentist's office to escape the weather, James's mother heads for the black section of town. They go to a warm café, where, because she feels obligated to spend something, Octavia orders milk and cookies for James and coffee for herself. She eats nothing. A man at the bar puts a coin in the juke box and asks Octavia to dance. The episode ends with Octavia pulling a knife on the pimp. She and James return to the cold street.

As Octavia and James again walk toward the dentist's they encounter an elderly white woman who asks if they have eaten. Octavia proudly answers that they "just finish," but the woman insists that they come into her store anyway. Her husband inquires from the back, where their living quarters are and whether she has found them yet, so the reader knows that she was on the street awaiting James and Octavia. Later she explains that she saw the two of them pass earlier, and waited for them to return. She tells them she has warm food on the stove; then, when Octavia seems ready to leave, she quickly adds that it is not free: she asks James to put her garbage out in return for the food. When James actually carries the can out to the street, it is so light that he is sure it is empty. Afterward he is allowed to wash up, and a meal is served him and his mother. Their hostess calls the dentist and arranges for James to see him as soon as the office opens.

As James and his mother leave, Octavia turns and asks the lady if she has salt meat, which she does. When Octavia asks for "two bits worth," Helena cuts off much too large a chunk. Asserting her fierce pride, Octavia refuses to accept this charity and turns to go. Only when Helena cuts off about half the chunk of meat does she accept it. On the street again, James turns his collar up against the sleet. His mother tells him to put it down again. "'You not a bum,' she says, 'you a man.'"

Themes and Meanings

"The Sky Is Gray" takes as its major theme the issue of black pride in the face of intolerable conditions of poverty. James and his family are reduced to poverty, ironically, by his father's service in the army. In the face of these hardships, James has been forced to sacrifice his childhood to the harsh realities of survival in a hostile, unforgiving world. The episode in which he is forced to kill the redbirds in order for the family to eat powerfully dramatizes the extent to which his mother must force him to overcome his own natural feeling for the sake of the family's need. As James comes to realize, there is no room for softness or gentleness in their world. What superficially appears to be cruelty on Octavia's part is her way of preparing him for a hard future.

Despite the grinding poverty of their lives, Octavia retains her pride and instills it in her son. James, like any child, cannot fully understand why his mother insists on paying her way when charity is offered, but the reader is aware that she is developing in him a sense of pride and character that will enable him to rise above his environment. Intuitively, he wants to be like the educated young black man he saw in the dentist's office, but he can become so only if he develops a sense of manhood based on self-reliance, self-respect, and pride. Octavia gives him that opportunity, even though her methods are hard. When, at the end of the story, she tells him that he is a man, she is refusing to allow him to be less.

Another theme of the story has to do with the kindness of Helena, whose generosity transcends the color line. As the young man says, it is by action rather than words that people should be measured. Even in the segregated South, simple human kindness can and does exist. After the callous disregard of the dentist and other whites in the story, Helena offers James an object lesson that people should be judged by what they do, not by who they are. Though this theme is never stated overtly, it is implicit throughout.

A last important meaning is the sense of a changing South implied by the conversation between the young black man and the preacher in the dentist's office. While the older man speaks of acceptance of suffering injustice as the duty of Christians, the young man represents a rising generation that will eventually throw off the shackles of segregation. Though James is still too young to understand these arguments, he is being reared to become one of that generation.

Style and Technique

Ernest J. Gaines is a master of the dialect of his home region of southern Louisiana, and he uses this skill to good advantage in "The Sky Is Gray." His use of the point of view and language of an eight-year-old boy, who narrates the story in his own words, is also an important stylistic device. The conversation between the preacher and the student which occurs in the dentist's office, for example, is presented without comment on the boy's part, because James lacks the intellectual capacity to analyze or even fully understand the significance of all that he sees and experiences. Abstractions such as the question of God's existence are beyond his intellectual range, so he simple repeats the dialogue as he heard it. Thus, the narrative is straightforward and simple; Gaines's themes and meanings are implicit rather than explicit, shown rather than told. The effective integration of language, theme, and narrative voice makes this story an excellent example of the literary realism for which Gaines is justly respected by critics and reviewers.

William E. Grant

THE SLIDE AREA

Author: Gavin Lambert (1924-   )
Type of plot: Social realism
Time of plot: The 1950's
Locale: Los Angeles
First published: 1959

> *Principal characters:*
> THE NARRATOR, a screenwriter
> ZEENA NELSON, the owner of a secondhand furniture store
> HENRIETTA "HANK" NELSON, her sister, a murder victim
> SISTER HERTHA, a nurse at St. Judith's Hospital
> COUNTESS OSTERBERG-STEBLECHI, a wealthy eccentric

The Story

The nameless narrator spends a late afternoon and night in the early summer drifting around the Los Angeles area. He is writing a film script without enthusiasm when he would rather be working "on the novel I am hoping to write and pretend is already under way." He leaves his office and wanders through the decaying sets on the back lot, then drives his battered 1947 Chevrolet to the ocean while meditating on the bizarre essence of Los Angeles: "not a city, but a series of suburban approaches to a city that never materializes." At the Pacific Palisades, he notices the omnipresent, ominous warning signs: DRIVE CAREFULLY; SLIDE AREA; BEWARE OF ROCKS. He watches as three elderly picnickers are rescued, apparently uninjured, from a huge pile of mud and stones.

In a Santa Monica bar, the narrator meets his friend Zeena Nelson, who is drunk and distraught because her sister, Henrietta, nicknamed "Hank," has been shot and the nuns at St. Judith's Hospital will not tell her about the woman's condition. He calls the hospital, and Sister Hertha informs him that Henrietta Nelson is dead. He leaves Zeena roaming the beach in a daze. Sister Hertha later telephones to ask him to come there to take away Zeena, who refuses to leave the hospital. The nun explains that Hank was shot in the head by an unidentified man whom she brought home.

The narrator remembers how he met Zeena and Hank at their secondhand furniture store and occasionally ran into them thereafter in bars or on the beach: "This is how everybody met them. This is how I am with Zeena today, by accident." He retrieves Zeena from the hospital and drives to her house in a seedy Venice neighborhood.

Themes and Meanings

Gavin Lambert has written extensively about films and Hollywood as the founder of *Sequence*, former editor of *Sight and Sound*, and author of *On Cukor* (1972) and *The Making of "Gone with the Wind"* (1973). He has written or cowritten such screenplays as *Bitter Victory* (1957), *Sons and Lovers* (1960), and *I Never Promised You a Rose Garden* (1977). The themes of "The Slide Area" are also examined in other stories in *The Slide Area: Scenes of Hollywood Life* (1959), his 1963 novel *Inside Daisy Clover*, and his screenplay for the 1965 film version of the latter. Lambert's Hollywood fiction is in the tradition of such British examinations of the Los Angeles scene as the novels *Prater Violet* (1945) by Christopher Isherwood and *The Loved One* (1948) by Evelyn Waugh and Paul Mayersberg's nonfiction *Hollywood: The Haunted House* (1967).

The protagonist of "The Slide Area" is less the narrator than Los Angeles itself, which Lambert sees as representative of America, a metaphor for the aimlessness of twentieth century life. Los Angeles lacks any definite identity because it is constantly in a state of flux, is "a comfortable unfinished desert" in which "between where you are and where you are going to be is a no-man's land." The crumbling cliffs of the Pacific Palisades perfectly embody the way in which chaos always lurks beneath the insubstantial surface. The narrator sees Los Angeles as having "nothing at all to do with living. It is a bright winking mirage in the desert; you are afraid to look away in case it has vanished when you look back." The narrator describes how a development site is built over where a prehistoric animal has recently been excavated, as if to ask whether all the history since this creature roamed the earth has led illogically to this.

Lambert comments frequently in "The Slide Area" on the nature of reality. On the back lot, the narrator considers the replica of a residential street to have "as much and perhaps more reality than the real thing." It is difficult to distinguish the real from the unreal, for the real world persists in imitating the world of film. Indeed, this phony world can almost be seen as superior, since the artificial canvas sky is bluer than the real one and spotlights are always standing by "to reinforce the sun."

Leaving the film sets does not lessen the narrator's sense of unreality; there is always something "almost supernatural" in the air, sometimes described by Los Angeles television weather forecasters as "neurotic." The physical and psychological spheres become inseparable. This lack of distinction is appropriate, according to the narrator, because "In America, illusion and reality are still often the same thing. The dream is the achievement, the achievement is the dream." With so little grasp on reality, even time becomes irrelevant. The narrator does not tear off the calendar leaves in his office: "Let time stand still or move back, it doesn't matter."

Lambert's themes are most effectively conveyed when the narrator goes to a drugstore and finds Countess Osterberg-Steblechi surveying the paperback crime novels. She is interested in *The Case of the Black-Eyed Blonde* but will not buy it because at thirty-five cents it is too expensive. The widow of a wealthy European banker, her chauffeur-driven Rolls Royce awaiting her, the countess claims that she is "heartrendingly poor." Swollen like a balloon, her dyed-red hair looking like a wig, she personifies the decadence and decay which Lambert associates with America.

Style and Technique

"The Slide Area" is almost an essay about Los Angeles, America, the state of civilization, and the nature of reality, with Lambert's thematic points illustrated by brief scenes involving his characters. The story is arranged as a series of snapshots of the people and places the narrator encounters, with his impressions of them as they relate to his view of the world. As is appropriate for a Hollywood story by a film critic and screenwriter, the style is cinematic: a series of seemingly random images which come clearly into focus with the Zeena scenes at the end. The film it most closely resembles and seems most influenced by is *Sunset Boulevard*, Billy Wilder's cynical 1950 vision of death and despair in Hollywood.

Lambert's cinematic style can be seen in the close-ups that he presents of his characters' faces to capture their emptiness. The countess' face "looks like the moon after an explosion, the features are blasted fragments." Zeena "has once been beautiful, but now her face has something ruined about it, as if she's been waiting too long, in vain, for the telephone to ring."

Michael Adams

A SMALL, GOOD THING

Author: Raymond Carver (1938-   )
Type of plot: Tragic realism
Time of plot: Late twentieth century
Locale: A town in the United States
First published: 1983

> *Principal characters:*
> HOWARD WEISS, a young executive
> ANN, his wife
> SCOTTY, their son
> A BAKER, unnamed

The Story

Ann Weiss is not pleased with the baker from whom she orders her son Scotty's eighth birthday cake. Though the baker is of an age to have children, and even grandchildren, he takes no interest in her son's birthday and seems to have no time for small talk. The transaction is direct and impersonal, and Ann leaves the bakery vaguely disgruntled by the man's coldness.

Two days later, on his birthday, Scotty and a friend are walking to school when Scotty is hit by a car and knocked to the pavement. The driver of the car stops, but drives on when Scotty gets up, shaken but apparently unharmed. Scotty returns home, lies down on the sofa, and loses consciousness. Alarmed because she cannot rouse him, Ann telephones her husband, Howard, who telephones an ambulance.

At the hospital, Howard and Ann are assured by their physician, Dr. Francis, that nothing serious seems to be wrong with Scotty. He is only in a deep sleep, not in a coma, and will soon awaken. That evening, while they await tests results, Howard goes home to bathe and change clothes. After he has reached the house, the phone rings, and the caller tells Howard that he has an unclaimed birthday cake. Impatient and confused, Howard denies any knowledge of a cake and hangs up, only to be disturbed by a second call a few minutes later. This time, the caller says nothing, then hangs up.

Back at the hospital, Howard discovers that Scotty, still unconscious, is being fed intravenously. Ann is anxious about his not waking up. Howard suggests that Ann go home for a while and tells her about the phone calls, but she refuses to leave Scotty. When Dr. Francis comes in on late-night rounds, Howard and Ann demand to know why Scotty has not yet awakened. The doctor assures them that Scotty is suffering from a hairline fracture of the skull and a mild concussion, but that he seems to be out of any real danger and should soon wake up. He is merely asleep, not in a coma. Later that night, another doctor, a radiologist, comes into the room and announces that a brain scan will be performed on Scotty. The increasingly anxious parents accompany their son downstairs to radiology and return with him to his room at dawn.

Scotty does not awaken the next day, despite Dr. Francis' assurances that he will do so. The exhausted Howard and Ann maintain their vigil in the hospital room. When Dr. Francis makes his second visit of the day, he expresses his bewilderment that Scotty has not awakened and this time calls the condition a coma. After the doctor leaves, Howard convinces Ann to go home to rest and feed the dog. No sooner has she arrived home, however, than the phone rings; the caller mentions Scotty's name and hangs up. Terrified, Ann calls the hospital and receives assurances from Howard that their son's condition has not changed.

Early the next morning (it is now Wednesday), after Ann has returned to the hospital, Howard tells her that the doctors have decided to operate on Scotty. Yet even as they are discussing the proposed surgery, Scotty opens his eyes, gazes blankly at his parents, suffers a spasm, and dies. Dr. Francis later attributes the death to a "hidden occlusion" and expresses sympathy. Dazed, Howard and Ann return home, and the phone rings yet again. Ann curses the caller and bursts into tears. Another call, this one late at night, prompts Ann to make the connection she has so far missed: The baker, angry about the unclaimed cake, has been making the calls.

The couple drive to the shopping center bakery to confront the baker. Though it is past midnight, he is still at work, and Ann pounds on the door to get his attention. When he opens the door, Ann pushes past him, identifies herself, and accuses him of making the calls. She angrily explains that her son is dead. Moved and ashamed, the baker asks them to sit down. He talks about the frustrations of his work, the disappointments of his life; he asks their forgiveness. He serves them coffee, cinnamon rolls, and fresh bread, explaining that, "Eating is a small, good thing in a time like this." Relaxed and contemplative, the three sit eating and talking until the break of day.

Themes and Meanings

Like many of Raymond Carver's stories, "A Small, Good Thing" is about bad things happening to good people and about how suddenly and irrevocably luck can change. Howard and Ann Weiss have done all the things expected of an upwardly mobile, middle-class couple; nothing has prepared them for a calamity of the magnitude of an only child's death, and both are at a loss about how to deal with it. As his son lies unconscious after the accident, Howard reflects on the remarkable good luck that has characterized his life thus far: his education and his marriage have gone without a hitch, and neither tragedy nor disgrace has touched his family. Still, he realizes that there are forces "that could cripple or bring down a man if the luck went bad, if things suddenly turned." During their son's stay in the hospital, both Howard and Ann find themselves wishing that things were back to normal—as though wishing could make it so. At one point, Ann longs for "a place where she would find Scotty waiting for her when she stepped out of the car, ready to say *Mom* and let her gather him in her arms."

There is every reason to believe, however, that Howard and Ann will survive the devastation of Scotty's death, and the story's most positive moments deal with the heightened sympathy for other human beings that often comes with personal tragedy. In a hospital waiting room, Ann meets a black family, one of whose members, Franklin, is being operated on after a knife fight. She becomes almost mystically bound to them through mutual suffering, telling them her story and listening to theirs. Scotty's death brings out the good side of the mostly unsympathetic Dr. Francis, as well: After the boy dies, the physician seems to Ann "full of some goodness she didn't understand." Howard and Ann become closer to each other through shared misfortune, and both become more magnanimous human beings. The story's final image— the grief-stricken parents and the childless baker awaiting the morning's light together—is clearly an affirmative one, illustrating as it does what the poet William Wordsworth called "the soothing thoughts that spring out of human suffering."

Style and Technique

Carver's clear, uncluttered syntax, short, simple sentences, and judicious use of repetition make comparisons with Ernest Hemingway inevitable. With Hemingway, Carver clearly represents the realist tradition in fiction, and the stories collected in *What We Talk About When We Talk About Love* (1981), *Will You Please Be Quiet, Please?* (1976), and *Cathedral* (1983, the collection in which "A Small, Good Thing" appears) established him as one of that tradition's foremost American practitioners.

The profundity of such stories as "A Small, Good Thing" resides in what lies beneath the uncomplicated surface of Carver's prose: complex and universal emotions with which even the most casual reader must instantly identify. In his quest for the *mot juste*, the right word that will trigger this sympathetic response, Carver does for twentieth century America what Gustave Flaubert did for France a century earlier: He exposes and records the emotional nuances, the tensions and the trials, of a troubled middle class.

J. D. Daubs

THE SMALLEST WOMAN IN THE WORLD

Author: Clarice Lispector (1925-1977)
Type of plot: Self-discovery
Time of plot: The twentieth century
Locale: Central Congo and a large metropolis
First published: "A menor mulher do mundo," 1960 (English translation, 1972)

> *Principal characters:*
> LITTLE FLOWER, the smallest woman in the world
> MARCEL PRETRE, an explorer, hunter, and man of the world

The Story

The action plot of the story is quite simple. The explorer, Marcel Pretre, while on an excursion into Equatorial Africa, comes across a tribe of extraordinarily small pygmies living in the forest. These pygmies tell him of an even smaller race of pygmies living deeper within the jungle. He travels even deeper into the heart of the luxuriant tropical forest and there discovers the smallest race of pygmies in the world. Among these minute creatures, he discovers "the smallest of the smallest pygmies in the world," a tiny woman no more than forty-five centimeters tall. She is mature; indeed, she is conspicuously pregnant, and she is quite black. She does not attempt to speak, and the reader learns that the tribe, the Likoualas, has only a very limited language and its members communicate primarily by gestures.

The explorer is awed by this unique creature, considering her the rarest and most extraordinary creature on the earth because of her diminutive size. He takes photographs of her, prepares a description, and sends the photograph and article on to a newspaper, which publishes the life-size photograph, together with the article, in the Sunday supplement.

As readers of the Sunday newspaper see the photograph, they react in different ways, and these reactions and the comments they make are explored in the story as the next part of the narrative. The scene then shifts back to the jungle, where the explorer and the tiny woman are regarding each other while he continues to gather data about her. He has named her Little Flower, and he gazes at her in wonder. Little Flower, herself, is feeling warm, safe, and happy, and within her arises spontaneously a feeling of love for the explorer. Yet the author notes that she loves Marcel Pretre in the same appreciative, admiring manner that she loves his ring and his boots.

She smiles at Marcel, and he responds by returning her smile. Yet he is not sure at all what she is smiling about or what response he is indicating with his own smile. Marcel's awareness of Little Flower's emotion, and some perception of his own feeling, increases. He becomes embarrassed by these feelings, and to reestablish his self-control he returns to taking notes very intently. This moment of awareness and self-discovery which Little Flower, the uncivilized, natural creature, has forced upon him reveals his own inner depths and so frightens him that he rejects the revelation and returns to the mechanical routine of gathering data and taking notes about her. He rejects the emotions that Little Flower reveals and his own emotions as well, because he is unable to handle and respond to the spontaneous and un-abashed natural emotions which his mannerly existence suppresses.

As a final note, rather like the "moral" at the end of a fable by Aesop, the scene shifts again to the metropolis, where an old woman reading about the tiny woman in the Sunday supplement responds with platitudes, commenting that "it just goes to show," meaning that unlikely things are indeed possible. "God," she adds, "knows what He's about."

The reader is left to ponder what God, Little Flower, Marcel Pretre, and the author are about. Clearly, the significance of the story does not lie in the story line. The action is so minimal as to qualify it for the designation "anti-story." Yet this lack of action is typical of the stories of Clarice Lispector and does not constitute an oversight or flaw in the construction of the narrative. She has a purpose to her writing which is far more important to her than re-counting the adventures of fictional characters: The story exists as a vehicle through which to demonstrate her philosophical convictions.

Themes and Meanings

Clarice Lispector, a thoroughgoing existentialist, explores in her stories the pain of ambiguity experienced by her fictional characters. Trivial moments generate confrontations with self-discovery which are wrenchingly sad, revealing to the characters their weakness in fearing freedom and the absurdity of human existence. The very triviality of the event, coupled with its profound impact, lends a grotesque incongruity to the moment and generates a flash of insight into the existentialist ambiguity of the human condition, which has been labeled the Absurd.

Marcel Pretre, explorer, hunter, and man of the world, moves from civilized, conventional surroundings into the equatorial jungle. This journey takes him into a setting of lush, rampant vegetation, where the jungle, the humidity, and the heat suggest the pervasive force of nature as one explores more and more deeply within the uncivilized jungle, and symbolically within the human personality. Yet Pretre ignores the lush presence of the untamed jungle as he probes deeper and deeper. When, in the deepest interior of the jungle, he discovers the ultimate human creature, the smallest woman in the world, Pretre feels awed almost to the point of giddiness at actually confronting nature's rarest product, a truly unique creation. Nature has derived this ultimate creature from a succession of smaller and smaller pygmies. Pretre has a sense that he has "arrived at the end of the line." He is enchanted by her rarity, charmed by her strangeness, and attracted to her as "a woman such as the delights of the most exquisite dream had never equaled."

Little Flower is the totally natural person, one who has never suffered the anguish of having to make choices and impose restrictions. She lives wholly in concord with her impulses and emotions and cares not at all for the acceptance or the indifference of humanity, since she scarcely comprehends the existence of the rest of the world. When Marcel sends her picture and description to the newspaper for publication in the Sunday supplement, he treats her as a curiosity for the amusement of the bored weekend reader. He describes her as "black as a monkey," and the picture he sends makes her look much like a dog. The identification with animal characteristics emphasizes the identification of Little Flower with nature, and her difference from the civilized people reading the paper. Her differences evoke in certain readers of the newspaper article a recognition of the uniqueness of each person, and the consequent alienation of every person from others. Readers are forced into moments of insight that strip away the conventional amenities and force them to recognize their own character and the implications of their own condition within the scope of civilized humanity.

The comment of the old woman at the end of the story gains force as one realizes that the author is suggesting that God (or Nature) knows what He is about in forcing people from time to time to acknowledge their natural feelings. Failure to acknowledge and fulfill these impulses and emotions represents a choice to restrict and thwart one's own personality, leading to a loss of touch with one's own self and a failure, because of weakness and fear, to achieve one's full potential.

Style and Technique

The author employs limited physical description, but detailed omniscience when she explores the thoughts and feelings of the characters in the story. She describes the characters sometimes from the internal perspective of their thoughts and feelings, and at other times simply by describing their behavior, letting the reader determine the implications.

Lispector uses humor as a contrast to the overarching themes of failure and isolation that inform the story. An example of her humor occurs in the scene in which Little Flower scratches herself "where one never scratches," while the explorer is regarding her with awestruck adoration, and he modestly averts his gaze.

The author uses symbolism constantly. The jungle, the animal references, the newspaper supplement, the explorer and his long search leading to his discovery, his helmet, his notes, the treetop home, and the name Little Flower are all conspicuous symbols in this story. Lispector's intense exploration of the emotional moments of crisis and discovery, and the contrast of this intensity with the surface calm of the action, give the story a special focus on the inner conflict of the characters. None of the characters is particularly well developed. They are all, except for Little Flower, intended to represent deep psychological complexities, and the author forces recognition of their ambiguities and the meaning, or meaninglessness, of their existence.

Betty G. Gawthrop

THE SMELL OF DEATH AND FLOWERS

Author: Nadine Gordimer (1923-   )
Type of plot: Psychological realism
Time of plot: The early 1950's
Locale: Johannesburg, South Africa
First published: 1956

> *Principal characters:*
> JOYCE McCOY, a pretty young white woman, the main
>   protagonist
> JESSICA MALHERBE, a white antiapartheid political activist
> EDDIE NTWALA, a black man who attends the multiracial
>   party
> DEREK ROSS, the host of the multiracial party
> RAJATI, Jessica Malherbe's Indian husband
> MATT SHABALALA, a black participant in the act of civil
>   disobedience
> MALCOLM BARKER, Joyce McCoy's brother-in-law

The Story

The story is told by an omniscient narrator in the third person. Although the narrator occasionally looks inside the mind of another character, the story is told chiefly from the point of view of the female protagonist, Joyce McCoy.

Joyce McCoy, a pretty and somewhat shallow young white woman of twenty-two, returns to South Africa from England, where she has lived for five years. As the story begins, Joyce, accompanied by her brother-in-law Malcolm Barker, is attending a party in Johannesburg. Because members of all races are present, this social affair is most unusual for South Africa. There, Joyce dances with a black man, Eddie Ntwala; this is the first time in her life that she has ever done such a thing.

A fateful step is taken by Joyce at the very beginning of the story, when she catches sight of Jessica Malherbe. Jessica is a white antiapartheid activist who has rebelled against her traditional Afrikaans family background by both her political choices and by her choice of an Indian, Rajati, for a husband. As the party finally draws to a close, Joyce, on the spur of the moment, asks for permission to take part in an act of civil disobedience planned by Jessica: a protest march, by a group composed of members of all of South Africa's races, into the segregated African section of the town; such a march is illegal under the South African apartheid system.

Joyce's initial request, made at the party, gets no reply; she gains Jessica's reluctant permission to join the march only after visiting her on separate occasions in the days following the party. When Joyce does go to Jessica's apartment on the day of the protest, to gather with the other marchers, she feels a strong sense of panic, which she overcomes with difficulty; only after having overcome this panicky sensation is she able to get into the car with the other demonstrators. Once the demonstrators have marched into the African section, Joyce is, like all the other demonstrators, placed under arrest for having violated the rules of apartheid.

Themes and Meanings

The main theme of the story is the possibility of a radical leap from political apathy to wholehearted involvement in a just cause. At the beginning of the story, the protagonist is a pretty but shallow woman; at the end of the story, she has been arrested for an act of civil disobedience and has come to feel the righteousness of the blacks' fight against apartheid, and to make their cause her own. Such a conversion to political activism is, for Joyce, not a matter of intellectual ratiocination; nobody tries to convince her to join the demonstration. Instead, the struggle takes place almost entirely within Joyce's emotions.

The first milestone in Joyce's move toward emotional involvement in the black cause is her dance with a black man at the multiracial party. As Joyce dances with Eddie Ntwala, the author looks inside Joyce's mind, showing both the protagonist's anxious queries to herself about what she is feeling and her relief that she still feels "nothing." Here, in this moment of introspection, the reader sees the beginning of the struggle for Joyce's soul between apathy and commitment. The second milestone is Joyce's inner struggle with her emotions at Jessica's apartment, a struggle that leads to her final decision to keep her earlier promise to take part in the demonstration. The third and final milestone occurs just after her arrest, when the police are taking down the names of the demonstrators. By this time, the author relates, Joyce no longer feels "nothing"; instead, she feels what the black onlookers are feeling at the sight of her, a young white woman, being arrested. For Joyce, a genuine sense of solidarity with the oppressed has finally triumphed over her earlier indifference to the larger world; she now knows how the blacks feel when they are oppressed by white authority.

In "The Smell of Death and Flowers," Gordimer strongly suggests that the motives for undertaking acts of political courage are not always purely idealistic ones. Taking part in an antigovernment demonstration, while indeed dangerous, can be a means whereby an individual can, through involvement in the camaraderie of political activism, break out of personal isolation and a crippling inability to feel anything strongly; such a dangerous act thus provides psychological benefits to the participant.

Although she evidently has faith in South African whites' ability to travel down the road to multiracial political activism by achieving genuine empathy with the plight of the blacks, Nadine Gordimer has no illusion that the path to fellow feeling with the victims of oppression is an easy one to tread. In her narration of the gathering of the protesters for the march into the African location, Gordimer points out that Matt Shabalala, the black participant, knows that he is taking far greater risks than Joyce—for he, a married man, is endangering his future hopes for employment, thereby placing his entire livelihood at risk. Joyce, Gordimer pointedly notes, thinks that she, in her excited anticipation of what will happen, is feeling exactly what Shabalala is feeling, but she is not. Even here, then, in the midst of the common struggle, Gordimer shows that there is a gap in empathy between the races that only shared experiences can close.

Style and Technique

Gordimer relies heavily on imagery to illuminate certain aspects of Joyce McCoy's character. When Gordimer first introduces Joyce McCoy, she compares Joyce to a pink, cold porcelain vase, compares Joyce's face to the type of face found in a Marie Laurencin painting, and describes Joyce's prettiness as "two-dimensional." When Joyce conducts her banal, almost incoherent conversation with her black dancing partner, the author describes her voice as "small" and "flat." The reader's impression of Joyce's superficiality is further reinforced by her initial remarks concerning Jessica Malherbe; an observation of how "nice" the antiapartheid activist looks, and of how good that woman's perfume is. The author again mentions how Jessica looks, using Joyce's original words, when Joyce first puts the question to Jessica about joining the demonstration; the author thereby implies that the original sensory impression is still uppermost in Joyce's mind. When Joyce first puts the question to Jessica, Joyce's face is described as "blank" and "exquisite," and her manner of making the request is compared to that of someone requesting an invitation to a dinner party. With such techniques, the author gives a vivid picture of a young woman who is all pretty surface and no intellectual depth.

In charting Joyce's road to political commitment, Gordimer plays again and again on olfactory imagery. Twice in the story, Joyce becomes aware of the smell of death and flowers, identified with the odor of incense. The first time that this aroma comes into Joyce's consciousness is when she is at the multiracial party. In a flashback, Joyce suddenly remembers having noticed this particular smell years earlier, when she had been shopping at an Indian shop in Johannesburg and had been followed by a mysterious stranger who tried to molest her. In the same flashback, Joyce suddenly remembers the same smell of death and flowers as having pervaded the funeral of her English grandfather. The second time that Joyce becomes aware of the smell is during her difficult struggle, while at Jessica's apartment on the day of the march, to suppress her own anxieties about taking part in the planned antigovernment demonstration.

The author uses this aromatic imagery to symbolize the influence exerted upon Joyce's decision-making processes by psychic elements of which the protagonist is hardly aware. The imagery of smell looms in Joyce's consciousness whenever she faces something new or shocking or when she is contemplating a leap into the unknown, a decision from which there is no turning back. The smell is to some extent associated with Joyce's deeply buried anxieties about miscegenation. Thus, she first becomes aware of the smell when she learns, at the party, that Jessica has an Indian husband; her mind then flashes back to when that mysterious man of vaguely Indian appearance had tried to molest her. The smell returns to Joyce's consciousness on the day of the march, in Jessica's apartment, at precisely the moment when Joyce meets Jessica's husband.

The smell of incense, of death and flowers, is also associated with the code of good manners inherited from Joyce's family background and, by extension, from the English mother country. At the funeral for her grandfather, Joyce had first noticed this smell. The smell returns to her consciousness during the crucial inner struggle in Jessica's apartment, when Joyce decides that good manners require her to take part in the demonstration as she had promised. The smell of death and flowers thus represents not only the lifeless code of formal politeness inherited from England but also the possibility of new life (flowers) arising from this inherited tradition: a symbol of resurrection as well as of death.

Paul D. Mageli

THE SMILES OF KONARAK

Author: George Dennison (1925-   )
Type of plot: Realism
Time of plot: The 1960's
Locale: New York City
First published: 1979

> *Principal characters:*
> TAGGART, who is a playwright, poet, and reviewer
> KARLA, Taggart's lover
> EVERETT WILDER, an aging neighborhood activist

The Story

At the beginning of this story, set in New York during the early 1960's, a time of beatnik literature and social consciousness among intellectuals, a writer, Taggart, meets Karla at a party given in honor of Taggart's latest play. Its success is a gauge of Taggart's ripening as a writer in his thirties. Blessed with inherited money, he has spent years developing his craft without the bind of an ordinary job. While Taggart's destiny of success is apparent, that of his casual but intimate acquaintance Karla is less clear. She has known much frustration in her few years since taking degrees in teaching and social work. These conventional paths to careers merely exposed her to the miseries of working amid bureaucratic agencies which defeated Karla's intention to solve society's many problems. She quit her teaching job and, early in the story, resigns her position as a social worker.

After their first night together, Karla asks Taggart's advice. He has no solution for her problem, knowing already through other friends' experiences the pitfalls of the "helping fields." Characteristic of Taggart, however, he argues the sublime negativity of such occupations, urging Karla to temper her passionate need for instant and permanent effects with a dose of detached realism. Karla's spirit will not be so appeased. Prostitution, she imagines, will be the answer, allowing her to minister to human needs and earn a living. Taggart is shocked at her idealism, if not her impulsive obliviousness, and when her work leads to a painful disillusionment, unspecified in the story, he feels bitterly righteous. She ignored his counseling, which she had sought during their first night together.

While Karla's dreams of "the right job" are dispelled, Taggart's self-esteem as a writer is challenged, not by any personal failure to create literature but by Karla's irreverence for the beatnik poetry writing and readings he values and through meeting Luis Fontana, a young Puerto Rican gang leader with literary aspirations. Luis is charged with possession of narcotics and receives a three-year sentence. In prison he is murdered, a crime the officials feebly attempt to rig as a suicide. After promises of further investigation, the Luis issue dies nearly as swiftly as did the boy himself. Luis, Taggart senses, was the real-life embodiment of the human energies—assertiveness, pride, intelligence—which Taggart imaginatively ascribes to his literary characters, who, precisely because they are imaginary, are privileged, enjoying immunity from the fate that befalls Luis. That Luis as a playwright lacked the skills to embody the experience of "life on the edge" in the violent city puts Taggart's own unique gifts in an ironic light, as he writes successfully of things of which he is not truly part.

Nevertheless, Taggart does *feel* the reality of such harshness abrading the human soul. Karla feels it as well, and her intention has been to lessen its force. She accepts the leadership of a reading clinic organized by Taggart's friend Everett, the aging political activist who has spent a lifetime adjusting his politics to reality. Taggart's stance toward the harshness, while sharing in the actual clinic work, and reuniting with Karla in the process, is through his art: "How mysterious it was that artistic form should absorb and recreate the spirit!" Despite the sadness, the grimness of things, the artist exists, and if not triumphant, mysteriously persistent. The story's final scene has Taggart suddenly remembering that he is scheduled to read at the Eiffel, a community center for beat poets. Karla assures him that they will read to themselves if he does not show, but impelled by his difficult-to-explain connection to the brotherhood, Taggart heads for the center, Karla at his side, and "every ten steps or so he broke into a trot, and she would shrug and smile and run beside him."

Themes and Meanings

The story's title alludes to a central theme. Midway through the story, Taggart has a nostalgic reverie featuring his wife Naomi, from whom he is now divorced. She was extremely beautiful. She appears clearly in his sad reflections, smiling at him while the present Karla sleeps beside him. He has a vision of photographs that once fascinated him, pictures of "sculptured orgiasts" from the Indian Temple of Konarak, abode of the sun god. In their erotic abandonment the figures smile smiles which, in Taggart's perception, "were not images of private bliss, but presupposed a community of trust, perhaps even a community of love." Taggart, citizen of New York City, where Puerto Ricans, blacks, Italians, Slavs, Mexicans, and Jews make a disharmonious cultural hash, senses that the orgiasts' smiles are utopian, their orgy "a visionary hope of trust." The seemingly perfect fit of Taggart's relationship with Naomi was only seeming. Still, Taggart is assailed by the vision of her beauty, her smile, her ravishing appeal, and the memory of those first hours with Naomi endures despite the disharmony and disappointment that followed.

George Dennison suggests that the dream of compatibility is truer than the acknowledged incompatibility, whether among New York's many races or between a man and a woman. He injects Karla into Taggart's life as an antidote to disillusionment, for Karla, a Texas girl with a Southerner's ingenuous frankness, is not a native of the community of the disillusioned. Her continuing love, her calling up from the street to Taggart's apartment ("'Heyyyy, TAAA-gart!' He had never before been hailed like this in the vast city of New York"), enacts for Dennison the possibility which the smiling figures ideally represent. Karla may not perfectly complement Taggart or agree with him on every point, but she is with him in an unprecendented communion, creating for the moment something of the harmony which the photos of the orgiasts so attractively advertise: "The small voice rang up confidently out of the vastness, and he began to smile and feel buoyant."

Style and Technique

"The Smiles of Konarak," published in 1979, details a period nearly twenty years before the date of publication. The first sentence reads: "Early in the nineteen sixties a group of New York poets built a diminutive theater in a Lower East Side settlement house and proceeded to produce their own plays." The focus narrows rapidly to one playwright, Taggart, but the ambience of the early 1960's is itself a considerable presence in the story. Billie Holiday records play during the dance at Taggart's celebration; beat poets drink cappuccinos and compose lines of poetry "by the laws of chance." Dennison seems intent on that time when the hopes which sustained the revolutionary 1960's, era of free and brotherly love, were at their freshest. What has happened since that time, "history," has neither fulfilled those hopes nor definitively discredited them.

To enhance the historical feeling, Dennison leaves his characters in states of limbo, neither granting their dreams nor arguing their impotence. The success of Taggart, an isolated and definitely fortuitous fact—he is lucky enough to have a share of genius—is juxtaposed to Karla's frustrations, and those of other characters, such as the political activist Everett and his friend Luis Fontana. The characters with the greatest enthusiasm for changing the world are frustrated, while the more detached Taggart earns nothing but praise for his writing. The plot contains no development to a climax, but is composed through a series of dramatized scenes which collectively form a sense of culmination. Dennison's style seeks gently to embody the spectacle of life free of literary comment. One example of this is the closing scene, when Taggart and Karla attend an outdoor play in a park. Of all plays to perform, the company has picked *Coriolanus* (1607-1608): "Had ever Shakespeare such an audience as this!? . . . Their speech was a babble of contending phrases." Life is more a spectacle than literature. The comings and goings of Ukranians, Poles, Puerto Ricans, and one particularly belligerent negress, "with red hair and dully gleaming sores on her legs," who stands onstage before the play shaking her fist at the audience are, Taggart admits, more interesting than the performance of the "real" actors.

Through the story's re-creation of an era, the reader feels both the distance of the past and its still-forceful presence, much as Taggart experiences the still-living smiles of his long gone wife, Naomi.

Bruce Wiebe

THE SNAKE CHARMER

Author: Varlam Shalamov (1907-1982)
Type of plot: Social realism
Time of plot: Sometime between the mid-1930's and the mid-1950's
Locale: A forced-labor camp in the Kolyma region of northeastern Siberia
First published: "Zaklinatel zmei," 1978 (English translation, 1980)

> *Principal characters:*
> THE NARRATOR, a political prisoner in one of Joseph Stalin's
>   work camps
> PLATONOV, a fellow political prisoner, a former screenwriter
> FEDYA, a criminal

The Story

Two political prisoners are sitting on a fallen tree during a work break. One of them, a former screenwriter named Platonov, is telling the narrator the story of his "second life," his life in the camps. It turns out that Platonov has spent a year at the Jankhar mine, a place notorious even by the standards of Kolyma, a region of northeastern Siberia.

Platonov explains, however, that only the first few months were bad. The only political prisoner—therefore the only educated one—among common criminals, he survived the year at Jankhar by telling the stories of Alexandre Dumas, *pere*, Arthur Conan Doyle, and H. G. Wells, and in return was fed, clothed, and protected by the thieves. He assumes that the narrator has also made use of this, the one advantage of the literate prisoner.

The narrator has never been a "novelist," however, and in fact opines that "novel-telling" is the lowest form of humiliation. At the same time, he does not find fault with Platonov and says only that a starving man can be forgiven much.

Platonov plans, if he lives long enough, to write a story about his own storytelling career, and he has even thought of a title, "The Snake Charmer." Yet he dies too soon—three weeks after this conversation, he collapses while breaking rock and dies as so many have died, of hunger, weakness, and heart failure. The narrator, who liked Platonov for his curiosity and lively interest in the world outside, decides to tell the snake charmer's story.

The snake charmer's story begins as Platonov finishes his first, exhausting day at Jankhar. He waits for the roll to be called and while waiting reflects on the fact that the end of the working day is not really the end, that they all must return their tools, fall in for yet another roll call, march five kilometers to gather firewood, then haul the logs back to camp. No vehicles are used for hauling wood, and the horses are too ill and weak to leave the stable—which leads Platonov to thoughts about human endurance and human instinct, the instinct (not will) that makes even a dying man cling tenaciously to life. Man, he thinks, is tougher than any animal.

When he finally gets to the barracks, he sees that not everyone has worked that day. A group is perched on the top bunks, watching a card game. Platonov barely has time to sit down on the edge of a bunk when one of the toughs addresses him as a generic "Ivan Ivanovich." When Platonov answers that that is not his name, he is shoved over to the chief thug, threatened, and then slugged in the face. The thug, Fedya, orders him to sleep by the slop bucket, the foulest spot in the barracks.

Platonov knows that these thugs are not joking—he has already seen two thieves strangled to settle scores. He does as he is told, but Fedya is bored and restless; Fedya wants his feet scratched, but is not satisfied with the way the young thief Mashka does it. He rouses Platonov again with orders to carry out the bucket and stoke the stove.

Most of the prisoners are asleep by this time, but Fedya wants a story. The thieves roust Platonov out one more time and almost ingratiatingly ask him if he can "tell novels." Platonov considers, doubts racing through his mind over the bargain he is about to make—and agrees. Fedya immediately brightens, gives him some bread and a cigarette, and asks him his name.

Platonov offers a selection, then begins the tale chosen by Fedya. It is dawn by the time he finishes the first part. Fedya is delighted and lets Platonov sleep in the best bunks with the thieves.

When the prisoners are leaving the barracks the next morning, a big country boy gives Platonov a vicious shove and curses him. Yet all it takes is one word from another prisoner, and the big one apologizes, asking Platonov not to tell Fedya what has happened. Platonov promises not to tell.

Themes and Meanings

An ordinary political prisoner in the forced-labor camps of Kolyma might survive cold, hunger, and disease; he might survive overwork and lack of sleep; he might survive brutal beatings by the camp guards. Yet even if he lived through all these things, he might not make it through the encounter with one group of his fellow prisoners—the common criminals, or "urkas." Thieves, murderers, and rapists in the outside world, they exercise their talents in the camps as well.

The urka subculture—and here that term is frighteningly literal—dates back to brigand gangs of the seventeenth century and has lived on through revolution and social upheaval. Often bizarrely and profusely tattooed, maimed, and scarred, speaking their own argot, rewarding and punishing according to their own code, the urkas have seemed barely human to many a new arrival in the camps. Yet their position is a privileged one. They receive better food, warmer clothing, lighter work—and steal or extort whatever they cannot get "legally." Anything a political owns is fair game. The urkas live in an uneasy truce—not alliance—with the camp administration, not only because the administration fears them, not only because their absolute amorality terrifies the other prisoners, but also because they are useful in enforcing official policy. They are one more means of breaking the politicals' spirit. The urkas are told that though they might be guilty, erring, prodigal sons and daughters of the Soviet motherland, they are nevertheless still part of the family, not yet the lowest of the low. The politicals, however, are total outcasts, traitors, filth. An urka can thus rob, brutalize, or even murder a political with virtual impunity—he is actually helping the administration do its job.

Yet there is one urka custom which has saved many a "friar," or intellectual. The urkas love hearing novels, preferably adventure tales or mysteries, and preferably as close to the original as possible. For a lump of bread, some soup, a blanket, and immunity from beatings, an educated prisoner can play Scheherazade to the criminal court, telling and retelling *The Count of Monte Cristo*, *Les Miserables*, and other stories.

Hence, Platonov's dilemma: Are the compromises that make physical survival possible always the same ones that make moral survival impossible? This is the central question of the story, and this is what races through Platonov's mind before he gives Fedya his answer. He toys with the idea that perhaps even here he can be useful, can educate, enlighten in the noble old tradition of the Russian intelligentsia. Yet both he and the reader realize immediately that these are the terms of Platonov's old life, not his new one. He will be saving only himself, and some other unfortunate will be the butt of jokes, curses, and abuse. Is "novel-telling," then, really any more noble than carrying out the slop bucket? Or is it the moral equivalent of scratching a thug's feet?

Platonov does not answer the question for himself or for the reader, but he makes his choice and tells his tale. His final words do not resolve the ambivalence, but they do speak in his favor, just as the narrator's introduction did. Platonov is now safe, albeit temporarily and precariously, and high enough in the hierarchy to exercise some tiny bit of power himself. He can, with a word, arrange for someone else to be beaten, but he chooses not to.

Style and Technique

One of the chief sources of irony in all of Shalamov's stories is his narrative method itself—horrific events recited in calm, undramatic fashion, an objective account of murderous absurdity. In "The Snake Charmer," he adds a more explicitly moral dimension to that irony by prefacing Platonov's story with a conversation between Platonov and the narrator, and by letting the narrator inform the reader of Platonov's death.

When Platonov tells the narrator that he wants to write a story about his "novelist" days, he automatically begins his sentence with a camp formula, a cautionary charm. If he lives, he will write the story. While the narrator agrees that Platonov's title is a good one, he reminds him that the main thing is to survive to write it. Platonov, the "novelist," dies before he can write anything down, and the narrator, who has avoided becoming just such an entertainer, is left to tell his story, the story of a man who did what he himself refused to do.

Thus the reader already knows this narrator's point of view and his attitude toward Platonov and his choice. Platonov's doubts and waverings are filtered through the mind of a man who would not have done what he did. Yet Shalamov himself refuses to turn that irony into either self-righteousness or sarcasm. His narrator has his own storytelling code, and he does not betray it, but tells the truth.

Jane Ann Miller

THE SNIPER

Author: Liam O'Flaherty (1896-1984)
Type of plot: Adventure
Time of plot: The early 1920's
Locale: Dublin, Ireland
First published: 1923

> *Principal characters:*
> A SNIPER, a Republican
> ANOTHER SNIPER, a Free Stater
> A MAN IN AN ARMORED CAR
> AN OLD WOMAN

The Story

"The Sniper" relates an encounter in downtown Dublin near the O'Connell Bridge between a sniper for the Republicans and a sniper for the Free Staters. Guns roar in the distance as the Republican sniper lies on a rooftop. He is a young boy. "His face was that of a student—thin and ascetic, but his eyes had the cold gleam of a fanatic . . . the eyes of a man who is used to look at death."

It is a June evening, and the sniper, who has had nothing to eat since morning, hungrily wolfs down a sandwich and takes a short drink from the flask of whiskey he carries in his pocket. He desperately wants a cigarette and finally risks showing his position by igniting a match and lighting one. Instantly, a bullet hits the wall near him. He takes two puffs of the cigarette and snuffs it. He raises himself to look over the parapet, but another bullet whizzes by his head, and he flattens himself against the roof.

An armored car crosses O'Connell Bridge and stops just below the sniper's position. An old woman with a tattered shawl around her head comes out of a side street to talk with a man in the turret of the armored car. The sniper wants to shoot at the armored car, but he knows that his bullets will not penetrate its fortified exterior. The old woman points in the direction of the sniper, who now realizes that she is an informer. When the man inside opens the turret to talk with her, the sniper shoots, and the man slumps over lifeless. The woman hurries toward the side street, but the sniper shoots again. The old woman shrieks and falls into the gutter. The car speeds away, the man in the turret still slumped there. More shooting is heard, and the sniper knows that it is coming from the roof across the way. He has been hit in his right arm, in which he has lost all feeling.

The sniper takes out his knife and uses it to rip open his shirt. He sees that a bullet has gone into his arm but has not emerged from the other side. He takes out his field-dressing kit, breaks off the top of the iodine bottle that he pulls from it, and pours the dark liquid into his wound. Then he applies the bandages from his kit, using his teeth to tie the knot.

The sniper knows that he must get off the roof by morning or else the enemy sniper will kill him. He realizes that the sniper on the roof across the way is watching him every minute and will not let him get away. Taking his rifle, which is useless to him because his wounded arm makes it impossible for him to fire it, he puts his army cap on the muzzle and raises it slightly above the parapet. A shot rings out and the cap falls to the earth far below. The sniper lets his left arm hang lifelessly over the parapet, holding his rifle in it. Then he lets the rifle fall and rolls over.

The opposing sniper, assuming that his enemy is dead, relaxes his vigilance and stands up on the roof. The Republican sniper aims his revolver at his opponent and fires. The enemy sniper reels over the parapet in his death agony, then falls to the earth. The Republican sniper is suddenly revolted by what he sees and by what he has done. "His teeth chattered. He began to gibber to himself, cursing the war, cursing himself, cursing everybody." He drains his whiskey flask in one draught.

The sniper leaves the roof. When he gets to the street, his curiosity overcomes him and forces him to steal over to see whom he has shot. He attracts machine-gun fire as he goes toward the dead sniper, but he is not hit. He flings himself down beside the body of the man he has killed, then turns it over. He finds himself staring into his own brother's face.

Themes and Meanings

"The Sniper" emphasizes one of the greatest ironies of civil war: Brother is pitted against brother. In this story, O'Flaherty deals with a strife that has divided Ireland for more than sixty years and still shows few signs of moderating. The Republican sniper in the story is young, and his youth is emphasized. Yet under conditions of war, this youth is growing up fast, probably too fast. He has the look of a fanatic, and he is forced to develop the cunning of a seasoned warrior. If he fails to develop that cunning, he will not live.

In the course of two hours, the young sniper kills three people, one his own brother—who, ironically, is poised to kill him if he is given the opportunity. The Republican sniper outwits the Free Stater into being careless, and this carelessness costs the Free Stater his life.

In a sense, carelessness also costs the man in the turret of the armored car his life. He should not have responded to the old woman who came to give him information. Had he not exposed his head, he could not have been killed, because the car's armor would have protected him. In a moment of relaxed security, he makes himself vulnerable and loses his life. In the next instant, the sniper kills an old woman.

O'Flaherty demonstrates the impersonality of war: One shoots the Enemy, not people. When the sniper is doing his killing, it is the Enemy at whom he is firing. The Enemy, however, becomes a person when the protagonist sees the opposing sniper's body fall to the ground. He is sickened at the thought of what he has done, and one can only speculate on the implications for him of discovering, ultimately, that it is his own brother he has killed.

O'Flaherty is saying that soldiers grow up fast or not at all. There is no question that the sniper does what he has to do, and at the beginning, there is a great adventure in what he is doing. The adventure, however, depends upon anonymity. No one in this story has a name, and everyone, even, to an extent, the protagonist, is seen from a distance. Once one is killing people, the whole impact of what war is about crowds in on the killer.

Although one perhaps cannot go so far as to call "The Sniper" a pacifist tract, certainly it depicts several of the worst horrors of war. It shows that war makes life seem cheap. It shows that war also hardens the hearts of those who participate in it. In the end, the story shows the absurdity and futility of fighting against individual human beings.

Both snipers in this story are pawns of forces larger than themselves, and these forces split families, shatter loyalties, and pervert the very causes that they purport to be fighting to preserve. The first irony is that men will kill other men. The second and greater irony in the O'Flaherty story is that in this case the two men are of the same parents.

Style and Technique

Fear and tension pervade "The Sniper." O'Flaherty, making full use of his tight unity of place, builds tension steadily and systematically in several ways. The reader is told that one can hear the thunder of ammunition exploding in the distance. In the immediate milieu that the author creates, bullets whiz by and every simple act, such as lighting a cigarette, must be weighed carefully for its potential danger. The sniper is essentially a schoolboy caught up in a situation over which he must gain control. If he fails, he dies.

O'Flaherty creates a feeling of tension by his skillful use of short, clipped sentences and simple, direct vocabulary. As the tension is built, each sentence reveals only one bare fact:

> The turret opened. A man's head and shoulders appeared, looking towards the sniper. The sniper raised his rifle and fired. The head fell heavily on the turret wall. The woman darted toward the side street. The sniper fired again. The woman whirled around and fell with a shriek into the gutter.

The beat of these sentences is like the beating of one's heart. To read a paragraph so tightly controlled and structured as this one is to have one's breath taken away.

O'Flaherty, because he has to emphasize how totally on his own the young sniper is, cannot have dialogue in this story. The sniper must be on the roof alone. The omniscient observer must tell everything that happens without being intrusive. O'Flaherty thus keeps a tight rein on a story that is highly dramatic but whose dramatic impact must be made through understatement.

R. Baird Shuman

THE SNIPER

Author: Alan Sillitoe (1928-   )
Type of plot: Psychological realism
Time of plot: 1914-1918 and 1964
Locale: Nottingham, England, and Gommecourt, France
First published: 1981

> *Principal characters:*
> NEVILL, a farm laborer, a sergeant in World War I, and a
>   mechanic
> AMY, his wife
> A FANCYMAN, Amy's lover

The Story

The patrons at The Radford Arms pub are astonished to see an old man suddenly leap on one of the tables and begin to dance. Everyone looks at the man's feet, expecting him to fall down. Some continue to find the performance amusing, but others start to ignore him, more interested in consuming their last drinks, since it is near closing time. The man still hops around and, at the same time in a sort of singsong voice, talks about a murder he has committed a half century ago. The dancer, crushed by guilt and fear, wants to confess publicly, now that his life is near its end. Few people are listening, however, and those who do hear nothing that makes much sense. Had they been able to figure out what the old man was saying, they would have heard how he killed his wife's lover in 1914.

The story is told in flashback. Nevill, suspecting that his spouse is unfaithful, lies in wait for her in the woods, where he believes she and her fancyman will have their rendezvous. From his hiding place, he watches Amy follow her lover into the shelter of the trees. Nevill waits while the two make love, considering that it might be best to go home, but his compulsion for retribution is strong. When her passion is spent, Nevill's wife leaves to return home, but her lover remains behind to smoke a cigarette. Nevill stalks him and batters his neck with the butt of a shotgun, giving him the *coup de grâce*, when he is on the ground, by smashing his temple. Nevill then hides the body.

Before Nevill leaves the wood, he kills a rabbit and sells the dead animal at a local bar; he then drinks a beer with the proceeds and listens to some other patrons talk about the war. Nevill thinks that they do not know what life is all about. The next day, he returns to the wood and buries the body, making sure that he disguises the grave with dead twigs and rotting leaves. Afterward, he goes down to the recruiting office and enlists, believing "that the army would be as good a place to hide as any." Amy is so distraught at the prospect of her husband's departure that for a moment Nevill regrets having joined the army, but he puts this out of his mind.

He leaves to fight in France, but the memory of the murder follows him. Ironically, his fear that he might be apprehended at any moment contributes to his proficiency as a soldier, "for he did not live from day to day like most of the platoon.... [H]e existed by the minute because everyone contained the possibility of him being taken off and hanged." He becomes a lance corporal and, because of his superior marksmanship, is made a sniper, a job that obliges him to remain concealed, quietly scanning the enemy lines for quarry, "letting his body into complete repose so as to make no move," picking off those careless enough to show their heads around a parapet in an unguarded moment. He remains like this throughout the day, trying to remain undetected. After nightfall, a new sniper's post will be built, and tomorrow he will "be in a different position and, corked face invisible, could start all over again." The memory of his past continues to haunt him. Each morning, when he awakes, he realizes that he has not yet been "taken up" for the one he has killed in Nottingham. Sometimes he sees the murdered man's likeness in the opposite trenches.

Nevill's sniping days come to an end through a fluke. He is behind the lines with his company at the communal bathhouse, where the water is only a few degrees above freezing. The men are complaining bitterly about the icy spray, but Nevill makes light of this and begins to shout, "It's too hot! It's scalding me to death. Turn it off! I'm broiled alive. Put some cold in, for Christ's sake." The men begin laughing, and the tension breaks. Nevill has no idea what prompted him to act as he did, but his captain admires his performance, thinking that this is a man who can control men through firmness and display of wit. The captain promotes Nevill to sergeant.

Becoming a noncommissioned officer makes Nevill's life more dangerous. Now he will fight with his platoon in the front ranks in the forthcoming big assault. When the day arrives, Nevill tries to give his men courage, walking along the trench asking them if they have drunk their allotment of rum. Before they go over the top, Nevill's lieutenant tells him that he is wanted at Battalion Headquarters. The reason, unknown to the lieutenant and Nevill, is to ask Nevill why he applied for so many ration allotments the previous week, but Nevill automatically assumes that this is his long-awaited summons to be arrested for the murder he committed in Nottingham, and he begs the lieutenant to allow him to participate in the attack with his men. He says he will go to Battalion Headquarters afterward. The lieutenant agrees.

The attack is a debacle. Most of the platoon is cut to pieces, the survivors dispersed all over the battlefield. Nevill finds himself isolated in a shell-hole with a man called Jack Clifford. In trying to knock out a German machine-gun nest which has them pinned down, Clifford is mortally wounded. With the bullets and shrapnel flying overhead, Nevill tells the blood-soaked Clifford about how he murdered his wife's lover. "It's on'y one you killed, sarge.

Don't much matter," says the dying man. Nevill tries to carry Clifford to safety, "thinking that as long as he hung on to him he need never consider the hangman again." He manages to bring him in, but he is not rewarded for his bravery, because the wounded man is already dead.

Nevill is demobilized in 1919, and he returns to Nottingham to find Amy, who welcomes him back. During the war, Amy has been a munitions worker, filling shells in a factory at Chilwell. She wrote him letters in which she said that she loved him and would always love him. She told him that she was having a baby. Yet Nevill realized that the child could hardly be his. Nevertheless, when he returns, he pretends to be the child's father. Amy and Nevill have two sons of their own. Nevill is never brave enough to tell her what he told Jack Clifford in that shell-hole in France. He senses that if he does, it would mean the end of their relationship.

Now, years later and nearly eighty, Nevill tries to tell the strangers at The Radford Arms pub. Even those who hear his words refuse to believe him and think that he is senile. Several good souls drive him back home to his wife. He does not live long after that. Amy finds him dead one morning, sitting fully dressed by the fireplace. Some of his neighbors, who come to the funeral, are not surprised. They have heard about his dancing on the table and assume that after that, the end could not have been far away.

Themes and Meanings

Nevill, like many of Sillitoe's heroes, is an outsider, but his alienation is in large part self-imposed. Although he comes from the lower classes (in a society where "lower class" means no class), social problems are only incidental to this story. Nevill's crime, the quintessential antisocial act, does not flow from the class struggle, nor from feelings of rage against economic exploitation or political oppression, nor is it conditioned by any societal code of honor. Even among the lower classes in England in 1914, it was not considered particularly good form for a husband to punish a sexual transgression with death. Unless intended as an act of independence against a sort of sexual exploitation, the deed might be considered part of a desire to preserve one's territory against a poacher. Nevill fully realizes what he is doing: "Now that he knew for certain, there seemed no point in pursuing them, for he could call the tune any time he liked." Yet he believes that he is compelled to bring the affair to an end, as if by coming this far retreat would be unconscionable, "the deliberate putting forward on the grass of one foot after another was as if he advanced on a magnetised track impossible to sidestep."

In the army, he is directed by no such emotion. He becomes a cold, methodical hit man, accepting his sniper job as a normal part of a day's work. He is proud of his professionalism, each of his kills being proof of his expertise, his cleverness, and his self-discipline. He feels less concern about exterminating Germans than about those rabbits he had shot in order to buy a few drinks. His country's laws, which prohibit murder on the small scale, now condone and bless it on the grand scale. Thus, Nevill's routine slaughter, directed against strangers, becomes more horrific than his *crime passionnel* and is all the more chilling for its abstraction. The war provides a means for Nevill to remove the memory of the man he killed in Nottingham. "In pushing aside the image of the hangman coming to get him across no-man's-land . . . he had only to punctuate his counting of the minutes by a careful shot at some flicker on the opposite sandbags." Nevill, however, finds it impossible to free himself socially and psychologically.

The deed directs his life to greater dependence, conformity, and regulation. Haunted by fear of discovery, he seeks escape in the most restricted of societies. After the army, his attempt at catharsis unsuccessful, he returns home and decides to lead a life of complete domesticity, remaining with the woman who was impregnated by the man he had slain. His nightmare continues, as does his search for relief, finally culminating in a desperate attempt to achieve resolution in an absurd dance on the table in a pub, an act of liberation manqué. Here is a hero whose desire is not for the transformation of society, but for peace of mind.

Style and Technique

Though Sillitoe was born a decade after the end of the Great War, his descriptions of the effects of trench warfare on the lives of the participants make one recall the poems of Siegfried Sassoon:

> Shells of shrapnel balls exploded above their heads. They stopped silently, or rolled against the soil as if thrown by an invisible hand. Or they were hidden in a wreath of smoke and never seen again. The wire was like a wall. The guns had cut only one gap so they were like a football crowd trying to get off the field through a narrow gate on which machine guns were trained.

Sillitoe relies on such compelling passages to keep the reader moving through his story.

He also sustains interest through the skillful interaction of nature with the mind of his character. Consider the way in which he sets up the murder itself, a murder which the reader has already been informed has taken place. Nevill's bloody thoughts blend with the locale in which they will be translated into action. All living things and natural phenomena seem to be one with the character's primitive determination to seek justice: "A breeze which carried the smell of grass made him hungry." "The last of the sun flushed white and pink against his eyes." "A platoon of starlings scoured back and forth on a patch of grass to leave no worm's hiding place unturned." "The odour of fungus and running water on clean pebbles was sharpened by the cool of the evening."

Sillitoe creates grand suspense by his use of the flashback. The beginning of the story reveals exactly enough about the protagonist to compel interest. (The narrative hook of an octogenarian dancing on a table is by itself intriguing and inventive.) What motivates his activity? Why, after half a century, does the old man want to speak his peace? Nevill is not Sillitoe's usual proletarian hero, who attempts to fight external forces beyond his control. Nevill's struggle is within himself, and Sillitoe seems to convey that he, too, is seeking to find answers to the same questions that he poses. Sillitoe has learned that the less a character is made to appear a victim of society, the less he becomes a stereotype, the more compelling and interesting he can be as an individual. Nevill, despite all one is told about his actions, still remains distant and aloof. Sillitoe allows the reader to share his anxieties, but keeps his distance, surrounding him with an imagery of pessimism and gloom.

Wm. Laird Kleine-Ahlbrandt

THE SNOW-STORM

Author: Leo Tolstoy (1828-1910)
Type of plot: Romantic realism
Time of plot: The 1850's
Locale: The Russian Caucasus
First published: "Metel," 1856 (English translation, 1889)

Principal characters:
THE UNNAMED NARRATOR
ALYËSHKA, the narrator's manservant
SLEDGE DRIVERS

The Story

The unnamed narrator of the story (probably meant to be Leo Tolstoy himself) and his manservant Alyëshka start on an evening trip by sledge from Novocherkassk in the Caucasus to a destination in central Russia. As they ride, a winter storm begins, and soon the road becomes covered with heavy, thick snow. The narrator becomes concerned about getting lost and queries his driver about their chances of making it safely to the next post station. The driver is somewhat vague and fatalistic concerning the rest of the journey, suggesting that they may or may not get through. The narrator has little confidence in the driver, who seems inexperienced and sullen.

A few minutes later, the driver stops the sledge, gets down, and starts searching for the road which they have lost. Disturbed by this situation, the narrator orders the phlegmatic driver to turn back, giving the horses their head to seek out the post station from which they started out. To add to the anxiety, the driver tells a story of some recent travelers who got lost and froze to death in a similar storm.

Soon they hear the bells of three mail-express sledges coming toward them and going in the opposite direction. The narrator orders his driver to turn around and follow the fresh tracks of the mail sledges. The tracks and road markers quickly disappear in the drifting snow. The narrator himself now gets out of the sledge to look for the road, but soon loses sight of even the sledge. Finding his driver and sledge, a decision is again made to turn back and return to the station from which they started out.

Again they hear the bells of the mail express, which is now returning to their original starting point, having delivered the mail and changed horses. The narrator's driver suggests that they follow them back. As the narrator's driver tries to turn around, his shafts hit the horses tied to the back of the third mail *troyka*, making them break their straps, bolt, and run. The post driver goes off in search of the runaway horses, while the narrator follows the first two sledges at full gallop. In better spirits now that he has somebody to follow, the narrator's driver converses with his passenger affably, telling about his life and family circumstances.

Soon they run across a caravan of wagons, led by a mare without help from the driver who is sleeping. They almost lose sight of the mail sledges, and the driver wants to turn around again, but they go on.

The old driver who went to get the runaway horses returns with all three and loses little time in reprimanding the narrator's driver, whose inexperience created the problem in the first place.

The narrator begins to daydream, losing himself in the monotonous and desolate snowstorm and musing lyrically about the snow and wind: "Memories and fancies followed one another with increased rapidity in my imagination." The narrator conjures up stream-of-consciousness images of his youth: the old family butler on their baronial estate, summers in the country, fishing, languid July afternoons, and finally a peasant drowning in their pond and nobody being able to help.

The narrator's driver announces that his horses are too tired to go on, and he proposes that the narrator and his servant go with the post sledges. The baggage is transferred, and the narrator is glad to get into the warm, snug sledge. Inside, two old men are telling stories to pass the time. They give very short, blunt answers to the narrator's suggestion that they all might freeze to death if the horses give out: "To be sure, we may. . . ." After driving a while longer, the men in the sledge begin arguing about whether what they see on the horizon is an encampment. The narrator becomes sleepy and thinks that he is freezing to death. He has hallucinations about what it must be like to freeze to death, dozing and waking alternately.

The narrator wakes in the morning to find that the snow has stopped and he has arrived at a post station. He treats all the men to a glass of vodka and, having received fresh horses, continues on the next leg of his journey.

Themes and Meanings

"The Snow-Storm" is based on an actual event from Tolstoy's life. While traveling in the Caucasus in 1854, Tolstoy became lost and had to spend the night in a snowstorm. He gives a fictional account of his ordeal in the present story two years later.

"The Snow-Storm" is Tolstoy's Russian version of the classical mythic theme of exile and travel. The story is very topical and specific in regard to time and place. Nevertheless, the narrator, whose experiences the story describes, can be seen as a kind of universal hero or Everyman. The journey thus becomes life; the snowstorm, life's unpredictable mortal dangers which must be faced. Tolstoy goes on to elaborate the conceit on a symbolic level. The powerful snowstorm begins suddenly and without warning. It is a force of nature against which man, alone or in congregation, becomes important and ultimately vulnerable. It is sheer good fortune which permits one man to survive while another perishes. This is why Tolstoy has the characters in the story exhibit a kind of Oriental fatalism toward the snowstorm and the danger it represents. Like so many implacable, impersonal misfortunes to which man is subject, the snowstorm renders philosophy and religion, as well as human strength and cunning, useless at a moment of great peril.

Russian snowstorms have a special place in Tolstoy's writings. They are frequently used by Tolstoy as a symbol of the elemental, powerful, and uncontrollable force of nature. Unlike his Romantic precursors, however, Tolstoy does not imbue the storm with any sentimental or poetic significance. His approach is realistic, almost scientific. The snowstorm is for Tolstoy but another meterological phenomenon, characteristic of Russia and other places with similar winter seasons. The accuracy and descriptive power of the young Tolstoy are noteworthy and typical for his whole literary career.

Style and Technique

The story is told in the first person by an unnamed narrator, who probably represents Tolstoy himself. "The Snow-Storm" contains little suspense and almost no adventure. Nothing extraordinary happens—a man gets lost while sleighing in a snowstorm and finds his way to shelter with the help of some mail-express drivers. The main point of interest in the story is the narrator's psychological contemplation of things around him: his driver, the horses' behavior, the storm, the night, and himself.

The language of the story is neutral, unmarked, and stylistically classical. The one literary device characteristic to Tolstoy in the story is the narrator's ability to associate images from the reality around him to his dreams as he alternately dozes and wakes up during the long night of travel.

Although there are no real sociological complications between the nobleman narrator and the serf drivers, there is a hint of distrust between the representatives of two different classes.

R. E. Richardson

A SOLDIER'S EMBRACE

Author: Nadine Gordimer (1923-   )
Type of plot: Social realism
Time of plot: The twentieth century
Locale: An unnamed African country
First published: 1980

> *Principal characters:*
> THE LAWYER, a white liberal, displaced by the revolution
> SHE, his wife, the central consciousness in the story
> CHIPANDE, their African friend, recently returned from
>   political exile
> FATHER MULUMBUA, also a friend, a black priest sympathetic
>   to the revolution
> MUCHANGA, their black servant

The Story

The very fact that the woman and her lawyer husband are not given names in this story is significant, for although they are the central characters, they are anonymous colonials whose lives must change, even though they are liberals sympathetic to the freedom fighters, now that native blacks have taken over this unnamed African country. This story, like many others by Nadine Gordimer, a white South African writer, is about the changing world of African society, a world always at tension between the often silent world of the blacks and the increasingly dislodged world of the white colonials. Dislodgement is indeed what "A Soldier's Embrace" is about.

The story begins with the event of the embrace itself, an experience of the lawyer's wife confronting two celebrants of the cease-fire, one white, one black. In an abruptly frozen moment, she kisses them both on the cheek, and as the story progresses and the revolutionaries take more and more control of the city, she remembers that embrace in an obsessively symbolic way—the convergence of the two soldiers with her own confused self symbolizing the dilemma in which she and her well-meaning, liberal husband are caught. She kisses one on the left cheek and one on the right cheek as if they were two sides of one face, and this Janus image of the two faces of African society is the central one which dominates the story.

The two-faced nature of the story centers on the gradual sense of fear and alienation that the couple feel in a world in which they once felt at home. Three former native friends whose attitudes change with the revolution add to this feeling of isolation. First, there is Father Mulumbua, a priest from the slums who has gone to prison in the past for shouting freedom slogans; the couple are proud of their friendship with Mulumbua. Now he feels uncomfortable in their home and says little. Then there is Chipande, who has come in out of the bush after being forced to leave by the old white regime. Now with a job in the new order, he comes to visit but is also uncomfortable, restless, and curt. Finally, there is Muchanga, an old servant, who, although they keep him on because they believe that he will not survive alone, causes them to feel somehow guilty.

Gradually, the lawyer loses clients as more and more of the white colonials move across the border; reluctantly he realizes that there is no longer a place for him in this country that he has called his home, for he knows that he will be at risk in the university and will be unwanted as a consultant in the new government. The story comes to an inevitable climax when the lawyer and his wife realize that they must go, and the lawyer accepts a position in the neighboring country. At this point, Chipande, the young friend whom they have known for years, comes, with tears in his eyes, to beg them to stay. At the story's close, the wife sets up Muchanga with a hawker's license and a handcart, realizing that he cannot survive. As she waves good-bye to him, she does not know what to say, for the right words, whatever they were, she feels are left behind forever.

Themes and Meanings

"A Soldier's Embrace" has a curious sense of reflecting the same kind of ambiguous relationship between blacks and whites in Africa with the arrival of independence that must have been experienced by blacks and whites in some areas of the American South after the Civil War. The white couple are liberals and proud of it, taking special pride in welcoming into their home the radical black priest and befriending the poor black Chipande; they also feel a paternalistic attitude toward the servant Muchanga. What the story seems to emphasize is the double face of black-white relations, in which even as the white couple are innocent of a conscious prejudicial attitude toward the blacks, they inevitably seem to manifest such a prejudice. Regardless of what they do, they seem somehow to feel their superiority to the blacks. Even when they exhibit their liberal values, they are too self-conscious of their liberal gestures. This is not to make them particularly culpable, but rather to expose the difficult ambiguity of the white attitude toward the black in Africa. The lawyer and his wife are not named because they represent the white liberal relationship with blacks in Africa that seems somehow inescapable.

There is no reason that the lawyer and his wife should leave the country except the simple fact that they are white, for they have supported the revolution in belief throughout. Gradually, however, they begin to feel more and more uncomfortable, which suggests that they felt comfortable before only because, even though they never expressed the desire for domination, they were in the dominant position. It is easy to feel liberal toward someone different when one is in a position of power over the other—not so easy when the tables are turned. The subtle revelation that the turning of the tables manifests is what this story is really about.

Style and Technique

The method of the story is typical of many of Gordimer's short stories; it is lean and spare, like the stories of her early modernist precursors, Anton Chekhov and Katherine Mansfield. The story communicates by implication rather than by direct statement. It begins with the embrace which gives it its title and then develops that minor but symbolically dramatic encounter into a metaphor that obsesses the lawyer's wife, but which she herself does not really understand. Throughout the story, the image of her face between the white face and the black face of the two soldiers continually recurs to her, standing for the inescapable dilemma of the white man in Africa.

The point of view of the story is that of an unidentified omniscient narrator, but it sticks closely to the perspective of the lawyer's wife. One curious element of the story is that although the lawyer seems the central liberal white caught in the revolution of black freedom fighting, it is actually his wife who serves as the reflector of the growing discomfort that the couple feel in their home.

The structure of "A Soldier's Embrace" moves back and forth between the personal experiences of the wife, beginning with the embrace and ending with her attitude toward her servant, and the more general problems of the lawyer trying to hold on to his place. These shifts are treated in an abrupt, elliptical fashion by Gordimer; the two faces of the story itself—one personal and one political—are separated by blank spaces in the text. Finally, the technique of the story is gradually to develop the embrace—the white soldier and the black soldier, with the white liberal woman caught in between—into a metaphor of the subtle ambiguity of the Janus-faced reality of black-white relations in modern Africa. It is an ambiguity that is never resolved, for at the end of the story the haughty Chipande comes and begs them to stay with tears in his eyes, like a truant child asking his parents to forgive him and not to leave. Thus, from Gordimer's point of view, moving from childlike dependence to equal friendship is a difficult transition to make. The fact that the wife does not know what to say to her old servant Muchanga means she knew what to say before only because of his role as a servant. Now that is he not, that relationship is left behind, and she truly does have nothing to say. Only with the overthrow of white supremacy does even the white liberal realize how complex his relationship with blacks in their own country has been.

Nadine Gordimer had always been a staunch champion of the short-story form, claiming that it is a genre better equipped to capture the nature of human reality than the novel. Basically, Gordimer believes that the coherence of tone necessary to hold a novel together is false to what can really be grasped of human reality, whereas short-story writers practice the art of the present moment, the epiphanic realization that comes sometimes abruptly and sometimes gradually and is good only for that moment. "A Soldier's Embrace" is a good example of Gordimer's view of what the short story does best—reflect an ambiguous state of things that cannot be captured either by the prolonged coherence of tone of the novel or by the conceptual straight-forward statement of the essay, but which can be realized indirectly by subtle suggestion.

Charles E. May

SOLDIER'S HOME

Author: Ernest Hemingway (1899-1961)
Type of plot: Psychological realism
Time of plot: The 1920's
Locale: A small town in Oklahoma
First published: 1925

Principal characters:
HAROLD KREBS, a soldier
MRS. KREBS, his mother

The Story

The title of this story suggests a familiar American landmark and symbol: The soldier's home, a place for retired military to live and relive their war experiences. In this tale, however, the soldier's home is neither a haven for ex-soldiers nor an environment for reminiscing. It is the place to which Harold Krebs, a Marine who fought in World War I, returns to be alone and to face the lies that he and others utter about the war.

When Krebs returns to his hometown in Oklahoma, after having fought in various European arenas, he discovers that he has changed but that nothing in the town has changed. This dramatic difference between the returnee and those who stayed home sets up the basic conflict in the story: the dishonesty that is demanded for survival. It is demonstrated most clearly in the retelling of war stories, for the townspeople do not want to hear the truth about the atrocities of battle, preferring, instead, lies about the heroics of war. Krebs finds himself telling these lies because dishonesty is the path of least resistance, even though it causes a "nausea in regard to experience that is the result of untruth or exaggeration."

Alienated from his family and the local people, Krebs spends his days aimlessly, sleeping late, reading, practicing the clarinet, playing pool. He makes no effort to relate seriously with anyone, including women, because he does not want the complications or consequences of relationships. He is home, but it is no soldier's home to which he has returned.

The climax of the story occurs during a conversation between Krebs and his mother. Initiating a discussion with her son about religion and a job—predictable maternal and Midwestern topics—Mrs. Krebs leads Harold to tell still another lie. She asks him, "Don't you love your mother, dear boy?" Harold responds with total honesty, "I don't love anybody," causing Mrs. Krebs to cry and revealing her inability and unwillingness to hear the truth. Nauseated by his next statement but believing that it is the only way to stop her crying, he lies and tells her that he did not mean what he said; he was merely angry at something. Mrs. Krebs reasserts her maternal role, reminding her son that she held him next to her heart when he was a tiny baby, reducing Krebs to the juvenile lie: "I know, Mummy. . . . I'll try and be a good boy for you." Mother and son then kneel together, and Mrs. Krebs prays for Harold.

After this emotional lie, Harold Krebs decides to leave the Oklahoma town, go to Kansas City for a job, and live his life simply and smoothly. The soldier leaves his home.

Themes and Meanings

One of the story's central concerns might be described by a term that was once fashionable: "the generation gap." In "Soldier's Home," the gap is more like a chasm that separates the ex-Marine from the townspeople. Krebs returns from the war, changed by his experiences, but the local citizenry are exactly what they were before the war—sure of themselves and their values. To stay in the town, to survive this time warp, Krebs must compromise his integrity; he must lie if he is to live among people who do not want to hear the truth.

Krebs represents the transformation brought about by World War I, and in this sense his metamorphosis reflects America's changed face. Before the war, the conventional values of Krebs's hometown had been, for the most part, America's values. After World War I, however, those values were challenged, and the war's returnees were among the chief challengers. In "Soldier's Home," the conflict is between challenger and challenged—the tension between Americans moving into the modern world and Americans protecting Victorian values.

Style and Technique

Ernest Hemingway's understated, detached style is suited to this story of a soldier whose reaction to his environment is itself understatement and detachment. The narrative technique, sentence structure, dialogue, lack of symbolism and imagery—all these strategies create a marriage between form and content in "Soldier's Home."

Told in the journalistic style of a third-person narrator, the story appears to be a simple, objective, disinterested report of Harold Krebs's return from the war. The first paragraph sets up this expectation of objectivity when the narrator describes a photograph of Krebs and his fraternity brothers in college. What the reader notes, however, are the details that this journalistic narrator chooses to include. Stating, for example, that it was a Methodist college and that all the men in the picture were "wearing exactly the same height and style collar," the narrator is pointing to the conformist mentality of prewar, Midwestern America.

The sentence structure is also suited to the message of restraint, of the famous Hemingway code of "grace under pressure." In both the narrator's explanations and the dialogue itself, the clipped sentences imply a control, a sense of holding on and holding in. Thus, a series of sentences might use the same syntactical structure: "He did not want to get into the intrigue and the politics. He did not want to have to do any courting. He did not want to tell any more lies." Brief, simple, repetitious, this series of "he did not wants" catalogs the ways in which Harold Krebs intends to remain uninvolved, detached, restrained.

Absent from "Soldier's Home" is imagery that might add an inappropriate complexity to the story. This tale is about one man's efforts to recover a simplicity he once knew; the style of the story, lean and unadorned, reinforces Krebs's struggle to regain the honesty he had known in the war when he had felt "cool and clear inside himself . . . when he had done the one thing, the only thing for a man to do, easily and naturally. . . ." Regarding words, sentences, and images in "Soldier's Home," less is definitely more.

Marjorie Smelstor

SOME LIKE THEM COLD

Author: Ring Lardner (1885-1933)
Type of plot: Comedy
Time of plot: c. 1920
Locale: Chicago and New York City
First published: 1921

> *Principal characters:*
> CHARLES F. LEWIS, an aspiring songwriter in New York City
> MABELLE GILLESPIE, a "working girl" in Chicago

The Story

Though "Some Like Them Cold" is told in an unorthodox way, its plot is quite simple. Charles Lewis and Mabelle Gillespie meet by chance in the Lasalle Street train station in Chicago. Charles is about to travel to New York City in order to pursue his fortune as a songwriter. Mabelle is waiting for her sister to arrive for a visit. Charles and Mabelle converse until Charles's train arrives. Before leaving, Charles makes a bet with Mabelle that he will write to her from New York. This he does. Mabelle writes back, and the two carry on their flirtation by means of the United States Postal Service.

At first all goes well. Charles masks his loneliness and uncertainty in New York City by describing his adventures to Mabelle. These adventures fall into two categories: first, the quest for success in the songwriting business, and second, resistance against sexual temptation. Repeatedly, Charles resists the advances of overly aggressive, "painted" women. At the same time, though he teases and flatters Mabelle, he is careful not to cast doubt on her virtue. Mabelle is quite sensitive on this issue. She refers to herself as a "bad" girl for speaking to Charles without a "proper introduction," and she assures Charles that she is not in the habit of doing such a thing. Definitely viewing her own aspirations as secondary to Charles's grandiose ambitions, she passes over most of her own trials and tribulations as a single working girl in Chicago. Instead, through the eyes of her sister and friends, she provides a self-portrait for Charles's inspection. A "great home girl," Mibs (as her friends call her) is "a great talker," has a humorous nature, likes a good book, and loves to bathe. She goes out to dance or see a show only occasionally. In sum, Mabelle presents herself as modest, sociable, and wholesome. She also expresses boundless confidence in Charles's songwriting ability and repeatedly assures him of his ultimate success.

During the exchange of the first few letters, Charles and Mabelle seem to be pleasant, perhaps slightly silly young people carrying on an ambiguous but harmless flirtation. There is a steady diet of flattery and ego stroking on both sides, with Mabelle in particular providing the moral support needed for Charles to fight "the battle of Broadway." In addition, Mabelle has mentioned a fantasy about some "rich New Yorker" who might bring her there to live. Yet exactly what the outcome of the relationship between Charles and Mabelle will be is not clear.

Within a few weeks, that is no longer true. Charles's interest in Mabelle is plainly waning as he makes some personal connections in New York City and begins to fall into the rhythm of the town. More specifically, Charles meets a lyricist named Paul Sears, with whom he begins to collaborate. He does send Mabelle the lyrics from their first song together, "When They're Like You."

> Some like them hot, some like them cold.
> Some like them when they're not too darn old.
> Some like them fat, some like them lean.
> Some like them only at sweet sixteen.
> Some like them dark, some like them light.
> Some like them in the park, late at night.
> Some like them fickle, some like them true,
> But the time I like them is when they're like you.

Although the lyric might not seem particularly impressive to the reader, Mabelle is "thrilled to death over the song." The tide has turned, however, and Charles no longer needs Mabelle's encouragement. Whereas Charles described New York City as dirty and hot at the outset of the story, he now calls it a "great town" and seems willing to burn his bridge back to Chicago. He has found a new home, and because of this Mabelle is shunted to the periphery of his life. Soon Charles's letters become sketchy and much less attentive to Mabelle. "Dear Girlie" becomes "Dear Miss Gillespie." (In return, "Dear Mr. Man" becomes "Dear Mr. Lewis.") The end comes when Charles, rather insensitively, announces that he has become engaged to Paul Sears's sister Betsy, whom he has described as being "ice cold" (thus the story's title). Though Betsy enjoys the nightlife and is just about everything else that Charles has said he does not like, he seems completely infatuated. Charles offers to keep up his correspondence with Mabelle. Mabelle refuses his offer, however, citing a jealous "man friend." She closes her last letter by congratulating Charles and wondering exactly how Betsy is going to "run wild" on the sixty-dollar salary that he will be earning as a musician in Atlantic City. With this, the story comes to an end less than two months after it began.

Themes and Meanings

Ring Lardner is known primarily as a humorist, and humor has provided an important avenue for American self-expression. Mark Twain is perhaps the best example of this. Humor has enabled Americans to poke fun at themselves in a way that is often quite revealing but not as threatening as other forms of social criticism. "Some Like Them Cold" is a humorous story, particularly in its portrayal of the linguistic and behavioral foibles of its characters and their culture. Yet this humor cloaks serious themes.

Indeed, the story's resolution is sad rather than amusing. This is understandable, since the story is a study of profound disappointment. Mabelle has thrown herself into conversation and then correspondence with a romantic stranger who might offer a way out of her unfulfilling existence, but she ends up only with a fantasy "man friend" and the specter of becoming an old maid. Charles fails to achieve success as a songwriter and at the story's close has been reduced to the grind and insecurity of being a professional musician. In addition, one gets the definite idea that his marriage will offer little in the way of consolation, if, indeed, it even lasts very long. Thus, the story begins with high hopes but ends with the defeat of both main characters.

A number of other pessimistic themes also emerge from the story. Self-delusion and, correspondingly, the absence of self-knowledge pave the way for the disappointments suffered by Charles and Mabelle, as does the fickleness of infatuation. All these things taken together add up to an exposé of American manners and morals in the early twentieth century. One might also interpret the story in the light of feminist concerns, paying special attention to the lyrics of "When They're Like You."

Yet the story is not completely gloomy. Neither Charles nor Mabelle is necessarily down for the count. One senses that both of the main characters are resilient enough to bounce back, though probably not into each other's arms. These ships have passed in the night and are not likely to renew their encounter.

Style and Technique

The core of Lardner's style and the source of much of his humor lies in his mastery of various American dialects. More specifically, Lardner's characters, most of whom reside in the lower reaches of the middle class or below, use ordinary language rather than the idealized speech of much literature. This usually means that they slaughter grammar, diction, and all else that is sacred in language. Yet Lardner's characters also speak colorfully, employing delightful slang expressions and revealing the soul of American society. In this, Charles Lewis and Mabelle Gillespie are no exception. What is different about "Some Like Them Cold" is the fact that the entire story is told through letters. This allows Lardner to have a field day with his characters' spelling, particularly that of Charles, who ends his first letter to Mabelle as follows: "In the mean wile girlie au reservoir and don't do nothing I would not do." (Mabelle seems to be slightly more literate.)

In Lardner's work, the language employed is not primarily an instrument for moving the story along. It is itself the story, providing a window not only into Lardner's characters, but also into American society and into the very depths of human nature.

Ira Smolensky

SOME OF US HAD BEEN THREATENING OUR FRIEND COLBY

Author: Donald Barthelme (1931-   )
Type of plot: Absurdist fable
Time of plot: c. 1973
Locale: The United States
First published: 1973

> *Principal characters:*
> COLBY WILLIAMS, the protagonist, who has committed an
>   unspecified crime
> COLBY WILLIAMS' FRIENDS, who have decided to punish him

The Story

The story concerns the punishment of Colby Williams by his friends. Colby, it seems, has "gone too far"—when, how, and at what, the reader is not told. He readily admits that he has done this, claiming, however, that "going too far... was something everybody did sometimes." His friends, an anonymous, all-male group, are unswayed by his reasoning and remain firm in their benevolent conviction that as his "dear friends" they have an obligation to punish him for his transgression by hanging him.

The hanging itself will be the climax of a gala social affair, and the bulk of the story centers on the arrangements which have to be made. Luckily, Colby's friends are a cosmopolitan, multitalented group. They count among their ranks a conductor, an architect, people knowledgeable about printing and about the history of executions, environmental activists, and the owner of a car-and-truck rental business. Everyone's talents are called upon and everyone's opinions are consulted, even Colby's. The group is committed to bringing off the affair with éclat, and much of their discussion turns on setting the correctly festive tone for the event and making sure the day will be a success.

Colby shows his tendency to "go too far" when, graciously consulted about his preference for music for the occasion, he suggests Charles Ives's Fourth Symphony, a gargantuan work that would "put [the friends] way over the music budget." Disagreement about this choice threatens to disrupt the arrangements until Colby is sternly admonished to "be reasonable" and "think of something a little less exacting." Once the question of the music is solved, the friends discuss the appearance and wording of the invitations. They dismiss some slight qualms about the illegality of the proceedings by claiming that "we had a perfect *moral* right [to hang Colby] because he was our friend, *belonged* to us in various important senses, and he had after all gone too far." Referring to the hanging ambiguously as "An Event Involving

Mr. Colby Williams," they determine, will help them to evade unwelcome attention from the law. They decide to serve drinks and magnanimously assure Colby that he can drink, too, before the finale.

The mechanics of the hanging are a more complicated matter, but the friends pool their knowledge to overcome their lack of experience with such things. In a debate between building a gibbet or using a tree, they choose a tree for reasons of ease, economy, and most important, aesthetics—this will be a "June hanging" and the full-leafed tree will "add a kind of 'natural' feeling." Aesthetic and environmental considerations lead the friends to dismiss the idea of a hangman or a firing squad (the latter is Colby's suggestion, his last attempt at "going too far," prudently rejected by Howard as an "ego trip" and as "unnecessary theatrics"). Instead, they decide, the guest of honor will jump off a large rubber ball considerately painted a deep green to blend in with the surroundings. For the noose, rope is selected over wire, for although the latter would be "more efficient," it "would injure the tree."

The friends' scrupulous planning pays off, for at the end the reader is told that "everything went off very smoothly." Not only is the event a social success ("a 'bang-up' production right down to the wire"), but also, perhaps most important, it succeeds in its punitive aim, for "nobody has ever gone too far again."

Themes and Meanings

Meaning is closely allied to style in this story's mock-serious, deadpan consideration of a clearly absurd situation. The friends are a tightly knit group whose strong allegiance to one another and willingness to substitute their own law for the law of the land recall the *esprit de corps* and modus operandi of the Ku Klux Klan, the Mafia, the Central Intelligence Agency, and other organizations engaged in covert activities. Less ominously, this group is reminiscent of such all-male fraternal organizations as the Masons and the Shriners, which use costumes, codes, and procedures known only to their initiates; college fraternities with their hazing rituals; and less formal clubs which nevertheless impose behavioral norms on their members.

The apparent reasonableness with which this group claims the right to chastise their "dear friend" and fellow member is undercut by the gruesomeness and extremity of their chosen method. In short, they make friendship the rationale for murder. The group is fully aware that they are taking the law into their own hands, but rather than finding this a deterrent to action, like many a vigilante group they proceed regardless, taking precautions only to avoid calling undue attention to themselves.

Published in the wake of the Watergate revelations and the controversial nomination of William E. Colby to be promoted from deputy director of the CIA to its head, the story can be read as a commentary on the extralegal operation of such secret organizations. Exactly how such groups "go too far"

Barthelme leaves the reader to imagine. In such a reading, however, Colby would be seen as an operative who botched a mission or whose indiscretion threatened to blow the group's cover; the group takes action against him of necessity to protect itself.

While such topical parallels are suggested by the story, they do not account for the friends' show of spirit and commitment to making the affair a success, and a semipublic one at that, since others will be invited to join the festivities. Yet just as killing is an extreme form of discipline, the loving planning lavished on this "June hanging" is equally exaggerated. In detailing how the event is planned, Barthelme satirizes such clubby virtues as devotion and sacrifice for the good of the group and love for each of "the boys." Friendship entails obligations, and every character in the story, Colby included, willingly surrenders his autonomy to the group. Colby himself, after a brief defense, accedes to the notion that he should be disciplined. Basically a good team player despite his previous indiscretion, he cheerfully puts his fate into his friends' hands and participates with them in planning his end. His reward for such selflessness: proof of his friends' esteem and a convivial drink with them before his demise. For their part, his friends sacrifice many hours to serious discussion and careful planning. In further token of their devotion to the group, they both put themselves to considerable expense and also donate their respective professional services to make the event a success, thus upholding the reputation of their organization while showing their loyalty to a fellow member. They take the responsibility of membership in this group very seriously—it is a valued privilege—and are glad that the ritual hanging has the desired admonitory effect on the behavior of their members so that the future of their organization will be secure.

Style and Technique

The story includes many traditional elements of a fable: simple, straightforward narration; one-dimensional characters; uncomplicated, black-and-white logic; a morally satisfying, didactic ending. Yet unlike classic fables, which teach useful lessons, in this story the gap between the extreme action (hanging) and the vague offense it purports to correct (going "too far") makes it difficult to take the lesson literally, or even, it would seem, seriously.

Colby is told to "be reasonable," to conform to the commonsense norm of his friends. Reasonableness does indeed seem to be one of the group's leading traits, as is seen in their even-tempered discussion of the numerous practical arrangements for the hanging, with its democratic weighing of pros and cons. Yet reason in the service of brutality is reason debased. While they may be reasonable about some matters, for example in providing a tent in case of rain, they are notably unreasonable about others, as when concern for protecting a tree ironically obscures concern for human life. The friends appear to be logical as well as reasonable, moving directly from cause to effect ("And now he'd gone too far, so we decided to hang him"). Their logic, however, is as perverted as their reasoning. After all, they never consider any form of punishment less extreme than murder. The speciousness of this logic originates in the subtle capacity of language as they use it to disguise the nature of reality; hence their self-deluding wit, as when Colby jokes about his friends' being "a little Draconian." In the hands of this group, both language and logic are distorted, as if in illustration of George Orwell's famous dictum that "if thought corrupts language, language can corrupt thought."

The alliance of pseudologic and clever wordplay produces an artificial matter-of-factness of tone, a jocose, tongue-in-cheek collusion between readers and the future murderers that invites the reader to play along with the absurd notion of this hanging as social ritual, as wedding/graduation party/ Bar Mitzvah. Rather than feel repulsion or moral outrage at the impending killing, the reader finds himself worrying about the affair along with Howard, Victor, Hugh, and the others, sympathetically identifying with their concerns about unpredictable weather, transporting guests, exceeding the budget. The reader shares Paul's distaste for having Colby jump off a chair ("that would look . . . extremely tacky—some old kitchen chair sitting out there under our beautiful tree") and approves Tomás' considered judgment that instead Colby should stand on a large rubber ball that "would afford a sufficient 'drop' and would also roll out of the way if [he] suddenly changed his mind after jumping off." After the party, the reader rejoices with the hosts that "it didn't rain, the event was well attended, and we didn't run out of Scotch, or anything." Thus caught up in the group's practical concerns narrated in a flat, unemotional manner, the reader is lulled into forgetting the viciousness of their act of "friendship." Ordinariness of tone and focus on the mundane mask the grotesque; the reader responds uncritically by finding it palatable and involving.

It is a sly maneuver on Barthelme's part that he winds up placing the reader in the position of Colby's friends. Just as their distorted, inside-out "reason" carries them inexorably from one decision to the next, their humor and mock logic obscure rational thinking and overcome moral faculties so that the reader, too, tolerates and enjoys the perpetration of a legally indefensible, morally repugnant act. In fact, more than merely identifying with the characters in the story, Barthelme suggests, we actually mimic them, for in much the same way we are gulled by the reasoning and behavior of Colby's friends, we passively accept and comply with the actions of a government that also on occasion tends to "go too far." The fable thus operates on more than one level. Literally, it may be absurd, a game, an entertainment, but despite the dislike of the present age for moral teaching, it also speaks to a particular condition of the world. At the end, the fable presents the moral learned by Colby's surviving friends, but since Barthelme has inveigled his readers into recognizing that they share their capacity for easy self-delusion, it offers a lesson to everyone.

Nancy Sorkin

SOMETHING OUT THERE

Author: Nadine Gordimer (1923-   )
Type of plot: Social realism
Time of plot: The 1980's
Locale: Johannesburg, South Africa, and its suburbs
First published: 1984

> *Principal characters:*
> JOY, a young white revolutionary
> CHARLES, her former lover, also a revolutionary
> VUSI, a black revolutionary
> EDDIE, a black revolutionary
> MRS. NAAS (HESTER) KLOPPER, the wife of an affluent white
>   realtor

The Story

A strange, apelike creature is terrorizing the affluent white suburbs of Johannesburg, South Africa. It strikes at night, killing and maiming pets and frightening the many citizens who have seen it. Only young Stanley Dobrow has tried to photograph it, but the photograph turned out badly, revealing only some movement in the treetops. The bizarre happenings occasion much speculation and many letters to the editors of the white newspapers. It is a novel news story and a welcome one, providing as it does relief from the usual depressing fare: labor strikes, student riots, and international sanctions against the white-controlled South African government. To the white citizens of Johannesburg, the ape story seems to be something more immediately applicable to their own lives than does the racial conflict that is dividing their country.

One such citizen is Mrs. Naas (Hester) Klopper, the wife of a prosperous realtor, a fastidious woman proud of her fine house and of her skill at maintaining it. When her husband unexpectedly brings home a prospective client and his wife, Mrs. Klopper is ready with tea and sweetbreads to offer them. Charles and Joy Rosser seem shy, but quite pleasant: Mrs. Rosser is expecting their first child, and the couple are interested in the old Kleynhans place, a secluded farm that has stood empty for three years. Later, Naas Klopper shows them the place, and they take it on the condition that they can rent it with the option to buy. Though it seems unorthodox to him, Klopper is impressed with their offer of six months' advance rent, and he agrees to their terms.

The Rossers are not, however, the ordinary young newlyweds they appear to be. Unknown to the Kloppers, and to the rest of the white community, the couple (they are not married, nor are they any longer lovers) have rented the

Kleynhans place as a base from which to plan a revolutinary operation against the government. With the help of Vusi and Eddie, black revolutionaries posing as farm laborers, they set about transforming an abandoned shed into an ammunition warehouse and making other preparations for their strike. All four of them are careful to maintain appearances, observing by day the traditional social conventions between white masters and their black servants. Inside the house, however, and under cover of night, they live as equals, coping as best they can with the boredom and restlessness that come from confinement.

Meanwhile, the ape continues its raids on the northern suburbs of Johannesburg, and sightings of it continue to cause anxiety and speculation. Some say that the creature is a baboon; others insist that it is a chimpanzee. At various times, it is spotted by a group of doctors on a golf course, a pair of lovers trysting in a secluded cottage, a black servant in an affluent white household, and a young white policeman's wife (she does not actually see the animal, but it steals a leg of venison that her husband has hung in the kitchen window). Citizens protest that it should be trapped, even killed; the SPCA protests such moves. Still, the sightings remain brief and momentary, with no witness getting a good enough look at the creature to say precisely what it is.

Life goes on at the Kleynhans place. Charles rounds up "necessities" (their word for munitions); Vusi, the older and more experienced of the blacks, instructs Eddie in the use and maintenance of weapons. The four talk politics, analyze the media, read, and wait. Eddie takes a secret trip into the city; Vusi fashions a makeshift saxophone from scrap metal. A complication arises when the black man who had worked for the late Mr. Kleynhans arrives to ask after his mealie patch, which he had planted before his old boss's death. Vusi and Eddie manage to placate him by telling him that they will tend the patch, and he goes away. His visit, however, combined with Eddie's ill-advised trip to the city, creates nervousness and a certain amount of friction among the four revolutionaries as the date of their operation approaches. The tension is finally broken by Eddie and Joy, who begin to dance together one evening to the music of Eddie's tape player. Vusi joins in on his saxophone, and Charles watches them contentedly.

Soon, according to plan, Vusi and Eddie leave the Kleynhans place and move to a rural cave, where they undertake the final stages of their mission. Charles and Joy are visited by the black farmhand, who wonders what has become of the two blacks. Uncertain about what to do, Joy tells him that he may tend the mealie patch himself; her decision makes Charles uneasy, but both of them realize that they will soon be gone. Not long afterward, a massive power failure cripples the city, the result of the bombing of a power station. The Kloppers and the farmhand are questioned about Charles and Joy, who have by now disappeared. The police uncover the facts about the Rossers (which is not their real name) but are unable to apprehend either them or Vusi. Only Eddie is caught and killed by the police as he tries to escape into Swaziland.

The ape, too, is killed, wounded in the arm by a white householder and later found dead. It turns out to have been a common baboon, gone berserk for some unknown reason. Its death is not covered extensively by the newspapers, since public interest has been usurped by the attack on the power station.

Themes and Meanings

"Something Out There" is, above all else, a harsh indictment of the South African government's policy of apartheid, under which blacks are segregated from whites, forced to live in slumlike black "homelands," made to carry identification papers at all times, and subjected to various other indignities. This novella-length story explores the tensions of apartheid at the personal, everyday level; the government policy is viewed here, as in much of Nadine Gordimer's work, as a direct result of individual will.

Consequently, while Vusi and Eddie and their white supporters are treated sympathetically, the white suburbanites are often the subject of bitter satire. Representative of this group is Mrs. Naas Klopper, a woman so taken with the comfortable life-style that her husband's prosperity affords her that she has for years neglected her own given name, always referring to herself as "Mrs." An essentially well-meaning woman, she is nevertheless bigoted and shortsighted in the extreme, offering to find the Rossers a new black "boy" to replace the one who had worked for Mr. Kleynhans and taking a generally maternal attitude toward the young white couple. She is a woman unable to connect the political and the personal, incapable of appreciating either the inhumanity of apartheid or her own role in its maintenance. On a symbolic level, her share of responsibility for the violence threatening her society is brought home to her near the end of the story: while searching the Kleynhans place, the police discover that a cookie box in which Charles and Joy have stored munitions is the very box that Mrs. Klopper brought them earlier, filled with her own homemade sweetbreads. It is characteristic, however, of Mrs. Klopper and her kind that this irony escapes her.

This inability to connect also characterizes the whites who figure in the parallel story of the ape attacks. Concerned with the creature only insofar as it threatens their own lives and homes ("so long as it attacked other people's cats and dogs, frightened other people's maids—that was other people's affair," says the narrator), they are unable to band together to find a solution to their common problem. Thus, the ape becomes an appropriately ominous symbol of apartheid itself, "something out there" that serves to expose the amorality of an entire nation.

Style and Technique

This long short story is double-plotted; that is, it is actually two stories that enhance and comment upon each other. While the story of the events at the Kleynhans place receives the most attention, it is frequently interrupted by abrupt and often darkly comic sections devoted to the ape attacks. Only gradually does it become clear that the two plots are related in that they both illuminate, albeit in very different ways, the cancerous intolerance at the core of South African society.

The characters of Charles, Eddie, Vusi, and especially Joy, are fully rounded, replete with complex motivations and very human shortcomings. The white suburbanites of the ape sections, on the other hand, are frequently stereotypes, monsters of egotism and self-absorption whose personalities are exposed rather than developed. Through her manipulation of these interlocking plots, Gordimer manages to mimic in her fiction what she sees the South African government doing in fact: treating one segment of society as a community of responsible, dignified individuals, the other segment as a collection of simpleminded, inflammatory, and potentially dangerous rabble.

J. D. Daubs

SONNY'S BLUES

Author: James Baldwin (1924-   )
Type of plot: Social realism
Time of plot: The 1940's and 1950's
Locale: Harlem and Greenwich Village, New York
First published: 1958

> *Principal characters:*
> THE NARRATOR, an unnamed high school math teacher
> SONNY, his younger brother, a jazz pianist

The Story

The narrator, a teacher in Harlem, has escaped the ghetto, creating a stable and secure life for himself despite the destructive pressures which he sees destroying so many young blacks. He sees black adolescents discovering the limits placed upon them by a racist society at the very moment when they are discovering their abilities. He tells the story of his relationship with his younger brother, Sonny. That relationship has moved through phases of separation and return. After their parents' deaths, he tried and failed to be a father to Sonny. For a while, he believed that Sonny had succumbed to the destructive influences of Harlem life. Finally, however, they achieved a reconciliation in which the narrator came to understand the value and the importance of Sonny's need to be a jazz pianist.

The story opens with a crisis in their relationship. The narrator reads in the newspaper that Sonny has been taken up in a drug raid. He learns that Sonny is addicted to heroin and that he will be sent to a treatment facility to be "cured." Unable to believe that his gentle and quiet brother could have so abused himself, the narrator cannot reopen communication with Sonny until a second crisis occurs, the death of his daughter from polio. When Sonny is released, the narrator brings him to live with his family.

The middle section of the story is a flashback. The narrator remembers his last talk with his mother, in which she made him promise to "be there" for Sonny. Home on leave from the army, he has seen little of Sonny, who is then is school. His mother tells him about the death of his uncle, a story she had kept from him until this moment. His uncle, much loved by his father, was killed in a hit-and-run accident by a group of drunken whites who miscalculated in an attempt to frighten the young man. The pain, sorrow, and rage this event aroused colored his father's whole life, especially his relationship with Sonny, who reminded him of his brother. She tells the narrator this story partly in order to illustrate that there is no safety from suffering in their world. The narrator cannot protect Sonny from the world any more than his father could protect his own brother. Such suffering is a manifestation of the general chaos of life out of which people struggle to create some order and meaning. Though suffering cannot be avoided, one can struggle against it, and one can support others in their struggles.

From this conversation, the narrator brings the story forward through his marriage and return to the army, Sonny's announcement at their mother's funeral that he intends to be a jazz pianist, Sonny's attempt to live with the narrator's wife's family, teaching himself piano while the narrator is away at war, the failure of this arrangement, Sonny's term in the navy, and, after the war, a final break between the brothers because of the narrator's inability to accept Sonny's way of life. The narrator then explains the suffering he and his wife felt at the death of their daughter, suffering which made him want to write to Sonny at the treatment center and which finally began to make him appreciate the importance of having someone to talk to, a source of comfort in suffering.

In the final third of the story, the narrator and Sonny come to an understanding which seems to reconcile them. The narrator is very worried that Sonny will return to heroin. Sonny invites the narrator to hear him play piano with a group in a Greenwich Village club. When the narrator accepts this invitation, Sonny tries to explain why he took heroin. Heroin is a way to try not to suffer, a way to take control of inner chaos and to find shelter from outer suffering. Though he knows that ultimately heroin cannot work, he also knows that he may try it again. He implies that with someone to listen to him, he may succeed in dealing with "the storm inside" by means of his music:

> You walk these streets, black and funky and cold, and there's not really a living ass to talk to, and there's nothing shaking, and there's no way of getting it out, that storm inside. You can't talk it and you can't make love with it, and when you finally try to get with it and play it, you realize *nobody's* listening. So *you've* got to listen. You got to find a way to listen.

At the nightclub, the narrator understands what Sonny means when he finally hears him play. He sees that Sonny's music is an authentic response to life. He sees that one who creates music, "is dealing with the roar rising from the void and imposing order on it as it hits the air." He understands that his brother's music is an attempt to renew the old human story: "For while the tale of how we suffer, and how we are delighted, and how we may triumph is never new, it always must be heard. There isn't any other tale to tell, it's the only light we've got in all this darkness." Having witnessed Sonny's struggle to play "his blues," the narrator recognizes that those blues are mankind's blues, that Sonny's music gives the narrator and all people a way of finding meaning in their pains and joys. This perception enables the narrator to accept his brother, the life he has chosen, and the risks he must incur.

Themes and Meanings

As the narrator feels united with his brother and, by implication, with all mankind in shared sorrows, he reflects, "And I was yet aware that this was only a moment, that the world waited outside, as hungry as a tiger, and that trouble stretched above us, longer than the sky." This opposition between moments of meaning in loving community and the terrifying, troubled, and apparently meaningless outside world pervades the story in theme and in technique.

The opposition appears in multiple guises. It appears in the housing project where the narrator lives, an attempt to impose order on the old dangerous neighborhood which fails when the project is transformed into merely a new version of the old dangerous neighborhood. The opposition is reflected in his memories of childhood, of being secure in families, not having yet to deal with the horrors of the world, and yet being aware even as children, that with each passing moment, they come closer to having to live unprotected in the dark, chaotic world. It appears in the story of the death of his uncle; on a warm, beautiful night when the brothers were walking, enjoying each other's company, a wild car suddenly swooped over a hill, to destroy a beloved brother. For American blacks in the middle of the twentieth century, racism is another of the dark forces of destruction and meaninglessness which must be endured. Beauty, joy, triumph, security, suffering, and sorrow are all creations of community, especially of family and familylike groups. They are temporary havens from the world's trouble, and they are also the meanings of human life.

The narrator and Sonny have found alternative ways of making meaning and order. The narrator makes a literal family and a conventional career, as his father did. Sonny becomes an artist, one who expresses for himself and his community and to himself and his community the passions which unite them. By expressing these passions, giving them order in articulation and making them meaningful, he also makes and sustains a kind of family, a community of shared moments of meaning.

James Baldwin often deals with these themes in his fiction and other prose, especially with the problems of the black artist or intellectual trying to find or create a sustaining community.

Style and Technique

Baldwin emphasizes the theme of opposition between the chaotic world and the human need for community with a series of opposing images, especially darkness and light. The narrator repeatedly associates light with the desire to articulate or give form to the needs and passions which arise out of inner darkness. He also opposes light as an idea of order to darkness in the world, the chaos which adults endure, but of which they normally cannot speak to children.

The opposition of light and darkness is often paired with the opposition of inside and outside. Sonny's problem as an artist is that inside himself he feels intensely the storm of human passion; to feel whole and free, he must bring this storm outside by gaining artistic control over it, by articulating it for some listener. Inside is also the location of the family, the place of order which is opposed to outside, the dark and predatory world.

These and other opposing images help to articulate Baldwin's themes of opposition between the meaningless world and the meaning-creating community. The artist, by giving voice to the inner chaos of needs and passions, unites mankind in the face of the outer chaos of random and continuous suffering. The artist helps to create a circle of light in the midst of surrounding darkness.

Terry Heller

SORROW-ACRE

Author: Isak Dinesen (Baroness Karen Blixen-Finecke, 1885-1962)
Type of plot: Fable
Time of plot: c. 1775
Locale: A Danish manor
First published: 1942

> *Principal characters:*
> ADAM, a young Danish nobleman returning to his ancestral
>   home after nine years in England
> ADAM'S UNCLE, the old lord of the manor
> THE LORD'S YOUNG WIFE, Adam's step-aunt
> GOSKE PIIL, a serf accused of setting fire to one of the lord's
>   barns
> ANNE-MARIE, Goske's widowed mother

The Story

"Sorrow-Acre" opens with a leisurely description of the Danish landscape, and it is clear that the setting is to be as strong a character in this folktale as any of the humans populating its stage.

It is the end of the eighteenth century, and at the opening of the story, everything is still in its time-honored place, from manor house through the church to the peasant huts in the village. The winds of change are beginning to blow, however (the serfs will be freed here in 1887), and enlightened ideas from England and the Continent are just beginning to be heard in this semi-feudal land.

Adam has been serving in the Danish Legation to the Court of King George, but now he has returned to his ancestral home "to make his peace with it." In his long absence, his sickly cousin and the heir to this estate has died, leaving Adam, for the moment, as the heir himself: The old lord has now married his son's betrothed, and he hopes to perpetuate his line with another son. During the day of the action of "Sorrow-Acre," Adam spends most of his time in the company of his young step-aunt, and the indication is that he himself will marry her after his uncle's death.

Early in the morning after his arrival, Adam is strolling the grounds and meets his uncle, who, in Adam's childhood, was a second father to him. The uncle is up early, even for this first day of the harvest, but, as he explains, "a matter of life and death" is being acted out that day. It seems that a young peasant has been accused of setting fire to one of the lord's barns. His guilt is not clear, for those who have accused him have other reasons to be jealous. Anne-Marie, the boy's mother, has intervened, however, and the lord has struck a bargain with her: If Anne-Marie can mow a field of rye by herself, her son will be freed.

When Adam returns that afternoon to the field where his uncle has remained all day, all other work has ceased, and the other peasants are following Anne-Marie in her slow and painful progress. Adam sees that she is close to death, and he urges his uncle to end this "tragic and cruel tale," but the old lord, who believes in the retributive justice of the old order and argues that "tragedy is the privilege of man, his highest privilege," refuses. "I gave Anne-Marie my word," he says simply. In anger, Adam says that he must leave the estate: "I shall go to America, to the new world."

At this very moment, when Adam has apparently given up any opportunity for reconciliation with his homeland, a strange pity takes hold of him. He sees his uncle as a tyrant close to death himself, a man who has lost his only son (as Anne-Marie is killing herself to save hers) and whose own semi-feudal world is breaking up. Adam's "forgiveness" of his uncle leads to a "sudden conception of the unity of the universe" and "a surrender to fate and to the will of life." Adam tells his uncle that he will stay, and a clap of thunder sounds: "The landscape had spoken." Adam has been reconciled to his homeland; he now has a "feeling of belonging to this land and soil."

Adam returns to the manor house and does not witness the final act of this tragedy. Several minutes before sunset, Anne-Marie finishes the field, the old lord frees her son, and she dies in her son's arms. The story closes, as it has opened, with a sense of place:

> In the place where the woman had died the old lord later on had a stone set up, with a sickle engraved on it. The peasants on the land then named the rye field "Sorrow-Acre." By this name it was known a long time after the story of the woman and her son had itself been forgotten.

Themes and Meanings

"Sorrow-Acre" is based on a Danish folktale, and, like that older, didactic form, it carries overt lessons. Isak Dinesen has deepened the story's mystery and thereby made its meaning more ambiguous.

At the center of "Sorrow-Acre" is a debate, both real and dramatic, between two ways of life, the past and the present. The old lord is like a god in this aristocratic world, while Adam represents a newer, more liberal view and "the great new ideas of the age: of nature, of the right and freedom of man, of justice and beauty." Adam's view, surprisingly, does not prevail, and it is the uncle who is left at the end watching the close of this tragedy. Adam actually gains his reconciliation with the land by accepting his uncle's sense of justice and order. Eventually, the reader suspects, he may inherit this manor; for now, the old lord is still firmly in control. The reader's sympathy has similarly shifted from an easy identification with the modern ideas of Adam to a recognition of the essential harmony and unity of this almost medieval world.

Yet nothing in Dinesen's work is ever so simple. A series of overlapping parallels deepens the mystery and tragedy of the story. Anne-Marie is toiling to save her son, which is exactly what the old lord was unable to do for his own. Ironically, Goske Piil was his son's only playmate; now he is being accused of setting the fire by a wheelwright who suspects him "with his young wife" (as the reader suspects Adam with the young wife of the lord). Finally, Anne-Marie had another "child and did away with it." These overlapping parallels—actually triangles reminiscent of medieval religious paintings— deepen the structure of the story and reveal the complex web of human life.

This meaning is further complicated by the religious symbolism of the story. Adam is the "new man" returning to Eden, perhaps with the original sin of enlightened knowledge with him. His innocence, however, is no match for the justice of the old gods such as his uncle. Similarly, Anne-Marie is a Christ figure in her superhuman task of freeing her son (and mankind—the serfs will one day be freed) from the justice of the old order. Her effort lives on in the name of the field, "Sorrow-Acre," which is also a reminder of the agony and anguish of human life.

What Dinesen has done, in following out the fateful lines of human inter- action and playing with their religious connotations, is to make the meaning of the story ambiguous and complex. At the beginning, the reader naturally condemns the cruel notion of justice in this semifeudal society; by the end, the reader's sympathy has shifted and, as Adam senses, the order and har- mony of this world seem to be acted out in the tragedy of Anne-Marie. It is not so easy, Dinesen is saying, to pass judgment on the past.

Style and Technique

Like the story's meaning, the form of "Sorrow-Acre" reveals its folktale origins but takes on the complexity of modern fiction. The story is divided into four parts. The opening section is a leisurely description of the Danish landscape and an exposition of all the elements of this medieval world. In the second part, Adam and his uncle meet and begin their debate. Part 3 is a romantic reprieve, a description of the lovely young mistress of the manor as she awakens alone and observes the fertility of this spring morning. The main action of the story takes place in the last part, where the two men argue, are reconciled, and then part, and where Anne-Marie's tragedy is played out.

If the pace of the story is almost stately, the descriptions are rich and pas- sionate. Dinesen lingers over these figures in her landscape and, like some writing god herself, paints all the characters (including the setting) with equal fullness. The shift in the reader's loyalty, from an identification with Adam at the beginning to a recognition of the rightness of the lord's justice at the end, is carried off without calling attention to itself; even Dinesen's religious symbolism seems natural and unobtrusive in the unified fabric of her story.

Style, in short, helps to enhance the power and poignancy of "Sorrow-

Acre." By the end of the story, most readers will agree with Adam: "For to die for the one you loved was an effort too sweet for words." Dinesen's words are exactly what make this story one of her most beautiful, as most critics agree—and as this passage on the last page amply illustrates:

> At the sound of his voice she lifted her face to him. A faint, bland shadow of surprise ran over it, but still she gave no sign of having heard what he said, so that the people round them began to wonder if the exhaustion had turned her deaf. But after a moment she slowly and waveringly raised her hand, fumbling in the air as she aimed at his face, and with her fingers touched his cheek. The cheek was wet with tears, so that at the contact her fingertips lightly stuck to it, and she seemed unable to overcome the infinitely slight resistance, or to withdraw her hand. For a minute the two looked each other in the face. Then, softly and lingeringly, like a sheaf of corn that falls to the ground, she sank forward onto the boy's shoulder, and he closed his arms round her.

Like very few writers before or after her, Isak Dinesen captures a moment of human tragedy and beauty in words.

David Peck

THE SOUTH

Author: Jorge Luis Borges (1899-1986)
Type of plot: Magical realism
Time of plot: 1939
Locale: Buenos Aires and the southern plains of Argentina
First published: "El Sur," 1944 (English translation, 1962)

> *Principal characters:*
> JUAN DAHLMANN, the secretary of a municipal library in
>   Buenos Aires
> THREE YOUNG RUFFIANS
> AN OLD GAUCHO

The Story

Juan Dahlmann works in a library in Buenos Aires. Like many Argentines, he is of mixed heritage. His paternal grandfather was a German minister who emigrated to Argentina in 1871. His maternal grandfather was a famous Argentine military man who suffered a violent death at the hands of Indians on the frontier. In spite of Dahlmann's bookish life-style, he prefers to think of himself as more closely linked to his military-hero grandfather, "his ancestor of romantic death." Because of this, Dahlmann keeps some souvenirs that remind him of the more heroic side of his heritage. One of these is a run-down ranch in the South which belonged to his mother's family. Dahlmann is an absentee landowner, however, as his work at the library keeps him in the city.

Dahlmann's life changes dramatically on a February evening in 1939. Anxious to examine a rare edition of *The Arabian Nights' Entertainments*, which he has just obtained, Dahlmann elects not to wait for the elevator in his apartment building but instead rushes up the dark stairs, where he accidentally runs into the edge of an open door. The injury to his head is such that he is forced to spend several feverish days at home in bed. When he does not improve, he is taken to a sanatorium, where he endures a battery of neurological tests. Sometime later, the doctors reveal to him that "he had been on the point of death from septicemia." After several months in the sanatorium, he is told that he should go to his ranch in the South to convalesce.

Dahlmann sets out for the ranch, acutely aware that he who travels to the South "enters a more ancient and sterner world." Once on the train, he attempts to read his still-untouched copy of *The Arabian Nights' Entertainments*, but now, free of the sanatorium, he finds himself distracted by the "joy of life" and pays little attention to the book. He instead gazes out the window at the passing countryside. Though able to recognize much of what he watches go by, he is not intimately familiar with anything in this part of the country, for his firsthand knowledge of the region is "quite inferior to his nostalgic and literary knowledge." As the train moves deeper into the South, Dahlmann dozes.

Because of a ticket mix-up, Dahlmann is forced to disembark at a stop short of his destination. While waiting for further transportation to arrive, he decides to eat in the local general store. There he is harrassed by three young ruffians. Though he does his best to ignore them, he is finally forced to acknowledge their taunts. He confronts them. One of them pulls a knife and challenges Dahlmann to a fight outside. When the store owner points out that Dahlmann is unarmed, an old gaucho, "a summary and cipher of the South," throws Dahlmann a dagger, which lands at his feet. Although he knows that he is no match for his opponent, Dahlmann picks up the weapon and, in so doing, accepts the challenge. He views his impending death as "a liberation, a joy, and a festive occasion," for were it between dying a violent and heroic death in the South and dying in the sanatorium, it is the more romantic death that "he would have chosen or dreamt." The story ends as Dahlmann, holding a knife that will probably be of little use to him, goes out to fight.

Themes and Meanings

This story focuses on several significant concerns in the fiction of Jorge Luis Borges. One of these is the Argentine concept of "the South." The southern region of Argentina has both a history and a reputation similar to those of the western region of the United States; the term "the South" carries virtually the same connotations for Argentines as the term "the old West" does for Americans. Virtually every aspect of the region, from its landscape to its colorful characters to its code of honor, has been romanticized in music, literature, and film. As is the case of the American West, much of the truth about the Argentine South has been replaced by myth. At the same time, much of what is no longer true about the South is still held to be true by many Argentines. It is the romantic, the mythical vision of the region and of those who inhabit it that Dahlmann clings to while living in Buenos Aires. It is also that vision that draws this library employee to the region and compels him to stand up courageously to his aggressors, something he probably would never do under similar circumstances in the city.

Of more profound thematic interest in "The South" is the concept of "real" reality versus "imagined" reality. It is necessary to describe reality as either "real" or "imagined" in the world of Borges' fiction, for the author not only utilizes two types of reality but also deliberately makes little or no effort to distinguish between them. For example, "The South" can be read in two ways. A straightforward reading shows that Dahlmann indeed travels to the South, where he is about to meet a violent death at the hands of a challenger. Another reading, however, implies that Dahlmann never makes the trip at all but, in fact, dies in the sanatorium. This alternative reading suggests that Dahlmann's heroic death is only an illusion, a fever-induced dream, an imagined fulfillment (perhaps even at the point of his death in the sanatorium) of what he would like to have happen in real life. Here, as in other stories, Borges suggests that whether reality is "real" or only "imagined" does not matter; what does matter is the perception of that reality by the person or persons involved. Therefore, whether Dahlmann's heroic demise actually occurs or is merely self-illusion is of no real consequence to Dahlmann himself. In either case, he is allowed to die a death in keeping with the romantic image in which he likes to view himself.

Style and Technique

The technical strength of "The South" lies in the deliberately inserted elements that suggest more than one interpretation of the events presented in the text. The story contains several subtly presented clues that imply that Dahlmann's trip to the South is a product of his feverish delirium. All these clues are found in the second half of the story, which depicts Dahlmann's actions after his supposed release from the sanatorium. For example, when Dahlmann pets a black cat while waiting for the train, he thinks his contact with the cat is "an illusion." Once on the train, he feels as if he were "two men at the same time," one of these free to travel, the other still "locked up" in the sanatorium. The train ride itself is unconventional, as it appears to be a trip "into the past and not merely south." Later, Dahlmann thinks that he recognizes the owner of the general store, but he then realizes that the man simply bears a remarkable resemblance to an orderly at the sanatorium. When the ruffians begin to taunt Dahlmann, he is surprised to learn that the store owner already knows his name, even though Dahlmann has never entered the store in his life. Additionally, the gaucho who tosses Dahlmann the dagger is not a gaucho typical of the 1930's but one whose appearance is more in line with the protagonist's own romantic vision of the region. Finally, there are the words of the narrator as Dahlmann prepares to fight: "He felt that if he had been able to choose, then, or to dream his death, this would have been the death he would have chosen or dreamt." This statement is skillfully worded so as to leave open the possibility of both the "imagined" reality and the "real" reality.

These and other clues that Borges places in the story do not provide definitive evidence that what happens to Dahlmann once he appears to leave the sanatorium occurs only in the protagonist's imagination. They do indeed imply that such may be the case, but they stop short of fully supporting one version of the story and fully eliminating the possibility of the other. This lack of definitiveness is in no way an error, however. It is all perfectly Borgesian, totally in keeping with Borges' view of reality. Owing to the author's subtle clues, the story can be viewed as neither completely realistic nor completely fantastic. To support fully one version of the story would mean denying the existence of the other, thereby ignoring the author's suggestions about the nature of reality itself, for in Borges' fictional world anything is possible.

"The South" is a masterfully written narrative that can be appreciated both as a piece of realistic fiction and as an intriguingly subtle mixture of realism and illusion. It is a work that, because of its double-edged reality, adds another dimension to the term "magical realism."

Keith H. Brower

THE SOUTHERN THRUWAY

Author: Julio Cortázar (1914-1984)
Type of plot: Fantasy
Time of plot: c. 1966
Locale: The main highway connecting Southern France with Paris
First published: "La autopista del sur," 1966 (English translation, 1973)

Principal characters:
AN ENGINEER, who is in a Peugeot 404
A YOUNG WOMAN, who is in a Dauphine
TWO NUNS, who are in a 2CV
A PALE MAN, who is driving a Caravelle and who commits suicide
A COUPLE and
A LITTLE GIRL, who are in a Peugeot 203
TWO BOYS, who are in a Simca
TWO MEN and
A BOY, who are in 2 Taunus
AN ELDERLY COUPLE, who are in an ID Citroën
A FARM COUPLE, who are in an Ariane
A SOLDIER and
HIS YOUNG WIFE, who are in a Volkswagen
A TRAVELING SALESMAN, who is in a DKW
AN OLDER WOMAN, who is in a Beaulieu
A FAT MAN, who is driving a Floride and who deserts
AN AMERICAN TOURIST, who is in a DeSoto
A FORD MERCURY and
A PORSCHE, black-market dealers

The Story

"The Southern Thruway" begins with a traffic jam on the main highway back to Paris from Southern France, on a summer Sunday afternoon. It seems to be a perfectly ordinary occurrence as cars slow to a crawl, stop, and start up again. The drivers and passengers look irritably at their watches and begin to exchange comments with those in neighboring cars. As the traffic inches along in increasingly infrequent moves forward, the same group of cars stays together and their occupants gradually become acquainted. Although written in the third person, the story focuses upon the experiences and thoughts of an engineer in a Peugeot 404.

Rumors circulate as to the cause of the traffic jam:

No one doubted that a serious accident had taken place in the area, which could be the only explanation for such an incredible delay. And with that, the government, taxes, road conditions, one topic after another, three yards, another commonplace, five yards, a sententious phrase or a restrained curse.

They stay in or near their cars, sweltering in the sun, waiting for the police to dissolve the bottleneck, impatient to move along and get to Paris. The cars continue to move ahead as a group, their drivers chatting to pass the time as they suffer "the dejection of again going from first to neutral, brake, hand brake, stop, and the same thing time and time again."

By the time night falls, the new rumors brought by "strangers" to their group seem remote and unbelievable. The group shares food and drink; surreptitiously, they relieve themselves by the roadside. Time begins to blur; "there was so little to do that the hours began to blend together, becoming one in the memory."

The next day, they advance a few yards and continue to hope that the road will soon be clear. Again a stranger brings them hopeful news, but then they realize the "the stranger had taken advantage of the group's happiness to ask for and get an orange" and they become wary and more conscious of their cohesiveness as a group. The cars beyond their primitive commune are also forming themselves into survival units. Those in the group pool their food and water, choose a leader, and send out exploratory parties to seek supplies and information.

The members of the group adapt to their situation. Thefts of communal supplies are punished, care for the children and the ailing is arranged, and even a suicide (the strained man in the Caravelle) is taken in stride and the body sealed into his car trunk with glue and Scotch tape. Days go by and the weather turns cold. Inexplicably, the farmers who live near the highway are hostile. They beat and threaten anyone who trespasses, and they refuse to sell food. "It was enough to step out of the thruway's boundaries for stones to come raining in from somewhere. In the middle of the night, someone threw a sickle that hit the top of the DKW and fell beside the Dauphine."

As winter sets in, new ingenuities are necessary. A Ford Mercury and a Porsche sell supplies, at a price, and people make warm clothes out of seat covers, fear for the lives of their car batteries, and huddle together. They help one another through times of desperation and illness. A doctor trudges through the snow to visit the sick. There is happiness in survival, in the security of repeated routines, and in the discreet alliances managed by many of them, including the engineer and the girl in the Dauphine.

With the coming of mild spring days, more sociable relationships with neighbors are restored. Human rhythms accord with the changing seasons: The girl in the Dauphine tells the engineer she is pregnant and the old lady in the ID dies. Suddenly, "when nobody expected it anymore," traffic begins to move again, slowly at first and then faster. Yearning for Paris—for hot water and clean sheets and white wine—the drivers advance eagerly, but when the engineer looks over into the next lane, the Dauphine is no longer beside him. Trapped in the flow of various traffic lanes, the members of the commune are separated. The group is irrevocably dispersed as the cars move faster and faster and the engineer realizes sadly that "the everyday meetings would never take place again, the few rituals, and war councils in Taunus' car, Dauphine's caresses in the quiet of night, the children's laughter as they played with their little cars, the nun's face as she said her rosary." The engineer tries to stop and find his friends, but it is impossible as the cars go racing along. He cannot believe that the simple communal joys are left behind as they rush along "at fifty-five miles an hour toward the lights that kept growing, not knowing why all this hurry, why this mad race in the night among unknown cars, where no one knew anything about the others, where everyone looked straight ahead, only ahead."

Themes and Meanings

Julio Cortázar bases his story upon an experience common to everyone, a traffic jam, and upon a common response: an impatient, exasperated "I feel as though I've been here for days." Well, speculates Cortázar, what if it *were* days, what if the figure of speech became literally true? The traffic jam becomes an emergency situation which brings out the best in everyone (leadership qualities, compassion, generosity, fairness) as the group collectively fights for survival. Stripped of possessions, of acquired social status and influence, of all the qualities and barriers which would normally isolate them from one another, the denizens of the freeway form close bonds with their companions. There is real satisfaction in contributing to the primitive tribal society where each member of the group has a function and is essential, where each member is cared for and recognized. Twentieth century technology is reduced to a collection of metal boxes and radios which cease to convey any message relevant to their actual situation. The individuals discover resilience and dormant primitive skills within themselves and take pleasure in this meaningful connection with their ancestral heritage. Positive human values are revealed when these superficial overlayers of materialism, technology, and the rush of contemporary life are stripped away. These are twentieth century men and women, and when traffic does move they must inevitably go with it, however regretful they may feel. The metaphors of the river (or highway) of life and the medieval dance of death (of which one is explicitly reminded by the sickle, symbol of death) are metaphors of inexorable progression; once cars enter the thruway they must move along to their destinations.

Style and Technique

The narrative device of the enclosure (placing the characters in a confining situation which isolates them) serves a variety of functions. The behavior of the characters as they interact with one another may be more easily observed in a situation in which there are minimal outside influences, ensured in "The Southern Thruway" by the hostility of the neighboring cars and farmers. The group is a microcosm of society in general; as in a medieval religious drama, also meant to symbolize the world, the characters include children, youths (the boys in the Simca), and old people, representatives of the Church (the nuns), the military (the soldier), business (the traveling salesman), professions (the engineer, the doctor), and farmers. It includes all aspects of the human life cycle, from conception (Dauphine's child) to death, both natural and suicidal. The situation encompasses summer and winter, hope and despair. The technique of identifying individuals only by the names of their cars depersonalizes them and emphasizes their function in the microcosm. It recalls the origin of surnames, when people were called John the Tailor or Paul the Shoemaker. Thus, it is a part of the transition to a primitive communal world of basic need fulfillment where the inessential is stripped away, and "the girl in the Dauphine" becomes simple Dauphine. It is also appropriate to the highway world where driver and car are referred to as one unit ("Watch out for that Ford up there"), where identity is defined by the car. It is also a reminder of the depersonalization of the twentieth century world where individuals are labeled by their social security, registration, or hospital admission numbers.

The sentence rhythms are adapted to the events of the story. While the cars are still moving along, the long sentences flow along, broken by series of jerky clauses as the cars begin to stop and start. As the traffic speeds up at the end, again long breathless sentences hurtle the reader through the night toward Paris.

The traffic jam symbolizes the breakdown of twentieth century technology and the consequent rediscovery of age-old human instincts and values. With warmth and humor, the story presents an optimistic view of basic human nature. It contrasts twentieth century impersonality and hurry with a primitive tribal society and reflects upon the differences, returning to the contemporary world in the end.

Mary G. Berg

THE SPINOZA OF MARKET STREET

Author: Isaac Bashevis Singer (1904-   )
Type of plot: Psychological realism
Time of plot: 1914
Locale: Warsaw
First published: "Der Spinozist," 1944 (English translation, 1961)

>   *Principal characters:*
>   DR. NAHUM FISCHELSON, the protagonist and a doctor of
>   philosophy
>   BLACK DOBBE, a spinster

The Story

   Dr. Nahum Fischelson is a Jewish intellectual who has studied in Switzerland and has achieved some fame as a commentator on the works of Benedict
de Spinoza, the seventeenth century Dutch philosopher. As the story opens,
Fischelson is a poor old man with a stomach ailment that the doctors cannot
diagnose. He lives on an annuity of five hundred marks provided by the Jewish community of Berlin. In an attic room overlooking Market Street in Warsaw, he pursues his study of Spinoza's *Ethics*, brooding on the great philosopher's ideas about the divine laws of reason and about the infinite extension
of God. He views the stars through his telescope, seeing in them examples of
Spinoza's insight and vision, while below him in the street mankind, blind to
Spinoza's sense of ethical propriety, pursues its finite passions.
   The chaotic crowd on Market Street is composed of shopkeepers, ped-
dlers, thieves, prostitutes, thugs, policemen, and drunks. Across the street,
Jewish boys are toiling over books in the study house. Fischelson is remote
from them all, having become more and more isolated over the years. When
he first returned from Zurich as a doctor of philosophy, much was made
of him in his community. He became the head librarian of the Warsaw synagogue and more than one rich girl was offered to him for marriage. He would
not marry, however, preferring to remain as free as his idol Spinoza, and he
lost his job as librarian because his ideas clashed with those of the rabbi. He
supported himself as a tutor in Hebrew and German, but then he became
sick and had to give it up. He no longer goes to the café as he had, for intellectual stimulation and the company of his peers. The Revolution of 1905,
moreover, brought such chaos to the society with which he was familiar that
it further isolated him. Ideas and even language have changed for the worse,
as far as he is concerned, and the crowd-pleasing philosophy of the time in-
furiates him, despite Spinoza's warning against emotions.
   Then World War I starts, and fear is added to Fischelson's illness. Military

convoys pass through Market Street, and his subsidy from Berlin is abruptly cut off. He returns to the café he once frequented, but no one there is familiar to him. He seeks out the rabbi of the synagogue where he was head librarian, but the rabbi and his wife have left, ostensibly on vacation. He considers suicide, but he remembers that Spinoza equates it with madness. Thinking that the world has gone mad, he takes to his bed, convinced that his own end is near. He has a confusing dream then about being ill as a boy, being kept away from a Catholic procession passing by his childhood house, and about the end of the world.

At this point, Black Dobbe, an ugly spinster who lives next door to him in the attic, enters his room to get him to read a letter to her from her cousin, a shoemaker who emigrated to New York. Black Dobbe used to peddle bread in the street, but she quarreled with the baker and now sells cracked eggs there. She was engaged three times; each time, though, the engagement was broken. The two boys she was going to marry backed out, and the rich old man to whom she was engaged turned out to be married. She has a low opinion of men—not simply because of her bad luck with them, but because she knows how the underworld on Market Street treats women, sometimes kidnaping them to be prostitutes in foreign countries, a fate she herself once escaped.

At first thinking that Fischelson is dead, Black Dobbe throws a glass of water in his face when she discovers that he is not. She undresses him and makes his bed, then cooks soup for him and cleans his room, which she finds rather tidy to begin with. That evening she cooks for him again and, though briefly imagining that he might be in league with evil powers, asks him if he has converted from Judaism. He assures her that he has not.

Fischelson's health takes a turn for the better. Black Dobbe continues to visit him and cook for him. She keeps him up to date on the progress of the war, and he, having told her about his own background, questions her about hers. This is the first time that anyone has ever done this to her. When Fischelson asks her if she believes in God, she says that she does not know. He says that he himself does, and that God's presence is not restricted to the synagogue. Black Dobbe then shows him the trousseau she has collected and carefully preserved.

A short time later, Fischelson and Black Dobbe, much to the amusement of the neighbors who attend the ceremony in the rabbi's chambers, are married. That night, despite his prior warning to Black Dobbe that he is an old man in ill health, Fischelson makes love to her with the feeling and vigor of a young man. Afterward, while she sleeps, he looks at the stars out his window as he did at the beginning of the story, and as he concentrates on the aspect of heat, diversity, and change in Spinoza's divinely determined universe, he asks the spirit of the great philosopher to forgive him for giving in to the world of passion—this source, it seems, of joy and health.

Themes and Meanings

At the heart of this story is the conflict between the world of ideas and the world of passion, between the rational and the irrational, the ideal and the actual, the mind and the body, eternity and time. Fischelson and Black Dobbe dramatize both sides of this equation— Fischelson the intellectual side, and Black Dobbe the physical and emotional. Isaac Bashevis Singer painstakingly shows that each side needs the other, especially that the mental requires its opposite for survival. Fischelson's problem is that he has isolated himself in the ideal through his all but idolatrous devotion to Spinoza, and in so doing—in not paying attention to the other side of his humanity—he has become ill. The story makes a point of showing that his illness has no physical source; that is, his commitment to the mind has caused it, for the doctors whom Fischelson consults cannot attribute his chronic indigestion and stomach pains to anything more concrete than a nervous disorder. Fischelson emphasizes the general over the specific, thereby neglecting many of his needs as a specific human being, and it is this emphasis which provides the context for his impending death. He decides that he is dying, not because of something he has done as an individual but because the Great War has started. His logic is that if destruction has come in general, then his own life is finished. In short, he sees survival in general, not personal, terms.

Black Dobbe, on the other hand, has not had the luxury of looking at life and survival as Fischelson does. She is not supported by a subsidy as he is, and without the support of a man or the backing of a family, it has been particularly difficult for her to make her way in the world as a woman. She has had to rely on the nonintellectual virtues of thrift, courage, and persistence, and on her practical knowledge of how life in the gutter operates, to stay alive. Fischelson can afford to die, since death for him is an escape from the chaos of a life from which he has long been traveling away. Black Dobbe cannot afford to die, for life is all that she has.

What Black Dobbe has done is to bring life itself to Fischelson—not life from the point of view of Spinoza's God, but life as it is lived by God's tumultuous creatures. The marriage of Fischelson and Black Dobbe, absurd as it may seem at first, is no more absurd than life itself, which is paradoxical, confusing, and difficult. Moreover, the marriage of these two characters is the story's way of suggesting that human contact, passion, and love define human life at its best.

Style and Technique

One of the major devices of *The Spinoza of Market Street* is the placement of the main characters in a way that dramatizes their condition. Fischelson lives in a room high above the street, cut off from its turmoil, and Black Dobbe lives in a room cut off from sunlight. Fischelson lives between the sky and the earth, descending to the latter only once a week to buy his food, preferring to look at the former through his telescope. The light of vision, of intellectual insight, comes through his window, as it were. Black Dobbe has no window, no intellectual light, and she spends most of her time down in the street, struggling to make a living, her feet firmly on the earth. Fischelson's room, however, is the more important of the two rooms in the end, for it does more than embody isolation. It helps to highlight the fact that man is neither a beast (as the events in the street below seem to assume) nor divine (as the events in the night sky seem to suggest to the mind), but in between. Fischelson's room is where the two extremes meet, bringing new life to the philosopher and a sense of value and meaning to the ignorant peddler. Viewed as a stage, Fischelson's room is where the two components of human destiny—the need to eat and feel and the need to envision life's meaning—play out their importance to each other.

Mark McCloskey

SPLIT CHERRY TREE

Author: Jesse Stuart (1907-1984)
Type of plot: Psychological realism
Time of plot: The 1930's
Locale: Rural Kentucky
First published: 1939

> *Principal characters:*
> DAVE SEXTON, the narrator, a high school student
> LUSTER SEXTON (PA), Dave's father, a feisty backwoods
> Kentucky farmer
> PROFESSOR HERBERT, Dave's principal

The Story

The title of the story identifies the incident that animates the action of this masterful piece of short fiction. Dave Sexton, together with five of his classmates, climbs a neighbor's cherry tree to capture a lizard while on a field trip with his high school biology class. The tree is broken and the six boys must pay for the damage. Unfortunately, Dave Sexton is unable to come up with his dollar. The principal, Professor Herbert, contributes the money for Dave but makes him stay after school to work off the debt. It is at this point that the story begins.

Dave would rather take a whipping than stay after school, because he must help his father with the farm chores. Professor Herbert, however, believes that Dave is too big to be punished in this fashion. When Dave gets home two hours late, Luster Sexton, Dave's father, is furious with his son, as well as with the high school principal, modern education, and society in general. Luster vows to go to school with Dave and put a stop to such foolishness as "bug larnin'." He declares, "A bullet will make a hole in a schoolteacher same as it will anybody else." Before Luster leaves with his son the next morning, he straps on his gun and holster.

Naturally, Luster causes a commotion in the school with his rustic ways and his revolver. He confronts the principal and, after placing his gun on the seat beside him, demands an explanation. Professor Herbert is taken aback and then explains that he had no other choice than to punish Dave in the way he did. He also tells Luster that education has changed since the days when he attended school. When Herbert offers to show Luster what really goes on in high school, he accepts accompanying the principal on an extended tour for the whole day, and eventually showing up in his son's biology class, where he sees germs under a microscope for the first time.

In the end, Luster understands that the world has changed considerably from the time when he was a boy, and that there is a need to learn more than "readin', writin', and cipherin'." When Professor Herbert excuses Dave from the two hours of work yet remaining from him to pay his debt, Luster will not hear of it. So changed is his attitude that he volunteers to help his son sweep the school, insisting now that Dave get all the education he can.

Themes and Meanings

This story demonstrates Jesse Stuart's concern with both education of and the difficulty of life for rural Americans, especially those out of the mainstream of cultural change. While the story seems on the surface to be about Dave Sexton, it is really the story of Dave's father, Luster: the inappropriateness of his untutored response to the modern world, his anger caused by ignorance, and his willingness to change when given the opportunity to see the facts for himself. Stuart sympathizes, and would have the reader sympathize, too, with those who hold on to ways of life that are no longer quite appropriate—especially if their roughshod ways are redeemed by virtues that tend to be undervalued in more recent times. Luster represents country folk in general. He is ignorant and stubborn, but he is not unreasonable and uncompromising. He finally comes to recognize the value and the importance—indeed, the necessity—of the kind of education his son is receiving, especially Dave's more detailed knowledge of the natural world. The isolation of rural life quickly makes social knowledge obsolete, but it nevertheless keeps those who lead this life in contact with the more elemental knowledge of life and death, of honesty and virtue.

Dave represents young people in rural society. He lives in two worlds at the same time: the outdated world of his parents and the more current world of his school environment and friends. His struggle, the tension of his character, is to keep these two worlds together, functioning harmoniously. That he is willing to do so, that he makes such an effort to lead both lives successfully, is a sure sign of Stuart's optimism and his faith in the young. In one sense, "Split Cherry Tree" is an example of a recurring fictional pattern, the coming-of-age story. Frequently in this pattern, adolescents must solve problems of sexuality or identity in order to become fully functioning adults, though other problems of adulthood are common in this form. For example, many of Ernest Hemingway's young characters learn to deal with the existence of evil. Stuart's variation on the coming-of-age theme requires Dave to solve the dilemma of the old versus the new, the home and the world. In resolving this conflict, Dave becomes ready to assume a mature place in both his family and society.

Above all, Jesse Stuart is concerned with the lives of those about whom he writes. In literary terms, this concern makes him a writer who emphasizes character above either plot or theme, though in this story all three elements are superbly coordinated, a major reason why "Split Cherry Tree" is one of Jesse Stuart's best.

Style and Technique

While the coming-of-age theme is important in understanding the meaning of this story, it is Jesse Stuart's handling of character that has made "Split Cherry Tree" one of the classics of the American short-story form. Luster, for example, is finely delineated. For the story to be successful, the reader must see him as a man who is fully capable of carrying out the violence that his threats against Professor Herbert promise. Without that element in his personality, the reader would know far too early that the story is going to have a happy ending, and the drama of the tale would be lost. At the same time, Luster cannot appear so violent and unregenerate that he becomes an out-and-out villain, for this would completely destroy Stuart's theme and ruin his aim of developing sympathy for rural people. Stuart strikes this subtle balance in Luster Sexton's character with a masterful handling of details. Most essential, he imbues Luster with a strong sense of justice and fair play, and this characteristic is evident in Luster's early tirade against the school and its principal. By building in this trait from the beginning, Stuart prepares the reader unconsciously to see the positive side of Luster's character, which will gain much more prominence in the ending. Luster's character is further enhanced by his love of the natural world. The only thing that he cannot finally forgive about the new school is its killing and dissecting of black snakes. When Professor Herbert offers to choloroform and dissect a snake to show Luster that germs are to be found everywhere, Luster urges him not to, explaining that he does not allow people to kill them on his farm. Dave, the narrator, notices that "the students look at Pa. They seem to like him better after he said that." Without this sort of careful preparation for the reversal of the reader's attitude toward Luster in the closing part of the work, "Split Cherry Tree" would have the kind of trick ending that mars the work of lesser writers, the kind of endings that feature prominently in some of the weaker stories of O. Henry.

Customarily, the short-story form does not allow writers the freedom to tell stories in which a change of character (or a different interpretation of character by the reader) is featured so prominently. That sort of narrative is usually the province of the novel, which, because of its greater length, can show a gradual change of personality over time. It is a mark of Stuart's mastery of technique that he is able to encapsule a trait of the longer form and use it with success in a short story.

The character of Dave is also finely drawn. As stated earlier, he lives simultaneously in both the contemporary world and the outdated world of his parents. Were he completely to reject the values of his family—more specifically, to rebel against his father's country ways and attitudes—the story would not be able to carry its meanings and themes. Instead, Stuart places Dave at the fulcrum of both value systems. Dave is embarrassed that his father goes to school with him, but he is not mortified at his father's presence in the high school. Dave enjoys a wider social sphere than his parents. While he seems to enjoy learning as well, especially learning about nature, he does not reject the farming life that nurtured and formed him. On the other hand, he is not solely the child of his parents; the modern world has a strong appeal for him, and he wants to participate in it as fully as he wants to maintain his contact with the hearth and the hollows of his native Kentucky. In the end, his father's acceptance of the school and its modern ideas is a victory for Dave, for it allows him to live a richer, more complete life—sharing the love of his family and enjoying the fruits of the contemporary world as well.

Jesse Stuart took an incident he had heard about when he himself served as the principal of a rural Kentucky school and transformed it, through his genius in creating character, into a struggle between the old and the new, the familiar and the exciting. In doing so, Stuart used the short-story technique he had mastered so well, pinpoint characterization, to create a tale in a style that was distinctively his own—masterfully orchestrated, spare of ornamentation, and tightly focused on the lives and tribulations of rural Americans, a group he knew and loved.

Charles Hackenberry

SPOTTED HORSES

Author: William Faulkner (1897-1962)
Type of plot: Comic realism
Time of plot: Early twentieth century
Locale: Mississippi
First published: 1931

> *Principal characters:*
> FLEM SNOPES, the owner of the horses and one of the
>   principal personages in the town of Frenchman's Bend
> BUCK HIPPS, Flem's partner
> HENRY ARMSTID, an unlucky purchaser of one of the horses
> ECK SNOPES, the cousin to Flem and another purchaser of a
>   horse
> VERNON TULL, who is injured by one of the runaway horses

The Story

Flem Snopes returns to Frenchman's Bend after an absence of many months in Texas, accompanied by Buck Hipps and a string of wild spotted horses. The horses are confined in a lot next to the town hotel and put up for auction. On the day of the auction, people from the farms and surrounding countryside gather around the lot but at first are generally reluctant to bid on the animals, which have several times shown that they are unbroken and frankly dangerous. Hipps taunts the audience to no avail but finally succeeds in getting the auction going by giving Eck Snopes one horse for free if Eck will agree to purchase another for five dollars. At this moment, Henry Armstid arrives and demands to be allowed the same terms as Eck, but ends up bidding five dollars for another of the wild animals. Mrs. Armstid begs Hipps not to take her husband's money, since it is the last five dollars they possess.

The auction proceeds until all the horses are spoken for and Hipps has collected all the money. When Mrs. Armstid renews her plea, Hipps tells her that she should apply to Mr. Snopes on the following day for the money. In the meantime, the new owners of the horses have gathered to put ropes around the necks of their latest purchases, but the lot gate is left open, and the horses escape and go running through the town and on into the country-side. One of Eck's horses encounters the Tulls crossing a bridge and causes Vernon Tull to fall off his wagon and receive serious, though not fatal, in-juries. The rest of the horses, with the exception of the one that Eck pur-chased (which is upended and breaks its neck), escape, and no one is able to retrieve either his horse or his money. Mrs. Armstid applies to Flem Snopes for the five dollars promised her by Hipps, but Snopes assures her that he never owned the horses and that he does not have her money—although the story is generally disbelieved by everyone in the town.

Ultimately, court suits are brought against Flem and against Eck for reckless endangerment and for damages suffered as a result of the horses' having got loose. None of the suits is successful, however, since ownership of the horses is denied by Flem (with another cousin's corroborating testimony), and the judge rules that since the horse which did the damage to the Tulls was given to Eck and his possession of it was never established (since he never actually was in control of it), in the eyes of the law, Eck technically never owned the horse and thus could not be held liable for any damage inflicted by the animal. The story comes to an end with the adjournment of the court and the judge in exasperation, but with Flem presumably having received the profits from the sale of the horses—although, as V. K. Ratliff might have said, " That ain't been proved yet neither."

Themes and Meanings

"Spotted Horses" is among a series of short stories which Faulkner wrote from the late 1920's to the end of the 1930's and which would subsequently become part of his trilogy of novels about the rise and fall of Flem Snopes and the general infestation of the country by the Snopes family. First published in 1931 in *Scribner's Monthly*, it was later incorporated in the fourth section of *The Hamlet* (1940), entitled "The Peasants." By itself, the story is a riotous comic portrayal of a shady horse deal, but positioned near the end of *The Hamlet* at the point at which Flem is about to complete his takeover of Frenchman's Bend before moving on to the town of Jefferson, it assumes ominous overtones which are only weakly apparent in Flem's ruthless treatment of Mrs. Armstid.

The horses themselves are several times referred to as "that Texas disease," and it is the image of plague sweeping over the countryside which dominates this and other of the stories in the Snopes saga. Faulkner himself once compared the arrival of the Snopeses to a plague of locusts, and it is clear that he himself viewed the rise of Flem Snopes to a position of power with something like the alarm evinced by V. K. Ratliff, the itinerant sewing machine salesman who opposes Flem throughout the three volumes in which he figures. The story of the wild horses, symbolizing the unleashing of chaos upon the world of the novel, resonates with the earlier comic episode in the novel, related by Ratliff, in which Ab Snopes (Flem's father) is bested in a horse trade by the incomparable Pat Stamper, a legendary trader never known to have been defeated in a deal for anything that walks on four legs. The signal difference between the two episodes, however, lies in the intent of Ab merely to redeem the honor of the land by besting Stamper in a trade, in comparison to Flem's wish simply to acquire as much money as he can as quickly and efficiently as possible. The two different stories thus figure two different historical and socioeconomic periods in the world of the novel: a precapitalist moment of barter economy, as opposed to the properly capitalist world of the cash nexus. The career of Flem Snopes is Faulkner's most telling version of the emergence of the petty bourgeois class which came to dominate the South in the wake of Reconstruction and the transformation of the Southern economy from an agrarian-based to a partially industrialized one. Faulkner's great theme, the betrayal of the natural virtues of the land for the sake of financial gain, is depicted here in its most naked form. The abandonment of the moral economy of the precapitalist world is something that Faulkner consistently condemned, and Flem Snopes is merely the most infamous incarnation of a character-type that Faulkner frequently realized: the ruthless entrepreneur.

Style and Technique

Faulkner's prose is legendary for its complexity and its violation of the ordinary constraints of syntax. In addition, as has often been remarked, Faulkner captures the idiom of the Southern rural poor with great acuteness, reproducing not only their diction and pronunciation but also the very rhythms of their speech.

"Spotted Horses" is unusual among most of the other episodes in *The Hamlet* for not featuring V. K. Ratliff, the archetypal raconteur who figures prominently in early sections and who is generally on hand to attempt to prevent Flem's doing grave harm to the community. His steadfast refusal to intervene in this episode, even on behalf of the Armstids, differentiates this section from the others thematically, as the episode is distinct technically for its placing Ratliff largely to the side of the action. One can surmise that this relative absence of Ratliff from the action suggests something about the stage in the plot that has been attained at this point. It is plausible to read here the beginning of the end, in this novel at least, for any principled attempt to stop the onward march of the Snopeses into the country. The next and final episode in *The Hamlet* involves Ratliff's being easily bilked by Flem into purchasing a worthless piece of property and thereby providing Flem with his entrée into the town of Jefferson. Thus, the temporary disappearance of Ratliff from the foreground of the narrative would seem the preliminary to the ultimate triumph of Flem over the community of Frenchman's Bend.

The story itself harks back to a long tradition of tall tales and Western humor, of which Mark Twain is probably the most representative and famous figure. The hyperbole in Faulkner's descriptions of the horses derives from this tradition, as does the general tone of comic excess. Faulkner's humor, like Twain's, is scarcely innocent, and the inordinate violence which the story depicts is allowed full scope when the reader finds himself roaring over the antics of the horses and the incapacity of the men to tame them. This tone is continued in the next novel in the Snopes trilogy, *The Town* (1957), but the humor becomes increasingly difficult to sustain. One might say that *The Hamlet* marks a terminus of sorts for Faulkner (although the spirit of this novel would be briefly revived in his final novel, *The Reivers*, 1962), in that he would never quite be able to summon up the comic genius which this novel, and in particular "Spotted Horses," exhibits in abundance. As an example of this characteristic Faulknerian comedy, "Spotted Horses" is probably without peer in the Faulkner canon.

Michael Sprinker

SPRING VICTORY

Author: Jesse Stuart (1907-1984)
Type of plot: Psychological realism
Time of plot: 1918
Locale: Rural Kentucky
First published: 1942

> *Principal characters:*
> THE BOY, the central character and narrator, ten years old
> SAL, his mother
> MICK, his father

The Story

During the dead of winter in 1918, a rural farm family faces starvation. After a summer in which the crops failed, the father is sick in bed with a protracted case of the flu, and the four children are all very young, by modern standards, to be of much help. It is left to the narrator's mother to find a path through the dilemma.

Her solution is to resume a craft she learned as a girl, basket weaving, and to enlist the older children in the enterprise. The unnamed narrator, who is ten years old, supplies the raw materials for his mother. Through bitter cold he trudges to a nearby bluff to cut white oak saplings so that they can later be cut, quartered, and splintered to serve as basket-making materials. In addition to his new responsibilities in the basket-making venture, which include taking the finished products to the closest town and selling them, the boy labors on the farm from early morning until night. Much of the description of the story centers on the details of his chores: milking the cow, feeding the stock, and tending the fires. One of his major responsibilities on the farm is cutting, hauling, and splitting firewood, a task with which his mother helps him in the early and middle parts of the tale—but which she leaves entirely to him in the final section of the story.

By any standards, the young boy's lot is a difficult one, but he accepts all of his responsibilities without complaint and carries out each one with surprising success. He relishes the tasks that would customarily be a man's work, and he especially likes selling the baskets that his mother makes each day to his neighbors and the townsfolk. One of the boy's most mature accomplishments is negotiating the purchase of fodder and corn, which will keep the stock alive until the pasture grass returns in the spring. In all things, the lad follows his mother's instructions precisely, selling the baskets for the price she establishes and buying the food that they need to see them through the difficult winter. Through the mother's careful planning, they are even able to put a small sum aside. The father's illness lingers, but all the children do what they can to reduce their mother's household burdens so that she can continue to increase her production of the wares that are sold to provide the food they sorely need. Both the mother and the children develop a sense of pride in their self-reliance, and she cheers her family by reminding them often that even as the snow deepens on the ground, the violets are budding underneath.

Through much of the story, the reader waits for the tragedy that will shatter the stoic bliss of the brave little family. When the narrator's mother sends him to fetch the doctor, it seems as if the ax has finally fallen, and that they will be overwhelmed by nature, snow, and cold, as is the family in Nathaniel Hawthorne's tale "The Ambitious Guest," a narrative that bears comparison to both "Spring Victory" and a similar Jesse Stuart story, "Dark Winter."

The story's surprise ending is that the doctor has been summoned, not to treat the ailing father, but to deliver the mother's baby. Spring finally returns, the father gets well, and their close scrape with disaster draws the family even closer together.

Themes and Meanings

Jesse Stuart's paean to rural courage and human love extolls the somewhat opposing virtues of self-reliance and family unity. The individual members of the family, from the resourceful mother to the newborn child, can survive only by uniting their efforts against the forces that threaten them, which in this story take the form of a violent winter and the sickness that incapacitates the father. The central character, the ten-year-old son, does whatever is required of him, and he does it without complaint or opposition of any kind. His concerns center on the well-being of his parents, the illness of his father, and the possible threat to his mother's health through overwork as she makes the baskets that temporarily earn the living for all of them. So, too, does his mother focus her thoughts on the survival of her husband and children, the good of the whole, paying as little attention as does her son to her own comfort and convenience. Only by striving to ensure the survival of the whole family can the members do their utmost to provide for their own continuance, though this is not the level on which the family lives its life during this time of trial.

Their efforts are concerted and expended through an unstated love of one another, a love that has existed before the opening of the story and one that will continue, the ending reassures the reader, throughout the life of each family member. Few short stories in American literature reverberate with such a positive view of human ties and affection, and few celebrate quite so wholeheartedly what have come to be considered traditional American values.

Above all, this tale of a poor farming family expresses a deep optimism about the possibilities of life, the peace and solace to be found in fortitude, and the benefits of a cheerful stoicism. One should take life as it comes, the story teaches, and do the best one can with what one has. Love one another and everything will be all right.

Style and Technique

Short-story writers or novelists undertake few challenges as difficult as telling their tale by using an immature narrator. Entrusting the boy to tell the story related in "Spring Victory" was a venture full of pitfalls for Jesse Stuart, and his ability to sidestep so many of them is one mark of his accomplishments as a writer of short fiction. The primary problem of this device is that the narrator cannot seem more mature than his years allow, yet he or she must be capable of giving the insights that the writer wants to convey—about the people in the story, about the interpretation of their actions, and about life in general. A story concocted by a real child is full of childishness, but readers of serious fiction expect a story to be coordinated and meaningful. Satisfying the expectations of readers while giving the illusion that the story is actually being told by a child creates a situation in which the believability of the action, let alone the believability of the narrator's character, is constantly in danger of rupture.

Through a careful manipulation of the narrator's language, through his tone of voice as well as through what he merely implies, Stuart makes both the action of the story and the character of the young narrator seem real. The narrator's terseness shows a child not yet very proficient in his use of language, yet his observations are keen and vivid nevertheless. Stuart balances the boy's personality, which at times is almost too good to be true, with his ignorance of life. It comes as a shock to the narrator that the doctor has been summoned to assist his mother with the birth of a child. His sister is surprised to learn that the boy never noticed that his mother was pregnant, yet the reader understands the limitations of inexperience better than she, and such details bring the boy alive and compensate for those times when the reader would have been lazy or complaining if he had been asked to do the narrator's chores or suffer his privations.

One need only try to imagine the story told by the mother or the father (or by an omniscient narrator) to see the harvest that Stuart reaped by putting the words in the mouth of the boy. What Stuart learned about life, about love, and about family from his experience of the grueling winter of 1918 was apparent to even a child, and it was the kind of lesson that would stay with him through adolescence, through the time when he would learn his native tongue well enough to tell others what he found valuable enough, many years later, to turn into literary art.

Charles Hackenberry

SREDNI VASHTAR

Author: Saki (Hector Hugh Munro, 1870-1916)
Type of plot: Horror
Time of plot: The early 1900's
Locale: England
First published: 1911

Principal characters:
CONRADIN, a very imaginative, sick ten-year-old boy
MRS. DE ROPP, his cousin and guardian

The Story

Conradin, a ten-year-old boy whom the doctor has given less than five years to live, is antagonized by his cousin and guardian, Mrs. De Ropp, who seems to take delight in thwarting him under the guise of taking care of him. Conradin finds escape in his vivid imagination and in an unused toolshed, in which he keeps two pets—a Houdan hen, on which he lavishes affection, and a ferret, which he fears and comes to venerate as a god.

Conradin names the ferret Sredni Vashtar and worships the beast as his god, bringing it flowers in season and celebrating festivals on special occasions, such as when his cousin suffers from a toothache. When his cousin notices him spending too much time in the shed, she discovers the Houdan hen and sells it. She is surprised when Conradin fails to show any emotion at the news, but Conradin changes his usual worshiping ritual. Instead of chanting Sredni Vashtar's praises, he asks an unnamed boon of his god. Every day he repeats his request for the one wish from the ferret. Mrs. De Ropp, noticing his frequent visits to the toolshed, concludes that he must have something hidden there, which she assumes to be guinea pigs. She ransacks his room until she finds the key to the cage and goes out to the shed.

As she goes to the shed, Conradin watches her and imagines her triumph over him and his subsequent declining health under her oppressive care. He does not see her emerge from the shed for a long time, however, and he begins to hope, chanting to Sredni Vashtar. Finally, he notices the ferret coming out of the shed with dark, wet stains around its mouth and throat.

The maid announces tea and asks Conradin where his cousin is. He tells her that Mrs. De Ropp has gone to the shed, and the maid goes to announce tea to her. Conradin calmly butters his toast, relishing every moment as he hears the scream of the maid and the loud sobs and talk of the kitchen help, followed by the footsteps of someone carrying a heavy burden. Then he hears the kitchen help discussing who will tell the young boy the news as he takes another piece of toast to butter.

Themes and Meanings

This short, macabre story is chilling in its portrayal of the fiendish young boy. Saki takes the boy's point of view toward the annoying, officious cousin, who, the boy believes, delights in tormenting him. The boy lives almost entirely in his imagination. The real world is that which is ruled by adults such as his cousin, who are most disagreeable to him. In this aspect, Conradin seems to be a perfectly normal child at odds with the demands of the cruel outside world. What sets Conradin apart from other children is his almost pathological escape from reality and his achieving his revenge through the agency of the wild animal. What is usually only imaginary to a child is carried to fruition, and the child relishes it.

Conradin's veneration of the ferret comes to take up more and more of his waking hours after his cousin has sold his beloved hen. It becomes an obsession with him, and the reader finally comes to understand that he prays that the beast will kill his cousin. When the ferret actually kills the cousin, the most shocking thing is the boy's nonchalant, almost happy acceptance of the event. It is the boy's reaction to the killing which takes the story out of the realm of reality.

Although Conradin's condition is unusual in that he has been diagnosed as having a short time to live, he could, to an extent, be perceived as a typical boy escaping in his imagination from the cold world. Even his adoration of the ferret seems to differ only in degree from what could be considered normal. Even normal children imagine killing their adult antagonists, and in this case, it could be considered accidental that his cousin is killed (although Conradin makes no effort to warn her, he fully expects her to emerge from the shed victorious, as she usually does when in conflict with him). Yet the realization that his prayers have been answered and his cold, calm acceptance of the accomplished fact are shocking.

In a sense, then, the story can be seen as a child's fantasy of getting even with the nonunderstanding world of adults. It is a kind of wish fulfillment of which many children dream. The horror is that Saki presents it as a reality, and the boy as fully enjoying the event.

Style and Technique

All of Saki's short stories are very short and to the point, and "Sredni Vashtar" is no exception. Many of his stories are also as macabre as this one. What distinguishes Saki's stories is his ability to capture the feelings and attitudes of children toward their elders. That he was reared by two aunts, one of whom acted sadistically toward children, is probably what motivated Saki to fill so many of his stories with young children and sadistic elder guardians. His purpose is usually achieved by a quasi-objective narrative stance, in which the narrator interprets events from the point of view of the young protagonist but pretends to relate events objectively, as in this story.

The narrator at the beginning depicts the situation as Conradin views it. To him, Mrs. De Ropp represents "those three-fifths of the world that are necessary and disagreeable and real," while "the other two-fifths, in perpetual antagonism to the foregoing, were summed up in himself and his imagination." The fruit trees in the "dull cheerless garden" are described as being "jealously apart from his plucking, as though they were rare specimens of their kind blooming in an arid waste." It is an adult narrating the perceptions of a child.

Mrs. De Ropp becomes for the boy the epitome of all that is respectable, and thus the antithesis of all that he holds dear. When she has sold his beloved hen, he refuses to let her see how deeply he feels the loss, but he is described as hating the world as represented chiefly by Mrs. De Ropp. His antipathy takes the form of his devoting his energies to praying more fervently to his animal god.

Saki cleverly omits mentioning the subject of Conradin's supplication to Sredni Vashtar, and while the cousin is in the toolshed to get rid of the ferret, the narrator describes Conradin's imagining his cruel cousin's final triumph over him by extirpating the one creature he so venerates. Then, as Saki obliquely informs the reader of the demise of the hated guardian, his description of Conradin calmly eating and enjoying his butter and toast heightens the reader's sense of shock.

Roger Geimer

THE STATION-MASTER

Author: Alexander Pushkin (1799-1837)
Type of plot: Satire
Time of plot: The 1830's
Locale: A country station and St. Petersburg
First published: "Stantsionnyi smotritel'," 1831 (English translation, 1875)

> *Principal characters:*
> SAMSON VYRIN, the station-master
> DUNYA, his daughter
> MINSKY, an officer
> THE NARRATOR, a traveler

The Story

After an irrelevant introduction about station-masters in general, the narrator tells about one in particular. Samson Vyrin, a widower, is the harried station-master at a remote location visited by the narrator. The operation runs smoothly because his beautiful fourteen-year-old daughter, Dunya, knows how to calm irritated customers, organize the business of the station, and keep her father on an even keel.

The weary narrator presents his papers to the station-master, who copies them in a log book, a bureaucratic necessity in czarist Russia. As the narrator looks around the station during this process, he notes the presence of paintings on the wall depicting the tale of the prodigal son. The first painting portrays the leave-taking of the son, the second his dissolute behavior as he wastes his inheritance, the third his subsequent poverty and tending of swine, and the fourth the joyous reception of the son by the father as the boy returns to his senses and to the paternal home.

As the station-master completes the recording of the orders, Dunya enters the room with a samovar; the three sit down for a chat and tea. The narrator is very impressed by Dunya and, when he is ready to leave, he asks for a kiss, which he receives. The narrator remembers this kiss even to this day.

A few years later, the narrator is again in the area and stops at the same station. The paintings depicting the parable of the prodigal son are still on the wall, but the station is unkempt and the master has aged. After a few preliminary remarks, Samson tells the narrator what has happened since their last meeting.

A young officer, a certain Minsky, stopped at the station and fell in love with Dunya. In order to prolong his visit, he feigned an illness and Dunya served as his nurse. When Minsky had apparently recovered and was ready to leave, he offered to drive Dunya to church; Dunya was reluctant, but her father, who liked the young officer, persuaded her to accept the ride. When

Dunya did not return later in the morning, Samson went to the church and discovered that Dunya had not been there. Going on to the next station, his fear was confirmed; his daughter had run away with Minsky, according to the master of that station. Samson returned home and fell ill.

When he had recovered, Samson decided to travel to St. Petersburg and try to rescue his daughter from a life of shame. The station-master was sure that the officer meant only to use his daughter and then discard her, thus forcing her to become a prostitute in the large city. He found Minsky and implored him to return his daughter; the officer, however, replied that he and Dunya were in love, what was done was done, and, having handed the old man a sum of money, pushed him out into the street.

In a state of despair, Samson walked around St. Petersburg in a daze and accidentally discovered Minsky's coach before a house. Correctly surmising that his daughter lived there, he told a maid that he had a message for her mistress, brushed past her, and found his daughter in a beautifully appointed room. Dunya was sitting next to Minsky, looking at him tenderly and winding her fingers through his hair. When she saw her father, Dunya fainted and Minsky expelled Samson from the house. The old man returned to his station, took to drink, and wallowed in self-pity. He concludes his story by telling the narrator that he has not heard from Dunya, but he is sure that she has wound up like other women in her position: poor and discarded, living off the streets. He had punctuated this sad tale with frequent sobbing and glasses of rum. The narrator leaves the station, but he has been deeply touched by the story; he remembers Samson and his story for a long time.

Many years later, the narrator is again in the vicinity of the station. He discovers that the station has been closed and that Samson has died of drinking. He also learns that the master's grave was visited by a beautiful lady with three children, a nurse, and a dog. The lady arrived in a beautiful carriage with six horses, spent time crying over the old man's grave, and liberally tipped the little boy who told her of her father's death. Dunya had finally come home.

Themes and Meanings

Alexander Pushkin's attitude toward religion was skeptical, to say the least; among his writings are works which would be considered blasphemous or irreverent by any standard. In this story, the author uses two New Testament parables—those of the prodigal son and the good shepherd—as contrasts to the reality of the station-master's life.

On his first visit, the narrator sees the four pictures depicting the tale of the prodigal son and recalls the story behind each picture. On his second visit, the narrator again notes the presence of the pictures, thus reminding the reader of the parable. Dunya's experiences and character are quite different from those of the errant son; while the latter is a fool who contributes nothing to his father's work and desires only to spend his inheritance in riotous living, Dunya is the mainstay of her father's station and goes to St. Petersburg reluctantly. The son is depicted with loose women, while Dunya maintains a monogamous relationship with the man she loves. When the son runs out of money, his friends abandon him; he is forced to live with pigs and to eat their food. Dunya, on the other hand, is not abandoned, but rather lives comfortably with a man who loves her very deeply.

The big difference between Pushkin's story and the parable is the delusion of the father, perhaps caused by his viewing of the pictures every day and presuming that reality will parallel what he has read in the Scriptures. Samson persists in believing that his daughter will come to the same end as the prodigal son. He does not wait for his daughter to come home, but seeks her out. When his attempts are unsuccessful, he returns home and drinks himself to death. Dunya does return home, but in finery and with children, not seeking forgiveness and not degraded. The prodigal son realized that he had been foolish and sought to rectify his errors; Dunya has always been independent and has always known what to do under any circumstances. She has not been foolish. Her father has fallen into ruin rather than her. Even upon her return to the village, she is in control of her children and tells the young boy that she does not need a guide to the cemetery. She is not the lost person that her father imagines, but rather an assertive young woman in control of her life.

Is this tale, then, a polemic with the parable of the prodigal son, an attack of filial piety and religion? It may only be the use of a tale familiar to all Russian readers of the time in order to make other points, such as the complexity of life or the danger of simply transferring one's reading to reality without thought. On the other hand, given Pushkin's attitude toward religion, it may well have been an attempt on his part to demonstrate the shortcomings of biblical morality.

Samson refers to his daughter as the "lost sheep" and seeks her, just as the good shepherd sought the one lost sheep in the New Testament parable. Samson, however, is unsuccessful, and Pushkin seems to ridicule the efforts of the old man. The officer, who on one occasion is contrasted to a wolf by the station-master (before the flight to St. Petersburg), lures the lost sheep away, while the shepherd returns home empty-handed. Moreover, the reader knows that Samson's effort is ill-advised and not the praiseworthy search of the shepherd; the "lost sheep" is better off with the wolf than with her father at the station. Thus, Pushkin seems to contradict the wisdom of another parable.

Despite the religious symbolism, it is possible that Pushkin was attempting to scuttle a literary myth, not religion. The author wrote this story as Romanticism was giving way to realism as the predominant literary influence. One of the typical plots of sentimental novels was the doomed love of social unequals, usually a noble male and peasant female. In this story Pushkin portrays such a situation, but with a completely different ending; the love is enduring. The use of religious symbolism may have been only to buttress his point that established dogma—in this case, literary—had to give way to alternative positions.

Style and Technique

Pushkin stands as an example of the transition from Romanticism to realism; his poetry, especially his early verse, is usually viewed as part of Romanticism, while his prose is seen as the beginning of Russian realism. In this story, Pushkin employs the precision and economy of words which serve as ingredients of realism, but he also begins with a windy introduction which is completely irrelevant to the story. Perhaps Pushkin wanted to demonstrate the two styles within one story in order to point out the great difference between them and to show the superiority of a precise style, telling a story quickly, over a list of irrelevancies.

Philip Maloney

THE STEPPE
The Story of a Journey

Author: Anton Chekhov (1860-1904)
Type of plot: Lyrical realism
Time of plot: The 1870's
Locale: Southern Russia
First published: "Step: Istoriya odnoi poezdki," 1888 (English translation, 1915)

>   *Principal characters:*
>   YEGORUSHKA KNYAZEV, the protagonist, a fatherless nine-
>   year-old boy
>   IVAN KUZMICHOV, a provincial wool merchant and the boy's
>   uncle
>   FATHER CHRISTOPHER, a Russian Orthodox priest
>   PANTELEY, the elderly, ailing peasant in charge of the train of
>   carts
>   YEMELYAN, one of the carters, formerly a choir singer
>   DYMOV, a handsome, boisterous, and sometimes malicious
>   carter, about thirty
>   MOSES, a poor Jewish innkeeper
>   SOLOMON, his half-demented brother
>   VARLAMOV, a provincial tycoon

The Story

Southern Russia is covered by a vast, prairielike grassland, "the steppe." Anton Chekhov's story recounts the experiences of the young hero, Yegorushka, during his journey of several weeks across the steppe to the great city of Kiev. His uncle, Kuzmichov, and a family friend, Father Christopher, are accompanying a cart train of sheep wool being taken to market. They are also charged with taking Yegorushka and arranging for his lodging and schooling in Kiev. It is the boy's first time away from his mother, the widow of a civil-service clerk.

The two men, in high spirits, set out early one July morning. Yegorushka is in tears as the dilapidated carriage leaves the familiar town and cemetery where his father and grandmother lie. The men chide the crybaby and discuss the questionable merits of further education, but soon fall silent, subdued by the monotony of the limitless steppe. Yegorushka's feeling of desolation and loneliness deepens.

That evening the party briefly stops at an isolated inn to inquire about their wagon train, which has preceded them, and about the powerful Varlamov, with whom they have business. They are effusively greeted by Moses, the obsequiously affable Jewish innkeeper. While the two friends talk, Moses takes Yegorushka into his squalid quarters, where the boy meets the obese wife and several sickly children. Overcome at the plight of the orphan, the wife, after an intense discussion in Yiddish, gives Yegorushka a honeycake, a treat the family can ill afford. The boy returns to find the men talking with the half-mad Solomon. The bizarrely ill-clothed brother, as rudely arrogant as Moses is fawning, points out that as a poor Jew, he is doubly damned. Had he great wealth, however, even Varlamov would fawn on him. Their rest over, the party sets out again and soon overtakes the wagon train. Finding all well, they transfer Yegorushka to one of the wool carts and to the care of the head wagoner, old Panteley, while they, in search of Varlamov, will travel separately and meet in Kiev.

Yegorushka awakes in the morning to find himself high atop the last of the twenty carts in the train. A commotion soon brings the spread-out carters together. One, Dymov, has brutally killed a harmless grass snake. The older men are troubled by the needless violence and talk of Dymov's character. When the wagon stops at a well, Dymov, noticing the boy, jokingly accuses Panteley of having given birth to a baby boy overnight. Offended, Yegorushka takes a strong dislike to the laughing carter. This dislike intensifies some days later when Dymov attempts to dunk the boy while the younger men are happily swimming and net-fishing in a river.

The wagons again move out in the cool dusk, and Yegorushka stares at the stars, troubled by feelings of his own insignificance and isolation. He thinks of death. At a rest halt the men gather around the campfire and tell stories prompted by the roadside graves of travelers killed by brigands. These gruesome tales are interrupted by the arrival of a stranger, a hunter. He, too, has a story. After years of unsuccessful courtship, he has married the girl of his dreams. He is ecstatically happy. His account has a strangely depressing effect on the others. When Yegorushka awakes at dawn, he sees the men talking with the much-sought Varlamov, whose impatient figure radiates power and authority.

That night, the weather is oppressively close. The men are tired and ill-tempered, and Dymov picks a quarrel with the inoffensive Yemelyan. Yegorushka rushes to Yemelyan's defense and is derisively brushed aside by Dymov. "Hit him, hit him!" screams Yegorushka, before running away. After eating, Dymov gruffly apologizes to both Yemelyan and Yegorushka, inviting the boy to hit him. The long-threatened storm finally breaks. The constant lightning and thunderclaps terrify the shivering boy, who unsuccessfully tries to hide. Under way again the next day, Yegorushka feverishly dozes and fitfully dreams of his recent experiences. In the late afternoon they at last arrive in Kiev, where he is reunited with his uncle and Father Christopher, who are elated at the successful sale and impatient with Yegorushka's sullen, semi-delirious state.

Yegorushka awakens in the morning recovered and refreshed, but surprised not to see sodden wool bales under him. After breakfast a grumbling Kuzmichov takes the boy in search of his new lodgings. Advance arrangements have not been made, but it is hoped that an old friend of Yegorushka's mother will lodge the boy. At length, the widow is found, and with the departure of Kuzmichov and Father Christopher, "Yegorushka felt his entire stock of experiences had vanished with them like smoke. He sank exhaustedly on a bench, greeting the advent of his new and unknown life with bitter tears. What kind of life would it be?"

Themes and Meanings

The major theme of this story is Yegorushka's awakening to the complex and often harsh world beyond childhood. The boundless steppe is Chekhov's metaphor for life, and Yegorushka's journey through a portion of it is an important stage in his growing up. If Chekhov's steppe is life, it must have the same features: vast, incomprehensible, sometimes frightening, sometimes beautiful, often monotonous, and, most of all, desolate. Loneliness and isolation are the abiding essence of the steppe. The immensity of the landscape, the vastness of the sky, the infinite remoteness of the stars, all contribute to man's sense of his own insignificance, the despair and horror, the solitariness that awaits in the grave. Yegorushka is unable to establish rapport with any of his companions. Closely akin to the isolation theme is that of death. Although the boy cannot yet encompass the possibility of his own death, the subject is ever-present. Yegorushka encounters evil for the first time in the quarrelsome and combative Dymov. Even more frighteningly, he recognizes his own powerlessness in its presence. Dymov haunts his fevered dreams.

Yegorushka's education is social as well as moral, for he meets a wide variety of types ranging from the pathetic, disfigured, former singer Yemelyan to the ruthless, almost legendary provincial tycoon, Varlamov. The theme of social predjudice is also evoked in the encounter with the family of the Jewish innkeeper, especially the obsessed brother Solomon.

At journey's end, Yegorushka has had many new experiences. He remains a nine-year-old, but one who has painfully surmounted his first rite of passage. A new stage of his journey, his school years in Kiev, lies before him. He looks forward to them with anxiety, for the school of the steppe has taught him something of the nature of life.

Style and Technique

"The Steppe," like many Chekhov works, has little action or plot. It consists of a series of small, seemingly independent episodes linked by Yegorushka. Taken together, they portray a formative stage in his short life. The story is framed by Yegorushka's departure from home and his arrival in Kiev some weeks later, although only the opening and closing days of the journey are related.

Chekhov's third-person narrative technique is simple. After each of the formative episodes, Yegorushka tries to understand what has happened. Sometimes, he listens as others discuss the event; at other times, he reflects on his own; on still other occasions, the narrator's voice enters and (rather clumsily) "editorializes." "The Steppe" is narrated from two points of view: that of the omniscient author and that of the naïve, nine-year-old Yegorushka. Working on his first long, serious prose piece, Chekhov was not always successful in his effort to distinguish between the two viewpoints.

Chekhov is primarily an artist of mood and atmosphere rather than a social commentator. The story's main vehicle for the poetic evocation of mood is the steppe itself, which is its lyrical heroine, a protagonist no less important than Yegorushka. As the carts lumber on under the stars, the narrator is entranced by the beauty of the steppe:

> In this triumph of beauty, in this exuberance of happiness, you feel a tenseness and an agonized regret, as if the steppe knew how lonely she is, how her wealth and inspiration are lost to the world—vainly, unsung, unneeded, and . . . you hear her anguished, hopeless cry for a bard, a poet of her own.

In Chekhov, the great Russian steppe found her bard.

D. Barton Johnson

A STICK OF GREEN CANDY

Author: Jane Bowles (1917-1973)
Type of plot: Social realism
Time of plot: The mid-1950's
Locale: A town in the United States
First published: 1957

> *Principal characters:*
> MARY, the chief protagonist, a young girl
> FRANKLIN, a slightly younger boy
> MARY'S FATHER
> FRANKLIN'S MOTHER

The Story

Mary is a young girl, apparently about eleven years old, who undergoes a small, gentle rite of passage that forces her to take notice of the world of other children and adults. At the beginning of the story, she is a confirmed loner who stays away from other children, preferring to play in her own domain—a clay pit located a mile outside town. By the story's end, her seclusion sustains her less satisfactorily, and its security appears illusive.

Mary is a "scrupulously clean child" with "well-arranged curls"; her predominant characteristic, made immediately apparent in the story, is that she would like reality to be similarly orderly. She plays alone, because she perceives other children, whose games are noisy and hectic, to be a threat to the world of her imagination. That world is sustained by the clay pit, which Mary imagines is the barracks for a troop of soldiers that she commands. The military life suits her, for just as she cannot bear uncleanliness, she is a stickler for routine.

A mishap disrupts her routine, however, and leads her toward a series of experiences that will submit the world of her clay pit to the influence of the wider world beyond it. While playing in the pit, she slips, gets mud on her coat, and decides that she must wait until dark to go home. She thinks it necessary to concoct for her troops an explanation of why she has remained longer than usual, and tells them that she has decided to give them extra training to make them into a crack "mountain-goat fighting" unit. Despite this ready explanation, the unexpected mishap has worked cracks in her make-believe world. She is certain that her troops will accept her explanation, but she has difficulty accepting the deceit herself.

Other changes in her occur. She experiences new sensations: As night falls, she begins to feel uneasy, like an intruder in her own domain. She skulks home along the darkest streets to hide her dirty coat, somewhat ashamed and apprehensive about the possibility of a reprimand.

At home, her father does reprimand her and tells her to play at the playground like all the other children. The next day, Mary nevertheless returns to her clay pit, jubilant at feeling, for the first time, undaunted by her father's authority. She prepares her men for battle with the children on the playground. When her father drives by without stopping to chastise her again, she is perplexed to find her jubilation somewhat deflated.

A boy, Franklin, appears. He has come from the house above the clay pit. He is both similar to, and clearly different from, Mary. He is fastidious in a worldly sense—he looks "prudently" up and down the street as he crosses to the pit—but he is indifferent to smearing his coat with clay as he slides into the pit. Because Mary has not seen Franklin before, she scoffs dubiously at him when he says that he lives in the house. When he abruptly returns to the house, she follows him, her curiosity engaged by her righteous indignation at finding that she cannot command in him the same respect she does in her troops.

The state of the house, which is being repainted, challenges Mary's appetite for orderliness at the same time that Franklin's indifference to her challenges her egocentricity. The room into which she follows Franklin is so cluttered with furniture that she is forced to squeeze between two bureaus, "pinching her flesh painfully"—the challenge has an intrusive, tangible dimension. Oddly, however, the house also contrasts favorably with her clay pit in some respects. She sits in a chair "deeper and softer" than any she has experienced. With these and several other touches of detail, Bowles suggests that the attraction Mary finds in isolating herself from the world beyond the clay pit is being questioned and subverted.

With the appearance of Franklin's mother, this process quickens. She, like the bureaus, inadvertently demands Mary's attention. The room is so cramped that the mother's knees constantly touch Mary's as she addresses her in an adult, albeit immature and gossipy, fashion. She tells Mary, for example, that she would rather have had a girl than a boy; that would have permitted her to discuss her favorite topic—furnishings. Ironically, she also reveals that Franklin, who has led Mary out of her isolation, is himself a loner: "He sits in a lot and don't go out and contact at all."

The chat, in which neither Mary nor Franklin do any of the talking, is interrupted when the mother tells Franklin to fetch a tea box filled with candy. The social encounter ends when Mary selects a stick of green candy and abruptly leaves. While she continues to harbor an immature hostility toward other people, she also experiences subtle positive results from the encounter with Franklin and his mother. Her perspective on the area surrounding the clay pit has previously been from down in the pit, which she always approached from below; now, she commands a wider panorama from her position uphill from the pit: "She had never experienced the need to look at things from a distance before, nor had she felt the relief that it can bring."

The next day, she returns to the pit, but her make-believe world is now seriously jeopardized. She forgets for the first time to summon her men to order with a bugle call before addressing them. She cannot convince herself of the reality of her barracks.

It is only at this point, when Mary has begun to lose some of her imaginative independence and to incorporate some of the socialization that her father has tried to dictate to her, that her father appears, apparently to reprimand her again.

Themes and Meanings

Mary grows up to a certain extent in the course of the story's action, which takes place over three days. In a sense, however, the story also presents an example of the regrettable erosion of the child's ability to be sustained by imagination. Reality impinges upon Mary's imagined world, and once that influence has begun, its course cannot be reversed. At the end of the story, Mary finds how fragile is imagination, because the mere act of trying consciously to shore up her make-believe world erodes it further. She searches about to find a reason why her troops cannot practice their mountain-goat fighting on the steps up to Franklin's house, but "the reason was not going to come to her. She had begun to cheat now, and she knew it would never come."

Rather than suggest merely that this kind of erosion of imagination is a wholly negative thing, Bowles also suggests that it is a necessary compromise with the world that other people inhabit. Not to accept that fact, she suggests, is a failing. This view is made clear in her characterization of Mary, who, while she is scrupulously fair and almost egalitarian in dealing with her troops, is also petulant when dealing with Franklin. Similarly, while she is self-assured in her clay pit, she is uncomfortable in the presence of Franklin's mother. While any variance from the habitual is a threat to her narrowly construed picture of the world, every challenge to her make-believe world has a subtle maturing, socializing influence on her.

That Bowles considers this process of compromise to have its costs is clear in such things as her characterization of Franklin's mother as a gossipy and ill-finished adult who could hardly be considered a compelling model for Mary. This view is reinforced by the triumphant tone Bowles ejects into sentences that describe how satisfying Mary's egocentricity can be: "She was rapidly perfecting a psychological mechanism which enabled her to forget, for long stretches of time, that her parents existed."

Style and Technique

Bowles repeatedly uses physical details and descriptions of settings to suggest personality traits and to flesh out themes. At the opening of the story, for example, she pays close attention to the geometry of the clay pit in which

Mary plays. From the pit, Mary can see the "curved" highway, the steep "angle" of the hill in which the pit is dug, the "square" house above, whose steps lead to the curb, "dividing the steep lawn in two." The geometrical imagery describes the way Mary construes her surroundings to suit her needs—as tidy and regular. She has no patience with having to confront the geometry of the hill on its own terms; she finds it "tedious" to have to climb up a set of steep steps to follow Franklin. Once inside Franklin's house, she becomes anxious because the spaces there are cramped and dark, intimidating her so that she "looked around frantically for a wider artery."

A common feature of all of Bowles's writing is an arch, understated humor. That element is apparent here in her choice of a military make-believe world for Mary; such a fascination seems somewhat unusual for a young girl. The subtlety of Bowles's humor appears in such things as the description of the way that Mary walks home from her clay pit in her dirty coat: "She walked along slowly, scuffing her heels, her face wearing the expression of a person surfeited with food." Bowles does not say that Mary is pouting, but it is apparent from this sentence that that is what she is doing. The playground Mary dislikes intensely is called the Kinsey Memorial Grounds—the somber touch in the name supports humorously Mary's perception that it describes a place where the fantasy that sustains her is likely to be buried under the squealing of children who play with little apparent design or imagination.

If Bowles's humor is lightly sketched, so, too, is her theme. It finds its focus not in any token heavily laden with symbolism, but in a simple stick of green candy, an unlikely centerpiece of a rite of passage, but one that is in keeping with the changes Mary experiences.

Peter Monaghan

THE STONE BOY

Author: Gina Berriault (1926-   )
Type of plot: Psychological realism
Time of plot: The 1950's
Locale: A farm near a rural community in the United States
First published: 1957

Principal characters:

ARNOLD CURWING, a nine-year-old boy who accidentally kills
   his brother
EUGIE CURWING, his fifteen-year-old brother
MR. CURWING, his father
MRS. CURWING his mother
NORA CURWING, his sister

The Story

"The Stone Boy" is a story about a nine-year-old boy who accidentally kills his older brother as they are on their way to the garden to pick peas. The fact of the accidental killing of Eugie, however, is not the major question posed by the characters in this story. Rather, the question involves why Arnold, after having accidentally killed his brother, does not return home immediately to call for help from his parents, but instead spends an hour in the garden, picking peas. Arnold's father and mother and his Uncle Andy are unable to understand what kept Arnold in the garden while his brother lay dead. Arnold, himself, has no answer. All he can say is that the purpose of his trip to the garden in the first place was to pick peas, and the peas had to be picked while it was still cool, before the sun came up. The sheriff comes to the conclusion that the shooting was indeed an accident, that there was no malice intended, and that Arnold is either dim-witted or completely rational but unfeeling, like many criminals.

Under the circumstances, Arnold's father can think of nothing to do but take the gun away from the boy; Uncle Andy accepts the sheriff's explanation to the extent of making ironic and mean comments about Arnold's behavior to the farm people, who call upon the Curwings to express their sympathy. Arnold's mother can hardly bear to look at her son, and his sister, Nora, ignores his presence.

If the sheriff is correct in his explanation of Arnold's behavior, then Arnold is, indeed, a stone boy, unable to weep at a tragic accident, uncaring, and perhaps even cruel. On the other hand, one could argue that the boy is only nine, that his remaining in the garden to pick peas was the result of a trauma brought on by a sense of responsibility for the death of a brother who was his favorite companion. In this instance, a reader could question the motivation of the parents, relatives, and friends, who offer Arnold no solace or comfort in a time of intense need. Perhaps the author is demonstrating that "stone" parents create "stone" boys.

Answers to all these questions concerning the motivation of the characters must be found in the details of the story, since the point of view Berriault uses restricts the reader to Arnold's consciousness, and Arnold does not know why he behaves as he does. Moreover, since the plot is epiphanic, beginning *in medias res* without exposition and concluding without resolution, the author provides no explanation. In addition, the epiphanic ending of the story is even more puzzling than the unanswered questions concerning motivation. At the end of the story, Arnold's mother attempts to make some human contact with her son, but Arnold rejects her:

> "What'd you want?" she asked humbly.
> "I didn't want nothing," he said flatly.
> Then he went out of the door and down the back steps, his legs trembling from the fright his answer gave him.

This kind of epiphany at the end of the story throws a reader back to the beginning of the story to seek clarification and meaning.

Themes and Meanings

In "The Stone Boy," the roles of the various members of the family assume important dimensions. The father, clearly the stereotypical masculine presence, takes care of those activities outside the house. Mother and daughter are shown only tending to household tasks. Eugie, almost a man, has begun to assume many of the responsibilities of the father. Arnold's ties are still more to his mother, though he envies Eugie and unknowingly attempts to assert dominance. Arnold's attachment to his mother, his continuing need for her, and his subconscious desire to relate to her are as much a motivating factor as is Arnold's need to assert dominance. That Arnold feels a special sympathy for his mother is made evident by his knowledge of her intense discomfort as she tends to the canning in the kitchen where the heat from the wood stove would be almost unbearable. Sometimes, the reader is told, Arnold would come from out of the shade where he was playing and make himself as uncomfortable as his mother was in the kitchen by standing in the sun until the sweat ran down his body. The fear caused by Arnold's desire to emulate his father and older brother, while the nine-year-old is still too young to assume the role, causes Arnold to seek out his mother, especially so that he might express his fear and his hostility and receive from her solace and understanding.

The apparent need of a son to assume the role of patriarch, even if it means revolting against the father (or killing him as in Sophocles' *Oedipus*

Tyrannos, c. 429 B.C.), is a dominant theme in Western culture. Indeed, the patriarchal model of the culture, in which rule is passed from father to son who becomes father, sometimes creates a situation in which a son may want to rule before his time or in which a father may want to keep his son away from power. Such maneuverings among fathers and sons usually result in some kind of kind of violent behavior.

It is not likely that Berriault is saying that Arnold deliberately killed his brother. Yet the complex of events seems to suggest that the accident was accompanied by alternating feelings of submission and dominance. If this suggestion is true, then Arnold would subconsciously understand the reason for the accident and would assume a guilt too great for him to bear. These feelings of guilt, traumatizing the boy, would account for his strange behavior and the strange behavior of family and neighbors. Because they are unable to understand Arnold's needs, family and neighbors reject him in a cruel way, thus inflicting on him the punishment he believes that he deserves. After taking the step, after assuming the desired role, Arnold knows that he cannot go back. He is man enough to wrap around him a robe of pride to protect himself, but still boy enough to be frightened by the position he has unnaturally assumed.

Style and Technique

In "The Stone Boy," Berriault creates symbols within the context of the story to direct readers toward a meaning that is not apparent on the surface. For example, nowhere in the story does the author say that the roles assumed by members of the family are stereotypically patriarchal, resulting in the reenactment of old patterns of behavior, in which sons and fathers sometimes engage in violent actions to keep each other and "their" women in their "rightful" places, as the places are defined by the dominant culture. By creating patterns made up of various telling details in the story, however, the author points readers toward this kind of reading, which gives surface action a meaning far beyond itself and invests characters with motivations deeply embedded in their subconscious.

It is possible for the reader to ignore the elements of symbolic structure and to accept surface content as all there is. Such reading of a symbolic story will cause the reader to miss important, complex, and universal relationships. More depth of interpretation ensures understanding of concepts continually present, linking the past and possibly the future.

Mary Rohrberger

THE STORM

Author: Kate Chopin (1851-1904)
Type of plot: Domestic realism
Time of plot: 1898
Locale: Louisiana
First published: written 1898; published 1969

> *Principal characters:*
> BOBINÔT, an Acadian planter
> CALIXTA, his wife
> BIBI, his four-year-old son
> ALCÉE LABALLIÈRE, a rich Acadian planter and Calixta's
> former lover
> CLARISSE, Alcée's wife

The Story

While Bobinôt and his son, Bibi, are shopping at Friedheimer's store, the air becomes still. Dark clouds roll in from the west, and thunder rumbles in the distance. Father and son decide to wait inside until the storm passes instead of trying to reach home. When Bibi suggests that Calixta may be frightened to be alone, Bobinôt reassures him that she will be all right.

The approaching storm does not, in fact, worry her. She merely closes the doors and windows and then goes to gather the clothes hanging outside. As she steps onto the porch, she sees Alcée Laballière ride through the gate to seek shelter from the rain.

From "At the 'Cadian Ball," to which "The Storm" is a sequel, the reader knows that six years earlier Calixta and Alcée had gone to Assumption together in a fit of passion, and the following year they were about to have another romantic rendezvous in New Orleans when Clarisse intervened. In love with Alcée and suspecting his intentions, she had proposed marriage. He agreed, and Calixta had then yielded to Bobinôt's suit.

Despite the passage of time and their marriages, Calixta and Alcée's passion for each other has not abated. As they stand at a window, lightning strikes a chinaberry tree. Calixta, startled, staggers backward into Alcée's arms; this physical contact arouses "all the old-time infatuation and desire for her flesh." Alcée asks, "Do you remember—in Assumption, Calixta?" She does indeed. There they had kissed repeatedly; now, as the storm rages, they make passionate love. When the storm subsides, they know that they must separate, at least temporarily.

Bobinôt and Bibi walk home, pausing at the well outside to clean themselves as well as they can before entering the house. Calixta is a fastidious housekeeper, and they fear the reception they will receive after trudging home in the mud. Bobinôt is ready with apologies and explanations, but he needs none. Calixta is overjoyed to see her family and delighted with the can of shrimps that Bobinôt has brought her.

Alcée is as happy as Calixta. His wife has gone to Biloxi, Mississippi, for a vacation, and he writes her "a loving letter, full of tender solicitude" that night, telling her to stay as long as she wants. He says that he misses her, but he puts her pleasure above his own.

Clarisse is happy, too, when she receives the letter. She loves her husband, but the vacation is her first taste of freedom since her marriage. She intends to accept Alcée's offer to stay in Biloxi longer before returning home.

Themes and Meanings

When Kate Chopin prepared the collection "A Vocation and a Voice" for publication (the collection was, ultimately, not published), she excluded "The Storm" because she recognized it as too explicit and advanced for the period. Her description of passionate lovemaking would have been bad enough, but her endorsement of the adultery would have scandalized her readers.

Chopin depicts sex as liberating and enjoyable. Indeed, for Calixta, adultery with Alcée is more satisfying than sex with her husband; it is with Alcée that "her firm, elastic flesh knew for the first time its birthright." Lovemaking with Alcée touches "depths . . . that had never yet been reached."

Nor does this adultery end in tragedy—quite the reverse. Calixta, who would normally be upset with her husband and child for bringing dirt into the house, welcomes them warmly. She is truly happy to be reunited with her family. Because her physical needs have been met, she can share her newfound joy with others.

Alcée's marriage also benefits. He may be telling Clarisse to stay in Biloxi so he can pursue his affair with Calixta—though there is no evidence in the story that the two continue their liaison—but his letter is nevertheless filled with love and regard for his wife and children. Like Calixta, he is physically satisfied and so can be emotionally generous.

Clarisse eagerly snatches at Alcée's offer. For her, as, apparently, for Calixta, marriage is confining. Calixta escapes by having sex with Alcée; Clarisse escapes by forgoing "intimate conjugal life" with him for a while. She will return to her husband, just as Calixta will remain with Bobinôt, yet this innocent adultery has given everyone a breath of freedom, cleansing them as a summer storm freshens and purifies the air.

Chopin's characters here do not rebel against the institution of marriage; they object only to being confined by traditional roles. Given the freedom to satisfy their physical or spiritual needs, they are content with their spouses. In fact, for marriage to succeed, Chopin argues, such freedom is crucial. Far from threatening marriage, this liberty is its only means of salvation.

Style and Technique

The storm is the story's central metaphor, representing the passion of Calixta and Alcée. By linking the two, Chopin indicates that the lovers' feelings are natural and therefore not subject to moral censure. She reinforces this idea through other imagery drawn from nature, likening Alcée to the sun and Calixta to a lily and a pomegranate. Not only do these images come from nature, but they also derive from The Song of Songs, giving a kind of religious sanction to the lovers' union.

The storm is not only natural but also powerful, like the passions it symbolizes. While Calixta and Alcée make love, the thunder crashes and the elements roar; the passing of the storm indicates their physical exhaustion. While these passions, like the storm, are strong, they are not destructive. The storm does little damage, and when it passes the sun emerges, "turning the glistening green world into a palace of gems." The rain leaves the world a happier and more beautiful place, just as the lovers part with joy in their hearts. Alcée leaves with a smile, and Calixta answers him with laughter.

Chopin uses language to indicate that this joy derives from the lovers' equality. He is like the sun and she is a "white flame." She cushions but also clasps him, being both active and passive. His heart beats "like a hammer upon her" while she "strokes his shoulders." They "swoon together at the very borderland of life's mystery." In this union of true love there is neither master nor mastered—simply two partners who share desire and fulfillment. For Chopin, that is the only proper relationship between the sexes, the only one likely to bring happiness within marriage, or outside it.

Joseph Rosenblum

A STORY BY MAUPASSANT

Author: Frank O'Connor (Michael Francis O'Donovan, 1903-1966)
Type of plot: Psychological realism
Time of plot: The 1950's
Locale: A provincial town in County Cork, Ireland
First published: 1945

> *Principal characters:*
> TED MAGNER, the narrator and best friend of Terry Coughlan
> TERRY COUGHLAN, the childhood friend of Magner, a teacher
> in the monks' school
> TESS COUGHLAN, Terry's sister, the childhood friend of
> Magner
> PA HOURIGAN, a local policeman
> DONNELAN, a friend of Magner

The Story

Having grown up in a small, provincial town in Ireland, the narrator, Ted Magner, states that he has been best friends with Terry Coughlan since they were children. Terry has always been well-spoken and likes classical music and languages. "Whatever he took up, he mastered," says Magner of his friend. Magner remembers the friendly arguments that they had when they were young. "Maybe you don't remember the sort of arguments you had when you were young," the narrator fondly tells his readers, knowing that they do. The argument that he recalls, however, is the one he had with Terry about writers. Magner lists Guy de Maupassant as one of the greatest writers. Terry disagrees, however, saying that there is nothing "noble" about Maupassant's stories; rather, they are slick, coarse, and commonplace.

As they reach young manhood, the two friends drift away from close contact with each other, but Magner continues to be fond of Terry. Terry takes a job teaching in the monks' school, and Magner gets a job elsewhere, beginning to associate with a different crowd, people such as Donnelan, of whom Terry does not approve. Magner tells the reader that Terry slowly grows disillusioned by the behavior of the monks at the school and is discouraged by a form of cheating that the monks condone, allowing one boy to take a state examination using another boy's name. Magner later learns from Donnelan that Terry has begun to drink. His first reaction is, "A sparrow would have about the same consumption of liquor." Magner sees Terry drunk about six months later, however, and realizes that Terry drinks constantly, keeping his drinking a secret from his family and from his sister, Tess. Magner understands why Terry is so secretive: "You might almost say he was drinking unknown to himself. Other people could be drunkards but not he." He wonders whether he should confront Terry about his drinking but realizes that he cannot because "you couldn't talk like that to a man of his kind." He also comments that Terry is drinking himself to death.

When Terry is forty years old, his mother dies. That same year he visits Paris in the summer for the first time. At first, Magner hopes that Terry will begin to straighten out, but later he realizes that "it was worse he was getting."

Finally, Magner is surprised one day several years later to be visited by Pa Hourigan, a local policeman, who asks Magner to speak to Terry about his disreputable life. Magner, who thinks Hourigan is referring to Terry's drunkenness, is amazed to learn that Hourigan is concerned about Terry's consorting with prostitutes: "low, loose, abandoned women," says Hourigan. The policeman, who is worried about Terry's soul, asks Magner to intervene, saying, "Do what you can for his soul, Mr Magner. As for his body, I wouldn't like to answer." Magner comments about Terry in Latin, "Lilies that fester smell far worse than weeds."

Magner goes to Terry's house to confront him, speaking for a while with Terry and Tess. It reminds him of their old days together, until Tess leaves them alone. After a short time, Magner stands up to leave, realizing that he cannot discuss this situation with Terry: "There was something there you couldn't do violence to," Magner reasons. As he is leaving, Magner looks at Terry's bookcase, commenting, "I see you have a lot of Maupassant at last."

Somehow this remark cuts through the silence and reserve between the childhood friends, and Terry begins speaking honestly of his consorting with prostitutes and his drunkenness. He reveals that when he was first in Paris he took a prostitute to her room and discovered that she had her baby with her. After their transaction, the woman fell asleep; Terry remarks, "It's many years now since I've been able to sleep like that." This remark captures very well the kind of life in which Terry finds himself a prisoner. He continues to talk of the incident with this prostitute—one of many since then—because he remembers that after she awoke, they had a conversation about Maupassant. This conversation reminded Terry of his schoolboy arguments with Magner. Terry says that "it's only when you see what life can do to you" that one can appreciate Maupassant's stories.

Terry reads Magner's thoughts that this was indeed a strange conversation for a French prostitute and "a drunken waster" from the Irish countryside. Magner says sadly, "A man like you should have a wife and children." Yet clearly this is not to be, and Magner ends the story with the observation, "And life was pretty nearly through with Terry Coughlan."

Themes and Meanings

In this story, O'Connor is basically concerned with presenting a wasted life. He is especially concerned that despite a promising, bright, idealistic beginning, a person such as Terry Coughlan can allow something inside himself to die. The tragedy is that Terry, once interested in the nobility of human life and thought, can have reached the point where he is drinking himself to death. O'Connor shows clearly the horror of what life can do to certain individuals. The young Parisienne has entered into prostitution in order to earn a living; Terry Coughlan consorts with the lowest prostitutes rather than marry a good woman and rear a family.

A second tragedy that accompanies Terry's disintegration as a person is that Ted Magner is forced to witness the downfall of his best friend. Magner is helpless; there is nothing he can do to turn Terry around. Magner realizes this inability a number of times in the story when he seriously considers confronting Terry about his life situation. People such as Terry "stand or fall by something inside themselves," and no one else can help them, no matter how much they may wish to.

Style and Technique

O'Connor demonstrates his mastery of technique in several ways in this story. He makes special use of his first-person narrator, Ted Magner, to present the decay of Terry Coughlan from a highly personal perspective. Readers are not disinterested viewers of Terry's decay because of the way in which Magner tells the story. In addition, O'Connor makes effective use of colloquial Irish speech. Moreover, O'Connor displays the Irish sense of humor that one expects to find in his stories, having fun with such characters as Donnelan and with Pa Hourigan, who has a special respect for "education." The speech helps to convey the sense of warmth that exists in the personal relations in a small town where everyone knows everyone else and where it is particularly difficult to keep secrets, even those that one would like to keep in the dark.

The use of Maupassant in the story becomes an effective device in helping to organize the story and in presenting characterization and theme. First, the friends disagree about Maupassant—his coarseness and commonplaceness—at the story's beginning. Then, the last two pages conclude the discussion that started probably thirty years before. Both know that Maupassant would end Terry's story with Terry's death, and the narrator says that "life was pretty nearly through with Terry Coughlan" in the concluding sentence. In addition to organizing the story, the Maupassant material is appropriate to Terry because Terry's decay is typical of Maupassant's subject matter. It is moreover only in witnessing the hardships of life, the way life often does not follow one's plans or wishes, that Terry comes to appreciate Maupassant as a writer. Maupassant, according to Terry, may not deal with the noble, but then life itself often presents much that is ignoble.

A. Bruce Dean

THE STORY OF AN HOUR

Author: Kate Chopin (1851-1904)
Type of plot: Psychological realism
Time of plot: 1894
Locale: Natchitoches Parish, Louisiana
First published: 1894

> *Principal characters:*
> LOUISE MALLARD, the protagonist, a beautiful young woman
> BRENTLEY MALLARD, her husband
> JOSEPHINE, Mrs. Mallard's sister
> MR. RICHARDS, a newspaperman, Brentley Mallard's close
> friend

The Story

Because Louise Mallard suffers from a heart condition, her sister Josephine gently and carefully gives her the news of her husband's death. Mr. Richards, a close friend of her husband, Brentley Mallard, and the first to learn of the tragic railroad accident that claimed Mallard's life, has accompanied Josephine to help soften what they know will be a cruel blow.

Louise falls, sobbing, into her sister's arms, then retreats upstairs to her room. Josephine, who begs Louise to let her in, would be shocked if she knew what thoughts were racing through her sister's mind. Louise has loved her husband, who has in turn loved her and treated her kindly, but she is not crushed by his death, nor do her reflections make her sick.

Indeed, although she initially hesitates to admit to herself that she is not distressed, she begins to repeat one word: "free." Her life is her own again; no longer will she have to yield to her husband's wishes. Only yesterday she had regarded life as tedious and feared longevity. Now she yearns for long life.

Finally, she yields to her sister's repeated pleas to unlock her bedroom door. Louise embraces her sister, and together they go downstairs to rejoin Richards. As they reach the bottom of the stairs, Brentley comes through the door, unaware of the accident that supposedly has claimed his life. Richards tries to move between him and his wife to shield her from the shock, but he is too late; she has already seen Brentley. She screams and falls down dead. The doctors who examine her afterward say that her weak heart could not bear the sudden joy.

Themes and Meanings

Louise Mallard is Kate Chopin's strongest example of the self-assertive woman—so strong an example, in fact, that Richard Watson Gilder refused to publish the story in *The Century* because he regarded it as immoral. *Vogue*, which finally published it after the success of Chopin's *Bayou Folk* (1894), had initially rejected it for the same reason.

Mrs. Mallard certainly is a woman ahead of her time, for by the standards of the 1890's she should be happy. Her husband loves her and treats her well; she herself acknowledges that he "had never looked save with love upon her." Nor does she dislike Brentley.

However loving Brentley is, though, nothing can compensate Louise for the freedom that she has lost by marrying. Her face "bespoke repression"; no matter how kind Brentley has been, he has still imposed his will upon his wife. Hence, Brentley's death is not tragic to her, since it gives her own life back to her.

She therefore emerges from her room "like a goddess of Victory," with "a feverish triumph in her eyes." She has won back her freedom. Though Chopin does not specify how Louise will use that liberty, in "Lilacs," the next story she wrote, Mme Farival takes lovers, and Edna Pontellier in *The Awakening* (1899) also seeks sexual gratification outside marriage. Perhaps Louise, too, who resembles these women in her self-reliance, will seek sensual fulfillment.

Edna Pontellier also searches for her true vocation, which she believes is something other and more than mere wife and mother. Chopin regarded contemporary society as degrading to women, who were allotted limited roles in a male-dominated world. Just as the death of her husband sets Louise's body free, so, too, does it free her spirit to find happiness in any way that she wishes.

Her husband's return shatters her hopes. She is again a mere wife, subservient. This sudden reversal, the destruction of her dreams, kills her. Still, she is spared the living death of a stifling relationship, and before she thought her husband was dead she had dreaded a long life. The story's ending is therefore ironic but not tragic, since Louise does escape marriage in the only way now open to her.

Style and Technique

Nature imagery underlines the plot and meaning. Although authors typically associate death with autumn and winter, Brentley's supposed death occurs in the spring. The trees are "all aquiver" with new life. Rain has fallen, purifying the air, and now the clouds are parting to show "patches of blue sky." This scene mirrors Louise's situation. The death of Brentley marks the end of the winter of her discontent; her soul can awake from its torpor. She can realize the full potential of her life, so she, like the trees, feels aquiver with life. The clouds again represent her married life, which cast shadows on her happiness, but now the horizon of her life is clearing. As she contemplates her future, she imagines "spring days and summer days" only, not autumn or winter days, because she links herself to the seasons of rebirth and ripening.

In contrast to the world of nature is the cloistered, confining house, symbol of domesticity. In her own room she looks through an open window, another symbol of her freedom. The window does not intervene between her and nature and allows her the scope of infinite vision. She herself locks and unlocks the door to her room, admitting or excluding whomever she wants. She has what Virginia Woolf stressed as so important, a room of her own. Yet it is only a temporary, and finally an inadequate, refuge. She leaves it, as she must, to rejoin her sister and Richards; in unlocking her door she paradoxically consigns herself to the prison of her house. Nowhere else in the house is there even a glimpse of nature, and, in contrast to the open window, the front door is locked; only Brentley has the key. He can come and go as he pleases, but she remains trapped within.

Related to this contrast of nature and house is the imagery of up and down. Louise's room is upstairs, and from there she looks at the tops of trees and hears the songs of birds on the roof. Her freedom is thus literally elevating. Her leaving this refuge and going down the stairs foreshadows her loss of freedom. She descends from the heaven of solitude to the hell of marriage again, where she encounters her husband. Now death is her only salvation. Instead of soaring freely like the birds, she can escape only by sinking still lower, into the grave.

Joseph Rosenblum

THE STORY OF MY DOVECOT

Author: Isaac Babel (1894-1941)
Type of plot: Psychological realism
Time of plot: 1905
Locale: Nikolaev (near Odessa)
First published: "Istoriia moei golubiatni," 1925 (English translation, 1926)

> *Principal characters:*
> THE NARRATOR, the unnamed protagonist
> MOTHER and
> FATHER, the narrator's parents
> SHOYL BABEL, the narrator's granduncle, killed during the
> pogrom of October 20, 1905
> MAKARENKO, an anti-Semitic cripple who strikes the narrator
> KHARITON EFRUSSI, a wealthy Jew, the enemy of the Babel
> family
> KARAVAYEV and
> PYATNITSKY, two Russian teachers who are friendly toward
> the boy

The Story

"The Story of My Dovecot" describes the effect of the notorious pogrom of October 20, 1905, on the Babel family and particularly on the author himself as a boy of eleven. It is one of Babel's most autobiographical stories. Nevertheless, the author changes a number of crucial details, including even his age, to yield greater drama. The story is thus clearly a work of fiction, yet the author rightly maintains the verisimilitude of autobiography for its powerful effect on the reader.

The situation of the boy, as the story opens, is precisely delineated: His father will build him a dovecot and buy him three pigeons for it if he gets top marks in the Russian language and arithmetic exams. He needs the very highest scores, because the quota system will admit only two Jewish boys from his form into the preparatory class. If he is accepted into the higher school, his father, with his "pauper pride," will enjoy vicarious success. The pressures on the boy, all ultimately a result of Russian anti-Semitism at every level in the society, are sufficient to keep him in a state of permanent, anxious daydream and reverie.

The boy fails to make the quota because the wealthy Jew Khariton Efrussi, a wheat exporter, bribes the school authorities to admit his own son instead of Babel. Such betrayal by a fellow Jew is unbearable (Babel senior wants to bribe two longshoremen to beat up Efrussi)—but, again, Russian anti-Semitism is the root cause.

In the following year, young Babel succeeds in his aim, befriended by a Russian teacher, Karavayev, who gives him the A+ grade he actually earns, and by Assistant Curator Pyatnitsky, for whom the boy, in a kind of exalted trance, recites from the works of Alexander Pushkin. After the examination, Pyatnitsky makes a point of protecting young Babel from some menacing Russian schoolboys. These two Russian humanitarians are important exceptions to the widespread anti-Semitism.

The "pauper's ball" that follows the boy's admission into the first class offers insight into the ways that the Babel family copes with life. While Father is delirious with victory (prematurely, as always), Mother is in despair, unable to see the future except as disaster. The reader learns that Grandfather had been a rabbi, was "thrown out for blasphemy," and is now starting to go insane. One uncle had died in a house of ill-fame; another is crazy. Granduncle Shoyl is full of wonderful, lying stories about his past; he now sells fish at the market. All dance and sing while young Babel pictures himself as David having defeated Goliath: "the Russian boys with their fat cheeks" as well as the sons of Jewish parvenus.

At last, the day comes to visit the market and buy pigeons from Ivan Nikodimych. The young lad's joy is destroyed, however, when he hears that Shoyl is perhaps dead. The pogrom, which has grown out of celebrations following the Constitutional Manifesto of October 17, has begun. While policeman look the other way, hordes of Russian scum, many poorer even than Jews, loot Jewish homes and businesses. (The Russian government connived in such pogroms, which sometimes led to the injuring and killing of hundreds of Jews, because they took people's minds away from revolution.)

Young Babel approaches his friend Makarenko, a cripple in a wheelchair, to ask about Shoyl. Makarenko, however, is in a fit of rage because he and his wife are unable to steal all the things that they believe they deserve to have. Doubly angered because the boy has nothing more valuable than pigeons, he smashes the boy on the head with one of the birds. The boy lies on the ground in a daze, with pigeon entrails running down his face.

In the moment of violence, as he overhears Makarenko's wife remark, "Their spawn must be wiped out," young Babel comes to a deep understanding of life. The author as narrator writes that he walked home, "weeping bitterly, full and happily as I never wept again in all my life." A certain genius is required to find the word "happily" here; it denotes that the boy will no longer live in a state of illusion—and that he knows it. In his new awareness, he is able to accept the shocking and ignominious death of Shoyl, who, as he died, had cursed his killers thoroughly—"a wonderful damning and blasting it was."

Themes and Meanings

The most important theme in the story is that of overcoming illusion. Not only the boy but also his entire family avoid facing reality. While it is largely anti-Semitism that leads them to this condition, it is also anti-Semitism in its most vicious form that shocks the boy out of his illusions. The narrator recalls what it was like for him as he lay on the ground with "tender pigeon guts" sliding down over his forehead: "I closed my solitary unstopped-up eye so as not to see the world that spread out before me. This world was tiny and it was awful. A stone lay just before my eyes, a little stone so chipped as to resemble the face of an old woman with a large jaw." The detail here is so precise that one is convinced that the author experienced it exactly so—and that it was then permanently etched in his memory. These minute details impel the reader to enter the boy's consciousness.

Still lying on the ground, "in his new overcoat," the boy hears hoofbeats in the distance—the pogrom: "Somewhere far way Woe rode across [the trampled earth] on a great steed. . . ." He becomes aware of the very dirt beneath his nose: "The earth smelled of raw depths, of the tomb, of flowers. I smelled its smell and started crying, unafraid."

All this description evokes in the reader a perception equal to that of the boy. It has the character of an awakening, a revelation—an epiphany. It includes the disturbing realization that violence and death are necessary to produce true understanding. For the boy, the experience becomes also a rite of passage, parallel to Bar Mitzvah. On that day, he became a man.

The pogrom takes on an unreal aspect as Babel describes Russians (and Ukrainians) happily looting and smashing or carrying aloft in processions icons, the Cross, a portrait of the czar. There is almost an invitation here to see the point of view of those others. Yet the key to Babel's true attitude lies in his treatment of Makarenko, whom the boy had actually looked upon as a friend. The illusion of that friendship is the first illusion the boy loses, as the cripple turns on him like a snake. Although the reader might feel some slight inclination to pity the man bound to a wheelchair, Babel removes that inclination when he has Makarenko say, lamenting his inability to obtain all the booty he wants, "God's picked on me, I reckon." What he means is that God has picked on him to suffer. There might even be something noble in it—a supposition confirmed by Makarenko's next utterance: "I'm a son of man, I reckon." The phrase "son of man" is Jesus' usual manner of referring to Himself in the Gospels. The vicious Makarenko is thus transformed by Babel into a grotesque Christ-figure, and anti-Semitism is revealed for what it is: an attribute of the Christian religion.

This story was dedicated to the writer Maxim Gorky because it was Gorky who published Babel's first stories in 1916.

Style and Technique

The most important stylistic feature of "The Story of My Dovecot" is the epiphany described in detail above. This is a device often used by Babel—

but never more successfully than in this particular story. At its best, the literary epiphany brings into focus all of the main elements of the story in which it appears. It becomes a "showing forth."

Interestingly, Babel echoes the major epiphany of this story with a minor one that acts as an ode to the joy of a young Russian peasant as he smashes the house of a Jew: "Sighing, he smiled all around with the amiable grin of drunkenness, sweat, and spiritual power. The whole street was filled with a splitting, a snapping, the song of flying wood." This epiphany truly reflects the happiness of the peasant, but it is ironic to such a degree that it qualifies as black humor. There is irony also in the fact that the peasant is smashing the house of Khariton Efrussi, thus acting as the instrument of the Babel's family desired vengeance on the hated parvenu. Such a linking of early and late elements in the story lends artistic unity to the work.

Surprisingly, this story contains much humor, required both for emotional relief and as a device for maintaining detachment in the narrating author. An example of such humor is the remark, "Like all Jews I was short, weakly, and had headaches from studying." The exaggeration qualifies as self-deprecating Jewish humor. Yet there is also truth in it; many Jews really were short and weak, owing to poverty and poor diet—the consequence of anti-Semitism.

Babel employs a number of effective images that are relatively low-key, not so "ornamental" as in most of his other stories of the early 1920's. An example is his description of the Russian Pyatnitsky, as he walks down a corridor, hemmed in by the shadowy walls, and "moving between them as a barge moves through a deep canal. . . ." This positive image of a good Russian is needed in the story—as is the dedication to Gorky—but it cannot make up for the anti-Semitism that is shown in the story to be ubiquitous.

Donald M. Fiene

THE STORY OF SERAPION

Author: E. T. A. Hoffmann (1776-1822)
Type of plot: Gothic tale
Time of plot: Early nineteenth century
Locale: Germany
First published: "Die Serapionsbrüder," 1819-1821 (English translation, 1886)

> *Principal characters:*
> THE STORYTELLER, an amateur psychologist
> PRIEST SERAPION, a hermit who escaped from a lunatic asylum

The Story

Lost in a thick forest somewhere in the South of Germany, the storyteller happens upon a long-bearded hermit, from whom he asks directions to the nearby village of B———. He is puzzled by the reply, though, for the hermit refers to the forest as a desert and recommends that he follow a friend to Alexandria, which is in Egypt, not Germany.

From a traveler on the road he later learns that the odd fellow is known to the villagers as Priest Serapion, a kindly gentleman who is "not quite right in his head." Dr. S———provides more background, explaining that the hermit, once one of the most brilliant men in the town of M———, was about to be sent on a diplomatic mission when he mysteriously disappeared. At nearly the same time a hermit calling himself Priest Serapion suddenly appeared in the vicinity. Then one day Count P———of M———recognized him as his lost nephew. Arrested after a violent struggle, he was committed to a lunatic asylum in B———.

The medical men there found only one thing wrong with his mind: the fixed idea that he was the same Serapion who fled the Theban desert in the days of the Emperor Decius (in the third century) and suffered martyrdom in Alexandria. Probably with the help of Dr. S———, he escaped from the asylum and was allowed to live in a hut he built in the forest.

Himself an amateur psychologist, the storyteller decides to go back to the forest and cure Serapion by attacking his fixed idea at its source. The story reaches its climax in their debate. Serapion insists that centuries ago he had survived a gruesome martyrdom, "his limbs being torn asunder at the joints, and his body thrown down from a lofty rock." Even now there are reminders, he says, "a severe headache, and occasional violent cramps and twitchings in my limbs."

At that point, the storyteller attempts his cure. First he explains the malady of the fixed idea, citing the case of Abbot Molanus, "who conversed most rationally upon every subject, but would not leave his room because he thought he was a barleycorn, and the hens would swallow him." At last he stands up, takes Serapion by both hands, and cries loudly, "Count P——, awake from the pernicious dream."

Serapion, however, is not moved. Instead he responds by reducing his adversary's position to an absurdity with the observation that only a lunatic would try to reason another lunatic out of his lunacy, if it were lunacy, or if it were not. Since time and space themselves are relative and not fixed, their conquest is a feat his mind can perform.

Overwhelmed by "the very rationality of his irrationality," the storyteller realizes the folly of his own undertaking and begins to understand how the madman can consider his madness "a priceless gift from heaven." Serapion goes on to describe several supernatural visits from geniuses who died long ago, and he further demonstrates the power of his imagination by relating several spellbinding romances before their encounter comes to an end.

Converted from cynicism to fascination, the storyteller returns often to Serapion's hut, though he never again tries to play the role of a psychological doctor. Then one day, after an absence of three years, he returns to the forest one last time, only to find the amazing man dead.

Themes and Meanings

The storyteller's debate with Serapion epitomizes the conflict between Romanticism and rationalism. Based largely on the scientific theories of Isaac Newton, Francis Bacon, and René Descartes, rationalism exalted reason over emotion, and empirical knowledge over faith. Rejecting supernatural explanations, it sought to describe nature as a set of material substances governed by a set of scientific laws revealed by experiments rather than the divine. The new science of psychology was finding its first empirical and experimental bases in E. T. A. Hoffmann's time. With his methodical cynicism, his advanced degree, and his scholarly inquiries, the storyteller embodies the follies of rationalism, as he soon discovers.

In Serapion the storyteller finds his nemesis. No rational man would claim to be a martyr who died centuries ago, but Serapion does. For him, a firm conviction can make something so, since mind controls matter and not the other way around, as some scientists suppose.

Serapion espouses a kind of religious idealism. "If it is the mind only which takes cognizance of events around us," he argues, "it follows that that which it has taken cognizance of *has* actually occurred." Further, he declares that the mental power of men is not their own, but only "lent to them for a time by that Higher Power." Several times he chides the storyteller for underrating the omnipotence of God. He ridicules the rationalistic concept of a watchmaker-God who wound up the universe only to watch it run down without interfering.

His chosen name, Priest Serapion, associates him with the beginnings of a religion called Christianity. Surviving martyrdom like the Savior himself,

Serapion remembers awakening from death when "the spirit dawned, and shone bright within me." Even the rationalistic storyteller recognizes in him a "lofty, invulnerable higher spirit."

Serapion emerges from the story as a portrait of the Romantic artist. At first sight the storyteller likens him to a figure in one of painter-poet Salvator Rosa's wild mountain scenes. He tells the storyteller tales "only the most imaginative poet could have constructed." Dr. S——finds in him "remarkable poetical gifts" and "a most brilliant fancy." The departed spirits who visit him are fit companions, Ludovico Ariosto, Petrarch, and Dante, early heroes of Romantic sensibilities in literature.

For artists such as Serapion, faith, art, and imagination are synonymous. All command a prophetic power which penetrates material reality to expose deeper, unexpected truths. Serapion's notion that time and space are relative, for example, was considered hopelessly visionary and impractical until, almost a century later, Albert Einstein demonstrated its truth.

Serapion's isolation from society typifies the predicament of the Romantic artist. Art in the Age of Reason had been, for the most part, more concerned with public life, common sense, and general truths than with cultivating private fantasies and personal eccentricities. Romantic artists' obsessions with introspection and personal visions, however, cut them off from society. Serapion's hermitage symbolizes the Romantic artist's alienation from society.

Serapion goes back to nature as many Romantics have longed to do since Jean-Jacques Rousseau explained how under such natural, primitive conditions, devoid of the corrupting influence of society, man could enjoy his innate goodness in simple happiness. Serapion does live a placid, cheerful life in his hut. Yet he is not quite the untutored noble savage Rousseau had in mind. Indeed, his return to nature is an ironic enterprise, undertaken as an alternative to incarceration in a lunatic asylum. His whole attitude toward nature is ambivalent. He considers it a desert. Like many Romantic artists, he loves the immortal spirit more than mortal nature. His death occurs not in the Theban desert but in a German forest.

Style and Technique

Hoffmann helped make the short story a viable literary genre. His influence on Washington Irving and Edgar Allan Poe was profound. Brief prose narratives and tales had been around longer than the written language, but before the nineteenth century they were usually written down in ways as unstructured, rambling, and episodic as the stories themselves happened to be. Hoffmann was among the first generation of writers who deliberately set about to give those amorphous forms more artistic shape.

The conflict between Serapion and the storyteller follows a pattern which became virtually definitive of the short story as a literary form. First comes a complicating incident (the puzzling reply in the forest) which draws the opposing forces into conflict. The action mounts to a climax (their debate) where the forces do decisive battle. Then the action falls to a point of final resolution (Serapion's death).

The tales of Hoffmann have been called the culmination of gothicism. The Romantic revival of emotionalism, supernatural faith, noble savagery, and the like precipitated in Europe a craving for things gothic. Dark forests, melancholy, superstitious peasants, misty ruins, mystery, and other obstacles to rationalism came back into vogue. The gothic style can be felt in the forest setting, supernatural events, numerous medieval allusions, and the eerie, supernal tone that pervades this story.

Hoffmann cleverly uses an unnamed narrator to enlist the reader's sympathy for Serapion. Namelessness suggests a lack of individuality, which is appropriate to an avatar of rationalism, and it helps make his clash with Serapion philosophical rather than personal in nature. He is the Everyman of rationalism who adopts a cynical attitude toward imagination. Ordinarily, most readers would share his initial reaction to Serapion's madness. Thus, when he begins to appreciate the madman, the reader is tempted to do the same.

Because this story is a mental adventure, philosophical dialogue plays a greater role in it than action. Even the lively details of an atrocious martyrdom, the capture and escape from the lunatic asylum, are rendered narratively rather than dramatically. Serapion's astonishing character is revealed by words and scarcely developed through action, while the storyteller's character is developed largely through dialogue.

John L. McLean

THE STRANGE RIDE OF MORROWBIE JUKES

Author: Rudyard Kipling (1865-1936)
Type of plot: Horror
Time of plot: The 1880's
Locale: A city of the living dead in the desert between Pakpattan and
 Mubarukpur, India
First published: 1885

> *Principal characters:*
> MORROWBIE JUKES, a British civil engineer stationed in India
> GUNGA DASS, a Brahman, formerly a telegraph master
> DUNNOO, Jukes's dog boy

The Story

 Morrowbie Jukes's strange ride occurs when he is weakened by a fever.
Baying dogs disturb his sleep. He kills one of them and displays its body,
hoping to deter the other dogs from their baying. Instead, they devour the
body "and, as it seemed to me, sang their hymns of thanksgiving afterwards
with renewed energy." Morrowbie tries to shoot the loudest of the dogs, but
the light-headedness that accompanies his fever makes him miss the offending dog even though he unloads both barrels of his shotgun in its direction.

 Finally, Morrowbie decides to go after the dog with his boar spear. He has
his pony, Pornic, saddled and sets out. The pony runs at breakneck speed in
a straight line, galloping past the baying dog and running for several miles
beyond it. Suddenly Morrowbie sees the waters of the river Sutlej before
him; then his pony stumbles and the two roll down a slope. Morrowbie loses
consciousness.

 When he awakes, he is inside a horseshoe-shaped crater, three sides of
which are enclosed by high slopes slanting at about sixty-five degrees. The
river provides the remaining boundary. Morrowbie tries to ride out of the
crater, but he cannot conquer its steep slopes. Then he hears a gunshot from
across the river, and a bullet lands close to Pornic's head.

 Some time passes before Morrowbie becomes aware that other people inhabit this wilderness. Slowly, about sixty-five people emerge from badger
holes that Morrowbie thought were untenanted. Among them is Gunga
Dass, a Brahman and a former telegraph master, whom Morrowbie once
knew. Gunga Dass cries, "Sahib! Sahib!" Morrowbie recognizes him only by
a scar on his cheek for which Morrowbie was apparently responsible. Gunga
Dass commences to tell Morrowbie about this city of the living dead on
which he has stumbled.

 The crater and its barrows are inhabited by people who, thought to be
dead from cholera, had been taken away for hasty cremation. Some of them

were not dead, and when they stirred, those who were to have cremated them plastered their noses and mouths with mud. Those who did not die from suffocation as a result of this ministration were set loose, and many of them, including Gunga Dass, who almost died, ended up in this crater. A gunboat cruises the Sutlej by daylight to make sure that no one escapes from the place.

Gunga Dass takes all of Morrowbie's money and wants to take his boots as well. He tells Morrowbie that he will look after him for a while but suggests that in time Morrowbie should wait on him, a suggestion that Morrowbie rejects. All at once, however, Morrowbie finds himself in the middle of a role reversal. He is no longer master. Gunga Dass controls him. On Morrowbie's first night in the crater, its residents kill his pony to use as food, a meat much better than the crow that they usually catch and roast for their daily meal.

Morrowbie learns that there is only one way out of the crater, an intricate course along the riverbank, most of which is composed of deadly quicksand. He also learns that one other Briton has stumbled into the crater and that Gunga Dass murdered him.

Morrowbie gets possession of the murdered man's mummified body and buries it in the quicksand, but not before he has secured the man's possessions, including his journal. Out of the journal's binding falls a piece of paper on which the dead man has written the secret of how to escape from the crater. Just as Morrowbie discovers this piece of paper with its burned edges, Gunga Dass appears, knows that Morrowbie has found the piece of paper for which he himself has been searching, and takes it from Morrowbie.

When Gunga Dass drops it, calculatedly, Morrowbie rushes to pick it up and Gunga Dass hits him in the head from behind. When he regains consciousness, Morrowbie is aware that someone is calling, "Sahib! Sahib!" He looks up to see the face of his dog boy, Dunnoo, staring down at him from a considerable distance. Dunnoo knots together a few leather punkah ropes with a loop at one end. He lowers them to Morrowbie, who puts the loop under his arms. Dunnoo hauls him up the side of the crater and tells him that he has followed Pornic's hoof prints fourteen miles to this place to save his life.

Themes and Meanings

"The Strange Ride of Morrowbie Jukes" is rich in meaning. One theme that Kipling explores here is that of the social stratifications that exist both within Indian society, with its caste system, and between the Indian natives and their British masters. One is reminded of the exploration of similar themes in Sir James Barrie's *The Admirable Crichton* (1902) and in William Golding's *Lord of the Flies* (1954). In the Kipling story the master prevails, but not without the help of the faithful servant.

Morrowbie must prove his mastery to the people confined in the crater: "I have been accustomed to a certain amount of civility from my inferiors, and on approaching the crowd naturally expected that there would be some rec- ognition of my presence." These people, however, first laugh at Morrowbie and cackle after him. He thrashes one or two of them, and then they keep a respectful distance. Morrowbie realizes, "I had left the world, it seemed, for centuries. I was as certain then as I am now of my own existence, that in the accursed settlement there was no law save that of the strongest."

When Morrowbie's pony is killed, Gunga Dass explains to him that horse is "better than crow, and 'greatest good of greatest number' is political maxim. We are now Republic, Mister Jukes, and you are entitled to a fair share of the beast." This political statement, written in the 1880's, must have been startling for its time.

This story is in many ways a commentary on all humanity. The microcosm that Kipling creates in the crater is a discouraging one. Gunga Dass torments the representative of the ruling class because in the crater the classes that exist outside have little meaning. Gunga Dass reminds Morrowbie of a schoolboy who enjoys watching the death agonies of a beetle impaled upon a pin, but Morrowbie is not much better than Gunga Dass in this respect. One must remember that life does not mean much to him. He kills a dog because it disturbs his sleep. He has no feeling for the Indians, whom he regards as his inferiors.

The human race, Kipling seems to be saying, feeds on itself, just as the baying dogs eat the dog that Morrowbie has slain. Gunga Dass uses live crows, Judas crows, to attract other crows so that he can capture them and eat them. Survival for the British, according to this philosophy, can be as- sured only if, figuratively, they feed on their own species, the Indians and other colonials.

In the crater, Morrowbie depends upon Gunga Dass for his survival, and Gunga Dass moves toward assuming the role of master. Yet Morrowbie also depends upon his Indian servant, Dunnoo, for his escape from the crater and from the city of the living dead. Once Morrowbie is back in his own world, Dunnoo will be the inferior, Morrowbie the master.

Style and Technique

At the center of "The Strange Ride of Morrowbie Jukes" is a pattern of reversals: Servants become masters, and the dead rise up to live again. Morrowbie Jukes seems almost to be living through a bad dream, except that the horrors he experiences are real. Kipling achieves a plausible basis for this dreamlike atmosphere, however, by presenting his readers with a protagonist who has been suffering from a fever that has weakened him and left him dis- oriented, as one sees when he tries to shoot the baying dog.

"The Strange Ride of Morrowbie Jukes" can be seen as the strange ride of mankind. The galloping pony takes Morrowbie to the brink of the crater, and they both fall in. Morrowbie is powerless to control the force that takes him to the crater, just as people, perhaps, are powerless to control the forces that direct their destinies.

R. Baird Shuman

THE STREET OF CROCODILES

Author: Bruno Schulz (1892-1942)
Type of plot: Fantasy
Time of plot: Early twentieth century
Locale: A small town anywhere in the Western world
First published: "Ulica krokodyli," 1934 (English translation, 1963)

> *Principal characters:*
> A TOWN
> THE INHABITANTS OF THE TOWN
> A STORE CLERK
> OTHER SALESCLERKS, young women
> CITY CABS
> TROLLEYS
> TRAINS
> PROSTITUTES

The Story

A discussion of "The Street of Crocodiles" must begin with the difficulty of identifying its central figure or hero. The first sentence reads in a deceptively clear and straightforward fashion: "My father kept in the lower drawer of his large desk an old and beautiful map of our city." Later, very little is clear. As in the works of Franz Kafka, a "terrible ambiguity" seems to hang over the story. It is not a story about the father, nor is it really a story about the narrator's town, even though that town is the principal character. It is a story about modern life, its degeneration as a result of the triumph of commercialism and cheap values (see the metaphoric title), a story about the "degradation of reality" as a modern Polish critic (Artur Sandauer) has called it. There may not even be an actual city—at least none is ever named, and its geographic location would be difficult to pinpoint except to say that it is a city in the Western world where Western goods are traded. The reader knows no more of it except that an "old and very beautiful map" exists of this city where the engraver entered with great care every significant detail: "streets and alleyways, the sharp lines of cornices, architraves, archivolts, and pilasters. . . ." The city has an old and a new section, and it is the new section with its "pseudo-Americanism" and its "shops with the stigma of some wild Klondike" which the author uses as his metaphor for the decrepitude and illusoriness of life in the twentieth century. Here, starting with the vegetation, everything is cheap and shoddy. There are no individual distinctions, but a pervasive grayness and barrenness reigns everywhere. The goods in the outfitters' shops are gray and colorless and the bales of cloth form "imaginary jackets and trousers." The young salesman drowns the shopper with his "cheap sales talk."

The outfitters' shops, however, are nothing but a disguise for antiquarian bookstores with "collections of highly questionable books and private editions." They are façades of a world of corruption underneath where the young salesclerk and the saleswomen play out erotic poses in front of one another. The narrator, who has observed these activities, uses the moment of their absorption in one another's suggestive poses to escape out into the street in order to view the larger panorama of the new district of the city.

What he saw in miniature in the outfitters' stores, alias pornographic bookstores, now is viewed in the larger dimension of street life. It is a "reality as thin as paper." It is a sham reality without substance where cabdrivers do not drive cabs but cavort through the town with their fares, engaging in meaningless and dangerous antics; the trolleys are not trolleys but conveyances made of papier-mâché and lacking a front section, and the trains stop in the middle of a street and temporarily transform the street into a cavernous railroad station. Nothing is certain here, nothing can be depended on, not even the normal purchase of railroad tickets. Around it all—the cabs, trolleys, and trains—prostitutes wend their way, women who are not a special group but could be the wives of the barbers, the coffeehouse conductors, or anyone else.

The narrator asks in conclusion, is this corruption, this sham reality, only imaginary? Where does it go once it has reached its apogee? It recedes, he says, like an ocean wave. Corruption, like virtue, is too banal to last. Nothing, not even vice, can endure. It, too, comes and goes, impermanent like everything else. "The Street of Crocodiles" is a phantasmagoria created of corruptible material like papier-mâché, which disintegrates when confronted with the true reality. What is the true reality? That question is not answered. The world is like papier-mâché; it came to life and died in the imagination that produced it.

Themes and Meanings

The central theme in "The Street of Crocodiles" is an examination of the nature of twentieth century life. The mode of presentation is surrealistic and the title an extended metaphor. Life in the new district is a caricature of life in the old; it has degenerated to the extent that it has lost what was once called reality. It is not real. Life in the city which the narrator examines by looking at a "beautiful map," which is extended over a "sheaf of parchment pages," is illusory. It presents a mere "bird's eye panorama." The narrator's imagination fills it with life, peoples its stores and streets, permits motion and activity to flow through its boulevards and alleys, observes and assesses. This observation and assessment reveal the vanity of life, its illusoriness, its deceptiveness (the outfitters' shops as façades of pornographic bookstores), its impotence. Its reality is a sham, for it exists, after all, only on a map, despite the beauty of its engraving.

Does this view of "The Street of Crocodiles" not possess any reality at all? It does. The grotesque possesses elements of the real, but its forms are misshapen as in a distortion mirror. Great predecessors of Bruno Schulz in the art of the grotesque were the painter Hieronymus Bosch (1450?-1516), the Russian writer Nikolai Gogol (1809-1852), and the Austrian writer Franz Kafka (1883-1924). The upheavals of the twentieth century gave further impetus to a presentation of the grotesque in painting (George Grosz, 1893-1959), in literature (Stanisław Ignacy Witkiewicz, 1885-1939), and even music (aleatory music and its practitioners, such as Karlheinz Stockhausen, born 1928). The presentation of reality in grotesque forms raises questions about the nature of reality itself. Where does it exist if not in the human mind, and does one not create it for oneself every moment of one's life again and again? It may appear to one appealing or unappealing. The artist Schulz saw his reality and transformed it through his imagination and creative talent. He made it "strange," so that the familiar should once again become unfamiliar to his readers and should rouse their own imaginative sensibility. Finally, reality is ambiguous.

Style and Technique

The artist proceeds as a painter by addressing first and above all the visual sense. The design of the map from which he creates his city is shown in precise visual detail. Such visual detail applies to aspects of the city, its people and transport. Since the proportions are out of shape, what one sees is grotesque. Schulz makes rich use of adjectives that refer to decay and disintegration. The most widely used color epithet is "gray": a gray day, gray-glassed display windows, that gray, impersonal crowd, those dirty gray squares. The author pays special attention to his language (the use of adjectives is only one element), and by means of certain pronouns tries to create the effect of an oppressive atmosphere, of the hopeless treadmill of life, of delusion and irreality. His paratactic syntax carries the effect of a certain monotony, appropriate to the setting of unrelieved grayness, of life beyond redemption. The story is very short (eight pages in the original Polish), yet its power rests on its concentrated linguistic texture, the incongruity of its pictures, and the unique and hypnotic imaginative flight of its creator.

Joachim T. Baer

STRONG HORSE TEA

Author: Alice Walker (1944-   )
Type of plot: Social realism
Time of plot: Mid-twentieth century
Locale: The rural American South
First published: 1968

Principal characters:

RANNIE MAE TOOMER, the protagonist, a poor Southern black woman

SNOOKS, her dying infant son

"AUNT" SARAH, a local expert in country medicine and home remedies

THE MAILMAN, a white man in whom Rannie places her trust

The Story

Snooks, Rannie Mae Toomer's infant son, is dying of double pneumonia and whooping cough. Rannie has no one else in the world, is unmarried, and lives in an unheated, drafty shack somewhere in the South.

Sarah, a neighbor who is expert in country medicine and home remedies, suggests that one of these remedies might help Snooks, but Rannie will have none of it. She has supreme confidence in white medicine and wants a white doctor for her son. She is also certain that the white mailman whom she has begged to call for the doctor will send him as soon as possible. Despite the drenching rain and bone-chilling winds which enter the shack, Rannie is sure that the doctor will soon arrive and give Snooks an injection which will make him well again.

Rannie recalls two past meetings with the mailman. Once, she had inquired whether the advertising circulars she received meant that someone would come later to deliver the things she needed: sweaters, shoes, rubbing alcohol, a heater for the house, a fur bonnet for Snooks. When he explained to her the meaning of the word "sale," which was always written on the circulars in red capital letters, Rannie was amazed, for she could never afford to buy any of the items advertised. Her conclusion was that this was simply the way things were; no one could do anything about it.

She met the mailman again on the morning Snooks was so ill. She had waited in the winter rain, had no umbrella, and had only leaky plastic shoes. At this second meeting she insisted that he send her a real doctor. The mailman first suggested Sarah's home remedies, but when Rannie remained adamant that a real doctor give Snooks real medicine, he said that he would do what he could and stuffed a new consignment of advertising circulars in Rannie's hand. Rannie recalls that she had once asked the mailman for any extra circulars he had so she could patch the drafty walls of her house with them.

A doctor finally arrives, but it is Sarah, not the white doctor whom Rannie has expected. Sarah is the "doctor" the mailman sent. At this point, Rannie realizes that no white doctor will come, and she places all the confidence she can muster in "Aunt" Sarah. Sarah frankly tells Rannie that Snooks is dying but suggests that she has one remedy if Rannie has the stomach to help. Snooks must drink some "strong horse tea," and Rannie must collect it.

Once again Rannie ventures outside in rain, thunder, and lightning. She waits for nearly an hour in the pouring rain before the gray mare begins to spread its legs, only to realize that she has brought nothing in which to catch the "tea." Nevertheless, Rannie is determined to save Snooks, so she quickly slips off one of her plastic shoes and runs after the mare. When she realizes the shoe leaks, she places her mouth over the tiny crack so as not to lose any of the precious "medicine." Even as Rannie slips and slides through the mud to return with the "tea" that Sarah needs, the reader is told that Snooks's frail breathing has already stopped with the thunder.

Themes and Meanings

Rannie Mae Toomer is twice a victim of her own childlike need to trust. Her naïveté is clear from her belief that the items in the advertising circulars she receives will be delivered to her house for free if only she requests them. Significantly, the items she most wants are hardly luxuries (rubbing alcohol, sweaters, shoes, a heater, a baby's bonnet); they are not even for herself but for her child. The mailman and the circulars he brings are Rannie's only contacts with the world of white people, a world which seems infinitely superior to her own.

As Rannie waits in the drenching winter rain to beg the mailman to send a real doctor for Snooks, she has the same innocent confidence that all will be well once she makes her request, but to the mailman she merely appears "more ignorant than usual." Indeed, Rannie is ignorant, but only in the sense that she possesses the childlike simplicity that most people quickly lose. Ironically, as a poor black woman living in a remote country shack, Rannie stands as little chance of getting the doctor her son requires as she does of receiving for free the items she sees advertised in the circulars the mailman brings. Clearly, the word "ignorant" more accurately applies to the mailman, who never sees beyond Rannie's unkempt appearance to the desperate nature of her plight. He does not understand that Rannie's request for a white doctor is implicitly a rejection of Sarah's home remedies and, by extension, of her own background. Rannie has told Sarah that she does not want "witch's remedies" for her son and is therefore at the mercy of whoever might help.

Still, Rannie is victimized a second time, in this instance by Sarah.

Though Sarah probably does believe that "strong horse tea" might help Snooks, she nevertheless exploits Rannie's courage when for a second time Rannie ventures into the rain and waits, this time for a mare to urinate. The final irony is Rannie's use of her leaky plastic shoe to catch the "tea" and her sealing the crack by holding her mouth to the toe. All at once, ignorance is triumphant, and Snooks is dead.

Style and Technique

Alice Walker often writes works in which a black protagonist, usually a woman, is caught between black and white cultures and inevitably becomes the victim of both. At her best, Walker neither indulges in polemics nor seeks to blame; indeed, here, as third-person narrator, she distances herself from her characters and allows the story to tell itself. The effect of this technique is akin to high tragedy. The reader of "Strong Horse Tea," for example, knows that the white doctor will not come, that either Sarah will refuse to help once Rannie has rejected "witch's remedies" or that Sarah's help will probably come too late. What comes as a surprise is the grotesque indignity to which Rannie submits in order to do what she desperately hopes will help her child. Here, most of all, Rannie's guileless innocence comes into its sharpest focus.

The winter storm, which continues in varying degrees of fury, serves as an important symbol. Rannie cannot escape; it pours through the walls of her shack, and it drenches her on her two errands to help Snooks. All the while, tears pour down Rannie's face, left unwashed for five days because of her concern for her son, and leave "whitish snail tracks." This is a late winter rain, and the death which that season brings is matched in the death of Snooks, whose breathing stops with the thunder.

Those who have read Walker's celebrated novel *The Color Purple* (1982) will recognize similarities between its narrator, Celie, and Rannie, the protagonist of "Strong Horse Tea." The common humanity and simple faith of these country women are easy to recognize, and Walker's skill in portraying these qualities gives her work a lyricism which is far above the racial polemic that might have come from a less gifted author.

Robert J. Forman

THE SUICIDE CLUB

Author: Robert Louis Stevenson (1850-1894)
Type of plot: Suspense
Time of plot: Late nineteenth century
Locale: London and Paris
First published: 1878

> *Principal characters:*
> PRINCE FLORIZEL, the heir apparent to the Bohemian throne
> COLONEL GERALDINE, the Master of the Bohemian Horse and
> aide-de-camp to Prince Florizel
> THE PRESIDENT OF THE SUICIDE CLUB, a notorious villain
> DR. NOEL, an English expatriate in Paris, a former associate
> of the president, now assisting the prince

The Story

Three related stories make up the larger plot of "The Suicide Club," although each of the separately titled stories might be understood if read alone. The larger plot concerns the work of the hero, Prince Florizel of Bohemia, and his assistant, Colonel Geraldine, in pursuing and finally destroying the unnamed president of the Suicide Club, an organization that provides desperate men with ways to escape unhappy or disastrous lives without the scandal of overt self-destruction.

The first part, "The Story of the Young Man with the Cream Tarts," establishes the personalities of the major characters and the nature of the club. The prince and the colonel, both of whom are visiting London and are interested in life's more eccentric opportunities, are seeking adventures in an oyster bar near Leicester Square. Among the pair's many attributes is the capacity to disguise their true characters so as to meet and talk with all classes of people—the prince being less proficient in disguise than his assistant because the nobility of his nature makes it impossible to hide its quality altogether. As they are enjoying the bar's fare, the young man enters, accompanied by two men carrying trays of cream tarts, a rich pastry. The young man proceeds to offer tarts to each of the patrons in the bar, including the Bohemian pair; by the rules of the sport he has invented, he eats any tart that is rejected by the person to whom he first offers it. The prince and Geraldine accept his offer on the condition that the young man join them for supper after the remainder of the tarts are consumed. The young man agrees, and the three soon find themselves in the private dining room of a Soho restaurant.

After a pleasant meal, the prince and Geraldine persuade the young man to explain his unusual sport with the cream tarts. He tells of an insufficient fortune, of an excessive love that could not be returned, and, finally, of bankruptcy. Playing to the young man's apparently morbid concern, the Bohemian pair succeed in discovering that he is actually preparing himself to die by suicide, although he tells them that he is not going to commit the act himself. Intrigued and alarmed, they convince the young man that they are in the same circumstances themselves, and they persuade him to take them along as he visits the club where the matter will be taken care of.

Once they arrive, the prince and Geraldine are admitted as members only after an elaborate interview with the president, which includes the signing of a solemn pledge not to violate the secrecy of the club or to fail in completing the tasks assigned to them as members. Afterward, they enter the club room to find what appears to be an ordinary party of men talking, drinking, and playing at cards, although with a particularly feverish air. Many of the members are quite young or in the prime of life, but the attention of the prince is arrested by a crippled man of considerable age, Mr. Malthus, who, although apparently suffering from many afflictions, is nevertheless intensely interested in the affairs of all the members. After a period of conversation and gaming, doors at the end of the room are opened and the company retires to another room containing a large table at which the president sits, carefully shuffling a deck of cards.

As soon as the members take their seats around the table, the prince and Geraldine find out how the business of the club is transacted: by dealing out, one at a time to the members, the whole pack of cards until the ace of clubs and the ace of spades have been turned over. The man receiving the spade will die that night at the hands of the man receiving the club, who will follow the plans laid out by the president. Both Bohemians are suddenly concerned that, should chance turn against them, the prince might be put in a position that would be intolerable, for either his honor or his life would suffer. As it happens, however, the spade falls to Mr. Malthus—who almost collapses when he sees his fate—and the club to the young man with the cream tarts. The prince and Geraldine extricate themselves as quickly as possible and depart, discovering in the papers the next day the news of Mr. Malthus' death by accident in Trafalgar Square. The prince decides to return to the club the next evening in order to destroy it, hoping in that way to help the young man work through his guilt for the death of Malthus.

In the evening's hand, however, the worst happens: The prince is dealt the ace of spades and prepares to meet his doom because of his word of honor to follow the rules of the club. Following the instructions of the president, he sets out, only to be captured and stolen away by a gang of apparent thugs, who turn out to be his own servants under the direction of Geraldine. The colonel tells the prince that all has been taken care of, and the two return to Box Court, the location of the club, where the prince metes out justice. He invites the president to take a trip to the Continent with the younger brother of Geraldine—an implicit sentence of execution, since the younger Geraldine is under instructions to dispose of the man by duel. With that, the first and most elaborate of the stories concludes.

The second part, "The Story of the Physician and the Saratoga Trunk," continues the story from a somewhat different perspective. Mr. Silas Q. Scuddamore, a wealthy New Englander visiting Paris, is tricked by a series of strange coincidences into keeping an assignation with a woman who never appears at the rendezvous. When he returns to his lodging, he is horrified to find on his bed the body of a man recently killed. In his horror and fright, he attracts the attention of a neighbor, Dr. Noel, who promises to help him out of the obvious difficulty that the body represents. The next day the doctor departs for a while to make arrangements while Scuddamore keeps grisly watch over the body. When the doctor returns, he tells Scuddamore that he can transport the body to England and dispose of it there, the transportation being possible because Dr. Noel has arranged to convey his luggage through diplomatic channels, where it will not be opened at customs inspection, and the disposal of the body being possible because of Dr. Noel's connections in England. Scuddamore is too much in a state of shock to notice how quickly and easily this serious problem is solved; in this period of shock, his only real response is a feeling of disgust when the doctor tells him that the body must be transported in the Saratoga trunk that stands in his room and that Scuddamore himself must load the body into the trunk.

Scuddamore discovers the next day that he will be traveling in the suite of Prince Florizel. Despite great anxiety, he arrives in England without trouble and tries to take the Saratoga trunk to the address that Dr. Noel has given him; the prince's servants, who drive him to the address, evidence surprise when he instructs them to go to Box Court. Returning to his hotel and made anxious by a man who appears to be trailing him, he keeps the trunk with him overnight, then tries again to deliver it. He is immensely surprised when the occupant at Box Court turns out to be the prince himself, who has taken over these quarters as he tries to dismantle the damage done by the club. The prince is even more surprised, however, when he opens the trunk to find the dead body of Geraldine's brother. After hearing Scuddamore's account, the prince explains that Dr. Noel is an erstwhile colleague of the president and that the entire coincidence seems providential in the matter of punishing the wicked. Recognizing his own implicit guilt in the death of the younger Geraldine, the prince announces that he will even more steadfastly undertake to bring the president to vengeance, upon which note this second section closes.

The final part, "The Adventure of the Hansom Cab," introduces Lieutenant Brackenbury Rich, a young war hero who has returned to England after his service in India. Feeling out of place upon his arrival in London, the lieutenant sets out to explore the streets of the city and to familiarize himself with a scene from which he has long been absent. A sudden downpour of rain drives him into the shelter of an unoccupied cab, and he instructs the driver to drive about as he will, for lack of a better destination. The driver immediately sets off to a large and well-lighted house, where a party of gentlemen is being entertained. Assured that he will be well received, the lieutenant finds there a group of strangers who nevertheless have in common an air of independence and self-sufficiency. When only a half-dozen guests remain, the host declares his purpose: He is looking for courageous and iron-willed men who will assist him in a matter of honor. Four of those remaining decline to participate and retire, leaving the lieutenant and Major O'Rooke, another war hero, to accompany the host.

As the three make their way to the rendezvous for the duel, the host—who is in fact Colonel Geraldine—explains that the masquerade at the house was a device by which he hoped to acquire the services of the most courageous and most honorable men. On arrival at a large but dilapidated house in extensive grounds, they are introduced to their host's principal, whom the major recognizes as Prince Florizel. The prince explains that he is now about to conclude the dangerous business of destroying the president of the Suicide Club, with the assistance of Geraldine and Dr. Noel, who is also present. The two war heroes are to serve as seconds in the duel between the prince and the president, who attempts to ambush the prince but is forestalled by the party. The principals and seconds in the duel retire to the grounds, leaving Geraldine and Dr. Noel to wait anxiously. The prince and the heroes soon return with word that the president has been dispatched, and thus the story ends.

Themes and Meanings

"The Suicide Club" is an interesting representative of the so-called sensational fiction of the nineteenth century, in which peculiar circumstances and exciting action sometimes replaced narrative and psychological realism. As a result, the story lacks some of the more intensely conceived ideas and themes that mark other, perhaps more serious, fiction in the period. In this story, one recurrent idea appears in all three sections as a unifying motif: the idea of personal honor. Florizel's situation, as Geradline frequently reminds him, requires that the prince consider not only his own interest but also the interest of Bohemia, the throne of which he is to inherit. In the exciting events of the story, the prince is thus constantly placing himself at risk, and he seems to depend on his wit, strength, and honor to defend him. In the first and third parts, however, the prince is actually in danger of sacrificing his life for the sake of his honor, the result being that his personal virtue will remain intact, although his country will then be without a fitting successor to the crown. Geraldine, as the active partner in this relationship, is always having to place his own interest and safety at the disposal of the prince. As the story develops, one may reasonably ask whether the continual reference to and discussion of honor is not a device by which the author ironically points out the ephemerality of honor in the kind of extreme behavior that the prince both confronts and represents.

Style and Technique

"The Suicide Club" was included in a collection called *The New Arabian Nights* (1882). As the title would appear to suggest, the stories in the collection are highly mannered and artificial in character. Stevenson does not represent either the life of Victorian London or the character of a crown prince with any psychological reality; his intention seems rather to have been the production of a story with peculiar and exciting incidents, however unlikely the circumstances they depict might actually have been.

In structure and technique, the story has the same superficial character. Besides the elaborate and peculiar events of the plot, Stevenson indulges the habit of introducing characters without developing them beyond the few bold strokes in which they are drafted at their first appearance. As a result, recognizable stereotypes—the completely amoral villain, the young man disappointed in love, the miserly New Englander, the war hero—predominate in the action of each story. Even the prince (the name and country of whom Stevenson borrows from William Shakespeare's *The Winter's Tale*) is conspicuously lacking in developed personality, serving for the most part as a mere representative of an extraordinary notion of honor. The only significantly developed character is Colonel Geraldine, who must be more fully represented if his actions are to be at all credible. Nevertheless, the absence of any explicit indications of his grief at the death of his brother suggests that even in his case, Stevenson had in mind not a portrait of human beings as they actually are but an exciting story that would engage and entertain readers with a taste for suspense.

Dale B. Billingsley

SUMMER EVENING

Author: Kay Boyle (1903-   )
Type of plot: Psychological realism
Time of plot: The late 1940's
Locale: Germany
First published: 1949

> *Principal characters:*
> MAJOR HATCHES, a military officer and host
> LIEUTENANT PEARSON, a guest
> THE YOUNG MAN IN THE BLUE SUIT, an intelligence agent and another guest
> THE HAUSMEISTER (POP), a houseboy or servant

The Story

Like many of Kay Boyle's stories written while she was a foreign correspondent for *The New Yorker*, the events of "Summer Evening" take place during the post–World War II reconstruction of Germany under the American occupation. The story relates the events of a cocktail party given by one Major Hatches and his wife. Their guests include military officers, government personnel, and their spouses. Although little action occurs during the course of the story, as the party progresses, the reader is introduced to a variety of sharply etched characters and is permitted to overhear their various conversations.

As the story opens, Major Hatches comments to Lieutenant Pearson about choosing a *Hausmeister*: "You have to be as careful about who you take as a *Hausmeister* as who you marry. . . . You have him underfoot twenty-four hours every day of the week." Hatches is cruel in his remarks concerning the *Hausmeister*'s desperation, exemplified by his having to retrieve cigarette stubs for his own use. Pearson continues the discussion by relating the story of a fellow in Nuremberg who would drop his butts out the window so that his *Hausmeister* would have to crawl through the shrubbery for them.

Marcia Cruickshank, the flirtatious wife of Captain Cruickshank, is one of the lonely, unhappy Americans among this ensemble of characters. Unlike another member of this party, Wendy Forsythe, who is unhappy in her realization of man's cruelty to his fellow creatures, Mrs. Cruickshank is unhappy because of her own empty life. She gets so drunk, as she does at all the social gatherings she attends, that she openly seduces the young man in the blue suit, an "intelligence" operative whose name is never revealed. Disgusted, her husband eventually must carry her to their car.

Captain Pete Forsythe, as he views the castle across the valley, is forced to think of the war: "There's a tank, a big Sherman tank, rusted and gutted and turned on its back, with field flowers growing through the carcass of it," an example of "the meaningless paraphernalia of war." As Forsythe remembers the Americans' defeat of the Germans, he maintains a strong conviction against further humiliating the former enemy. It is his wife Wendy's sensitivity to the extinction of the whooping crane which stimulates his thoughts: "The wheat growers came down across the plains and the marshes and the open prairies, . . . and the whooping crane lost its breeding ground. Like the Indian, the bison, the poets, their time is finished. There is no role left for them to play." Like other creatures similarly exploited by Americans, the Germans are made to feel like foreigners in their own land.

The Americans' exploitation of the Germans is further exemplified by the last conversation between Hatches, Pearson, and the intelligence agent, regarding the museum-quality treasures—the Biedermeier silver coffee set which had been in a German family for generations, the seventy-four-piece Dresden dinner service with gold inlay, the tablecloth which took a professor's wife twenty years to make—all bought "for a song." They are amused that the hungry Germans are willing to trade their "back teeth" for coffee and lard.

The Americans not only have cheated the Germans out of their material possessions but also proceed to strip them of any dignity that they may have left. At the end of the story, Hatches, Pearson, and the intelligence agent play their cruelest prank on the *Hausmeister*. When he is invited by Major Hatches to partake of a nightcap, the *Hausmeister* divulges his American background. He was born in "New Joisey" and desires to return to his homeland. The *Hausmeister* is led to believe that the young intelligence agent is the General Consul and that a golf-score card is a passport. To their embarrassment, the *Hausmeister* breaks down in tears of joy. Hatches expresses his disgust at what they have become during their stay in Germany: "*What are we doing here, any of us?* he asked himself, in sudden bewilderment, almost in fright. *What has become of the lot of us here?*" Boyle's stories typically end in this kind of revelation, rather than in resolution.

Themes and Meanings

"Summer Evening" portrays man's injustice to his fellowman. The references to the Americans' mistreatment of the Indians and to the German's systematic annihilation of the Jews both echo the Americans' present exploitation of the Germans. The character of the *Hausmeister* and the Americans' ridicule of him particularize the general helplessness of Germany. The major's statement that the *Hausmeister* will "make enough out of what's left in the ashtrays after one of these shindigs to keep him in luxury six months" not only belittles the subservience of the *Hausmeister* but also alludes to the falling social status of the entire German population.

The *Hausmeister* is a broken old man who must resort to alcohol to escape his pain. He has no purpose in life because of the destruction of the war ("Everything bombed out. Everything lost. Nothing left to Pop"). Although Boyle does not sympathize with the Nazis, she exhibits compassion for a proud and defeated people. While the *Hausmeister* symbolizes the broken spirit of Germany, the young man in the blue suit (the intelligence agent) represents the strength of America. He is naïve about the frailty of human feelings, just as the Americans were practically taking over a country which did not belong to them. He exhibits no conscience in his taking advantage of Mrs. Cruickshank's loneliness or his taking part in the practical joke played on the *Hausmeister*.

The setting is not merely background for the story, but further supports its theme. The party is held on "a dreamy, bluish summer evening" in a terraced villa overlooking an eleventh century Hessian town. The villa and the wealth associated with it symbolize America's exploitation of postwar Germany. Across the valley, the ancient castle, which appears "to watch, as it had watched for century after century, for armored knights on horseback . . . or for armored vehicles and low-flying planes," represents an ennobled German past. Unfortunately, the view of the castle elicits sympathy only from Captain Forsythe. The others are interested in filling themselves with Scotch-and-sodas and chopped-egg-and-anchovy canapés. The absence of German guests and the presence of German musicians and a German servant indicate that the Americans are interested, not in socializing with the Germans, but in using them for their entertainment and service.

Style and Technique

Although the story does not contain a plot in the traditional sense, "Summer Evening" does contain a coherent structure and well-developed characterization. It is framed by two incidents which humiliate the *Hausmeister*: the discussion of his collecting cigarette stubs and the prank of the make-believe passport. Within this frame, Boyle moves in and out of various conversations, in the manner of tracing shots by a motion-picture camera. These conversations take place between a few individuals whose lives are unfolded by Boyle's delicate touch. The characters are first introduced by third-person description. Mrs. Hatches, for example, is described as one who "flew at her guests with cries of pleasure, her bosom swollen like a pigeon's in her flowered dress." The words "flew" and "cries" make vivid Mrs. Hatches' image as a pigeon. Similarly, Lieutenant Pearson is described as a good-natured, youthful man who has been "larded" since childhood with excessive fat. This quintessential "ugly American" is so fat, in fact, that he has three rolls of flesh overlapping his jacket collar. It is no wonder that Boyle has a strong reputation as a stylist, a manipulator of language in her striking metaphors and her ability to create sharp, vivid pictures.

What the characters say also supports the narrator's description of them.

Mrs. Hatches' own statements reveal her personality: "That's twice you-all gave you' wud you'd come on ovah and play bridge with the Majah and me!" "You promised me that lemon-meringue recipe two weeks ago . . . an' you nevah kep' you' wud!" Not only do these lines portray Boyle's keen ear for dialect, but also the trivial, cocktail-party subject matter exposes Mrs. Hatches as the superficial person she is. It is not surprising that Mrs. Hatches, unlike her husband, achieves no moral growth during the course of the story.

Boyle once stated in a lecture that, more than technique, it is the writer's profound belief in something which is essential in creating a story. Boyle's belief in the need for pity and understanding is evident in "Summer Evening."

Patricia A. Posluszny

SUMMER NIGHT

Author: Elizabeth Bowen (1899-1973)
Type of plot: Psychological realism
Time of plot: World War II
Locale: Ireland
First published: 1941

> *Principal characters:*
> EMMA, an errant wife
> THE MAJOR, her husband
> FRAN, the Major's aunt
> DI and
> VIVIE, Emma's daughters
> ROBINSON, Emma's lover
> JUSTIN CAVEY, a city man visiting the small town
> QUEENIE CAVEY, Justin's sister, who is completely deaf

The Story

An unnamed, bare-legged young woman, who later turns out to be Emma, is driving rapidly south, alone, on an Irish road. She pulls into a "Do Not Park" space in order to make a long-distance call from a hotel. She has a brief conversation with an unnamed man, who is later called Robinson. He cautions her not to drive too fast in the treacherous light because they have the whole night before them, and he inquires about the Major, Emma's husband.

Robinson, having hung up rather abruptly, returns smiling slightly to the two guests in his living room: a pretty, middle-aged, deaf woman named Queenie Cavey, and her brother, Justin Cavey, who, because of the war in Europe, is spending his vacation visiting his sister in their native town. Tonight for the first time they have taken up Robinson's invitation to call at Bellevue any evening. Queenie sits by the window drinking tea and enjoying the view of the distant beeches of the old feudal domain while Justin discourses on the war, life, identity, and love, and Robinson keeps glancing at the clock. Robinson is a factory manager who arrived in town only three years ago and does not socialize with the townspeople. The local ladies, having discovered that he is a married man living apart from his wife and that he frequently disappears for the weekend, whisper that Bellevue is a Bluebeard's castle. Suddenly Justin asks: "What's love like?" Robinson utters a short, temporizing, and unnaturally loud laugh that reaches Queenie.

Justin is angered, and Robinson apologizes; to change the subject, he asks if Queenie is fond of children. "You mean why did she not marry? There was some fellow once . . ." Justin answers. Robinson takes photos of his two sons over to Queenie, who says that it is a wonder that he has no little girl. He returns for a third photo, passes his hand "as though sadly expunging something, backwards and forwards across the glass." He does not know how to tell Queenie that the child is dead.

Without transition, the Major is introduced in his orchard sixty miles away: a tall, unmilitary-looking man with a stoop, whose frown has intensified in the last months. He is called to the phone by Aunt Fran. Emma has rung up ostensibly to say goodnight. He asks if the people with whom she is going to stay will be waiting up for her. Aunt Fran protests that Emma said goodnight before she left and comments that she seemed undecided about going all afternoon.

The Major goes up to the bedroom of his daughters, Di and Vivie: The latter is a miniature of his wife. Di reports that Aunt Fran is frightened that something will happen. Vivie says that her mother likes things to happen and was whistling all the time she was packing. She suggests that her mother may not come back.

When Di is asleep, Vivie prowls through the house naked, her body covered with chalk drawings of stars and snakes. Her bouncing on the bed in her mother's room causes the chandelier in the drawing room to tinkle. Aunt Fran insists on investigating. Told to kneel and pray, Vivie objects: "In my skin?" Aunt Fran rolls Vivie up like a great sausage in the pink taffeta eiderdown.

Again with no transition, the reader is back at Bellevue, where Justin and Queenie are taking their leave. At this moment a car pulls up at the gate and its lights go off. Emma has arrived.

Robinson is very much at ease, while Emma is nervous and asks for a drink. This is her first visit to Bellevue. She says that the friends expecting her have no phone and that he will have to think of something that went wrong with her car. She remarks that she hardly knows Robinson and asks if she was wrong to come. During a visit to his garden, Emma is intrigued by the domain in the distance and its destroyed castle. When Robinson observes that they do not want to stay outdoors all night, Emma becomes frightened by his experienced delicacy on the subject of love. He has ruined her fairy tale.

On his return to the hotel, Justin writes a lengthy, accusatory letter to Robinson and adds that he prefers they should not meet again. "Justin, trembling, smote a stamp on this letter," and walks toward Bellevue to post it. "On his way back he still heard the drunken woman sobbing against the telegraph pole."

Queenie happily undresses in the dark. "This was the night she knew she would find again. On just such a summer night, once only, she had walked with a lover in the demesne . . . That had been twenty years ago, till to-night when it was now. To-night it was Robinson who, guided by Queenie down leaf tunnels, took the place on the stone seat by the lake."

Themes and Meanings

The psychological complexities of life and of social intercourse, especially the interactions between the public and the secret lives of the characters, are vividly evoked in this story. The "European war" is vaguely upsetting even in neutral Ireland. Emma wants excitement, Robinson wants to enjoy fully his time away from work, Aunt Fran feels threatened on all sides, and Justin, the sensitive thinker, sums up: "Now that there's enough death to challenge being alive we're facing it that, anyhow, we don't live."

Emma's bid for excitement disturbs everyone except Queenie. The Major is apprehensive and worried by her departure from home; her daughters think that she may not return; Aunt Fran urges Vivie to pray after rolling the child up in a protective eiderdown as if she were on fire; Justin is outraged; Robinson evidently has some scruples because he twice suggests that Emma should return to her home. Only Queenie does not react, probably because she has not heard the town gossip or the war talk and apparently does not understand the significance of Emma's car at the gate of Bellevue. Queenie has been touched by Robinson's kindness to her and lives in her own dream-world.

Critics often mention Elizabeth Bowen's sense of social comedy, but there is no comedy in this story except Aunt Fran's efforts to ward off evil. It is the somber record of humans hurting one another. The author has managed to catch her people at the moment when, through action or speech, their inner lives are exposed.

Style and Technique

"Summer Night" is considered to be one of the best of Elizabeth Bowen's scores of short stories. The style is taut: Every word counts; no detail is unimportant. Tension is created in the very first paragraph by small details. One does not know who the excited young woman is or where she is going at sunset in such a mad rush, but one feels her mood of expectancy because she glances at her watch and reads the mileage on the yellow signposts.

The reader can see the characters as they move about and talk to one another despite the economy of description of the rooms. In the main scene, an open window, easy chairs, and a fireplace mantel with a clock and silver-framed photos suffice. The author displays her extraordinary talent for the creation of atmosphere when she pictures Aunt Fran's room with its feeling of transitoriness.

It is the characters who unfold the plot, not the narrator. Elizabeth Bowen wrote that the action of a character should be unpredictable before it has been shown, inevitable when it has been shown. She does not explain what prompts the actions of her characters. Understanding this story requires the same technique demanded by an Impressionist painter: The reader must synthesize for himself. He must conjecture what has happened.

The most striking symbolism in the story is the use of light and darkness to mark the difference between public and secret lives. Emma watches the sun set on her ride to her rendezvous. It is dark when she arrives, and as soon as she enters the house she wants the top light turned off. When she and Robinson are in the garden and she is still living her fairy tale, there is the light from his flashlight, but no moon. Justin writing the angry letter in his small harsh hotel room is bothered by the hot light. It is well past twelve o'clock on this dark night when he sees the woman sobbing by the telegraph pole. Queenie goes happily to bed in the dark. Since light and darkness also have a moral connotation throughout the tale, one wonders if Queenie will be Robinson's next victim. This lack of conclusion is typical of Elizabeth Bowen's short stories.

Dorothy B. Aspinwall

THE SUMMER OF THE BEAUTIFUL WHITE HORSE

Author: William Saroyan (1908-1981)
Type of plot: Comic anecdote
Time of plot: Early twentieth century
Locale: The Central Valley of California
First published: 1940

Principal characters:
ARAM GAROGHLANIAN, a nine-year-old boy
MOURAD, Aram's cousin
UNCLE KHOSROVE, Aram and Mourad's uncle
JOHN BYRO, a neighbor

The Story

"The Summer of the Beautiful White Horse" is narrated by nine-year-old Aram Garoghlanian, a member of an Armenian community living among the lush fruit orchards and vineyards of California. One morning Aram is awakened before dawn by his older cousin Mourad, who everyone thinks is crazy. Aram is astonished to see that Mourad is sitting on a beautiful white horse. Aram has always wanted to ride a horse, but his family is too poor to afford one. Yet the Garoghlanian family is noted not only for its poverty but also for its honesty, so it is unthinkable that Mourad could have stolen the horse.

Nevertheless, Aram asks Mourad if he has stolen the horse, and Mourad invites him to jump out the window if he wants to go for a ride. Now Aram is sure that Mourad has stolen the horse, but he jumps up behind Mourad, and the two of them begin to ride out of the little town in which they live.

As they ride, Mourad begins to sing. Everybody in the family thinks that Mourad has inherited his crazy behavior from Uncle Khosrove, a huge man who can stop all discussions and arguments by bellowing at the top of his loud voice, "*It is no harm; pay no attention to it.*" Khosrove once said this when told that his house was on fire. Although Mourad is not Khosrove's son, this fact does not matter to the Armenians. They think that it is Khosrove's spirit that Mourad has inherited, not his flesh.

When they reach the open country, Aram wants to ride the horse by himself, but Mourad reminds him that it is up to the horse. Mourad can ride because, he says, "I have a way with a horse." When Aram tries to ride the horse, he cannot control the animal, and it throws him. The two boys find the runaway horse, hide him in an abandoned barn, and go home.

That afternoon, Uncle Khosrove comes to Aram's house to smoke cigarettes and drink coffee. John Byro, an Assyrian farmer, also comes by for a visit and complains that his white horse was stolen last month. Uncle Khosrove roars, "Pay no attention to it." John Byro says that he walked ten miles to get to Aram's house, causing pains in his legs, and Uncle Khosrove again bellows that he should pay no attention to it. John Byro points out that he paid sixty dollars for the horse, and Uncle Khosrove shouts, "I spit on money." John Byro stalks out of the house.

Aram runs to his cousin Mourad's house and finds him fixing the wing of a hurt bird. His cousin has a way with birds. Aram explains that John Byro visited and that he wants his horse back. He also reminds Mourad that Mourad had promised to keep the horse until Aram could learn how to ride. Mourad says that it might take a year for Aram to learn how to ride, so Aram suggests that they keep the horse for a year. Mourad roars that the horse must go back to its owner and that no Garoghlanian could ever steal. He says they will keep the horse for only another six months.

For two weeks, the boys take the horse out in the mornings for rides, and every morning Aram is thrown, but he never gives up hope that he will learn to ride like his cousin. One morning the boys meet John Byro as they are putting the horse away. Mourad explains that he will handle the situation, as he has a way with farmers. John Byro asks the name of the horse, and Mourad tells him that it is My Heart. The farmer says that he looks exactly like the horse that was stolen from him and, after inspecting the horse's teeth, says that the boy's horse could be his horse's twin. As he leaves them, he points out that, "A suspicious man would believe his eyes instead of his heart."

The next morning, the boys return the horse to John Byro's barn. The farmer's dogs do not bother them because Cousin Mourad has a way with dogs. He presses his nose against the horse's nose, and the boys leave. That afternoon John Byro rides by Aram's house in his surrey to show Aram's mother the horse that has been returned. He says that the horse is stronger and better-tempered than ever. Uncle Khosrove shouts, "Your horse has been returned. Pay no attention to it."

Themes and Meanings

In this gentle story from the collection *My Name Is Aram* (1940), William Saroyan calls into question the nature and the value of conventional morality and even of reality itself. Faced with a situation in which the first impulse of most people would be to punish the thieves, the people of this slow-moving, rural Armenian community (which undoubtedly was modeled on the author's hometown, Fresno, California) do more than recognize that boys will be boys. They also understand that the value and thereby the use of property belong to those with spirit and understanding, not only money. A horse, after all, is a living being, not a thing like the burning house which Uncle Khosrove so easily dismisses. John Byro knows who has taken his horse, and he hints not to the boys but to the boy's relatives that he knows, but he does not force the issue by demanding his horse back. To insult the honor of the

Garoghlanian family would cause much more trouble than the loss of a horse, disrupting the peace of the community. Even when Byro catches the boys red-handed, he does not condemn them. When he mentions that he believes with his heart, not with his eyes, he is telling the boys that he knows that they are basically good boys who do not intend him or the horse injury. Ironically, all turns out for the best. The daily morning exercise has improved the health of the animal, and he is better than ever, so the boys have done John Byro a favor with their mischief. No harm to it, as Uncle Khosrove would say.

The importance of spirit in Saroyan's writings is shown in the characters of Uncle Khosrove and Mourad. No one is upset because both are crazy, for craziness has its strong points. Mourad really does have a way with animals, perhaps because of his unusual approach to the world, and Uncle Khosrove really is able to calm every conflict, even those involving himself, so who is to say who is crazy or even what is crazy?

Style and Technique

Saroyan adds to the warmth and gentleness of the story of the borrowed horse by making the narrator a child, a technique which also suggests that the story might be viewed by a child as a lesson in human relations to be carried into and acted on in adulthood. Saroyan does not sugarcoat his view of childhood, however, as Aram's continuing inability to ride the horse both reminds the reader that all childhood dreams do not come true and enlists the sympathy of the reader through the technique of the self-deprecating narrator. As such a narrator is not threatening to the reader, it is easier to believe in and participate in his experiences.

Perhaps "listener" is a better term than "reader" when discussing the audience of Saroyan's stories, as the folk tradition from which his works come suggests an oral presentation which is often missing in the modern, media-dominated world. It is much easier to understand the power of a character such as Uncle Khosrove, for example, if the listener can hear the storyteller bellow his remarks, and the emotions behind the apparently off-center conversations of the people in the story can be better grasped if the teller reads the story aloud with an ear and a voice for the underlying meanings.

James Baird

SUN

Author: D. H. Lawrence (1885-1930)
Type of plot: Psychological realism
Time of plot: The 1920's, or possibly earlier
Locale: Sicily
First published: 1926

Principal characters:
JULIET, a New York matron
MAURICE, her husband, a stuffy, conventional businessman with "a grey city face"
JOHNNY, their son
MARININA, a Sicilian woman more than sixty years old, probably of Greek descent
A SICILIAN PEASANT, about thirty-five years old

The Story

Divided into five parts, D. H. Lawrence's story of initiation into rites of the healing, vital process of connection with the universe begins with the doctor's command: "Take her away, into the sun." Juliet, a middle-class young matron, leaves behind her tepid-souled husband Maurice as she travels by ocean passage with her son, a nurse, and her mother to the south, to Sicily. There, in a landscape known to ancient Greek colonists of the Italian isle, she strips off her clothes—symbolic of her former prudish conventions—to be naked in the sun. In part 1, by the roots of a cypress tree, she feels the sun warm her into renewed physical consciousness; revitalized, she invites her young son, Johnny, to play in the sun.

In part 2, mother and son make a ritual of sunbathing by the cypress tree. Marinina, a wise old Sicilian woman in whose veins probably flows the Greek blood of her ancestors, acts as priestess of the sun cult, encouraging Juliet to appreciate the beauty of her nude body. Part 3 treats Johnny's encounter with a golden-brown snake, which slithers to escape into the rocks, unharmed by Juliet. In part 4, Maurice visits his wife and son; his pale, unhealthy appearance contrasts with the sun-brown vitality of his wife and son. Ashamed to cast aside the clothes that represent his civilized constraints, he is an awkward presence, and Juliet senses an estrangement between themselves. In part 5, Juliet fantasizes of an affair with a healthy, "rather fat, very broad fellow of about thirty-five," a married Sicilian peasant, but she rejects her fantasy to have the peasant father her next child. Instead, she will—with regret—return to Maurice, who will give her a pallid child. "The fatal chain of continuity would cause it."

Themes and Meanings

Unlike most of Lawrence's fiction, "Sun" avoids the basic conflicts arising from problems of mating (or of erotic selection and fulfillment). Although Juliet and Maurice are temperamentally estranged throughout the story, the wife decides finally (although unenthusiastically) to resume her marriage and, after a time, to conceive another child by her listless husband. Attracted to the "quick animal" vitality of the Sicilian peasant, she nevertheless rejects this man as a lover, following the dictates of prudence and convention rather than the impulses of her emotions. Head wins over heart, and the narrative line of this story deviates—in a pattern not typical for Lawrence—from one that has an end result in erotic fulfillment. Instead, the pattern resembles that of such late fiction by the author as "The Woman Who Rode Away" and *St. Mawr* (1925), in which the female protagonist similarly discovers spirituality by merging her ego with the universe, thus attaining a substitute gratification for physical passion.

In this story, the substitute "lover" for Juliet is the animating force of the sun. This force provides more than the healthful values of sunbathing or physical culture: It provides a close contact with blood consciousness. Warmed by the sun, Juliet is restored in her blood to a consciousness of her essential nature, so that her body is in harmony with external Nature.

Lawrence contrasts the physical and emotional well-being of Juliet and her child, devotees of the sun, with the pallor of Maurice. With his "grey city face," Maurice represents effete civilization, the brain instead of the instincts, a man who smells "of the world and all its fetters and its mongrel cowardice." Compared to the Sicilian peasant, healthy in his vitality and "quick energy," Maurice is "like a worm that the sun has never seen." Unlike the snake, which Juliet and the boy observe with fascination but do not disturb, Maurice is wormlike in his fear of the sun.

To Lawrence, the golden-brown snake, a fertility (indeed, phallic) symbol, is perfectly at home in both worlds—that of the sun and that of the underworld (the dark or blood consciousness). In his poem "Snake," Lawrence develops in much greater complexity his concept of the snake as a "lord of life," symbol of the deepest instinctual and procreative powers. In this episode of the story, the snake simply represents the unity of all creatures, unself-conscious in their natural roles. The snake is "part of the place, along with her and the child." By accepting the "place," Juliet also becomes part of the whole design of nature, a "worshiper" not only of the sun but also of the harmonizing force that unites mankind with the source of vitality in all life— the anima.

Style and Technique

To express the theme of revitalization, Lawrence uses symbols for a rite of initiation into the "mysteries" of the anima. His major symbols are the golden-brown snake, symbol of the unconscious that can return to the rocks, the "underworld" of blood instinct, after sunning itself in the external (conscious) world; the orange and the lemons, symbols of the vitality of the sun; and, above all, the cypress tree. The cypress was sacred to the ancient Greeks who once colonized Sicily and whose descendants, such as Marinina, still carry their racial traits. For example, in the sanctuary of Aesculapius at Kos, Greeks of the classic age were forbidden to cut down cypress trees. Once sacred both to Osiris, the "Dying and Reviving God," and to Dionysus, worshiped for his vitality and ecstatic excesses, the cypress is also significant in this story as a link between the sun and the earth. Being fully aware of the classical-mythological attributes of the tree, Lawrence symbolizes the cypress as "a low, silvery candle whose huge flame was darkness against light: earth sending up her proud tongue of gloom." Like the snake, at home in both the underworld and the sun-heated rocks, the cypress is treated as though it were a "candle," kin to the sun, but whose flame is "darkness" from the underworld (subconsciousness). Similarly, in the great poem "Bavarian Gentians," Lawrence describes a dark-blue flower with "torch-like" points that serve as a connection between the consciousness and the subconsciousness, that serve to illuminate the rites of the "marriage of the living dark."

Through means of ritual—suggested, not directly stated, by the writer— Juliet first takes off her clothes as she sits by the cypress tree, as though she were an acolyte to the god. When her child has similarly been initiated into the sacred rites, he also responds to the tree. By that sacred place, mother and son are made whole, and "she herself, her conscious self, was secondary, a secondary person, almost an onlooker." Ruled by the sun, she is re-animated; the true Juliet is "this dark flow from her deep body to the sun."

Leslie B. Mittleman

THE SUPPER AT ELSINORE

Author: Isak Dinesen (Baroness Karen Blixen-Finecke, 1885-1962)
Type of plot: Gothic tale
Time of plot: 1841
Locale: Elsinore and Copenhagen, Denmark
First published: 1934

> *Principal characters:*
> MADAME BAEK, an old servant of the De Coninck family
> FERNANDE (FANNY) DE CONINCK, the eldest daughter of the
> family
> ELIZA DE CONINCK, her sister
> MORTEN DE CONINCK, their handsome, fashionable brother, a
> privateer

The Story

Madame Baek, who lives as the caretaker in the now empty De Coninck house in Elsinore, reflects on her memories. She has spent most of her life with the De Coninck children and senses the doom which hangs over the breed.

For the two sisters, this doom takes the form of restless dispositions, which causes them to be bitterly unhappy despite their great beauty, family wealth, and social success. As young ladies growing up in the family home, they were the leading lights of Elsinore society, surrounded by admiring friends and beaux and much in demand at parties, balls, and outings.

Yet even as young women they were obsessed with the dark side of life and gave themselves up to bitter tears in the privacy of their own rooms, dwelling on the sham and hypocrisy about them. At the time of the story, they are "old maids" of fifty-two and fifty-three, for they have found it impossible to accept any of their numerous suitors.

As a young man, their brother, Morten, exceptionally handsome and elegant, was pursued by every girl in Elsinore. He became engaged to Adrienne Rosenstand, a friend of his sisters, but then he went to serve in the Napoleonic Wars. As the commander of a privateer, he engaged in many thrilling encounters with British ships, which earned for him public adulation. When privateering was finally prohibited, everyone thought that he would marry his sweetheart and settle down. On the morning of the wedding, however, the bridegroom was discovered missing, and he has never again been seen in Elsinore.

In the ensuing years, however, strange rumors of him drifted back to Denmark. It was rumored that he was a pirate, that he had distinguished himself in wars in America, that he had become a wealthy landowner in the Antilles.

Eventually, the townspeople came to think of him as a legendary figure, much like Bluebeard or Sindbad the Sailor.

Fanny and Eliza, initially overcome with grief and shame at the sudden disappearance of Morten, inflated the rumors into portents of great honors that would befall him. As years have passed, however, they have come to accept the worst. Someone has seen Morten in New Orleans, poor and sick, and the last news that the sisters hear is that he has been hanged. As for Adrienne, she waited fifteen years for Morten to return, then finally married another. At her wedding, the two De Coninck sisters appeared for the last time as the belles of Elsinore.

Now, in the present time of the story, Madame Baek begins to decline, with fainting, shrieking, and deep, silent spells. Her friends believe that she is near death, but she rallies and sets off for Copenhagen, where the two sisters now live. She arrives on the day of Fanny's birthday and waits in the kitchen. Upstairs, the two maiden ladies entertain their guests, talking happily of the past, on which they love to dwell. They also enjoy talking about their married friends with pity and contempt, as those whose fates are sealed. Eliza, particularly, is as lovely as ever, and wears an air of expectation, as if extraordinary things might still happen.

When the guests leave, the sisters meet with Madame Baek. She tells them that Morten has returned to Elsinore, that he "walks in the house." She has seen him seven times. The sisters journey to Elsinore and assemble in the room in which they shared so many secret suppers with their brother in the old days. He appears and takes the chair between them, as he had in the past. His noble forehead bears a strange likeness to a skull, but he is quiet and considerate, as always. He soon reveals that he comes from Hell.

Morten questions his sisters about their lives, then tells them of his five wives. What he loved best, however, was his life as a pirate on the finest schooner that ever flew over the Atlantic, the loveliest thing he ever saw. He was sent to buy the schooner by a wealthy old shipowner, but fell in love with it and kept the ship himself. That was the beginning of his downfall. He named the ship *La Belle Eliza*. Eliza now admits that she knew of the ship, having heard of it from a merchant captain of her father. She has guarded the secret from all the world, and it has kept her happy throughout the years.

Fanny asks Morten to tell her one or two things he knows that they do not. He tells them that he has learned one thing, "that you cannot eat your cake and have it." Morten was eventually hanged for stealing the ship. Before he died, he asked the priest for one more minute of life, to "think, with the halter around my neck, for one minute of *La Belle Eliza*."

Fanny, exhausted from the strain, turns on Morten and bitterly complains that he has at least lived. She is always cold, she says, so cold that her warming pans in bed do not warm her. When the clock strikes midnight, Fanny stretches out her arms to Morten, but at the last strike he is gone. Eliza, in great pain or joy, repeats Morten's last wish on earth, "to think, with the halter around my neck, for one minute of *La Belle Eliza*."

Themes and Meanings

Isak Dinesen set her gothic tales in the past because, as she said, "Here, no temptation for me to fall back into realism, nor for my readers to look for it." She explained that the word "gothic" in the title of the collection in which this tale appears refers to her affinity with the Romantic age of Lord Byron. The erotic heroes and demonic daredevils of Romantic literature gave Dinesen her earliest notions of emotional freedom, the theme which is embodied in the three main characters.

Morten, although of an aristocratic family and hero to all Elsinore, abandons his fiancée and his place in society for the wandering life of a pirate. When he loses his heart to a ship, the essence of his heart's desire, he seals his doom by stealing it. In this way, he lives out an unconventional, heroic morality that is based on the freedom to incur risk and take the consequences. The individual is free to fulfill his destiny, to become himself. Although this act eventually leads to his hanging, he has lived his dream. About to be hanged, he is not repentant but wishes only for another moment of life to think of *La Belle Eliza*.

Eliza has also lived out her Romantic destiny. Although she has remained an "old maid," her beauty and grace are realized by her namesake, *La Belle Eliza*. When she thinks about the ship, imagining it with its full white sails billowing, "She looked once more like a girl, and the white streamers of her cap were no longer the finery of an old lady, but the attire of a chaste, flaming bride."

Although Fanny seems to be the only one unfulfilled at the end of the story, she has nevertheless kept the faith by refusing to tread the path of mediocrity. When Morten must finally return to Hell, she begs him to take her with him. He cannot, but there is a strong suggestion that she will soon join him in the nether world, which is her own Romantic destiny.

Style and Technique

The Romantic mode has left its mark on the style of Dinesen's story no less than on its theme. The two sisters are described in hyperbolic terms, as befits Romantic heroines. Not only are they the "heart and soul of all the gayety in town," but also "When they entered its ballrooms, the ceilings of sedate old merchants' houses seemed to lift a little, and the walls to spring out in luminous Ionian columns, bound with vine." Morten, a match for his sisters in all things, is "the observed of all observers, the glass of fashion and the mold of form."

Even nature conspires to set the stage for the return of the hero. It is not until the unusually severe winter of 1841, when the "flatness and whiteness of the sea was very strange, like the breath of death over the world," that Madame Baek sees Morten returned from the dead.

The first part of the story, which recounts the early years of the three De Coninck siblings, is told primarily from the point of view of Madame Baek. Her speculations on their strange behavior serve to heighten the air of mystery that surrounds them. After she has unburdened herself of her secret, however, "A weight and a fullness had been taken from her, and her importance had gone with it."

Her importance is gone structurally, as well, for now the point of view changes, and a new omniscient narrator relates the reunion of the three siblings. While the reader has glimpses of the inner thoughts of both Fanny and Eliza, Morten is revealed solely through his dialogue and the reactions of his sisters. All three main characters are embodiments of Romantic ideals rather than the fully realized, rounded characters that are typical of more realistic fiction. Dinesen has resurrected the Romantic short story and given it philosophical overtones.

Sheila Golburgh Johnson

THE SUPREMACY OF THE HUNZA

Author: Joanne Greenberg (1932-   )
Type of plot: Social realism
Time of plot: The 1970's
Locale: A Western American mountain region
First published: 1971

>   *Principal characters:*
>   TED MARGOLIN, a professor of anthropology
>   REGINA MARGOLIN, his wife
>   LARRY WESTERCAMP, a civic activist and conservationist

The Story

Ted Margolin, an anthropologist and university professor, commutes to work from his home in the mountains because he enjoys the unspoiled surroundings. His serenity is suddenly broken by the installation of ninety-foot power lines across the countryside. He protests through his lawyer, to no avail. Then he is invited to a citizens' protest meeting, where Larry Westercamp, an avid campaigner for citizens' rights, tries to enlist his active support in helping to fight the installation of the lines. On the way home, Westercamp fumes to Margolin about how he is especially angry at having been made the butt of a humorous television newsclip in which he was seeding a stream with trout while the state's governor was fishing downstream.

During the next weeks, Margolin is besieged with telephone calls and mail seeking his support for various causes. He becomes irritated with what he sees as an infringement on his personal life. When he speaks to Westercamp again, he is curt and evasive about his unwillingness to become personally involved in the protest over the power lines. In the course of the conversation, Westercamp explains to Margolin how civilization has ruined the harmony enjoyed by primitive societies such as the Chontal Indians. Margolin, with superior knowledge of ancient settlements, counters Westercamp's Utopian vision with hard facts about the primitive life-style that Westercamp idolizes.

The power lines continue to disturb Margolin, but he goes on with life during the fall; he learns later from Westercamp that the protest movement is almost dead. In December, Margolin goes to the state hospital to help therapists there on three cases involving Indians. He leaves home believing that his knowledge of ancient cultures may be of some help; he returns sobered, realizing that the Indians he sees are far removed from their culture and have become victims of "civilization" in its worst form. Almost immediately upon returning, he calls Westercamp, who is now trying to solicit support to stop water pollution. On this occasion, Westercamp laments modern society by comparing it to the civilization of the Hunza, a Tibetan group. Though Margolin knows that this vision is flawed, he says nothing to change Westercamp's opinion. The conversation disturbs him so that, unable to sleep all night, he rises early in the morning and begins hurling a primitive spear, which he keeps to show his classes, to release the tension he has built up inside himself.

Themes and Meanings

Greenberg's main concern in "The Supremacy of the Hunza" is with the encroachment of civilization and technology on human society. The central question raised by the events of the story is: What role can, or should, an individual take to preserve a way of life about which he or she feels strongly? The simplicity of the question belies the complexity of the answers suggested by this story. The central characters, Margolin and Westercamp, present two contrasting attitudes toward the question.

Westercamp is an idealist, but his idealism appears at first to be founded in a kind of blind naïveté. He has only a superficial knowledge of more primitive civilizations. They exist for him not as real communities but as symbols of a pristine form of human society which has become overwhelmed by the march of progress. He comes alive when he is working for a cause; he wastes away when he cannot generate enthusiasm for his ideals. His vision is Utopian, and he is willing to work to bring about his ideal society in the real world.

Margolin perceives Westercamp's activism as folly. Unlike his neighbor, Margolin takes only those steps that he believes will not interfere with his own routines: He calls his lawyer and he calls the power company. These are clearly civilized responses. On the other hand, Margolin has what he believes is a firmer understanding of societies such as the Chontal and the Hunza. His anthropological studies have provided him some insight, it is true: He knows, for example, that such societies were racked with disease, that hard work caused the population to age prematurely, that living in these communities often amounted to no more than grubbing out a day-to-day existence against the harsh elements of nature.

His experience with the young Indian in the mental hospital shocks Margolin into realizing that the heritage of these primitive societies is in fact disappearing; civilization has indeed destroyed what was good in these peoples as it alleviated their physical deprivations. Further, he realizes that his own knowledge of such societies is also defective. His wife's observation that he does not "know primitive man any more than" Westercamp does hits home. As a result, as he comes to understand the commitment that drives Westercamp to continue his activism in the face of defeat and disappointment, he realizes that such beliefs are necessary if modern man is not to be overwhelmed by his own inventions.

Style and Technique

The narrative style of this story belies the complexity of its construction. Greenberg balances major scenes carefully, pivoting them on the central experience of Margolin's visit to the state mental hospital. The story opens with Margolin's measured protest against the construction of the towers. After an encounter with Westercamp, he feels annoyed at what he perceives as an intrusion into his private life by someone trying to get him involved in a movement for social change. His frustration is exhibited in his curt response to Westercamp's description of the Chontal society. When he has chastised his neighbor, he feels smug and satisfied.

Margolin's interview with the Indian at the mental hospital shows him the hubris that lies at the center of his own personality. That scene is followed quickly by another encounter with Westercamp, one in which Margolin refrains from criticizing his neighbor's mistaken views of the Hunza. Feeling upset and irritable, he ends up making a primitive response to release his frustrations: He begins hurling the spear he had hitherto used only for classroom demonstrations, making this symbolic gesture as a protest against the towers.

The balanced structure is supported by carefully crafted descriptions of scenery that focus on the beauty of the countryside and the imposing, ugly towers. Greenberg portrays the towers as animate objects that have invaded the countryside. They symbolize all that is wrong with the encroachment of technology and civilization upon nature. Further, since the point of view is limited to Margolin's vision, the reader is led only gradually to realize that there is much merit in Westercamp's view and that the story is really about Margolin's conversion to appreciate the supremacy, in a sense, of communities such as that of the Hunza.

Laurence W. Mazzeno

SUR
(A Summary Report of the *Yelcho* Expedition to the Antarctic, 1909-1910)

Author: Ursula K. Le Guin (1929-   )
Type of plot: Adventure
Time of plot: 1909-1910
Locale: Antarctica
First published: 1982

> *Principal characters:*
> THE NARRATOR, the unnamed "Supreme Inca" of the
>   expedition
> JUANA, the narrator's cousin
> ZOE, the one with a gift for naming
> BERTA, a sculptor, "La Araucana" of the expedition
> EVA, with Berta the chief architect and builder of Sudamérica
>   del Sur
> TERESA, the mother of Rosa del Sur
> CARLOTA, "The Third Mate" of the expedition
> LUIS PARDO, the captain of the *Yelcho*

The Story

Despite its apparent objectivity as "A summary report of the *Yelcho* expedition to the Antarctic, 1909-1910," the story "Sur" is a surprising piece of gently subversive fiction, narrated by an unnamed woman some years after the events of the story take place. The surprise and the subversion result from the story's feminist stance and from the attendant replacement of the value of "achievement" by "what is large."

In the early paragraphs of the story, its feminism remains latent, hinted at only by the items with which the report will be kept—children's clothes and toys, wedding shoes and finneskos—and by the atypical purpose stated for the expedition: "[T]o go, to see—no more, no less." Further, the trouble encountered in gathering an expeditionary force hints at the narrator's dissatisfaction with what women are or have been made to be, with the stark limits imposed on the average woman by her socially determined role: "So few of those we asked even knew what we were talking about—so many thought we were mad, or wicked, or both!" The following sentences, with their references to parents, husbands, children, and the responsibilities to family that are traditionally a woman's concern, prepare the reader for the first explicit indication that this is to be an all-female expedition: the list of its participants. The knowledge of this expedition's special character colors the rather ordinary story of travel and exploration that follows.

The report of the expedition itself proceeds naturally enough with accounts of the voyage to Antarctica on the Chilean vessel *Yelcho*, the choice of a site for base camp and the building of "Sudamérica del Sur," the sledge-journey to the South Pole, and the return to base and, finally, to civilization. Each part of this report, however, reveals in various ways its feminist character. During the initial voyage, for example, the *Yelcho* is nicknamed *la vaca valiente* (the valiant cow) in memory of the "far more dangerous cows" of Juana's past, and the members of the expedition find themselves "oppressed at times by the kindly but officious protectiveness of the captain and his officers." Such details are embedded in expected surroundings: discussion of the best route for the voyage, celebration of the first iceberg sighted, descriptions of the Ross Sea and the Great Ice Barrier.

Male superiority is subverted in the report's next stage by contrasting the slovenly housekeeping found at Captain Robert Falcon Scott's base hut with the home built by the women of the *Yelcho* Expedition. Having described the surroundings of Scott's camp as "a kind of graveyard," the narrator details the dirtiness and "mean disorder" of the hut's interior: an open tin of tea, empty meat tins, spilled biscuits, even "a lot of dog turds" on the floor. The narrator's excuse for the men who have left this mess is scathing: "[H]ouse-keeping, the art of the infinite, is no game for amateurs." By contrast, the home created by the women provides "as much warmth and privacy as one could reasonably expect," then becomes at the hands of Berta and Eva "a marvel of comfort and convenience," and is the setting, finally, of the "beautiful forms" Berta sculpts from the ice.

After the *Yelcho* steams north, leaving the women "to ice, and silence, and the Pole," the southern journey is a model of good planning, good practice, and amazing perseverance. The narrator meticulously details the establishment of supply depots, the superiority of the food they carry, the organization of the southern party, the pain, weariness, even craziness of the terrible trek to the Pole. Even in this account, so fact-filled, the narrator's condescension toward men is clearly revealed: "I was glad . . . that we had left no sign there, for some man longing to be first might come some day, and find it, and know then what a fool he had been, and break his heart."

The story draws swiftly to its close with the return to base and the laconic report of the return to civilization: "We came back safe." Two feminist moments color these final paragraphs. The matter of Teresa's pregnancy raises the central biological fact of femininity—menstruation and childbearing. The narrator's response of "anger—rage—fury" is directed first at Teresa for apparently having concealed her pregnancy, but the emotions are quickly directed away from Teresa to the society that has kept her ignorant of what it means to be a woman. In the wider context of the story's feminism, the anger is both self-directed and competitive: The narrator's earlier frustration with female ignorance becomes anger at an unavoidable fact of normal female life, and her anger at Teresa is also recognition that the party's womanhood could have caused the expedition to fail. The story ends, though, on a lighter note, ostensibly added as a postscript years later, but still echoing the narrator's condescension toward other explorers; her grandchildren, she says, may enjoy the secret of her expedition, "but they must not let Mr. [Roald] Amundsen know! He would be terribly embarrassed and disappointed."

Themes and Meanings

The subversion of male superiority that colors the story's progress is balanced by its aim of personal fulfillment and freedom and by its positive feminine acts, revealed in the expedition's command structure, in its making of a home, and in its emphasis on forethought over prowess.

The narrator's natural human curiosity—the sort that might begin any story of travel—provides the first impetus to the *Yelcho* Expedition; she is drawn to "that strange continent, last Thule of the South, which lies on our maps and globes like a white cloud, a void, fringed here and there with scraps of coastline, dubious capes, supposititious islands, headlands that may or may not be there: Antarctica." The expedition's real justification, however, seems more specifically personal and feminine, the desire to break out of biologically and socially imposed limitations; this sense is revealed in the narrator's grief for "those we had to leave behind to a life without danger, without uncertainty, without hope." The freedom the women find on the ice of Antarctica is a freedom achieved by shedding familiar securities and points of reference, a freedom that leaves them with only themselves: "It was overcast, white weather, without shadows and without visible horizon or any feature to break the level; there was nothing to see at all. We had come to that white place on the map, that void, and there we flew and sang like sparrows."

The women's establishment of a command structure that is never used, their delight in making a home in the ice, and their patient preparation for the trek to the South Pole are possible because of a fundamental difference between their expedition and those of male explorers. Their goal contrasts with the "scientific accomplishments" of earlier and later explorers, with their desire "to be first." This contrast is explained partly by the narrator's sense that as women the members of the *Yelcho* Expedition are "by birth and upbringing, unequivocally and irrevocably, all crew" rather than officers, and it is provided with a more explicit rationale as the narrator comments on the ugly traces left by earlier expeditions. She muses that "the backside of heroism is often rather sad; women and servants know that. They know also that the heroism may be no less real for that. But achievement is smaller than men think. What is large is the sky, the earth, the sea, the soul." If her final words, written years later, contain any regret, she hides it well: "We left no footprints, even."

Style and Technique

In her introduction to *The Left Hand of Darkness* (1969), Ursula K. Le Guin wrote, "A novelist's business is lying." She noted further that novelists may "use all kinds of facts to support their tissue of lies" and that "this weight of verifiable place-event-phenomenon-behavior makes the reader forget that he is reading a pure invention. . . ." Her story "Sur" foregrounds this "peculiar and devious" practice, for in it the factive and the fictive, explorer's log and wanderer's yarn, strive for dominance. The fictive wins.

The level, reportorial tone of "Sur" is established partly by the narrator's distance in time from the events she reports—memory, like reflections in a glass, levels what would in fact be three-dimensionally alive—but more concretely by the selection and organization of details in the story told. The account of the origin of the expedition, for example, carefully outlines the sequence of the narrator's growing interest in Antarctica, naming names, indicating dates, supplying the reader with the sources of her knowledge. Yet these are also the sources of her desire, and the reader cannot miss the vocabulary of emotion that laces the list of facts ("my imagination was caught," "I . . . followed with excitement," "filled me with longing"), the telling hyperbole of "reread a thousand times," and the romantic inversion of the world in the phrase "last Thule of the South," appropriating centuries of geographic lore in a single act of the making mind.

Careful indications of position, records of temperatures and other weather conditions, meticulous accounting for distances traveled, even the qualification of the accuracy of such measurements with a note that "our equipment was minimal"—these details enforce the illusion of factuality that the story seeks to create, yet even a quasi-scientific explanation may in this narrator's hands become the occasion for metaphor. Her explanation for "footprints standing some inches above the ice," for example, segues into a logically unnecessary simile, then checks the aesthetic impulse with a neutral remark:

In some conditions of weather the snow compressed under one's weight remains when the surrounding soft snow melts or is scoured away by the wind; and so these reversed footprints had been left standing all these months, like rows of cobbler's lasts—a queer sight.

The narrator is quite conscious of the fictive role she and her companions play in Antarctica and later at home. Zoe, with her "gift for naming," for example, begins to fill "that white place on the map" with names that the women recognize as having effective factual status only for them. The "invisible cattle, transparent cattle pastured on the spindrift snow" are recognized, too, as products of minds "a little crazy," but this is the insanity of art, more formally realized in later years as the narrator's children hear stories of "a great, white, mad dog named Blizzard . . . and other fairy tales."

Like Berta's ice sculptures the narrator's experience of Antarctica can be preserved only in stories. Because its truth—more human, at last, than strictly feminine—cannot be truly said in words, it cannot be brought north: "That," says the narrator with sadness, perhaps, but also with a sense of freedom, "is the penalty for carving in water."

Jonathan A. Glenn

SWEAT

Author: Zora Neale Hurston (1903-1960)
Type of plot: Psychological realism
Time of plot: The 1920's
Locale: A village in Florida
First published: 1926

> *Principal characters:*
> DELIA JONES, a black washwoman
> SYKES JONES, her husband of fifteen years
> BERTHA, his mistress

The Story

The story covers several weeks in the lives of Delia Jones and her husband, Sykes, from a Sunday evening to a Monday morning, with a brief flashback to the course of their relationship during fifteen years of marriage. The action begins at a crucial moment that is to lead to Sykes's death and Delia's liberation. For the first time, Delia stands up to Sykes's abuse. She has just returned from church and has begun her week's work as a laundry woman for white people, sorting out the clothes that she collected the day before. Sykes, who has spent the day with his mistress, Bertha, lays a bullwhip across her shoulders to frighten her. She is deathly afraid of snakes. He also kicks her clothes around, grinding dirt into them, and complains not only about her working for white people but also about her hypocrisy, for she goes to church and receives the Sacrament but still works on Sunday. This irreligious, adulterous man, making such accusations and physically and psychologically abusing her, suddenly causes her to alter the relationship: She drops the meek posture of the subservient wife, takes up a heavy frying pan as a weapon, and threatens Sykes with retaliation. She declares herself willing to defend not only her person but also the house that she has paid for with "sweat" for the past fifteen years. She refuses to let him drive her out to make room for his new woman.

The following Saturday, Delia takes the laundered clothes to town. During this second segment of the story, Hurston chooses to present her heroine's situation from the town's point of view, as an assortment of men gossip on the porch of a general store. The men sympathize with Delia, recognize the abuse she has suffered from Sykes, and condemn Bertha as the dregs of a neighboring town, the only woman during the past fifteen years who would succumb to Sykes's advances. Sykes and Bertha show up at the store to buy groceries. Sykes flouts his importance before the townspeople and before Delia, who is passing by on her way home. Such public indignity heightens the conflict.

The third and final section of the story takes place several weeks later. No longer able to intimidate Delia with physical abuse, he plays upon her fears by bringing home a real snake, a six-foot rattler in a soap box. After living with the snake for two or three days, Delia's Christian patience reaches the breaking point: She declares that she is moving her church membership to another town, because she does not want to take the Sacrament with her husband, and that she hates this man she married. The next day being Sunday, she goes off to church and does not come home until evening. As she passes the soap box and notices that the snake is gone, she imagines that perhaps Sykes has taken seriously her threat to seek justice from the white community. As she prepares to begin the week's washing, however, she discovers, to her shock, the rattlesnake at the bottom of the clothes hamper. Frightened almost senseless, she runs out to the barn to spend the night. When Sykes returns later in the evening, he finds no matches left to light the candles. As he stumbles about drunk in the dark, the rattlesnake bites him. Hearing his cries, Delia ventures out from the barn and watches through a window as Sykes dies from poison. Unable to endure the final moments before death, and unable or unwilling to help him, she goes to sit under a chinaberry tree to imagine the look on Sykes's face.

Themes and Meanings

Hurston's story derives from the black folk tradition that she first came to know in her hometown, the black community of Eatonville, Florida. Christianity was a part of that tradition; her father was a Baptist preacher. Even after her years of study under anthropologist Franz Boas, her fieldwork as an anthropologist collecting folklore among her own people and in the Caribbean, and the consequent influence of Voodoo on her thinking, Christianity remained a living part of Hurston's work. She continued to prefer biblical settings and stories; a character in *Jonah's Gourd Vine* (1934) calls the Bible a "hoodoo" book. "Sweat," one of her earliest stories, records her thinking before the Voodoo period. It assumes a Christian cosmology, as yet unmodified by Voodoo traditions, but adapted to the perceptions of a folk culture— that of poor blacks in the American South.

Hurston's theme of extreme love and extreme hate within the black family acquires, in the story "Sweat," the magnitude of a cosmic struggle between good and evil, God and Satan. The central principle, which almost has the force of a moral, Hurston pronounces through the voice of Delia: "Whatever goes over the Devil's back, is got to come under his belly. Sometime or ruther, Sykes, like everybody else, is gointer reap his sowing." Faith in a Providence that will reward good and punish evil is a refuge of people who on earth know nothing but suffering.

Within the religious scheme of this fictional world, Sykes is the representative of those who defy the Christian God. He rebels against the principles of love and compassion, and, hence, his soul becomes hardened. A proud, vengeful creature, he is already damned. He cannot see goodness in others and elevates himself to the role of god. In an ironic assertion of his own powers, he claims, "Ah aint got tuh do nothin' but die," disclaiming responsibility to anyone on earth. He brags to Bertha that "this was his town and she could have it if she wanted it."

The reader knows where his sympathies ought to lie. Sykes is clearly wrong throughout the story, and Delia is right in living out the principles of Christian love, tolerance, and humility. In addition, she has those virtues closely associated with Christian principles in America, hard work and "sweat." She earns her way in life. The ending bears out her prediction of poetic justice. God does not forget the faithful.

Nevertheless, the ending of the story struggles against a strictly Christian reading. The pattern does not go so far as to challenge the Christian order. The man who plays with snakes and defies Christian ethics is not a hero, a conjure man of another cultural order, but a villain. Yet Hurston does not allow the Christian scheme to dictate the psychology of her heroine. She has Delia at last defy her husband, call him the same names that he has called her, and in the end disclaim any responsibility for him. When he is dying of poison, she feels compassion but refuses to aid him. In the sense that Sykes is pure evil, one can see this as consistent with Christian eschatology, but in the sense that he is a man, one may read it as human, female vengeance. She not only does nothing to help him but also wills his destruction. She must live with the knowledge, too, that he sees her and knows that she lets him die.

"Sweat" is thus one of many literary accounts of Christianity's impact on the black psyche and its modifications under the stress of psychological pressures. It is also, perhaps, an indirect comment on the economic consequences of a racially split society. What is more noticeable, however, is the absence of white society. The story pits black against black. Whites are far in the background. They appear only once, in Delia's threat to complain to them if Sykes ever beats her again. In this respect, Hurston anticipates by forty years the fiction of Alice Walker and Toni Morrison: She affirms black culture by ignoring or subordinating the white; she allows the culture to speak for itself; she subordinates the male to the female consciousness. This last characteristic in itself dictates a modification of the Christian tradition.

Style and Technique

Though written in a Southern folk idiom, "Sweat" has none of the humor of Hurston's predecessor in the genre, Charles Waddell Chestnutt. Her message is somber from beginning to end. What the story offers is a naturalistic slice of life combined with some heavy Christian symbolism. The most potent symbol is the rattlesnake, known for its ubiquitous ("ventriloquist") death rattle. Having already introduced evil into their house, Sykes next brings the snake itself. Delia's known fear of worms and snakes and Sykes's vain belief that he possesses a magic power over them are both symbolic attitudes toward evil. When he releases the snake from the box, gives it free rein in the house in order to drive out Delia (goodness), he only prepares the scene for his own destruction. Worked into this major symbol is that of the matches, Sykes's practice of using up all the matches (light) without ever replacing them. When Delia returns home there is only one left, but it is enough. When he returns there is no light for him to see the rattlesnake. In total darkness "Satan" kills him.

Other symbols complete the Christian scenario. The experience of the Passion—suffering and triumph over it—is central. Delia's whole life is the Passion experience, yet Hurston does not use the symbolism explicitly until Delia goes through the agonizing months of Sykes's affair with Bertha: It is then that "Delia's work-worn knees crawled over the earth in Gethsemane and up the rocks of Calvary. . . ." On returning home from church on the fatal Sunday evening, Delia sings of the River Jordan that *"Chills de body, not de soul."* The sacramental experience has begun her resurrection. (Another "cold river," the poison of the snake, destroys both Sykes's body and his soul.) Delia's actual resurrection, however, comes in another symbolic place, the barn behind the house, clearly a reminder of the stable. There she ends her suffering and momentarily achieves peace.

Even the structure of the story at first seems to insist on a Christian salvation. It begins on a Sunday and the final act begins on another Sunday. Delia's symbolic rebirth in the barn comes before Sykes's death on Sunday evening. In fact, however, consistent with the psychological turn already noted, Hurston adds a twist to the symbolism in the final paragraph, for the real ending to the story comes not on Sunday, but on Monday morning. Life is not over for Delia. She must bear up under the knowledge that Sykes still had hope. The sun has revealed to Sykes signs that Delia had returned home and that she was close by watching. Though it seems clear that Delia is helpless—the doctors are too far away, and her fear of snakes keeps her from entering the house—the torment of imagining Sykes's plaintive and accusing eye in the final moment of life gives the closing statement of the story the psychological horror of the macabre rather than the peace of resurrection. On that symbolic Monday morning, the agony of the Passion continues. The Passion is not simply a biblical story; it is human experience.

Thomas Banks

THE SWIMMER

Author: John Cheever (1912-1982)
Type of plot: Psychological realism
Time of plot: The early 1960's
Locale: Bullet Park, a fictional suburb of New York
First published: 1964

> *Principal character:*
> NED MERRILL, a youthful-looking man of middle age

The Story

In "The Swimmer," Cheever experiments with narrative structure and chronology. Apparently realistic on the surface, the story is eventually revealed as reflecting the disordered mind of the protagonist. When the story opens, Ned Merrill is youthful, strong, and athletic; by the end, he is a weak and broken man, unable to understand the wreckage of his life. Proud of his wife and his four beautiful daughters, Merrill at first seems the picture of health and contentment. This initial image quickly disintegrates as Merrill weakens and is confronted with his loss. Yet the action of the story takes only a few hours.

One summer day, Ned decides to swim a series of pools between the home of his friends the Westerhazys and his own home eight miles away. He imagines the string of pools as a river, a "quasi-subterranean stream that curved across the county," and names it Lucinda, after his wife. He begins his peculiar trip with great gusto, imagining himself "a legendary figure" or "a pilgrim, an explorer, a man with a destiny." As Ned begins his journey, Cheever establishes the social context of a typical Sunday in Bullet Park. People go to church, it seems, but once there they commiserate with one another about their hangovers. Once home from church, most of their activities are athletic: golf, swimming, tennis, and perhaps some bird-watching at the wildlife preserve. Ned's desire to swim across the country is presented as the quintessence of the athletic optimism that characterizes his whole community. Yet the ubiquitous hangovers undercut the otherwise rosy picture of life in this beautiful suburb. Similarly, Ned's apparent health and vigor mask the reality of his psychological distress.

At first Ned's trip goes well. He swims unnoticed through people's backyards, or is welcomed by surprised friends who are enjoying a Sunday swim, or entertaining at poolside. At several houses he accepts drinks. By the time he has swum half the Lucinda, he is tired but satisfied. Yet the second half of the journey goes less well. He is caught in a sudden storm, which turns the weather cooler and creates an autumnal feeling. He is disappointed when a friend's pool is empty of water, the bathhouse locked, and a "For Sale" sign nailed to a tree. When he has to cross a highway, he is embarrassed to be seen in his swim trunks by passing motorists, some of whom throw beer cans or jeer at him. He considers returning to the Westerhazys, but finds rather to his surprise that he feels unable to return. Somehow it is impossible to go back.

The worst part of the trip is yet to come. First, he must swim with distaste through the crowded, unclean public pool. Then, as he travels from yard to yard, old friends and neighbors make strange remarks to him. One couple, who happen to believe in nude sunbathing, offer sympathy for his recent misfortunes—yet Ned has no sense of what they mean. In two places, rude comments are made about his financial situation. His former mistress, who cried when he broke off their affair, now scorns him. He even perceives rebuff at the hands of a bartender working at one of the parties through which he passes. At the last few pools he can barely swim and must stop repeatedly, holding on to the side. When he reaches his own house, he finds the garage doors rusty, the rain gutters loose, and the door locked. Looking in the windows, he sees that the house is empty.

Themes and Meanings

"The Swimmer" has as its primary theme the power of the mind to deny unpleasant truths, or, to put it more positively, the determination of the ego to preserve itself in the face of events which might erode or obliterate one's self-confidence. In order to grasp this theme, the reader must figure out roughly what has happened to Ned and how he has responded to those events.

The recent events of Ned Merrill's life can be tentatively reconstructed once the story has been read. Evidently a few years past he had been living a comfortable suburban life with his wife, Lucinda, his four daughters, and a house boasting not only a cook and a maid but also a tennis court. When the story opens, the reader accepts Ned's description of such a life as reflecting his present condition. Yet clues quickly begin to mount that something has happened to Ned—a financial ruin which led to social ostracization and eventually to a psychological breakdown. Even while his journey is going well, he shows signs of dislocation. He cannot remember whether a neighbor had been in Japan last year or the year before. Another family, the Lindleys, has dismantled their riding ring, but he has only a vague memory of having known this. He asks another friend for a drink only to be told that "there hasn't been anything in this house to drink since Eric's operation. That was three years ago." When he arrives at the house of his former mistress, he cannot remember how long ago their affair ended, and he has apparently lost all memory of having sold his house. In the last paragraph of the story, he still clings to the idea that his wife and daughters are due to return home at any moment.

Ned is determined to hold on to his past despite the many signs that his former life has disappeared. This determination underscores the theme of the mind's willfulness in the face of disaster. Ultimately, however, this strength of mind is impressive without being admirable, since Ned's conviction cannot restore to him his former happy life.

Style and Technique

Despite the many realistic details included in the story, from the detailed descriptions of the various pools (specifying, for example, whether they are fed by a well or a brook) to the nuances of suburban social climbing, the story contains an element of fantasy. Although the action of the story covers at most several hours, Ned seems to age appreciably. Midway through the journey, he notices that his swim trunks are loose, and wonders if he could have lost weight in the space of the afternoon. The youthful vigor he exhibits in the early pages of the story gives way to a fatigue that leaves him unable to swim even one length of his last pool.

In addition to his own sense of aging, the summer itself gives way with inappropriate suddenness to autumn. After he is caught in the rainstorm (an event which exhilarates rather than depresses him), he notices a maple bare of leaves and feels sad at this sign of autumn, even while rationalizing that the tree must be blighted to have lost its foliage in midsummer. Yet the signs of autumn persist. He smells wood smoke and wonders who would be burning wood at this time of year. Toward the end of his trip, the water of one pool has a "wintry gleam," he smells the autumn flower chrysanthemum, and the constellations of the oncoming night are those of the winter sky.

In "The Swimmer," then, Cheever veers from conventional realism to experiment with a style that emphasizes psychological veracity. Although the structure of the narrative is unconventional, the story manages both to convey a conventional plot line (Ned's loss of money and status) and to reveal the complexity of a man's interior reaction to personal disaster. Cheever's juxtaposition of realistic detail and fantastic plot elements enables him to explore the workings of a mind out of touch with reality in a broad sense, yet acutely aware of the minor details and realities that comprise the social fabric of life in Bullet Park.

Diane M. Ross

THE TABLES OF THE LAW

Author: William Butler Yeats (1865-1939)
Type of plot: Metaphysical romance
Time of plot: The 1890's
Locale: Dublin
First published: 1896

> *Principal characters:*
> OWEN AHERNE, the protagonist, a mystic
> THE NARRATOR, Aherne's friend

The Story

After dinner and an evening of conversation, the narrator feels comfortable enough to ask his old friend Owen Aherne a question that has been troubling him for many years: For years Aherne has cared for nothing but theology and mysticism—why has he not followed through on his original vocation for the Church? Aherne considers his answer, meditatively holding a glass of red wine in his hand, "its deep red light dyeing his long delicate fingers," making him look as if he were "holding a flame in his naked hand." As he waits for Aherne's answer, the narrator reflects on the character of his friend. When the narrator and Aherne had been students in Paris, they had belonged to a group devoted to "speculations about alchemy and mysticism." Aherne, it seems to the narrator, has in his beliefs "a fanciful hatred of all life," and this hatred has ripened into a strange mélange of beliefs, in part self-created, in part borrowed, "that the beautiful arts were sent into the world to overthrow nations, and finally life herself, by sowing everywhere unlimited desires, like torches thrown into a burning city." It seems to the narrator that Aherne is the sort of person for whom "there is no order, no finality, no contentment in this world."

As the narrator so reflects, Aherne rises and offers to show the narrator the cause of his seeming loss of interest in the Church and of his apparent reserve and indifference of recent years. He leads the narrator down a long corridor to his private chapel, passing engravings and portraits that Aherne has acquired on his travels, pictures depicting "enraptured faces of the angels of Francesca," "sibyls of Michael Angelo," seeming to hold an "incertitude, as of souls trembling between the excitement of the spirit and the excitement of the flesh," and "faces like thin flames," wrought by the Symbolists and Pre-Raphaelites. As he looks, "that long, grey, dim, empty, echoing passage [has] become to my eyes a vestibule of eternity."

In the chapel, the narrator is shown the object that has changed Aherne's life: On the altar is a bronze box that stands before six unlighted candles and an ebony crucifix. The box, decorated with "gods and demons, whose eyes are closed to signify an absorption in the inner light," holds a secret book, the only surviving copy of a book written by Joachim of Flora, who had been an abbot in Cortale in the twelfth century. The book, *Liber inducens in Evangelium aeternum*, has been carefully hidden and guarded by generations of the family of Aretino after Pope Alexander IV had the original cast into the flames for its heretical views. Aherne has acquired the book from Giulio Aretano, an artist and a Cabalist. Aherne puts the book in the narrator's hands, and the narrator turns the "gilded, many-coloured pages." This book, claims Aherne, has "swept the commandments of the Father away," and it "goes to the heart." In it are the names of "great artists who made them graven things . . . and adored them and served them," as well as "the names of the great wits who took the name of the Lord their God in vain. . . ." It praises the "breakers of the seventh day and wasters of the six days" and tells of "men and women who railed upon their parents." Those "heavy with love and sleep and many-coloured raiment" and "noble youths who loved the wives of others" fill the pages of this secret book. Murder, the violation of chastity, the bearing of false witness—all such deeds find their place in the book. Persons who had become "stars shaken out of the raiment of God" are its characters.

The narrator then sees that the ivory tables on which the Ten Command-ments were written, and which stood in the chapel, are now gone and have been replaced by blank tables, on which Aherne plans to write his "secret law." Aherne sees himself as the messiah for a new and terrible religion.

> Yes, I shall send out of this chapel saints, lovers, rebels, and prophets: souls that will surround themselves with peace, as with a nest made with grass; and others over whom I shall weep. The dust shall fall for many years over this little box; and then I shall open it; and the tumults, which are, perhaps, the flames of the last day, shall come from under the lid.

The narrator tries to dissuade Aherne, pointing out the danger of such beliefs, but Aherne is adamant: "How then can the pathway which will lead us into the heart of God be other than dangerous?" he asks. The first part of the story ends at this point, as the narrator expresses his regret and sorrow for not having tried more forcefully to dissuade Aherne.

The second part finds the narrator walking along a quay in Dublin ten years later. Suddenly he sees Aherne, his face a "lifeless mask with dim eyes." Aherne seems to see the narrator but turns away, hurries down a side street, and disappears. The narrator searches for him for weeks, then again spots him in a narrow street behind the Four Courts and follows him to his house. He seems, to the narrator, like a man "whose inner life had soaked up the outer life." At first, Aherne tries to keep him away ("I am lost, and must be hidden!") but finally allows the narrator to come into his house. Again the narrator follows Aherne down the long corridor, now "choked with dust and cobwebs," the pictures "grey with dust and shrouded with cobwebs." Dust also covers the "ruby and sapphire of the saints on the window," making it very dim. Aherne points to the tablets, which are now "covered with small writing." "You have a right to hear," Aherne tells the narrator, "for since I have told you the ideas, I should tell you the extreme danger they contain, or rather the boundless wickedness they contain." The ideas had made him happy at first, he relates. He had felt "a divine ecstasy, an immortal fire in every passion, in every hope, in every desire, in every dream." He thought that he "was about to touch the Heart of God." Then everything changed, and he realized that "man can only come to that Heart through the sense of separation from it which we call sin, and I understood that I could not sin, because I had discovered the law of my being. . . ." Because he has learned to see the world from the perspective of the angels, he can no longer sin, for everything he does is in accordance with a self-given law. Thus, because he sees creation in its entirety, he is no longer "among those for whom Christ died. . . ." He has "lost my soul because I have looked out of the eyes of the angels."

Suddenly, the room darkens. As Aherne sits, listless and dejected, the narrator sees faint purple-robed figures, holding faint torches and sighing "with sorrow for his sorrow." The narrator, in terror, flees the house as a voice cries, "Why do you fly from our torches that were made out of the trees under which Christ wept in the Garden of Gethsemane?" The narrator realizes that if he turns back, "all that bound me to spiritual and social order, would be burnt up, and my soul left naked and shivering among the winds that blow from beyond this world and from beyond the stars." He thus leaves the house forever. As for Aherne, the narrator relates that he has been "driven into some distant country by the spirits whose name is legion, and whose throne is in the indefinite abyss, and whom he obeys and cannot see."

Themes and Meanings

The interest in matters mystical, and in their relation to destruction, derangement, or apocalypse is a strong element in Yeats's poetry, early and late. Owen Aherne, protagonist of "The Tables of the Law," is an important speaker in poems central to the Yeats canon, as well as playing a prominent part in *A Vision* (1925, 1937), the poet's prose summary of his own mystical divinations. The story's emphasis falls on the protagonist's daring, longing, loneliness, and ultimate desolation. The elapse of ten years between the close of the first part of the story and the opening of the second underlines a preoccupation with initiation and aftermath, with longing and its consequences. It also suggests that Aherne's experience will forever remain a mystery. It necessarily remains beyond the realm of collective and typical experience. The remoteness of Aherne's spiritual adventures is accentuated by the obvious psychological distance between him and the narrator during their second encounter. Reappearing in the second half of the story as a haunted, and haunting, travesty of his original ambitions, Aherne is less a neo-Mosaic legislator than an alarming caution against spiritual overreaching.

The quest for and desire to codify a new spiritual dispensation is a lofty goal, appropriately reserved for Aherne, "the supreme type of our race." Yet, for all of his learning, intensity, and commitment, he cannot escape his human limitations. His shockingly misguided but strangely exultant efforts to do so leave him the prisoner of an unending tragic dream, a hell of his own making.

The sense of ardent pursuit, the conception of an extreme, the possibility of swift, temporary uplift followed rapidly by a condition of endless deterioration and damnation—these and various ancillary preoccupations constitute the fabric of "The Tables of the Law." Such interests lend the story a distinct *fin de siècle* tinge. Aherne—in effect, a mind at the end of its tether—is reminiscent of such protagonists as the Duc des Esseintes of Joris-Karl Huysmans' *À rebours* (1884; *Against the Grain*, 1922) and Oscar Wilde's Dorian Gray.

Aherne conveys much perturbation of spirit. Despite excellent cultural credentials, he is rootless and disaffected. He is at pains to distinguish himself from "those . . . who have only the world." Yet his radical revision of contemporary orthodoxy in the name of one fabricated by himself and Joachim of Flora leads only to his coming face-to-face with himself. Aherne's inability to renounce or transcend his own nature, his incapacity to break the bonds of worldliness, his failure to inhabit a realm of pure spirit reveal a mind unable to consolidate its own impulses. "The Tables of the Law," then, may be seen as a precursor of the vision of cultural and spiritual dissolution central to the Modernist movement, a vision to which the more mature Yeats bore witness even as he abhorred it.

The story also strikes a contemporary note by appearing to create an association between decay of energy and decadence. Aherne is a would-be mythmaker, a seeker of paradise, a trustee of a sacred text, a sage who can declare, but not finally uphold, the belief that "the world only exists to be a tale in the ears of coming generations." Clearly, he possesses all the qualifications to bring out the revolution in consciousness which he envisages. Yet the greater his abilities, the more catastrophic their deployment. The more of himself he puts into his visionary enterprise, the more significant his losses. He ends up in exile, which in this case is a condition of spiritual entropy.

In addition, and perhaps as a corollary, the story offers a covert but elaborate reproof to the imagination. Here Yeats seems to be worrying tacitly about a dictum of one of his own imaginative ancestors, William Blake: "The road of excess leads to the palace of wisdom." Aherne's imaginative excess may lead him to a more profound assessment of his human destiny, but his habitation does not have the sense of ease and scope which "palace" and "wisdom" usually connote. Yet Aherne has appointed himself seer, visionary, seeker after strange gods, offices frequently arrogated to themselves by poets, particularly those of the Romantic tradition, as Yeats was. Ultimately, however, the imagination may not overrule the world. To coexist with it is a sufficient challenge.

Style and Technique

"The Tables of the Law" is much more obviously sustained by the sonorities of its style than it is by the accessibility of its ideas or the cogency of its plot. The story's rather elaborate prose is as inimitably part of Yeats's schooling by the leading stylists of the day, Walter Pater and Oscar Wilde, as anything else in this typical period piece. Yeats's protracted sentences, the rhetorical flair of Aherne's monologues, the pervasive sense of distracted brooding—all are the fruits of the fundamentally overripe, dandified prose of the author's stylistic mentors.

Yet style in the story is not merely a matter of language: The language's florid effects also influence other aspects of the material's presentation. Gesture, large and small, and invariably mannered, is a case in point. Aherne is a character of large gestures (all of them expressing repudiation and the usurpation of tradition), intended for dramatic effect and, ultimately, to influence public events. His presence, and particularly his conversation, has a theatrical aura—understandably, perhaps, given Yeats's growing interest in the theater and in its techniques of narration, which date roughly from the story's year of publication. Additional theatrical features are especially prominent in the first part of "The Tables of the Law"—the ritualized meal, the ceremonious initiation of the narrator into the secret history of Joachim, Aherne's declaration of heretical faith.

The story cunningly and critically contrasts this careful (perhaps too careful) orchestration of gestural effects in the opening section with the at once fugitive and overblown effects of part 2. Here, none of the evidently stabilizing factors of a familiar civilization (located by Yeats, typically, in the Aherne family home) is at work. On the contrary, the reader witnesses the ruins of thought's edifice, an apocalypse rendered primarily in fastidious and exalted prose. The witnessing, however, consists of monitoring the story's emotional atmosphere and registering the seismic shocks of Aherne's spiritual experiences. These attain imaginative plausibility as a result of the story's style and technique, its language and use of image and symbol.

George O'Brien

TATUANA'S TALE

Author: Miguel Ángel Asturias (1899-1974)
Type of plot: Legend
Time of plot: Probably the Spanish colonial period
Locale: Probably Guatemala
First published: "Leyenda de la Tatuana," 1930 (English translation, 1945)

> *Principal characters:*
> MASTER ALMONDTREE, a priest who can assume both human and tree form
> BLACK ROAD, who is granted part of the priest's soul
> THE MERCHANT OF PRICELESS JEWELS, who gains the priest's soul from Black Road
> TATUANA, a beautiful slave whom the merchant purchases with the priest's soul

The Story

This delightful legend, retold by Miguel Ángel Asturias, introduces the reader to the imagination of the Guatemalan Indian, an imagination that still reflects the worldview of the old Mayas. It is a worldview that seems at first totally strange, but its dissolving categories of time, place, and being are familiar to the modern Western mind in dreams, fairy tales, and surrealism.

Master Almondtree, the protagonist, can take either human or tree form. As a priest, he is so brilliantly arrayed that "the white men" think that he is "made of gold." Well-versed in curative herbs, he can also understand the messages of obsidian and the stars. He is old, with "a frosty beard," and as a tree, "the tree that walks," he mysteriously appeared in the forest already mature.

During the full Owl-Fisherman moon, Master Almondtree decides (no reason is given) to apportion his soul out to the four roads. Each road has a color and name: "the black one, sorcerer night; the green, spring torment; the red, Guaycamayo or tropical ecstasy; white, promise of new lands." The last three roads go off and meet something with a corresponding color—a white dove, a red heart, and a green vine—which tries to get their portions of the Master's soul from them, but the three roads refuse to listen and keep going. Not so careful is the Black Road, "speediest of all," which goes into town to the marketplace. There the Black Road meets the Merchant of Priceless Jewels and swaps him the Master's soul "for a little rest."

When the Master hears, he assumes human shape and heads for the city. In the marketplace he finds the Merchant of Priceless Jewels, who has the portion of his soul locked away in a box. The Master tries to buy it back, making numerous offers—"a hundred *arrobas* of pearls . . . a lake of emer- alds . . . amulets, deers' eyes to bring water, feathers against storms, marihuana for his tobacco"—but the Merchant will not sell. Instead, the Merchant intends to use the Master's soul to purchase a beautiful slave girl. The Master departs, leaving behind his curse.

A year later, the Merchant and thirty of his servants are traveling on horseback along the mountain highways, returning home with the purchased slave girl. She is naked except for long black hair sweeping to her feet, while the gold-clad Merchant sports "a mantle of goat's hair" on his shoulders. After telling her that she is worth her great price, the Merchant describes the life of ease they will enjoy together and the old woman who will tell their fortunes: "My destiny, she says, is the fingers of a gigantic hand." Not replying, the slave girl stares at the horizon. Then, out of the peaceful sky, a fierce storm breaks upon them. The horses spook, and the Merchant's horse falls, dumping him at the base of a tree hit just then by lightning: "It seized him by its roots as a hand picks up a stone and flung him into the abyss."

Back in the city, the Master has been roaming the streets during this time like a crazed man, speaking to animals, knocking on doors, and frightening people, who are "amazed at his green tunic and frosty beard as if confronted by an apparition." As the full Owl-Fisherman moon comes around again, he knocks on the Merchant's door. The beautiful slave, the only survivor of the terrible storm, answers. He twice asks her the question he has been asking everyone else: "For how many moons did the roads go traveling?" She does not reply; instead, they stand gazing deep into each other's eyes.

They are interrupted by rude sounds, followed by the authorities, who arrest them "in the name of God and the King." He is charged with "sorcery," she with "being possessed by a demon." After seven months in prison, they are sentenced to death by burning. The night before their scheduled execution, the Master comes to the beautiful slave girl, Tatuana, and uses his fingernails to tatoo the figure of a boat on her arm. He tells her to trace the same figure on the ground or in the air, step into it, and escape any danger. She will become as "free" and "invisible" as his thoughts. Following his instructions, Tatuana escapes. The next morning when the guards enter the prison, all they find is "a dry tree . . . on whose branches were two or three still frosty almond flowers."

Themes and Meanings

Characters who take different forms or become invisible appear in legends throughout the world. Legends summon up the prescientific mind, such as the European mind before Aristotelian logic decreed that one thing cannot be something else or in two places at the same time. In "Tatuana's Tale," the reader is back in a world similar to Homer's.

There is, however, an important difference. In European and Semitic legend, the legends themselves are a means of asserting man's control over nature, of bringing order out of chaos. Man imposes his personality on nature, viewing it anthropomorphically and slaying its monsters. In "Tatuana's Tale," the process works the other way. Man is not separate from nature but continuous with it, part of it. Instead of fighting nature, man joins it, reading its messages and learning its secrets. This view of nature, which undergirded Mayan worship of the corn god and possibly the later practice of human sacrifice, is embodied here in the old priest. He changes into human or tree form at will, and even in human form, wearing his "green tunic," he seems like "an apparition." Perhaps he distributes his soul to the four roads because, growing old, he desires to merge back into nature entirely, which seems to be all that death amounts to (at the end, the "dry tree" has apparently died).

In European and Semitic thinking, merging back into nature has never meant a consummation but rather a loss of personality and control, a return to night and chaos, home of John Milton's Satan. The Christian view is indicated by the ending of "Tatuana's Tale," where the Master and Tatuana are arrested "in the name of God and the King" for "sorcery" and "being possessed by a demon." This ending is like a coda to the legend, as though added at a later stage to deal with the colonial experience. It articulates a theory of liberation: People who can merge back into nature cannot be controlled. Trying to own or control them is like trying to own or control nature. The Merchant's fate should be adequate warning.

Style and Technique

The style of "Tatuana's Tale" shows the influence not only of a native surrealism, the tradition of *arte fantástico* stretching back to pre-Columbian times, but also of a superimposed European surrealism which Asturias picked up in Paris. The European surrealism is most apparent in several poetic descriptions, such as the following: "It was the hour of the white cats. They were walking back and forth. The rosebushes were amazed." Sheep return home "conversing with their shepherds," and "a thread of tobacco smoke separated reality from the dream, black cats from white cats. . . ." These descriptive touches hold up the action, but they also contribute to the story's strangeness and to its sense of continuity within nature.

Also strange are the legend's many references to numbers: the four roads, "the twenty months in the four-hundred-day year," the seven months in prison, and so forth. These references give the legend a ritualistic aspect, but their specific meanings are part of the mystery of the Mayas, who were geniuses with numbers. The Mayas' calendars and astronomical calculations indicate that they were obsessed with time, whose circular quality in nature might be suggested by the Master's reunion with his fragment of soul (Tatuana) precisely on the Owl-Fisherman full moon.

Harold Branam

TELL ME A RIDDLE

Author: Tillie Olsen (1913-   )
Type of plot: Realism
Time of plot: The 1950's
Locale: America
First published: 1961

> *Principal characters:*
> Eva, the protagonist, an elderly woman dying of cancer
> David, her husband
> Nancy,
> Hannah,
> Vivi,
> Clara,
> Lennie,
> Paul, and
> Sammy, their children
> Jeannie, the one grandchild who understands

The Story

"Tell Me a Riddle" is the story of an elderly immigrant couple who, after forty-seven years of marriage, disagree bitterly over how to live out their retirement. The wife looks forward to having her house to herself now that the children are all gone, "of being able at last to live within, and not move to the rhythms of others." The husband wants to sell the house and join his lodge's cooperative for the aged, where he hopes to find a "happy, communal life." As the bickering continues and threatens to "split the earth between them" now that they are no longer "shackled" together by the needs of the family, the children enter the dispute, siding with their father, whose jokes and sociability seem to be more reasonable than their mother's moodiness and introspection.

One night the wife, Eva, feeling strangely sick, asks her husband David to stay home with her. He has been planning to stay home anyway, watching television, but when she makes this request, he leaves, just to spite her. When he returns, she is asleep on the sun porch; this is the beginning of a week sleeping in separate beds, apparently for the first time in their married life. In the middle of Eva's last night on the porch, David awakes to her singing a Russian love song from their youth. "I can breathe now," Eva announces and finally returns to their bedroom. This passage marks an important turning point in the story. Though David proceeds to find a buyer for the house, the family soon discovers that Eva's body is riddled with cancer and that she has at best a year to live.

During the rest of the story, David rushes Eva around the country to visit each child in succession while she begs to return home. Though he worries about the money going quickly and fears his own weakness in coping with her disease, he does his best to hide her impending death from her, to cater to what he perceives to be her final needs.

At each stage of this journey, the reader learns more about Eva's past and the sources of the gap that separates her from her children. With Hannah it is religion; Eva associates her daughter's Judaism with the superstition and backwardness of prerevolutionary Russia, a world she fought to destroy. David is more accepting of Hannah's perspective as she defends the need for tradition and the pleasure of ritual.

With Vivi it is nurturance. Eva refuses to hold Vivi's new baby; she helps with ironing, with cleaning, "but to none tended or gave food." She had given everything to her own children, "had borne them to their own lives" and now fears a distraction which will draw her out of her self once again. Vivi responds to this unnatural behavior by "remembering out loud deliberately, so her mother would know the past was cherished" and that she appreciates the sacrifices Eva made despite her present strangeness. Instead of responding to these memories, Eva hides in a closet, where she returns to a more distant past, her own girlhood in Russia and the martyrdom of her beloved friend Lisa, "who killed one who betrayed many."

The final stage of their journey brings Eva and David to Los Angeles, where they move into an apartment set up for them by their granddaughter, Jeannie. Here they spend days at the ocean side where Eva marvels at the sand and stones, evenings visiting relatives and an old friend, Mrs. Mays, who lives in a one-room tenement, her husband dead, her children scattered. Though Tillie Olsen describes Los Angeles as the "dwelling place of the cast-off old" like Mrs. Mays, Eva finds peace in the rhythms of the sea and especially in the relationship she develops with her granddaughter Jeannie, who alone understands her needs and can speak openly to her of death. Most important, because of her refusal to report a Mexican family which is preparing a dead child for burial at home according to its own customs but in violation of United States health laws, Jeannie reminds Eva of Lisa.

Eva's last few days of life are filled with memories of the past; bits and pieces of songs and poems associated with the Russian Revolution pour out of her, "a girl's voice of eloquence that spoke their holiest dreams" but said nothing of her adult life in America. At first David feels betrayed by these memories which so totally exclude him, but then he realizes that he too once shared the same dreams, the same youthful idealism. He tries desperately to question her, to measure his loss of faith against her continued belief, but it is too late; she is too far gone to respond to him. Overcome by his own despair, David sees a sketch Jeannie has drawn of the two of them, "their hands . . . clasped, feeding each other" as "the tall pillar" feeds her veins:

And as if he had been instructed he went to his bed, lay down, holding the sketch (as if it could shield against the monstrous shapes of loss, of betrayal, of death) and with his free hand took hers back into his. So Jeannie found them in the morning.

That day, which is her last, Eva's body is wracked by convulsions of agony and members of her family must hold her down. David, who feels he cannot go on, leaves the room. Jeannie follows him, reassuring him that his wife is "not there," but is now "a little girl on the road of the village where she was born," reveling in the joy and music of a wedding. "Leave her there, Granddaddy. . . . Come back, come back and help her poor body to die."

Themes and Meanings

"Tell Me a Riddle," though it is simple in plot, is complex and rich thematically. It is at once a story about failed dreams, love and marriage, old age in America, the healing power of art, mothers and daughters, and the meaning of freedom. Above all, it is a powerful tale of a caged bird who longs to soar free and who recovers her youthful ability to sing only in dying. The key line is the repeated refrain "Of being able at last to live within," a poignant restatement of Virginia Woolf's famous call for a room of one's own. The story suggests that in loving and nurturing her seven children, Eva necessarily sacrificed her own personal needs. The few moments she found for herself and a book after the children were in bed were often snatched from her as David returned home and would coax her, "Don't read, put your book away." She does not resent those years, but now wants time and space for herself, freedom from living for other people.

Ironically, as Eva begins to break out of her cage and sing, the songs she recalls all date from the time when she may have been "free" of family responsibilities but was "imprisoned" by political repression. The story thus plays on the meaning of freedom. For the children it means the rights and liberties of American citizenship, freedom from poverty and anti-Semitism. For David, it also means to be "carefree," to have freedom in particular from constant worries about money. With Eva's death David remembers another freedom, "that joyous certainty, that sense of mattering, of moving and being moved, of being one and indivisible with the great of the past, with all that freed, ennobled," and that his struggle to be "carefree," to live the American dream, may have had as its price the loss of this more precious freedom.

Style and Technique

"Tell Me a Riddle" received the O. Henry Award as the best American short story of 1961 and continues to receive critical acclaim. By far the most ambitious and powerful of the four stories collected in the book *Tell Me a Riddle* (1961), it might be more appropriately labeled a novella. Its complex themes are supported by an equally rich narrative voice capable of modulating from bitter to funny, from sad to joyful, from serious to ironic. The lyricism of the language itself combined with her ability to involve and move her reader has earned Tillie Olsen high marks as a prose stylist.

Olsen deserves equal praise as a dramatist for her creation of character and dialogue. Eva and David, in all their pain and anguish, are brought to life with humor and affection. The authenticity apparently derives from Olsen's own familiarity with the world she describes and her careful rendition of the dialect her characters speak. David and Eva's English is filled with the colorful Yiddish metaphors they have brought to the New World from their native Russia. Whether used as a curse ("like the hide of a drum shall you be beaten in life, beaten in death") or in self-mocking honesty ("Vinegar he poured on me all his life; I am well marinated; how can I be honey now?"), such poetic language marks the distance between the generations. The generic English of the native American children suffers in comparison and seems to underline the aesthetic poverty with which they have paid for their material affluence.

Tillie Olsen sees herself as the spokeswoman for the uneducated, for the working classes, for all those whose creativity has been suppressed by the day-to-day pressures of earning a living and tending to the needs of a family. In her collection of essays, *Silences* (1979), she speaks of "the gifted" who have remained mute "because of circumstances, inner or outer, which oppose the needs of creation." Olsen's own work demonstrates how beautifully such voices can sing, once freed.

Jane M. Barstow

THE TELL-TALE HEART

Author: Edgar Allan Poe (1809-1849)
Type of plot: Gothic mystery and horror
Time of plot: The 1840's
Locale: An American town or village
First published: 1843

> *Principal characters:*
> THE NARRATOR, a man whose madness drives him to murder
> THE OLD MAN, the victim who is apparently cared for by the
> madman

The Story

This is a chilling tale of madness and murder. "True!—nervous—very, very dreadfully nervous I had been and am," admits the narrator, "but why *will* you say that I am mad?" In a vain effort to prove his sanity by detailing how carefully he planned the gruesome deed, the narrator makes it abundantly clear from the first that he is dangerously deranged. Little is revealed about him, or about the old man that he kills. He did not hate the old man; indeed, he says he loved him. Yet he had to kill him because he was tormented beyond distraction by the old man's eye—"a pale blue eye, with a film over it." In the first two paragraphs, the narrator draws the reader into the terrifying yet fascinating world of madness that has led him to murder.

Having decided to kill the old man, the narrator recalls with obvious pleasure how calculatingly he set about to do it. For seven successive nights, he slipped into the old man's room just after midnight. He moved ever so slowly, first lifting the latch and then gradually insinuating himself into the room. Once inside, he would open his darkened lantern so that a single ray of light fell upon his tormentor, that "vulture eye." On each of those nights, however, the eye remained closed when the light fell upon the old man's face, and the narrator found it "impossible to do the work; for it was not the old man who vexed me, but his Evil Eye." Although the old man possessed some wealth and was wary enough of robbers to have the shutters of his bed chamber nailed shut, the narrator insists that his victim suspected nothing. During the day, the narrator explains, he was kinder to the old man than ever before.

On the eighth night, the narrator was especially cautious, though almost ecstatic with feelings of power and triumph, certain that the old man knew nothing of what he was doing or planning to do. Reveling in the moment, he may well have laughed. At any rate, the old man startled in his bed. Moving steadily into the darkened bedroom, the narrator began to open the lantern, but his thumb slipped, and the old man cried out, asking who was there and sitting up in his bed. The narrator says that he did not move for more than an hour, for the room was pitch black; nor did the old man move. Finally, the old man groaned slightly, and the narrator knew that it was the sound of one overcome by deathly fear, for he too had experienced that terror deep in the night. "I knew what the old man felt," he claims, "and pitied him, although I chuckled at heart."

Slowly opening the lantern, the narrator found that its single ray fell directly upon the vulture eye—"all a dull blue, with a hideous veil over it that chilled the very marrow of my bones." No other part of the old man's face was visible, but presently he heard "a low, dull, quick sound, much such a sound as a watch makes when enveloped in cotton." He was sure it was the old man's heart, and as the beat grew louder, he feared the sound might be heard by the neighbors. Enraged by the thought, he threw open the lantern, sprang into the room with a yell, dragged the old man to the floor, and pulled the heavy bed over on him. He was shortly dead, and the heart beat no more. To conceal his crime, the narrator dismembered his victim and hid the corpse under the floor of the old man's chamber. A tub caught all the blood. The murderer asks if a madman would have been so sagacious.

It was about 4:00 A.M. when he finished doing away with the body. Shortly thereafter, there was a knock on the door, and, sure that no one could discover what he had done, the narrator was not at all worried when three police officers explained that a neighbor had heard a scream and suspected foul play. The narrator answered that he had cried out because of a bad dream. The old man was away visiting friends, he said, but the police should search the house, see that nothing was taken, and be assured that all was well. As they finished their work, the narrator bade them to sit down a few minutes, placing his own chair over the planks that covered the old man's remains. The pleasant conversation of the police convinced him that they suspected nothing. The officers seemed to be reluctant to leave, however, and the narrator began to feel uneasy. He then heard what sounded very much like the old man's heart beating again, and he became very anxious, talking loudly and moving about the room, hoping that the police would not hear the heartbeat. "I foamed—I raved—I swore! I swung the chair upon which I had been sitting, and grated it upon the boards, but the noise arose over all and constantly increased." He suddenly felt that the police knew, though they pretended to ignore him. In desperation, he admitted his crime and urged them to tear up the boards and uncover that "hideous heart."

Themes and Meanings

This is largely a study in human terror experienced on two levels, both horrifying to behold. First, there is the narrator, the maniac, driven by his compulsive hatred of the "evil eye" to kill a man he says he loved. He is a case study in madness, tormented by that satanic eye which he simply must destroy. His madness is quite convincing and profoundly disturbing because it seems so capricious and meaningless. Indeed, seldom has the mystery and the horror of mental illness been so vividly portrayed. The "eye" also has a double meaning. The narrator is driven to self-destruction, though his suicidal urges are objectified in the old man's diseased eye.

The other level of terror is that experienced by the old man. His terror is made all the more realistic because it is related from the perspective of his tormentor, the mad narrator, who takes sadistic delight in knowing that the old man is quaking in his bed. Given the appearance of three police officers not long after the murder, one is tempted to speculate that the old man knew more than the narrator thought he knew. Perhaps he had conveyed his suspicions to a neighbor, or perhaps the young man has been demented for years, and the old man has been caring for him. If he did suspect the narrator, the terror that the old man felt during the hour before his death must have been excruciating.

The story is replete with double meaning and irony. The narrator destroys the "evil eye," thus assuring his own destruction, or incarceration at least. Fearful that the neighbors would hear the heartbeat growing increasingly louder, the anxious maniac yells as he bludgeons the old man, and the neighbors certainly heard that. The arrival of three police officers suggests that they knew something was amiss and that the old man had tipped off someone, though the narrator is sure that his victim suspected nothing. There is also the beating of that tell-tale heart. Was it really the old man's heart, or was it the narrator's own heart betraying him? The mystery—and the story is to a considerable extent a mystery—is thus maintained to the very end. The irony is exquisite, a tribute to the literary genius of Poe.

Style and Technique

Poe had definite ideas about the style and composition of the short story. To begin with, despite his wonderfully realistic descriptions in this and other tales, he advocated art over reality and believed that the artifical contrivances of the writer's imagination could reveal more truth about the human condition than faithful adherence to observed reality. As Poe saw it, the short story was the ideal medium for conveying artistic insight because the reader was likely to give it his concentrated attention for the brief time it took to read it. Above all else, he insisted that the writer should make every part of the short story contribute to its total effect. "If his very initial sentence tend not to the outbringing of this effect," wrote Poe, "then he has failed in his first step." His devotion to that injunction is clearly demonstrated in "The Tell-Tale Heart." Indeed, he excels in creating and developing that fascinating mood of mystery and madness which makes the story so irresistible.

Poe had the ability to portray his protagonists, mad though they might be, in sympathetic terms. The reader comes to understand the demented narrator, or at least to pity him, because his obsession is so overpowering.

Poe was a master of the first-person narrator, and that technique, so treacherous in the hands of a lesser artist, makes for unusual intimacy between the
reader and the storyteller. Indeed, one is drawn into the tormented mind of
the madman. The mind is especially Poe's domain, with its interplay of emotions, its mixture of reality and fantasy, and its ultimate mystery. To convey
the impressions and feeling that he wanted, Poe relied upon a variety of rhetorical tools, and he carefully crafted every sentence. Yet "The Tell-Tale
Heart" is convincingly spontaneous and filled with those little details that
heighten the realism. Devoted to art for art's sake, Poe probed the limits of
human reality in stories shaped by both intuitive genius and literary craftsmanship.

Ronald W. Howard

THE TENDER SHOOT

Author: Colette (Sidonie-Gabrielle Colette, 1873-1954)
Type of plot: Psychological realism
Time of plot: May, 1940, and 1923
Locale: Paris, region of Doubs in Franche-Comté
First published: "Le Tendron," 1943 (English translation, 1959)

> *Principal characters:*
> THE NARRATOR, a woman
> ALBIN CHAVERIAT, the storyteller
> LOUISETTE, the young girl
> THE MOTHER, the mother of the young girl

The Story

The opening dialogue of "The Tender Shoot" introduces the reader to an unidentified woman and an old friend of hers to whom she gives the name Albin Chaveriat. Evidently this name is chosen to hide the real identity of the storyteller. The setting is Paris, in May of 1940. Over dinner, the woman persuades her seventy-year-old bachelor friend to tell her a story of his love life, a secret life which limited, for the woman at least, a deeper sense of their friendship.

The woman has just encouraged Chaveriat to spend his time in the country, while the war lasts, at the Hersent home, a home filled with young daughters and nieces. Chaveriat refuses to go there for that very reason. He has renounced the two great passions of his life, young girls and shooting. Chaveriat begins his story by telling the woman that it was because of the dissolution of a masculine friendship that he acquired his taste for young girls. Chaveriat considered his friend Eyrand's marriage a betrayal of their mutual affection, refused to forgive him, and the friendship ended. It was with this estrangement that he became unsociable with everyone but very young girls.

Chaveriat proceeds with his story by telling of a late summer in 1923 spent at the estate of a wealthy chemist friend in the region of Doubs. Though he no longer hunted, he still accepted his friends' hunting invitations. He is especially bored with the others present, their constant eating and drinking, and so he keeps to himself. Being an ardent walker, one day Chaveriat wanders outside the domain and finds himself at the top of a hill where a stream flows by. From the other side of a crumbling wall, the horned forehead of a she-goat nudges his hand. As he is about to touch the she-goat, a girl's voice warns him not to or the she-goat will chase him. He does so, and the she-goat bounds after him. The girl wrestles the she-goat to the ground and it runs off.

Chaveriat's passion for young girls is sparked by the presence of this lovely, nearly sixteen-year-old country girl named Louisette. A flirtation begins with very evident romantic intentions on the part of Chaveriat. Several times he offers Louisette trinkets to flatter and charm her. Each time she adamantly refuses, saying that her mother would disapprove, would not understand. After a week of these late-morning lovers' meetings, Chaveriat, because of a social conflict, invites Louisette to meet him in the evening.

More than two weeks of meetings follow when Louisette changes their meeting time to much later in the evening. By that time her mother will be in bed, and Louisette's work will be finished. One late evening, Chaveriat takes leave of his host to rendezvous with Louisette. The threatening weather prompts him to carry his mackintosh and his pocket torch. Their lovemaking is interrupted by a rainstorm, and Louisette leads him to the shelter of her nearby home, a run-down château. Quietly they sneak into the darkened château and settle on a sofa. The rain subsides and he is about to leave when the downpour redoubles. Chaveriat's uneasiness grows in this strange place, and he is eager to escape from these unfamiliar, eerie surroundings. Suddenly a candlelight appears on the staircase. Louisette's mother appears, a small, white-haired woman with a magnificent gaze, resembling her young daughter. To no avail Chaveriat attempts to explain his behavior with her daughter. She asks him how old he is and then rebukes him, a man of fifty with white hair and wrinkles under his eyes, for having forced himself upon her daughter. She could have understood such behavior with young boys but not with an old man.

With Louisette and her mother becoming increasingly enraged and threatening, Chaveriat streaks out of the house with them in pursuit. As he escapes down the dilapidated, stone-walled path, the two women push stones from the top of the wall which strike him on the shoulder, ear, and foot. Finally Chaveriat arrives at his host's home. After a long and violent bout with fever, he recovers to renounce his passion for all the Louisettes of the world.

Themes and Meanings

Estrangement and ensuing loneliness are the motivating forces which drive Chaveriat to find some sort of fulfillment in the arms of young girls—his tender shoots. It is with his boyhood friend Eyrand's betrayal of their friendship that Chaveriat enters into his world of solitude, never again to establish a truly meaningful bond with another person. Even the secrecy of Chaveriat's love life has limited an otherwise deeper relationship between him and his woman friend, the narrator. He confesses that he has been just like any other man in his involvement with women, his attraction toward a sensible marriage. Yet he rejects any close or permanent relationship in a kind of self-willed effort to remain separate and alone. The lonely world in which he has chosen to live has prevented him from entering into an adult relationship on an intimate basis. He was unwilling to give up the deep abiding friendship he had with Eyrand. Not wanting to be hurt again he substituted those to whom he would not and could not become deeply attached except on a superficial and physical basis. As Chaveriat stated, his friendship for Eyrand surpassed the faithful devotion of a lover for his mistress. Old boughs for tender shoots, he says to his woman friend, is the lie he tells to excuse himself for the lust he feels for young girls.

Though there appears at times to be some yearning for a deeper meaning in his relationship with young girls than simple sexual gratification, he has not been able to go beyond treating them as a species, as a sexual symbol which must be studied and then consumed. Louisette reinforces the theme of loneliness, for he sees her showing no fundamental gaiety and living in dangerous solitude. They increase in each other this sense of separateness in their game of mutual exploitation. He saw her exploiting him as a lecherous man who has found a willing girl and he saw himself as one relieving Louisette of her youthful boredom. Yet to give some kind of meaning to their relationship he wished she could show some affection, could treat her unselfish lover as a friend, perhaps the friend that Eyrand once had been. Chaveriat noted at their parting that no words of tenderness, desire, or friendliness had been exchanged. She would not let him into her secret life, and refused any show of affection, his gifts, and any attempts to know her better. In this way Louisette intensified his sense of rejection and loneliness. Their only intimacy was physical, and her only way to communicate with him was with kisses.

Chaveriat's hope for meaningful, adult intimacy ended at the time of his estrangement from Eyrand. He was left alone, rejected and abandoned. From that point in time Chaveriat did not mature psychologically in his relationship with women. In fact he confesses that Louisette's sensuality in a grown woman would have revolted him.

This conflict between his self-imposed loneliness and his escape from reality created a life for him of empty romantic intrigues, the shallowness of which is climaxed and revealed in his final amorous episode with Louisette. Chaveriat's reaction to his own story is one of sadness, this sadness he also felt emanating from Louisette. The result of his adventure with her was a feeling of disgust and a desire to reject all the Louisettes of his past. His compensation was freedom from this bondage of empty and meaningless sexual gratification with young girls. Finally healed, at least in part, of the loneliness that estrangement had thrust upon him, he could now turn to those other than the Louisettes of the world to comfort him.

Style and Technique

The writer of "The Tender Shoot," Colette, introduces Albin Chaveriat, the teller of the story, which is, in essence, a psychosexual study. If Colette, the writer, and Chaveriat, the teller, are the same person, then the interpretations of sexual inferences and connotations leave room for speculation. The relationship between Chaveriat and his Louisettes reflect a female rather than a male psychology. The implied meaning of the relationship is very much central to the mystical qualities of the story itself. Colette places the reader in two worlds, the real world of Chaveriat's woman friend and the chemist, and the illusory world of Louisette. These are the same two worlds in conflict in which Chaveriat finds himself. His Louisette world is that of sexual adolescence. His other world is finally that of adult reality.

The author's description of nature is lyric and evokes a sense of eerie loneliness that adds color and movement to the mystical tone of the story and intensifies Chaveriat's innermost feelings. Suspense and mystery are very much interwoven throughout the story. The web of intrigue concerning the secrets of Chaveriat's love life immediately engages the reader's attention. His friend's betrayal, the ensuing realization of loss, and his sudden hunger for young girls cement the reader's attention very early in the story. The suspense intensifies as the reader is drawn into the young girl's world. Who is Louisette? Does she symbolize and reinforce the empty, lonely, and nearly desperate nature of Chaveriat's essence? It is in this unreal world of the Louisettes that he is driven to choose and to accept the real world of Chaveriat.

David J. Quinn

TERRITORY

Author: David Leavitt (1961-   )
Type of plot: Domestic realism
Time of plot: The 1980's
Locale: California
First published: 1982

> *Principal characters:*
> NEIL CAMPBELL, a twenty-three-year-old homosexual, who is
> home visiting his mother
> MRS. BARBARA CAMPBELL, his mother
> WAYNE, his twenty-eight-year-old lover

The Story

After a two-year absence from home, Neil Campbell, a twenty-three-year-old homosexual, visits his mother with his current lover, Wayne. Mrs. Campbell, a beautiful, sophisticated, and politically committed woman, generously welcomes Neil and his lover, but the visit soon proves painful for both mother and son. Mrs. Campbell tries to maintain her normal schedule: playing music with her friends, caring for her three Airedales, and running errands, but her nonchalance soon dissolves into doubt and recrimination as lines are drawn between her and Neil. Neil's return sparks for him uncomfortable memories of his early sexual awakening and unresolved anger at his mother concerning how understanding she has always been about his sexual inclinations. He is embarrassed at how "she located and got in touch with an organization called the Coalition of Parents of Lesbians and Gays. Within a year she was president of it. . . . He winced at the thought that she knew all his sexual secrets and vowed to move to the East Coast to escape her."

Wayne, Neil's twenty-eight-year-old lover, is charming and natural; he gets along well with Mrs. Campbell. It is Wayne who reaches across the dinner table to take Neil's hand in plain sight of his mother, and later that evening, when Mrs. Campbell finds them in the garden where they have gone to make love, it is Wayne who "starts laughing" after being discovered. Wayne's ease with the situation, however, soon ends. The next day, when the three are returning from the dog groomer, one of the Airedales urinates on Wayne, and Mrs. Campbell responds by saying, " 'I'm sorry, Wayne. . . . It goes with the territory,' " using the word that effectively draws the boundaries between her life-style and that of her son.

Neil's "territory" is his sexual inclination, and in a flashback he reveals how his mother impinges on it. At Neil's first Gay Pride Parade, Mrs. Campbell manned a booth for the Coalition of Parents of Lesbians and Gays; "they had posted a huge banner on the wall behind them proclaiming: OUR

SONS AND DAUGHTERS, WE ARE PROUD OF YOU. She spotted him; she waved, and jumped up and down." Mrs. Campbell's territory is her house, an orderly environment that she shares with her three female dogs, Abigail, Lucille, and Fern. Her discovery of Neil and Wayne in the garden the night before has made her "very frightened—and worried," and she defends her territory by saying, "I lead a quiet life . . . I don't want to be a disciplinarian. I just don't have the energy for these—shenanigans." Neil accuses her of being uncomfortable with his "having a lover," and she responds by saying, "No, I'm not used to having other people around, that's all. Wayne is charming." Yet Mrs. Campbell is clearly disturbed by her son's arrangement. When the three of them go to an Esther Williams film and Neil attempts to put his arm on her shoulder, "it twitches spasmodically, and he jumps, as if he had received an electric shock." Neil, reaching out to her through a touch, unnerves Mrs. Campbell, and when they come home from the film, she rebukes Neil for "what you were doing at the movie," and admits that "I can only take so much. Just so much . . . I remember, and I have to stop remembering. I wanted you to grow up happy. And I'm very tolerant, very understanding. But I can only take so much." With all her good intentions gone and her hopes for her son put aside for all time, Mrs. Campbell returns to her house, to her territory, after Neil cautions her not to feel responsible for his life, but also not to make him responsible for hers.

On the plane trip home, Wayne, the outsider in this story, remarks to Neil that he has a "great mother and all you do is complain," but Neil responds by saying that no outsider would understand how "Guilt goes with the territory." As the plane nears New York City and the image of his mother fades, Neil settles back into the life that is right for him, into his self-defined territory of two men holding hands, eyes closed, and "breathing in unison."

Themes and Meanings

Mrs. Campbell's and Neil's relationship raises basic issues about parenting and sex, the boundaries of family love and obligation. In a family as liberal and understanding as the Campbells, there are still shame and thwarted expectations. Neil is ashamed of his own sexuality, while his mother treats it as a worthy political cause which she eventually loses. By coming to terms with each other's limitations, Neil and his mother reenact the painful but inevitable process of separation which takes place between parent and child. Since this is a mother-son separation, it has a sexual dimension. Since it involves a homosexual son, the usual separation rituals are inoperative; as much as Wayne is a part of Neil's life, a long-term partner perhaps, he can never be a potential daughter-in-law, and this fact must naturally bewilder Neil's mother and influence her responses.

Mrs. Campbell is not the kind of mother who shows anger toward her son for being homosexual, but one can speculate on the sublimated anger implied in her having three female dogs. Are Abigail, Lucy, and Fern daughters who will never betray her as her much-absent husband and her sexually deviant son have? Leavitt teases the reader to infer as much when he has Neil recount how his first dog, Rasputin (obviously male), licked his torso, thereby igniting his first sexual feelings. The respective sexual territories that Neil and his mother come to occupy were marked off at that moment.

Style and Technique

"Territory" is a third-person narration which alternates between the present action of Neil's visit and the past action of his sexual history, which is disclosed in a series of flashbacks. These flashbacks bring Neil into focus in a way that the present action of the story cannot. Certain information is divulged in these flashbacks to which only Neil and the reader are privy, Neil's sexual history, for example. By learning Neil's sexual history, the reader becomes more sympathetic to his situation. In fact, Neil's sexual behavior is no different from most heterosexual behavior; he has settled down with Wayne after a more promiscuous stage which he admits "had been brief and lamentable."

On another level, the flashback technique affords a more telling description of Mrs. Campbell. Though she is seen as gracious and liberal in the present action, a more fragile side of her character emerges in the flashbacks. During the gay pride march, her political savvy and her motherly good intentions crumble when confronted with "a sticklike man wrapped in green satin [whose] eyes were heavily dosed with green eyeshadow, and his lips were painted pink."

Finally, the alternating narrative structure is itself a territory of sorts. One moment the reader sees a group picture, something at a medium distance, the next moment a close-up, a memory, something more revealing and microscopic. Neil's consciousness acts as a lens, a focusing mechanism, a surveyor's tool that delineates for the reader where one boundary ends and another begins.

Sylvia G. O'Sullivan